EVERY MAN HIS WAY

EVERY MAN

PRENTICE-HALL, INC. ENGLEWOOD CLIFFS, NEW JERSEY

HIS WAY

Readings in Cultural Anthropology

ALAN DUNDES
University of California
Berkeley, California

PRENTICE-HALL ANTHROPOLOGY SERIES
David M. Schneider, Editor

EVERY MAN HIS WAY:
Readings in Cultural Anthropology

ALAN DUNDES

Current printing (last digit):
10 9 8 7 6 5 4

Library of Congress Catalog No.: 68-11339

PRENTICE-HALL INTERNATIONAL, INC., *London*
PRENTICE-HALL OF AUSTRALIA, PTY. LTD., *Sydney*
PRENTICE-HALL OF CANADA, LTD., *Toronto*
PRENTICE-HALL OF INDIA PRIVATE LTD., *New Delhi*
PRENTICE-HALL OF JAPAN, INC., *Tokyo*

PRINTED IN THE UNITED STATES OF AMERICA

If one were to offer men to choose out of all the customs in the world such as seemed to them the best, they would examine the whole number, and end by preferring their own; so convinced are they that their own usages surpass those of all others.

Herodotus, *The Persian Wars*, Book III, Chapter 38.

Preface

The study of cultural anthropology can be one of the most exciting of all intellectual experiences. In understanding how other men live and think, an individual can gain new insight into his own life and thought. Without some knowledge of other cultures, he may be unable to see that his way of doing things is not necessarily *the* way of doing things, but rather only one of the several alternatives devised by man.

It is difficult to doubt the validity of one's own native categories of cognition. Far too often such cultural categories are projected to the point where they are considered categories of nature rather than categories only of a single culture. Indeed, the study of the nature of nature is impeded by the nature of culture insofar as no human observer can be completely free from his native cultural categories. Cultures, in this sense, are barriers which stand between individual scientists and the objects of their study, barriers which channel perception and influence comprehension. Of equal importance is the fact that cultures also serve as barriers between peoples, often interfering with, if not preventing, meaningful communication. In a world shrunk by advances in rapid transportation and in a world where groups formerly considered to be exotic primitives have assumed the international status of emergent nationhood, it becomes even more imperative that men everywhere make a concerted effort to understand their neighbors and themselves. The study of cultural anthropology can assist those interested in making such an effort and it is to such individuals that this volume is dedicated.

This anthology contains some of the classic papers written on various topics of cultural anthropology. Many of the papers were written by professional anthropologists and appeared in leading anthropology periodicals. As a rule, articles that were especially lucid and well written were selected. Some of the articles were taken from non-anthropology journals because in these publications anthropologists had often made a special effort to avoid highly technical discussions. In most of the essays in this volume, one will find thoughtful and, hopefully, provocative pieces of the picture of man.

The organization of the essays consists of seven sections. The first essays come from what might be termed a prescientific period and are representative samples of early descriptions of "other" people. The second section reveals that a new era in the study of man dawned when anthropologists left the comfort of their library armchairs and went "into the field," that is, went to live among the people under investigation for the express purpose of studying their culture. The third group of essays concerns the concept of culture, a concept central to the thinking of cultural anthropologists. The fourth and longest section of the book deals with some, though by no means all, of the subdisciplines of cultural anthropology. These examinations of different aspects of culture are offered to illustrate the ways in which anthropologists pose problems and analyze data. The fifth section attempts to show what insights result when an anthropologist directs his professional energies and techniques toward the analysis of his own culture. Then follows a somewhat unusual sixth section in which members of different cultures, not professional anthropologists, describe themselves and their cultures. The final section explores the interesting question of what happens when cultures come in contact with one another. It is hoped that the readers of this anthology will come away with an idea of what culture is, how cultural anthropologists study it, and how this knowledge may be used to enrich human understanding and communication.

ACKNOWLEDGMENTS

I thank all the authors, editors, and publishers who were kind enough to give their permission to reprint copyrighted materials. I also wish to thank many of my colleagues and students, who were kind enough to recommend their favorite essays in cultural anthropology for me to consider. Among those who offered constructive suggestions are Jim Anderson, Dick Bauman, Gerry Berreman, Jan Petter Blom, Noel Chrisman, Elizabeth Colson, May Diaz, George Foster, Nelson Graburn, Gene Hammel, Bess Hawes, Dell Hymes, Ed Kahn, Bonnie Keller, Tom Kiefer, Pat Lyon, Grant McCall, Laura Nader, Mel Perlman, Herb Phillips, Jack Potter, Rosalind Ribnick, Robert Rodden, John Rowe, Bob Scholte, Alice Singer, Dale Valory, and Justine Walters. However, the selections were made by the editor and any criticism of them belongs to him and not to his friends, who in a few instances tried to dissuade him from including several of the items chosen.

I should like to express my gratitude to Bill Oliver of Prentice-Hall who arranged for me to convert my original idea for this reader into reality, to Richard Roe, the anthropology editor of Prentice-Hall for his encouragement, and to Vincent A. D'Arrigo and the other members of the Prentice-Hall staff who worked hard to produce an attractive format for the book. I wish to thank Robert E. Pfeiffer, Librarian, Art/Anthropology Library at the University of California, Berkeley, for taking enough time from his busy schedule to contribute his expertise to the final bibliographical essay. To Professor David Schneider of the University of Chicago, I am indebted for a reading of the entire manuscript. I owe special thanks to my wife Carolyn for all her help and for putting up with the bear that anyone who works on a book becomes.

ALAN DUNDES

Berkeley, California

Contents

EVERY MAN HIS WAY

The prescientific period

*A*lthough anthropology, the study of man, is a comparatively recent discipline, man has long been interested in himself and his fellows. Invariably, some men wrote down descriptions of themselves and their neighbors. Later, as travel became more common, men wrote about peoples and places quite far removed from themselves. It is true that not all of the early studies are of equal merit. Many suffer from enormous bias, but it is fair to say that almost all of them share a common interest in exploring the nature of the human animal.

By and large, the early reports tend to emphasize the bizarre and the exotic. (Some contemporary anthropologists have continued this emphasis.) This is in contrast to most modern studies in which there is more of a willingness to consider the mundane activities of everyday life. It was the search for the unusual and the extraordinary in the early ethnographic descriptions which probably accounts for the preponderance of studies of strange customs—tales of cruel punishments and apparently absurd rituals abound. Many of the early writings consist almost entirely of long lists of unrelated quaint practices. Unfortunately, this curio collecting usually did not result in any holistic picture of the culture concerned. It was not until the late nineteenth century that serious attempts were made to make sense of the vast number of isolated facts that had been reported.

In reading ethnographic studies from the prescientific period, it is well to remember when they were written. It is all too easy to pass judgment on a work of the past using standards of the present. Yet, even by present standards, some of the reporting of the past is of astonishingly high quality. In any case, it is important to realize that the study of man has ancient roots.

The Holy Bible

LEGAL ORDINANCES

The *Holy Bible* is much more than the primary source of the facts and inspiration for the Judeo-Christian religious tradition. The Bible is also literature, and it is quite properly studied as such. In addition, the Bible is an exceptionally valuable repository of ethnographic data. Many aspects of the culture of ancient Israel are discussed in great detail in various portions of the Old Testament.

In order to demonstrate the kinds of ethnographic information which are recorded in the Old Testament, two short sections of the Book of Exodus will be presented. In Exodus 21 and 22, which follow the chapter including the Ten Commandments, one finds a list of laws governing a variety of behavior ranging from the treatment of slaves to the punishment of witches. Possibly dating from as early as the eighth or ninth century B.C., the account is definitely prescriptive rather than descriptive— God is telling Moses what the people should or should not do. However, prescriptive dicta do, in fact, indicate by indirection what some of the customs and practices in common use were. If one is not supposed to allow a sorceress to live, then it is clear that there must have been such individuals present. If one is required to put to death anyone who lies with a beast, then it is obvious that such sexual activities must have occurred. Any "Thou shalt not" statement implies that there is or was some desire to perform the forbidden act or there would be no point in making the "shalt not" statement.

There is a fairly extensive literature studying the Bible as ethnographic source material. Samples include P. Saintyves, *Essais de Folklore Biblique: Magie, Mythes et Miracles dans L'Ancien et le Nouveau Testament* (Paris, 1923) and James George Frazer's three volume *Folklore in the Old Testament* (London, 1918). For a more recent detailed account of the incredible amount of ethnographic data in the Old Testament, see Roland de Vaux, *Ancient Israel,* 2 vols. (New York, 1965).

Chapter 21

"Now these are the ordinances which you shall set before them. When you buy a Hebrew slave, he shall serve six years, and in the seventh he shall go out free, for nothing. If he comes in single, he shall go out single; if he comes in married, then his wife shall go out with him. If his master gives him a wife and she bears him sons or daughters, the wife and her children shall be her master's and he shall go out alone. But if the slave plainly says, 'I love my master, my wife, and my children; I will not go out free,' then his master shall bring him to God, and he shall bring him to the door or the doorpost; and his master shall bore his ear through with an awl; and he shall serve him for life.

7 "When a man sells his daughter as a slave, she shall not go out as the male slaves do. If she does not please her master, who has designated her for himself, then he shall let her be redeemed; he shall have no right to sell her to a foreign people, since he has dealt faithlessly with her. If he designates her for his son, he shall deal with her as with a daughter. If he takes another wife to himself, he shall not diminish her food, her clothing, or her marital rights. And if he does not do these three things for her, she shall go out for nothing, without payment of money.

12 "Whoever strikes a man so that he dies shall be put to death. But if he did not lie in wait for him, but God let him fall into his hand, then I will appoint for you a place to which he may flee. But if a man willfully attacks another to kill him treacherously, you shall take him from my altar, that he may die.

15 "Whoever strikes his father or his mother shall be put to death.

16 "Whoever steals a man, whether he sells him or is found in possession of him, shall be put to death.

17 "Whoever curses his father or his mother shall be put to death.

18 "When men quarrel and one strikes the other with a stone or with his fist and the man does not die but keeps his bed, then if the man rises again and walks abroad with his staff, he that struck him shall be clear; only he shall pay for the loss of his time, and shall have him thoroughly healed.

20 "When a man strikes his slave, male or female, with a rod and the slave dies under his hand, he shall be punished. But if the slave survives a day or two, he is not to be punished; for the slave is his money.

22 "When men strive together, and hurt a woman with child, so that there is a miscarriage, and yet no harm follows, the one who hurt her shall be fined, according as the woman's husband shall lay upon him; and he shall pay as the judges determine. If any harm follows, then you shall give life for life, eye for eye, tooth for tooth, hand for hand, foot for foot, burn for burn, wound for wound, stripe for stripe.

26 "When a man strikes the eye of his slave, male or female, and destroys it, he shall let the slave go free for the eye's sake. If he knocks out the tooth of his slave, male or female, he shall let the slave go free for the tooth's sake.

28 "When an ox gores a man or a woman to death, the ox shall be stoned, and its flesh shall not be eaten; but the owner of the ox shall be clear. But if the ox has been accustomed to gore in the past, and its owner has been warned but has not kept it in, and it kills a man or a woman, the ox shall be stoned, and its owner also shall be put to death. If a ransom is laid on him, then he shall give for the redemption of his life whatever is laid upon him. If it gores a man's son or daughter, he shall be dealt with according to this same rule. If the ox gores a slave, male or female, the owner shall give to their master thirty shekels of silver, and the ox shall be stoned.

33 "When a man leaves a pit open, or when a man digs a pit and does not cover it, and an ox or an ass falls into it, the owner of the pit shall make it good; he shall give money to its owner, and the dead beast shall be his.

35 "When one man's ox hurts another's, so that it dies, then they shall sell the live ox and divide the price of it; and the dead beast also they shall divide. Or if it is known that the ox has been accustomed to gore in the past, and its owner has not kept it in, he shall pay ox for ox, and the dead beast shall be his.

Chapter 22

"If a man steals an ox or a sheep, and kills it or sells it, he shall pay five oxen for an ox, and four sheep for a sheep. He shall make restitution; if he has nothing, then he shall be sold for his theft. If the stolen beast is found alive in his possession, whether it is an ox or an ass or a sheep, he shall pay double.

2 "If a thief is found breaking in, and is struck so that he dies, there shall be no bloodguilt for him; but if the sun has risen upon him, there shall be bloodguilt for him.

5 "When a man causes a field or vineyard to be grazed over, or lets his beast loose and it feeds in another man's field, he shall make restitution from the best in his own field and in his own vineyard.

6 "When fire breaks out and catches in thorns so that the stacked grain

or the standing grain or the field is consumed, he that kindled the fire shall make full restitution.

7 "If a man delivers to his neighbor money or goods to keep, and it is stolen out of the man's house, then, if the thief is found, he shall pay double. If the thief is not found, the owner of the house shall come near to God, to show whether or not he has put his hand to his neighbor's goods.

9 "For every breach of trust, whether it is for ox, for ass, for sheep, for clothing, or for any kind of lost thing, of which one says, 'This is it,' the case of both parties shall come before God; he whom God shall condemn shall pay double to his neighbor.

10 "If a man delivers to his neighbor an ass or an ox or a sheep or any beast to keep, and it dies or is hurt or is driven away, without any one seeing it, an oath by the LORD shall be between them both to see whether he has not put his hand to his neighbor's property; and the owner shall accept the oath, and he shall not make restitution. But if it is stolen from him, he shall make restitution to its owner. If it is torn by beasts, let him bring it as evidence; he shall not make restitution for what has been torn.

14 "If a man borrows anything of his neighbor, and it is hurt or dies, the owner not being with it, he shall make full restitution. If the owner was with it, he shall not make restitution; if it was hired, it came for its hire.

16 "If a man seduces a virgin who is not betrothed, and lies with her, he shall give the marriage present for her, and make her his wife. If her father utterly refuses to give her to him, he shall pay money equivalent to the marriage present for virgins.

18 "You shall not permit a sorceress to live.

19 "Whoever lies with a beast shall be put to death.

20 "Whoever sacrifices to any god, save to the LORD only, shall be utterly destroyed.

21 "You shall not wrong a stranger or oppress him, for you were strangers in the land of Egypt. You shall not afflict any widow or orphan. If you do afflict them, and they cry out to me, I will surely hear their cry; and my wrath will burn, and I will kill you with the sword, and your wives shall become widows and your children fatherless.

25 "If you lend money to any of my people with you who is poor, you shall not be to him as a creditor, and you shall not exact interest from him. If ever you take your neighbor's garment in pledge, you shall restore it to him before the sun goes down; for that is his only covering, it is his mantle for his body; in what else shall he sleep? And if he cries to me, I will hear, for I am compassionate.

28 "You shall not revile God, nor curse a ruler of your people.

29 "You shall not delay to offer from the fulness of your harvest and from the outflow of your presses.

"The first-born of your sons you shall give to me. You shall do likewise with your oxen and with your sheep: seven days it shall be with its dam; on the eighth day you shall give it to me.

31 "You shall be men consecrated to me; therefore you shall not eat any flesh that is torn by beasts in the field; you shall cast it to the dogs.

Herodotus

THE PERSIANS
AND THE SCYTHIANS

Herodotus (484–425 B.C.) is sometimes considered to be the father of history, but he is also regarded by some anthropologists as the father of anthropology. (It is, of course, a commentary upon our own culture that we insist upon searching for "fathers" of disciplines!) Although, like writers both before and after him, Herodotus relied on hearsay reports, he did base some of his writing on data which he gathered himself. His description of the Persians, he claims, comes from his own observation. Herodotus was sufficiently critical to notice what he thought were significant differences between peoples. For example, he remarked that the Persians readily adopted foreign customs whereas the Scythians did not. Whether he was correct or not, he did try to distinguish differences.

For further consideration of the contributions of the classics to anthropology, see R. R. Marett, *Anthropology and the Classics* (Oxford, 1908), E. E. Sikes, *The Anthropology of the Greeks* (London, 1914), and Clyde Kluckhohn, *Anthropology and the Classics* (Providence, 1961). M. I. Finley in *The World of Odysseus* (New York, 1954) provides ethnographic data reconstructed from literary sources. It should also be noted that there were some Roman writers who contributed to the ethnographic literature. These include *De Rerum Natura* by Lucretius (*c.* 94–55 B.C.) and the exceptionally interesting *Germania* by Tacitus (*c.* A.D. 55–120), who described the German people in considerable detail.

Now the Persian nation is made up of many tribes. Those which Cyrus assembled and persuaded to revolt from the Medes, were the principal ones on which all the others are dependent. These are the Pasargadae, the Maraphians, and the Maspians, of whom the Pasargadae are the noblest. The Achaemenidae, from which spring all the Perseid kings, is one of their clans. The rest of the Persian tribes are the following: the Panthialaeans, the Derusiaeans, the Germanians, who are engaged in husbandry; the Daans, the Mardians, the Dropicans, and the Sagartians, who are Nomads....

The customs which I know the Persians to observe are the following.

Reprinted from *The Greek Historians*, Vol. I, ed. Francis R. B. Godolphin (New York, 1942), pp. 56, 58–61, 230, 247–52. Copyright 1942 by Random House, Inc. Reprinted by permission. The translation of *The Persian Wars* by Herodotus was made by George Rawlinson.

They have no images of the gods, no temples nor altars, and consider the use of them a sign of folly. This comes, I think, from their not believing the gods to have the same nature with men, as the Greeks imagine. Their wont, however, is to ascend the summits of the loftiest mountains, and there to offer sacrifice to Zeus, which is the name they give to the whole circuit of the firmament. They likewise offer to the sun and moon, to the earth, to fire, to water, and to the winds. These are the only gods whose worship has come down to them from ancient times. At a later period they began the worship of Aphrodite, which they borrowed[1] from the Arabians and Assyrians. Mylitta is the name by which the Assyrians know this goddess, whom the Arabians call Alitta, and the Persians Mitra.[2]

To these gods the Persians offer sacrifice in the following manner: they raise no altar, light no fire, pour no libations, there is no sound of the flute, no putting on of chaplets, no consecrated barley-cake; but the man who wishes to sacrifice brings his victim to a spot of ground which is pure from pollution, and there calls upon the name of the god to whom he intends to offer. It is usual to have the turban encircled with a wreath, most commonly of myrtle. The sacrificer is not allowed to pray for blessings on himself alone, but he prays for the welfare of the king, and of the whole Persian people, among whom he is of necessity included. He cuts the victim in pieces, and having boiled the flesh, he lays it out upon the softest grass that he can find, trefoil especially. When all is ready, one of the Magi comes forward and chants a hymn, which they say recounts the origin of the gods. It is not lawful to offer sacrifice unless there is a Magus present. After waiting a short time the sacrificer carries the flesh of the victim away with him, and makes whatever use of it he pleases.

Of all the days in the year, the one which they celebrate most is their birthday. It is customary to have the board furnished on that day with an ampler supply than common. The richer Persians cause an ox, a horse, a camel, and an ass to be baked whole and so served up to them: the poorer classes use instead the smaller kinds of cattle. They eat little solid food but abundance of dessert, which is set on table a few dishes at a time; this it is which makes them say that "the Greeks, when they eat, leave off hungry, having nothing worth mention served up to them after the meats; whereas, if they had more put before them, they would not stop eating." They are very fond of wine, and drink it in large quantities. To vomit or obey natural calls in the presence of another, is forbidden among them. Such are their customs in these matters.

It is also their general practice to deliberate upon affairs of weight when they are drunk; and then on the morrow, when they are sober, the decision to which they came the night before is put before them by the master of

[1]The readiness of the Persians to adopt foreign customs, even in religion, is very remarkable.

[2]This identification is altogether a mistake. The Persians, like their Vedic brethren, worshipped the sun under the name of Mithra. His worship became most important in the later developments of the Persian religion. [For further information on the Mithra cult, see Franz Cumont, *The Mysteries of Mithra* (New York, 1956).—*Ed. Note.*]

the house in which it was made; and if it is then approved of, they act on it; if not, they set it aside. Sometimes, however, they are sober at their first deliberation, but in this case they always reconsider the matter under the influence of wine.

When they meet each other in the streets, you may know if the persons meeting are of equal rank by the following token; if they are, instead of speaking, they kiss each other on the lips. In the case where one is a little inferior to the other, the kiss is given on the cheek; where the difference of rank is great, the inferior prostrates himself upon the ground. Of nations, they honour most their nearest neighbours whom they esteem next to themselves; those who live beyond these they honour in the second degree; and so with the remainder, the further they are removed, the less the esteem in which they hold them. The reason is, that they look upon themselves as very greatly superior in all respects to the rest of mankind, regarding others as approaching to excellence in proportion as they dwell nearer to them; whence it comes to pass that those who are the farthest off must be the most degraded of mankind. Under the dominion of the Medes, the several nations of the empire exercised authority over each other in this order. The Medes were lords over all, and governed the nations upon their borders, who in their turn governed the States beyond, who likewise bore rule over the nations which adjoined on them.[3] And this is the order which the Persians also follow in their distribution of honour; for that people, like the Medes, has a progressive scale of administration and government.

There is no nation which so readily adopts foreign customs as the Persians. Thus, they have taken the dress of the Medes, considering it superior to their own; and in war they wear the Egyptian breast-plate. As soon as they hear of any luxury, they instantly make it their own: and hence, among other novelties, they have learned pederasty from the Greeks. Each of them has several wives, and a still larger number of concubines.

Next to prowess in arms, it is regarded as the greatest proof of manly excellence, to be the father of many sons. Every year the king sends rich gifts to the man who can show the largest number: for they hold that number is strength. Their sons are carefully instructed from their fifth to their twentieth year, in three things alone,—to ride, to draw the bow, and to speak the truth. Until their fifth year they are not allowed to come into the sight of their father, but pass their lives with the women. This is done that, if the child die young, the father may not be afflicted by its loss.

To my mind it is a wise rule, as also is the following—that the king shall not put any one to death for a single fault, and that none of the Persians shall visit a single fault in a slave with any extreme penalty; but in every case the services of the offender shall be set against his misdoings; and, if the latter be found to outweigh the former, the aggrieved party shall then proceed to punishment.

The Persians maintain that never yet did any one kill his own father or mother; but in all such cases they are quite sure that, if matters were sifted

[3]It is quite inconceivable that there should have been any such exact system of government, either in Media or Persia, as Herodotus here indicates.

to the bottom, it would be found that the child was either a changeling or else the fruit of adultery; for it is not likely they say that the real father should perish by the hands of his child.

They hold it unlawful to talk of any thing which it is unlawful to do. The most disgraceful thing in the world, they think, is to tell a lie; the next worse, to owe a debt: because, among other reasons, the debtor is obliged to tell lies. If a Persian has the leprosy he is not allowed to enter into a city, or to have any dealings with the other Persians; he must, they say, have sinned against the sun. Foreigners attacked by this disorder, are forced to leave the country: even white pigeons are often driven away, as guilty of the same offence. They never defile a river with the secretions of their bodies, nor even wash their hands in one; nor will they allow others to do so, as they have a great reverence for rivers. There is another peculiarity, which the Persians themselves have never noticed, but which has not escaped my observation. Their names, which are expressive of some bodily or mental excellence, all end with the same letter—the letter which is called San by the Dorians, and Sigma by the Ionians. Any one who examines will find that the Persian names, one and all without exception, end with this letter.[4]

Thus much I can declare of the Persians with entire certainty, from my own actual knowledge. There is another custom which is spoken of with reserve, and not openly, concerning their dead. It is said that the body of a male Persian is never buried, until it has been torn either by a dog or a bird of prey.[5]

According to the account which the Scythians themselves give, they are the youngest of all nations. Their tradition is as follows. A certain Targitaus was the first man who ever lived in their country, which before his time was a desert without inhabitants. He was a child—I do not believe the tale, but it is told nevertheless—of Zeus and a daughter of the Borysthenes. Targitaus, thus descended, begat three sons, Leipoxais, Arpoxais, and Colaxais, who was the youngest born of the three. While they still ruled the land, there fell from the sky four implements, all of gold,—a plough, a yoke, a battle-axe, and a drinking-cup. The eldest of the brothers perceived them first, and approached to pick them up; as he came near, the gold took fire, and blazed. He therefore went his way, and the second coming forward made the attempt, but the same thing happened again. The gold rejected both the eldest and the second brother. Last of all the youngest brother approached, and immediately the flames were extinguished; so he picked up the gold, and carried it to his home. Then the two elder agreed together, and made the whole kingdom over to the youngest born.

[4]Here Herodotus was again mistaken. The Persian names of men which terminate with a consonant end indeed invariably with the letter s, but a large number of Persian names of men were pronounced with a vowel termination, not expressed in writing, and in these the last consonant might be almost any letter.
[5]This strange custom, still prevails among the Parsees wherever they are found, whether in Persia or in India.

From Leipoxais sprang the Scythians of the race called Auchatae; from Arpoxais, the middle brother, those known as the Catiari and Traspians; from Colaxais, the youngest, the Royal Scythians, or Paralatae. All together they are named Scoloti, after one of their kings: the Greeks, however, call them Scythians. . . . Their manners and customs come now to be described. They worship only the following gods, namely, Hestia, whom they reverence beyond all the rest, Zeus and Earth, whom they consider to be the wife of Zeus; and after these Apollo, Celestial Aphrodite, Heracles, and Ares. These gods are worshipped by the whole nation: the Royal Scythians offer sacrifice likewise to Poseidon. In the Scythic tongue Hestia is called *Tabiti,* Zeus (very properly, in my judgment) *Papaeus,* Earth *Apia,* Apollo *Oetosyrus,* Celestial Aphrodite *Artimpasa,* and Poseidon *Thamimasadas.* They use no images, altars, or temples, except in the worship of Ares; but in his worship they do use them.

The manner of their sacrifices is everywhere and in every case the same; the victim stands with its two fore-feet bound together by a cord, and the person who is about to offer, taking his station behind the victim, gives the rope a pull, and thereby throws the animal down; as it falls he invokes the god to whom he is offering; after which he puts a noose round the animal's neck, and, inserting a small stick, twists it round, and so strangles him. No fire is lighted, there is no consecration, and no pouring out of drink-offerings; but directly that the beast is strangled the sacrificer flays him, and then sets to work to boil the flesh.

As Scythia, however, is utterly barren of firewood, a plan has had to be contrived for boiling the flesh, which is the following. After flaying the beasts, they take out all the bones, and (if they possess such gear) put the flesh into boilers made in the country, which are very like the cauldrons of the Lesbians, except that they are of a much larger size; then, placing the bones of the animals beneath the cauldron, they set them alight, and so boil the meat. If they do not happen to possess a cauldron, they make the animal's paunch hold the flesh, and pouring in at the same time a little water, lay the bones under and light them. The bones burn beautifully, and the paunch easily contains all the flesh when it is stripped from the bones, so that by this plan the ox is made to boil himself, and other victims also to do the like. When the meat is all cooked, the sacrificer offers a portion of the flesh and of the entrails, by casting it on the ground before him. They sacrifice all sorts of cattle, but most commonly horses.

Such are the victims offered to the other gods, and such is the mode in which they are sacrificed; but the rites paid to Ares are different. In every district, at the seat of government, there stands a temple of this god, whereof the following is a description. It is a pile of brushwood, made of a vast quantity of faggots, in length and breadth 600 yards; in height somewhat less, having a square platform upon the top, three sides of which are precipitous, while the fourth slopes so that men may walk up it. Each year 150 waggon-loads of brushwood are added to the pile, which sinks continually by reason of the rains. An antique iron sword is planted on the top of every such mound, and serves as the image of Ares; yearly sacrifices of cattle and of horses are made to it, and more victims are offered thus than to all the rest of their gods. When prisoners are taken in war, out of every hundred men they sacrifice one, not however with the same rites as the cattle, but with different. Libations of wine are first poured upon their heads, after which they are slaughtered over a vessel; the vessel is then carried up to the top of the pile, and the blood poured upon the scimitar. While this takes place at the top of the mound, below, by the side of the temple, the right hands and arms of the slaughtered prisoners are cut off, and tossed on high into the air. Then the other victims are slain, and those who have offered the sacrifice depart, leaving the hands and arms where they may chance to have fallen, and the bodies also, separate.

Such are the observances of the Scythians with respect to sacrifice. They never use swine for the purpose, nor indeed is it their wont to breed them in any part of their country.

In what concerns war, their customs are the following. The Scythian soldier drinks the blood of the first man he overthrows in battle. Whatever number he slays, he cuts off all their heads, and carries them to the king; since he is thus entitled to a share of the booty, whereto he forfeits all claim if he does not produce a head. In order to strip the skull of its covering, he makes a cut round the head above the ears, and, laying hold of the scalp, shakes the skull out; then with the rib of an ox he scrapes the scalp clean of flesh, and softening it by rubbing between the hands, uses it thenceforth as a napkin. The Scyth is proud of these scalps, and hangs them from his bridle-rein; the greater the number of such napkins that a man can show, the more highly is he esteemed among them. Many make themselves cloaks, like the sheepskins of our peasants, by sewing a quantity of these scalps together. Others flay the right arms of their dead enemies, and make of the skin, which is stripped off with the nails hanging to it, a covering for their quivers. Now the skin of a man is thick and glossy, and would in whiteness surpass almost all other hides. Some even flay the entire body of their enemy, and, stretching it upon a frame, carry it about with them wherever they ride. Such are the Scythian customs with respect to scalps and skins.

The skulls of their enemies, not indeed of all, but of those whom they most detest, they treat as follows. Having sawn off the portion below the eyebrows, and cleaned out the inside, they cover the outside with leather. When a man is poor, this is all that he does; but if he is rich, he also lines the inside with gold: in either case the skull is used as a drinking cup. They do the same with the skulls of their own kith and kin if they have been at feud with them, and have vanquished them in the presence of the king. When strangers whom they deem of any account come to visit them, these skulls are handed round, and the host tells how that these were his relations who made war upon him, and how that he got the better of them; all this being looked upon as proof of bravery.

Once a year the governor of each district, at a set place in his own province, mingles a bowl of wine, of which all Scythians have a right to drink by whom foes have been slain; while they who have slain no enemy are not allowed to taste of the bowl, but sit aloof in disgrace. No greater shame than this can happen to them. Such as have slain a very large number of foes, have two cups instead of one, and drink from both.

Scythia has an abundance of soothsayers, who foretell the future by means of a number of willow wands. A large bundle of these wands is brought and laid on the ground. The soothsayer unties the bundle, and places each wand by itself, at the same time uttering his prophecy: then, while he is still speaking, he gathers the rods together again, and makes them up once more into a bundle. This mode of divination is of home growth in Scythia. The Enarees, or woman-like men, have another method, which they say Aphrodite taught them. It is done with the inner bark of the linden-tree. They take a piece of this bark, and, splitting it into three strips, keep twining the strips about their fingers, and untwining them, while they prophesy.

Whenever the Scythian king falls sick, he sends for the three soothsayers of most renown at the time, who come and make trial of their art in the mode above described. Generally they say that the king is ill, because such or such a person, mentioning his name, has sworn falsely by the royal hearth. This is the usual oath among the Scythians, when they wish to swear with very great solemnity. Then the man accused of having forsworn himself is arrested and brought before the king. The soothsayers tell him that by their art it is clear he has sworn a false oath by the royal hearth, and so caused the illness of the king—he denies the charge, protests that he has sworn no false oath, and loudly complains of the wrong done to him. Upon this the king sends for six new soothsayers, who try the matter by soothsaying. If they too find the man guilty of the offence, straitway he is beheaded by those who first accused him, and his goods are parted among them: if, on the contrary, they acquit him, other soothsayers, and again others, are sent for, to try the case. Should the greater number decide in favour of the man's innocence, then they who first accused him forfeit their lives.

The mode of their execution is the following: a waggon is loaded with brushwood, and oxen are harnessed to it; the soothsayers, with their feet tied together, their hands bound behind their backs, and their mouths gagged, are thrust into the midst of the brushwood; finally the wood is set alight, and the oxen, being startled, are made to rush off with the waggon. It often happens that the oxen and the soothsayers are both consumed together, but sometimes the pole of the waggon is burnt through, and the oxen escape with a scorching. Diviners—lying diviners, they call them—are burnt in the way described, for other causes besides the one here spoken of. When the king puts one of them to death, he takes care not to let any of his sons survive: all the male offspring are slain with the father, only the females being allowed to live.

Oaths among the Scyths are accompanied with the following ceremonies: a large earthen bowl is filled with wine, and the parties to the oath, wounding themselves slightly with a knife or an awl, drop some of their blood into the wine; then they plunge into the mixture a scimitar, some arrows, a battle-axe, and a javelin, all the while repeating prayers; lastly the two contracting parties drink each a draught from the bowl, as do also the chief men among their followers.

The tombs of their kings are in the land of the Gerrhi, who dwell at the point where the Borysthenes is first navigable. Here, when the king dies, they dig a grave, which is square in shape, and of great size. When it is ready, they take the king's corpse, and, having opened the belly, and cleaned out the inside, fill the cavity with a preparation of chopped cypress, frankincense, parsley-seed, and anise-seed, after which they sew up the opening, enclose the body in wax, and, placing it on a waggon, carry it about through all the different tribes. On this procession each tribe, when it receives the corpse, imitates the example which is first set by the Royal Scythians; every man chops off a piece of his ear, crops his hair close, makes a cut all round his arm, lacerates his forehead and his nose, and thrusts an arrow through his left hand. Then they who have the care of the corpse carry it with them to another of the tribes which are under the Scythian rule, followed by those whom they first visited. On completing the circuit of all the tribes under their sway, they find themselves in the country of the Gerrhi, who are the most remote of all, and so they come to the tombs of the kings. There the body of the dead king is laid in the grave prepared for it, stretched upon a mattress; spears are fixed in the ground on either side of the corpse, and beams stretched across above it to form a roof, which is covered with a thatching of twigs. In the open space around the body of the king they bury one of his concubines, first killing her by strangling, and also his cup-bearer, his cook, his groom, his lackey, his messenger, some of his horses, firstlings of all his other possessions, and some golden cups; for they use neither silver nor brass. After this they set to work, and raise a vast mound above the grave, all of them vying with each other and seeking to make it as tall as possible.

When a year is gone by, further ceremonies take place. Fifty of the best of the late king's attendants are taken, all native Scythians—for, as bought slaves are unknown in the country, the Scythian kings choose any of their subjects that they like, to wait on them—fifty of these are taken and strangled, with fifty of the most beautiful horses. When they are dead, their bowels are taken out, and the cavity cleaned, filled full of chaff, and straitway sewn up again. This done, a number of posts are driven into the ground, in sets of two pairs each, and on every pair half the felly of a wheel is placed archwise; then strong stakes are run lengthways through the bodies of the horses from tail to neck, and they are mounted upon the fellies, so that the felly in front supports the shoulders of the horse, while that behind sustains the belly and quarters, the legs dangling in midair; each horse is furnished with a bit and bridle, which latter is stretched out in front of the horse, and fastened to a peg. The fifty strangled youths are then mounted severally on the fifty horses. To effect this, a second stake is passed through their bodies along the course of the spine to the neck; the lower end of which projects from the body, and is fixed into a socket, made in the stake that runs lengthwise down the horse. The fifty riders are thus ranged in a circle round the tomb, and so left.

Such, then, is the mode in which the kings are buried: as for the people, when any one dies, his nearest of kin lay him upon a waggon and take him round to all his friends in succession: each receives them in turn and entertains them with a banquet, whereat the dead man is served with a portion of all that is set before the others; this is done for forty days, at the end of which time the burial takes place. After the burial, those engaged in it have to purify themselves, which they do in the following way. First they well soap and wash their heads; then, in order to cleanse their bodies, they act as follows: they make a booth by fixing in the ground three sticks inclined towards one another, and stretching around them woollen felts, which they arrange so as to fit as close as possible: inside the booth a dish is placed upon the ground, into which they put a number of red-hot stones, and then add some hemp-seed.

Hemp grows in Scythia: it is very like flax; only that it is a much coarser and taller plant: some grows wild about the country, some is produced by cultivation: the Thracians make garments of it which closely resemble linen; so much so, indeed, that if a person has never seen hemp he is sure to think they are linen, and if he has, unless he is very experienced in such matters, he will not know of which material they are.

The Scythians, as I said, take some of this hemp-seed, and, creeping under the felt coverings, throw it upon the red-hot stones; immediately it smokes, and gives out such a vapour as no Grecian vapour-bath can exceed; the Scyths, delighted, shout for joy, and this vapour serves them instead of a water-bath,[6] for they never by any chance wash their bodies with water. Their women make a mixture of cypress, cedar, and frankincense wood, which they pound into a paste upon a rough piece of stone, adding a little water to it. With this substance, which is of a thick consistency, they plaster their faces all over, and indeed their whole bodies. A sweet odour is thereby imparted to them, and when they take off the plaster on the day following, their skin is clean and glossy.

The Scythians have an extreme hatred of all foreign customs, particularly of those in use among the Greeks.

Ahmed ibn Fadlān

SCANDINAVIANS
ON THE VOLGA IN 922

From classical antiquity to the Renaissance there were numerous pseudo-ethnographic writings, the majority of which were not

[6]Herodotus appears in this instance to have confounded together two things in reality quite distinct, intoxication from the fumes of hemp-seed or hashish, and indulgence in the vapour-bath.

Reprinted from Albert Stanburrough Cook, "Ibn Fadlān's Account of Scandinavian Merchants on the Volga in 922," *Journal of English and Germanic Philology,* **22** (1923), 54–63, by permission of the publisher.

based upon empirical observation but rather upon unsubstantiated reports of travelers. However, occasionally a traveler wrote his own ethnographic report. Such is the case of Ahmed ibn Faḍlān who left Bagdad in 921 to visit the king of Bulgaria. His description of the Scandinavian merchants he met en route is a most interesting example of early ethnographic reporting. His eyewitness account of a funeral is one of the high points of his contribution. Especially valuable is his recording of a Scandinavian informant's defense of cremation and criticism of ground burial. It is a beautiful example of ethnocentric reasoning (in which one's own way is the "natural" and "right" way, while the other person's way it "unnatural" and "wrong"). The slightly pedantic introductory headnote by Yale Professor Cook has been left intact inasmuch as it shows how early ethnographic writings moved from country to country and how the processes of translation and editing caused inaccuracies.

Yākūt ibn Abdallah, an Arabic writer of the first decades of the thirteenth century, has left us a geographical lexicon,[1] in which occur the subjoined passages, the greater part of which embodies a brief account of the Northmen—by his author, Ahmed ibn Faḍlān, called Russians—whom the latter encountered on the Volga in the year 921 or 922. Being sent as ambassador by Al-Muktadir[2] (894–932), caliph of Bagdad from 907 to 932, to the king of Bulgaria, he left Bagdad in June, 921, and arrived at the king's residence on May 11, 922. The occasion of the embassy was a request from the king of the Bulgars that Al-Muktadir would send Mohammedan missionaries to teach his people the faith of Islam, to erect Mohammedan temples, and, incidentally, to construct for him a fortress which should defend him against his enemies. The journey was a roundabout one, by way of Bokhara and the region between the Caspian and the Aral Sea, to southeastern Russia, north of the Caspian. Frähn (see below) conjectures that the Scandinavians met had reached the Volga by way of the Black Sea, the Sea of Azof, the Don, and thence overland, by a comparatively short portage, to the neighborhood of Tzaritzin.

The whole passage, as embodied in Yākūt's treatise, was published by the St. Petersburg Academy in 1823, with the title: "Ibn Fosslan's und Anderer Berichte über die Russen Alterer Zeit. Text and Übersetzung, mit Kritisch-Philologischen Anmerkungen, . . . von C. M. Frähn." Previous to the issue of Frähn's edition, a Danish translation had appeared, and from

[1]Edited by Wüstenfeld in 1866, from the MSS. of St. Petersburg, Copenhagen, and Oxford, as Jāqūt's *Geographisches Wörterbuch.*
[2]According to Muir (*The Caliphate,* 1915, pp. 365–7), he was a weak voluptuary, the mere tool of a depraved and venal court, and at the mercy of foreign guards. He was twice deposed, and finally slain in opposing a loyal officer whom he had called to his support. See also Weil, *Geschichte der Khalifen.*

this were made a Swedish and an English one, a version into French being made from the English rendering. The Danish version was published by J. L. Rasmussen in the *Athene* (ed. Molbech, Copenhagen) of April, 1814 (2.305–318); the Swedish one, by J. Adlerbeth, appeared at Stockholm in 1817; the English rendering, made by Mexander (?) Nicoll, appeared in *Blackwood's Magazine* for January, 1819 (4.460–4). The English version is quite untrustworthy, besides omitting certain passages; some of the inaccuracies, however, are due to Rasmussen's Danish rendering, or to his imperfect original, a manuscript at Copenhagen. Another Danish translation appeared in the *Forhandlinger et i Christiania Videnskabs-Selskab* for 1869 (pp. 270–280), the translator being C. A. Holmboe, and the title, "Ibn Fozlân, om nordiske Begravelses-skikke, fra det Arabiske oversat og med Anmærkninger oplyst." This contained the portion represented below by page 19, paragraph one, to page 21, paragraph three, inclusive, with two brief excisions. According to Holmboe, the French rendering referred to above was published in the *Journal Asiatique*, Vols. 4 and 6 (1824, 1825). The part relating to the voluntary victim is epitomized in Williams' *Social Scandinavia in the Viking Age* (New York, 1920), pp. 420–1. References to the tract may occasionally be found in other books—Keary's *The Vikings* (where the authorship is wrongly attributed to Ibn Haukal), Weinhold's *Altnordisches Leben,* etc.[3] The basis of the following translation is the German of Frähn, opposite the Arabic text of his edition. My rendering has had the inestimable advantage of being revised by my colleague, Professor Charles C. Torrey, who has followed the text of Wüstenfeld's edition (2.834[18]—840[12]).

Translation

Yākūt's Introduction

Rus, written also Rs, is a people whose country borders on that of the Slavs and Turks. They have their own language, a religion, and a divine law, in all of which they have nothing in common with any other people. Mukaddesi says that they live on a pestilential island,[4] which is surrounded by a lake, and which serves them as a stronghold against those who seek to molest them. Their number is estimated at a hundred thousand. They have no crops nor herds. The Slavs conduct expeditions against them, and despoil them of their goods. When a son is born to one of them, he flings down a sword, saying, "Only that is yours which you win with your sword." When their king pronounces judgment between two contestants, and they are not satisfied, he says to them, "Decide it for yourselves with

---

[3]Cf. Paul, *Grundriss der Germanischen Philologie,* 2d ed. 3.428; W. Thomsen, *Der Ursprung des Russischen Staates* (Gotha, 1879), pp. 29–36 (including translation), 52–3; Georg Jacob, *Der Nordisch-Baltische Handel der Araber im Mittelalter,* pp. 86–93; Jacob Grimm, *Kleine Schriften* 2. 288–94 (= *Abh. der Berl. Akad.* für 1849, pp. 253–8).

[4]Professor Torrey's correction. He adds: "There is no proper name 'Wabia.' I do not think that Frähn's 'Dania' is at all probable; it is hardly safe to insist on the geographical conditions which *we* know."

your swords." He whose sword proves the sharpest is then the victor. It was these Northmen[5] who held possession of the city of Barda'a for a year,[6] and dealt grievously with it, until God rescued it from them, and destroyed them.

I have read a brief account by Ahmed ibn Fadlān,[7] ibn Abbās, ibn Rāshid, ibn Hammād, the retainer of Mohammed ibn Suleimān, an ambassador of Al-Muktadir to the king of the Slavs, in which he relates everything that he saw on his journey from Bagdad and his return. What he relates I report, because of my amazement at it, exactly as it there stands.

Ibn Fadlān's Account

I saw how the Northmen[8] had arrived with their wares, and pitched their camp beside the Volga. Never did I see people so gigantic; they are tall as palm trees, and florid and ruddy of complexion. They wear neither camisoles nor *chaftans,* but the men among them wear a garment of rough cloth, which is thrown over one side, so that one hand remains free. Every one carries an axe, a dagger, and a sword, and without these weapons they are never seen. Their swords are broad, with wavy lines, and of Frankish make. From the tip of the finger-nails to the neck, each man of them is tattooed with pictures of trees, living beings, and other things. The women carry, fastened to their breast, a little case of iron, copper, silver, or gold, according to the wealth and resources of their husbands. Fastened to the case they wear a ring, and upon that a dagger, all attached to their breast. About their necks they wear gold and silver chains. If the husband possesses ten thousand dirhems, he has one chain made for his wife; if twenty thousand, two; and for every ten thousand, one is added. Hence it often happens that a Scandinavian woman has a large number of chains about her neck. Their most highly prized ornaments consist of small green shells, of one of the varieties which are found in [the bottoms of] ships.[9] They make great efforts to obtain these, paying as much as a dirhem for such a shell, and stringing them as a necklace for their wives.

They are the filthiest race that God ever created. They do not wipe themselves after going to stool, nor wash themselves after a nocturnal pollution, any more than if they were wild asses.

They come from their own country, anchor their ships in the Volga, which is a great river, and build large wooden houses on its banks. In every such house there live ten or twenty, more or fewer. Each man has a couch, where he sits with the beautiful girls he has for sale. Here he is as likely as not to enjoy one of them while a friend looks on. At times several of them will be thus engaged at the same moment, each in full view of the others. Now and again a merchant will resort to a house to purchase a girl, and

---

[5]Where a literal rendering would have been "Russians," I have uniformly rendered by "Northmen" or "Scandinavians."

[6]So C. C. T.

[7]"*Fadlān* is right. *Fozlan* or *Fŭzlan* is the modern *Turkish* pronunciation."—C.C.T.

[8]Probably Swedes, particularly of the eastern coast; see Thomsen, *op. cit.,* pp. 52–3, 86 ff., 105 ff.; Williams, *op. cit.,* p. 420.

[9]So C.C.T. A different opinion is expressed by Jacob, *op. cit.,* p. 146.

find her master thus embracing her, and not giving over until he has fully had his will.[10]

Every morning a girl comes and brings a tub of water, and places it before her master. In this he proceeds to wash his face and hands, and then his hair, combing it out over the vessel. Thereupon he blows his nose, and spits into the tub, and, leaving no dirt behind, conveys it all into this water. When he has finished, the girl carries the tub to the man next him, who does the same. Thus she continues carrying the tub from one to another, till each of those who are in the house has blown his nose and spit into the tub, and washed his face and hair.

As soon as their ships have reached the anchorage, every one goes ashore, having at hand bread, meat, onions, milk, and strong drink, and betakes himself to a high, upright piece of wood, bearing the likeness of a human face; this is surrounded by smaller statues, and behind these there are still other tall pieces of wood driven into the ground. He advances to the large wooden figure, prostrates himself before it, and thus addresses it: "O my lord, I am come from a far country, bringing with me so and so many girls, and so and so many pelts of sable" [or, marten]; and when he has thus enumerated all his merchandise, he continues, "I have brought thee this present," laying before the wooden statue what he has brought, and saying: "I desire thee to bestow upon me a purchaser who has gold and silver coins, who will buy from me to my heart's content, and who will refuse none of my demands." Having so said, he departs. If his trade then goes ill, he returns and brings a second, or even a third present. If he still continues to have difficulty in obtaining what he desires, he brings a present to one of the small statues, and implores its intercession, saying: "These are the wives and daughters of our lord." Continuing thus, he goes to each statue in turn, invokes it, beseeches its intercession, and bows humbly before it. If it then chances that his trade goes swimmingly, and he disposes of all his merchandise, he reports: "My lord has fulfilled my desire; now it is my duty to repay him." Upon this, he takes a number of cattle and sheep, slaughters them, gives a portion of the meat to the poor, and carries the rest before the large statue and the smaller ones that surround it, hanging the heads of the sheep and cattle on the large piece of wood which is planted in the earth. When night falls, dogs come and devour it all. Then he who has so placed it exclaims: "I am well pleasing to my lord; he has consumed my present."

If one of their number falls sick, they set up a tent at a distance, in which they place him, leaving bread and water at hand. Thereafter they never approach nor speak to him, nor visit him the whole time, especially if he is a poor person or a slave. If he recovers and rises from his sick bed, he returns to his own. If he dies, they cremate him; but if he is a slave they leave him as he is, till at length he becomes the food of dogs and birds of prey.

If they catch a thief or a robber, they lead him to a thick and lofty tree,

---

[10]A sentence of Frähn's translation is here omitted, since "it is wanting in the best MSS. and in the printed text (835[17]), and is evidently secondary."—C. C. T.

fasten a strong rope round him, string him up, and let him hang until he drops to pieces by the action of wind and rain.

I was told that the least of what they do for their chiefs when they die, is to consume them with fire. When I was finally informed of the death of one of their magnates, I sought to witness what befell. First they laid him in his grave—over which a roof was erected—for the space of ten days, until they had completed the cutting and sewing of his clothes. In the case of a poor man, however, they merely build for him a boat, in which they place him, and consume it with fire. At the death of a rich man, they bring together his goods, and divide them into three parts. The first of these is for his family; the second is expended for the garments they make; and with the third they purchase strong drink, against the day when the girl resigns herself to death, and is burned with her master.[11] To the use of wine they abandon themselves in mad fashion, drinking it day and night; and not seldom does one die with the cup in his hand.[12]

When one of their chiefs dies, his family asks his girls and pages: "Which one of you will die with him?" Then one of them answers, "I." From the time that he utters this word, he is no longer free: should he wish to draw back, he is not permitted. For the most part, however, it is the girls that offer themselves. So, when the man of whom I spoke had died, they asked his girls, "Who will die with him?" One of them answered, "I." She was then committed to two girls, who were to keep watch over her, accompany her wherever she went, and even, on occasion, wash her feet. The people now began to occupy themselves with the dead man—to cut out the clothes for him, and to prepare whatever else was needful. During the whole of this period, the girl gave herself over to drinking and singing, and was cheerful and gay.

When the day was now come that the dead man and the girl were to be committed to the flames, I went to the river in which his ship lay, but found that it had already been drawn ashore. Four corner-blocks of birch and other woods had been placed in position for it, while around were stationed large wooden figures in the semblance of human beings. Thereupon the ship was brought up, and placed on the timbers above mentioned. In the meantime the people began to walk to and fro, uttering words which I did not understand. The dead man, meanwhile, lay at a distance in his grave, from which they had not yet removed him. Next they brought a couch, placed it in the ship, and covered it with Greek cloth of gold, wadded and quilted, with pillows of the same material. There came an old crone, whom they call the angel of death, and spread the articles mentioned on the couch. It was she who attended to the sewing of the garments, and to all the equipment; it was she, also, who was to slay the girl. I saw her; she was dark (?),...thick-set,[13] with a lowering countenance.

[11]Cf. Thomsen, *op. cit.*, p. 53.
[12]Cf. Goethe's *Der König in Thule.*
[13]Professor Torrey comments: "What the true reading of the Arabic is here, is still an unsolved riddle. Frähn's guess, 'devil,' has nothing to support it. Wüstenfeld conjectures two Persian words, and wishes to render them by 'witch'; but, as other scholars have remarked, they do not mean (nor could mean) anything of the sort. What can plausibly be got out of the reading of the MSS. is [the rendering above]. The word 'thickset' is in two of the three MSS."

When they came to the grave, they removed the earth from the wooden roof, set the latter aside, and drew out the dead man in the loose wrapper[14] in which he had died. Then I saw that he had turned quite black, by reason of the coldness of that country. Near him in the grave they had placed strong drink, fruits, and a lute; and these they now took out. Except for his color, the dead man had not changed. They now clothed him in drawers, leggings, boots, and a *kurtak* and *chaftan* of cloth of gold, with golden buttons, placing on his head a cap made of cloth of gold, trimmed with sable. Then they carried him into a tent placed in the ship, seated him on the wadded and quilted covering, supported him with the pillows, and, bringing strong drink, fruits, and basil, placed them all beside him. Then they brought a dog, which they cut in two, and threw into the ship; laid all his weapons beside him; and led up two horses, which they chased until they were dripping with sweat, whereupon they cut them in pieces with their swords, and threw the flesh into the ship. Two oxen were then brought forward, cut in pieces, and flung into the ship. Finally they brought a cock and a hen, killed them, and threw them in also.

The girl who had devoted herself to death meanwhile walked to and fro, entering one after another of the tents which they had there. The occupant of each tent lay with her, saying, "Tell your master, 'I [the man] did this only for love of you.' "

When it was now Friday afternoon, they led the girl to an object which they had constructed, and which looked like the framework of a door.[15] She then placed her feet on the extended hands of the men, was raised up above the framework, and uttered something in her language, whereupon they let her down. Then again they raised her, and she did as at first. Once more they let her down, and then lifted her a third time, while she did as at the previous times. They then handed her a hen, whose head she cut off and threw away; but the hen itself they cast into the ship. I inquired of the interpreter what it was that she had done. He replied: "The first time she said," 'Lo, I see here my father and mother'; the second time, 'Lo, now I see all my deceased relatives sitting'; the third time, 'Lo, there is my master, who is sitting in Paradise. Paradise is so beautiful, so green. With him are his men and boys. He calls me, so bring me to him.' " Then they led her away to the ship.

Here she took off her two bracelets, and gave them to the old woman who was called the angel of death, and who was to murder her. She also drew off her two anklets, and passed them to the two serving-maids, who were the daughters of the so-called angel of death. Then they lifted her into the ship, but did not yet admit her to the tent. Now men came up with shields and staves, and handed her a cup of strong drink. This she took, sang over it, and emptied it. "With this," so the interpreter told me, "she is taking leave of those who are dear to her." Then another cup was handed her, which she also took, and began a lengthy song. The crone admonished

---

[14]Or, "waist-cloth." The word may be rendered by either of these two, or by "winding-sheet."—C.C.T.
[15]So C.C.T.

her to drain the cup without lingering, and to enter the tent where her master lay. By this time, as it seemed to me, the girl had become dazed [or, possibly, crazed][16]; she made as though she would enter the tent, and had brought her head forward between the tent and the ship, when the hag seized her by the head, and dragged her in. At this moment the men began to beat upon their shields with the staves, in order to drown the noise of her outcries, which might have terrified the other girls, and deterred them from seeking death with their masters in the future. Then six men followed into the tent, and each and every one had carnal companionship with her.[17] Then they laid her down by her master's side, while two of the men seized her by the feet, and two by the hands. The old woman known as the angel of death now knotted a rope around her neck, and handed the ends to two of the men to pull. Then with a broad-bladed dagger she smote her between the ribs, and drew the blade forth, while the two men strangled her with the rope till she died.

The next of kin to the dead man now drew near, and, taking a piece of wood, lighted it, and walked backwards[18] toward the ship, holding the stick in one hand, with the other placed upon his buttocks (he being naked), until the wood which had been piled under the ship was ignited. Then the others came up with staves and firewood, each one carrying a stick already lighted at the upper end, and threw it all on the pyre. The pile was soon aflame, then the ship, finally the tent, the man, and the girl, and everything else in the ship. A terrible storm began to blow up, and thus intensified the flames, and gave wings to the blaze.

At my side stood one of the Northmen, and I heard him talking with the interpreter, who stood near him. I asked the interpreter what the Northman had said, and received this answer: " 'You Arabs,' he said, 'must be a stupid set! You take him who is to you the most revered and beloved of men, and cast him into the ground, to be devoured by creeping things and worms. We, on the other hand, burn him in a twinkling, so that he instantly, without a moment's delay, enters into Paradise.' At this he burst out into uncontrollable laughter, and then continued: 'It is the love of the Master [God] that causes the wind to blow and snatch him away in an instant.' " And, in very truth, before an hour had passed, ship, wood, and girl had, with the man, turned to ashes.

Thereupon they heaped over the place where the ship had stood something like a rounded hill, and, erecting on the centre of it a large birchen post, wrote on it the name of the deceased, along with that of the king of the Northmen. Having done this, they left the spot.

---

[16]So C.C.T.

[17]Professor Torrey comments: "There is no uncertainty in the Arabic. I must say that the reading of the text seems to me very improbable, however. Instead of [Arabic quoted], one would expect [Arabic quoted], 'they lifted up.' The translation would then be, 'and they all together lifted up the girl,' the two words resembling each other very closely."

[18]Cf. Virgil, *Aen.* 6.223–4 (at the funeral of Misenus):
Subjectam, more parentum,
Aversi tenuere facem.

It is the custom among the Northmen that with the king in his hall there shall be four hundred of the most valiant and trustworthy of his companions, who stand ready to die with him or to offer their life for his. Each of them has a girl to wait upon him—to wash his head, and to prepare food and drink; and, besides her, he has another who serves as his concubine. These four hundred sit below the king's high seat, which is large, and adorned with precious stones. Accompanying him on his high seat are forty girls, destined for his bed, whom he causes to sit near him. Now and again he will proceed to enjoy one of them in the presence of the above mentioned nobles of his following. The king does not descend from his high seat, and is therefore obliged, when he needs to relieve himself, to make use of a vessel. If he wishes to ride, his horse is led up to the high seat, and he mounts from there; when he is ready to alight, he rides his horse up so close that he can step immediately from it to his throne. He has a lieutenant, who leads his armies, wars with his enemies, and represents him to his subjects.

Yākūt's Conclusion

These are the accounts which I have drawn literally from Ibn Faḍlān's narrative. For their veracity the author himself must vouch; God alone knows the truth. As for the Northmen of the present time, it is well known that they profess the Christian religion.

Katherine George

THE CIVILIZED WEST LOOKS AT
PRIMITIVE AFRICA: 1400–1800,
A STUDY IN ETHNOCENTRISM

Here is a cogent analysis of some of the bias found in "traveler ethnography." Despite the areal and temporal limitations (Africa, 1400–1800), many of Katherine George's comments apply to both earlier and later reports dealing with other parts of the world. Ethnocentrism, which is almost a dirty word in cultural anthropological circles, continues to interfere with the description and understanding of cultures different from that of the observer. Yet ethnocentrism, the notion that one's own culture is preferable or more natural than all others, cannot be avoided. And the very best trained anthropologists provide no exception. When a Western anthropologist joins his informants for a meal that includes ant larvae or insect grubs, it is difficult for him not to make a value judgment about the relative merits of such fare

Reprinted from *Isis*, **49** (1958), 62–72, by permission of the History of Science Society, Inc.

vis-à-vis a sirloin steak from his own culture. With the anthropological "philosophy" of cultural relativism, according to which elements of a culture are evaluated and understood in relation to that culture rather than some other culture (e.g., the culture of the observer), one can only do one's best to reduce the amount of ethnocentric bias. One cannot eliminate it altogether. The idea that one can totally eliminate ethnocentrism is itself an example of ideal culture, an ideal of "anthropological" culture, that is, the culture of anthropologists, as opposed to real culture. Ethnocentrism is found in all cultures. All peoples have "we" as opposed to "they," and, at least in some respects, "we" do things properly and "they" do not. Incidentally, the distinction between ideal culture (what we think is or should be the correct behavior in a given situation) and real culture (what in fact is the actual behavior in that situation) helps pinpoint another cause of ethnocentric judgments. Too often the tendency to compare the *real* culture of the people under study with one's own *ideal* culture results in the belief, that one's own culture is vastly superior to the culture observed. If one does insist on cultural comparisons (and the crucial question here is what and whose value system is to be employed in making evaluative comparisons), one should at least compare the real culture of the people under study with one's own real culture (or the ideal culture with one's own ideal culture). The point is that ethnocentrism exists whether we like it or not and that people judge other people whether we like it or not. However, given our cultural value bias, which insists that more rather than less intercultural communication and understanding is good and necessary, it makes sense for us to make an attempt to reduce the ravages of ethnocentric thinking.

To be born into a culture has generally implied being supported by it, being upheld, as it were, on a pedestal, from which one might look down with varying degrees of disinterest or antagonism upon other, alien cultures. Hence, the observer of alien cultures has tended to be prejudiced, in the simple sense that he has preferred his own to all other existent cultures and has viewed the strange as a malformed deviant from the familiar. The ego-flattering naïveté of the Aristotelian division of the world's population into Greeks and barbarians, or freemen by nature and slaves by nature, has formed the usual pattern into which men have fitted their observation of human differences.

The category of barbarism is for Aristotle notably inclusive, and without distinction as to region, people, or custom; but in the writings of most commentators upon human affairs variations in the extent of cultural difference have been associated with variations in the kinds of observational judgments made. The greater the extent of cultural difference, the greater is the amount of antagonism or scorn expressed. Primitive cultures, as described by the civilized observer, have suffered in particular, therefore, from the fashion of disparaging the alien; and the commandment, "Thou shalt not bear false witness," has proven particularly difficult of observance in this area of cultural description.

It is the purpose of this paper to analyze in one segment of the literature about primitive cultures something of the precise nature of the prejudices involved and the extent to which they were obstructive of adequate and truthful description. First, as to the total literature susceptible of this type of investigation, a geographical limitation has been set: this paper is concerned only with the literature of European contacts with primitive Africa, particularly with Negro Africa. There is also a temporal limitation: intensive reading has been done only in literature written from the fifteenth through the eighteenth centuries. To provide background and comparison, however, the principal classical and medieval sources have also been considered. As an analysis of the total sum of writings existent even within these limitations, this study does not presume to be exhaustive. Nevertheless, the well over a hundred reports of African travel or relevant geographical treatises which have been consulted constitute a sufficient sampling of the whole literature to enable sound generalizations as to content.[1]

Classical accounts of the primitive inhabitants of Africa are in general scattered and brief, and tend consistently to emphasize the strange, the shocking, and the degrading qualities of the peoples and cultures they deal with, and thus to emphasize the gulf between the civilized and the primitive worlds. Something of the nature of such accounts is due, of course, to the extreme inadequacy of the information on which they were based, for effective classical knowledge of Africa was limited to the Mediterranean littoral, principally to the two recognized civilizations which flourished there, the Egyptian and the Carthaginian. But more than a mere scantiness of data limits these accounts of the African primitive; they are characterized, too, by a selection of data on the basis of an attitude of superiority and dis-

[1]Two bibliographies are of particular service in regard to this literature: first, Edward Godfrey Cox, *A Reference Guide to the Literature of Travel* (Seattle, 1935), vol. I, *The Old World*, section XIII, "Africa," pp. 354–401; and second, Monroe N. Work, *A Bibliography of the Negro in Africa and America* (New York, 1928), part I, "The Negro in Africa," section I, "Discovery and Exploration in Africa from Ancient Times to 1800," pp. 1–17. Though their coverage in period and area is different from that of this paper, two book-length treatments of similar travel material ought to be mentioned here: Geoffroy Atkinson, *Les Relations de Voyages du XVIIe Siècle et l'Evolution des Idées* (Paris, 1924); and Roy H. Pearce, *The Savages of America: A Study of the Indian and the Idea of Civilization* (Baltimore, 1953). [The author surveyed these materials originally as part of her doctoral work. See Katherine Beverly Oakes, "Social Theory in the Early Literature of Voyage and Exploration in Africa," unpublished doctoral dissertation in Social Institutions at the University of California at Berkeley, 1944, for a fuller treatment of the topic. For additional consideration of the "anthropology" of this period, see John Howland Rowe, "The Renaissance Foundations of Anthropology," *American Anthropologist*, 67 (1965), 1–20.—*Ed. Note.*]

approval, and by the reporter's increasing propensity, as he moves farther from the sections of the continent relatively familiar to him at first or second hand, to substitute antagonistic fantasy for fact. Thus, even that most noted of classical geographers, Herodotus, in describing the native peoples of the Great Sahara, comes at last to the hazy realms of far western Libya, where "the huge serpents are found, and the lions...and the creatures without heads whom the Libyans declare to have their eyes in their breasts, and also the wild men, and the wild women...."[2] And Diodorus makes the following statement in introducing a discussion of certain Ethiopian primitives:

> The majority of them...are black in colour and have flat noses and woolly hair. As for their spirit, they are entirely savage and display the nature of a wild beast...and are as far removed as possible from human kindness to one another; and speaking as they do with a shrill voice and cultivating none of the practices of civilized life as these are found among the rest of mankind, they present a striking contrast when considered in the light of our own customs.[3]

This statement adequately conveys the tone of the descriptions which succeed, for the long list of primitive groups whom Diodorus here considers (most of whom were presumably situated in the area between the Nile and the Red Sea) are generally said to be strange and miserable folk who barely exist in continual hunger and fear, ruthlessly kill their aged and their sick, and practice sexual promiscuity.

The classical consensus, then, is that these peoples in the hidden interior and on the farthest shores of Africa not only lack civilization but any worthy ethic of social organization or conduct as well. Anarchic, promiscuous, and cruel, they live the life of beasts rather than that of men. The most remote, in addition, are often denied the possession of a truly human form. The dominant attitude in these accounts conceived of civilization—Graeco-Roman civilization in particular—as an essential discipline imposed upon the irregularities of nature: as nature—blind nature—without restraint and guidance, runs to monstrosities, so culture without civilization runs to disorder and excess. There was established thus early the pattern of thought which for many future centuries formed a basis for approach to the primitives of Africa, and which defined them primarily not in terms of what they were and what they had, but in terms of what they presumably were not and had not—in terms, that is, of their inhumanity, their wildness, and their lack of proper law.

In the fifteenth century direct and consistent European contact with the Africa beyond the Mediterranean littoral is initiated, and the travel reports

[2]Herodotus, *The History*. Translated and edited by George Rawlinson (London, 1910), I, p. 362. (Book II, Ch. 191.)
[3]Diodorus Siculus [Works], trans. by C. H. Oldfather (London, 1935), II, pp. 103–105. (Book III, Ch. 8.) Ethiopia proper has been viewed since antiquity as a civilized land, and reports of its inhabitants and their culture will therefore not be considered in this study.

with which this study is principally concerned begin to be written.[4] From the fifteenth century itself come only a handful of such accounts, all either of Portuguese or Italian authorship.

The great physical extension of European contact with Africa inevitably produces an increase of knowledge about the area, an increase of knowledge chiefly about African geography, but about African peoples and cultures to some extent as well. The end of the century sees an outline map of the continent closely approximate to the present form, and the monsters of classical imaginings have largely disappeared from the more distant shores and even from the as yet unpenetrated interior. But the pressures of an aggressive civilization, even then embarking upon a more ambitious program of exploiting the alien and primitive than any previously known, are still at work shaping what the observer sees and what he reports. The problem of ethnocentrism is still present.

Ethnocentrism exerts its influence in these reports in a variety of ways. First and most importantly, it makes for that negative prejudice toward the primitive and his culture whose power for distortion has already been discussed. Second, it makes for indifference toward the primitive and his culture, so that little time or care is given to the reportage of such matters, and for every item which is described many other items easily within reach of the observer are ignored. Such sins of omission are inherent in the very nature of this early modern travel literature; they are perhaps more significant, indeed, than the sins of commission which are more easily cited. Third, the ethnocentric bias induces a too ready and too complete identification with the familiar cultural background of anything in the new cultural situation found to be sufficiently similar. This identification, which does not necessarily imply approval of the trait in question, and most definitely not of its cultural context, is probably ascribable merely to that indifference to the characteristics of an alien culture referred to above. Finally, ethnocentrism, which is itself a tradition and a habit, also encourages the persistence of other traditions or habits of reporting, since it tends to focus the observer's attention not so much on what he sees in an alien culture as on what he has heard about it in his own culture. Thus, particular kinds of prejudice, particular items of description, and even particular turns of phrase become established and persist, often through centuries, and lend the weight of specific instances of statement to the impression of continuity which this literature conveys.

The descriptions of the political institutions of African primitives in the accounts of the fifteenth century contain elements both of change and of persistence, but themselves set up a tradition to be followed in future reports.

---

[4]Because of limitations in space, medieval accounts, whether Arabic or Christian, will not be considered here. Arabic reports of North African places and peoples beyond the confines of old and well known centers of civilizations are based for the most part on first-hand knowledge and are therefore greatly superior to both classical and contemporary Christian accounts; but they are products of an intensely militant culture in the heyday of expansion, and even the best of them (Ibn Battuta's *Travels*, for example) are overburdened and limited by the political concerns and religious judgments of the writers.

For the complex political structure of West African Negro societies in particular was too obvious to be ignored by those engaged in mercantile negotiations in the region. In the case of such societies, the classical stereotype of
the lawless primitive had to be abandoned, but it has been replaced by only
a somewhat lesser distortion, since their political institutions, without regard
to differences from tribe to tribe, are identified with those of contemporary
Europe. One hears not only of African kings and an African nobility but
also of African dukes and counts and knights.[5] On the other hand, the more
remote African primitives, in the fifteenth century, the "tawnie Moores" of
the Sahara especially, are still reported to be ignorant of all law and order,[6]
and between the two political extremes little if any ground is given to
subtleties of variation.

The charge of bestiality, so much the mark of the primitive among
classical geographers, is abundantly encountered in these fifteenth-century
accounts. The absence of recognized institutional formalities is in the traditional view an absence of an important adjunct of humanity, hence bestial.
The society without law, regulations of sexual conduct, or religion is, in
respect to each of these lacks, a bestial society, and several African societies
are declared by writers of the century to be without one or another such
institutional forms. One traveler asserts that certain Negroes living in a
vaguely identified area south of the Sahara "are in carnal acts like the
beasts, the father has knowledge of his daughter, the son of his sister."[7]
Cannibalism is, in the traditional view, a bestial practice, too, and the same
traveler asserts that the same Negroes are "eaters of human flesh."[8] Any
peculiarity of dress, diet, or manner which was distressing to European
sensibilities could be made to contribute to this image of African bestiality.[9]
The following statement well illustrates this: the writer is endeavoring to
justify the Portuguese slave trade (this trade depended in its early years
upon the slave raid), and he has spoken first of the "happy" situation of
the kidnapped Africans, now enslaved, in Portugal:

> And so their lot was now quite contrary of what it had been; since before they
> had lived in perdition of soul and body; of their souls, in that they were yet
> pagans, without the clearness and the light of holy faith; and of their bodies, in
> that they lived like beasts, without any custom of reasonable beings—for they

[5]See Gomes Eannes de Azurara, *The Chronicle of the Discovery and Conquest of
Guinea,* trans. by C. Beazley and E. Prestage (London: Hakluyt Society, 1896),
I, pp. 48, 281, 284. It should be noted that the placing of each account in its century
grouping is based in this study upon the date at which the journey in question was
made and/or the account was written, rather than upon the date even of initial
publication.
[6]*Ibid.,* II, p. 233; also Alvise da Cadamosto, *The Voyages of Cadamosto and Other
Documents on Western Africa,* trans. by G. R. Crone (London: Hakluyt Society,
1937), p. 54.
[7]Antoine Malfante, "The Letter of Antoine Malfante from Tuat, 1447," in Cadamosto, *op. cit.,* p. 89.
[8]*Ibid.*
[9]For references to certain African customs of eating and dressing as "bestial," see
Azurara, *op. cit.,* II, pp. 231–232; and Cadamosto, *op. cit.,* p. 41.

had no knowledge of bread or wine, and they were without the covering of clothes, or the lodgment of houses; and worse than all, through the great ignorance that was in them, in that they had no understanding of good, but only knew how to live in a bestial sloth.[10]

This statement presents the issue of Christianity's influence upon the civilized view of the primitive, and upon the problem of the present study, that of ethnocentrism. For the classical dichotomy between Greek and barbarian Christianity did substitute a more generous and more flexible measure by which to divide humanity—the measure of a faith, which its adherents were constantly endeavoring to expand. Nevertheless, no more than does the rigid exclusiveness of the Greek view does this proselytizing character of Christianity provide a basis for a favorable or objective interest in the qualities of man or of man's culture which lie outside the pale. And the judgments which arise from either position fall likewise with special displeasure upon the primitive way of life. Raw nature, "fallen" nature, which for the Greek was disorder, is for the Christian even worse: it is sin. In addition, Christianity did not eliminate older hierarchies based on race, nationality, class or occupational status, but it rather collaborated with such hierarchies and more frequently than not strengthened instead of weakening them—though it did introduce the complicating idea of a possible restatement of human relations in the society of another world. The availability of salvation to all properly indoctrinated souls alike, despite bodily inequalities —we find this gift of Christianity in the previously cited passage. But does it lessen the writer's prejudice? To the contrary. It enables him instead to commend actions (the kidnapping of helpless people) as morally virtuous, actions which to classical observers would have seemed merely expedient.

Christianity, or the religious frame of reference in general, also tends to foster the atmosphere of moral judgment which pervades this travel literature. Whatever else may or may not be reported about an African people, some statement regarding their "character" is almost always made. Usually it consists of a listing of vices, though an occasional virtue may also be acknowledged. The vice most consistently noted is thievishness;[11] the virtue, hospitality.[12] In both judgments an ethnocentric bias is the guiding principle: the reporter considers the Africans, not in terms of how they deal with one another, but in terms of how they deal with Europeans.

The physical attributes of the African primitive are likewise subjected to this parochial appraisal and, typically, are measured against the esthetic standard of the European Caucasoid. The physical traits peculiar to the Negro, his thick lips and his dark skin, are always thought ugly; a Negro is only

---

[10]Azurara, *op. cit.*, I, pp. 84–85.

[11]See Cadamosto, *op. cit.*, p. 19.

[12]*Ibid.*, p. 33. The initial reception of the intruding Europeans by African primitives was almost invariably non-hostile. So friendly were the natives at one spot on the southeast coast of Africa where the ships of da Gama's first expedition were anchored for a period that the country was called "Terra da Boã Gente" (land of good people) by the Portuguese. *A Journal of the First Voyage of Vasco da Gama, 1497–1499*, trans. and ed. by E. G. Ravenstein (London: Hakluyt Society, 1897), pp. 17–18.

said to be less ugly as he is less Negroid. The absolute nature of this judgment is striking; it is made without the smallest consciousness of its relativity. Indeed, the esthetic judgment assumes in time the dimensions of a moral judgment too. For when the traditional climatic explanation of Negro skin coloration has been replaced by the genetic, which in these accounts has occurred by the sixteenth century,[13] the rationale is generally provided by the presumed descent of the Negro from Ham, the accursed. The dark skin of the Negro becomes more than esthetically displeasing; it becomes the symbol and the product of a moral taint as well.[14]

One further notable feature of the reporting is the tendency to view the culture of the primitive African as poverty-stricken in material skills and resources, and to make any reference to material culture a basis for invidious comparison with the achievements of Western civilization.[15] Fact and prejudice no doubt coincide more nearly in this than in most areas of comparison. But again, the nature of the prejudice prevents adequate observation or adequate description of what is observed, for it brings into primary focus the absence rather than the presence of cultural qualities.

Inevitably, the emphasis of a paper such as this is upon what is "wrong" with the accounts in question, rather than upon what is "right." But to maintain that these early accounts are inadequate from any standpoint is not to deny that they contain a considerable amount, and a steadily growing amount, of accurate information concerning the cultures with which they deal. One must take full cognizance, too, of the sheer physical enormity of the task of making contact with, and coming even superficially to know the peoples of this vast and hitherto inaccessible continent. The difficulties of encountering in relatively rapid succession a large number of new cultures and strange languages should certainly excuse much. Still, such considerations do not entirely serve to explain the fact that whereas by the end of the fifteenth century the outline map of Africa was accurately delineated, no similarly reliable sketch of African primitive cultures existed or was to exist for a very long time to come. In the one field, knowledge kept pace with experience; in the other, aggressive factors were at work to perpetuate ignorance.

The reports of contacts with primitive Africa of the sixteenth century are still few in number. Though still primarily of Italian or Portuguese authorship, they are no longer exclusively so. A spreading interest in African trade has induced other nationalities, notably the English, to make occasional contributions to the accounts.

Much of the spirit and content of these accounts continue as in the century before. The West African political structure is again described in terms of its kings and nobility, and one also hears something of East African

---

[13]The climatic theory is still found in Malfante, *op. cit.*, p. 86. For the biological theory in the sixteenth century, see Duarte Lopez, *A Report of the Kingdom of Congo and the Surrounding Countries*, trans. by Margarite Hutchinson from the Italian account of Philip Pigafetta (London, 1881), pp. 16–17.

[14]See Father Jerom [Girolamo] Merolla da Sorrento, "A Voyage to Congo," in John Pinkerton, *A General Collection of...Voyages and Travels....* (London, 1808–1814), XVI, p. 267.

[15]See Cadamosto, *op. cit.*, p. 31.

Negro potentates, of an emperor of Monomotapa, for example, who maintains a ceremonious court, possesses great wealth, and has among the most valiant of his armed supporters a troop of Amazons.[16] Less patently organized primitive Africans are still said to be lawless, to lack religion, to be sexually promiscuous, and to live "like with beasts."[17] The charge of cannibalism is frequently made, and acquires the colorful details which take it well out of the realm of fact and into the realm of slander. One writer declares that a certain Negro people of the interior, about whom he knows only by hearsay, "have a shambles for human flesh, as we have of animals" and devour the bodies not only of enemies taken in battle, but also those of their "friends, subjects, and even relations,"[18] a description which becomes one of the stock tales of African travel. One ideological addition appears in the accounts of the sixteenth century, for by this time the West African coastal Negroes, at least, had experienced considerable exposure to civilizing influences; and the Western writers of reports about these people are therefore able to document their complacency regarding the superiority of their own to a primitive culture by citing instances of improvement in Negro customs brought about by European example.[19]

The seventeenth century sees a marked increase in the number of accounts of travel to primitive Africa and in the number of nationalities represented by the authors. South Africa becomes in this century the one area of real European colonization on the continent, and two little known peoples, the Bushmen and Hottentots, are thereby exposed to view.

The accounts of the seventeenth century evince a quality of transition between a definite viewpoint of the past (as embodied in fifteenth- and sixteenth-century accounts) and an equally definite, though very different, viewpoint of the future (as embodied in eighteenth-century accounts). But it is the dominance of the past which is first and most forcibly apparent. The negative portrait of African character is more emphatically and fully drawn than before,[20] and the opinion still prevails that the African primitive

[16]See Duarte Barbosa, *The Book of Duarte Barbosa. An Account of the Countries Bordering on the Indian Ocean and Their Inhabitants*, trans. by M. L. Dames (London: Hakluyt Society, 1918), I, pp. 12–13. The non-existent Amazons of eastern Africa are mentioned several times in accounts of the sixteenth and seventeenth centuries; the female soldiers who actually formed part of the retinue of the rulers of Dahomey are not remarked upon until the eighteenth century.

[17]*Ibid.*, p. 16; and Duarte Lopez, *op cit.*, p. 125.

[18]Duarte Lopez, *op. cit.*, pp. 28–29. Cannibalism is or has been practiced by certain peoples of Africa, but it has been almost entirely limited to ceremonial occasions. With a few possible exceptions, human flesh appears never to have been the common article of diet which the early voyagers assumed it to be.

[19]*Ibid.*, p. 72; also João de Barros, "Extracts from the 'Decadas da India,' " Cadamosto, *op. cit.*, pp. 107–108. Leo Africanus, a Moroccan-born Arab, in his sixteenth-century account of travel in North Africa, attributes to the extension of Moslem influence such improvement as has occurred in the bestial ways of the primitive Africans who have come within his purview. See Leo Africanus, *History and Description of Africa*, trans. by John Pory (London: Hakluyt Society, 1896), III, p. 820.

[20]See Jacques Joseph Le Maire, *A Voyage of the Sieur Le Maire to the Canary Islands, Cape Verd, Senegal and Gamby* (London, 1696; translated from the French original), pp. 79–82; and William Bosman, *A New...Description of the Coast of Guinea* (London, 1705; translated from the Dutch original), p. 117.

is improved in character and customs by contact with the European. The tendency to deny to certain primitive African cultures the possession of some one or another of the institutional forms likewise persists. Religion is particularly apt to such eliminating from the tally of African cultural equipment. In one highly antagonistic account of Hottentot culture, this simple people is indeed brought perilously close to the ancient prototype of the altogether brutish primitive. "These lawless barbarians and immoral pagans," the author writes, "practice only those habits to which a blind impulse of nature irresistibly impels them."[21] The boldest forms of such a concept are now found, however, not in accounts directly attributable to specific travelers, but in that more backward form of travel literature, the digest of the accounts of others. In one such treatise on Africa we are told of "the Caffers, or Libertines, who hold many Atheisticall Tenets, live together promiscuously...following their...unbridled lust...."[22] And here too we meet again that first fifteenth-century conception of the two political systems existent among African primitives:

> As for their Governments, some of them know none, neither ever scarce heard of any, but live in a confused Ataxy, sway'd on all occasions like tumultuous Herds, and at other times like tame Cattel feeding, and following their idle pleasures. But the rest are all Monarchical, living under Laws, Order and Princes.[23]

But, despite the fact that cultural parochialism and negative prejudice are still the major features of the accounts of the seventeenth century, new elements deserve acknowledgment. These accounts are on the whole considerably more informative than those of the past; they tend to be longer, fuller, and more concerned with cultural matters. This improvement should be credited in part to the increase of data about African cultures almost inevitably consequent upon extension and repetition of contacts with them. But new ideas and influences are also involved. As befits a century in which Europe saw a great growth in interest in voyage literature, there is to some extent an emergence of a consciousness of contributing to a specific literary genre, of a certain pride in workmanship, and of a sense of responsibility to the standards of their task. To be the eyewitness of a fact and to tell the truth about it—these requirements to which writers of earlier centuries paid scarcely any heed are seriously invoked by occasional seventeenth-century travelers as guides to proper reporting.[24]

Only one account from the century, however, sharply departs from most

---

[21]Willem ten Rhyne, "A Short Account of the Cape of Good Hope" (translated from the Latin original) in Isaac Schapera, *The Early Cape Hottentots, Described in the Writings of Olfert Dapper (1668), Willem ten Rhyne (1686), and Johannes Gulielmus de Grevenbroek (1695)*, (Cape Town, 1933), p. 127.
[22]John Ogilby, *Africa* (London, 1670), p. 34. This treatise appears to be in the main a translation of Olfert Dapper, *Beschreibung von Africa und den gehörigen Königreichen und Landschaften* (Amsterdam, 1670).
[23]*Ibid.*, p. 318.
[24]See Bosman, *op. cit.*, Preface.

of the tendencies of the past and breaks a new pathway of approach to primitive African culture: that written by Grevenbroek, who became the first champion of the natives of South Africa before the world. One quotation from his report (in the form of a long letter to a European friend, and hence rather disorganized) sufficiently indicates the revolutionary quality of his outlook:

> I am astonished that...those half-truths that are spread about our Africans should have reached even your ears. I found this people with one accord in their...daily life living in harmony with nature's law, hospitable to every race of men, open, dependable, lovers of truth and justice, not utterly unacquainted with the worship of some God, endowed...with a rare nimbleness of mother wit, and having minds receptive of instruction...it is through the faults of our countrymen...that the natives have been changed for the worse.... From us they have learned...misdeeds unknown to them before, and, among other crimes of deepest die, the accursed lust for gold.[25]

The important fact about this remarkable statement is that Grevenbroek's report, despite its casual letter form, is certainly one of the two or three best of the century.

Thus we come to the end of the seventeenth century, with two new principles beginning to influence writers about African culture: one, a new insistence on the responsibility of the traveler to check the accuracy of reports, preferably by eyewitness observation, and the other, the wholly fresh idea of viewing primitive life and customs in terms of their positive values and virtues.

Accounts of African travel in the eighteenth century are more numerous than in any previous era, and they are also more various in respect to the nationalities, the interests, the training, and the professions of the travelers writing them. There are missionaries, traders, and officials, as in the past, but in addition there are numbers of an entirely different breed, men who, with a considerable background of education in the philosophical and scientific thought of the day, came to Africa primarily to explore and to observe. It is in the reports of such men as these, Thunberg, Sparrman, Le Vaillant, Bruce, Mungo Park, and others, that the new spirit, barely indicated in seventeenth-century accounts, achieves its full development. So persuasive and powerful was this new spirit, however, that almost all eighteenth-century reports of travel to primitive Africa show it.

The two components of this spirit, an increased regard for accuracy of reporting, and an unprecedented sympathy for the primitive and his culture, which consistently tend to reinforce one another, cooperate in stimulating active criticism of previous prejudice and error, so commonly found in eighteenth-century accounts. The mistakes of classical geographers had occasionally been indicated by earlier writers, but not until this century does

[25]Johannes Gulielmus de Grevenbroek, "An Elegant and Accurate Account of the... Hottentots" (translated from the Latin original), in Schapera, *op. cit.*, p. 173.

criticism of past inadequacies of reporting become wholesale, consistent, and searching. The superiority in obtaining and conveying sound knowledge on the part of the "new man" on the African scene, the explorer and student of natural history, over the merchant, the conqueror, and the missionary, who had hitherto monopolized the field, the proneness to exaggeration and outright falsehood of the latter, and their excessive dependence upon that enemy of truth, the hearsay report—these ideas appear repeatedly in these accounts.

As the debris of old error is thrust aside, new patterns of description are constructed. The "character" of the African primitive is quite rebuilt. Added to his one traditional virtue, his hospitality, which had stood so long alone amid a sea of vices, are other virtues—his willingness to share, his emphasis on the equality of all members of the group in feast or famine[26]—insights that derive not from the sole concern for relationships between African and European but from an interest in relationships within African society itself. Even the traditional "vice" of the African primitive, his propensity to steal from Europeans, is explained away in terms of the enormous relative wealth of the European traveler, his externality to the rules of the tribal unit, and the consequent strength of temptation to which native is exposed.[27] The charge of cannibalism ceases to be a prominent part of the accounts; the tale of the bloody shambles of human flesh is not repeated.[28] Not that the African primitive is made to seem a saint; he still is assigned his share of vices and foolish ways. But the eighteenth-century traveler typically conceives of his own culture, too, as often vicious and wrong-minded. He can look at himself and say, as does one writer, "that we Christians have as many idle ridiculous Notions and Customs as the Natives of *Guinea* have, if not more."[29]

In this new atmosphere of thought, what happens to the hitherto characteristic modes of description of African institutions? In the first place, with the disappearance of the concept of the bestial African primitive, the lawless promiscuous society peculiarly associated with him also disappears. The universality of regulations of sexual conduct is recognized. An effort is made to describe more accurately the social or political organization, both of the "monarchies" of the West Coast and of the "free republics" or "independent hordes" elsewhere in Africa; and on the whole the weight of preference and interest swings away from the former to the latter. Though in an occasional eighteenth-century account some African group is said to lack religion,[30] the

[26]See Peter Kolben, *The Present State of the Cape of Good-Hope* (London, 1731; translated from the German original), p. 165.

[27]Mungo Park, "Travels," in Pinkerton, *op. cit.*, XVI, p. 871.

[28]Two writers of eighteenth-century accounts declare that all assertions of African cannibalism have been based on hearsay evidence, and categorically deny the existence of such a custom. John Atkins, *A Voyage to Guinea, Brasil and the West Indies* (London, 1735), Preface; and Thomas Winterbottom, *Nachrichten von der Sier-raleona-Kuste und ihren Bewohnern,* aus dem Englischen...herausgegeben von T. F. Ehrmann (Weimar, 1805), pp. 218–219. (Translation of Winterbottom's *An Account of the Native Africans in the Neighborhood of Sierra Leone* [London, 1803].)

[29]William Smith [fl. 1726], *A New Voyage to Guinea* (London, 1744), p. 267.

[30]Andrew Sparrman, *A Voyage to the Cape of Good Hope...1772–1776* (London, 1786; translated from the Swedish original), I, p. 207.

tendency is to be more generous in attributing religious beliefs to African peoples, and far more often than in the past they are asserted to have achieved some sort of faith in a single deity.

The institutions and customs of the African primitive are not merely accepted with a new tolerance by the eighteenth-century traveler; they are even fairly often upheld as models to be admired and emulated by the civilized world. For the "noble savage" is indubitably a personage in these accounts. We cannot take time now to explore the nature and history of the ideas behind this image, but at least two ingredients are inherent in it: first, a definite dissatisfaction with the inadequacies and injustices of Western civilization; and second, the citing of some actual primitive group or culture as an instance of a presumed improvement or remedy.[31] The qualities of primitive African character particularly apt to such selection are his hospitality, his love of his fellows and his generous sharing with them, his lack of envy and avarice. The qualities of primitive African society which tend to be similarly exalted are its freedom, its equalitarianism, its responsiveness to the needs and desires of all its members. One also often hears of the absence among primitive Africans of some foolish prohibition or unnatural restriction which in civilized society obstructs the course of life.

On the basis of such an approach to the African primitive one would expect that the charge barely heard in earlier writings, that contact with European civilization corrupts rather than benefits, would become the dominant opinion in eighteenth-century reports. And so it is. The whole European effort in Africa of conquering, trading, and colonizing is for the first time brought to the bar of judgment for analysis and attack. In all the major accounts of travel in South Africa from this century are many passages critical of colonial policies. The slave trade is no longer taken for granted but becomes a subject for debate. Several writers argue for its abolition, but even those who continue to accept it as necessary are driven to seek a new and more persuasive rationale.

It must, of course, be acknowledged that the entire complex of impulses to defend and exalt the primitive which we have been discussing—particu-

---

[31]The idea of the "noble savage," which, though it has foreshadowings in scattered references such as those of Tacitus, first appears in developed form in an essay by Montaigne, must be carefully distinguished from the superficially similar concept of the Golden Age. The latter idea also begins, to be sure, in discontent with the restraints and tensions of a given civilization, and also plays with equalitarian and libertarian sentiments; but, instead of encouraging admiration for existent primitive society (more often than not it is linked with a marked scorn for such society) it leads to a yearning contemplation of a never-never land of fancy somewhere in the remote origins of civilization. The gulf that separates the two concepts is nicely illustrated in Shakespeare's play of shipwreck and romantic wilderness, *The Tempest*. Gonzallo, the noble councillor, worn with the wickedness of the world he knew, alludes to the Golden Age when he talks of a society without private property, class distinctions, or authoritarian coercion, a society very like the Stoic state of ideal nature, or the Christian Garden of Eden. But Caliban, the monster, who emerges even from Shakespeare's somewhat pitying treatment as bestial in body and corrupt in soul—here is the actual primitive as Shakespeare and the majority of Shakespeare's time still saw him.

larly the vision of the "noble savage"—is itself a kind of prejudice, a kind of ethnocentrism even, which springs from a dynamic operating in the home-land environment of the traveler, and which is essentially extraneous to the data he observes; it is a romanticism, which in its extremer forms, at least, can and does distort objectivity.[32] But all the errors to be chalked up against this new positive prejudice in favor of the African primitive are as nothing beside the almost countless errors of commission and omission attributable to the earlier negative prejudice.

The concept of the "noble savage," it must be further remembered, emerged in the same period and from many of the same influences as the idea of progress. Its real purport was not to assert the superiority of primi-tivism as a whole to civilization as a whole, nor yet to return civilization to a primitive condition, but, by an appeal both to new concepts of natural right and to the concrete facts of primitive life, to remove or reform certain specific abuses—certain social inequalities and political tyrannies in par-ticular—which, it was thought, had intruded into civilized society and were interfering with its continued growth. In terms of these very functions, however, the concept of the "noble savage" became of necessity a friend rather than an enemy to the advance of knowledge about the primitive. A bias it might remain, with capacities to distort; but, whereas the older prejudice had obstructed the study of primitive culture, this new prejudice instead introduced a compulsion to go forth and observe.

The accounts of the eighteenth century—even the best of them—when viewed according to the standards of modern anthropological research and writing, still appear limited and crude. Beside a Herskovits or a Schapera, even a Sparrman is clumsy and uninformative in the cultural field. There is, to begin with, a primary preoccupation with botanical, zoological, and geo-graphical data. In so far as observation of really scientific calibre is present in eighteenth-century accounts, it concerns the physical and biological much more than cultural or human material. In regard to cultural data, moreover, there is still too much involvement with issues of moral judgment. Any judgment, whether positive or negative, is ethnocentric in its emphasis, and derogates from the dignity of primitive cultures by refusing to grant their right to exist and to be studied as entities independent of all value systems. The concept of the "noble savage" may have been a door to objectivity; it is not objectivity itself.

If one considers these eighteenth-century accounts, however, in com-parison with the earlier literature, one is struck by a crucial change. A deci-sive expansion of human interests and sympathies has occurred. Real progress in the direction of a fuller understanding of man and his culture has been made. Indeed, I know of no body of data which compels one more forcibly and directly to an admiration for the intellectual and moral magni-cence of the eighteenth century.

[32]François Le Vaillant, *Travels from the Cape of Good Hope into the Interior Parts of Africa* (London, 1790; translated from the French original); and *New Travels into the Interior Parts of Africa* (London, 1796; translated from the French original).

Charles Darwin

THE TIERRA DEL FUEGIANS

Not everyone realizes that the celebrated naturalist Charles Darwin made a modest contribution to the ethnographic descriptive literature. Sailing on the famous *Beagle,* Darwin arrived at Tierra del Fuego in 1832. On board with Darwin were three Yahgans (Indians of Tierra del Fuego) whom Captain Fitz Roy of the *Beagle* was transporting back to their native land. Captain Fitz Roy had brought them to England from Tierra del Fuego on an earlier voyage of the *Beagle*. Darwin's description of these Indians and their reception by their family and friends upon their return to Tierra del Fuego is a moving account of this naïve nineteenth-century experiment in "civilizing" savages!

Although Darwin, keen observer that he was, did record some bona fide ethnographic data, it is his passing remarks and gratuitous commentaries that are of primary interest to the modern reader. Remembering that Darwin holds an honored position in the history of science, one can see with some surprise how much a child of his century he was. Looking down at lowly savages from the lofty vantage point of high civilization was a favorite pastime of nineteenth-century English (and other European) intelligentsia. Not even Darwin's great interest in zoology completely explains his numerous comparisons of the Tierra del Fuegians with "wild animals"! Moreover, it is clear that Darwin did not understand some of what he observed. For example, he reported that a piece of cloth given to one individual was torn into shreds and distributed to others. Darwin remarks that no one individual becomes richer than another (as contrasted to what happens in our capitalist culture). Yet this principle of distributing and sharing goods is found all over the world and, from the perspective of group solidarity, it makes a good deal of sense. Each distribution of freshly killed game or of a gift provides an opportunity to review and reinforce the various tie-lines of relationship and obligation. X must give something to Y who in turn is obliged to give something to Z, etc. Such distribution techniques reveal critical relationship patterns much as the standard experiment in elementary botany classes in which dipping a petiole in a red dye solution reveals the venation patterns in leaves. Yet in the end, Darwin grudgingly admits that the Tierra del Fuegians are not without some redeeming features. Damning with faint praise, he suggests, for example, that they might not be mentally inferior to the aborigines of Australia!

Reprinted in abridged form from *Journal of Researches into the Natural History and Geology of the Countries Visited During the Voyage of H.M.S. Beagle Round the World, Under the Command of Capt. Fitz Roy,* by Charles Darwin. Copyright 1896 by The Century Company. Reprinted by courtesy of Appleton-Century-Crofts.

For a short sketch of Darwin's influence in anthropology, mostly with respect to the impact of his theory of evolution, see Abram Kardiner and Edward Preble, *They Studied Man* (New York, 1963), pp. 15–32. For a more ethnographically sophisticated survey of Yahgan culture, see Elman R. Service, *Profiles in Ethnology* (New York, 1963), pp. 27–43. For further references on the Yahgan, see Timothy J. O'Leary, *Ethnographic Bibliography of South America* (New Haven, 1963), pp. 195–99.

December 17th, 1832.—Having now finished with Patagonia and the Falkland Islands, I will describe our first arrival in Tierra del Fuego. A little after noon we doubled Cape St. Diego, and entered the famous strait of Le Maire. We kept close to the Fuegian shore, but the outline of the rugged, inhospitable Statenland was visible amidst the clouds. In the afternoon we anchored in the Bay of Good Success. While entering we were saluted in a manner becoming the inhabitants of this savage land. A group of Fuegians partly concealed by the entangled forest, were perched on a wild point overhanging the sea; and as we passed by, they sprang up and waving their tattered cloaks sent forth a loud and sonorous shout. The savages followed the ship, and just before dark we saw their fire, and again heard their wild cry. The harbour consists of a fine piece of water half surrounded by low rounded mountains of clay-slate, which are covered to the water's edge by one dense gloomy forest. A single glance at the landscape was sufficient to show me how widely different it was from anything I had ever beheld. At night it blew a gale of wind, and heavy squalls from the mountains swept past us. It would have been a bad time out at sea, and we, as well as others, may call this Good Success Bay.

In the morning the Captain sent a party to communicate with the Fuegians. When we came within hail, one of the four natives who were present advanced to receive us, and began to shout most vehemently, wishing to direct us where to land. When we were on shore the party looked rather alarmed, but continued talking and making gestures with great rapidity. It was without exception the most curious and interesting spectacle I ever beheld: I could not have believed how wide was the difference between savage and civilized man: it is greater than between a wild and domesticated animal, inasmuch as in man there is a greater power of improvement. The chief spokesman was old, and appeared to be the head of the family; the three others were powerful young men, about six feet high. The women and children had been sent away. These Fuegians are a very different race from the stunted, miserable wretches farther westward; and they seem closely allied to the famous Patagonians of the Strait of Magellan. Their only garment consists of a mantle made of guanaco skin, with the wool outside: this they wear just thrown over their shoulders, leaving their persons as often exposed as covered. Their skin is of a dirty coppery red colour.

The old man had a fillet of white feathers tied round his head, which partly confined his black, coarse, and entangled hair. His face was crossed by two broad transverse bars; one, painted bright red, reached from ear to ear and included the upper lip; the other, white like chalk, extended above and parallel to the first, so that even his eyelids were thus coloured. The other two men were ornamented by streaks of black powder, made of charcoal. The party altogether closely resembled the devils which come on the stage in plays like Der Freischutz.

Their very attitudes were abject, and the expression of their countenances distrustful, surprised, and startled. After we had presented them with some scarlet cloth, which they immediately tied round their necks, they became good friends. This was shown by the old man patting our breasts, and making a chuckling kind of noise, as people do when feeding chickens. I walked with the old man, and this demonstration of friendship was repeated several times; it was concluded by three hard slaps, which were given me on the breast and back at the same time. He then bared his bosom for me to return the compliment, which being done, he seemed highly pleased. The language of these people, according to our notions, scarcely deserves to be called articulate. Captain Cook has compared it to a man clearing his throat, but certainly no European ever cleared his throat with so many hoarse, guttural, and clicking sounds.

They are excellent mimics: as often as we coughed or yawned, or made any odd motion, they immediately imitated us. Some of our party began to squint and look awry; but one of the young Fuegians (whose whole face was painted black, excepting a white band across his eyes) succeeded in making far more hideous grimaces. They could repeat with perfect correctness each word in any sentence we addressed them, and they remembered such words for some time. Yet we Europeans all know how difficult it is to distinguish apart the sounds in a foreign language. Which of us, for instance, could follow an American Indian through a sentence of more than three words? All savages appear to possess, to an uncommon degree, this power of mimicry. I was told, almost in the same words, of the same ludicrous habit among the Caffres: the Australians, likewise, have long been notorious for being able to imitate and describe the gait of any man, so that he may be recognized. How can this faculty be explained? is it a consequence of the more practised habits of perception and keener senses, common to all men in a savage state, as compared with those long civilized?

When a song was struck up by our party, I thought the Fuegians would have fallen down with astonishment. With equal surprise they viewed our dancing; but one of the young men, when asked, had no objection to a little waltzing. Little accustomed to Europeans as they appeared to be, yet they knew and dreaded our fire-arms; nothing would tempt them to take a gun in their hands. They begged for knives, calling them by the Spanish word "cuchilla." They explained also what they wanted, by acting as if they had a piece of blubber in their mouth, and then pretending to cut instead of tear it.

I have not as yet noticed the Fuegians whom we had on board. During the former voyage of the Adventure and Beagle in 1826 to 1830, Captain Fitz Roy seized on a party of natives, as hostages for the loss of a boat, which had been stolen, to the great jeopardy of a party employed on the survey; and some of these natives, as well as a child whom he bought for a pearl-button, he took with him to England, determining to educate them and instruct them in religion at his own expense. To settle these natives in their own country, was one chief inducement to Captain Fitz Roy to undertake our present voyage; and before the Admiralty had resolved to send out this expedition, Captain Fitz Roy had generously chartered a vessel, and would himself have taken them back. The natives were accompanied by a missionary, R. Matthews; of whom and of the natives, Captain Fitz Roy has published a full and excellent account.[1] Two men, one of whom died in England of the small-pox, a boy and a little girl, were originally taken; and we had now on board, York Minster, Jemmy Button (whose name expresses his purchase-money), and Fuegia Basket. York Minster was a full-grown, short, thick, powerful man: his disposition was reserved, taciturn, morose, and when excited violently passionate; his affections were very strong towards a few friends on board; his intellect good. Jemmy Button was a universal favourite, but likewise passionate; the expression of his face at once showed his nice disposition. He was merry and often laughed, and was remarkably sympathetic with any one in pain: when the water was rough, I was often a little sea-sick, and he used to come to me and say in a plaintive voice, "Poor, poor fellow!" but the notion, after his aquatic life, of a man being sea-sick, was too ludicrous, and he was generally obliged to turn on one side to hide a smile or laugh, and then he would repeat his "Poor, poor fellow!" He was of a patriotic disposition; and he liked to praise his own tribe and country, in which he truly said there were "plenty of trees," and he abused all the other tribes: he stoutly declared that there was no Devil in his land. Jemmy was short, thick, and fat, but vain of his personal appearance; he used always to wear gloves, his hair was neatly cut, and he was distressed if his well-polished shoes were dirtied. He was fond of admiring himself in a looking glass; and a merry-faced little Indian boy from the Rio Negro, whom we had for some months on board, soon perceived this, and used to mock him: Jemmy, who was always rather jealous of the attention paid to this little boy, did not at all like this, and used to say, with rather a contemptuous twist of his head, "Too much skylark." It seems yet wonderful to me, when I think over all his many good qualities, that he should have been of the same race, and doubtless partaken of the same character, with the miserable, degraded savages whom we first

[1][Captain Fitz Roy describes the Fuegians who visited England in his *Narrative of the Surveying Voyages of His Majesty's Ships Adventure and Beagle, Between the Years 1826 and 1836, Describing Their Examination of the Southern Shores of South America, and the Beagle's Circumnavigation of the Globe,* II (London, 1839), 4–13. He also (pp. 175–201) gives an excellent ethnographic survey of the Yahgans in addition to providing details of other South American Indian peoples. Actually, Darwin's *Journal,* from which the present selection was taken, is the third volume in the three volume report begun by Captain Fitz Roy. However, Darwin's volume published originally in 1840 has been reprinted many times while Fitz Roy's two have not. Anyone interested in seeing the number of editions of this and other works of Darwin should consult R. B. Freeman, *The Works of Charles Darwin; An Annotated Bibliographical Handlist* (London, 1965).—*Ed. Note.*]

met here. Lastly, Fuegia Basket was a nice, modest, reserved young girl, with a rather pleasing but sometimes sullen expression, and very quick in learning anything, especially languages. This she showed in picking up some Portuguese and Spanish, when left on shore for only a short time at Rio de Janeiro and Monte Video, and in her knowledge of English. York Minster was very jealous of any attention paid to her; for it was clear he determined to marry her as soon as they were settled on shore.

Although all three could both speak and understand a good deal of English, it was singularly difficult to obtain much information from them, concerning the habits of their countrymen: this was partly owing to their apparent difficulty in understanding the simplest alternative. Every one accustomed to very young children, knows how seldom one can get an answer even to so simple a question as whether a thing is black *or* white; the idea of black or white seems alternately to fill their minds. So it was with these Fuegians, and hence it was generally impossible to find out, by cross-questioning, whether one had rightly understood anything which they had asserted. Their sight was remarkably acute: it is well known that sailors, from long practice, can make out a distant object much better than a landsman; but both York and Jemmy were much superior to any sailor on board: several times they have declared what some distant object has been, and though doubted by every one, they have proved right, when it has been examined through a telescope. They were quite conscious of this power; and Jemmy, when he had any little quarrel with the officer on watch, would say, "Me see ship, me no tell."

It was interesting to watch the conduct of the savages, when we landed, towards Jemmy Button: they immediately perceived the difference between him and ourselves, and held much conversation one with another on the subject. The old man addressed a long harangue to Jemmy, which it seems was to invite him to stay with them. But Jemmy understood very little of their language, and was, moreover, thoroughly ashamed of his countrymen. When York Minster afterwards came on shore, they noticed him in the same way, and told him he ought to shave; yet he had not twenty dwarf hairs on his face, whilst we all wore our untrimmed beards. They examined the colour of his skin, and compared it with ours. One of our arms being bared, they expressed the liveliest surprise and admiration at its whiteness, just in the same way in which I have seen the ourang-outang do at the Zoological Gardens. We thought that they mistook two or three of the officers, who were rather shorter and fairer, though adorned with large beards, for the ladies of our party. The tallest amongst the Fuegians was evidently much pleased at his height being noticed. When placed back to back with the tallest of the boat's crew, he tried his best to edge on higher ground, and to stand on tiptoe. He opened his mouth to show his teeth, and turned his face for a side view; and all this was done with such alacrity, that I dare say he thought himself the handsomest man in Tierra del Fuego. After our first feeling of grave astonishment was over, nothing could be more ludicrous than the odd mixture of surprise and imitation which these savages every moment exhibited....

The Fuegian wigwam resembles, in size and dimensions, a haycock. It merely consists of a few broken branches stuck in the ground, and very imperfectly thatched on one side with a few tufts of grass and rushes. The whole cannot be the work of an hour, and it is only used for a few days. At Goeree Roads I saw a place where one of these naked men had slept, which absolutely offered no more cover than the form of a hare. The man was evidently living by himself, and York Minster said he was "very bad man," and that probably he had stolen something. On the west coast, however, the wigwams are rather better, for they are covered with seal-skins. We were detained here several days by the bad weather. The climate is certainly wretched: the summer solstice was now passed, yet every day snow fell on the hills, and in the valleys there was rain, accompanied by sleet. The thermometer generally stood about 45°, but in the night fell to 38° or 40°. From the damp and boisterous state of the atmosphere, not cheered by a gleam of sunshine, one fancied the climate even worse than it really was.

While going one day on shore near Wollaston Island, we pulled alongside a canoe with six Fuegians. These were the most abject and miserable creatures I anywhere beheld. On the east coast the natives, as we have seen, have guanaco cloaks, and on the west they possess seal-skins. Amongst these central tribes the men generally have an otter-skin, or some small scrap about as large as a pocket-handkerchief, which is barely sufficient to cover their backs as low down as their loins. It is laced across the breast by strings, and according as the wind blows, it is shifted from side to side. But these Fuegians in the canoe were quite naked, and even one full-grown woman was absolutely so. It was raining heavily, and the fresh water, together with the spray, trickled down her body. In another harbour not far distant, a woman, who was suckling a recently-born child, came one day alongside the vessel, and remained there out of mere curiosity, whilst the sleet fell and thawed on her naked bosom, and on the skin of her naked baby! These poor wretches were stunted in their growth, their hideous faces bedaubed with white paint, their skins filthy and greasy, their hair entangled, their voices discordant, and their gestures violent. Viewing such men, one can hardly make one's self believe that they are fellow-creatures, and inhabitants of the same world. It is a common subject of conjecture what pleasure in life some of the lower animals can enjoy: how much more reasonably the same question may be asked with respect to these barbarians! At night, five or six human beings, naked and scarcely protected from the wind and rain of this tempestuous climate, sleep on the wet ground coiled up like animals. Whenever it is low water, winter or summer, night or day, they must rise to pick shell-fish from the rocks; and the women either dive to collect sea-eggs, or sit patiently in their canoes, and with a baited hair-line without any hook, jerk out little fish. If a seal is killed, or the floating carcass of a putrid whale is discovered, it is a feast; and such miserable food is assisted by a few tasteless berries and fungi.

They often suffer from famine: I heard Mr. Low, a sealing-master intimately acquainted with the natives of this country, give a curious account of the state of a party of one hundred and fifty natives on the west coast, who were very thin and in great distress. A succession of gales prevented the women from getting shell-fish on the rocks, and they could not go out in their canoes to catch seal. A small party of these men one morning set out, and the other Indians explained to him, that they were going a four day's journey for food: on their return, Low went to meet them, and he found them excessively tired, each man carrying a great square piece of putrid whale's-blubber with a hole in the middle, through which they put their heads, like the Gauchos do through their ponchos or cloaks. As soon as the blubber was brought into a wigwam, an old man cut off thin slices, and muttering over them, broiled them for a minute, and distributed them to the famished party, who during this time preserved a profound silence. Mr. Low believes that whenever a whale is cast on shore, the natives bury large pieces of it in the sand, as a resource in time of famine; and a native boy, whom he had on board, once found a stock thus buried. The different tribes when at war are cannibals. From the concurrent, but quite independent evidence of the boy taken by Mr. Low, and of Jemmy Button, it is certainly true, that when pressed in winter by hunger, they kill and devour their old women before they kill their dogs: the boy, being asked by Mr. Low why they did this, answered, "Doggies catch otters, old women no." This boy described the manner in which they are killed by being held over smoke and thus choked; he imitated their screams as a joke, and described the parts of their bodies which are considered best to eat. Horrid as such a death by the hands of their friends and relatives must be, the fears of the old women, when hunger begins to press, are more painful to think of; we are told that they then often run away into the mountains, but that they are pursued by the men and brought back to the slaughter-house at their own firesides!

Captain Fitz Roy could never ascertain that the Fuegians have any distinct belief in a future life. They sometimes bury their dead in caves, and sometimes in the mountain forests; we do not know what ceremonies they perform. Jemmy Button would not eat land-birds, because "eat dead men:" they are unwilling even to mention their dead friends. We have no reason to believe that they perform any sort of religious worship; though perhaps the muttering of the old man before he distributed the putrid blubber to his famished party, may be of this nature. Each family or tribe has a wizard or conjuring doctor, whose office we could never clearly ascertain. Jemmy believed in dreams, though not, as I have said, in the devil: I do not think that our Fuegians were much more superstitious than some of the sailors; for an old quartermaster firmly believed that the successive heavy gales, which we encountered off Cape Horn, were caused by our having the Fuegians on board. The nearest approach to a religious feeling which I heard of, was shown by York Minster, who, when Mr. Bynoe shot some very young ducklings as specimens, declared in the most solemn manner, "Oh, Mr. Bynoe, much rain, snow, blow much." This was evidently a retributive punishment for wasting human food. In a wild and excited manner he also related, that his brother, one day whilst returning to pick up some dead birds which he had left on the coast, observed some feathers blown by the wind. His brother said (York imitating his manner), "What that?" and crawling onwards, he peeped over the cliff, and saw "wild man" picking his birds; he crawled a little nearer, and then hurled down a great stone and killed him. York declared for a long time afterwards storms raged, and much rain and snow fell. As far as we could make out, he seemed to consider the elements themselves as the avenging agents: it is evident in this case, how naturally, in a race a little more advanced in culture, the elements would become personified. What the "bad wild men" were, has always appeared to me most mysterious: from what York said, when we found the place like the form of a hare, where a single man had slept the night before, I should have thought that they were thieves who had been driven from their tribes; but other obscure speeches made me doubt this; I have sometimes imagined that the most probable explanation was that they were insane.

The different tribes have no government or chief; yet each is surrounded by other hostile tribes, speaking different dialects, and separated from each other only by a deserted border or neutral territory: the cause of their warfare appears to be the means of subsistence. Their country is a broken mass of wild rocks, lofty hills, and useless forests: and these are viewed through mists and endless storms. The habitable land is reduced to the stones on the beach; in search of food they are compelled unceasingly to wander from spot to spot, and so steep is the coast, that they can only move about in their wretched canoes. They cannot know the feeling of having a home, and still less that of domestic affection; for the husband is to the wife a brutal master to a laborious slave. Was a more horrid deed ever perpetrated, than that witnessed on the west coast by Byron, who saw a wretched mother pick up her bleeding dying infant-boy, whom her husband had mercilessly dashed on the stones for dropping a basket of sea-eggs! How little can the higher powers of the mind be brought into play: what is there for imagination to picture, for reason to compare, for judgment to decide upon? to knock a limpet from the rock does not require even cunning, that lowest power of the mind. Their skill in some respects may be compared to the instinct of animals; for it is not improved by experience: the canoe, their most ingenious work, poor as it is, has remained the same, as we know from Drake, for the last two hundred and fifty years.

Whilst beholding these savages, one asks, whence have they come? What could have tempted, or what change compelled a tribe of men, to leave the fine regions of the north, to travel down the Cordillera or backbone of America, to invent and build canoes, which are not used by the tribes of Chile, Peru, and Brazil, and then to enter on one of the most inhospitable countries within the limits of the globe? Although such reflections must at first seize on the mind, yet we may feel sure that they are partly erroneous. There is no reason to believe that the Fuegians decrease in number; therefore we must suppose that they enjoy a sufficient share of happiness, of whatever kind it may be, to render life worth having. Nature by making habit omnipotent, and its effects hereditary, has fitted the Fuegian to the climate and the productions of his miserable country. . . .

January 15th, 1833.—The Beagle anchored in Goeree Roads. Captain Fitz Roy having resolved to settle the Fuegians, according to their wishes, in Ponsonby Sound, four boats were equipped to carry them there through the Beagle Channel. This channel, which was discovered by Captain Fitz Roy during the last voyage, is a most remarkable feature in the geography of this, or indeed of any other country: it may be compared to the valley of Lochness in Scotland, with its chain of lakes and friths. It is about one hundred and twenty miles long, with an average breadth, not subject to any very great variation, of about two miles; and is throughout the greater part so perfectly straight, that the view, bounded on each side by a line of mountains, gradually becomes indistinct in the long distance. It crosses the southern part of Tierra del Fuego in an east and west line, and in the middle is joined at right angles on the south side by an irregular channel, which has been called Ponsonby Sound. This is the residence of Jemmy Button's tribe and family.

19th.—Three whale-boats and the yawl, with a party of twenty-eight, started under the command of Captain Fitz Roy. In the afternoon we entered the eastern mouth of the channel, and shortly afterwards found a snug little cove concealed by some surrounding islets. Here we pitched our tents and lighted our fires. Nothing could look more comfortable than this scene. The glassy water of the little harbour, with the branches of the trees hanging over the rocky beach, the boats at anchor, the tents supported by the crossed oars, and the smoke curling up the wooded valley, formed a picture of quiet retirement. The next day (20th) we smoothly glided onwards in our little fleet, and came to a more inhabited district. Few if any of these natives could ever have seen a white man; certainly nothing could exceed their astonishment at the apparition of the four boats. Fires were lighted on every point (hence the name of Tierra del Fuego, or the land of fire), both to attract our attention and to spread far and wide the news. Some of the men ran for miles along the shore. I shall never forget how wild and savage one group appeared: suddenly four or five men came to the edge of an overhanging cliff; they were absolutely naked, and their long hair streamed about their faces; they held rugged staffs in their hands, and, springing from the ground, they waved their arms round their heads, and sent forth the most hideous yells.

At dinner-time we landed among a party of Fuegians. At first they were not inclined to be friendly; for until the Captain pulled in ahead of the other boats, they kept their slings in their hands. We soon, however, delighted them by trifling presents, such as tying red tape round their heads. They liked our biscuit: but one of the savages touched with his finger some of the meat preserved in tin cases which I was eating, and feeling it soft and cold, showed as much disgust at it, as I should have done at putrid blubber. Jemmy was thoroughly ashamed of his countrymen, and declared his own tribe were quite different, in which he was wofully mistaken. It was as easy to please as it was difficult to satisfy these savages. Young and old, men and children, never ceased repeating the word "yammerschooner," which means "give me." After pointing to almost every object, one after the other, even to the buttons on our coats, and saying their favourite word in as many intonations as possible, they would then use it in a neuter sense, and vacantly repeat "yammerschooner." After yammerschoonering for any article very eagerly, they would by a simple artifice point to their young women or little children, as much as to say, "If you will not give it me, surely you will to such as these."

At night we endeavoured in vain to find an uninhabited cove; and at last were obliged to bivouac not far from a party of natives. They were very inoffensive as long as they were few in numbers, but in the morning (21st) being joined by others they showed symptoms of hostility, and we thought that we should have come to a skirmish. An European labours under great disadvantages when treating with savages like these, who have not the least idea of the power of fire-arms. In the very act of levelling his musket he appears to the savage far inferior to a man armed with a bow and arrow, a spear, or even a sling. Nor is it easy to teach them our superiority except by striking a fatal blow. Like wild beasts, they do not appear to' compare numbers; for each individual, if attacked, instead of retiring, will endeavour to dash your brains out with a stone, as certainly as a tiger under similar circumstances would tear you. Captain Fitz Roy on one occasion being very anxious, from good reasons, to frighten away a small party, first flourished a cutlass near them, at which they only laughed; he then twice fired his pistol close to a native. The man both times looked astounded, and carefully but quickly rubbed his head; he then stared awhile, and gabbled to his companions, but he never seemed to think of running away. We can hardly put ourselves in the position of these savages, and understand their actions. In the case of this Fuegian, the possibility of such a sound as the report of a gun close to his ear could never have entered his mind. He perhaps literally did not for a second know whether it was a sound or a blow, and therefore very naturally rubbed his head. In a similar manner, when a savage sees a mark struck by a bullet, it may be some time before he is able at all to understand how it is effected; for the fact of a body being invisible from its velocity would perhaps be to him an idea totally inconceivable. Moreover, the extreme force of a bullet, that penetrates a hard substance without tearing it, may convince the savage that it has no force at all. Certainly I believe that many savages of the lowest grade, such as these of Tierra del Fuego, have seen objects struck, and even small animals killed by the musket, without being in the least aware how deadly an instrument it is. . . .

Jemmy was now in a district well known to him, and guided the boats to a quiet pretty cove named Woollya, surrounded by islets, every one of which and every point had its proper native name. We found here a family of Jemmy's tribe, but not his relations: we made friends with them; and in the evening they sent a canoe to inform Jemmy's mother and brothers. . . .

The next morning after our arrival (the 24th) the Fuegians began to pour in, and Jemmy's mother and brothers arrived. Jemmy recognised the stentorian voice of one of his brothers at a prodigious distance. The meeting was less interesting than that between a horse, turned out into a field, when he joins an old companion. There was no demonstration of affection; they simply stared for a short time at each other; and the mother immediately went to look after her canoe. We heard, however, through York that the mother has been inconsolable for the loss of Jemmy, and had searched everywhere for him, thinking that he might have been left after having been taken in the boat. The women took much notice of and were very kind to Fuegia. We had already perceived that Jemmy had almost forgotten his own language. I should think there was scarcely another human being with so small a stock of language, for his English was very imperfect. It was laughable, but almost pitiable, to hear him speak to his wild brother in English, and then ask him in Spanish ("no sabe?") whether he did not understand him.

Everything went on peaceably during the three next days, whilst the gardens were digging and wigwams building. We estimated the number of natives at about one hundred and twenty. The women worked hard, whilst the men lounged about all day long, watching us. They asked for everything they saw, and stole what they could. They were delighted at our dancing and singing, and were particularly interested at seeing us wash in a neighbouring brook; they did not pay much attention to anything else, not even to our boats. . . .

On the 5th of March, we anchored in a cove at Woollya, but we saw not a soul there. We were alarmed at this, for the natives in Ponsonby Sound showed by gestures, that there had been fighting; and we afterwards heard that the dreaded Oens men had made a descent. Soon a canoe, with a little flag flying, was seen approaching, with one of the men in it washing the paint off his face. This man was poor Jemmy,—now a thin, haggard savage, with long disordered hair, and naked, except a bit of blanket round his waist. We did not recognize him till he was close to us, for he was ashamed of himself, and turned his back to the ship. We had left him plump, fat, clean, and well-dressed;—I never saw so complete and grievous a change. As soon however as he was clothed, and the first flurry was over, things wore a good appearance. He dined with Captain Fitz Roy, and ate his dinner as tidily as formerly. He told us that he had "too much" (meaning enough) to eat, that he was not cold, that his relations were very good people, and that he did not wish to go back to England: in the evening we found out the cause of this great change in Jemmy's feelings, in the arrival of his young and nice-looking wife. With his usual good feeling, he brought two beautiful otter-skins for two of his best friends, and some spear-heads and arrows made with his own hands for the Captain. He said he had built a canoe for himself, and he boasted that he could talk a little of his own language! But it is a most singular fact, that he appears to have taught all his tribe some English: an old man spontaneously announced "Jemmy Button's wife." Jemmy had lost all his property. He told us that York Minster had built a large canoe, and with his wife Fuegia,[2] had several months since gone

2Captain Sulivan, who, since his voyage in the Beagle, has been employed on the survey of the Falkland Islands, heard from a sealer in (1842?), that when in the western part of the Strait of Magellan, he was astonished by a native woman coming on board, who could talk some English. Without doubt this was Fuegia Basket. She lived (I fear the term probably bears a double interpretation) some days on board.

to his own country, and had taken farewell by an act of consummate villainy; he persuaded Jemmy and his mother to come with him, and then on the way deserted them by night, stealing every article of their property.

Jemmy went to sleep on shore, and in the morning returned, and remained on board till the ship got under way, which frightened his wife, who continued crying violently till he got into his canoe. He returned loaded with valuable property. Every soul on board was heartily sorry to shake hands with him for the last time. I do not now doubt that he will be as happy as, perhaps happier than, if he had never left his own country. Every one must sincerely hope that Captain Fitz Roy's noble hope may be fulfilled, of being rewarded for the many generous sacrifices which he made for these Fuegians, by some shipwrecked sailor being protected by the descendants of Jemmy Button and his tribe! When Jemmy reached the shore, he lighted a signal fire, and the smoke curled up, bidding us a last and long farewell, as the ship stood on her course into the open sea.

The perfect equality among the individuals composing the Fuegian tribes must for a long time retard their civilization. As we see those animals, whose instinct compels them to live in society and obey a chief, are most capable of improvement, so is it with the races of mankind. Whether we look at it as a cause or a consequence, the more civilized always have the most artificial governments. For instance, the inhabitants of Otaheite, who, when first discovered, were governed by hereditary kings, had arrived at a far higher grade than another branch of the same people, the New Zealanders, —who, although benefited by being compelled to turn their attention to agriculture, were republicans in the most absolute sense. In Tierra del Fuego, until some chief shall arise with power sufficient to secure any acquired advantage, such as the domesticated animals, it seems scarcely possible that the political state of the country can be improved. At present, even a piece of cloth given to one is torn into shreds and distributed; and no one individual becomes richer than another. On the other hand, it is difficult to understand how a chief can arise till there is property of some sort by which he might manifest his superiority and increase his power.

I believe, in this extreme part of South America, man exists in a lower state of improvement than in any other part of the world. The South Sea Islanders, of the two races inhabiting the Pacific, are comparatively civilized. The Esquimaux, in his subterranean hut, enjoys some of the comforts of life, and in his canoe, when fully equipped, manifests much skill. Some of the tribes of Southern Africa, prowling about in search of roots, and living concealed on the wild and arid plains, are sufficiently wretched. The Australian, in the simplicity of the arts of life, comes nearest the Fuegian: he can, however, boast of his boomerang, his spear and throwing-stick, his method of climbing trees, of tracking animals, and of hunting. Although the Australian may be superior in acquirements, it by no means follows that he is likewise superior in mental capacity: indeed, from what I saw of the Fuegians when on board, and from what I have read of the Australians, I should think the case was exactly the reverse.

Frank Hives

IBO PUNISHMENTS FOR ADULTERY

Although the prescientific period has ended, prescientific attitudes still persist among those observers who have not had the advantages of anthropological training. Missionaries and other representatives of Western societies continue to describe the peoples with whom they work and live. Thus the ethnocentric biases of the earlier reports continue unabated. Frank Hives was a District Commissioner in Nigeria around the turn of the century, when part of the "white man's burden" entailed the recording of native customs. The rationale was that such collections would facilitate the implementation of colonial administrative policies. It should be noted that anthropologists sometimes have difficulty in establishing rapport with prospective informants because of the existence of such a philosophy. Informants fear (and perhaps rightly so) that the information they provide anthropologists will come back to haunt them in the form of oppressive governmental regulations. Add to this the fallacious notion that anthropologists study only "primitive peoples"—and what modern African would delight in being described by such an epithet—and one can see what some of the many obstacles confronting the contemporary anthropologist in the field are.

For further information about the Ibo, who number more than four million and are one of the largest of Nigeria's ethnic groups, see Daryll Forde and G. I. Jones, *The Ibo and Ibibio-speaking Peoples of South-eastern Nigeria* (London, 1950), M. M. Green, *Ibo Village Affairs* (London, 1947), Simon Ottenberg, "Supplementary Bibliography on the Ibo-speaking People of South-eastern Nigeria," *African Studies*, **14** (1955), 63–85, and Ottenberg, "The Present State of Ibo Studies," *Journal of the Historical Society of Nigeria*, **2** (1961), 211–30.

I propose now to describe some of the horrible customs practised under the native customary code for adultery with a chief's wife, before officials of the Government put a stop to such atrocities. Readers who are distressed by the reading of gruesome and repulsive details are seriously advised to pass over this chapter.

I gathered information regarding the punishments for adultery with chiefs' wives from some of the chiefs themselves who had become enlight-

Reprinted from Frank Hives, *Justice in the Jungle* (London, 1932), pp. 31–39, by permission of The Bodley Head, Ltd.

ened. This was part of the collection of data about native laws and customs which the District Commissioners were instructed by the Government to make, with a view to publishing it in book form. If I am not mistaken, the work for some reason or other was never completed.

My informants made no bones whatever about describing these punishments to me down to the most minute details. They evidently considered the tortures meted out quite right and proper, especially as they had no other form of redress, and as examples had to be made so as to deter others.

Although no actual cases were brought to my notice—which was not surprising—I was shown the ju-ju pool[1] where the "sacred" crocodiles grew fat on the bodies of poor wretches supplied to them from time to time. I also saw the sacrificial trees upon which the guilty parties were offered up. These trees were grown for this particular purpose. They were generally planted on the edge of one of the main roads leading into the market-place, so that all who passed by could see and take warning. Then there were the posts outside the ju-ju, or meeting-house to which the man and the woman were bound until they had practically eaten each other alive.

The customs I am about to describe were observed in those days in the Bende District. The Ibo tribe which lived there was then very much under the thumb of the Aros, but it is quite a different people now. Before I left the country a Mission Church stood near the site of the ju-ju house which had been torn down years previously. The sacrificial trees were no longer used for the evil purpose for which they were originally grown. The pool, I presume, is still in existence, but the loathsome creatures which disported themselves there, fed with such gruesome food, must have long since died out.

One of the punishments was as follows, carried out after the parties accused of adultery had been arraigned before the chiefs, elders and ju-ju priests of the town, and found guilty. The man and the woman were stripped naked. Then, in the presence of their judges, their accusers and the assembled audience, to the noise of drums and the chanting of the crowd, they were made to lie on the floor in the centre of the ju-ju house and repeat the act for which they were found guilty. If they refused to comply with this order of their own will and accord the executioners forced them into position. While they were committing the act, or while they were presumed to be doing so, the executioners bound them together in that posture with tie-tie ropes around their bodies.

---

[1][Hives uses "ju-ju" essentially as a synonym for "sacred." A ju-ju is a charm or fetish. See Frank Hives, *Ju-ju and Justice in Nigeria* (London, 1930) for further examples. Interestingly enough, the concept of ju-ju figures prominently in an unusual novel. The unlikely plot involves a man who mates with a newly discovered "missing link" female. When a "son" is born, the man is so repulsed that he kills it. The novel is concerned with the trial of the man. Was the fruit of this union an animal or a human? If the latter, then the man is guilty of murder. Since man had not ever been defined by English law, the trial was an attempt to do so. One of the key factors is that the "missing link" creatures do *not* have ju-ju's, the implication being that ju-ju's or religion are a human characteristic. See Vercors, *You Shall Know Them* (Boston, 1953) for this literary exercise in defining man.—*Ed. Note.*]

There was a lapse of time while the beating of tom-toms and the singing of the assembly became louder and quicker, and the people executed a dance around the trussed pair. Then, at a signal from the ju-ju priest, the executioners advanced with a sharp, hard, wooden stake, about five feet long, and a heavy billet of wood. The sharpened end of the stake was placed on the middle of the bound man's back, held in position there by one of the executioners, and slowly hammered into the body by another executioner with the wooden billet. The stake went through the man's body and then through the woman's, the screams of the victims being drowned by the beating of tom-toms and yells from the dancing crowd around them.

When the stake protruded a foot or two from the woman's body, the executioners seized it by either end, and lifting the writhing couple from the ground, proceeded to carry them to the sacred pool. They were followed by the crowd which took delight in catching the victims by the hair of their heads and pulling it downward so that the bodies rotated on the stake.

The procession having arrived at the sacred pool, the ju-ju priest called upon its denizens to come forth and receive their sacrifice. Then, with a heave from the strong arms of the executioners, and amidst the final yells of the crowd, the bound victims were thrown together into the pool where the loathsome reptiles awaited them. There was a splash, a disturbance of the water, a few bubbles rose to the surface, and the face of the pool became calm once more.

Or there was another punishment. After the couple had been found guilty they were stripped of what scanty clothing they might have on and were led through the village, preceded by the village crier, who would "cry" the offence of which the unfortunate couple had been found guilty as well as the punishment decreed for them. They were soon surrounded by a dancing and yelling crowd who were permitted to cuff, to beat with sticks, and in other lewd and disgusting ways to manhandle, the guilty couple on their way to the sacrificial trees.

These young and supple trees, or straight saplings, had been planted three or four feet apart. The female victim was thrown face upward on the ground, her legs and arms stretched out to their fullest extent. She was held there while the man was being treated in the same manner. He was then lifted up and placed on top of the woman, in such a way that his face came between her thighs and hers between his.

In this position they were lashed to the trees, their limbs fully extended, forming a figure like the letter X. Together in this ghastly and lewd position they were left to starve, in a broiling tropical sun, tormented by the bites of ants, mosquitoes and other insects, parched with thirst. They were in full view of the hundreds of passers-by, not one of whom would dare defy the ju-ju by giving them release from their sufferings or by offering them a sip of water. They were pariahs, outcasts, being punished for the outrageous crime they had committed.

There they hung until death freed them from their agonies. My informants told me that the man usually died first because, I presume, he was hanging head downwards. The woman often lingered about two days more, lashed to a putrefying corpse, until she also died. Even then it was a crime for anyone to touch the bodies which hung on the trees until they rotted and fell to the ground to become food for the wandering half-wild pigs and scavenger dogs of the village.

One might imagine that no more horrible torture and death could be devised by mortal man, savage or civilised. Yet the third form of punishment inflicted on these adulterers was the most diabolical of them all, and it seems hardly possible that even the most debased savage could invent anything so fiendish.

The guilty couple having been sentenced, they were each tied to a post about five feet high which was sunk in the ground. These posts were erected in the ju-ju house or somewhere near it. The condemned wretches were stripped naked and tightly bound so that they could not move hand or foot; the posts about four feet apart and the victims facing one another.

Executioners and guards, relieved at intervals, were put in charge of them. The man and the woman were allowed nothing whatever to eat, but they could have as much water to drink as they desired, and the water was always well salted. After perhaps twenty-four hours or more, when they were both ravenously hungry, one of the torturers would ask the man if he wanted food and he would naturally say yes. Whereupon the torturer would draw his matchet and proceed to hack off a portion of the woman's breasts with it, putting the piece of flesh into the man's mouth to eat. As his hands were tied to the posts he could not resist. Another torturer meanwhile applied a mixture of clay and chalk to the wound in the woman's breast so as to stop the bleeding.

Then the woman would be asked if she were hungry. Upon a reply in the affirmative a piece of flesh was cut off some part of the man's body, care being taken that none of the arteries and big veins were severed in the operation. The flesh was put into the woman's mouth while clay and chalk was being applied to the man's wound.

So the ordeal went on until they had practically devoured each other alive. The survivor continued to be fed on the flesh of the dead partner for so long as life remained.

A number of other details connected with this ghastly torture were given me by my informants without the slightest qualm, but they are too horrible to repeat. Even at that I doubt whether I was told them all. I had heard quite enough and took care not to press for more.

It is something to know that these dreadful practices were put a stop to years ago. Though some of the chiefs may still make use of their wives for profit. . . , even that is better than a continuance of such devilish tortures. It must be remembered that among savage races life is of no consequence at all. The killing of a slave, a malefactor or an enemy means nothing to them.

From the
library to the
field

$\mathcal{T}$he beginning of the scientific study of man might be said to have occurred when individual scholars started to survey the rapidly increasing amount of ethnographic data gathered by travelers, missionaries, and others. Most of these scholars were strictly armchair anthropologists who rarely, if ever, forsook the comforts of their libraries. It was in this tradition that Edward B. Tylor and James George Frazer worked. From the incredible assortment of ethnographic bits and pieces, these scholars, along with their colleagues, tried to find order. Sometimes theories were constructed and imposed upon the data; sometimes the theories came from the data. But regardless of the validity of individual theories, it was the intellectual ferment stimulated by men like Tylor and Frazer that eventually led to cultural anthropologists' going to the field.

Leaving the library to go into the field was a step in the study of man, the importance of which cannot be exaggerated. True, travelers and missionaries had been in the field before this time, but they did not go into the field for the express purpose of studying man. This is the critical point. It was only when individuals went into the field to study—rather than convert or exploit—a people that the modern scientific approach to cultural anthropology really began to develop. Fieldwork is the hallmark of the professional anthropologist. Often he becomes an acknowledged expert on "his" people. (Typically, the anthropologist assumes a proprietary attitude toward the people he has studied!) In contrast, the amateur has visited peoples of the world only through the pages of books written by others. It should be noted, however, that library and fieldwork are not mutually exclusive. They are both necessary and are, in fact, reciprocally enriching. Before the anthropologist goes into the field, he normally reads up on his people or on his proposed topic (assuming there is anything in print). Then he goes into the field for one or two years to live among a people. Upon his return, he may well go to library sources to see how the data he has gathered confirms or corrects what has previously been written on the subject. In this way, each generation of anthropologists adds to our total knowledge of man and culture.

Edward B. Tylor

ON A METHOD OF INVESTIGATING THE DEVELOPMENT OF INSTITUTIONS: APPLIED TO LAWS OF MARRIAGE AND DESCENT

This is a classic paper. In it, Edward B. Tylor, one of the founders of modern anthropology, attempts to find meaningful correlations between hitherto unrelated facts. These correlations, or adhesions as Tylor terms them, are not mere guesses on Tylor's part, for he tested statistically each proposed correlation. Even though Tylor did not have data available from a majority of the peoples of the world, he did use approximately 350 cultures, and, in any case, his methodology, given the limited nature of his data, was exemplary. In this brilliant exposition, Tylor takes a custom like avoidance behavior (in which an individual is required to avoid seeing or speaking to a certain relative) and attempts to correlate it with the pattern of residence after marriage.

Tylor's concern is primarily with what he calls laws of marriage and descent. These topics are normally considered by contemporary anthropologists to fall under the rubric of what

Reprinted from the *Journal of the Royal Anthropological Institute of Great Britain and Ireland*, 18 (1889), 245–72, by permission of the Royal Anthropological Institute.

is termed social organization or social structure. If there is one aspect of culture which has challenged the imagination of anthropologists more than any other, that aspect is social structure in general and the study of kinship groups and terminology in particular. The ways in which human groups are organized and the implications of such systems of organization for behavior continue to remain a principal area of anthropological inquiry and analysis.

One part of the study of social organization concerns the definition of "family." Who is family or kin and who is not is a question answered differently by different peoples. Nowhere is it easier to demonstrate cultural relativism than in cross-cultural comparisons of family definitions. One must take care to distinguish biological and cultural categories here. Biologically, of course, a child is produced by two parents, but culturally speaking, he may belong to the family of just one parent. It is the latter practice that interested Tylor. The majority of the peoples of the world trace their descent through one parent, rather than both. Thus an individual child belongs either to his mother's family *or* to his father's family. Groups tracing their descent through mothers employ what anthropologists term *matrilineal descent*. Groups tracing their descent through fathers employ *patrilineal descent*. Both matrilineal and patrilineal descent, depending as they do upon one line rather than two, are unilateral schemes. Some societies, including our own, have bilateral descent in which a child belongs to both his father's and his mother's family. (However, even in our culture there is something of a patrilineal bias insofar as we take as surname or family name the cognomen of our fathers.)

It is not easy for people brought up under a bilateral system to grasp the significance of a unilateral descent system. For example, in a matrilineal descent system, the family head is usually not the biological father *since he does not belong to his child's mother's family* (except by marriage). Rather, the family head is frequently the child's mother's brother. It is therefore the child's mother's brother (the child's maternal uncle) who may make key decisions in the life of the child. Moreover, the system of inheritance may be closely related to the descent pattern. Thus, commonly in a matrilineal descent system, a son does not inherit the goods of his father, but rather the goods of his mother's brother. His father's goods in such a system would pass to a paternal uncle or a cousin. (From the son's perspective, his biological father's goods might be inherited by his father's sister's son.)

Another example of the importance of the descent system concerns marriage rules, and this is one of Tylor's great interests. In a matrilineal system where the children belong to the family of their mothers, but not their fathers, there may be a "preferred marriage" rule in which a male is expected to marry his mother's brother's daughter. In such a system, a man and his mother's brother's daughter are *not* members of the same family. The girl in this case would belong to *her mother's family*, not to her father's. Note that under our system this would be a first-cousin marriage, which, in fact, is considered incestuous by some and is forbidden by law in a number of areas. (This suggests that incest, which is a sexual relationship between persons too closely related to marry legally is defined differently in different cultures.) Notice also that such a preferred marriage in a matrilineal descent system neatly circumvents the inheritance rule previously mentioned. A man has to give his goods to his sister's son, but if that sister's son married the man's own daughter, this ensures that his goods remain in his "biological" family.

Among the first clues that indicated that families were defined differently in different cultures were the terms used to address and the terms used to refer to members of one's family. For example, in some societies, a man calls his mother and his mother's sisters by one and the same term. Such a kinship terminology is what Tylor and other anthropologists called a "classificatory" system. In such a system, generation is often the most important of several critical factors—another factor might be the sex of the individuals concerned. Thus, to cite one example, a man's mother and all her female relatives *of the same generation* are "classified" together under one term. A problem here is the translation of that term into the English term "mother." This is misleading because the native system may not involve an extension of our notion of mother to other relatives. Rather, the term refers to a whole category of female relatives of which one's biological mother is but one example. Certainly the people who have such a kinship terminology are well aware of the difference between biological mothers and these mothers' sisters or female cousins.

In reading Tylor's essay, one must remember that Tylor was deeply committed to evolutionary thinking. It is easy to see that his work is full of various evolutionary schemes. One of these is the theory that all peoples have evolved or are evolving in a one line (unilinear) evolutionary sequence, which consists of three successive stages: savagery, barbarism, and civilization. According to nineteenth-century unilinear evolutionary theory, all peoples passed or were passing through *identical* stages. Because the stages were identical, an ingenious type of historical reconstruction was possible. Nineteenth-century English culture was clearly an example of civilization. Since one of the goals of the anthropology of this period was historical reconstruction of the past, there was great interest in discovering what the ancestors of the English (and other civilized peoples) were like. The fact that there were no savage Englishmen running around didn't matter because any savage was as good as any other for purposes of study. The Australian aborigines, for example, were savages, and since the stage or state of savagery was considered to be a constant, one could know what the ancestors of the English must have been like by studying the present-day Australian aboriginals! This type of narrow Procrustean evolutionary scheme is no longer held by American anthropologists, who are more likely to believe in multilinear (many lines) than unilinear evolution. There are many possible paths of human development and there is no reason to equate Australian aboriginals with the ancestors of contemporary English gentlemen.

Another example of Tylor's evolutionary bias is his insistence that there were three successive stages of descent: matrilineal, matrilineal-patrilineal, and patrilineal (his terms are maternal, maternal-paternal, and paternal). Such an evolutionary scheme, speculative as it is, cannot be easily proven or disproven. At any rate, the interest in social organization (and other areas of cultural anthropology) today is not so much in origins (Where did such and such a custom start?), but in structure (What are the constituent units of the system and what are their interrelationships?) and in function (How does the system operate and what does it do for the people who live under it?).

If one can put aside some of Tylor's evolutionary extravagances (which are not at all unreasonable considering the time at which the paper was written), one can appreciate the exceptional insight Tylor had. It is a testament to his genius that many of the terms he proposed in this paper, e.g., teknonymy (the practice of addressing an adult in terms of the name of the adult's child—"mother of Carolyn" would be an example), have become standard terms.

Those who wish to read more of Tylor's work should definitely look at his *Primitive Culture: Researches into the Development of Mythology, Philosophy, Religion, Language, Art and Custom* which appeared in 1871 and is available in a paperback edition (New York, 1958). For a convenient sketch of Tylor's life and contributions to anthropology, see Abram Kardiner and Edward Preble, *They Studied Man* (New York, 1963), pp. 50–68. For further information about the study of social organization, see such works as George Peter Murdock, *Social Structure* (New York 1949), Claude Lévi-Strauss, *Les Structures Élémentaires de la Parenté* (Paris, 1949), and Elman R. Service, *Primitive Social Organization: An Evolutionary Perspective* (New York, 1962). For more recent attempts to discover adhesions or correlations between various cultural variables, see John W. M. Whiting and Irvin L. Child, *Child Training and Personality: A Cross-Cultural Study* (New Haven, 1953), William N. Stephens, *The Oedipus Complex: Cross-Cultural Evidence*

(New York, 1962), and the essays contained in Frank W. Moore, *Readings in Cross-Cultural Methodology* (New Haven, 1961).

For years past it has become evident that the great need of anthropology is that its methods should be strengthened and systematised. The world has not been unjust to the growing science, far from it. Wherever anthropologists have been able to show definite evidence and inference, for instance, in the development series of arts in the Pitt-Rivers Museum, at Oxford, not only specialists but the educated world generally are ready to receive the results and assimilate them into public opinion. Strict method has, however, as yet only been introduced over part of the anthropological field. There has still to be overcome a certain not unkindly hesitancy on the part of men engaged in the precise operations of mathematics, physics, chemistry, biology, to admit that the problems of anthropology are amenable to scientific treatment. It is my aim to show that the development of institutions may be investigated on a basis of tabulation and classification. For this end I have taken up a subject of the utmost real as well as theoretical interest, the formation of laws of marriage and descent, as to which during many years I have been collecting the evidence found among between three and four hundred peoples, ranging from insignificant savage hordes to great cultured nations. The particular rules have been scheduled out into tables, so as to ascertain what may be called the "adhesions" of each custom, showing which peoples have the same custom, and what other customs accompany it or lie apart from it. From the recurrence or absence of these customs it will be our business to infer their dependence on causes acting over the whole range of mankind.

Years since, long before my collection of data approached its present bulk, and could be classified into the elaborate tables now presented, I became naturally anxious to know whether the labour had been thrown away, or whether this social arithmetic would do something to disclose the course of social history. The question was how to make the trial. I remembered a story I had once heard of Horace Vernet, that a friend asked him how he planned out his huge battle-pieces. The painter took the inquirer into his studio and began a picture for him by first touching in a bayonet in one corner of his canvas, then drawing the arm and sabre of the trooper slashing over the bayonet-thrust, and so on from one overlapping figure to the next till he reached the central group. It seemed to me that it would be well to begin thus in one corner of the field. The point I chose was a quaint and somewhat comic custom as to the barbaric etiquette between husbands and their wives' relatives, and *vice versâ:* they may not look at one another, much less speak, and they even avoid mentioning one another's names. Thus, in America, John Tanner, the adopted Ojibwa, describes his being taken by a friendly Assineboin into his lodge, and seeing how at his companion's entry the old father and mother-in-law covered up their heads in their blankets till their son-in-law got into the compartment reserved for him, where his wife brought him his food. So in Australia, Mr. Howitt relates how he inadvertently told a native to call his mother-in-law, who was passing at some little distance; but the blackfellow sent the order round by a third party, saying reproachfully to Mr. Howitt, "You know I could not speak to that old woman." Absurd as this custom may appear to Europeans, it is not the outcome of mere local fancy, as appears on reckoning up the peoples practising it in various regions of the world, who are found to be about sixty-six in number, that is, more than one-sixth of the whole number of peoples catalogued, which is roughly three hundred and fifty. Thus:—

Avoidance

Between H. and W.'s Rel.	Mutual.	Between W. and H.'s Rel.
45	8	13

Now, on looking out from the schedules the adhesions of this avoidance-custom, a relation appears between it and the customs of the world as to residence after marriage. This is seen in the following computation of the peoples whose habit is for the husband to take up his abode with the wife's family permanently, or to do so temporarily and eventually to remove with her to his own family or home (the reverse of this does not occur), or for the husband at once to take home the wife.

Residence

H. to W.	Removal	W. to H.
65	76	141

Now, if the customs of residence and the customs of avoidance were independent, or nearly so, we should expect to find their coincidence following the ordinary law of chance distribution. In the tribes where the husband permanently lives with his wife's family (sixty-five out of three hundred and fifty), we should estimate that ceremonial avoidance between him and them might appear in nine cases, whereas it actually appears in fourteen cases. On the other hand, peoples where the husband at marriage takes his wife to his home (one hundred and forty-one out of three hundred and fifty), would rateably correspond with avoidance between him and her family in eighteen cases, whereas it actually appears in nine cases only. Also, if the thirteen cases of avoidance between the wife and the husband's family were divided rateably among the different modes of residence, two or three cases should come among the peoples where the husband lives with the wife's family, but there are no such cases. On the other hand, five cases should be found among the peoples where the wife lives in the husband's home or family, but actually there are eight. Thus there is a well marked preponderance indicating that ceremonial avoidance by the husband of the wife's family is in some way connected with his living with them; and *vice versa* as to the wife and the husband's family. Hereupon, it has to be enquired whether the facts suggest a reason for this connexion. Such a reason readily presents itself, inasmuch as the ceremony of not speaking to and pretending not to see some well-known person close by, is familiar enough to ourselves in the social rite which we call "cutting." This, indeed, with us implies aversion, and the implication comes out even more strongly in objection to utter the name ("we never mention her," as the song has it). It is different, however, in the barbaric custom we are considering, for here the husband is none the less on friendly terms with his wife's people because they may not take any notice of one another. In fact, the explanation of this ceremonial cutting may be simpler and more direct than in civilised Europe. As the husband has intruded himself among a family which is not his own, and into a house where he has no right, it seems not difficult to understand their marking the difference between him and themselves by treating him formally as a stranger. So like is the working of the human mind in all stages of civilisation, that our own language conveys in a familiar idiom the same train of thought; in describing the already mentioned case of the Assineboin marrying and taking up his abode with his wife's parents who pretend not to see him when he comes in, we have only to say that they do not *recognise* him, and we shall have condensed the whole proceeding into a single word. In this first example, it is to be noticed that the argument of a causal connexion of some kind between two groups of phenomena brings into view, so far at least as the data prove sound, a scientific fact. But we pass on to less solid ground in assigning for this connexion a reason which may be only analogous to the real reason, or only indirectly corresponding with it, or only partly expressing it, as its correlation with other connexions may eventually show. This important reservation, once stated, may be taken as understood through the rest of the enquiry.

Let us now turn to another custom, not less quaint-seeming than the last to the European mind. This is the practice of naming the parent from the child. When Moffat, the missionary, was in Africa among the Bechuana, he was spoken to and of, according to native usage, as Ra-Mary = father of Mary. On the other side of the world, among the Kasias of India, Colonel Yule mentions the like rule; for instance, there being a boy named Bobon, his father was known as Pabobon. In fact there are above thirty peoples spread over the earth who thus name the father, and, though less often, the mother. They may be called, coining a name for them, *teknonymous* peoples. When beginning to notice the wide distribution of this custom of *teknonymy*, and setting myself to reckon its adhesions, I confess to have been fairly taken by surprise to find it lying in close connection with the custom of the husband's residence in the wife's family, the two coinciding twenty-two times, where accident might fairly have given eleven. It proved to be still more closely attached to the practice of ceremonial avoidance by the husband of the wife's relatives, occurring fourteen times, where accident might have given four. The combination is shown on the diagram, Fig. 1, the (approximate) numbers on which give the means of estimating the

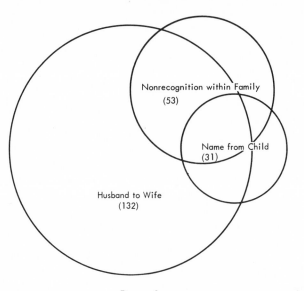

Nonrecognition within Family
(53)

Name from Child
(31)

Husband to Wife
(132)

Figure 1.

probable closeness of causal connection. Were the three customs so distantly connected as to be practically independent, the product of the corresponding fractions $\frac{132}{350} \times \frac{53}{350} \times \frac{31}{350}$, multiplied into the three hundred and fifty peoples would show that their concurrence might be expected to happen between once and twice in the list of peoples of the world. In fact it is found eleven times. Thus, we have their common causation vouched for by the heavy odds of six to one. Many of the firmest beliefs of mankind rest, I fear, on a less solid basis. In tracing out the origin of the group of customs in conformity with these conditions, it is not necessary to invent a hypothesis, as an account of the proceedings of the Cree Indians will serve as a "luminous instance" to clear up the whole situation. Among these Indians the young husband, coming to live with his wife's parents, must turn his back on them, not speaking to them (especially not to his mother-in-law), being thus treated as a stranger till his first child is born; whereupon he takes its name, and is called "father of So-and-so," and thenceforth attaches himself to his parents-in-law rather than to his own parents. That is to say, he is ceremonially treated as a stranger till his child, being born a member of the family, gives him a status as father of a member of the family, whereupon they consistently leave off the farce of not recognising him. When I brought this argument to the knowledge of Dr. G. A. Wilken, of Leyden, he pointed out to me that in his series of papers on "Primitive Forms of Marriage,"[1] where he gives instances of the naming of fathers from children, he had stated this practice to be an assertion of paternity.

[1]G. A. Wilken, "Over de primitieve vormen van het huwelijk, &c.," in "Indische Gids," 1880, &c.

Undoubtedly it is so on the father's part, and its being so is quite compatible with its being a recognition of him by the wife's kinsfolk, the two aspects belonging to one social fact.

Taking the connection between residence and ceremonial avoidance to be substantiated by their relative adhesions, it is necessary to notice that there are cases where the husband, although he carries the wife away from the home of her parents, nevertheless goes through the form of avoiding them. This, under the circumstances, seems a motiveless proceeding, but is intelligible as a survival from a time when he would have lived with them. These cases belong mainly to the Malay District and to Australia. In the Malay District the habit of residence in the wife's family is still a notable institution of the country, though being fast superseded by householding on the Arab and European models. In Australia, the native custom is described as being that the husband takes his wife to his own home, while at the same time he carries out the etiquette of cutting his mother-in-law to a ludicrous extreme, with slight traces of the avoidance of the father-in-law. It appeared to me that on the present explanation this must indicate a recent habit of residence on the wife's side, and reference showed a law of the Kurnai tribe of Gippsland,[2] that when a native kills game, certain parts of the meat (of a kangaru, the head, neck, and part of the back) are the allotted share of the wife's parents. As the duty of supplying game to the wife's household when the husband lives there is one of the best-marked points of matriarchal law, I wrote to Mr. Howitt, as the leading authority on Australian anthropology, suggesting that further enquiry would probably disclose evidence hitherto unnoticed as to the maternal stage of society subsisting in Australia. After examination made, Mr. Howitt replied:— "I am now satisfied that your surmises are quite correct," and therewith he sent details bearing on the question, especially an account by Mr. Aldridge, of Maryborough, Queensland, as to the practice of the tribes in his neighbourhood. This I will quote, as being a strongly marked case of residence on the wife's side. "When a man marries a woman from a distant locality, he goes to her tribelet and identifies himself with her people. This is a rule with very few exceptions. Of course, I speak of them as they were in their wild state. He becomes part of and one of the family. In the event of a war expedition, the daughter's husband acts as a blood-relation, and will fight and kill his own blood-relations if blows are struck by his wife's relations. I have seen a father and son fighting under these circumstances, and the son would most certainly have killed his father if others had not interfered."

The relative positions of the two groups of customs, residence and avoidance, may now be more completely shown, by the aid of the diagram, Fig. 2.

Here the space representing residence is divided into three sections, viz., residence on the wife's side; the transitional stage of removal (where the couple begin married life in the wife's house, but eventually move); resi-

[2]Fison and Howitt, "Kamilaroi and Kurnai," p. 207.

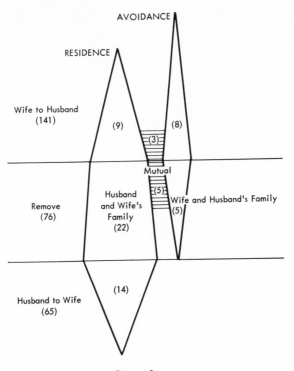

Figure 2.

dence on the husband's side. According to the previous arguments, the ceremonial avoidance between the husband and the wife's family is taken to have arisen within the periods when he and they lived permanently or temporarily in contact, and to have continued by survival into the period after this co-residence had ceased. There next appear the small group of eight cases of mutual avoidance, at once between the husband and the wife's family, and the wife and the husband's family. These consistently are found in the removal stage, where both kinds of residence meet, surviving into the stage of residence on the husband's side. Avoidance between the wife and the husband's family has the same range, but here the conditions producing it belong to both stages of residence, and there is no question of survival.

From this distribution of the avoidance-customs, it appears that in the parts of the world open to the present inspection, the three stages of residence have tended to succeed one another in the upward order of the diagram. Residence on the wife's side appears earliest, after this the removal stage, and latest, residence on the husband's side. For if it be supposed that the course of society was in the reverse direction, as would be represented by turning the diagram upside down, avoidance between the husband and the wife's family would be represented as arising in the stage when the husband lived away from it, while avoidance between the wife and the husband's family, which ought on this supposition to continue by survival into the stage of residence on the wife's side, is not found there. The avoidance-customs, though practically so trifling, are thus signals showing the direction of a movement, of which we shall more fully see the importance, namely, the shifting of habitual residence from the wife's family to the husband's.

Let us now proceed to apply a similar method to the investigation of the great division of society into matriarchal and patriarchal. In the matriarchal system, descent in the family or clan is reckoned from the mother; authority is mainly on her side, the mother's brother being habitually guardian of the childen; succession to rank and office, and inheritance of property, follow the same line passing to the brother or to the sister's son. In the patriarchal system descent is from the father; he has the power over wife and children; succession and inheritance are from him to his offspring. Between these extreme stages lies an intermediate or transitional stage in which their characteristics are variously combined. The terms patriarchal and matriarchal not being quite appropriate, I shall use in preference for the three stages the terms maternal, maternal-paternal, and paternal. The classification is necessarily somewhat vague, but I think will be found to have sufficient precision for the problem of determining the direction in which mankind has tended to move from one of the stages to another. In dealing with this problem certain customs relating to marriage law will be used as indicators.

Among a large proportion of the nations of the world up to the middle levels of culture, the re-marriage of widows is arranged, and more or less enforced, but the regulations are framed on two distinct principles. On the first principle the widow becomes the wife of her husband's brother, or near kinsman, according to some recognized order of precedence of claim. The word "levirate," from *levir* = husband's brother, has become the accepted term for this institution, but its sense must in most cases be extended to take in a series of kinsmen, among whom the brother-in-law only ranks first. Unfortunately, it has seldom been thought worth while to ascertain this precise order, which might throw light on family structure, as in an account drawn up by Mr. Howitt of the practice in Australian tribes where any man is eligible to succeed to the widow, if he stands in the relation of elder or younger brother to the deceased, beginning with actual brothers on the male or female side, according to the rule of descent in the tribe, and extending to tribal brothers who are in our terminology cousins, more or less near. The levirate appears in its various forms among one hundred and twenty peoples in my list, or about one in three in the world. On taking out its adhesions it seems sufficiently accounted for as a custom of substitution, belonging to the period when marriage is a compact not so much between two individuals as between two families, often made when the couple are infants unable to understand it, in fact sometimes before their birth. That the levirate forms part of this family transaction is consistent with other customs more or less associated with it, viz., that when a wife dies or turns out ill her family are bound to replace her by another, a rule which sometimes even holds for betrothal, and that the widow is not allowed to marry out of her husband's family unless by leave of his kinsmen, who have the choice of keeping her, or parting with her, usually for a price. The social distribution of the levirate is shown in Fig. 3

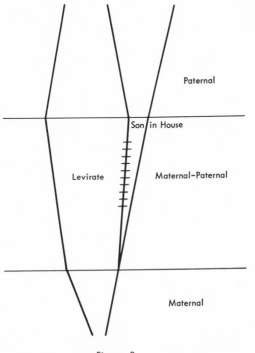

Figure 3.

to extend through all three social stages. It is in the maternal-paternal stage that it comes into competition with the second principle, unknown in the maternal stage, in which the father's widows pass by inheritance to his sons, especially the eldest son taking his stepmothers. A small but important group of cases forms a bridge between the two principles of levirate and filial succession, combining both in the same nation. This combination is well shown in Africa, where on a chief's death the head wife will pass by levirate to his brother, while her son, the new chief, will inherit a crowd of stepmothers, a less onerous legacy indeed than may seem, as they are practically slaves who hoe and grind corn for their own living. Looking at the distribution of these groups of customs, it is seen to be only compatible with the view that the paternal rule followed the maternal, bringing with it even while its prevalence was but partial, the principle of paternal widow-inheritance.

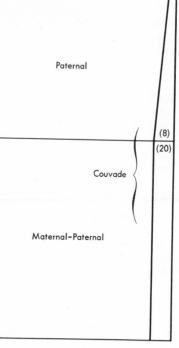

Paternal

(8)

(20)

Couvade

Maternal–Paternal

Maternal

Figure 4.

The quaint custom of the couvade[3] has now to be considered from the same point of view. In this the father, on the birth of his child, makes a ceremonial pretence of being the mother, being nursed and taken care of, and performing other rites such as fasting and abstaining from certain kinds of food or occupation, lest the new-born should suffer thereby. This custom is known in the four quarters of the globe. How sincerely it is still accepted appears in a story of Mr. Im Thurn, who on a forest journey in British Guiana noticed that one of his Indians refused to help to haul the canoes, and on enquiry found that the man's objection was that a child must have been born to him at home about this time, and he must not exert himself so as to hurt the infant. In the Mediterranean district it is not only mentioned by ancient writers, but in Spain and France, in or near the Basque country, it went on into modern times; Zamacola, in 1818, mentions, as but a little time ago, that the mother used to get up and the father take the child to bed. Knowing the tenacity of these customs, I should not be surprised if traces of couvade might be found in that district still. Now examining the distribution of the couvade by the diagram, Fig. 4, we see

[3]The reader should bear in mind that to the extent that the subject matter and the discipline of cultural anthropology are international in scope, the scholarship is equally international. The essays in the present volume have been selected principally from the Anglo-American literature. However, there are often important references

that this farcical proceeding does not appear in the maternal stage, but arising in the maternal-paternal, at once takes its strongest development of twenty cases; in the paternal the number falls to eight cases, leading to the inference that here it is only kept up in dwindling survival.

Looking at this position, I must now argue that the original interpretation of the couvade given by Bachofen in his great treatise[4] in 1861, and supported by Giraud-Teulon, fits substantially with the facts, and is justified by them. He takes it to belong to the turning-point of society when the tie of parentage, till then recognised in maternity, was extended to take in paternity, this being done by the fiction of representing the father as a second mother. He compares the couvade with the symbolic pretences of birth which in the classical world were performed as rites of adoption. To his significant examples may be added the fact that among certain tribes the couvade is the legal form by which the father recognizes a child as his. Thus this apparently absurd custom, which for twenty centuries has been the laughing-stock of mankind, proves to be not merely incidentally an indicator of the tendency of society from maternal to paternal, but the very sign and record of that vast change.

The distribution of customs in figs. 3 and 4 is only compatible with a tendency of society to pass from the maternal to the paternal systems, the maternal being placed as earliest from the absence of survivals from other stages extending into it, as they freely do into the paternal, which is therefore placed as latest. The argument is a geological one. Just as the forms of life,

---

in other languages. As an example, consider the following limited sampling of some of the couvade discussions: H. H. Ploss, *Die Maennerkindbett (Couvade), seine geographische Verbreitung und ethnographische Bedeutung* (Leipzig, 1871); G. A. Wilken, "De Couvade bij de Volken den Indisch-Archipel," *Bijdragen voor de Taal, Land, en Volkerkunde,* Series V, 4 (1889), 250–66; H. Ling Roth, "On the Signification of Couvade," *Journal of the Anthropological Institute,* 22 (1893), 204–43; H. Kunike, "Das sogenannte Männerkindbett," *Zeitschrift für Ethnologie,* 43 (1911), 546–63; M. J. Bouwman, "La Couvade," *Revue Anthropologique,* 35 (1925), 49–70; Warren R. Dawson, *The Custom of Couvade* (Manchester, 1929); Theodor Reik, "Couvade and the Psychogenesis of the Fear of Retaliation," in *Ritual: Four Psychoanalytic Studies* (New York, 1946); Raffaele Corso, "La 'Couvade' y su interpretacion," *Runa,* 6 (1953–54), 133–99; Wayland D. Hand, "American Analogues of the Couvade," in *Studies in Folklore,* ed. W. Edson Richmond (Bloomington, 1957), pp. 213–29; Robert L. Munroe, "Couvade Practices of the Black Carib: A Psychological Study," unpublished doctoral dissertation, Harvard University, 1964; and Harriet J. K. Kupferer, "Couvade: Ritual or Real Illness," *American Anthropologist,* 67 (1965), 99–102. Each of these references has further references!—Ed. Note.]

[4] J. J. Bachofen, "Das Mutterrecht," pp. 17, 255; Giraud-Teulon, "Les Origines du Marriage," p. 138. In my account of the couvade, "Early History of Mankind," Chap. x, I have laid stress on the magical-sympathetic nature of a large class of couvade rites as implying a physical bond between parent and child; thus an Abipone would not take snuff lest his sneezing might hurt his newborn baby, and a Carib father must abstain from eating sea-cow lest his infant should get little round eyes like it. This motive, which is explicitly or implicitly recognised by the savages themselves, certainly forms part of the explanation of the couvade. It is, however, secondary, being due to the connexion considered as subsisting between parent and child, so that these sympathetic prohibitions may be interpreted as originally practised by the mother only, and afterwards adopted by the father also.

and even the actual fossils of the Carboniferous formation, may be traced on into the Permian, but Permian types and fossils are absent from the Carboniferous strata formed before they came into existence, so here widow-inheritance and couvade, which, if the maternal system had been later than the paternal, would have lasted on into it, prove by their absence the priority of the maternal. Thus the present method confirms on an enlarged and firm basis the inference as to the antiquity of the maternal system arrived at by the pioneers of the investigation, Bachofen and McLennan, and supported by the later research of a generation of able investigators— Morgan, Lubbock, Bastian, Giraud-Teulon, Fison, Howitt, Wilken, Post, Lippert, and others. By this it is not, however, meant to imply that the maternal form of family as here set forth represents the primitive condition of mankind, but that it is a stage through which the inhabitants of a great part of the world now in the paternal appear to have passed, and which still continues in force over considerable tracts of every part of the globe except Europe. It seems probable that this maternal system arose out of an earlier and less organised and regulated condition of human life. As to this problem, however, though the present schedules are not devoid of information, I have not been able to bring the general evidence into shape sufficiently to justify my offering a theory here.

The analogy has already come into view between the division of society according to residence, and according to the maternal and paternal systems. This relation, the reality of which is evident from mere consideration of the difference as to family life which must ensue from the husband living in the wife's house or the wife living in the husband's, may be corroborated from the schedules. Thus the number of coincidences between peoples where the husband lives with the wife's family and where the maternal system prevails, is naturally large in proportion, while the full maternal system as naturally never appears among peoples whose exclusive custom is for the husband to take his wife to his own home. But as I have pointed out, the maternal and paternal systems are not each a definite institution, but combinations in which more or less strictly the authority, descent, succession, inheritance follow the female or the male side. The imperfection of my schedules makes it desirable for me to postpone an attempt to work out numerically the intricate problem of the mutual relations of these social rules till more perfect data are accessible. I have made, however, a rough sketch illustrative of the hypothesis suggested by the diagrams figs. 3 and 4, namely that in the one simple fact of residence we may seek the main determining cause of the several usages which combine to form a maternal or paternal system. This sketch, Fig. 5, is meant to suggest the social movement which the schedules seem to imply. Division according to residence on the female or male side is taken as the fundamental fact, and the lines show the institutions of female descent, avuncular authority, &c., arising in the stage of residence on the female side, and extending into the stages of removal and residence on the male side. Within these two latter stages it is that male descent, paternal authority, &c., arise and extend onward in history. This direction is indeed consistent with what our own knowledge of human nature would lead us to expect. We can well understand how

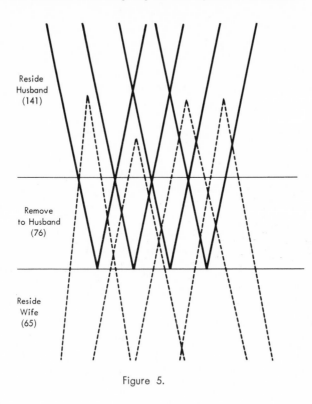

Reside
Husband
(141)

Remove
to Husband
(76)

Reside
Wife
(65)

Figure 5.

when the man lives in his wife's family his power will count for little against the combined authority of her maternal uncles and brothers, whereas when he takes her to his own home, he is apt to become master of the household; and we should expect the rules of descent, succession, and inheritance to follow the same order. Actual record of such transition is very rare, but at any rate one observer, the Hon. J. W. Powell, of the Bureau of Ethnology at Washington, has had both the opportunity to see and the skill to see what he was seeing, with the result of convincing himself that the transition from maternal to paternal society has in great measure depended on residence. I quote a passage of a letter from him:—"It would seem from such opportunities as I have had to collect facts in the field that hunting and other parties are frequently organised in such a manner that the male members of a clan group proceed together in company with their wives and children. Under such circumstances the control of the family necessarily falls into the hands of the husbands and fathers." This happens among the Pueblo Indians, a matriarchal people with female descent, whose clans, in consequence of the scarcity of water for irrigation in their desert region, are obliged to separate widely for the cultivation of lands at a distance from the central Pueblo. The result is that the control of families and the training of children are temporarily taken out of the hands of their own kin on the mother's side, and with the acquisition of cattle in these new homes comes the tendency to settle there permanently. Observation of these facts led Major Powell to adopt the hypothesis that clanship by female descent passed in this way into clanship by male descent by the segregation of clans for industrial purposes.

The next diagram, Fig. 6, throws more light on the great social transformation. It shows the distribution of the practice of marriage by capture. When the accounts of national custom are classified they show that capture (which belongs to over one hundred of the peoples scheduled) can be more or less accurately divided into three kinds:—Hostile capture, when warriors of one tribe bring away as captives women of another tribe, is a feat of arms praised in history short of the highest levels of culture. There were fierce Indians of the Pampas who held that their god, the Great Eagle, told them to live by making war on all other tribes, slaying their men and carrying off their women and children. The same spirit is heard in the hopes of Sisera's host to divide the spoil, to every man a damsel or two. Looking at hostile capture from the anthropological point of view, we have to notice that it exists equally through the three stages of society, from maternal to paternal. Now it obviously conflicts with full matriarchal institutions that a man should bring in a captive wife, for he cannot take her home to his mother-in-law. To understand such a custom appearing within the range of matriarchy at all, we must remember that a captive has no rights, so that what happens to her does not immediately affect the regular custom of

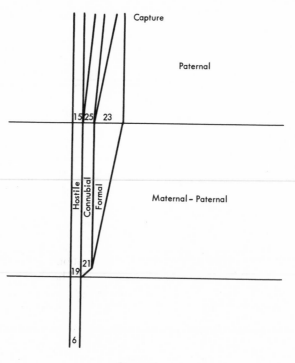

Figure 6.

the tribe, which applies to native free women. Yet even here the tendency of capture must always have been to upset the maternal arrangements. When capture comes to be an accepted mode of marriage between or among tribes or clans who live at peace and habitually intermarry, it is evident that such "connubial capture," as it is described on the diagram, can only consist with the paternal system, inasmuch as the husband necessarily carries the wife to his own home, thereby setting on foot a paternal household. This is true also of the cases where the capture has become a merely formal ceremony, accompanying a marriage settled beforehand, for the very form of capture involves the bridegroom coming with his friends to carry the bride to his home. This is the interpretation of the fact, made evident in the diagram, that connubial and formal capture belong only to the intermediate stage where paternal institutions are arising, and to the later stage where they are fully established. The effect of capture in breaking up the maternal system, and substituting the paternal for it, has thus to be taken into account as a serious factor in social development. There is at least one region of the world where the operation may be seen going on at this day—the Malay Islands. To quote the concise description by Riedel of the matrimonial arrangements of the Babar Archipelago:— "The men follow the women, and live in their houses. The children also belong to the wife's family. If a man is rich enough he may marry seven wives, who all remain in the houses of their parents. A man who has many wives is respected. The robbery of a wife from another clan (*negari*) is an honour, and the children follow the father, with or without payment of the fine attached to the deed. Smaller or weaker clans even demand no fine."[5] In the Kisar and Wetar island groups a like state of things appears, the maternal system being the recognised rule, but always liable to pass into the paternal system by capture, which brings wife and children into the husband's hands.

At this point it will be convenient to examine two institutions of early marriage law, namely, exogamy and classificatory relationship. The principle of exogamy was brought prominently into view fifty years ago, by Sir George Grey,[6] when he described the native Australian rule for a man not to marry a woman of the same family name or bearing the same animal-crest or kobong as himself; and called attention to the coincidence of this with the North American system of clans named from totem animals, a man being bound to marry outside his own totem or clan. Mr. J. F. McLennan[7] gave these customs the name of exogamy or "marrying-out," and showed them to belong to "a most widely prevailing principle of marriage law among primitive races." Much information has since then come in, with the result of showing that exogamy has hardly to do with the capture of wives in war between alien nations, but rather with the regulation of marriages within groups of clans or tribes who have connubium; such

[5]Riedel, "De Sluik- en Kroesharige Rassen tusschen Selebes en Papua," p. 351; see 415, 448.
[6]Grey, "Journals of Two Expeditions in N.W. and W. Australia," Vol. II, p. 225.
[7]J. F. McLennan, "Primitive Marriage," pp. 48, 130.

clans or tribes may be more or less at strife, but they acknowledge ties of kindred and are usually allied by language. It is now also understood that a people may at once practice endogamy or "marrying-in" within its borders, and exogamy or "marrying-out" of its clans with one another. The situation may be understood among the Hindus, where a man must marry in his caste, but within that caste must not marry in his own gotra or clan. The effect of an exogamic rule is similar whether clanship follows the female or male line of descent. Next, as to the principle of classificatory relationship, an early mention of this is by Father Lafitau,[8] above one hundred and fifty years ago, who states that "among the Iroquois and Hurons all the children of a cabin regard all their mother's sisters as their mothers, and all their mother's brothers as their uncles, and for the same reason they give the name of fathers to all their father's brothers, and aunts to all their father's sisters. All the children on the side of the mother and her sisters, and of the father and his brothers, regard each other mutually as brothers and sisters, but as regards the children of their uncles and aunts, that is, of their mother's brothers and father's sisters, they only treat them on the footing of cousins. . . . In the third generation this changes, the great uncles and great aunts become again grandfathers and grandmothers of the children of those whom they called nephews and nieces. This continues always in the descending line according to the same rule." In our own time, Lewis H. Morgan, living among the Iroquois as an adopted Indian, was struck with this system of relationships, so unlike what he had been brought up among, and which he at first thought to be a peculiar invention of his Iroquois. But finding, on enquiry, that it extended to other North American tribes, he eventually by circulating interrogatories succeeded in collecting a great series of systems of relationship, in which he established the wide prevalence of classificatory systems, as he called them from the relatives being grouped in classes.[9] Under the term classificatory systems, Mr. Morgan included not only those approximating to the Iroquois type, but a much simpler and ruder plan prevalent in Polynesia; it is, however, convenient for me to confine my remarks here to the former group only. This system, as found among the American Indians, Mr. Morgan showed to be closely analogous to that of the Dravidian nations of Southern Hindustan. This latter is a well-known source of perplexity to a newly appointed English civilian, who may be told by a witness that his father was sitting in the house, but presently the same witness mentions his father as coming in from the field; the native is sharply reproved by the judge for contradicting himself, whereupon he explains, it was my "little father," by which he means his father's younger brother.

I am placing together the two institutions, exogamy and classificatory relationship, inasmuch as they are really connected, being in fact two sides

[8]Lafitau, "Mœurs des Sauvages Ameriquains," Paris, 1724, Vol. I, p. 552. [For further discussion of the principles of classificatory relationship, see the famous analysis by Alfred Kroeber, "Classificatory Systems of Relationship," which is reprinted in this volume.—Ed. Note.]

[9]L. H. Morgan, "Systems of Consanguinity and Affinity of the Human Family" (Smithsonian Contributions, 1871).

of one institution. This was made out eight years ago, by the Rev. Lorimer Fison, in the work on the Kamilaroi and Kurnai tribes of Australia by him and Mr. Howitt.[10] This important explanation is still scarcely known to anthropologists, nor indeed, have I much right to reproach others with neglecting it, for I reviewed Fison and Howitt's book without distinctly realising the bearing of this argument on the theory of exogamy, which only came round to me lately in a way which I had better now describe, as it will enable me to explain shortly and plainly the whole problem. In tabulating the nations of the world, I found a group of twenty-one peoples whose custom as to the marriage of first cousins seemed remarkable; it is that the children of two brothers may not marry, nor the children of two sisters, but the child of the brother may marry the child of the sister. It seemed obvious that this "cross-cousin marriage," as it may be called, must be the direct result of the simplest form of exogamy, where a population is divided into two classes or sections, with the law that a man who belongs to Class A can only take a wife of Class B. Such a division, for instance, is familiar in Melanesia. Dr. R. H. Codrington describes it in the Banks Islands, where the natives have two families, called *veve* = mother, which implies that descent follows the mother's side, and a man must marry a wife of the other mother from himself, or as they say, not on his own side of the house but on the other. Thus, taking A, a, B, b, as males and females of the class A and B, and bearing in mind that the mother's children are of her class, but the father's children of the opposite class to his, we have:—

Two sisters, a, a,	Two brothers, A, A,	Brother and sister, A, a,
their : :	their : :	their : :
Children, A, a,	Children B, b,	Children B, a,
are of	are of	are of
Same class = tribal	Same class = tribal	different class = tribal
brother and sister	brother and sister	cousins
= unmarriageable	= unmarriageable	= marriageable

Figure 7.

Having come to this point, it seemed to me that I had seen something like it elsewhere, and on looking back to "Kamilaroi and Kurnai" I found that Fison had thus worked out the origin of the Turanian classificatory system, as Morgan calls that including the above-mentioned systems of North America and India, with others. Fig. 8 puts concisely the main features of the argument as to a man's kin.

Though not proposing to enter fully into the deduction of classificatory relationships in all their varieties from the rule of exogamy, it is necessary to point out that the form of exogamy here contemplated is the simplest

[10]Fison and Howitt, "Kamilaroi and Kurnai," 1880, p. 76.

His
    father's brother's child
        or   } is (tribal) brother or sister
    mother's sister's child

Therefore
    father's brother is (tribal) father,
    mother's sister is (tribal) mother,

His
    father's sister's child
        or   } is tribal (cousin)
    mother's brother's child

Therefore
    father's sister is (tribal) aunt
    mother's brother is (tribal) uncle

Figure 8.

or dual form, in which a people is divided into two intermarrying classes. Systems of exogamy which are dual in their nature, that is, consisting of two classes or groups of classes, stand in direct connection with cross-cousin marriage and classificatory relationship. But if the number of exogamic divisions is not dual, if there are for instance three clans, and a man of one clan may take a wife of either of the other two clans, it is readily seen that the argument of fig. 7 breaks down. Although at present only prepared to deal with exogamy and classificatory relationship in their dual form, I may notice that the treatment of the problem by the method of adhesions strengthens the view, not wanting in other evidence, that the dual form of exogamy may be considered the original form. In reckoning from the present schedules the number of peoples who use relationship names more or less corresponding to the classificatory systems here considered, they are found to be fifty-three, and the estimated number of these which might coincide accidentally with exogamy were there no close connexion between them, would be about twelve. But in fact the number of peoples who have both exogamy and classification is thirty-three, this strong coincidence being the measure of the close causal connexion subsisting between the two institutions. The adherence is even stronger as to cross-cousin marriage, of which twenty-one cases appear in the schedules, no less than fifteen of the peoples practising it being also known as exogamous. Here, indeed, the relation is not one of derivation, but of identity, the cross-cousin rule being actually a partial form or imperfect statement of the law of exogamy itself. Such adhesions between two or more customs have been already recognised as proving the existence of causal connexion, but it has now to be pointed out that they serve another purpose. The connexion, when proved, reacts on the evidence by which it was proved. When once it has been shown that cross-cousin marriage is part and parcel of exogamy, it may be argued that all the twenty-one peoples practising cross-cousin marriage are to be set down as exogamous. Now as only fifteen of them are expressly recorded to be so, the list of exogamous nations of the world has to be increased by six. So, classificatory relationship being evidence that the peoples practising it are or have been exogamous, this will add some twenty more to the list of nations among whom further investigation will probably disclose record that exogamic society once prevailed or still prevails. Even if no direct record is forthcoming, the indirect proof may with due caution be sufficient for placing them in the exogamous group, which may thus number above one hundred peoples out of the three hundred and fifty of the world. Those who remember the sharp discussion between McLennan and Morgan years ago, and the view that the classificatory relationships were a mere system of addresses, will be struck with the way in which the controversy is likely to end. For myself I hardly know whether I feel more glad or sorry that my old friend McLennan to the day of his death never knew that Morgan and he, who believed themselves adversaries, were all the while allies pushing forward the same doctrine from different sides.

It thus appears that the number of nations who have the system of intermarrying clans is larger than has been known. But even this by no means measures the full importance of exogamy as a factor in the constitution of society. Anthropologists have long had before them the problem of determining how far clan-exogamy may have been the origin of the prohibited degrees in matrimony so variously defined in the laws of nations. The yet larger problem has been opened, how far laws of permission and prohibition of marriage may have led nations to define relationships and give them names, distinguishing for instance uncles from fathers, and cousins from brothers. It may, I think, conduce to the solution of these problems to notice two ways in which the collation of the present tables bears on the meaning and origin of exogamy.

There are conditions of society under which exogamy is found side by side with wife-capture, so that a barbaric marriage often involves both in one and the same act, as when a Tatar and a party of his friends, all armed to the teeth, ride off to the tents of a distant clan, and thence with simulated or even real violence carry off a bride. But on reckoning up the peoples among whom this combination of capture and exogamy is found, the number, though enough to show that they co-exist freely, falls short of what would justify the inference that they are cause and effect. Moreover, it appears that this co-existence belongs especially to the paternal stage of society, and to the maternal-paternal, in which paternal influence is partly established. This is intelligible enough from what has been already said as to the effect of capture in setting on foot paternal institutions, from its very outset, by bringing the wife into the husband's hands and home. We are thus led to a more fundamental test of the position of exogamy, by enquiring whether it existed in the earliest known stage of the maternal system of society, where the husband lives in the wife's family. The schedules show that there are in different parts of the world twelve or thirteen well-marked exogamous peoples whose habit of residence is for the husband to join the wife's family.[11] This state of things seems to me to prevent our regarding exogamy as a result of capture, it being plain that the warrior

[11]Kasia, Garo, Menangkabau and Padang, Banks Islands, Mortlock Islands, Chiroki, Delaware, Iroquois, Mandan and Minitari, Moqui, Tlinkit, Arawak.

who has carried a wife captive from a hostile tribe does not take up his abode in her family. If capture leads to any form of exogamy, this must, I think, be a paternal form, and if it be admitted that the maternal form is earlier, then it follows that capture is inadmissible as the primary cause of exogamy.

More than twenty years ago, in compiling a list of nations practising this custom of marrying out of the tribe or kin, I noticed that in any full discussion of the subject would have to be considered the wish to bind different tribes together in friendship by intermarriage.[12] Compiling the present tables has brought together observations to this effect. Morgan, describing how the alliance of the Iroquois tribes, made up of intermarrying clans, formed a bond of union throughout the national league, writes: "It was the boast of the Iroquois that the great object of their confederacy was peace; to break up the spirit of perpetual warfare, which had wasted the red race from age to age."[13] Another group of North American tribes, the Tinneh, on the Arctic circle, are divided into three castes, their rule being that, for instance, a Chit-sangh may not marry a Chit-sangth. When this does take place, the persons are ridiculed and laughed at, the man is said to have married his sister, even though she may be from another tribe, and there be not the slightest connection by blood between them. Hardisty, who gives these details, remarks:—"One good thing proceeded from the above arrangement, it prevented war between two tribes who were naturally hostile."[14] The Bogos of Abyssinia are exogamous, and of them Munzinger reports that they are closely bound together by reciprocal marriages, "so that internal war is almost impossible. Blood-quarrels among the Bogos are always settled very quickly, whilst the smallest collision with the adjoining tribes leads to everlasting wars."[15] Du Chaillu writes of Ashango-land, "tribes and clans intermarry with each other and this brings about a friendly feeling among the people. People of the same clan cannot intermarry with each other."[16] Thus, it seems that when Plutarch asks in the "Roman Questions," "Why do they not marry women near of kin?" he has some reason in setting down as one possible answer, "Whether from their wishing to increase friendships by marriages, and to acquire many kinsfolk, giving wives to others and receiving (wives) from them."[17]

On looking at the distinction between endogamy and exogamy from this point of view, it will be seen that there is a period in the growth of society when it is a political question of the first importance. While the vast forest or prairie still affords abundant food for a scanty population, small hordes may wander, or groups of households may be set up, each little tribe or settlement cut off from the rest, and marrying within its own border. But when tribes begin to adjoin and press on one another and quarrel, then

[12]"Early History of Mankind," p. 286.
[13]Morgan, "League of the Iroquois," p. 91.
[14]"Smithsonian Report," 1866, p. 315.
[15]Munzinger, "Sitten und Recht der Bogos," p. 10.
[16]Du Chaillu, "Journey to Ashango-land," p. 427.
[17]Plutarch, "Quæst. Rom.," cviii.

the difference between marrying-in and marrying-out becomes patent. Endogamy is a policy of isolation, cutting off a horde or village, even from the parent-stock whence it separated, if only a generation or two back. Among tribes of low culture there is but one means known of keeping up permanent alliance, and that means is intermarriage. Exogamy, enabling a growing tribe to keep itself compact by constant unions between its spreading clans, enables it to overmatch any number of small intermarrying groups, isolated and helpless. Again and again in the world's history, savage tribes must have had plainly before their minds the simple practical alternative between marrying-out and being killed out. Even far on in culture, the political value of intermarriage remains. "Matrimonial alliances increase friendship more than aught else," is a maxim of Mohammed. "Then will we give our daughters unto you, and we will take your daughters to us, and we will dwell with you, and we will become one people," is a well known passage of Israelite history.

Exogamy lies far back in the history of man, and perhaps no observer has ever seen it come into existence, nor have the precise conditions of its origin yet been clearly inferred. Even the historical relation between exogamy and the system of classes known as totemism is not fully cleared up; whether as Prof. Robertson Smith takes it,[18] totemism supplied the necessary machinery for working a law of exogamy, or whether exogamy itself led to totemism. But as to the law of exogamy itself, the evidence shows it in operation over a great part of the human race as a factor of political prosperity. It cannot be claimed as absolutely preventing strife and bloodshed, indeed, it has been remarked of some peoples, such as the Khonds and the Banks Islanders, that the intermarrying clans do nevertheless quarrel and fight. Still by binding together a whole community with ties of kinship and affinity, and especially by the peacemaking of the women who hold to one clan as sisters and to another as wives, it tends to keep down feuds and to heal them when they arise, so as at critical moments to hold together a tribe which under endogamous conditions would have split up. Exogamy thus shows itself as an institution which resists the tendency of uncultured populations to disintegrate, cementing them into nations capable of living together in peace and holding together in war, till they reach the period of higher military and political organisation. Seen from this point of view, the remarkable fact is more easily understood that exogamy, passing on from the maternal to the paternal stage of society, shifts its prohibitions from the female to the male line of descent, now allowing marriages which it treated formerly as incestuous, while prohibiting others which it formerly allowed without scruple. This transformation has been taking place within recent times among Malay and American tribes, and seems to be even going on still, it making no difference politically whether kinship follows the female or male line, if only marrying-out causes the requisite intermixture of the clans. In this connexion it is worth while to notice that there are a small number of peoples in different parts of

18W. Robertson Smith, "Kinship and Marriage in Early Arabia," p. 184.

the world, who have a rule of exogamy not depending on kinship at all. For instance, Piedrahita[19] relates of the Panches of Bogota, that those of one town did not marry any woman thereof, as all held themselves brothers, and the impediment of kinship was sacred to them, but such was their ignorance that if a sister were born in a different town from her brother, he was not prevented from marrying her. An anthropologist, with the list before him of the peoples who prohibit a man from marrying in his own village, might explain this not as a result of ignorance, but as an extreme case of what may be called "local exogamy."

The results here brought forward make no approach to exhausting the possible inferences to be drawn from the tables. These need not even be confined to working out the development of customs found in existence somewhere on the globe, but may in some measure restore the knowledge of forms of society now extinct. Interesting, however, as these problems are, I am more anxious to bring under discussion the method by which they are here treated, how imperfectly I am well aware. The interpretations offered will have to be corrected, the tabulated material improved in quantity and quality, and the principles it involves brought out more justly, yet at any rate it will remain clear that the rules of human conduct are amenable to classification in compact masses, so as to show by strict numerical treatment their relations to one another. It is only at this point that speculative explanation must begin, at once guided in its course and strictly limited in its range by well-marked lines of fact to which it must conform. The key of the position is, as that veteran anthropologist, Prof. Bastian, of the Berlin Museum, is never weary of repeating, that in statistical investigation the future of anthropology lies. As soon as this is systematically applied, principles of social development become visible. Even the diagrams of this paper may suffice to show that the institutions of man are as distinctly stratified as the earth on which he lives. They succeed each other in series substantially uniform over the globe, independent of what seem the comparatively superficial differences of race and language, but shaped by similar human nature acting through successively changed conditions in savage, barbaric, and civilised life.

The treatment of social phenomena by numerical classification will, it must be added, react on the statistical material to which the method is applied. It is in classifying the records of tribes and nations that one becomes fully aware of their imperfect and even fragmentary state. The descriptions happily tend to correct one another's errors, but the great difficulty is blank want of information. As for extinct tribes, and those whose native culture has been re-modelled, there is nothing to be done. But there are still a hundred or more peoples in the world, among whom a prompt and minute investigation would save some fast vanishing memory of their social laws and customs. The quest might be followed up internationally, each civilised nation taking in hand the barbaric tribes within its purview. The future will, doubtless, be able to take care of itself as to most branches of knowledge,

[19]Piedrahita, "Historia General de las Conquistas del Nuevo Reyno de Granada," 1688, page 11.

but there is certain work which if it is to be done at all, must be done by the present.

James George Frazer

THE ROOTS OF MAGIC

James George Frazer's curiosity about an alleged classical practice reported at the sacred grove of the Roman goddess Diana at Nemi in Italy led to the writing of the *Golden Bough,* which became one of the best known works in anthropology. In the grove, a priest-king stood guard next to a certain tree. He stood guard because he could retain his office only so long as he was not slain by a successor. (He himself had taken office by slaying his predecessor.) A candidate for this priesthood could not, however, begin the combat unless he had first succeeded in plucking a golden bough from the tree that the priest was guarding. Frazer's gloss on the plucking of the bough appeared in 1890 as a two-volume work. By 1915, the third edition had swelled to twelve volumes, surely the longest footnote in the history of scholarship!

In the *Golden Bough,* Frazer presented thousands of examples of what he considered to be man's evolution from savagery through barbarism to civilization and from magic through religion to science. In the light of present knowledge, there are many things wrong with the *Golden Bough.* Frazer's theories, upon which he hung the ethnographic snippets gleaned from countless reports, have not survived. Frazer used sources uncritically, bad mixed with good, and he lifted material out of its cultural context. Yet the vision of man that Frazer had was a noble one and his forceful style of writing has influenced men of letters as well as men of science.

One of the portions of Frazer's work which is still esteemed by many anthropologists concerns his analysis of magic. Frazer's two principles of sympathetic magic: homeopathic magic and contagious magic, appear to have cross-cultural validity. Although Frazer invariably used more examples than he needed to illustrate a point, there is a certain fascination in wading through them to admire how thoroughly Frazer ransacked ethnographic reports from all over the world. (Frazer's footnotes have been included to show the wide range of his sources.) Reading in Frazerian anthropology is an experience, an aesthetic experience. But the reader should realize that Frazer's work was probably the high

Reprinted from *The New Golden Bough,* ed. Theodor H. Gaster (Garden City, 1961), pp. 5–21, 58–62, 73–77. Reprinted by permission of S. G. Phillips, Inc., and Trinity College, Cambridge. Copyright © 1959 by S. G. Phillips, Inc.

point of library-literary bits-and-pieces anthropology. Once anthropologists began to go into the field and learn how holistic magical systems worked in individual cultures, Frazer's multi-volume masterpiece lay in the library to be used only by other armchair anthropologists.

For a sketch of Frazer's contribution to anthropology, see Abram Kardiner and Edward Preble, *They Studied Man* (New York, 1963), pp. 69–94. For a moving tribute to the power of Frazer's inspiration, which led him into the field of anthropology, see Bronislaw Malinowski's dedication to Frazer in his *Myth in Primitive Psychology* (New York, 1926), reprinted in the paperback, *Magic, Science and Religion* (Garden City, 1954).

[5.] Analysis shows that magic rests everywhere on two fundamental principles: first, that *like produces like,* effect resembling cause; second, that *things which have once been in contact continue ever afterwards to act on each other.* The former principle may be called the Law of Similarity; the latter, that of Contact or Contagion. From the one the magician infers that he can produce any effect he desires merely by imitating it in advance; from the other, that whatever he does to a material object will automatically affect the person with whom it was once in contact. Practices based on the Law of Similarity may be termed Homoeopathic Magic; those based on the Law of Contact or Contagion, Contagious Magic. Both derive, in the final analysis, from a false conception of natural law. The primitive magician, however, never analyzes the mental assumptions on which his performance is based, never reflects on the abstract principles involved. With him, as with the vast majority of men, logic is implicit, not explicit; he knows magic only as a practical thing, and to him it is always an art, never a science, the very idea of science being foreign to his thinking.

Homoeopathy

[6.] Perhaps the most familiar application of the principle that like produces like is the attempt which has been made by many peoples in many ages to injure or destroy an enemy by injuring or destroying an image of him. For thousands of years this practise was known to the sorcerers of ancient India, Babylon and Egypt, Greece and Rome;[1]* and it is still employed by cunning and malign savages in Australia, Africa, and America. When, for example, an Ojibway Indian desires to work evil on anyone, he

---

*[Frazer's notes as well as the additional notes by Theodor H. Gaster are listed by paragraph following the essay. Frazer's notes begin on page 108; Gaster's on page 114. —Ed. Note.]

makes a little wooden image of his enemy and runs a needle into its head or heart, or he shoots an arrow at it, believing that wherever the needle pierces or the arrow strikes the image, his foe will at the same instant be seized with sharp pain. If he intends to kill the person outright, he burns or buries the puppet, uttering magic words as he does so.[2] So when a Cora Indian of Mexico wishes to kill a man, he makes a figure of him out of burnt clay, strips of cloth, and so forth, and then, muttering incantations, runs thorns through its head or stomach.[3] Similarly, the Peruvian Indians used to mould images of fat mixed with grain to imitate persons whom they disliked or feared, and then burn the effigy on the road where the intended victim was to pass.[4] Again, in the Torres Straits a mode of encompassing a man's death was to prick a wax model of him with the spine of a sting-ray; when he next went fishing, it was believed, a sting-ray would puncture him in the corresponding part of his body.[5]

If an Aino of Japan desires to destroy an enemy, he fashions a likeness of him out of mugwort or the guelder-rose and buries it upside down in a hole or under the trunk of a rotten tree, with a prayer to the demons to carry off the man's soul or make his body rot along with the tree. Sometimes, indeed, an Aino woman will try to get rid of her husband in this way by wrapping up his head-dress in the shape of a corpse and burying it deep in the ground, while she prays that he may rot and die with it.[6] The Chinese too profess the belief that you can harm a man by maltreating or cursing an image of him, especially if you have first taken care to write on it his name and horoscope.[7]

In Burma a rejected lover sometimes resorts to a sorcerer and engages him to make a small image of the scornful fair one, containing a piece of her clothes or something which she has been in the habit of wearing. Then, to the accompaniment of certain charms, the doll is cast into the water. As a consequence the girl is supposed to go mad.[8]

The ancient books of the Hindus attest the use of similar practices among their remote ancestors. To destroy his foe a man would fashion a figure of him in clay and transpierce it with an arrow which had been barbed with a thorn and winged with an owl's feathers. Or he would mould the figure of wax and melt it in a fire.[9]

Analogous devices are employed by the Moslems of North Africa. Thus an Arabic treatise on magic directs that if you wish to deprive a man of the use of his limbs you should make an image of him out of wax and engrave on it both his own and his mother's name, using for the purpose a knife the handle of which must be made of the same substance; then you must strike that limb of the image which answers to the one you wish to disable; straightway the latter will be paralyzed.[10]

Among the Ibo and Ijebu of Southern Nigeria, "a mud or wax image is modelled in the rough semblance of the man whom it is desired to injure and, while incantations are made, this is damaged by being pierced with a nail or spear, or it is decapitated."[10a] In Loango the magician fashions an image of his victim out of a root, pith, or wood, and with appropriate incantations throws it into a river or the sea or the wilderness, holds it in the fire, or hangs it in the smoke. As the image rots, shrivels up, or is reduced to ashes, the victim suffers a corresponding fate.[10b] The same practice is recorded also in a Greek inscription of the fourth century B.C. from Cyrene, in North Africa. Cyrene was founded by Greek colonists from the island of Thera in the Aegean, and in founding it the Therans passed a very stringent decree directed against all such recreants as either refused to sail with the colonists or having sailed with them might later desert and return to their native soil. Waxen images of all such traitors were to be made and burned, doubtless for the purpose of bringing down destruction on their heads.[10c]

[7.] Nowhere, perhaps, were the magic arts more carefully cultivated, nowhere did they enjoy greater esteem or exercise a deeper influence on the national life than in the land of the Pharaohs. Little wonder, therefore, that the practice of enchantment by means of images was familiar to the wizards of Egypt. A drop of a man's blood, some clippings of his hair or parings of his nails, a rag of the garment which he had worn, sufficed to give a sorcerer complete power over him. These relics of his person the magician kneaded into a lump of wax, which he moulded into the likeness and dressed after the fashion of his intended victim, who was then at the mercy of his tormentor. If the image was exposed to the fire, the person whom it represented straightway fell into a burning fever; if it were stabbed with a knife, he felt the pain of the wound.[1] Thus, for instance, a certain superintendent of the king's cattle was once prosecuted in an Egyptian court of law for having made figures of men and women in wax, thereby causing paralysis of their limbs and other grievous bodily harm. He had somehow obtained a book of magic which contained the spells and directions how to act in reciting them. Armed with this powerful instrument the rogue had shut himself up in a secret chamber, and there proceeded to cast spells over the people of his town.

The use of the wax figures was not disdained by the priests of Amen-Ra at Thebes in Egypt, for they regularly burnt a wax figure of the fiend Apep, who daily endeavoured to prevent the sun from rising. This figure was in the form of a serpent of many folds, on which the name Apep was written or cut. A case made of papyrus inscribed with spells containing curses was prepared, and, the wax figure having been placed inside it, both case and figure were cast into a fire made of a special kind of plant. Whilst they were burning the priest recited curses, and stamped upon them with his left foot until they were rendered shapeless and were finally destroyed. This magical ceremony was believed to be very helpful to Ra, the Sun-God, who uttered over the real Apep spells which paralysed him, and then killed him by the fiery darts of his rays, and consumed him.[1a]

In ancient Babylonia also it was a common practice to make an image of clay, pitch, honey, fat, or other soft material in the likeness of an enemy, and to injure or kill him by burning, burying, or otherwise ill-treating it. Thus in a hymn to the fire-god Nusku we read:

"Those who have made images of me, reproducing my features,
Who have taken away my breath, torn my hairs,
Who have rent my clothes, have hindered my feet from treading the dust,
May the fire-god, the strong one, break their charm."[2]

[8.] But both in Babylon and in Egypt this ancient tool of superstition, so baneful in the hands of the mischievous and malignant, was also pressed into the service of religion and turned to glorious account for the confusion and overthrow of demons. In a Babylonian incantation we meet with a long list of evil spirits whose effigies were burnt by the magician in the hope that, as their images melted in the fire, so the fiends themselves might melt away and disappear.[1] Every night when the Egyptian sun-god Ra sank down to his home in the glowing west he was assailed by hosts of demons under the leadership of the arch-fiend Apepi. All night long he fought them, and sometimes by day the powers of darkness sent up clouds even into the blue sky to obscure his light and weaken his power. To aid the sun-god in this daily struggle, a ceremony was daily performed in his temple at Thebes. A figure of his foe Apepi, represented as a crocodile with a hideous face or a serpent with many coils, was made of wax, and on it the demon's name was written in green ink. Wrapt in a papyrus case, on which another likeness of Apepi had been drawn in green ink, the figure was then tied up with black hair, spat upon, hacked with a stone knife, and cast on the ground. There the priest trod on it with his left foot again and again, and then burned it in a fire made of a certain plant or grass. When Apepi himself had thus been effectually disposed of, waxen effigies of each of his principal demons, and of their fathers, mothers, and children, were made and burnt in the same way. The service, accompanied by the recitation of certain prescribed spells, was repeated not merely morning, noon, and night, but whenever a storm was raging, or heavy rain had set in, or black clouds were stealing across the sky to hide the sun's bright disc. The fiends of darkness, clouds, and rain felt the injuries inflicted on their images as if they had been done to themselves; they passed away, at least for a time, and the beneficent sun-god shone out triumphant once more.[2]

[9.] If homoeopathic or imitative magic, working by means of images, has commonly been practised for the spiteful purpose of putting obnoxious people out of the world, it has also, though far more rarely, been employed with the benevolent intention of helping others into it. In other words, it has been used to facilitate childbirth and to procure offspring for barren women. Thus among the Esquimaux of Bering Strait a barren woman desirous of having a son will consult a shaman, who commonly makes, or causes her husband to make, a small doll-like image over which he performs certain secret rites, and the woman is directed to sleep with it under her pillow.[1] Amongst the many ceremonies which a Thompson Indian girl of British Columbia had formerly to perform at puberty was the following. She had to run four times in the morning, carrying two small stones which had been obtained from underneath the water. These were put in her bosom; and as she ran, they slipped down between her body and her clothes and fell to the ground. While she ran, she prayed to the Dawn that when she should be with child she might be delivered as easily as she had been delivered of these stones.[2] Similarly among the Haida Indians of the Queen Charlotte Islands a pregnant woman would let round stones, eels, chips, or other small objects slip down over her abdomen for the sake of facilitating her delivery.[3] Among the Nishinam Indians of California, when a woman is childless, her female friends sometimes make out of grass a rude image of a baby and tie it in a small basket after the Indian fashion. Some day, when the woman is away from home, they lay this grass baby in her hut. On finding it she holds it to her to nurse it, and sings it lullabies. This is done as a charm to make her conceive.[4] The Huichol Indians of Mexico believe in a certain Mother who is the goddess of conception and childbirth, and lives in a cave near Santa Catarina. A woman desirous of offspring deposits in this cave a doll made of cotton cloth to represent the baby on which her heart is set. After a while she goes back to the cave, puts the doll under her girdle, and soon afterwards is supposed to be pregnant.[5] With a like intent Indian women in Peru used to wrap up stones like babies and leave them at the foot of a large stone, which they revered for this purpose.[6] Among the Makatisses, a Caffre tribe of South Africa, a traveller observed a woman carefully tending a doll made out of a gourd, adorned with necklaces of glass beads, and heavily weighted with iron ore. On enquiry he learned that she had been directed by the medicine-man to do this as a means of obtaining a child.[7] Among the Basutos childless wives make rude effigies of clay, and give them the name of some tutelar deity. They treat these dolls as if they were real children, and beseech the divinity to whom they have dedicated them to grant them the power of conception.[8] In Anno, a district of West Africa, women may often be seen carrying wooden dolls strapped, like babies, on their backs as a cure for sterility.[9] In Japan, when a marriage is unfruitful, the old women of the neighbourhood come to the house and go through a pretence of delivering the wife of a child. The infant is represented by a doll.[10] The Maoris had a household god whose image was in the form of an infant. The image was very carefully made, generally life-size, and adorned with the family jewels. Barren women nursed it and addressed it in the most endearing terms in order to become mothers.[11]

[10.] Magical images have often been employed for the amiable purpose of winning love. Thus to shoot an arrow into the heart of a clay image was an ancient Hindu method of securing a woman's affection;[1] while the Chippeway Indians used to prick the hearts of images of those whose love they wished to win and insert magical powders into the punctures, meanwhile addressing the effigies by the names of the persons they represented and bidding them requite their affection.[2] Similarly too ancient witches and wizards used to melt wax in fire in order to make the hearts of their sweethearts melt of love.[3] Such customs, still commonly observed in some parts of Catholic Europe, are interesting because they shew how in later times magic comes to be incorporated with religion. The moulding of wax images of ailing members is in its origin purely magical: the prayer to the Virgin or to a saint is purely religious: the combination of the two is a crude, if pathetic, attempt to turn both magic and religion to account for the benefit of the sufferer.

[11.] The natives of New Caledonia make use of effigies to maintain or restore harmony between husband and wife. Two spindle-shaped bundles, one representing the man and the other the woman, are tied firmly together to symbolise and ensure the amity of the couple. They are made up of various plants, together with some threads from the woman's girdle and a piece of the man's apron; a bone needle forms the axis of each. The talisman is meant to render the union of the spouses indissoluble, and is carefully treasured by them both. If, nevertheless, a domestic jar should unfortunately take place, the husband repairs to the family burying-ground with the precious packet. There he lights a fire with a wood of a particular kind, fumigates the talisman, sprinkles it with water from a prescribed source, waves it round his head, and then stirring the needle in the bundle which represents himself he says, "I change the heart of this woman, that she may love me." If the wife still remains obdurate, he ties a sugar-cane to the bundle, and presents it to her through a third person. If she eats of the sugar-cane, she feels her love for her husband revive. On her side she has the right to operate in like manner on the bundle which represents herself, always provided that she does not go to the burying-ground, which is strictly forbidden to women.[1]

[12.] Another beneficent use of homoeopathic magic is to heal or prevent sickness. In ancient Greece, when a man died of dropsy, his children were made to sit with their feet in water until the body was burned. This was supposed to prevent the disease from attacking them.[1] Similarly, on the principle of water to water, among the natives of the hills near Rajamahall in India, the body of a person who has died of dropsy is thrown into a river; they think that if the corpse were buried, the disorder would return and carry off other people.[2]

The ancient Hindus performed an elaborate ceremony, based on homoeopathic magic, for the cure of jaundice. Its main drift was to banish the yellow colour to yellow creatures and yellow things, such as the sun, to which it properly belongs, and to procure for the patient a healthy red colour from a living, vigorous source, namely a red bull.[3] Pliny tells of the stone-curlew or some similar bird to which the Greeks gave their name for jaundice, because if a jaundiced man saw it, the disease left him and slew the bird.[4] He mentions also a stone which was supposed to cure jaundice because its hue resembled that of a jaundiced skin.[5] In modern Greece jaundice is called the Golden Disease, and very naturally it can be healed by gold. To effect a perfect cure, take a piece of gold and put it in a measure of wine. Expose the latter to the stars for three nights; then drink three glasses of the mixture daily till it is used up.[6] In Germany yellow turnips, gold coins and rings, saffron and other yellow things are still esteemed remedies for jaundice, just as a stick of red sealing-wax carried on the person cures the red eruption popularly known as St. Anthony's fire, or the blood-stone allays bleeding.[7]

Similarly, the Toradyas of Central Celebes employ rings of red stones to staunch the bleeding of wounds of all sorts.[7a] The same principle of homoeopathic magic is employed by the Brahuis of Baluchistan to save the wheat crop when it is attacked by red rust;[7b] while in Europe there is an old superstition that if scarlet fever or smallpox were epidemic, red flannel worn around the neck, or next to the skin on any part of the body, warded away the disease. Even in the present day the peasantry of Wales cling very closely to the old superstition about a bit of red flannel as a preventive against fever, smallpox, and rheumatism.[7c]

[13.] One of the great merits of homoeopathic magic is that it enables the cure to be performed on the person of the doctor instead of on that of his victim, who is thus relieved of all trouble and inconvenience, while he sees his medical man writhe in anguish before him. For example, the peasants of Perche, in France, labour under the impression that a prolonged fit of vomiting is brought about by the patient's stomach becoming unhooked, as they call it, and so falling down. Accordingly, a practitioner is called in to restore the organ to its proper place. After hearing the symptoms he at once throws himself into the most horrible contortions, for the purpose of unhooking his own stomach. Having succeeded in the effort, he next hooks it up again in another series of contortions and grimaces, while the patient experiences a corresponding relief. Fee five francs.[1] In like manner a Dyak medicine-man, who has been fetched in a case of illness, will lie down and pretend to be dead. He is accordingly treated like a corpse, is bound up in mats, taken out of the house, and deposited on the ground. After about an hour the other medicine-men loose the pretended dead man and bring him to life; and as he recovers, the sick person is supposed to recover too.[2] A cure for a tumour, based on the principle of homoeopathic magic, is prescribed by Marcellus of Bordeaux, court physician to Theodosius the First, in his curious work on medicine. It is as follows. Take a root of vervain, cut it across, and hang one end of it round the patient's neck, and the other in the smoke of the fire. As the vervain dries up in the smoke, so the tumour will also dry up and disappear. If the patient should afterwards prove ungrateful to the good physician, the man of skill can avenge himself very easily by throwing the vervain into water; for as the root absorbs the moisture once more, the tumour will return.[3] The same sapient writer recommends you, if you are troubled with pimples, to watch for a falling star, and then instantly, while the star is still shooting from the sky, to wipe the pimples with a cloth or anything that comes to hand. Just as the star falls from the sky, so the pimples will fall from your body; only you must be very careful not to wipe them with your bare hand, or the pimples will be transferred to it.[4]

[14.] Further, homoeopathic and in general sympathetic magic plays a great part in the measures taken by the rude hunter or fisherman to secure an abundant supply of food. On the principle that like produces like, many things are done by him and his friends in deliberate imitation of the result which he seeks to attain; and, on the other hand, many things are scrupulously avoided because they bear some more or less fanciful resemblance to others which would really be disastrous.

Nowhere is the theory of sympathetic magic more systematically carried into practice for the maintenance of the food supply than in the barren regions of Central Australia. Here the tribes are divided into a number of totem clans, each of which is charged with the duty of propagating and multiplying their totem for the good of the community by means of magical ceremonies and incantations. The great majority of the totems are edible animals and plants, and the general result supposed to be accomplished by these magical totemic ceremonies or *intichiuma,* as the Arunta call them, is that of supplying the tribe with food and other necessaries. Often the rites consist of an imitation of the effect which the people desire to produce; in other words, their magic is of the homoeopathic or imitative sort.

Thus among the Arunta the men of the witchetty grub totem perform a series of elaborate ceremonies for multiplying the grub which the other members of the tribes use as food. One of the ceremonies is a pantomime representing the fully-developed insect in the act of emerging from the chrysalis. A long narrow structure of branches is set up to imitate the chrysalis case of the grub. In this structure a number of men, who have the grub for their totem, sit and sing of the creature in its various stages. Then they shuffle out of it in a squatting posture, and as they do so they sing of the insect emerging from the chrysalis. This is supposed to multiply the numbers of the grubs.[1] Again, in order to multiply emus, which are an important article of food, the men of the emu totem in the Arunta tribe proceed as follows. They clear a small spot of level ground, and opening veins in their arms they let the blood stream out until the surface of the ground, for a space of about three square yards, is soaked with it. When the blood has dried and caked, it forms a hard and fairly impermeable surface, on which they paint the sacred design of the emu totem, especially the parts of the bird which they like best to eat, namely, the fat and the eggs. Round this painting the men sit and sing. Afterwards performers, wearing head-dresses to represent the long neck and small head of the emu, mimic the appearance of the bird as it stands aimlessly peering about in all directions.[2] Again, men of the hakea flower totem in the Arunta tribe perform a ceremony to make the hakea tree burst into blossom. The scene of the ceremony is a little hollow, by the side of which grows an ancient hakea tree. In the middle of the hollow is a small worn block of stone, supposed to represent a mass of hakea flowers. Before the ceremony begins, an old man of the totem carefully sweeps the ground clean, and then strokes the stone all over with his hands. After that the men sit round the stones and chant invitations to the tree to flower much and to the blossoms to be filled with honey. Finally, at the request of the old leader, one of the young men opens a vein in his arm and lets the blood flow freely over the stone, while the rest continue to sing. The flow of blood is supposed to represent the preparation of the favourite drink of the natives, which is made by steeping the hakea flower in water. As soon as the stone is covered with blood the ceremony is complete.[3] Again, the men of the kangaroo totem in the Arunta tribe perform ceremonies for the multiplication of kangaroos at a certain rocky ledge, which, in the opinion of the natives, is full of the spirits of kangaroos ready to go forth and inhabit kangaroo bodies. A little higher up on the hillside are two blocks of stone, which represent a male and female kangaroo respectively. At the ceremony these two blocks are rubbed with a stone by two men. Then the rocky ledge below is decorated with alternate vertical stripes of red and white, to indicate the red fur and white bones of the kangaroo. After that a number of young men sit on the ledge, open veins in their arms, and allow the blood to spurtle over the edge of the rock on which they are seated. This pouring out of the blood of the kangaroo men on the rock is thought to drive out the spirits of the kangaroos in all directions, and so to increase the number of the animals. While it is taking place, the other men sit below watching the performers and singing songs which refer to the expected increase of kangaroos.[4] In the Kaitish tribe, when the headman of the grass seed totem wishes to make the grass grow, he takes two sacred sticks or stones (*churinga*) of the well-known bullroarer pattern, smears them with red-ochre, and decorates them with lines and dots of down to represent grass seed. Then he rubs the stick or stones together so that the down flies off in all directions. The down is supposed to carry with it some virtue from the sacred stick or stone whereby the grass seed is made to grow. For days afterwards the headman walks about by himself in the bush singing to the grass seed and carrying one of the sacred bull-roarers (*churinga*) with him. At night he hides the implement in the bush and returns to camp, where he may have no intercourse with his wife. For during all this time he is believed to be so full of magic power, derived from the bull-roarer, that if he had intercourse with her the grass seed would not grow properly and his body would swell up when he tasted of it. When the seed begins to grow, he still goes on singing to make it grow more, but when it is fully grown he brings back the sacred implement to his camp hidden in bark; and having gathered a store of the seed he leaves it with the men of the other half of the tribe, saying, "You eat the grass seed in plenty, it is very good and grows in my country."[5]

[15.] The Indians of British Columbia live largely upon the fish which abound in their seas and rivers. If the fish do not come in due season, and the Indians are hungry, a Nootka wizard will make an image of a swimming fish and put it into the water in the direction from which the fish generally appear. This ceremony, accompanied by a prayer to the fish to come, will cause them to arrive at once.[1] The islanders of Torres Straits use models of dugong and turtles to charm dugong and turtle to their destruction.[2] The Toradjas of Central Celebes believe that things of the same sort attract each other by means of their indwelling spirits or vital ether. Hence they hang up the jawbones of deer and wild pigs in their houses, in order that the spirits which animate these bones may draw the living creatures of the same kind into the path of the hunter.[3] In the island of Nias, when a wild pig has fallen into the pit prepared for it, the animal is taken out and its back is rubbed with nine fallen leaves, in the belief that this will make nine more wild pigs fall into the pit, just as the nine leaves fell from the tree.[4] In the East Indian islands of Saparoea, Haroekoe, and Noessa Laut, when a fisherman is about to set a trap for fish in the sea, he looks out for a tree, of which the fruit has been much pecked at by birds. From such a tree he cuts a stout branch and makes of it the principal post in his fish-trap; for he believes that just as the tree lured many birds to its fruit, so the branch cut from that tree will lure many fish to the trap.[5]

The western tribes of British New Guinea employ a charm to aid the hunter in spearing dugong or turtle. A small beetle, which haunts coco-nut trees, is placed in the hole of the spear-haft into which the spear-head fits.

This is supposed to make the spear-head stick fast in the dugong or turtle, just as the beetle sticks fast to a man's skin when it bites him.[6] When a Cambodian hunter has set his nets and taken nothing, he strips himself naked, goes some way off, then strolls up to the net as if he did not see it, lets himself be caught in it, and cries, "Hillo! what's this? I'm afraid I'm caught." After that the net is sure to catch game.[7] A pantomime of the same sort has been acted within living memory in our Scottish Highlands. The Rev. James Macdonald, now of Reay in Caithness, tells us that in his boyhood when he was fishing with companions about Loch Aline and they had had no bites for a long time, they used to make a pretence of throwing one of their fellows overboard and hauling him out of the water, as if he were a fish; after that the trout or silloch would begin to nibble, according as the boat was on fresh or salt water.[8] Before a Carrier Indian goes out to snare martens, he sleeps by himself for about ten nights beside the fire with a little stick pressed down on his neck. This naturally causes the fall-stick of his trap to drop down on the neck of the marten.[9] Among the Galelareese, who inhabit a district in the northern part of Halmahera, a large island to the west of New Guinea, it is a maxim that when you are loading your gun to go out shooting, you should always put the bullet in your mouth before you insert it in the gun; for by so doing you practically eat the game that is to be hit by the bullet, which therefore cannot possibly miss the mark.[10] A Malay who has baited a trap for crocodiles, and is awaiting results, is careful in eating his curry always to begin by swallowing three lumps of rice successively; for this helps the bait to slide more easily down the crocodile's throat. He is equally scrupulous not to take any bones out of his curry; for, if he did, it seems clear that the sharp-jointed stick on which the bait is skewered would similarly work itself loose, and the crocodile would get off with the bait. Hence in these circumstances it is prudent for the hunter, before he begins his meal, to get somebody else to take the bones out of his curry, otherwise he may at any moment have to choose between swallowing a bone and losing the crocodile.[11]

[16.] This last rule is an instance of the things which the hunter abstains from doing lest, on the principle that like produces like, they should spoil his luck. For it is to be observed that the system of sympathetic magic is not merely composed of positive precepts; it comprises a very large number of negative precepts, that is, prohibitions. It tells you not merely what to do, but also what to leave undone. The positive precepts are charms: the negative precepts are taboos. In fact the whole doctrine of taboo, or at all events a large part of it, would seem to be only a special application of sympathetic magic, with its two great laws of similarity and contact. Though these laws are certainly not formulated in so many words nor even conceived in the abstract by the savage, they are nevertheless implicitly believed by him to regulate the course of nature quite independently of human will. He thinks that if he acts in a certain way, certain consequences will inevitably follow in virtue of one or other of these laws; and if the consequences of a particular act appear to him likely to prove disagreeable or dangerous, he is naturally careful not to act in that way lest he should incur them. In other words, he abstains from doing that which, in accordance with his mistaken notions of cause and effect, he falsely believes would injure him; in short, he subjects himself to a taboo. Thus taboo is so far a negative application of practical magic. Positive magic or sorcery says, "Do this in order that so and so may happen." Negative magic or taboo says, "Do not do this, lest so and so should happen." The aim of positive magic or sorcery is to produce a desired event; the aim of negative magic or taboo is to avoid an undesirable one. But both consequences, the desirable and the undesirable, are supposed to be brought about in accordance with the laws of similarity and contact. And just as the desired consequence is not really effected by the observance of a magical ceremony, so the dreaded consequence does not really result from the violation of a taboo. If the supposed evil necessarily followed a breach of taboo, the taboo would not be a taboo but a precept of morality or common sense. It is not a taboo to say, "Do not put your hand in the fire"; it is a rule of common sense, because the forbidden action entails a real, not an imaginary evil. In short, those negative precepts which we call taboo are just as vain and futile as those positive precepts which we call sorcery. The two things are merely opposite sides or poles of one great disastrous fallacy, a mistaken conception of the association of ideas. Of that fallacy, sorcery is the positive, and taboo the negative pole. If we give the general name of magic to the whole erroneous system, both theoretical and practical, then taboo may be defined as the negative side of practical magic.

[17.] Several examples of such negative magic can be cited. Thus, it is a rule with the Galelareese that when you have caught fish and strung them on a line, you may not cut the line through, or next time you go a-fishing your fishing-line will be sure to break.[1] Among the Esquimaux of Baffin Land boys are forbidden to play cat's cradle, because if they did so their fingers might in later life become entangled in the harpoon-line.[2] Here the taboo is obviously an application of the law of similarity, which is the basis of homoeopathic magic: as the child's fingers are entangled by the string in playing cat's cradle, so they will be entangled by the harpoon-line when he is a man and hunts whales. Again, among the Huzuls, who inhabit the wooded north-eastern slopes of the Carpathian Mountains, the wife of a hunter may not spin while her husband is eating, or the game will turn and wind like the spindle, and the hunter will be unable to hit it.[3] Here again the taboo is clearly derived from the law of similarity. So, too, in most parts of ancient Italy women were forbidden by law to spin on the highroads as they walked, or even to carry their spindles openly, because any such action was believed to injure the crops.[4] Probably the notion was that the twirling of the spindle would twirl the corn-stalks and prevent them from growing straight. So, too, among the Ainos of Saghalien a pregnant woman may not spin nor twist ropes for two months before her delivery, because they think that if she did so the child's guts might be entangled like the thread.[5] For a like reason in Bilaspore, a district of India, when the chief men of a village meet in council, no one present should twirl a spindle; for they think that if such a thing were to happen, the discussion, like the spindle, would move in a circle and never be wound up.[6] In the East Indian islands of Saparoea, Haroekoe, and Noessa Laut, any one who comes to the house of a hunter must walk straight in; he may not loiter at the door, for were he to do so, the game would in like manner stop in front of the hunter's snares and then turn back, instead of being caught in the trap.[7] For a similar reason it is a rule with the Toradjas of Central Celebes that no one may stand or loiter on the ladder of a house where there is a pregnant woman, for such delay would retard the birth of the child;[8] and in various parts of Sumatra the woman herself in these circumstances is forbidden to stand at the door or on the top rung of the house-ladder under pain of suffering hard labour for her imprudence in neglecting so elementary a precaution.[9] Malays engaged in the search for camphor eat their food dry and take care not to pound their salt fine. The reason is that the camphor occurs in the form of small grains deposited in the cracks of the trunk of the camphor-tree. Accordingly it seems plain to the Malay that if, while seeking for camphor, he were to eat his salt finely ground, the camphor would be found also in fine grains; whereas by eating his salt coarse he ensures that the grains of the camphor will also be large.[10] Some of the Brazilian Indians would never bring a slaughtered deer into their hut without first hamstringing it, believing that otherwise they and their children would never be able to run down their enemies.[11] Apparently they thought that by hamstringing the animal they at the same stroke deprived their foemen of the use of their legs. No Arikara Indian would break a marrow bone in a hut; for they thought that were he to do so, their horses would break their legs in the prairie.[12]

[18.] Among the taboos observed by savages none perhaps are more numerous than the prohibitions against eating certain foods, and many of these are demonstrably derived from the law of similarity and are accordingly examples of negative magic. Just as the savage eats many animals or plants in order to absorb desirable qualities with which he believes them to be endowed, so he avoids eating many others lest he acquire *un*desirable qualities which he attributes to them. In Madagascar, for example, soldiers are forbidden to taste the flesh of hedgehog, "as it is feared that this animal, from its propensity of coiling into a ball when alarmed, will impart a timid shrinking disposition to those who partake of it." Again, no soldier is allowed to eat an ox's knee, lest like an ox he become weak in the knees and unable to march.[1] So too a Caffre has been known to refuse to eat two mice caught at the same time in a single trap, alleging that if he were to do so his wife would give birth to twins; yet he would eat freely of mice caught singly.[2] Among the Zulus pig's flesh is not eaten by girls on any account; for they think that if they eat it, a resemblance to the pig will appear among their children; nor will Zulu men consume the entrails of cattle, lest their enemies stab them in the bowels.[3]

[19.] The reader may have observed that in some of the foregoing examples the magical influence is supposed to operate at long distance. Whatever doubts science may entertain as to the possibility of action at a distance, magic has none; faith in telepathy is one of its basic principles. Hence on important occasions the behaviour of friends and relatives at a distance is often regulated by a more or less elaborate code of rules, the neglect of which by the one set of persons would, it is supposed, entail misfortune or even death on the absent ones. In particular when a party of men are out hunting or fighting, their kinsfolk at home are often expected to do certain things or abstain from doing certain others, for the sake of ensuring the safety and success of the distant warriors or hunters.

In setting out to look for the rare and precious eagle-wood on the mountains, Cham peasants enjoin their wives, whom they leave at home, not to scold or quarrel in their absence, for such domestic brawls would lead to their husbands' being rent in pieces by bears and tigers.[1] In Yule Island, Torres Straits, when the men are gone to fetch sago, a fire is lit and carefully kept burning throughout their absence; for the people believe that if it went out the voyagers would fare ill.[2] At the other end of the world the Lapps similarly object to extinguishing a brand in water while any of the family are out fishing, since to do so would spoil their luck.[3]

[20.] Among the Esquimaux of Alaska similar notions prevail. During the whaling season the women remain in comparative idleness, since it is considered inauspicious for them to sew while the men are out in the boats.[1] Moreover, even in England there may be found traces of this primitive belief that the good luck of fishermen at sea can be directly influenced by the conduct of their wives at home. Thus, at Flamborough in Yorkshire, while the men are at sea, their wives and other women disguise themselves in various ways, often wearing the clothes of their male relatives, and go about the village with music and laughter, receiving alms or wishes of God-speed from their neighbors.[1a] Similarly, while a Gilyak hunter is pursuing the game in the forest, his children at home are forbidden to make drawings on wood or sand; for they fear that if the children did so, the paths in the forest would become as "crossed up" as the lines in the drawings, so that the hunter would lose his way and never return.[2] Again, when a Nuba of north-eastern Africa goes to El Obeid for the first time, he tells his wife not to wash or oil herself and not to wear pearls round her neck during his absence, because she would thus draw down on him the most terrible misfortunes.[3]

Elephant-hunters in East Africa believe that, if their wives prove unfaithful in their absence, this gives the elephant power over his pursuer, who will accordingly be killed or severely wounded. Hence if a hunter hears of his wife's misconduct, he abandons the chase.[4]

Many of the indigenous tribes of Sarawak are firmly persuaded that were the wives to commit adultery while their husbands are searching for camphor in the jungle, the camphor obtained by the men would evaporate.[5] Further, the wives dare not touch a comb while their husbands are away collecting the camphor; for if they did so, the interstices between the fibres of the tree, instead of being filled with the precious crystals, would be empty like the spaces between the teeth of a comb.[6] While men of the Toaripi or Motumotu tribe of eastern New Guinea are away hunting, fishing, fighting, or on any long journey, the people who remain at home must observe strict chastity, and may not let the fire go out. Those of them who stay in the men's clubhouses must further abstain from eating certain foods and from touching anything that belongs to others.[7]

[21.] Where beliefs like these prevail as to the sympathetic connexion between friends at a distance, we need not wonder that above everything else war, with its stern yet stirring appeal to some of the deepest and tenderest of human emotions, should quicken in the anxious relations left behind a desire to turn the sympathetic bond to the utmost account for the benefit of the dear ones who may at any moment be fighting and dying far away. Hence, to secure an end so natural and laudable, friends at home are apt to resort to devices which will strike us as pathetic or ludicrous, according as we consider their object or the means adopted to effect it. Thus in some districts of Borneo, when the men are away on a warlike expedition, their mats are spread in their houses just as if they were at home, and the fires are kept up till late in the evening and lighted again before dawn, in order that the men may not be cold. Further, the roofing of the house is opened before daylight to prevent the distant husbands, brothers, and sons from sleeping too late, and so being surprised by the enemy.[1] While a Malay of the Peninsula is away at the wars, his pillows and sleeping-mat at home must be kept rolled up. If any one else were to use them, the absent warrior's courage would fail and disaster would befall him. His wife and children may not have their hair cut in his absence, nor may he himself have his hair shorn.[2]

Among the Shans of Burma the wife of an absent warrior has to observe certain rules. Every fifth day she rests and does no work. She fills an earthen goblet with water to the brim and puts flowers into it every day. If the water sinks or the flowers fade, it is an omen of death. Moreover, she may not sleep on her husband's bed during his absence, but she sweeps the bedding clean and lays it out every night.[3] In the island of Timor, while war is being waged, the high-priest never quits the temple; his food is brought to him or cooked inside; day and night he must keep the fire burning, for if he were to let it die out, disaster would befall the warriors and would continue so long as the hearth was cold. Moreover, he must drink only hot water during the time the army is absent; for every draught of cold water would damp the spirits of the people, so that they could not vanquish the enemy.[4]

An old historian of Madagascar informs us that "while the men are at the wars, and until their return, the women and girls cease not day and night to dance, and neither lie down nor take food in their own houses. And although they are very voluptuously inclined, they would not for anything in the world have an intrigue with another man while their husband is at war, believing firmly that if that happened, their husband would be either killed or wounded. They believe that by dancing they impart strength, courage, and good fortune to their husbands; accordingly during such times they give themselves no rest, and this custom they observe very religiously."[5] In the Babar Archipelago, and among the Wagogo of East Africa, when the men are at the wars the women at home are bound to chastity, and in the Babar Archipelago they must fast besides.[6] Under similar circumstances in the islands of Leti, Moa, and Lakor the women and children are forbidden to remain inside of the houses and to twine thread or weave.[7] When the men of the Yuki tribe of Indians in California were away fighting, the women at home did not sleep; they danced continually in a circle, chanting and waving leafy wands. For they said that if they danced all the time, their husbands would not grow tired.[8] At Masset the Haida women danced and sang war-songs all the time their husbands were away at the wars, and they had to keep everything about them in a certain order. It was thought that a wife might kill her husband by not observing these customs.[9] In the Kafir district of the Hindu Kush, while the men are out raiding, the women abandon their work in the fields and assemble in the villages to dance day and night. The dances are kept up most of each day and the whole of each night.[10]

Among the Bantu people of Southern Nigeria, while the men were away at the war their wives at home were forbidden to wash, and they remained very quiet and anxious, and held no festivities of any kind. If any of them during this time had illicit intercourse, it was believed that her husband would surely be killed, and if any of them had previously sinned in this way and had not confessed her fault before his departure, it was believed that he would incur great danger and would hear a shot whistle by his ears. If he, after all, returned in safety, he would sell his faithless wife into another country.[10a]

[22.] Among the many beneficent uses to which a mistaken ingenuity has applied the principle of homoeopathic or imitative magic is that of causing trees and plants to bear fruits in due season.

In the interior of Sumatra rice is sown by women who, while sowing, let their hair hang loose down their backs, in order that the rice may grow luxuriantly and have long stalks.[1] And Thomas Hardy was once told that the reason why certain trees in front of his house did not thrive was that he looked at them before breakfast on an empty stomach!

Among the Huzuls of the Carpathians, when a woman is planting cabbages, she winds many cloths about her head, in order that the heads of the cabbages may also be thick. And as soon as she sows parsley, she grasps the calf of her leg with both hands, saying, "May it be as thick as that!"[2] By similar reasoning the Malagasy think that only people with an even set of teeth should plant maize, for otherwise there will be empty spaces in the cob corresponding to those in the planter's teeth.[3]

[23.] In many parts of Europe dancing or leaping high in the air are approved homoeopathic methods of making the crops grow high. Thus in Swabia and among the Transylvanian Saxons it is a common custom for a man who has sown hemp to leap high on the field in the belief that this will make the hemp grow tall.[1] All over Baden until recently it was the custom that the farmer's wife gave the sower a dish of eggs or a cake baked with eggs either before or after the sowing, in order that he might be strengthened to leap as high as possible.[2] Of the same import, too, was the rule at Quellendorf, in Anhalt, that the first bushel of seed-corn had to be heaped up high;[3] while when Macedonian farmers have done digging their fields, they throw their spades into the air and, catching them again, exclaim "May the crops grow as high as the spade has gone!"[4]

[24.] The notion that a person can influence a plant homoeopathically by his act or conditions comes out clearly in a remark made by a Malay woman. Being asked why she stripped the upper part of her body naked in reaping the rice, she explained that she did it to make the rice-husks thinner, as she was tired of pounding thick-husked rice.[1] Clearly, she thought that the less clothing she wore the less husk there would be on the rice. Among the Minangkabauers of Sumatra, when a rice barn has been built a feast is held, of which a woman far advanced in pregnancy must partake. Her condition will obviously help the rice to be fruitful and multiply.[2] Among the Zulus a pregnant woman sometimes grinds corn, which is afterwards burnt among the half-grown crops in order to fertilise them.[3] For a similar reason in Syria when a fruit-tree does not bear, the gardener gets a pregnant woman to fasten a stone to one of its branches; then the tree will be sure to bear fruit, but the woman will run a risk of miscarriage,[4] having transferred her fertility, or part of it, to the tree. In Bohemia for a similar purpose the first apple of a young tree is sometimes plucked and eaten by a woman who has borne many children, for then the tree will be sure to bear many apples.[5] In the Zürcher Oberland, Switzerland, they think that a cherry-tree will bear abundantly if its first fruit is eaten by a woman who has just given birth to her first child.[6] In Macedonia the first fruit of a tree should not be eaten by a barren woman but by one who has many children.[7] The Nicobar Islanders think it lucky to get a pregnant woman and her husband to plant seed in gardens.[8] Among the Ilocans of Luzon the men sow bananas, but the sower must have a young child on his shoulder, or the bananas will bear no fruit.[9] When a tree bears no fruit, the Galelareese think it is a male, so they put a woman's petticoat on it in order to change its sex and render it naturally prolific.[10]

[25.] This belief in the noxious and infectious nature of certain personal qualities or accidents has given rise in turn to a number of prohibitions or rules of avoidance: people abstain from doing certain things lest they should homoeopathically infect the fruits of the earth with their own undesirable state or condition. Thus the Indians of Santiago Tepehuacan suppose that if a single grain of the maize which they are about to sow were eaten by an animal, the birds and the wild boars would come and devour all the rest, and nothing would grow. And if any of these Indians has ever in his life buried a corpse, he will never be allowed to plant a fruit-tree, for they say that the tree would wither. Moreover, they will not let such a man go fishing with them, for the fish would flee from him.[1] Clearly these Indians imagine that anybody who has buried a corpse is thereby tainted, so to say, with an infection of death, which might prove fatal to fruits and fish. In Nais, the day after a man has made preparations for planting rice he may not use fire, or the crop would be parched; he may not spread his mats on the ground, or the young plants would droop towards the earth.[2] When the Chams of Cochinchina are sowing their dry rice-fields and desire that no rain should fall, they eat their rice dry instead of moistening it, as they usually do, with the water in which vegetables and fish have been boiled. That prevents rain from spoiling the crop.[3]

On the principle of homoeopathic magic: the plant can infect the man just as much as the man can infect the plant; action and reaction are equal and opposite. The Cherokee Indians are adepts in practical botany of the homoeopathic sort. The wiry roots of the catgut plant or devil's shoestring (*Tephrosia*), for instance, are so tough that they can almost stop a plough-share in the furrow. Hence Cherokee women wash their heads with a decoc-tion of the roots to make the hair strong, and Cherokee ball-players wash themselves with it to toughen their muscles.[4] The Guarani Indians of South America thought that a woman would become a mother of twins if she ate a double grain of millet.[5] Among the Lkuñgen Indians of Vancouver Island an infallible means of making your hair grow long is to rub it with fish oil and the pulverised fruit of a particular kind of poplar (*Populus trichocarpa*). As the fruit grows a long way up the tree, it cannot fail to make your hair grow long, too.[6] At Allumba, in Central Australia, there is a tree to which the sun, in the shape of a woman, is said to have travelled from the east. The natives believe that if the tree were destroyed, they would all be burned up; and that were any man to kill and eat an opposum from this tree, the food would burn up all his inward parts so that he would die.[7] Near Charlotte Waters, in Central Australia, there is a tree which sprang up to mark the spot where a blind man died. It is called the Blind Tree by the natives, who think that if it were cut down all of the people of the neighbourhood would become blind. A man who wishes to deprive his enemy of sight need only go to the tree by himself and rub it, muttering his wish and exhorting the magic virtue to go forth and do its baleful work.[8]

[26.] These examples introduce us to a fruitful branch of homoeopathic magic, namely, to that department of it which works by means of *the dead;* for just as the dead can neither see nor hear nor speak, so you may on homoeopathic principles render people blind, deaf, and dumb by the use of dead men's bodies or of anything that is tainted by the infection of death.

Burglars in all ages and many lands have been patrons of this species of magic, which is very useful to them in the exercise of their profession. Thus a South Slavonian housebreaker sometimes begins operations by throwing a dead man's bone over the house, saying, with pungent sarcasm, "As this bone may waken, so may these people waken"; after that not a soul in the house can keep his or her eyes open.[1] Similarly, in Java the burglar takes earth from a grave and sprinkles it round the house which he intends to rob; this throws the inmates into a deep sleep.[2] With the same intention a Hindu will strew ashes from a pyre at the door of the house;[3] Indians of Peru scatter the dust of dead men's bones;[4] and Ruthenian burglars remove the marrow from a human shin-bone, pour tallow into it, and having kindled the tallow, march thrice round the house with this candle burning, which causes the inmates to sleep a death-like sleep.[5]

In Europe similar properties were ascribed to the Hand of Glory, which was the dried and pickled hand of a man who had been hanged. If a candle made of the fat of a malefactor who had also died on the gallows was lighted and placed in the Hand of Glory as in a candlestick, it rendered motionless all persons to whom it was presented; they could not stir a finger any more than if they were dead.[6] Often it is prescribed that the thief's candle should be made of the finger of a new-born or, still better, unborn child; sometimes it is thought needful that the thief should have one such candle for every person in the house, for if he has one candle too little somebody in the house will wake and catch him. Once these tapers begin to burn, there is nothing but milk that will put them out. In the seventeenth century robbers used to murder pregnant women in order thus to extract candles from their wombs.[7] An ancient Greek robber or burglar thought he could silence and put to flight the fiercest watchdogs by carrying with him a brand plucked from a funeral pyre.[8]

[27.] Again, Servian and Bulgarian women who chafe at the restraints of domestic life will take the copper coins from the eyes of a corpse, wash them in wine or water, and give the liquid to their husbands to drink. After swallowing it, the husband will be as blind to his wife's peccadilloes as the dead man was on whose eyes the coins were laid.[1] The Belep of New Caledonia think that they can disable an enemy from flight by means of the legbone of a dead foe.[2] The ancient Greeks seem to have thought that to set a young male child on a tomb would be to rob him of his manhood by infecting him with the impotence of the dead.[3] And as there is no memory in the grave the Arabs think that earth from a grave can make a man forget his griefs and sorrows, especially the sorrow of an unhappy love.[4]

[28.] Again, *animals* are often conceived to possess qualities or properties which might be useful to man, and homoeopathic or imitative magic seeks to communicate these properties to human beings in various ways. Thus some Bechuanas wear a ferret as a charm, because, being very tenacious of life, it will make them difficult to kill.[1] In Morocco a fowl or a pigeon may sometimes be seen with a little red bundle tied to its foot; the bundle contains a charm, and it is believed that as the charm is kept in constant motion by the bird, a corresponding restlessness is kept up in the mind of him or her against whom the charm is directed.[2] When a Galla sees a tortoise, he will take off his sandals and step on it, believing that the soles of his feet are thereby made hard and strong like the shell of the animal.[3] The Wajaggas of Eastern Africa think that if they wear a piece of the wing-bone of a vulture tied round their leg they will be able to run and not grow weary, just as the vulture flies unwearied through the sky.[4] The Esquimaux of Baffin Land fancy that if part of the intestines of a fox is placed under the feet of a baby boy, he will become active and skilful in walking over thin ice like a fox.[5] The Lkuñgen Indians of Vancouver Island believed that the ashes of wasps rubbed on the faces of warriors before going to battle will make them as pugnacious as wasps, and that a decoction of wasps' nests or of flies administered internally to barren women will make them prolific like insects.[6] The Baronga of Delagoa Bay carry the powdered ashes of a serpent in a little bag as a talisman which guards them from snake-bites.[7] The Cholones of eastern Peru think that to carry the poison tooth of a serpent is a protection against the bite of a serpent, and that to rub the cheek with the tooth of an ounce is an infallible remedy for toothache and face-ache.[8] In order to strengthen her teeth some Brazilian Indians used to hang round a girl's neck at puberty the teeth of an animal which they called *capugouare,* that is "grass-eating."[9] When a thoroughbred mare has drunk at a trough, an Arab woman will hasten to drink any water that remains in order that she may give birth to strong children.[10] If a South Slavonian has a mind to pilfer and steal at market, he has nothing to do but to burn a blind cat, and then throw a pinch of its ashes over the person with whom he is higgling; after that he can take what he likes from the booth, and the owner will not be a bit the wiser, having become as blind as the deceased cat with whose ashes he has been sprinkled. The thief may even ask boldly "Did I pay for it?" and the deluded huckster will reply, "Why, certainly."[11] The ancient Greeks thought that to eat the flesh of the wakeful nightingale would prevent a man from sleeping; that to smear the eyes of a blear-sighted person with the gall of an eagle would give him the eagle's vision; and that a raven's eggs would restore the blackness of the raven to silvery hair. Only the person who adopted this last mode of concealing the ravages of time had to be most careful to keep his mouth full of oil all the time he applied the eggs to his venerable locks, else his teeth as well as his hair would be dyed raven black, and no amount of scrubbing and scouring would avail to whiten them again.[12] The hair-restorer was in fact a shade too powerful, and in applying it you might get more than you bargained for.

[29.] On the principle of homoeopathic magic, inanimate things, as well as plants and animals, may diffuse blessing or bane around them, according to their own intrinsic nature and the skill of the wizard to tap or dam, as the case may be, the stream of weal or woe. Thus, for example, the Galelareese think that when your teeth are being filed you should keep spitting on a pebble, for this establishes a homoeopathic connexion between you and the pebble, by virtue of which your teeth will henceforth be as hard and durable as a stone. On the other hand, you ought not to comb a child before it has teethed, for if you do, its teeth will afterwards be separated from each other like the teeth of a comb.[1] Nor should children look at a sieve, otherwise they will suffer from a skin disease, and will have as many sores on their bodies as there are holes in the sieve.[2] In Samaracand women give a baby sugar candy to suck and put glue in the palm of its hand, in order that, when the child grows up, his words may be sweet and precious things may stick to his hands as if they were glued.[3] The Greeks thought that a garment made from the fleece of a sheep that had been torn by a wolf would hurt the wearer, setting up an itch or irritation in his skin.[4] Among the Arabs of Moab a childless woman often borrows the robe of a woman who has had many children, hoping with the robe to acquire the fruitfulness of its owner.[5] The Caffres of Sofala, in East Africa, had a great dread of being struck with anything hollow, such as a reed or a straw, and greatly preferred being thrashed with a good thick cudgel or an iron bar, even though it hurt very much. For they thought that if a man were beaten with anything hollow, his inside would waste away till he died.[6] Again, the Galelareese think that, if you are imprudent enough to eat while somebody is sharpening a knife, your throat will be cut that same evening, or next morning at latest.[7] At critical times the Mahakam Dyaks of Central Borneo seek to strengthen their souls by biting on an old sword or setting their feet upon it.[8] At initiation a Brahman boy is made to tread with his right foot on a stone, while the words are repeated, "Tread on this stone; like a stone be firm";[9] and the same ceremony is performed, with the same words, by a Brahman bride at her marriage.[10]

The common custom of swearing upon a stone may be based partly on a belief that the strength and stability of the stone lend confirmation to an oath. Thus the Old Danish historian Saxo Grammaticus tells us that "the ancients, when they were to choose a king, were wont to stand on stones planted in the ground, and to proclaim their votes, in order to foreshadow from the steadfastness of the stones that the deed would be lasting."[11] There was a stone at Athens on which the nine archons stood when they swore to rule justly and according to the laws.[12] In Laconia an unwrought stone was shewn which, according to the legend, relieved the matricide Orestes of his madness as soon as he had sat down on it;[13] and Zeus is said to have often cured himself of his love for Hera by sitting down on a certain rock in the island of Leucadia.[14] In these cases it may have been thought that the wayward and flighty impulses of love and madness were counteracted by the steadying influence of a heavy stone.

[30.] But while a general magical efficacy may be supposed to reside in all stones by reason of their common properties of weight and solidity, special magical virtues are attributed to particular stones, or kinds of stone, in accordance with their individual or specific qualities of shape and colour. Thus in the Banks Islands a stone with little discs on it is deemed good for bringing in money; and if a man found a larger stone with a number of small ones under it, like a sow among her litter, he was sure that to offer money upon it would bring him pigs.[1]

The ancients set great store on the magical qualities of precious stones; indeed it has been maintained, with great show of reason, that such stones were used as amulets long before they were worn as mere ornaments.[2] Thus the Greeks gave the name of tree-agate to a stone which exhibits tree-like markings, and they thought that if two of these gems were tied to the horns or neck of oxen at the plough, the crop would be sure to be plentiful.[3] Again, they recognized a milk-stone which produced an abundant supply of milk in women if only they drank it dissolved in honey-mead.[4] In Lechrain down to modern times German women have attempted to increase their milk by stroking their breasts with a kind of alum which they call a milk-stone.[5] Again, the Greeks believed in a stone which cured snake-bites, and hence was named the snake-stone; to test its efficacy you had only to grind the stone to powder and sprinkle the powder on the wound.[6] The wine-coloured amethyst received its name, which means "not drunken," because it was supposed to keep the wearer of it sober.[7] In Albania people think that if the blood-stone is laid on a wound it will stop the flow of blood.[8]

[31.] Dwellers by the sea cannot fail to be impressed by the sight of its ceaseless ebb and flow, and are apt, on the principles of that rude philosophy of sympathy and resemblance which here engages our attention, to trace a subtle relation, a secret harmony, between its tides and the life of man, of animals, and of plants. In the flowing tide they see not merely a symbol, but a cause of exuberance, of prosperity, and of life, while in the ebbing tide they discern a real agent as well as a melancholy emblem of failure, of weakness, and of death. The Breton peasant fancies that clover sown when the tide is coming in will grow well, but that if the plant be sown at low water or when the tide is going out, it will never reach maturity and that the cows which feed on it will burst.[1] Another ancient belief, attributed to Aristotle, was that no creature can die except at ebb tide. The belief, if we can trust Pliny, was confirmed by experience, so far as regards human beings, on the coast of France.[2] Philostratus also assures us that at Cadiz dying people never yielded up the ghost while the water was high.[3] A like fancy still lingers in some parts of Europe. On the Cantabrian coast of Spain they think that persons who die of chronic or acute disease expire at the moment when the tide begins to recede.[4] In Portugal, all along the coast of Wales, and on some parts of the coast of Brittany, a belief is said to prevail that people are born when the tide comes in, and die when it goes out.[5] Dickens attests the existence of the same superstition in England. "People can't die, along the coast," said Mr. Peggotty, "except when the tide's pretty nigh out. They can't be born, unless it's pretty nigh in—not properly born till flood."[6] The belief that most deaths happen at ebb tide is said to be held along the east coast of England from Northumberland to Kent.[7] Shakespeare must have been familiar with it, for he makes Falstaff die "even just between twelve and one, e'en at the turning o' the tide."[8] We meet the belief again on the Pacific coast of North America among the Haidas of the Queen Charlotte Islands. Whenever a good Haida is about to die he sees a canoe manned by some of his dead friends, who come with the tide to bid him welcome to the spirit land. "Come with us now," they say, "for the tide is about to ebb and we must depart."[9] At the other extremity of America the same fancy has been noted among the Indians of Southern Chile. A Chilote Indian in the last stage of consumption, after preparing to die like a good Catholic, was heard to ask how the tide was running. When his sister told him that it was still coming in, he smiled and said that he had yet a little while to live.[10] At Port Stephens, in New South Wales, the natives always buried their dead at flood tide, never at ebb, lest the retiring water should bear the soul of the departed to some distant country.[11]

In San Cristoval, one of the Solomon Islands, a woman of the noble Araha clan may not leave the house in her pregnancy. Pregnant women of other clans may leave their houses, but only at high tide, because they believe that it is only at high tide that women give birth to offspring successfully.[11a] In Loango it is believed that people do not die when the tide is flowing, but only when it is ebbing.[11b] Similarly the coast-dwellers of the North Andaman Islands believe that the soul of a dying man goes out with the ebbing tide.[11c]

[32.] To ensure a long life the Chinese have recourse to certain complicated charms, which concentrate in themselves the magical essence emanating, on homoeopathic principles, from times and seasons, persons and things. The vehicles employed to transmit these happy and beneficial influences are no other than grave-clothes. These are provided by many Chinese in their lifetime, and most people have them cut out and sewn by an unmarried girl or a very young woman, wisely calculating that, since such a person is likely to live a great many years to come, a part of her capacity to live long must surely pass into the clothes, and thus stave off for many years the time when they shall be put to their proper use. Further, the garments are made by preference in a year which has an intercalary month; for to the Chinese mind it seems plain that grave-clothes made in a year which is unusually long will possess the capacity of prolonging life in an unusually high degree. Amongst the clothes there is one robe in particular on which special pains have been lavished to imbue it with this priceless quality. It is a long silken gown of the deepest blue colour, with the word "longevity" embroidered all over it in thread of gold. To present an aged parent with one of these costly and splendid mantles, known as "longevity garments," is esteemed by the Chinese an act of filial piety and a delicate mark of attention. As the garment purports to prolong the life of its owner, he often wears it, especially on festive occasions, in order to allow the influence of longevity, created by the many golden letters with which it is bespangled, to work their full effect upon his person. On his birthday, above all, he hardly ever fails to don it, for in China common sense bids a man lay in a large stock of vital energy on his birthday, to be expended in the form of health and vigour during the rest of the year. Attired in the gorgeous pall, and absorbing its blessed influence at every pore, the happy owner receives complacently the congratulations of friends and relations, who warmly express their admiration of these magnificent cerements, and of the filial piety which prompted the children to bestow so beautiful and useful a present on the author of their being.[1]

[33.] Sometimes homoeopathic or imitative magic is called in to annul an evil omen by accomplishing it in mimicry. The effect is to circumvent destiny by substituting a mock calamity for a real one. It is related, for instance, that two missionaries were once journeying through Central Celebes, accompanied by some Toradjas. Unfortunately the note of a certain bird called *teka-teka* was heard to the left. This boded ill, and the natives insisted that they must either turn back or pass the night on the spot. When the missionaries refused to do either, an expedient was hit upon which allowed them to continue the journey in safety. A miniature hut was made out of a leafy branch, and in it were deposited a leaf moistened with spittle and a hair from the head of one of the party. Then one of the Toradjas said, "We shall pass the night here," and addressing the hair he spoke thus: "If any misfortune should happen through the cry of that bird, may it fall on you." In this way the evil omen was diverted from the real men and directed against their substitute the hair, and perhaps also the spittle, in the tiny hut.[1] When a Cherokee has dreamed of being stung by a snake, he is treated just in the same way as if he had really been stung; otherwise the place would swell and ulcerate in the usual manner, though perhaps years might pass before it did so. It is the ghost of a snake that has bitten him in sleep.[2] One night a Huron Indian dreamed that he had been taken and burned alive by his hereditary foes the Iroquois. Next morning a council was held on the affair, and the following measures were adopted to save the man's life. Twelve or thirteen fires were kindled in the large hut where they usually burned their prisoners to death. Every man seized a flaming brand and applied it to the naked body of the dreamer, who shrieked with pain. Thrice he ran round the hut, escaping from one fire only to fall into another. As each man thrust his blazing torch at the sufferer he said, "Courage, my brother, it is thus that we have pity on you." At last he was allowed to escape. Passing out of the hut he caught up a dog which was held ready for the purpose, and throwing it over his shoulder carried it through the wigwams as a sacred offering to the war-god, praying him to accept the animal instead of himself. Afterwards the dog was killed, roasted, and eaten, exactly as the Indians were wont to roast and eat their captives.[3]

Contagion

[34.] The most familiar example of Contagious Magic is the magical sympathy which is supposed to exist between a man and any severed portion of his person, such as his hair or nails; so that whoever gets possession of human hair or nails may work his will, at any distance, upon the person from whom they were cut.

Among the Australian tribes it was a common practice to knock out one or more of a boy's front teeth at those ceremonies of initiation to which every male member had' to submit before he could enjoy the rights and privileges of a full-grown man.[1] The reason of the practice is obscure; all that concerns us here is the evidence of a belief that a sympathetic relation continued to exist between the lad and his teeth after the latter had been extracted from his gums. Thus among some of the tribes about the river Darling, in New South Wales, the extracted tooth was placed under the bark of a tree near a river or water-hole; if the bark grew over the tooth, or if the tooth fell into the water, all was well; but if it were exposed and the ants ran over it, the natives believed that the boy would suffer from a disease of the mouth.[2] Among the Murring and other tribes of New South Wales the extracted tooth was at first taken care of by an old man, and then passed from one headman to another, until it had gone all round the community, when it came back to the lad's father, and finally to the lad himself. But however it was thus conveyed from hand to hand, it might on no account be placed in a bag containing magical substances, for to do so would, they believed, put the owner of the tooth in great danger.[3]

The Basutos are careful to conceal their extracted teeth, lest these should fall into the hands of certain mythical beings called *baloi,* who haunt graves, and could harm the owner of the tooth by working magic on it.[4] In Sussex some forty years ago a maid-servant remonstrated strongly against the throwing away of children's cast teeth, affirming that should they be found and gnawed by any animal, the child's new tooth would be, for all the world, like the teeth of the animal that had bitten the old one. A similar belief has led to practices intended, on the principles of homoeopathic magic, to replace old teeth by new and better ones. Thus in many parts of the world it is customary to put extracted teeth in some place where they will be found by a mouse or a rat, in the hope that, through the sympathy which continues to subsist between them and their former owner, his other teeth may acquire the same firmness and excellence as the teeth of these rodents. Thus in Germany it is said to be an almost universal maxim among the people that when you have had a tooth taken out you should insert it in a mouse's hole. To do so with a child's milk-tooth which has fallen out will prevent the child from having toothache. Or you should go behind the stove and throw your tooth backwards over your head, saying, "Mouse, give me your iron tooth; I will give you my bone tooth." After that your other teeth will remain good. German children say, "Mouse, mouse, come out and bring me out a new tooth"; or "Mouse, I give you a little bone; give me a little stone"; or "Mouse, there is an old tooth for you; make me a new one."[5] Jewish children in South Russia used to throw their cast teeth on the roof with the same request to the mouse to give them an iron tooth for one of bone;[6] just as a Singhalese will throw them on the roof, saying, "Squirrel, dear squirrel, take this tooth and give me a dainty one!"[7] In Bohemia a child will sometimes throw its cast tooth behind the stove, asking the fox to give it an iron one instead.[8] An Armenian generally buries his extracted teeth at the edge of the hearth with the prayer: "Grandfather, take a dog's tooth and give me a golden tooth."[9] In the light of the preceding examples, we may conjecture that the grand-father here invoked is not so much the soul of a dead ancestor as a mouse or a rat.

[35.] Other parts which are commonly believed to remain in a sympathetic union with the body, after the physical connection has been severed, are the navel-string and the afterbirth, including the placenta. So intimate, indeed, is the union conceived to be, that the fortunes of the individual for good or evil throughout life are often supposed to be bound up with one or other of these portions of his person, so that if his navel-string or afterbirth is preserved and properly treated, he will be prosperous; whereas if it be injured or lost, he will suffer accordingly. Thus among the Maoris, when the navel-string dropped off, the child was carried to a priest to be solemnly named by him. But before the ceremony of naming began, the navel-string was buried in a sacred place and a young sapling was planted over it. Ever afterwards that tree, as it grew, was a *tohu oranga* or sign of life for the child.[1] Among the Arunta of Central Australia the navel-string is swathed in fur-string and made into a necklace, which is hung around the child's neck. The necklace is supposed to facilitate the growth of the child, keep it quiet and contented, and avert illness generally.[2] In like manner, in the Yabim tribe of New Guinea the mother ties the navel-string to the net which carries the child, lest any one should use the string to the child's hurt.[3] At Rotuma in Fiji it has become almost obligatory for a young man, who wants the girls to respect him, to make a voyage in a white man's vessel; and mothers come alongside ships anchored in the roadstead and fasten their boy's navel-string to the vessel's chainplates. This will make sure of a voyage for the child when it has grown up. This, of course, must be a modern development, but it has all the strength of an ancient custom.[4] In Ceram the child sometimes wears the navel-string round its neck as an amulet;[5] and in the islands of Leti, Moa, and Lakor he carries it as a talisman in war or on a far journey.[6] Similarly in the islands of Saparoea,

Haoekoe, and Noessa Laut, to the east of Amboyna, it is thought that a child born with a caul will enjoy in later years the gift of second sight.[7] So too in the Luang-Sermata islands a child born with a caul is counted lucky and can perceive and recognize the spirits of his ancestors.[8]

The people of Laos in Indo-China never consider the afterbirth as useless or throw it away in any corner: they believe that it remains in sympathetic connection with the individual, and according to its treatment will influence his lot in various ways. Attached to the highest branch of a tree in the courtyard, it becomes the prey of beneficent spirits, who will prepare for the child a happy life. Buried in the garden, it will secure the fidelity of the child to the house in which he was born: he will never leave it. Buried under the house ladder it will, oddly enough, secure the child from pains in his stomach.[8a]

In the Marshall Islands of the western Pacific the navel-string of a boy is thrown into the sea in order that he may become a good fisher: the navel-string of a girl is inserted in a leafy *pandanus* tree, in order that she may be diligent in plaiting *pandanus* fibre.[8b] In the Marquesas Islands, when a birth had taken place, the afterbirth was hastily buried under a frequented path in order that women passing over the spot might acquire from the afterbirth the gift of fecundity.[8c]

The Incas of Peru preserved the navel-string with the greatest care, and gave it to the child to suck whenever it fell ill.[9] In ancient Mexico they used to give a boy's navel-string to soldiers, to be buried by them on a field of battle, in order that the boy might thus acquire a passion for war. But the navel-string of a girl was buried beside the domestic hearth, because this was believed to inspire her with a love of home and a taste for cooking and baking.[10] Algonquin women hung the navel-string round the child's neck; if he lost it, they thought the child would be stupid and spiritless.[11]

[36.] Even in Europe many people still believe that a person's destiny is more or less bound up with that of his navel-string or afterbirth. Thus in Rhenish Bavaria the navel-string is kept for a while wrapt up in a piece of old linen, and then cut or pricked to pieces according as the child is a boy or a girl, in order that he or she may grow up to be a skilful workman or a good sempstress.[1] In Berlin the midwife commonly delivers the dried navel-string to the father with a strict injunction to preserve it carefully, for so long as it is kept the child will live and thrive and be free from sickness.[2] Again, in Europe children born with a caul are considered lucky;[3] in Holland, as in the East Indies, they can see ghosts.[4] The Icelanders also hold that a child born with a caul will afterwards possess the gift of second sight, that he will never be harmed by sorcery, and will be victorious in every contest he undertakes, provided he has the caul dried and carries it with him.[5]

[37.] A curious application of the doctrine of contagious magic is the relation commonly believed to exist between a wounded man and the agent of the wound, so that whatever is subsequently done by or to that agent must correspondingly affect the patient either for good or evil. Thus Pliny tells us that if you have wounded a man and are sorry for it, you have only to spit on the hand that inflicted the wound, and the sufferer's pain will be instantly relieved.[1] So, too, among the Lkuñgen Indians of British Columbia it is a rule that an arrow, or any other weapon that has wounded a man, must be hidden by his friends, who have to be careful not to bring it near the fire until the wound is healed. If a knife or an arrow which is still covered with a man's blood were thrown into the fire, the wounded man would suffer very much.[2] In the Yerkla-mining tribe of south-eastern Australia it is thought thát if any one but the medicine-man touches the flint knife with which a boy has been subincised, the boy will thereby be made very ill. So seriously is this belief held that if the lad chanced thereafter to fall sick and die, the man who had touched the knife would be killed.[3] "It is constantly received and avouched," says Bacon, "that the anointing of the weapon that maketh the wound will heal the wound itself. In this experiment, upon the relation of men of credit (though myself, as yet, am not fully inclined to believe it), you shall note the points following: first, the ointment wherewith this is done is made of divers ingredients, whereof the strangest and hardest to come by are the moss upon the skull of a dead man unburied, and the fats of a boar and a bear killed in the act of generation." The precious ointment compounded out of these and other ingredients was applied, as the philosopher explains, not to the wound but to the weapon, and that even though the injured man was at a great distance and knew nothing about it. The experiment, he tells us, had been tried of wiping the ointment off the weapon without the knowledge of the person hurt, with the result that he was presently in a great rage of pain until the weapon was anointed again. Moreover, "it is affirmed that if you cannot get the weapon, yet if you put an instrument of iron or wood resembling the weapon into the wound, whereby it bleedeth, the anointing of that instrument will serve and work the effect."[4] Remedies of the sort which Bacon deemed worthy of his attention are still in vogue in the eastern counties of England. Thus in Suffolk if a man cuts himself with a bill-hook or a scythe he always takes care to keep the weapon bright, and oils it to prevent the wound from festering. If he runs a thorn into his hand, he oils or greases it when extracted. If a horse wounds its foot by treading on a nail, your Suffolk groom will invariably preserve the nail, clean it, and grease it every day, to prevent the foot from festering. Arguing in the same way, a Suffolk woman whose sister had burned her face with a flat-iron, observed that "the face would never heal till the iron had been put out of the way; and even if it did heal, it would be sure to break out again every time the iron was heated."[5] Similarly Essex rustics opine that, if a man has been stabbed with a knife, it is essential to his recovery that the knife should be greased and laid across the bed on which the sufferer is lying,[6] while in the Harz mountains they say that if you cut yourself, you ought to smear the knife or the scissors with fat and put the instrument away in a dry place in the name of the Father, of the Son, and of the Holy Ghost. As the knife dries, the wound heals.[7]

In the Kagoro tribe of Northern Nigeria, if a man is wounded by a spear or sword and the place refuses to heal, the weapon, if it can be obtained, is washed with water, which is drunk by the patient, who is then supposed to recover.[7a]

The train of reasoning which thus commends itself to English and German rustics, in common with the savages of Melanesia and America, is carried a step further by the aborigines of Central Australia, who conceive that under certain circumstances the near relations of a wounded man must grease themselves, restrict their diet, and regulate their behaviour in other ways in order to ensure his recovery. Thus when a lad has been circumcised and the wound is not yet healed, his mother may not eat opossum, or a certain kind of lizard, or carpet snake, or any kind of fat, for otherwise she would retard the healing of the boy's wound. Every day she greases her digging-sticks and never lets them out of her sight; at night she sleeps with them close to her head. No one is allowed to touch them. Every day also she rubs her body all over with grease, as in some way this is believed to help her son's recovery.[8] Another refinement of the same principle is due to the ingenuity of the German peasant. It is said that when one of his pigs or sheep breaks its leg, a farmer of Rhenish Bavaria or Hesse will bind up the leg of a chair with bandages and splints in due form. For some days thereafter no one may sit on that chair, move it, or knock up against it; for to do so would pain the injured pig or sheep and hinder the cure.[9] In this last case it is clear that we have passed wholly out of the region of contagious magic and into the region of homoeopathic or imitative magic; the chair-leg, which is treated instead of the beast's leg, in no sense belongs to the animal, and the application of bandages to it is a mere simulation of the treatment which a more rational surgery would bestow on the real patient.

[38.] The sympathetic connexion supposed to exist between a man and the weapon which has wounded him is probably founded on the notion that the blood on the weapon continues to feel with the blood in his body. Strained and unnatural as this idea may seem to us, it is perhaps less so than the belief that magic sympathy is maintained between a person and his clothes, so that whatever is done to the clothes will be felt by the man himself, even though he may be far away at the time. That is the reason the Papuans of Tumleo search most anxiously for the smallest scrap which they may have lost of their scanty garments,[1] and why other Papuans, travelling through the thick forest, will stop and carefully scrape from a bough any clot of red pomade which may have adhered to it from their greasy heads.[2] The witch in Theocritus, while she melted an image or lump of wax in order that her faithless lover might melt with love of her, did not forget to throw into the fire a bit of the hem of his cloak which she had managed to acquire.[3] In Prussia they say that if you cannot catch a thief, the next best thing is to get hold of a garment which he may have shed in his flight; for if you beat it soundly, the thief will fall sick.[4] This belief is deeply rooted in the popular mind of primitives. Thus the Kai of Northern New Guinea believe that everything with which a man comes in contact retains something of his soul-stuff, by working on which a sorcerer may do the man himself grievous hurt. This is the great source of anxiety to the natives of New Guinea. Hence the native is at great pains to remove any traces of his presence from any object with which he has been in contact. If upon his way through the forest he leaves a lock of his hair or a thread of his girdle on a thorny bush, he goes not further until he has removed every trace of it. He throws nothing away. Even when he is a guest at a friendly village he gathers the shells of the betel-nuts carefully in his pouch which he always carries about with him; or he throws the remains in the fire. Even the places where he sits retain something of his soul-stuff, so on rising he is careful to efface the traces of his person, either by stamping with his feet, or by poking with his stick, or by sprinkling them with water from a stream. Or on the spot he places certain leaves which are believed to possess the property of driving away his soul-stuff. The soul-stuff is thought of itself soon to depart, but it is desirable to hasten its departure, for once a magician gets possession of the soul-stuff the original owner of it is often supposed to be a doomed man.[4a]

[39.] Again, magic may be wrought on a man sympathetically not only through his clothes and severed parts of himself, but also through the impressions left by his hand in sand or earth. In particular, it is a worldwide superstition that by injuring footprints you injure the feet that made them. Thus the natives of south-eastern Australia think that they can lame a man by placing sharp pieces of quartz, glass, bone, or charcoal in his footprints. Rheumatic pains are often attributed by them to this cause.

In New Britain it is thought that you can cause the sickness or death of a man by pricking his footprints with the sting of a sting-ray.[1] The Maoris imagine that they can work grievous harm to an enemy by taking up earth from his footprints, depositing it in a sacred place, and performing a ceremony over it.[2] On Savage Island a common form of witchcraft was to take up the soil on which an enemy had set his foot, and to carry it to a sacred place, where it was solemnly cursed, in order that the man might be afflicted with lameness.[3] The Galelareese think that if anybody sticks something sharp into your footprints while you are walking, you will be wounded in your feet.[4] In New Ireland a person who has been robbed looks for the footprints of the thief, and if he finds them he takes them up and performs ceremonies over them, which he supposes will disable the malefactor and so prevent him from doing further mischief.[4a]

In Izumo, a district of Japan, if a house has been robbed in the night while the inmates are asleep, when they wake in the morning they will look for the footprints of the burglars, and if they find them they will burn mugwort in them. By this operation it is hoped or believed that the burglar's feet will be made so sore that he cannot run far, and that the police may easily overtake him.[4b] The Ewe-speaking people of West Africa fancy they can drive an enemy mad by throwing a magic powder on his footprints.[5]

Similar practices prevail in various parts of Europe. Thus in Mecklenburg it is thought that if you drive a nail into a man's footprint he will fall lame; sometimes it is required that the nail should be taken from a coffin.[6] A like mode of injuring an enemy is resorted to in some parts of France.[7] It is said that there was an old woman who used to frequent Stow in Suffolk, and she was a witch. If, while she walked, any one went after her and stuck a nail or a knife into her footprint in the dust, the dame could not stir a step till it was withdrawn.[8] More commonly, it would seem, in Germany earth from the footprint is tied up in a cloth and hung in the chimney smoke; as it dries up, so the man withers away or his foot shrivels up.[9] The same practice and the same belief are said to be common in Matogrosso, a province of Brazil.[10] An old Danish mode of concluding a treaty was based on the same idea of the sympathetic connexion between a man and his footprints: the covenanting parties sprinkled each other's footprints with their own blood, thus giving a pledge of fidelity.[11] In ancient Greece superstitions of the same sort seem to have been current, for it was thought that if a horse stepped on the track of a wolf he was seized with numbness;[12] and a maxim ascribed to Pythagoras forbade people to pierce a man's footprints with a nail or a knife.[13]

[40.] But though the footprint is the most obvious it is not the only impression made by the body through which magic may be wrought on a man. The aborigines of south-eastern Australia believe that a man may be injured by burying sharp fragments of quartz, glass, and so forth in the mark made by his reclining body; the magical virtue of these sharp things enters his body and causes those acute pains which the ignorant European puts down to rheumatism.[1] To ensure the good behaviour of an ally with whom they have just held a conference, the Basutos cut and preserve the grass on which he sat during the interview.[2] Moors who write on the sand are careful to obliterate all the marks they have made, never leaving a stroke or dot in the sand when they have done writing.[3]

FOOTNOTES BY FRAZER

Abbreviations Used in Footnotes

AAA   *Annals of Archaeology and Anthropology*
ARW   *Archiv für Religionswissenschaft*
BTLVNI   *Bijdragen tot de Taal- Land- en Volkenkunde van Nederlandsch Indië*
JAI   *Journal of the [Royal] Anthropological Institute of Great Britain and Ireland*
JRAS   *Journal of the Royal Asiatic Society of Great Britian and Ireland*
KARI   *Keilschrifttexte aus Assur religiösen Inhalts, ed. E. Ebeling. Leipzig, 1919–*
KBo   *Keilschrifttexte aus Boghazköi*
NH   Pliny, *Naturalis Historia*
RA   *Revue d'assyriologie et d'archéologic orientale*
RHR   *Revue de l'histoire des religions*
SBE   *The Sacred Books of the East, ed. F. Max Muller. Oxford, 1879–1910*
ZDMG   *Zeitschrift der Deutschen Morgenländischen Gesellschaft*
ZDPV   *Zeitschrift der Deutschen Palaestina-Vereins*

[6]   1. See Theocritus, ii; Vergil, *Eclogues,* viii. 78–82; Ovid, *Heroides,* vi. 91 f.; id., *Amores,* iii. 7, 29 f.

     2. P. Jones, *History of the Ojebway Indians* (London n.d.), 146.

     3. C. Lumholtz, *Unknown Mexico* (London 1903), i. 485 f.

     4. P. J. de Arriaga, *Extirpacion de la Idolatria del Piru* (Lima 1621), 25 f.

     5. *Reports of the Cambridge Anthropol. Exped. to Torres Straits,* v (Cambridge 1904), 324 f.

     6. J. Batchelor, *The Ainu and Their*

Folklore (London 1901), 329–31.

7. J. J. M. de Groot, *The Religious System of China*, v (Leyden 1907), 920 f.

8. C. J. Forbes, *British Burma* (London 1878), 232.

9. A. Hillebrandt, *Vedische Opfer und Zauber* (Strasburg 1897), 117.

10. E. Doutté, *Magie et religion dans l'Afrique du Nord* (Algiers 1908) 61 f.

10a. P. A. Talbot, *The Peoples of Southern Nigeria* (London 1926), ii. 182.

10b. P. Güssfeldt, *et al., Die Loango-Expedition, 1873–1876* (Stuttgart 1909), III. ii, 337.

10c. A. D. Nock, in *Archiv für Religionswissenschaft,* 24 (1926), 172.

[7] 1. G. Maspero, *Histoire ancienne de l'Orient classique: les origines* (Paris 1895), 213 f.

1a. E. A. W. Budge, *Osiris and the Egyptian Resurrection* (London 1911), ii. 177 f.

2. M. Jastrow, *The Religion of Babylonia and Assyria* (Boston 1898), 268, 286.

[8] 1. Jastrow, *op. cit.,* 286 f.

2. E. A. W. Budge, *Egyptian Magic* (London 1899), 77 ff.

[9] 1. E. W. Nelson, in *Eighteenth Ann. Report of the Bureau of Amer. Ethnology* (1899), 435.

2. J. Teit, in *Memoirs of the Am. Mus. Nat. History: The Jessup North Pacific Expedition,* i., No. 4 (April 1900), 314.

3. J. R. Swanton, *Contributions to the Ethnology of the Haida* (Leyden-New York 1905), 47 ff.

4. S. Powers. *Tribes of California* (Washington 1877), 318.

5. C. Lumholtz, in *Mem. Am. Mus. Nat. History,* iii (May 1900), 52.

6. P. J. de Arriaga, *op. cit.,* 37.

7. A. Delegorgue, *Voyage dans l'Afrique Australe* (Paris 1847), ii. 325 f.

8. E. Casalis, *The Basutos* (London 1861), 251.

9. Capt. Binger, *Du Niger au golfe de Guinée* (Paris 1892), ii. 230.

10. W. G. Aston, *Shinto* (London 1905), 331.

11. R. Taylor, *Te Ika A Maui, or New Zealand and its Inhabitants*² (London 1870), 213.

[10] 1. W. Caland, *Altindisches Zauberritual* (Amsterdam 1900), 119; Hymns of the Atharva-Veda, tr. Blomfield (*SBE* xlii), 358 f.

2. W. H. Keating, *Narrative of an Expedition to the Source of St. Peter's River* (London 1825), ii. 159.

3. See Theocritus, ii. 28 f.; Vergil, *Ecl.,* viii. 81 f.

[11] 1. Father Lambert, *Moeurs et Superstitions des Néo-Calédoniens* (Nouméa 1900), 97 f.

[12] 1. Plutarch, *De sera numinis vindicta,* 14.

2. T. Shaw, in *Asiatic Researches,* 4 (1809), 69.

3. Caland, *op. cit.,* 75 ff.

4. Pliny, *NH,* xxx. 94.

5. *Ib.,* xxxvii. 170.

6. Personal communication from R. C. Bosanquet.

7. A. Wuttke, *Der deutsche Volksaberglaube*² (Berlin 1869), 302, ¶ 477.

7a. N. Adriani and A. C. Kruijt, *Die Bare'esprekende Toradja's van Midden-Celebei* (Batavia 1912), 350.

7b. D. Bray, in *Census of India,* 1911, iv. 68.

7c. M. Trevelyan, *Folk-Lore and Folk-Stories of Wales* (London 1909), 311.

[13] 1. P. Chapiseau, *Le Folk-lore de la Beauce et du Perche* (Paris 1902), i. 172 f.

2. H. Ling Roth, *The Natives of Sarawak and British North Borneo* (London 1896), i. 280.

3. Marcellus, *De medicamentis,* xv. 82.

4. *Ib.,* xxiv. 10.

[14] 1. B. Spencer and F. J. Gillen, *The Native Tribes of Central Australia* (London 1899), 176.

2. *Ib.*, 179 ff.
3. *Ib.*, 184 ff.
4. *Ib.*, 193 ff., 199 ff., 206 f.
5. *Id., The Northern Tribes of Central Australia* (London 1904), 291–94.

[15] 1. F. Boas, in *Sixth Ann. Report on the North-Western Tribes of Canada* (1890), 45.
2. A. C. Haddon, in *JAI*, 19 (1890), 427.
3. A. C. Kruijt, in *Vorslagen en Med. d. konink. Akad. v. Wetenschappen, Afdeeling Letterkunde*, IV. iii (1899), 203 f.
4. J. W. Thomas, in *Tijdschrift v. Indische Taal- Land- en Volkenkunde* 26 : 277.
5. Van Schmid, in *Tijdschrift voor Neerlands-Indië*, 1843, ii. 601 f.
6. B. A. Hely, in *British New-Guinea, Ann. Report for 1894–95*, p. 56.
7. E. Aymonier, in *Cochinchine francaise*, No. 16 (Saigon 1883), 157.
8. J. Macdonald, *Religion and Myth* (London 1893), 5.
9. A. G. Monce, *Au pays de l'Ours Noir* (Paris-Lyons 1897), 71.
10. M. J. van Baarda, in *Bijdragen tot de Taal- Land- en Volkenkunde van Nederl. Indië*, 45 (1895), 502.
11. W. W. Skeat, *Malay Magic* (London 1900), 300.

[17] 1. M. J. van Baarda, *op. cit.*, 507.
2. F. Boas, in *Bull. Am. Mus. Nat. History*, 15, i (1901), 161.
3. R. F. Kaindl, in *Globus*, 76 (1899), 273.
4. Pliny, *NH*, xxviii. 20.
5. B. Pilsudski, in *Anthropos*, 5 (1910), 763.
6. E. M. Gordon, *Indian Folk-Tales* (London 1908), 82 f.
7. Van Schmid, in *Tijdschr. v. Nederlands-Indië*, 1843, ii. 604.
8. A. C. Kruijt, in *Med. Zendel.*, 40 (1896), 262 f.; 44 (1900), 235.
9. C. Snouck Hurgronje, *De Atjehers* (Batavia-Leyden 1893–94), i. 409.

10. W. W. Skeat, *op. cit.*, 213.
11. A. Thevet, *Les Singularitez de la France Antarctique, autrement nommée Amérique* (Antwerp 1558), 93.
12. Maximilian zu Wied, *Reise in das innere Nord-America* (Coblenz 1839–41), ii. 247.

[18] 1. H. F. Standing, in *Antanarivo Annual and Madagascar Magazine*, 2 (reprinted 1896), 261.
2. D. Kidd, *Savage Childhood* (London 1906), 48.
3. H. Callaway, *Nursery Tales, Traditions and Histories of the Zulus*, i (Natal-London 1868), 280 ff.

[19] 1. E. Aymonier, in *RHR*, 24 (1891), 278.
2. A. C. Haddon, *Head-hunters* (London 1901), 259.
3. C. Leemius, *De Lapponibus Finmarchiae* (Copenhagen 1767), 500.

[20] 1. *Report of the Internat. Polar Exped. to Point Barrow, Alaska* (Washington 1883), 39.
1a. A. H. Armytage, *Flamborough, Village and Heathland* (Saffron Walden, 1880), 143.
2. P. Labbé, *Un Bagne Russe, l'Ile de Sakhaline* (Paris 1903), 268.
3. *Missions Catholiques*, 14 (1882), 460.
4. P. Reichard, *Deutsch-Ostafrika* (Leipzig 1892), 427.
5. Private communication from Dr. C. Hose, formerly Resident Magistrate of the Baram district, Sarawak.
6. W. H. Furness, *Home-life of the Borneo Head-hunters* (Philadelphia 1902), 169.
7. J. Chalmers, in *JAI*, 27 (1898), 327.

[21] 1. H. Ling Roth, in *JAI*, 22 (1893), 56.
2. W. W. Skeat, *op. cit.*, 524.
3. *Indian Antiquary*, 21 (1892), 120.
4. H. O. Forbes, in *JAI*, 13 (1884), 414.

5. De Flacourt, *Histoire de la Grande Isle Madagascar* (Paris 1658), 97 f.

6. H. Cole, in *JAI*, 32 (1902), 312, 317.

7. J. G. F. Riedel, *De sluik- en kroesharige rassen tusschhen Selebes en Papua* (The Hague 1886), 377.

8. S. Powers, *Tribes of California* (Washington 1877), 129 f.

9. J. R. Swanton, *Contributions to the Ethnology of the Haida* (Leyden-New York 1905), 55 f.

10. G. S. Robertson, *The Kafirs of the Hindu Kush* (London 1896), 335, 621–26.

10a. P. A. Talbot, *The Peoples of Southern Nigeria* (London 1926), iii. 856.

[22] 1. A. L. van Hasselt, *Volksbeschrijving van Midden-Sumatra* (Leyden 1882), 323.

2. R. F. Kaindl, in *Globus*, 76 (1899), 276.

3. H. F. Standing, in *Antanarivo Annual and Madagascar Magazine*, 2 (reprinted 1896), 257.

[23] 1. E. Meier, *Deutsche Sagen, Sitten und Gebräuche aus Schwaben* (Stuttgart 1852), 499.

2. E. H. Meyer. *Badisches Volksleben im 19ten Jahrhundert* (Strasburg 1900), 421 f.

3. O. Hartung, in *Zeitschrift d. Vereins für Volkskunde*, 7 (1897), 149 f.

4. G. F. Abbott, *Macedonian Folklore* (Cambridge 1903), 122.

[24] 1. W. W. Skeat, op. cit., 248.

2. J. L. van der Toorn, in *BTLVNI*, 39 (1890), 67.

3. D. Kidd. *Savage Childhood* (London 1906), 291.

4. Eijub Abela, in *ZDPV*, 7 (1884), 112, ¶ 202.

5. J. V. Grohman, *Aberglauben und Gebräuche aus Böhmen und Mähren* (Prague 1864), 143, ¶ 1053.

6. E. Hoffman-Krayer, in *Schweizer. Archiv f. Volkskunde*, 11 (1907), 263.

7. G. F. Abbott, op. cit., 122.

8. *Census of India, 1901*, iii. 206.

9. F. Blumentritt, in *Globus*, 48, No. 12, p. 202.

10. M. J. van Baarda, in *BTLVNI*, 45 (1895), 489.

[25] 1. *Bull. Soc. Geogr. de Paris*, IIme Sér., ii (1834), 181 ff.

2. E. Modigliani, *Un Viaggio a Nias* (Milan 1890), 590.

3. D. Grangeon, in *Missions Catholiques*, 28 (1896), 83.

4. J. Mooney, *Myths of the Cherokee* (Washington 1900), 425 ff.

5. R. Southey, *History of Brazil*, ii (London 1817), 37.

6. F. Boas, in *Sixth Ann. Report on the North-Western Tribes of Canada* (1890), 25.

7. B. Spencer and F. J. Gillen, *The Northern Tribes of Central Australia* (London 1904), 624 ff.

8. Id., *The Native Tribes of Central Australia* (London 1889), 552.

[26] 1. F. S. Krauss, *Volksglaube und religiöser Brauch der Südslaven* (Münster i.W. 1890), 146.

2. J. Knebel, in *Tijdschrift voor Indische Taal- Land- en Volkenkunde*, 40 (1898), 506.

3. W. Crooke, *Popular Religion and Folklore of Northern India* (Westminster 1896), i. 261.

4. P. J. de Arriaga, *Extirpacion de la Idolatria del Piru* (Lima 1621), 22.

5. R. F. Kaindl, in *Globus*, 61 (1892), 282.

6. J. Brand, *Popular Antiquities of Great Britain* (London 1882–83), iii. 278 f.

7. A. Wuttke, *Der deutsche Volksaberglaube*[2] (Berlin 1869), 126 f.

8. Aelian, *Nat. animalium*, i. 38.

[27] 1. F. S. Krauss, op. cit., 140.

2. Father Lambert, *Moeurs et Superstitions des Néo-Calédoniens* (Nouméa 1900), 30 f.

3. Hesiod, *Works and Days*, 750 ff. (But the lines are not free of ambiguity.)

4. E. Doutté, *Magie et religion dans l'Afrique du Nord* (Algiers 1908), 302 ff.

[28] 1. B. Shaw, *Memorials of South Africa* (London 1840), 66.

2. A. Leared, *Morocco and the Moors* (London 1876), 272.

3. P. Paulitschke, *Ethnographie Nordost-Afrika* (Berlin 1896), 27.

4. M. Merker, *Rechtsverhältnisse und Sitten der Wadschagga* (Gotha 1902), 21.

5. F. Boas, in *Bull. Am. Mus. Nat. Hist.*, 15, i (1901), 160.

6. Id., in *Sixth Ann. Report on the North-Western Tribes of Canada* (1890), 25.

7. H. A. Junod, *Les Ba-ronga* (Neuchatel 1898), 472.

8. E. Poeppig, *Reise in Chile, Peru und auf dem Amazonenstrome* (Leipzig 1835–36), ii. 323.

9. A. Thevet, *Cosmographie universelle* (Paris 1575), ii. 946 [980].

10. A. Jaussen, *Coutumes des Arabes au pays de Moab* (Paris 1908), 36.

11. F. S. Krauss, *op. cit.*, 147.

12. Aelian, *Nat. animalium*, i. 42, 43, 48.

[29] 1. M. J. van Baarda, in *BTLVNI*, 45 (1895), 483.

2. *Ib.*, 534.

3. E. Chavannes, *Documents sur les Tou-Kiue occidentaux* (St. Petersburg 1903), 134.

4. Aelian, *Nat. anim.*, i. 38.

5. Jaussen, *op. cit.*, 35.

6. J. Dos Santos, "Eastern Ethiopia," in G. McCall Theal's *Records of South-Eastern Africa* ([London] 1901), vii. 224.

7. M. J. van Baarda, *op. cit.*, 468.

8. A. W. Nieuwenhuis, *Quer durch Borneo*, ii (Leyden 1907), 173.

9. Grihya-Sútras, tr. Oldenberg (*SBE* xxx), 146.

10. Id., *SBE* xxix. 168, 282 f.

11. *The First Nine Books of . . . Saxo Grammaticus*, tr. O. Elton (London 1894), 16.

12. Aristotle, *Const. Ath.*, vii. 55;

Plutarch, *Solon*, 25; Pollux, viii. 86.

13. Pausanias, iii. 22,1. (Cp. ii. 31,4)

14. Ptolemaeus. *apud* Photius, Bibliotheca, 153 Bekker.

[30] 1. R. H. Codrington, *The Melanesians* (Oxford 1891), 181 ff.

2. W. Ridgeway, *The Early Age of Greece* (Cambridge 1901), i. 330.

3. Orphica, *Lithica*, 230 ff.

4. *Ib.*, 189 ff.

5. K. von Leoprechting, *Aus dem Lechrain* (Munich 1855), 92.

6. Orphica, *Lithica*, 335 ff.

7. Pliny, *NH*, xxxvii. 124.

8. J. G. von Hahn, *Albanesische Studien* (Jena 1854), i. 158.

[31] 1. P. Sébillot, *Légendes, croyances et superstitions de la mer* (Paris 1886), i. 136.

2. Pliny, *NH*, ii, 220.

3. Philostratus, *Vita Apolon.*, v. 2.

4. Sébillot, *op. cit.*, i. 132.

5. *Ib.*, i. 129–32; M. E. James, in *Folk-Lore*, 9(1898), 189.

6. *David Copperfield*, Chap. xxx.

7. W. Henderson, *Folk-Lore of the Northern Counties of England* (London 1879), 58.

8. *Henry V*, Act II, Scene 3.

9. C. Harrison, in *JAI*, 21 (1892), 17 f.

10. C. Martin, in *Zeitschrift für Ethnologie*, 4 (1877), 179.

11. A. W. Howitt, *The Native Tribes of S. E. Australia* (London 1904), 465.

11a. C. E. Fox, *The Threshold of the Pacific* (London 1924), 337.

11b. P. Güssfeldt, *et al.*, *Die Loango-Expedition, 1873–1876* (Stuttgart 1909), III. ii, 325.

11c. A. R. Brown, *The Andaman Islanders* (Cambridge 1922), 175.

[32] 1. J. J. M. de Groot, *The Religious System of China* (Leyden 1892–), i. 60–63.

[33] 1. N. Adriani and A. C. Kruijt, in *Med. Zendel.*, 42, (1898), 524.

2. J. Mooney, in *Seventh Ann. Report of the Amer. Bureau of Ethnology* (1891), 352; id., in

Nineteenth Ann. Report, i (1900), 295.

3. *Relations des Jésuites* (1642), 86 ff.

[34] 1. A. W. Howitt, op. cit., 538 ff.; B. Spencer and F. J. Gillen, *The Native Tribes of Central Australia* (London 1899), 213 f., 450 ff., id., *The Northern Tribes of Central Australia* (London 1904), 18, 329, 588 ff.

2. F. Bonney, in *JAI,* 13 (1884), 128.

3. Howitt. op. cit., 561.

4. Porte, in *Missions Catholiques,* 28 (1896), 312.

5. A. Wuttke, *Der deutsche Volksaberglaube*[2] (Berlin, 1869), 330. ¶ 526; F. Panzer, *Beitrag zur deutschen Mythologie* (Munich 1848–55), ii. 307.

6. S. Weissenberg, in *Globus,* 88 (1903), 317.

7. A. A. Perera, in *Indian Antiquary,* 32 (1903), 435.

8. J. V. Grohmann, *Aberglauben und Gebräuche aus Böhmen und Mähren* (Prague 1864), 55, 111, ¶ 825.

9. M. Abeghian, *Der armenische Volksglaube* (Leipzig 1899), 68.

[35] 1. R. Taylor, *Te Ika A Maui, or New Zealand and its Inhabitants*[2] (London 1870), 184.

2. B. Spencer and F. J. Gillen, *The Native Tribes of Central Australia* (London 1899), 467.

3. M. Krieger, *New Guinea* (Berlin [1899]), 165.

4. Personal communication from L. Fison (5/29/1901).

5. J. G. F. Riedel, *De sluik- en kroesharige rassen tusschen Selebes en Papua* (The Hague 1886), 135.

6. *Ib.,* 391.

7. Riedel, op. cit., 73 f.

8. *Ib.,* 326.

8a. G. Maupetit, in *Bull. et Mém. Soc. d'Anthropologie de Paris,* 6 (1912), 473.

8b. P. A. Erdland, *Die Marshall-Insulaner* (Münster 1914), 125, 338.

8c. M. Radiguet, *Les derniers sauvages* (Paris 1882), 173.

9. Garcilasso de la Vega, *Royal Commentaries on the Yncas,* tr. C. Markham (London 1867–71), i. 186.

10. B. de Sahagun, *Histoire générale des choses de la Nouvelle Empire,* tr. Jourdanet-Simeon (Paris 1880), 310.

11. *Relations des Jésuites* (1639), p. 44.

[36] 1. *Bavaria Landes- und Volkskunde des Königreichs Bayern,* IV. ii, 346.

2. E. Krause, in *Zeitschrift für Ethnologie,* 15 (1883), 84.

3. H. Ploss, *Das Kind*[2] (Leipzig 1884), i. 12 ff.

4. J. Grimm, *Deutsche Mythologie*[4] (Berlin 1875–78), ii. 728, n. 1.

5. M. Bartels, in *Zeitschrift für Ethnologie,* 32 (1900), 70 f.

[37] 1. Pliny, *NH,* xxviii. 36.

2. F. Boas, in *Sixth Ann. Report on the North-Western Tribes of Canada* (1890), 25.

3. A. W. Howitt, op cit., 667.

4. Francis Bacon, *Natural History,* cent. x, ¶ 998.

5. W. W. Groome, in *Folk-Lore,* 6 (1895), 126; E. S. Hartland, *The Legend of Perseus* (London 1894–96), ii. 169–72.

6. C. Partridge, *Cross River Natives* (London, 1905), 295.

7. H. Pröhle, *Harzbilder* (Leipzig 1855), 82.

7a. A. J. N. Tremearne, in *JAI,* 42 (1912), 161.

8. Spencer and Gillen, *Native Tribes,* 250.

9. F. Panzer, op. cit., ii. 302.

[38] 1. M. J. Erdweg, in *Mitt. d. Anthropol. Ges. in Wien,* 32 (1902), 287.

2. B. Hagen, *Unter den Papua's* (Wiesbaden 1899), 269.

3. Theocritus, ii. 53 f.

4. Hartland, op. cit., ii. 80 ff.

4a. R. Neuhauss, *Deutsch Neu-Guinea* (Berlin 1911), iii. 117.

[39] 1. R. Parkinson, *Dreissig Jahre in der Südsee* (Stuttgart 1907), 605.

2. E. Best, in *Journal of the Polynesian Society*, 9 (1900), 196.

3. B. C. Thomson, *Savage Island* (London 1902), 97.

4. M. J. van Baarda, in *BTLVNI*, 45 (1895), 512.

4a. P. F. Hess, in *Anthropos* 10–11 (1915–16), 48.

4b. Lafcadio Hearn, *Glimpses of Unfamiliar Japan* (London 1905), ii. 604.

5. A. B. Ellis, *The Ewe-Speaking Peoples of the Slave-Coast* (London 1890), 94.

6. K. Bartsch, *Märchen und Gebrauche aus Mecklenburg* (Vienna 1879–80), ii. 329 ff.

7. J. L. M. Nogués, *Les Moeurs d'autrefois en Saintonge et en Aunis* (Saintes 1890), 169 f.

8. Lady E. C. Gordon, ed., *County Folklore: Suffolk* (London 1893), 201.

9. Bartsch, *op. cit.*, ii. 330, 334; R. Andree, *Ethnographische Parallelen und Vergleiche*, N.F. (Leipzig 1889), 8, 11.

10. K. von den Steinen, *Unter den Naturvölkern Zentral-Brasiliens* (Berlin 1894), 558.

11. Saxo Grammaticus, tr. Elton (London 1894), 28 ff.

12. Aelian, *De natura animalium*, i. 36.

13. Mullach, ed., *Fragmenta Philosophorum Graecorum* (Paris 1875), i. 510.

[40] 1. Howitt, *op cit.*, 366.

2. E. Casalis, *The Basutos* (London 1861), 273.

3. J. Richardson, *Travels in the Great Desert of Sahara* (London 1848), ii. 65.

ADDITIONAL NOTES BY THEODOR H. GASTER

[5.] *Magic.* Among the recent studies of magic the following are especially significant: E. de Martino, *Il mondo magico* (Turin 1948); H. Webster, *Magic: A Sociological Study* (Stanford 1948); H. Aubin, *L'homme et la magie* (Paris 1952); K. Beth, *Religion und Magie*[2] (Leipzig 1927); S. Seligmann, *Die magischen-Heil-und Schutzmittel aus der unbelebten Natur* (Stuttgart 1927); L. Thorndike, *A History of Magic and Experimental Science during the First Thirteen Centuries of our Era* (New York 1929–38); L. Deubner, *Magie und Religion* (Freiburg i.B. 1922); C. Clemen, "Wesen und Ursprung der Magie" in *Archiv für Religionspsychologie*, 2–3 (1921), 108–35.

Homoeopathic Magic

Frazer's theory that in ceremonies where things desired are simulated in advance (e.g., rainfall by pouring water) or where an object employed somehow resembles that upon which it is to operate (e.g., yellow stones as a cure for jaundice), the underlying principle is *homoeopathy*, or a conviction that "like produces like," rests on assumptions which invite question.

In the first place, Frazer does not distinguish clearly between an act which is believed in itself to be automatically effective and one which is simply a dramatized petition addressed to a superior power. In several of the cases which he cites, the action involved is accompanied expressly by words of prayer. Hence, they are not magical acts at all, and no principle of magic, homoeopathic or other, can be said to inform them; they are simply indications to the gods or spirits of what the performer wants those gods or spirits to do for him. It is significant, for instance, that in the long Babylonian incantations recited during the act of burning images of one's enemies the verbs are usually in the optative, not the indicative, mood, i.e., "may such-and-such happen," rather than "such-and-such *will* happen," implying petition rather than automatic effect. Similarly, in Hittite ceremonies at the dedication or renovation of a house or temple, a piece of copper is deposited in the foundations with the recital of the words: "As this copper is firm and sound, so may the house (temple) be firm and sound." Here again no homoeopathic principle is involved; there is no automatic transference of properties from the object to the edifice; the procedure is purely symbolic.

Secondly, it should be observed that at that primitive stage of thought where the qualities and potentialities of things are attributed not (as by modern science) to their organic structure but to properties and "influences" conferred on them capriciously at separate occasions, it is "logical" enough to infer that such properties can be "borrowed" from one possessor of them and transferred to another object or person to meet a special demand. A red stone, for example, may be thought to have the property necessary to produce red blood, and when the production of red blood is demanded, the red stone naturally presents itself to the primitive mind as a potential source whence the redness may be borrowed. In all of this, however, there is no assumption of any law of homoeopathy—that is, of any intrinsic magical relationship between objects.

[6.] The practice of encompassing harm upon a person by maltreating (e.g., burning) images of him or things intimately connected with him, is known technically as *envoutement*. For further literature on the subject, see: A. Abt, *Apologie des Apuleius* (Giessen 1908), 80 f.; I. Scheftelowitz in *Archiv für Religionswissenschaft*, 17 (1914), 192; Skutsch, in *Festschrift d. schles. Ges. für Volkskunde* (1911), 529 f.; Pagenstecher, in *Archiv für Religionswissenschaft*, 15 (1912), 313 f.; Berkusky, in *Archiv f. Anthropol.*, N.F. 9 (1912), 88 ff.; Penquitt, *De Didonis Vergilianae exitu* (Diss., Königsberg, 1910), 35 ff.; W. Wundt, *Völkerpsychologie*, II. ii, 191 f.; E. A. W. Budge, *Amulets and Superstitions* (London 1930), 481–86; G. Kittredge, *Witchcraft in Old and New England* (Cambridge 1929),

73 ff., 411 ff.; nn. 1–71; Stith Thompson, *Motif-Index*, D 2061.2.2.–The practice is well attested in ancient Mesopotamia: R. C. Thompson, *The Devils and Evil Spirits of Babylonia* (London 1904), ii. 103; B. Meissner, *Babylonien und Assyrien* (Heidelberg 1920–25), ii. 210, 225. Prescriptions for making images for this purpose are given in a series of texts published by O. Gurney in *AAA* 22: 21–95: cf. also C. L. Wooley and S. Smith in *JRAS* 1926, 689–713, and S. Langdon in *RA*, 26 (1929), 39–42. The practise underlies the great Mesopotamian series of incantations known as Shurpu and Maqlu (both meaning "burning"); see H. Zimmern, *Die Beschwörungstafeln Surpu* (Leipzig 1901); G. Meier, *Die assyrische Beschwörungssammlung Maqlû* (Berlin 1937). Extracts are translated in I. Mendelsohn, *Religions of the Ancient Near East* (New York 1955), 211–19. In a text from Asshur, the ancient capital of Assyria, a cure for sickness is to fashion out of mud, pitch, chalk, or wood a figure of the offending witch or wizard, sprinkle it with "fish-oil" and burn it: E. Ebeling, *Quellen zur Kenntniss d. bab. Religion*, I (Leipzig 1918), 27–34.—A Hittite text (KBo. II. 3. ii, 47, 50) mentions an object called *nakkussis*, defined as "something that represents a person in sympathetic magic."— The Yoruba of W. Africa use a clay image called *shigidi* in both black and white magic: G. Parrinder, *La religion en Afrique occidentale* (Paris 1950), 189.—At Orissa, in India, it was customary to draw the figure of an enemy on the ground and then pierce it with a spear: *Notes and Queries*, III. xi (1867), 180.—Similarly, in nineteenth-century Scotland, Lady Fowlis had arrowheads shot at the portraits of two relatives: *ib.*, 180.—In March 1867, a *corp cré* or *criade*—that is, a human image made of clay and stuck with human nails, birds' claws, bones, and pins—was found in a stream near Inverness. It was believed that the person so represented would waste away: *ib.*, 375.—"The Irish, when anyone has been attacked with scarlet fever, are accustomed to cut off some of [his] hair, which they put down the throat of an ass. By this means the disease is

supposed to be charmed away from the patient and to attack the ass instead": N & Q, III. vi (1852), 600.—In April, 1950, the Appellate Division of the Superior Court of New Jersey denied a divorce to a woman who asserted that her husband "practiced voodooism" against her by sticking pins into a doll: New York *Herald Tribune*, April 28, 1950.

[17]   *Taboo on spinning*. An early Assyrian text (Ebeling, ZDMG 69 [1915], 93, lines 5–6) prescribes for the effectiveness of a magical praxis that "no male is to eat cress, no female to ply the spindle"; while in a menology from the ancient Assyrian capital of Asshur, it is enjoined, along with other restrictions, that "all weaving operations must cease" on the twenty-first day of the month of Nisan (Ebeling, *KARI*, 178, ii. 75).—In Swedish popular usage, spinning is taboo on Thursday nights: E. Clodd, *Tom Tit-Tot* (London 1898), 45.—In Germany, it is often proscribed during the Twelve Days from Christmas to Epiphany: P. Sartori, *Sitte und Brauch* (Leipzig 1910–14), ii. 46, n. 5; iii. 23, n. 2; or on St. Andrew's Eve (Schulenburg, *Wend. Volkskunde*, 126), December 31, Michaelmas, and St. Catherine's Day.—For the motif in folktales, see Stith Thompson, *Motif-Index*, G. 832.

[19]   *Animal flesh proscribed for homoeopathic reasons*. See on this: R. Andree, *Ethnographische Parallelen und Vergleiche*, i (Stuttgart 1878), 114–27; T. H. Gaster, *The Holy and the Profane* (New York 1955), 204 f.—The Loango proscribe the consumption of goat meat, lest the consumer's skin tend likewise to "scale": A. Bastian, *Die deutsche Expedition an der Loango-Küste* (Jena 1874–75), i. 185.—The Sea Dyaks of Borneo will not eat pork lest they contract a skin disease (scrofula?) to which pigs (cp. Italian *scrofa*) are thought to be liable: F. H. von Kittlitz, *Denkwürdigkeiten einer Reise* (1858), iii. 105. —The Caribs avoid pork for fear of getting "pig's eyes," and tortoises lest they become clumsy: T. Waitz, *Anthropologie der Naturvölker* (Leipzig 1860–77), iii. 384. —It is not improbable that some of these traditional taboos really underlie the dietary provisions of the Mosaic Code, though this is but one factor.

[21]   *Taboos during wartime*. See in general: Holsti, "Some Superstitious Customs in Primitive Warfare," in *Festskrift tillegnad Westermarck* (Helsingfors 1912), 137 f.; F. Schwally, *Semitische Kriegsaltertümer* (Leipzig 1901), 46 f.—Among the early Arabs, sexual intercourse was taboo to warriors: Aghāni, xiv. 67, xv. 161; Al-Ahtal, *Diwan*, 120.2; Mas'udi, vi. 63—65; *Frag. Hist. Ar.*, 247; W. R. Smith, *Religion of the Semites*[3] (London 1927), 455, 640 f.— Among the Hebrews, the word "consecrate" (q-d-sh) was used in the sense of "prepare for war": Jer. 22.7; 51.27 f.; Joel 4.9. Cp. also I Sam. 21.4—5; II Sam. 11.11. —The taboo upon consorting with women in wartime is but one application of the general idea that the very sight of women debilitates: see Stith Thompson, *Motif-Index*, C 212; T. H. Gaster, *Thespis* (New York 1950), 328.

[23]   *Leaping as a fertility-charm*. At Cambridge, England, it is still a popular folk custom that adults perform a ritual act of skipping on Good Friday: R. F. Rattray, *From Primitive to Modern Religion* (London [1949]), 25.—In a hymn to Zeus Kouros discovered at Palaikastro, in Crete, and dating from the third or second century B.C., the god is invoked to "leap for our herds and full pails," and some scholars have thought that this is an invitation to the deity to join his worshippers in a rite of leaping for fertility: see R. C. Bosanquet, in *Annual of the British School at Athens*, 15 (1908–09), 339 ff.; Gilbert Murray, *ib.*, 357ff.; Jane Harrison, *Themis* (Cambridge 1912), 3 ff.; Aly, in *Philologus*, 71 (1912), 469 ff.; W. M. L. Hutchinson, in *Classical Review*, 27 (1913), 132 ff.; Latte, *De saltationibus Graecorum* (1913), 21.—It has likewise been suggested that the real function of the Salii, i.e., leapers, who performed in the forum at Rome during the month of March, was to execute a ritual leaping for fertility.

[26]   *Use of corpses in magical practice*. For further literature see: T. J. Pettigrew, *On Superstitions connected with the History and Practise of Medicine and Sur-*

gery (Philadelphia 1844), 100; E. S. Mc Cartney, "Folklore Heirlooms," in *Papers of the Michigan Acad. of Science, Arts and Letters,* 16 (1931), 189–90; V. S. Lean, *Collectanea* (Bristol-London 1902–04), ii. 583; F. D. Bergen "Current Superstitions," *Memoirs of the American Folk-Lore Society,* 4 (1896), 131.—A popular recipe from Kentucky prescribes: "If you have a goitre on your neck, rub a dead person's hand over it three times. As the body decays, the goitre will disappear": D. L. and L. B. Thomas, *Kentucky Superstitions* (Princeton 1920), 105. This practise, which is also attested from Storington, England *(Folk-Lore Record* I [1878], 48), can be traced back to Pliny *(NH,* xxviii. 45).—In Thomas Hardy's story, "The Withered Arm" (included in *Wessex Tales),* touching the neck of a man who has been hanged is said to effect a cure. This finds a parallel in the belief of certain S. African primitives that the left hand and foot of a person ritually slain can, if decocted, prove effective for magical purposes. A trial for murder committed to this end was reported in the New York *Herald Tribune* of June 6, 1957. This, too, has an analogy in Pliny's statements that the hair of a crucified man protects from quartan fever *(NH,* xxviii. 41) and that the noose used by a suicide when applied to the temples, cures headache (xxviii. 49).

A magical papyrus in the British Museum says that in cases of theft by an unknown person, the culprit's eye will appear bruised and inflamed if a sorcerer taps his own ear with a hammer made out of the wood of a gibbet. A similar procedure survived in the seventeenth century at Holstein, Germany: E. Riess in *Trans. Am. Philological Association,* 25 (1895), 52. See on this subject: G. Kittredge, *Witchcraft in Old and New England* (Cambridge, 1929), 151, 470 f., n. 126; Stith Thompson, *Motif-Index,* D 1500.1.26.—The noose used by a suicide is likewise credited with the power of protecting from mishap: Kittredge, *op. cit.,* 142, 461, Stith Thompson, *op. cit.,* D 1384.2.

The idea underlying all these practices is that the vitality which quits the dead may be transferred to the living. Comparable therefore is the notion attested in Jewish folklore that a barren woman may induce conception by applying to her own person the water or soap with which a corpse has been washed: R. Patai in *Talpioth,* 5 (1953), 248, n, 2 [Hebrew]. The use for this purpose of criminals already condemned to death is simply a short cut in the interests of "economy." Analogous is the use of them as human scapegoats. . . .

[28] *Animal properties transferred to man.* Here belongs also the practice of giving newborn children the names of powerful or even of obnoxious animals as a means of warding off demons who might be seeking to attack them. For examples see: R. Andree, *Ethnographische Parallelen und Vergleiche,* i. (Stuttgart 1879), 177; *Zeitschrift d. Ges. f. Erdkunde zu Berlin,* 1 (1866), 386; Th. Bent, quoted in E. Clodd, *Tom Tit-Tot* (London 1898), 94. (It is quite mistaken to regard such names as evidence of totemism!)

[30] *Transference of properties from stones.* An arresting example of this is afforded by the widespread practice of supplying expectant mothers with a so-called eagle-stone *(aetites)* which they wear around their necks or carry upon their persons as a protective amulet. The object in question is a ferruginous pebble, usually found in streams, which, when rattled, reveals the presence of a smaller stone inside it and thus serves as a very natural symbol of pregnancy. See: Aelian, *De nat. animal.,* i. 35; Levret, *Essai sur les accouchements* (1776), 52; S. Seligmann, *Der böse Blick* (1910), 215–17; W. B. Mc-Daniel, *Birth and Infancy in Ancient Rome and Modern Italy* (Coconut Grove, Florida 1948), 12–13; *Notes and Queries,* VI, iii (1880), 327, 509; iv (1881), 297. The practice is mentioned by Plutarch (V. 95, Didot), and the properties of the stone are duly described by both Pliny *(NH,* xxx. 14; xxxvi. 39) and Dioscorides (v. 161). In Germany and Italy, it is not uncommon to bind it to the left hip of a pregnant woman: *Handwörterbuch deutsch. Abergl.,* v. 133 f.; McDaniel, *loc. cit.;* E. Canziani, in *Folk-Lore,* 39 (1928), 211. In the Middle

Ages, such a stone was carefully preserved in Durham Cathedral: Bede, *Historia Eccles. Gentis Angliae*, ed. Smith (1722), 740.

[31.] *Death at ebb-tide.* On this superstition, see further: F. D. Bergen, *Current Superstitions* (1896), 126, No. 1184 [New England]. Pliny says (*NH*, ii. 220) that the belief was tested along the "Gallic ocean" but found to hold true only for human beings. In Boulogne *s'en aller avec la marée* is a popular euphemism for "to die": A. S. Rapoport, *Superstitions of Sailors* (London 1928), 42. See also: P. Sébillot, *Folklore de la France* (Paris 1904–07), ii. 19 f.; Rutilius Benincasa, *Almanaco perpetuo*, pt. iv, tract. 5, c. 14; Ferraris, *Prompta Bibliotheca*, § 36; Tusser's *Five Hundred Points of Good Husbandrie* (1557), c. xiv, verse 4; *Notes and Queries*, V. vi (1876), 186, 305, 356; E. S. McCartney op. cit., 173 f.

Contagious Magic

Like his assumption of "homoeopathy," Frazer's theory of a Law of Contagion as a principle of magic is open to question. The practices which he cites in support of this contention can be otherwise explained.

What is really involved would seem to be the primitive notion of what we may call *the extended self.* The primitive believes that the self, or identity, of a person is not limited to his physical being but embraces also everything associated with it and everything that can evoke his presence in another person's mind. Thus, the shadow, name, footprint, gait, dress, excreta, portrait, etc., of a person are just as much an essential and integral part of him as his body, the more so since they can bear evidence of him even when he is corporeally absent. To "contact" any of these things is therefore just as effective a method of affecting him (for good or ill) as to work on his actual body. To bless or curse his name, for example, or to perform acts with portions of his clothing, will "touch" him—that is, "him" in his full, extended being—just as much as to punch him or caress him. Hence it is incorrect and oversimplified to say that one can use a man's garment in

magic because of some property attaching to it materially because, having once been in contact with him, it can ever afterwards "influence" him. The truth is rather that the garment is itself a part of him. In other words, it is a question not of conveyance of properties or influences, but rather of identity.

[34] *Hair as seat of the soul.* See further: Schredelseker, *De superstitionibus quae ad crines pertinent* (Heidelberg 1913); S. Reinach, *Samson* (1912), 23 ff.; Waser, in *ARW* 16 (1913), 381; Güntert, in *Sitzb. Heidelb. Akad. Wiss.*, 6 (1915), 11 f.; A. Abt, *Apologie des Apuleius* (Giessen 1908), 179 ff.; O. Gruppe, *Griech. Mythologie* (Munich 1906). 187 n. 2; 882, nn. 2 ff.; G. A. Wilken, *Ueber das Haaropfer* (Amsterdam 1886–87), 78 f.—According to L. Sommer, *Das Haar in Religion u. Aberglauben d. Griechen* (Munich 1918), this belief underlies the practice of swearing by the beard.

As to the belief that it is unlucky to cut a baby's hair, see the instances quoted in *Notes and Queries*, I. vi (1852), 312; II. xii (1861), 500; IV. vi (1870), 130, 204, 376; VI. vi (1882), 249, 416. Note also the superstition reported from Bottesford Moors, England, that if a child's nails are cut before it is one year old, it will grow up to be a thief: *N & Q.*, I. vi (1852), 71. This, of course, is simply a later rationalization of the time-honored taboo.

[36.] *Caul.* See further: H. Ploss, *Das Kind* (Leipzig 1911–12), i. 37 ff., 54 f.; G. F. Abbott, *Macedonian Folklore* (Cambridge 1903), 139; A. S. Rapoport, *Superstitions of Sailors.* (London 1928), 264; McCartney, op. cit., 113 ff. Medieval comments on the subject will be found in Levinius Lemnius, *De miraculis occultis naturae* (1593), Bk. ii, c. 8.—The caul is always regarded as beneficial in averting demons; E. Crawley, *The Mystic Rose*[2] (London 1927), i. 151–52; Van Gennep, *Les rites de passage* (Paris 1909), 72 f.; Ploss-Bartels, *Weib*[2], ch. 53; P. Sartori, *Sitte u. Brauch* (Leipzig 1910–14), i. 23; J. Trachtenberg, *Jewish Magic and Superstition* (New York 1939), 134.

[38.] *Sympathetic magic of clothes.* A striking example of the "sympathetic" quality popularly attached to garments is the Italian belief that if menstrual cloths are put in the wash above and not underneath the clothes of a man, the man will suffer atrocious pains: Z. Zanetti, *La medicina delle nostre donne* (Città di Castello 1892), 97 f., 101.—On the magic of clothes, see in general: E. Crawley, *Dress, Drink and Drums* (London 1931).

[39.] *Footprint.* Italian witches gather dust from footprints on Tuesdays and Fridays in order to work mischief with it:

M. Cox, *Introduction to Folk-Lore* (London 1897), 217.—An ancient German method of discomfiting a rival in love was to rub out his left footprint with one's right foot, and vice-versa, saying meanwhile, "I tread on thee and am over thee": W. Kroll, *Antiker Aberglaube* (Hamburg 1897), 23.— Not impossibly, superstitions of this kind underlie the legend in the Koran (Sura 20.96) that when Moses rebuked Aaron for his share in the incident of the Golden Calf, he accompanied his words by throwing dust from "the footprints of an angel" (i.e., Gabriel) at the offensive object.

Bronislaw Malinowski

ON THE METHODS AND AIMS
OF ETHNOGRAPHIC FIELDWORK

There is a mystique of Malinowski. No other anthropologist is more closely associated with the necessity for, and the techniques of, conducting fieldwork. His notion of living among a people rather than visiting them on occasional sorties from colonialist outposts fully equipped with the comforts of civilization marked a turning point in the gathering of ethnographic data. Specifically, his idea of participant observation in which the ethnographer participates as much as possible in the life of the people he is studying has served as an ideal for numerous young ethnographers. One reason for Malinowski's great influence is that he made explicit what the fieldwork experience was and what it should be. The introduction to his classic monograph on the Trobriand Islanders, *Argonauts of the Western Pacific,* first published in 1922, from which the present essay comes, is one of the clearest statements in the anthropological literature of what fieldwork is.

In view of Malinowski's contribution to fieldwork theory and methodology, it is somewhat astonishing to learn the circumstances of some of his field experiences. Caught in Australia at the outbreak of World War I, Malinowski, a native of Poland and citizen of Austria, was taken into custody for political reasons. Instead of sitting idly by under house arrest, he persuaded the Australian authorities to allow him to explore some of their territories during his internment. Part of Malinowski's

Reprinted from *Argonauts of the Western Pacific* (New York, 1922), pp. 4–25, 517–18, by permission of E. P. Dutton & Co., Inc., and Routledge & Kegan Paul, Ltd.

extensive fieldwork included two trips to the Trobriand Islands (1915–1916 and 1917–1918). Through the magic of his writing —and one must realize that English was not his native language —the Trobriand Islanders became one of the best known anthropologically described peoples of the world. Ethnography is not always interestingly written and, to be truthful, a good many ethnographies succeed all too well in transforming warm human behavior into cold lifeless facts. This makes Malinowski's achievement all the more unique, and it suggests that his mystique will not soon be forgotten.

For a sketch of Malinowski's life, see Abram Kardiner and Edward Preble, *They Studied Man* (New York, 1963), pp. 140–62. For some critical evaluation of his work, see Raymond Firth, ed., *Man and Culture: An Evaluation of the Work of Bronislaw Malinowski* (London, 1957). For further references of fieldwork techniques, see Buford H. Junker, *Field Work: An Introduction to the Social Sciences* (Chicago, 1960), *Notes and Queries on Anthropology,* 6th ed. (London, 1951), and Thomas Rhys Williams, *Field Methods in the Study of Culture* (New York, 1967). There are some manuals for special subjects. e.g., Kenneth S. Goldstein, *A Guide for Field Workers in Folklore* (Hatboro, Pennsylvania, 1964) and William J. Samarin, *Field Linguistics: A Guide to Linguistic Field Work* (New York, 1967). A recent insightful personalized account of what fieldwork is all about is Gerald Berreman's *Behind Many Masks: Ethnography and Impression Management in a Himalayan Village* (Ithaca, 1962). Two other classics on ethnographic field method are W. I. Thomas and F. Znaniecki, "Methodological Note," in *The Polish Peasant in Europe and America,* 1 (New York, 1918), 1–86, and William F. Whyte, "Methodological Appendix," in *Street Corner Society,* 2nd ed. (Chicago, 1955), pp. 279–358. Both these works are available in paperback (New York, 1958; Chicago, 1961). For an interesting analysis of the pattern of lies told by an informant, see Herbert Passin, "Tarahumara Prevarication: A Problem in Field Method," *American Anthropologist,* 44 (1942), 235–47. Actually, one of the most delightful introductions to anthropological fieldwork is Laura Bohannan's fictionalized account. See Elenore Smith Bowen (her *nom de plume*), *Return to Laughter: An Anthropological Novel* (New York, 1954), also available in paperback (Garden City, 1964).

III

Imagine yourself suddenly set down surrounded by all your gear, alone on a tropical beach close to a native village, while the launch or dinghy which has brought you sails away out of sight. Since you take up your abode in the compound of some neigh-bouring white man, trader or missionary, you have nothing to do, but to start at once on your ethnographic work. Imagine further that you are a beginner, without previous experience, with nothing to guide you and no one to help you. For the white man is temporarily absent, or else unable or unwilling to waste any of his time on you. This exactly describes my first initiation into field work on the south coast of New Guinea. I well remember the long visits I paid to the villages during the first weeks; the feeling of hopelessness and despair after many obstinate but futile attempts had entirely failed to bring me into real touch with the natives, or supply me with any material. I had periods of despondency, when I buried myself in the reading of novels, as a man might take to drink in a fit of tropical depression and boredom.

Imagine yourself then, making your first entry into the village, alone or in company with your white cicerone. Some natives flock round you, especially if they smell tobacco. Others, the more dignified and elderly, remain seated where they are. Your white companion has his routine way of treating the natives, and he neither understands, nor is very much concerned with the manner in which you, as an ethnographer, will have to approach them. The first visit leaves you with a hopeful feeling that when you return alone, things will be easier. Such was my hope at least.

I came back duly, and soon gathered an audience around me. A few compliments in pidgin-English on both sides, some tobacco changing hands, induced an atmosphere of mutual amiability. I tried then to proceed to business. First, to begin with subjects which might arouse no suspicion, I started to "do" technology. A few natives were engaged in manufacturing some object or other. It was easy to look at it and obtain the names of the tools, and even some technical expressions about the proceedings, but there the matter ended. It must be borne in mind that pidgin-English is a very imperfect instrument for expressing one's ideas, and that before one gets a good training in framing questions and understanding answers one has the uncomfortable feeling that free communication in it with the natives will never be attained; and I was quite unable to enter into any more detailed or explicit conversation with them at first. I knew well that the best remedy for this was to collect concrete data, and accordingly I took a village census, wrote down genealogies, drew up plans and collected the terms of kinship. But all this remained dead material, which led no further into the understanding of real native mentality or behaviour, since I could neither procure a good native interpretation of any of these items, nor get what could be called the hang of tribal life. As to obtaining their ideas about religion, and magic, their beliefs in sorcery and spirits, nothing was forthcoming except a few superficial items of folk-lore, mangled by being forced into pidgin English.

Information which I received from some white residents in the district, valuable as it was in itself, was more discouraging than anything else with regard to my own work. Here were men who had lived for years in the place with constant opportunities of observing the natives and communi-cating with them, and who yet hardly knew one thing about them really well. How could I therefore in a few months or a year, hope to overtake and go beyond them? Moreover, the manner in which my white informants spoke about the natives and put their views was, naturally, that of untrained minds, unaccustomed to formulate their thoughts with any degree of consistency and precision. And they were for the most part, naturally enough, full of the biassed and pre-judged opinions inevitable in the average practical man, whether administrator, missionary, or trader, yet so strongly repulsive to a mind striving after the objective, scientific view of things. The habit of treating with a self-satisfied frivolity what is really serious to the ethnographer; the cheap rating of what to him is a scientific treasure, that is to say, the native's cultural and mental peculiarities and independence— these features, so well known in the inferior amateur's writing, I found in the tone of the majority of white residents.[1]

Indeed, in my first piece of Ethnographic research on the South coast, it was not until I was alone in the district that I began to make some headway; and, at any rate, I found out where lay the secret of effective field-work. What is then this ethnographer's magic, by which he is able to evoke the real spirit of the natives, the true picture of tribal life? As usual, success can only be obtained by a patient and systematic application of a number of rules of common sense and well-known scientific principles, and not by the discovery of any marvellous short-cut leading to the desired results without effort or trouble. The principles of method can be grouped under three main headings; first of all, naturally, the student must possess real scientific aims, and know the values and criteria of modern ethnography. Secondly, he ought to put himself in good conditions of work, that is, in the main, to live without other white men, right among the natives. Finally, he has to apply a number of special methods of collecting, manipulating and fixing his evidence. A few words must be said about these three foundation stones of field work, beginning with the second as the most elementary.

IV

PROPER CONDITIONS FOR ETHNOGRAPHIC WORK.   These, as said, consist mainly in cutting oneself off from the company of other white men, and remaining in as close contact with the natives as possible, which really can only be achieved by camping right in their villages. It is very nice to have a base in a white man's compound for the stores, and to know there is a refuge there in times of sickness and surfeit of native. But it must be far enough away not to become a permanent milieu in which you live and from which you emerge at fixed hours only to "do the village." It should not even be near enough to fly to at any moment for recreation. For the native is not the natural companion for a white man, and after you have been

[1] I may note at once that there were a few delightful exceptions to that, to mention only my friends Billy Hancock in the Trobriands; M. Raffael Brudo, another pearl trader; and the missionary, Mr. M. K. Gilmour.

working with him for several hours, seeing how he does his gardens, or letting him tell you items of folk-lore, or discussing his customs, you will naturally hanker after the company of your own kind. But if you are alone in a village beyond reach of this, you go for a solitary walk for an hour or so, return again and then quite naturally seek out the natives' society, this time as a relief from loneliness, just as you would any other companionship. And by means of this natural intercourse, you learn to know him, and you become familiar with his customs and beliefs far better than when he is a paid, and often bored, informant.

There is all the difference between a sporadic plunging into the company of natives, and being really in contact with them. What does this latter mean? On the Ethnographer's side, it means that his life in the village, which at first is a strange, sometimes unpleasant, sometimes intensely interesting adventure, soon adopts quite a natural course very much in harmony with his surroundings.

Soon after I had established myself in Omarakana (Trobriand Islands), I began to take part, in a way, in the village life, to look forward to the important or festive events, to take personal interest in the gossip and the developments of the small village occurrences; to wake up every morning to a day, presenting itself to me more or less as it does to the native. I would get out from under my mosquito net, to find around me the village life beginning to stir, or the people well advanced in their working day according to the hour and also to the season, for they get up and begin their labours early or late, as work presses. As I went on my morning walk through the village, I could see intimate details of family life, of toilet, cooking, taking of meals; I could see the arrangements for the day's work, people starting on their errands, or groups of men and women busy at some manufacturing tasks. Quarrels, jokes, family scenes, events usually trivial, sometimes dramatic but always significant, formed the atmosphere of my daily life, as well as of theirs. It must be remembered that as the natives saw me constantly every day, they ceased to be interested or alarmed, or made self-conscious by my presence, and I ceased to be a disturbing element in the tribal life which I was to study, altering it by my very approach, as always happens with a new-comer to every savage community. In fact, as they knew that I would thrust my nose into everything, even where a well-mannered native would not dream of intruding, they finished by regarding me as part and parcel of their life, a necessary evil or nuisance, mitigated by donations of tobacco.

Later on in the day, whatever happened was within easy reach, and there was no possibility of its escaping my notice. Alarms about the sorcerer's approach in the evening, one or two big, really important quarrels and rifts within the community, cases of illness, attempted cures and deaths, magical rites which had to be performed, all these I had not to pursue, fearful of missing them, but they took place under my very eyes, at my own doorstep, so to speak. And it must be emphasised whenever anything dramatic or important occurs it is essential to investigate it at the very moment of happening, because the natives cannot but talk about it, are too excited to be reticent, and too interested to be mentally lazy in supplying details.

Also, over and over again, I committed breaches of etiquette, which the natives, familiar enough with me, were not slow in pointing out. I had to learn how to behave, and to a certain extent, I acquired "the feeling" for native good and bad manners. With this, and with the capacity of enjoying their company and sharing some of their games and amusements, I began to feel that I was indeed in touch with the natives, and this is certainly the preliminary condition of being able to carry on successful field work.

V

But the Ethnographer has not only to spread his nets in the right place, and wait for what will fall into them. He must be an active huntsman, and drive his quarry into them and follow it up to its most inaccessible lairs. And that leads us to the more active methods of pursuing ethnographic evidence. It has been mentioned at the end of Division III that the Ethnographer has to be inspired by the knowledge of the most modern results of scientific study, by its principles and aims. I shall not enlarge upon this subject, except by way of one remark, to avoid the possibility of misunderstanding. Good training in theory, and acquaintance with its latest results, is not identical with being burdened with "preconceived ideas." If a man sets out on an expedition, determined to prove certain hypotheses, if he is incapable of changing his views constantly and casting them off ungrudgingly under the pressure of evidence, needless to say his work will be worthless. But the more problems he brings with him into the field, the more he is in the habit of moulding his theories according to facts, and of seeing facts in their bearing upon theory, the better he is equipped for the work. Preconceived ideas are pernicious in any scientific work, but foreshadowed problems are the main endowment of a scientific thinker, and these problems are first revealed to the observer by his theoretical studies.

In Ethnology the early efforts of Bastian, Tylor, Morgan, the German Völkerpsychologen have remoulded the older crude information of travellers, missionaries, etc., and have shown us the importance of applying deeper conceptions and discarding crude and misleading ones.[2]

The concept of animism superseded that of "fetichism" or "devil-worship," both meaningless terms. The understanding of the classificatory systems of relationship paved the way for the brilliant, modern researches on native sociology in the field-work of the Cambridge school. The psychological analysis of the German thinkers has brought forth an abundant crop of most valuable information in the results obtained by the recent German expeditions to Africa, South America and the Pacific, while the theoretical works of Frazer, Durkheim and others have already, and will no doubt still for a long time inspire field workers and lead them to new

[2]According to a useful habit of the terminology of science, I use the word Ethnography for the empirical and descriptive results of the science of Man, and the word Ethnology for speculative and comparative theories.

results. The field worker relies entirely upon inspiration from theory. Of course he may be also a theoretical thinker and worker, and there he can draw on himself for stimulus. But the two functions are separate, and in actual research they have to be separated both in time and conditions of work.

As always happens when scientific interest turns towards and begins to labour on a field so far only prospected by the curiosity of amateurs, Ethnology has introduced law and order into what seemed chaotic and freakish. It has transformed for us the sensational, wild and unaccountable world of "savages" into a number of well ordered communities, governed by law, behaving and thinking according to consistent principles. The word "savage," whatever association it might have had originally, connotes ideas of boundless liberty, of irregularity, of something extremely and extraordinarily quaint. In popular thinking, we imagine that the natives live on the bosom of Nature, more or less as they can and like, the prey of irregular, phantasmagoric beliefs and apprehensions. Modern science, on the contrary, shows that their social institutions have a very definite organisation, that they are governed by authority, law and order in their public and personal relations, while the latter are, besides, under the control of extremely complex ties of kinship and clanship. Indeed, we see them entangled in a mesh of duties, functions and privileges which correspond to an elaborate tribal, communal and kinship organisation. Their beliefs and practices do not by any means lack consistency of a certain type, and their knowledge of the outer world is sufficient to guide them in many of their strenuous enterprises and activities. Their artistic productions again lack neither meaning nor beauty.

It is a very far cry from the famous answer given long ago by a representative authority who, asked, what are the manners and customs of the natives, answered, "Customs none, manners beastly," to the position of the modern Ethnographer! This latter, with his tables of kinship terms, genealogies, maps, plans and diagrams, proves the existence of an extensive and big organisation, shows the constitution of the tribe, of the clan, of the family; and he gives us a picture of the natives subjected to a strict code of behaviour and good manners, to which in comparison the life at the Court of Versailles or Escurial was free and easy.[3]

Thus the first and basic ideal of ethnographic field-work is to give a clear and firm outline of the social constitution, and disentangle the laws and regularities of all cultural phenomena from the irrelevances. The

[3]The legendary "early authority" who found the natives only beastly and without customs is left behind by a modern writer, who, speaking about the Southern Massim with whom he lived and worked "in close contact" for many years, says:— "...We teach lawless men to become obedient, inhuman men to love, and savage men to change." And again:—"Guided in his conduct by nothing but his instincts and propensities, and governed by his unchecked passions...." "Lawless, inhuman and savage!" A grosser misstatement of the real state of things could not be invented by anyone wishing to parody the Missionary point of view. Quoted from the Rev. C. W. Abel, of the London Missionary Society, "Savage Life in New Guinea," no date.

firm skeleton of the tribal life has to be first ascertained. This ideal imposes in the first place the fundamental obligation of giving a complete survey of the phenomena, and not of picking out the sensational, the singular, still less the funny and quaint. The time when we could tolerate accounts presenting us the native as a distorted, childish caricature of a human being is gone. This picture is false, and like many other falsehoods, it has been killed by Science. The field Ethnographer has seriously and soberly to cover the full extent of the phenomena in each aspect of tribal culture studied, making no difference between what is commonplace, or drab, or ordinary, and what strikes him as astonishing and out-of-the-way. At the same time, the whole area of tribal culture *in all its aspects* has to be gone over in research. The consistency, the law and order which obtain within each aspect make also for joining them into one coherent whole.

An Ethnographer who sets out to study only religion, or only technology, or only social organisation cuts out an artificial field for inquiry, and he will be seriously handicapped in his work.

VI

Having settled this very general rule, let us descend to more detailed consideration of method. The Ethnographer has in the field, according to what has just been said, the duty before him of drawing up all the rules and regularities of tribal life; all that is permanent and fixed; of giving an anatomy of their culture, of depicting the constitution of their society. But these things, though crystallised and set, are nowhere *formulated*. There is no written or explicitly expressed code of laws, and their whole tribal tradition, the whole structure of their society, are embodied in the most elusive of all materials; the human being. But not even in human mind or memory are these laws to be found definitely formulated. The natives obey the forces and commands of the tribal code, but they do not comprehend them; exactly as they obey their instincts and their impulses, but could not lay down a single law of psychology. The regularities in native institutions are an automatic result of the interaction of the mental forces of tradition, and of the material conditions of environment. Exactly as a humble member of any modern institution, whether it be the state, or the church, or the army, is *of* it and *in* it, but has no vision of the resulting integral action of the whole, still less could furnish any account of its organisation, so it would be futile to attempt questioning a native in abstract, sociological terms. The difference is that, in our society, every institution has its intelligent members, its historians, and its archives and documents, whereas in a native society there are none of these. After this is realised an expedient has to be found to overcome this difficulty. This expedient for an Ethnographer consists in collecting concrete data of evidence, and drawing the general inferences for himself. This seems obvious on the face of it, but was not found out or at least practised in Ethnography till field work was taken up by men of science. Moreover, in giving it practical effect, it is neither easy to devise the concrete applications of this method, nor to carry them out systematically and consistently.

Though we cannot ask a native about abstract, general rules, we can always enquire how a given case would be treated. Thus for instance, in asking how they would treat crime, or punish it, it would be vain to put to a native a sweeping question such as, "How do you treat and punish a criminal?" for even words could not be found to express it in native, or in pidgin. But an imaginary case, or still better, a real occurrence, will stimulate a native to express his opinion and to supply plentiful information. A real case indeed will start the natives on a wave of discussion, evoke expressions of indignation, show them taking sides—all of which talk will probably contain a wealth of definite views, of moral censures, as well as reveal the social mechanism set in motion by the crime committed. From there, it will be easy to lead them on to speak of other similar cases, to remember other actual occurrences or to discuss them in all their implications and aspects. From this material, which ought to cover the widest possible range of facts, the inference is obtained by simple induction. The *scientific* treatment differs from that of good common sense, first in that a student will extend the completeness and minuteness of survey much further and in a pedantically systematic and methodical manner; and secondly, in that the scientifically trained mind, will push the inquiry along really relevant lines, and towards aims possessing real importance. Indeed, the object of scientific training is to provide the empirical investigator with a *mental chart*, in accordance with which he can take his bearings and lay his course.

To return to our example, a number of definite cases discussed will reveal to the Ethnographer the social machinery for punishment. This is one part, one aspect of tribal authority. Imagine further that by a similar method of inference from definite data, he arrives at understanding leadership in war, in economic enterprise, in tribal festivities—there he has at once all the data necessary to answer the questions about tribal government and social authority. In actual field work, the comparison of such data, the attempt to piece them together, will often reveal rifts and gaps in the information which lead on to further investigations.

From my own experience, I can say that, very often, a problem seemed settled, everything fixed and clear, till I began to write down a short preliminary sketch of my results. And only then, did I see the enormous deficiencies, which would show me where lay new problems, and lead me on to new work. In fact, I spent a few months between my first and second expeditions, and over a year between that and the subsequent one, in going over all my material, and making parts of it almost ready for publication each time, though each time I knew I would have to re-write it. Such cross-fertilisation of constructive work and observation, I found most valuable, and I do not think I could have made real headway without it. I give this bit of my own history merely to show that what has been said so far is not only an empty programme, but the result of personal experience. In this volume, the description is given of a big institution connected with ever so many associated activities, and presenting many aspects. To anyone who reflects on the subject, it will be clear that the information about a phenomenon of such high complexity and of so many ramifications, could not be obtained with any degree of exactitude and completeness, without a constant interplay of constructive attempts and empirical checking. In fact, I have written up an outline of the Kula institution at least half a dozen times while in the field and in the intervals between my expeditions. Each time, new problems and difficulties presented themselves.

The collecting of concrete data over a wide range of facts is thus one of the main points of field method. The obligation is not to enumerate a few examples only, but to exhaust as far as possible all the cases within reach; and, on this search for cases, the investigator will score most whose mental chart is clearest. But, whenever the material of the search allows it, this mental chart ought to be transformed into a real one; it ought to materialise into a diagram, a plan, an exhaustive, synoptic table of cases. Long since, in all tolerably good modern books on natives, we expect to find a full list or table of kinship terms, which includes all the data relative to it, and does not just pick out a few strange and anomalous relationships or expressions. In the investigation of kinship, the following up of one relation after another in concrete cases leads naturally to the construction of genealogical tables. Practised already by the best early writers, such as Munzinger, and, if I remember rightly, Kubary, this method has been developed to its fullest extent in the works of Dr. Rivers.[4] Again, studying the concrete data of economic transactions, in order to trace the history of a valuable object, and to gauge the nature of its circulation, the principle of completeness and thoroughness would lead to construct tables of transactions, such as we find in the work of Professor Seligman.[5] It is in following Professor Seligman's example in this matter that I was able to settle certain of the more difficult and detailed rules of the Kula. The method of reducing information, if possible, into charts or synoptic tables ought to be extended to the study of practically all aspects of native life. All types of economic transactions may be studied by following up connected, actual cases, and putting them into a synoptic chart; again, a table ought to be drawn up of all the gifts and presents customary in a given society, a table including the sociological, ceremonial, and economic definition of every item. Also, systems of magic, connected series of ceremonies, types of legal acts, all could be charted, allowing each entry to be synoptically defined under a number of headings. Besides this, of course, the genealogical census of every community, studied more in detail, extensive maps, plans and diagrams, illustrating ownership in garden land, hunting and fishing privileges, etc., serve as the more fundamental documents of ethnographic research.

[4][For the contributions of W. H. R. Rivers, see "The Genealogical Method of Anthropological Inquiry," *The Sociological Review*, 3 (1910), 1–12, and *Kinship and Social Organization* (London, 1914).—*Ed. Note.*]
[5]See, for instance, C. G. Seligman, *The Melanesians of British New Guinea* (Cambridge, 1910), pp. 531, 532, where there are tables indicating the circulation of valuable axe blades.

A genealogy is nothing else but a synoptic chart of a number of connected relations of kinship. Its value as an instrument of research consists in that it allows the investigator to put questions which he formulates to himself *in abstracto,* but can put concretely to the native informant. As a document, its value consists in that it gives a number of authenticated data, presented in their natural grouping. A synoptic chart of magic fulfils the same function. As an instrument of research, I have used it in order to ascertain, for instance, the ideas about the nature of magical power. With a chart before me, I could easily and conveniently go over one item after the other, and note down the relevant practices and beliefs contained in each of them. The answer to my abstract problem could then be obtained by drawing a general inference from all the cases. I cannot enter further into the discussion of this question, which would need further distinctions, such as between a chart of concrete, actual data, such as is a genealogy, and a chart summarising the outlines of a custom or belief, as a chart of a magical system would be.

Turning for a moment to the question of methodological candour, discussed previously in Division II, I wish to point out here, that the procedure of concrete and tabularised presentation of data ought to be applied first to the Ethnographer's own credentials. That is, an Ethnographer, who wishes to be trusted, must show clearly and concisely, in a tabularised form, which are his own direct observations, and which the indirect information that form the bases of his account. The following Table will serve as an example of this procedure and help the reader of this book to form an idea of the trustworthiness of any statement he is specially anxious to check. With the help of this Table and the many references scattered throughout the text, as to how, under what circumstances, and with what degree of accuracy I arrived at a given item of knowledge, there will, I hope remain no obscurity whatever as to the sources of the book.

Chronological List of Kula Events Witnessed by the Writer

First Expedition, August, 1914—March, 1915.

> *March,* 1915. In the village of Dikoyas (Woodlark Island) a few ceremonial offerings seen. Preliminary information obtained.

Second Expedition, May, 1915—May, 1916.

> *June,* 1915. A Kabigidoya visit arrives from Vakuta to Kiriwina. Its anchoring at Kavataria witnessed and the men seen at Omarakana, where information collected.

> *July,* 1915. Several parties from Kitava land on the beach of Kaulukuba. The men examined in Omarakana. Much information collected in that period.

> *September,* 1915. Unsuccessful attempt to sail to Kitava with To'uluwa, the chief of Omarakana.

October—November, 1915. Departure noticed of three expeditions from Kiriwina to Kitava. Each time To'uluwa brings home a haul of *mwali* (armshells).

November, 1915—*March*, 1916. Preparations for a big overseas expedition from Kiriwina to the Marshall Bennett Islands. Construction of a canoe; renovating of another; sail making in Omarakana; launching; *tasasoria* on the beach of Kaulukuba. At the same time, information is being obtained about these and the associated subjects. Some magical texts of canoe building and Kula magic obtained.

Third Expedition, October, 1917—October, 1918.

November, 1917—*December*, 1917. Inland Kula; some data obtained in Tukwaukwa.

December—February, 1918. Parties from Kitava arrive in Wawela. Collection of information about the *yoyova*. Magic and spells of Kaygau obtained.

March, 1918. Preparations in Sanaroa; preparations in the Amphletts; the Dobuan fleet arrives in the Amphletts. The *uvalaku* expedition from Dobu followed to Boyowa.

April, 1918. Their arrival; their reception in Sinaketa; the Kula transactions; the big intertribal gathering. Some magical formulæ obtained.

May, 1918. Party from Kitava seen in Vakuta.

June, July, 1918. Information about Kula magic and customs checked and amplified in Omarakana, especially with regard to its Eastern branches.

August, September, 1918. Magical texts obtained in Sinaketa.

October, 1918. Information obtained from a number of natives in Dobu and Southern Massim district (examined in Samarai).

To summarise the first, cardinal point of method, I may say each phenomenon ought to be studied through the broadest range possible of its concrete manifestations; each studied by an exhaustive survey of detailed examples. If possible, the results ought to be tabulated into some sort of synoptic chart, both to be used as an instrument of study, and to be presented as an ethnological document. With the help of such documents and such study of actualities the clear outline of the framework of the natives' culture in the widest sense of the word, and the constitution of their society, can be presented. This method could be called *the method of statistic documentation by concrete evidence*.

VII

Needless to add, in this respect, the scientific field-work is far above even the best amateur productions. There is, however, one point in which the latter often excel. This is, in the presentation of intimate touches of native life, in bringing home to us these aspects of it with which one is made familiar only through being in close contact with the natives, one way or the other, for a long period of time. In certain results of scientific work— especially that which has been called "survey work"—we are given an excellent skeleton, so to speak, of the tribal constitution, but it lacks flesh and blood. We learn much about the framework of their society, but within it, we cannot perceive or imagine the realities of human life, the even flow of everyday events, the occasional ripples of excitement over a feast, or ceremony, or some singular occurrence. In working out the rules and regularities of native custom, and in obtaining a precise formula for them from the collection of data and native statements, we find that this very precision is foreign to real life, which never adheres rigidly to any rules. It must be supplemented by the observation of the manner in which a given custom is carried out, of the behaviour of the natives in obeying the rules so exactly formulated by the ethnographer, of the very exceptions which in sociological phenomena almost always occur.

If all the conclusions are solely based on the statements of informants, or deduced from objective documents, it is of course impossible to supplement them in actually observed data of real behaviour. And that is the reason why certain works of amateur residents of long standing, such as educated traders and planters, medical men and officials, and last, but not least, the few intelligent and unbiassed missionaries to whom Ethnography owes so much, surpass in plasticity and in vividness most of the purely scientific accounts. But if the specialised field-worker can adopt the conditions of living described above, he is in a far better position to be really in touch with the natives than any other white resident. For none of them lives right in a native village, except for very short periods, and everyone has his own business, which takes up a considerable part of his time. Moreover, if, like a trader or a missionary or an official he enters into active relations with the native, if he has to transform or influence or make use of him, this makes a real, unbiassed, impartial observation impossible, and precludes all-round sincerity, at least in the case of the missionaries and officials.

Living in the village with no other business but to follow native life, one sees the customs, ceremonies and transactions over and over again, one has examples of their beliefs as they are actually lived through, and the full body and blood of actual native life fills out soon the skeleton of abstract constructions. That is the reason why, working under such conditions as previously described, the Ethnographer is enabled to add something essential to the bare outline of tribal constitution, and to supplement it by all the details of behaviour, setting and small incident. He is able in each case to state whether an act is public or private; how a public assembly behaves, and what it looks like; he can judge whether an event is ordinary or an exciting and singular one; whether natives bring to it a great deal of sincere and earnest spirit, or perform it in fun; whether they do it in a perfunctory manner, or with zeal and deliberation.

In other words, there is a series of phenomena of great importance which cannot possibly be recorded by questioning or computing documents, but have to be observed in their full actuality. Let us call them *the inponderabilia of actual life*. Here belong such things as the routine of a man's working day, the details of his care of the body, of the manner of taking food and preparing it; the tone of conversational and social life around the village fires, the existence of strong friendships or hostilities, and of passing sympathies and dislikes between people; the subtle yet unmistakable manner in which personal vanities and ambitions are reflected in the behaviour of the individual and in the emotional reactions of those who surround him. All these facts can and ought to be scientifically formulated and recorded, but it is necessary that this be done, not by a superficial registration of details, as is usually done by untrained observers, but with an effort at penetrating the mental attitude expressed in them. And that is the reason why the work of scientifically trained observers, once seriously applied to the study of this aspect, will, I believe, yield results of surpassing value. So far, it has been done only by amateurs, and therefore done, on the whole, indifferently.

Indeed, if we remember that these imponderable yet all important facts of actual life are part of the real substance of the social fabric, that in them are spun the innumerable threads which keep together the family, the clan, the village community, the tribe—their significance becomes clear. The more crystallised bonds of social grouping, such as the definite ritual, the economic and legal duties, the obligations, the ceremonial gifts and formal marks of regard, though equally important for the student, are certainly felt less strongly by the individual who has to fulfil them. Applying this to ourselves, we all know that "family life" means for us, first and foremost, the atmosphere of home, all the innumerable small acts and attentions in which are expressed the affection, the mutual interest, the little preferences, and the little antipathies which constitute intimacy. That we may inherit from this person, that we shall have to walk after the hearse of the other, though sociologically these facts belong to the definition of "family" and "family life," in personal perspective of what family truly is to us, they normally stand very much in the background.

Exactly the same applies to a native community, and if the Ethnographer wants to bring their real life home to his readers, he must on no account neglect this. Neither aspect, the intimate, as little as the legal, ought to be glossed over. Yet as a rule in ethnographic accounts we have not both but either the one or the other—and, so far, the intimate one has hardly ever been properly treated. In all social relations besides the family ties, even those between mere tribesmen and, beyond that, between hostile or friendly members of different tribes, meeting on any sort of social business, there is this intimate side, expressed by the typical details of intercourse, the tone of their behaviour in the presence of one another. This side is different from the definite, crystalised legal frame of the relationship, and it has to be studied and stated in its own right.

In the same way, in studying the conspicuous acts of tribal life, such as ceremonies, rites, festivities, etc., the details and tone of behaviour ought to be given, besides the bare outline of events. The importance of this may be exemplified by one instance. Much has been said and written about survival. Yet the survival character of an act is expressed in nothing so well as in the concomitant behaviour, in the way in which it is carried out. Take any example from our own culture, whether it be the pomp and pageantry of a state ceremony, or a picturesque custom kept up by street urchins, its "outline" will not tell you whether the rite flourishes still with full vigour in the hearts of those who perform it or assist at the performance or whether they regard it as almost a dead thing, kept alive for tradition's sake. But observe and fix the data of their behaviour, and at once the degree of vitality of the act will become clear. There is no doubt, from all points of sociological, or psychological analysis, and in any question of theory, the manner and type of behaviour observed in the performance of an act is of the highest importance. Indeed behaviour is a fact, a relevant fact, and one that can be recorded. And foolish indeed and short-sighted would be the man of science who would pass by a whole class of phenomena, ready to be garnered, and leave them to waste, even though he did not see at the moment to what theoretical use they might be put!

As to the actual method of observing and recording in field-work these *imponderabilia of actual life and of typical behaviour,* there is no doubt that the personal equation of the observer comes in here more prominently, than in the collection of crystalised, ethnographic data. But here also the main endeavour must be to let facts speak for themselves. If in making a daily round of the village, certain small incidents, characteristic forms of taking food, of conversing, of doing work are found occurring over and over again, they should be noted down at once. It is also important that this work of collecting and fixing impressions should begin early in the course of working out a district. Because certain subtle peculiarities, which make an impression as long as they are novel, cease to be noticed as soon as they become familiar. Others again can only be perceived with a better knowledge of the local conditions. An ethnographic diary, carried on systematically throughout the course of one's work in a district would be the ideal instrument for this sort of study. And if, side by side with the normal and typical, the ethnographer carefully notes the slight, or the more pronounced deviations from it, he will be able to indicate the two extremes within which the normal moves.

In observing ceremonies or other tribal events, it is necessary, not only to note down those occurrences and details which are prescribed by tradition and custom to be the essential course of the act, but also the Ethnographer ought to record carefully and precisely, one after the other, the actions of the actors and of the spectators. Forgetting for a moment that he knows and understands the structure of this ceremony, the main dogmatic ideas underlying it, he might try to find himself only in the midst of an assembly of human-beings, who behave seriously or jocularly, with earnest concentration or with bored frivolity, who are either in the same mood as he finds them every day, or else are screwed up to a high pitch of excitement, and so on and so on. With his attention constantly directed to this aspect of tribal life, with the constant endeavour to fix it, to express it in terms of actual fact, a good deal of reliable and expressive material finds its way into his notes. He will be able to "set" the act into its proper place in tribal life, that is to show whether it is exceptional or commonplace, one in which the natives behave ordinarily, or one in which their whole behaviour is transformed. And he will also be able to bring all this home to his readers in a clear, convincing manner.

Again, in this type of work, it is good for the Ethnographer sometimes to put aside camera, note book and pencil, and to join in himself in what is going on.[6] He can take part in the natives' games, he can follow them on their visits and walks, sit down and listen and share in their conversations. I am not certain if this is equally easy for everyone—perhaps the Slavonic nature is more plastic and more naturally savage than that of Western Europeans—but though the degree of success varies, the attempt is possible for everyone. Out of such plunges into the life of the natives—and I made them frequently not only for study's sake but because everyone needs human company—I have carried away a distinct feeling that their behaviour, their manner of being, in all sorts of tribal transactions, became more transparent and easily understandable than it had been before. All these methodological remarks, the reader will find again illustrated in the following chapters.

VIII

Finally, let us pass to the third and last aim of scientific field-work, to the last type of phenomenon which ought to be recorded in order to give a full and adequate picture of native culture. Besides the firm outline of tribal constitution and crystallised cultural items which form the skeleton, besides the data of daily life and ordinary behaviour, which are, so to speak, its flesh and blood, there is still to be recorded the spirit—the natives' views and opinions and utterances. For, in every act of tribal life, there is, first, the routine prescribed by custom and tradition, then there is the manner in which it is carried out, and lastly there is the commentary to it, contained in the natives' mind. A man who submits to various customary obligations, who follows a traditional course of action, does it impelled by certain motives, to the accompaniment of certain feelings, guided by certain ideas. These ideas, feelings, and impulses are moulded and conditioned by the culture in which we find them, and are therefore an ethnic peculiarity of the given society. An attempt must be made therefore, to study and record them.

But is this possible? Are these subjective states not too elusive and shapeless? And, even granted that people usually do feel or think or experience certain psychological states in association with the performance of customary acts, the majority of them surely are not able to formulate these states, to put them into words. This latter point must certainly be granted, and it is perhaps the real Gordian knot in the study of the facts of social psychology. Without trying to cut or untie this knot, that is to solve the problem theoretically, or to enter further into the field of general methodology, I shall make directly for the question of practical means to overcome some of the difficulties involved.

First of all, it has to be laid down that we have to study here stereotyped manners of thinking and feeling. As sociologists, we are not interested in what A or B may feel *qua* individuals, in the accidental course of their own personal experiences—we are interested only in what they feel and

[6][Here is one of Malinowski's pleas for participant observation. It is one thing to *observe* and quite another to *participate and observe.—Ed. Note.*]

think *qua* members of a given community. Now in this capacity, their mental states receive a certain stamp, become stereotyped by the institutions in which they live, by the influence of tradition and folk-lore, by the very vehicle of thought, that is by language. The social and cultural environment in which they move forces them to think and feel in a definite manner. Thus, a man who lives in a polyandrous community cannot experience the same feelings of jealousy, as a strict monogynist, though he might have the elements of them. A man who lives within the sphere of the Kula cannot become permanently and sentimentally attached to certain of his possessions, in spite of the fact that he values them most of all. These examples are crude, but better ones will be found in the text of this book.

So, the third commandment of field-work runs: Find out the typical ways of thinking and feeling, corresponding to the institutions and culture of a given community, and formulate the results in the most convincing manner. What will be the method of procedure? The best ethnographical writers—here again the Cambridge school with Haddon, Rivers, and Seligman rank first among English Ethnographers—have always tried to quote *verbatim* statements of crucial importance. They also adduce terms of native classification; sociological, psychological and industrial *termini technici,* and have rendered the verbal contour of native thought as precisely as possible. One step further in this line can be made by the Ethnographer, who acquires a knowledge of the native language and can use it as an instrument of inquiry. In working in the Kiriwinian language, I found still some difficulty in writing down the statement directly in translation which at first I used to do in the act of taking notes. The translation often robbed the text of all its significant characteristics—rubbed off all its points —so that gradually I was led to note down certain important phrases just as they were spoken, in the native tongue. As my knowledge of the language progressed, I put down more and more in Kiriwinian, till at last I found myself writing exclusively in that language, rapidly taking notes, word for word, of each statement. No sooner had I arrived at this point, than I recognised that I was thus acquiring at the same time an abundant linguistic material, and a series of ethnographic documents which ought to be reproduced as I had fixed them, besides being utilised in the writing up of my account.[7] This *corpus inscriptionum Kiriwiniensium* can be utilised, not only by myself, but by all those who, through their better penetration and ability of interpreting them, may find points which escape my attention,[8] very much as the other *corpora* form the basis for the various interpretations of ancient and prehistoric cultures; only, these ethnographic inscriptions

---

[7]It was soon after I had adopted this course that I received a letter from Dr. A. H. Gardiner, the well-known Egyptologist, urging me to do this very thing. From his point of view as archæologist, he naturally saw the enormous possibilities for an Ethnographer of obtaining a similar body of written sources as have been preserved to us from ancient cultures, plus the possibility of illuminating them by personal knowledge of the full life of that culture.

[8][For a fascinating example of an analysis of Malinowski's linguistic data, an analysis which if valid would demonstrate Malinowski's point beautifully, see Dorothy Lee, "Codifications of Reality: Lineal and Nonlineal," in this volume.—*Ed. Note.*]

are all decipherable and clear, have been almost all translated fully and unambiguously, and have been provided with native cross-commentaries or *scholia* obtained from living sources.

IX

Our considerations thus indicate that the goal of ethnographic field-work must be approached through three avenues:

1. *The organisation of the tribe, and the anatomy of its culture* must be recorded in firm, clear outline. The method of *concrete, statistical documentation* is the means through which such an outline has to be given.

2. Within this frame, the *imponderabilia of actual life,* and the *type of behaviour* have to be filled in. They have to be collected through minute, detailed observations, in the form of some sort of ethnographic diary, made possible by close contact with native life.

3. A collection of enthnographic statements, characteristic narratives, typical utterances, items of folk-lore and magical formulæ has to be given as a *corpus inscriptionum,* as documents of native mentality.

These three lines of approach lead to the final goal, of which an Ethnographer should never lose sight. This goal is, briefly, to grasp the native's point of view, his relation to life, to realise *his* vision of *his* world. We have to study man, and we must study what concerns him most intimately, that is, the hold which life has on him. In each culture, the values are slightly different; people aspire after different aims, follow different impulses, yearn after a different form of happiness. In each culture, we find different institutions in which man pursues his life-interest, different customs by which he satisfies his aspirations, different codes of law and morality which reward his virtues or punish his defections. To study the institutions, customs, and codes or to study the behaviour and mentality without the subjective desire of feeling by what these people live, of realising the substance of their happiness—is, in my opinion, to miss the greatest reward which we can hope to obtain from the study of man.[9] . . .

What interests me really in the study of the native is his outlook on things, his *Weltanschauung,* the breath of life and reality which he breathes and by which he lives. Every human culture gives its members a definite vision of the world, a definite zest of life. In the roamings over human history, and over the surface of the earth, it is the possibility of seeing life and the world from the various angles, peculiar to each culture, that has always charmed me most, and inspired me with real desire to penetrate other cultures, to understand other types of life.

To pause for a moment before a quaint and singular fact; to be amused at it, and see its outward strangeness; to look at it as a curio and collect it into the museum of one's memory or into one's store of anecdotes—this

[9][The final paragraph from Malinowski's "Introduction" to *Argonauts of the Western Pacific* has been omitted. In its place have been substituted the closing paragraphs of the book. The reason for this is that the eloquent rhetoric of this latter passage states the ethnographer's credo with force, sincerity, and grace unequalled in the anthropological literature.—*Ed. Note.*]

attitude of mind has always been foreign and repugnant to me. Some people are unable to grasp the inner meaning and the psychological reality of all that is outwardly strange, at first sight incomprehensible, in a different culture. These people are not born to be ethnologists. It is in the love of the final synthesis, achieved by the assimilation and comprehension of all the items of a culture and still more in the love of the variety and independence of the various cultures that lies the test of the real worker in the true Science of Man.

There is, however, one point of view deeper yet and more important than the love of tasting of the variety of human modes of life, and that is the desire to turn such knowledge into wisdom. Though it may be given to us for a moment to enter into the soul of a savage and through his eyes to look at the outer world and feel ourselves what it must feel to *him* to be himself—yet our final goal is to enrich and deepen our own world's vision, to understand our own nature and to make it finer, intellectually and artistically. In grasping the essential outlook of others, with the reverence and real understanding, due even to savages, we cannot but help widening our own. We cannot possibly reach the final Socratic wisdom of knowing ourselves if we never leave the narrow confinement of the customs, beliefs and prejudices into which every man is born. Nothing can teach us a better lesson in this matter of ultimate importance than the habit of mind which allows us to treat the beliefs and values of another man from his point of view. Nor has civilised humanity ever needed such tolerance more than now, when prejudice, ill will and vindictiveness are dividing each European nation from another, when all the ideals, cherished and proclaimed as the highest achievements of civilisation, science and religion, have been thrown to the winds. The Science of Man, in its most refined and deepest version should lead us to such knowledge and to tolerance and generosity, based on the understanding of other men's point of view.

The study of Ethnology—so often mistaken by its very votaries for an idle hunting after curios, for a ramble among the savage and fantastic shapes of "barbarous customs and crude superstitions"—might become one of the most deeply philosophic, enlightening and elevating disciplines of scientific research. Alas! the time is short for Ethnology, and will this truth of its real meaning and importance dawn before it is too late?

Franz Boas

THE CONCEPT OF SOUL
AMONG THE VANDAU

Ninety-nine times out of a hundred the anthropologist goes to the field to obtain his data, but every once in a great while the field comes to the anthropologist. This field is usually in the

Reprinted from Franz Boas, *Race, Language and Culture* (New York, 1940), pp. 608–11, by permission of The Macmillan Company. Copyright 1940 by Franz Boas.

form of a foreign student attending a college or university in the United States. It should be noted, however, that anthropological orthdoxy cautions against relying upon information obtained from working with a single foreign student. The student may not be representative of his society; he may be a highly educated, ambitious, Westernized individual who may or may not have a thorough knowledge of the particular topic(s) the anthropologist would like to investigate. The informant may give ideal culture rather than real culture—ask a member of our own culture what he does when someone strikes his cheek and then watch what he really does when that happens—and since the ethnographer is not in the field, he cannot empirically observe whether the informant's behavior accords with the verbal testimony or not. In any case, it is always risky to generalize about a whole culture on the basis of what a single individual says or does.

Despite these legitimate objections to working with a single informant who is not living in his home environment, there are a number of advantages of ethnographic interviewing under these conditions. First, one could argue that the whole notion of participant observation as spelled out by Malinowski is partly wishful thinking on the part of ethnographers. Given the nature of the subtleties and nuances of culture patterning, it is virtually impossible for even the best trained cultural anthropologist to notice everything in the course of a one- or two-year visit. Often it may take almost that long to master the language well enough to speak fluently. It is for this reason that so many ethnographers come to rely upon prize informants and interpreters. What this amounts to in one sense is training the gifted informant to be an ethnographer, or at least to ask and answer the questions normally posed by cultural anthropologists. If, then, some of the valuable data obtained in the field is the product of a fruitful collaboration between ethnographer and a trusted informant, there is no reason why a similar fruitful collaboration should not be possible in the cultural context of the ethnographer. As a matter of fact, one reason why informants occasionally refrain from answering certain critical questions in the field is that they realize that it will soon become known who leaked the "secret" answers to the inquiring ethnographer. In a culture far removed from their own, the same informant may be much more willing to discuss the same taboo topics. This argument does not denigrate the value of the field experience as outlined by Malinowski. If nothing else, it is a formal *rite de passage* whereby a budding neophyte anthropologist becomes a full-fledged professional, and it is quite true that one cannot properly appreciate the task of studying and understanding another culture (as well as one's own) until one has been immersed in another culture. On the other hand, even the limited information one can obtain from working with a sensitive, intelligent foreign student is better than no information at all. In the case of the Ndau or Vandau, this is virtually the case.

In 1919 Franz Boas, perhaps the greatest name in American anthropology, worked with a young foreign student from Portuguese Southeast Africa. From the materials elicited, Boas published a number of short articles. In one instance, Boas listed the student as the coauthor of the article. In addition, Boas's student, Melville J. Herskovits, worked with the very same informant, work which led to a published paper. In fact, a fair share of our knowledge of this culture comes from a single informant.

There has been some vociferous criticism of Boas's field methods and the quality of his analysis of the data he collected. One persistent critic, clearly intent upon slaying the father figure—Boas was known affectionately to his favorite students as Papa Franz and it is a fact that many anthropologists trace their academic descent back to Boas or one of his students—has counted the total number of days Boas actually spent in the field (only thirty-three and one-half months) and the total number of pages of published ethnographic material contributed by a trained Kwakiutl and a trained Tsimshian Indian (4,165 pages), the implication being in the latter instance that Boas should have written up the material himself. However, it may be that Boas's methodology was a little too subtle for his critics. Above all, Boas realized the value of obtaining ethnographic data from the native point of view. One way of ensuring this was to train natives to record the data; another was to collect folklore and other "native documents"—Boas considered folklore to be "autobiographical ethnography." If Boas was right, then this brief study of the Vandau concept of the soul beautifully illustrates Boas's technique. He sticks close to the native language terms, avoiding any overly analytic hypothesizing and speculation. In this brief essay the reader can see that it is possible for one to obtain ethnographic information from the people around him. One does not have to travel thousands of miles at considerable expense in order to taste the flavor of ethnographic interviewing. As for the subject of Boas's inquiry, the reader can also see the fallacy of assuming that the Vandau (or any other people) probably have a concept of soul similar to our own.

Boas's other Vandau studies include "The Relationship of the Vandau," originally published in German in the *Zeitschrift für Ethnologie* in 1922 and later translated in *Race, Language, and Culture* (New York, 1940), pp. 384–96, "The Avunculate Among the Vandau," *American Anthropologist,* **24** (1922), 95–97, and the long joint article, Franz Boas and C. Kamba Simango, "Tales and Proverbs of the Vandau of Portuguese East Africa," *Journal of American Folklore,* **35** (1922), 151–204.

For Herskovits' study, see "Some Property Concepts and Marriage Customs of the Vandau," *American Anthropologist,* **25** (1923), 376–86. For other references on the Vandau, see the entries under "Ndau" in Ruth Jones, comp., *Africa Bibliography Series, South-East Central Africa and Madagascar* (London, 1961), p. 33. For a convenient biographical sketch of Boas, see Abram Kardiner and Edward Preble, *They Studied Man* (New York, 1963), pp. 117–39. For generally favorable evaluations, see Melville J. Herskovits, *Franz Boas: The Science of Man in the Making* (New York, 1953) and Walter Goldschmidt, ed., *The Anthropology of Franz Boas,* Memoir No. 89 of the American Anthropological Association (San Francisco, 1959). For vociferous criticism, see Leslie A. White, *The Ethnography and Ethnology of Franz Boas,* Bulletin of the Texas Memorial Museum, No. 6 (Austin, Texas, 1963) or White, *The Social Organization of Ethnological Theory,* Rice University Studies, 52, No. 4 (1966), 3–28.

The following is a description of the concepts relating to the soul among the Vandau of Portuguese Southeast Africa, as developed in conversations with K'amba Simango, a young Mundau who was studying in New York in 1919. He seemed to be well informed in regard to the customs and beliefs of his people. He speaks both Chindau and Zulu.

"Life" is called *vyomi*[1] (Zulu *ubutʿoŋgo*). The Zulu word is also used in

[1] *v, f*	bilabial
pʾ, tʾ, kʾ	glottalized surds
pʿ, tʿ, kʿ	strongly aspirated surds
ŋ	middle palatal nasal
γ	middle palatal fricative
ż	labialized sonant *z*, like a whispered *zü*
š	English *sh*
tš	English *ch*
dj	English *j*
ḷ	with strong vibration of sides of tongue
	long vowels
ᐧ	separates vowels that do not form diphthongs
e, o	always open

Chindau in the form *vutʿoŋgo*. The prefix shows that it is an abstract term. Living man has a body (*muvili* pl. *mivili*) and a *bvuli* (pl. *mabvuli;* Zulu *isitʿuʾndzi*). The *bvuli* is alive and indestructible. It is not indissolubly connected with the body. The shadow or reflection of an object is also called *bvuli.* The *bvuli* is an essential part of existence only in man. In dreams the *bvuli* appears or leaves the body, and both *bvuli* and body have "life" (*vyomi*). The *bvuli* is never sick. When a person dies the body is without "life" which stays with the *bvuli,* that is, the *bvuli* remains alive while the body is dead.

After the death of a person the *bvuli* becomes a *mulu·ŋgu* (pl. *valu·ŋgu*), synonym *mudjimu* (pl. *vadjimu*). The latter term may be derived from the stem *djima* (*k'udjima* to extinguish). The corresponding Zulu terms are *it'o·ŋgo* (pl. *amat'o·ŋgo*), used also in Chindau in the form *t'o·ŋgo* (pl. *mat' o·ŋgo*); synonym *isit'ut'a* (pl. *izit'ut'a*), used in Chindau in the form *tšit'ut'a* (pl. *zit'ut'a*). This term may be derived from Zulu *uk'ut'ut'a* to wander about. The *mulu·ŋgu* has the form and character of the deceased. The term *bvuli* is also used for the *mulu·ŋgu,* meaning that he is the shadowy, unsubstantial image of the dead one. With this meaning the *mulu·ŋgu* is also called *moya,* wind, air, and *mp'ep'o* wind, because, like the air, it cannot be touched and held. The *mulu·ŋgu* does not stay with the body but follows the family. The *mulu·ŋgu* retains the name of the deceased. He is immortal and cannot be reborn. Every family venerates its own *valu·ŋgu.*

When all the relatives of *mulu·ŋgu* are dead and his memory is forgotten, or when he goes to a strange tribe in which he has neither relatives nor friends, he wanders about and becomes a *tšilo·mbo* (pl. *zilo·mbo*) or a *dzok'a* (*k'udzok'a* to rattle in the throat), because a person possessed for the first time by a *dzok'a* produces a rattling noise in the throat. A synonym for *dzok'a* is *zint'ik'i* (pl. *mant'ik'i,* usually meaning "ceremonial song"; compare *k'unt'ik'inya* to throttle). The Zulu call the *tšilo·mbo idlozi* (pl. *amadlozi*) used in Chindau in the form *dlozi.* The Zulu call the *dzok'a muŋgo·ma.* Since all of these belong to persons who have been forgotten they have no known personal names, but they reveal their names when they come into personal contact with the living. The *tšilo·mbo* is similar to the *dzok'a,* but weaker. A *tšilo·mbo* who brings misfortune is also called *k'ombo,* i.e. bent, because he bends the straight road of life. The *tšilo·mbo* accompanies and directs the *beze* (pl. *madjibeze*), the experienced *naŋga* and the expert *dot'a.* These three are medical practitioners who by the use of herbs and by means of prophetic bones (*ze·mbe*) advise and cure the sick.

The *dzok'a* are unknown deceased persons who possess the *nyamsolo* (fuller form *nyamusolo*) and with whose assistance they take the scent (*k'ufemba*) of the *mulu·ŋgu* who causes sickness. The word *nyamsolo* (pl. *madjinyamsolo*), or in form of respect *vanyamsolo* may be derived from *solo* head. After the *dzok'a* has taken the scent of the *mulu·ŋgu,* he overpowers him, takes hold of him if he tries to escape and forces him into the body of the *nyamsolo.* Then the *mulu·ŋgu* speaks through the mouth of the *nyamsolo.* The *dzok'a* takes no part in these proceedings. By means of a slight indisposition of a person, his departed grandfather may wish to indicate his desire for attention. Then the *dzok'a* of the *nyamsolo* takes the scent of the *mulu·ŋgu* who is forced into the body of the *nyamsolo.* The *mulu·ŋgu* states his name and wishes. As soon as this is done the *nyamsolo* sneezes "*wensya*" and thus removes the *mulu·ŋgu* from his body. The *mulu·ŋgu* of a relative does not cause serious sickness. When the *mulu·ŋgu* of a person not a member of his own family attacks a person he is taken seriously ill. Then the *mulu·ŋgu* is bribed by presents to desist. After the *mulu῾ŋgu,* through the mouth of the *nyamsolo,* has expressed his willingness to accept the presents, the *nyamsolo* sends out his attendants (*muliša,* pl. *vališǎ*) who deposit the presents outside in the grass. Then the *nyamsolo* sneezes "*wensya*" and thus dismisses the *mulu῾ŋgu.* The *mulu῾ŋgu* who is sent out against a person attacks only the body, not the *bvuli.* He tries to throttle the patient, to break his neck or to kill him in some other way. The nature of his attacks is shown by the symptoms of the sickness. Often he tries to kill a person by the same sickness that killed him. A *dzok'a* belonging to a foreign tribe is designated by the word that belongs to the language of that tribe. Thus a Zulu *dzok'a* is called *muŋgo῾ma.* Others are simply indicated by tribal names, as, for instance, *lo῾zi,* a *dzok'a* of the Vandau of Rhodesia.

Generally a *dzok'a* is acquired unintentionally. A person who is walking about may accidentally pass *dzok'a* who will accompany him. Then the person feels ill. A *ŋaŋga* or *nyamsolo* is called who tries to drive away the *dzok'a.* If the person wishes to keep the *dzok'a* he will stay with him and after an initiation the person will be a *nyamsolo.*

Some *nyamsolo* have from ten to fifteen *dzok'a.* At the initiation, when the *dzok'a* enters the person's body for the first time, he fills the upper part of the body of the novice who breathes with rattling in the throat. At later times, when the *dzok'a* is asked to find the *mulu῾ŋgu* causing sickness he does not cause any discomfort.

The *bvuli* of children, old people, and mentally affected are called *nšimu* (sing. and pl.), synonym *salavusa* (pl. *masalavusa*) said to be derived from *k'usala* to stay, remain, and *vušwa* grass). They lie in the grass and attach themselves to anyone who happens to pass by. Their presence is indicated by a slight feeling of discomfort or by itching of the body. Therefore, when a person has these feelings it is said, *ndatšik'a salavusa,* "I stepped on a *salavusa.*" When a few crumbs of food are thrown to them they leave and repeat the same game with the next passer-by.

Several kinds of *mulu῾ŋgu* have special names. A *mupfukwa* is the *mulu῾ŋgu* of a person who has been murdered and who comes to take revenge. (*K'upfuk'a* means "to emerge", "to take revenge".) Other *mulu῾ŋgu* are instigated by witches, male or female (*valo῾yi*), to attack their enemies. The *mupfukwa* pursues his murderer at his own initiative.

Ba῾ndu is a special term for a particularly merciless *mulu῾ŋgu.*

The *mp῾o῾ŋgo* is the *mulu῾ŋgu* of a member of the chief's family, particularly of a past generation, presumably of an individual who has been forgotten. Some member of the chief's family, one who is observing the prescribed customs meticulously, is liable to be attacked by him. In this case he is also called *mp῾o῾ŋgo* because the *mp῾o῾ŋgo* speaks through him. The *mp῾o῾ŋgo* does not cause sickness of individuals but affects the welfare of the whole tribe.

My informant declares that the Vandau do not believe that dead ancestors turn into snakes. The *valu῾ŋgu* keep snakes in the way we keep dogs, and snakes are treated with respect because they are the property of the *valu῾ŋgu.* Groves are not venerated, but since graves are placed in groves they are feared and respected as property of the *valu῾ŋgu.*

Since "life" (*vyomi*) is considered as an abstract power, man, according to our informant, has only one soul which, according to its state and actions, is designated by various names:

During life of the owner	*bvuli* (shadow, reflection)
After death, but while the owner is remembered ..	*mulu·ŋgu* or *mudjimu*
On account of its unsubstantiality	*moya* or *mpʻepʻo* (wind)
Souls of children, old or mentally unsound persons	*nšimu* or *salavasa*
After death, when forgotten	*tšiloʻmbo* (if weak)
	dzokʼa (if strong)
The *mulu·ŋgu* of a member of the chief's family ..	*mpʻoʻŋgo*

Jaime de Angulo

SINGING FOR DAMAAGOMES AMONG THE PIT RIVER INDIANS

The ethnographer asks his prize informant to sing a medicine-song, but he refuses. Yet a moment before, he had sung on his own initiative a medicine-song belonging to a friend. If he could sing one medicine song, why could he not sing another? To understand why—and this is just one small sample of the kind of problem one runs into when one is engaged in fieldwork—one must know about personal guardian spirits, how they come when they are called, or rather when they are summoned by song, and how they may be stolen by other medicine men. Jaime de Angulo, a physician, who might be termed a "professional" amateur anthropologist, relates some of his adventures among the Achomawi whom he calls Pit River Indians of northern California.

For further information about the Achomawi, see the references in George Peter Murdock, *Ethnographic Bibliography of North American,* 3rd ed. (New Haven, 1960), pp. 85–86. Some of the standard ethnographic sources are by de Angulo, e.g., "The Background of the Religious Feeling in a Primitive Tribe," *American Anthropologist,* **28** (1926), 352–60.

I had gone into that house looking for an old fellow named Blind Hall, or Johnny Hall (his name, I found

Reprinted from Jaime de Angulo, "Indians in Overalls." Reprinted by permission from *The Hudson Review,* Vol. III, No. 3 (Autumn, 1950). Copyright © 1950 by The Hudson Review, Inc.

out later, was Tahteumi, meaning "red trail," or "red track," or "sunset trail"). They had told me he was one of the most powerful medicine-men around. But the tattooing girl said he wasn't there; this was his house, but he had gone to another camp. She said he was sick. "He was going to town the other day with his old woman; they were driving along in their old buggy; automobile come from behind; upset buggy; old Hall didn't know he was hurt, but he must have dropped his shadow; he went on to Hantiyu, but he got pretty sick; he is coming back today; he is going to doctor himself tonight."

That sounded interesting. I thought I would hang around. Maybe I would learn something. So I wandered around. About noon Blind Hall arrived in the old rattling creaking swaying buggy with his old woman and the old old decrepit horse. I knew right away I had seen him before somewhere, sometime; that massive face, the sightless eyes, the very thick lips and quite a lot of white beard for an Indian. "Hallo, white man, I remember you, you stop once, we camp side road, you give me can beans, bacon, you eat with us, you treat me good, you all right, I remember you, I remember your voice—I am pretty sick now, dropped my shadow on the road, can't live without my shadow, maybe I die, I dunno.... I doctor myself tonight. You stay, you help sing tonight."

Blind Hall called his medicine "my poison." The Indian word is *damaagome.* Some Indians translate it in English as "medicine," or "power," sometimes "dog" (in the sense of pet dog, or trained dog)....

Blind Hall was groaning and bellyaching about the pain in his ribs. We were sitting in the sun. "Give me a cigarette, white man. Mebbe I die. I dunno. That autocar he knock my shadow out of me; shadow he stay on the road now can't find me; can't live without my shadow!...It's too bad, mebbe I die...tonight I doctor myself, I ask my poisons...I got several poisons...I got Raven, he live on top mountain Wadaqtsuudzi, he know everything, watch everything.... I got Bullsnake, he pretty good too.... I got Louse, Crablouse, live with people, much friends, he tell me lots things.... I got Jim Lizard, he sit on rock all day, he pretty clever but not serious, he dam liar.... Sometime I doctor sick man, call my poisons come over my head, they fight, Raven he says that man poisoned, Bullsnake say no he not poisoned, he broke rule hunting...and then this here Jim Lizard he say, Oh! let's go home that man going to die anyhow!...Then Raven he shake his finger at him he say: Who ask you what you think? Why don't you help our father?" (The poisons call the medicine-man "my father," *ittu ai*—the medicine-man calls his poison *ittu damaagome* "my damaagome," or whatever you want to translate that word by: medicine, poison, power....) "You can go home if you want to, we will stay here and help our father. Then Jim Lizard mebbe he stay and help and mebbe he tell me lie. I can't depend on him.... Ohh...it hurt me inside here. Maybe I die. Everybody die sometime.... I ask my poison tonight. You white man, you help, you sing too. More people sing more good. Sometime my poison very far away, not hear. Lots people sing, he hear better."...

That evening we all gathered at sundown. Jack Steel, an Indian from

Hantiyu who usually acted as Blind Hall's "interpreter," had arrived. He went out a little way into the sagebrush and called the poisons. "Raven, you, my poison, COME! (*qaq, mi', ittu damaagome, tunnoo*).... Bull-snake, my poison, come.... Crablouse, my poison, cooome.... You all, my poisons, COOOME!!" It was kind of weird, this man out in the sagebrush calling and calling for the poisons, just like a farmer calling his cows home.

We all gathered around the fire; some were sitting on the ground, some were lying on their side. Blind Hall began singing one of his medicine-songs. Two or three who knew that song well joined him. Others hummed for a while before catching on. Robert Spring said to me: "Come on, sing. Don't be afraid. Everybody must help." At that time I had not yet learned to sing Indian fashion. The melody puzzled me. But I joined in, bashfully at first, then when I realized that nobody was paying any attention to me, with gusto.

Blind Hall had soon stopped singing, himself. He had dropped into a sort of brown study, or as if he were listening to something inside his belly. Suddenly he clapped his hands, the singing stopped abruptly. In the silence he shouted something which the "interpreter," Jack Steel, repeated. And before Jack Steel was through, Blind Hall was shouting again, which the interpreter also repeated, and so on, five or six times. It was not an exchange between Blind Hall and Jack Steel. Jack Steel was simply repeating word for word what Blind Hall was shouting. It was an exchange between Hall and his poison, Raven. First, Hall would shout a query which the inter-preter repeated; then Hall would listen to what Raven (hovering unseen above our heads) was answering—and he would repeat that answer of Raven which he, Hall, had heard in his mind—and the interpreter would repeat the repetition. Then Hall emitted a sort of grunted "Aaaah...," and relapsed into a brown study. Everybody else, Jack Steel included, relaxed. Some lit cigarettes; others gossiped. A woman said to me: "You did pretty good; you help; that's good!" Robert Spring said: "Sure, everybody must help. Sometimes the poisons are far away. They don't hear. Everybody must sing together to wake them up."

The woman who had praised me for singing said for my benefit: "He ask his Raven if he going to die. Raven say he don't know; ask the others." Blind Hall started humming another medicine-song, and everything went on like before. That way four or five times. At one time he got pretty excited and started to jump and dance, and fell down. It must be hell to be blind.

The whole performance lasted about a couple of hours. Then everybody dispersed.

The next morning Blind Hall felt much better. I asked Robert Spring about the "interpreter." They call it *astumage,* which literally means trans-lating or interpreting. According to Spring the medicine-man gets so excited that his speech often becomes quite unintelligible; but his interpreter is used to it and able to repeat it clearly. Quite so; he evidently performs that function. But I suspect something else, not so visible: the shaman is in a great state of excitement, it borders on hysteria, even catalepsy some-times; it seems to me that it would be pretty easy for the shaman to slip into the autistic stage of schizophrenia...and never come back to reality!

Is it not possible, perhaps, that the interpreter acts as a link, a life-line by which the shaman remains in contact with the reality of the material world?

Blind Hall was so pleased with my "helping" that he offered to make me some moccasins if I got him a piece of buckskin. Poor old blind fellow! *Some* moccasins!! They might have fitted the foot of a dinosaur, or some such beast, but not a human foot. However I assured him they fitted my feet like gloves and he was very proud.

It was Robert Spring who first made me understand about the *dinihowi*. "That's what we Indians call *luck*. A man has got to have luck, no matter for what, whether it's for gambling, or for hunting, for making love, for anything, unless he wants to be just a common Indian...like me."

We were lying flat on our backs under a juniper. After a silence he started again: "When a fellow is young, everybody is after him to go to the mountains and get himself a *dinihowi*. The old men say: "You'll never amount to anything if you don't go and catch a *dinihowi*. And then you hear other fellows brag about their luck at gambling, or how they got a good *dinihowi* for hunting. Well, there come a time when a young fellow starts to feel uneasy, kind of sad, kind of worried, that's just about the time he's getting to be a man grown up. Then he start to 'wander,' that's what we call it, wandering. They say: Leave him alone, he is wandering. That's the time you go to the hills, you don't come home, you stay out all night, you get scared, you cry; two, three days you go hungry. Sometime your people get worried, come after you, but you throw rocks at them: Go away, I don't want you, leave me alone. You get pretty hungry, you get dizzy, you are afraid of grizzly bears. Maybe you fall asleep and someone come wake you up, maybe a wolf, push your head with his foot, maybe bluejay peck at your face, maybe little fly get in your ear, he say: Hey! Wake up! What you doing here? Your people worrying about you! You better go home! I seen you wandering here, crying, hungry, I pity you, I like you. I help you. Listen, this is my song. Remember that song. When you want me, you come here and sing my song. I'll hear you. I'll come...."

I said to Robert Spring: "But then, I don't see what is the difference between the *dinihowi* and the *damaagome*...." "There is no difference. It's all the same. Only the *damaagome* that's for doctors." "How does the doctor get his *damaagomes?*" "Just like you and me get a *dinihowi*. He goes to the mountain. He cries. Then someone comes and says, this is my song, I'll help you." "Well then, I don't see any difference." "I am telling you there is no difference. Only the *dinihowi* that's for plain Indians like you and me, and the *damaagome* that's for doctors.... Well, I'll tell you, there is maybe some difference. The *damaagome* is kind of mean, quarrelsome, always fighting. The *dinihowi* is more peaceful."

There came a figure lurching toward us with a curious gait, something like an orangoutan, through the sagebrush. Robert Spring chuckled: "There comes your friend." Sure enough, it was Sukmit. "How did you know he and I were friends?" "Oh, Indians hear everything. It don't take long for news to travel in the sagebrush. I heard all about you stopping at his camp." Sukmit greeted me: "Hallo, Jaime!" (He was the only Pit River who ever called me by my first name. The others used my nickname in that country, Buckaroo Doc, or just Doc.) Then he and Robert Spring greeted each other: *Is, kaakaadzi* (Person, you are living). He sat down on one knee, which was his usual posture. "I heard Doctor Hall was sick, so I came to help," he said.

Now, that puzzled me. I had always heard that Indian shamans cordially detested each other. We told Sukmit that Hall had doctored himself and was now feeling better. "That's good," he said.

We all three went looking for the old man and found him sitting on a bench with his back to the shack and chewing tobacco. Robert Spring sat himself next to him and Sukmit and I on the ground in front, but careful to leave a clear space for the old blind man to spit into. Then there ensued the, to me, most amazing conversation about doctors and their poisons. Blind Hall started again on his pet subject of complaint: his pet *damaagome,* Jim Lizard, the lying sonofabitch he could never trust... but this time he had behaved himself, he wasn't mean enough to fool his own father when his father was sick, etc., etc. And Sukmit to corroborate: "Yes, some of them *damaagomes* is mean. When I started doctoring I tried a trick. I tried bringing my poison to a hand-game. Now, a doctor is not supposed to use his poison for gambling (this was addressed to me, not to Hall or Robert Spring). It's against the rules. But I thought I was smart, see. I thought to hell with the rules, I do like white man, see. Well, in the middle of the game I got awful thirsty, and I get up and go to the spring, and I take a long drink of water, and I got awful dizzy and sick, I got cramps, I puke.... See, my *damaagome* he do that, he mad because I bring him to hand-game, not supposed to do that." Blind Hall was roaring with laughter. "Ha, ha, ha. Your poison he make you sick. You bring him to hand-game, he make you sick. Ha, ha, ha."

Sukmit thought for a while, then he said: "Them *damaagomes* is dangerous things to handle. That's why I stick to my own and I don't try to steal other doctors' *damaagome.* But this old man here, Doctor Hall, he don't care, he steal other doctors' *damaagomes!*" Blind Hall guffawed: "Sure I do! I steal other doctors' *damaagomes.* They steal mine, too, if they can. They try to steal my Raven, but he won't follow them. Ha, ha!" Sukmit said: "That's a good one, your Raven. I would like to have him myself. But I don't like to fool with other people's poisons. It may be a bad one and you can't handle him and he make you sick." Blind Hall laughed again: "I am not afraid of them!"

Later on that day I asked Robert Spring: "How do the doctors steal each other's *damaagomes?*" "I dunno, Doc, I am not a doctor. But you heard Blind Hall say so himself. How do you steal another man's dog?"...

I was up again, the next year. This time I had a jalopy, myself. Progress. You can't defend yourself against progress. So this time I came up following the Pit River from Redding up. I was meeting more and more Indians after Montgomery Creek. I had never been through that territory before, only once, years before with a drove of horses, through a snowstorm. I didn't even recognize the country.

I got into the upper land. It was getting dark. I had a wolfish-looking bitch swaying on the back, on top of my camping stuff. I was getting tired driving that damned car. I hate them. When I got to Big Valley I couldn't stand the driving over the rough road any more. I saw a campfire a little south of the road. I was awfully tired. I thought: They must be Indians.

I got out and walked over, being careful to make a noise. There was no need for care. There comes Sukmit: "I have been watching for you. I got lonesome for you. I sent my poison after you. The old lady is there, in the camp. Old lady Gordon died. The other woman, my uncle, she is dead. We are all going to die. We can't help it. What have you got there? Is that a coyote? Looks a coyote. Don't growl at me, you son-of-a-bitch, I am Indian doctor. I ain't afraid of you. Want to be my poison? Say, Jaime, did you get my message? I got lonesome for you. You want to be a doctor? I teach you. I am Indian doctor. I teach you, pretty bad, get scared, I teach you, you no white man. . . ."

. . . I proposed to record some songs on my phonograph machine. I carried around one of those old Edison phonographs with a big horn. You made the records on wax cylinders with a special cutting jewel needle; then to play them you changed to a needle with a rounded point. The whole contraption was crude and primitive compared to modern methods. It was hard enough to operate in a laboratory; imagine it in the open, competing with the wind; the horn would swing around; we cursed. . . . How I sweated and labored over those Indian songs, and the fortune I spent on broken records! . . . That was before the days of amplification; later on new methods appeared; flat disks, unbreakable and permanent; wonderful improvements. . . but the Indians are gone, no more singing to record.[1]

Sukmit had a powerful voice of which he was vain. He was delighted to sing into the horn and then hear his own voice thrown back at him. We recorded several songs, mostly gambling songs and some puberty-dance songs. Then he said: "Let's record Old Blind Hall's medicine-song, you know, that one about digging up wild turnips and they all are rotten." So we put that on. It goes something like this:

> At Dalmo'ma near the spring
> I dig for wild turnips
> At Dalmo'ma in the evening
> I turn up but rotten ones.

Then I said to him: "Sukmit, let's record one of your own medicine-songs." The old lady had heard me, and she cried from where she was sitting

[1]The University would not help me; took no interest; would not even give me enough money to have the records transcribed and made permanent on modern disks. Decent anthropologists don't associate with drunkards who go rolling in ditches with shamans.

at the campfire. "Don't do it, Sukmit, don't do it, *tse-dutsee, tse-dutsee!!*"
He seemed dubious, torn two ways by his vanity and his fear of possible
consequences. "See, suppose I put my song in the machine; now you go
to Berkeley; sometime you play my song; my *damaagome* he hear it, he say:
Ha! my father is calling me, I'd better go and find him, maybe he needs
me.... So he come here to Berkeley, strange place, maybe he get lost,
maybe somebody steal him...then I get sick, maybe I die...." "Aw! he
couldn't hear that phonograph all the way from Alturas!" "Sure he can!
Just like 'lectricity, it goes underground, but it don't need no wires."[2]
"What do you know about electricity?! Electricity doesn't work that way!"
"Hell, what do you know about *damaagomes?* You are nothing but a
white man, a goddam tramp."[3] "No, I am not a white man!" "Yes, you
are a white man, you are a white man forever!!".

Old Mary chuckled from over the campfire "You two always quarreling
like two old men. You Indian, you white man, ha-ha-ha! You both crazy!"

So I took them down to Berkeley in my auto, Sukmit and old Mary
(she once told me her Indian name; it had something to do with tule
reeds at dawn; but I never heard any one call her by it; Sukmit called
her *niini*, baby-talk for *nen* "mother"; and I also called her that after a
while; other Indians called her "aunt," or "sister-in-law on the brother's
side," which is *wattulaawi*, or whatever the relationship term if they were
related; if not related to her they just called her *wiya'tsaale*, which is
equivalent to "old lady").

The city was a great disappointment to Sukmit. Didn't interest him at
all. "Too many people crawling around just like ants—makes me crazy...."
He spent most of his time wandering in the hills back of the University
campus. He looked sad and dejected. He didn't quarrel any more.

One day I said to him: "Sukmit, I know what's troubling you.... You
have been wandering in the hills and calling your *damaagomes*, and they
don't hear you!" He looked at me and I thought he was going to burst
into tears. "Yes," he said, "you and *niini*, you were right; they don't hear
me; they don't come! I am going to die if I stay here."

So I sent them back on the train. Funny-looking pair they made at the
station, bewildered, he with his long hair and his black sombrero, his long
arms and his hump; she clutching a bundle; and her gray hair under
a bright silk handkerchief we had just bought for her.

I spoke a word to the conductor for them. He smiled broadly: "Sure
I'll take care of them. I know Indians. I was raised in Oklahoma."

As the train pulled out, old Mary gave me the Pit River goodby: *Is tus'i
taakaadzee,* Man, live well! *Ittu toolol hakaadzigudzuma,* We also will live.

---

[2] This was before the days of wireless (at least before wireless became common knowledge)—an interesting example of so-called "primitive mentality."

[3] The Pit Rivers call the whites *enellaaduwi*, literally "wanderer," from the verbal
root *—llaa—* "to wander," plus the adverbial suffix *—duw—* "around." What struck the
Pit Rivers most about the first whites (prospectors, trappers, etc.) was that they
appeared to be homeless.

Alex Atkinson

AT HOME WITH ABORIGINES

In this parody of the anthropological field experience, a number of serious issues are raised. First of all, fieldwork is expensive and it is not always easy to obtain adequate financial support for a stay of one or two years. Then there is the matter of the privileged communication between ethnographer and informant. If an informant requests that certain information remain secret, does the professional ethnographer have the moral right to publish such data "in the interests of science"? Another ethical question concerns the ethnographer's selling of a work of primitive art for profit when he originally obtained it in exchange for a bauble. If there is profit, why should it not go in large measure to the artist-creator rather than to the middle-man ethnographer? Such questions and problems rarely find their way into the final polished monograph. Nor does one find mention of the difficulties of digesting all the delicacies of the native cuisine and the various recoveries. from relapses of different types of exotic diseases.

The spoof also provides pictures of contemporary stereotypic constructs. There is the stereotype of the anthropologist, the stereotype of the sophisticated native with his objections to the visit by anthropologists, the stereotype of the isolated romantic noble savage, and the stereotype of the despoiling evils of an automation-riddled civilization, among others. With regard to the stereotype of the anthropologist, one could maintain that in one sense the anthropologist may be said to have arrived when he is considered important enough to parody. On the other hand, some parts of the image, accurate or not, suggest that anthropologists are as human as anyone else and that there is such a thing as the culture of anthropologists.

When it comes to a question of really intensive fieldwork, carried out on the spot over a period of months or even years, one of the bitterest sources of disappointment for anthropologists to-day—apart from their steadily growing conviction that people all over the world are becoming more numerous, less different, and far dirtier—is the fact that there are hardly any quaint tribes left now who are prepared to extend hospitality indefinitely to a lot of subsidized professors with jeeps and notebooks.

"I might fit a party of three in for a week or so next February," wrote

Reprinted from *Punch,* Vol. **238** (June 1, 1960), by permission.

the chief of a tribe of unusual giants in Borneo,[1] to whom Mrs. Dyson had applied for digs, "but more than that I cannot promise. This place has been overrun with anthropologists during the last few years. They come here, insist on living as we do, eat us out of house and home, put ideas into our heads, take no active part in hunting or tree-felling, throw doubts on the validity and even the originality of our religion, complain about the sanitation, accuse us of having rickets, take flash-light photos during our Saturday night fertility rites, and generally disturb the even tenor of existence. Then they go home and put us into encyclopædias, and we don't make a brass farthing out of it. I remain yours etc."

You will therefore readily understand Mrs. Dyson's delight when we found the astonishing Mugus[2] in their mountain fastness deep in the interior of the largest of the three islands that form the Cocoranga Group, not very far from New Zealand, and were told, after a surprisingly brief parley, that we could stay as long as we liked provided that we promised never to divulge the secret password (*"Um t'ala groh,"* which means "Long is the claw of the land crab").

Mrs. Dyson had always felt confident that there were Mugus to be found on this particular island, chiefly on account of those intriguing references in Farringdon's *Chronicle of My Journeying In the Southern Oceans, With Some Accompt of Witches* to "men of but little tallness who, hauing no tools saue only mallets of stone and a kinde of wheel Barrow, yet raise up great Dwellings in the forest of this isle, where they do liue and thriue mightily." Farringdon's grasp of geography understandably left much to be desired, and for years controversy has raged about the exact location of his isle; but Mrs. Dyson never wavered in her belief that the Cocoranga Group was the place, quoting as her proof the following passage in the *Chronicle:*—

> Whereupon we did mooue forward in such small winde as did preuail from the Eastwards; altho we greatly doubted that our Mastes would long remain upright, being made fraile by the Storm; and in this sort we went onward. Now when we had trauelled three leags vpon our course, we did espy the greatest of the three Isles, being in the Middle, and in Shape like a Pidgeon, the head and Beake lying to the North, the rump and Taile at the South. Drawing neare, and hauing no longer any terrour that Worse might befall us, we did ground the Galley on the shore, and marching boldly forward, did meet at once a Company of strange Human creatures; who did fall vpon and eat Two of our number before we had made ready our Fowling pieces. In this and in diuers other matters they did shew such inciuility that we were presently resolued not to remain long in their midst, but to spy out whether there might be space here for a new Colony, and then depart.

"This is the place all right," said Mrs. Dyson, as we lurched up on to the beach in the surplus assault landing craft she had wheedled out of

[1] For the English translation of this letter I am indebted to Llewellyn Carfax of Hunstanton.
[2] Pronounced to rhyme with "fingers."

some anthropology-lover on the mainland. "You couldn't hope for a more pigeon-shaped isle. Now all we have to do is to poke about until we find the most inaccessible district there is. That's where the Mugus will be, you take my tip—otherwise some fool would have stumbled across them long before this. Well now, first of all we'd better have a roll-call and a brew-up."

There were five of us in the party. Mrs. Dyson's own main functions were to form irrevocable conclusions from the tentative findings of her experts, and to take the credit for whatever astounding scientific discoveries we were able to foist on to the public when we got back home. ("I may not be any great shakes as an anthropologist myself," she had said, "but *I* found the backers for this trip, and if anybody gets anything out of the Nuffied Trust or the *Reader's Digest* on the strength of it, it's going to be me." One of the backers, by the way, was a man named Harper who wanted us to try out a foolproof apparatus he had invented for snaring rhino, and when I pointed out to Mrs. Dyson that as we weren't likely to come within a thousand miles of any rhino it smacked a little of sharp practice to take the fellow's money, she said "Not at all. As a matter of fact it makes a very good hammock, and he'll probably become a millionaire as a result of my recommendation. Think of it—*Mrs. Dyson Sleeps On This Harper Hammock—Why Don't You?* After all, more people sleep on hammocks than snare rhino."—"Yes," I said, "but not *many* more"). Then there was a very old man by the name of Rossiter, whose special subject was somatology and who had to be helped up hills on account of his bones. He said they were brittle. Edwin Bothe was described on his passport as an ethnologist and once, in the course of his investigations, he had unfortunately been converted to animism by some people in Central Africa, which made him rather jumpy. On the other hand, as Mrs. Dyson was always quick to point out in his defence, he was a good plain cook and never threw away string. Then there was a Kamante Islander called John (it was short for something), who was alleged to be fluent in any of the dialects likely to be used by the Mugus. John was well over six feet tall, and very hungry. He also indulged in gruesome daydreams; he once confided to me that he wished his great-grandparents had been cannibals, so that he could have something to boast about around the camp-fire, like the white members of the party. I was the fifth member, and as a comparative beginner in the adventure business my duties were humdrum enough. They included seeing that nobody got lost, finding them if they did, reminding Mrs. Dyson when it was time for her medicine, fending off wild animals, helping Mr. Bothe to fasten his guy-ropes, taking notes about anything that seemed odd, and dealing with the daily list of complaints from the native bearers. As I believe Vasco da Gama once observed, *somebody* has to boil the cabbage, even in the middle of an epic.

The place where the Mugus live turned out to be so nearly inaccessible that I wondered at first why they didn't all go out of their minds.[3] We found them in a narrow cleft in the hills, four thousand feet above sea level, hemmed in on three sides by densely wooded slopes, with an active volcano

[3]I subsequently learned that seven of them had.

to the north, a haunted mountain to the east, three days of rain in a year, a week's tortuous journey to the coastal plain, and nothing to do when they got there.

For the last five miles old Mr. Rossiter was carried by the native bearers. (They liked nothing better than carrying Mr. Rossiter, because they got time and a quarter for it. Often they would snatch him up when no-one was looking and carry him, despite his protests, until they had earned enough for another booze-up when they got home, or until I happened to spot them, whichever was the sooner.) The rest of us managed to make it on foot, but we were in such bad shape when we finally reached the Mugu settlement that before we could even introduce ourselves we had to be rushed into the ju-ju house for treatment. There little men with *dumbali* feathers in their hair rubbed our feet with some kind of dirt, let a bit of our blood, and chanted incantations until we just couldn't bear it any longer, so we said we felt fine. I have often thought since that it was something of a triumph for witchcraft.

The average height of a Mugu is five foot five. (They smoke a good deal). They speak a kind of bastard *D'hoi*, with a few words of Helianthemum and more than a trace of Poinsettia, so that John was able to translate for us without much difficulty. They were also adept at making themselves understood by signs. At any rate I *hope* they were, because otherwise much of the information we brought back is not going to be worth a row of beans. The chief was a hundred and eight. He had been elected because everybody owed him so much money.[4] It was either that or cut him up in pieces, so they tossed for it. He had no teeth. He said white people had never been seen on the island before, although the Mugu had long suspected that such creatures might exist. One of their traditional songs, indeed, contains the lines:

> Then cream-visaged strangers
> With one wife each and haughty manners
> Came out of the sea to befriend us.
> O! Ah! O! Ah! O!

The chief expressed great interest in our wristwatches, our descriptions of life in Streatham, and our garments. (For all I know to the contrary he is still wearing the Jacqmar scarf that Mrs. Dyson gave him in exchange for a couple of rubies, and in the same unconventional place.) He said he would be delighted to put us up if we wouldn't mind sharing a hut with thirty-eight other people. And so we began our life with the aborigines.

From July to October we tasted their primitive existence, studying their culture, technology, hats, mortuary customs, folklore, methods of crop rotation, adult education schemes, sculpture, garbage disposal, and political economy; and when we'd finished Mrs. Dyson said she was very sorry but she didn't reckon much to them at all.

[4]The Mugu are inveterate gamblers. Their favourite game, played with three pieces of wood on which faces have been engraved with red-hot sticks, is called Find the She-goat.

She exaggerated, of course. The life of the Mugu had a simplicity which I found enchanting, although I'm bound to say that forty-three people in a hut sixty yards long is a mistake. The hour before the evening meal, for example, was apt to be tedious, what with the wives deep-frying grass and rabbits in the communal pot, the men piling the children in a corner and sluicing them down with buckets of water, Mrs. Dyson snoring in her hammock with a Chanel-soaked handkerchief over her face, old Mr. Rossiter crawling about measuring people's skulls with a pair of calipers and crying out "Brachycephalic!" or "Dolichocephalic!" in his piping voice, Mr. Bothe being taught the steps of some ritual dance by a crowd of giggling grandmothers, and the teenagers daubing one another with a mixture of river-sand and fish-glue in readiness for some festival or other. The sleeping arrangements too, were far from satisfactory, because there were always revellers who came in late and walked on people, singing the good old songs and drinking out of bamboo hip-flasks. Some nights there would be a rumbling noise in the hills and Mrs. Dyson would jump out of her hammock crying "There goes that damn volcano again!" Then she would hustle everybody out into the darkness and stampede them into the forest to escape the creeping horror of an avalanche of molten lava. Everyone in the hut resented this, because it was well known that there was never more than a trickle of lava, and it always went the other way. The native bearers refused to sleep in the hut at any price, explaining that they preferred to make their own arrangements if it was all the same to us. I'm not sure what it is about native bearers, but they always seem to know what's good for them, and you'll never find one short of a couple of pounds to send home to his mother at the week-end.

But what are a few petty discomforts compared with the thrill of uncovering the secrets of a people who could trace their descent in an unbroken line right back to the Stone Age if they only put their minds to it? Helping to investigate the Mugu was one of the most rewarding experiences of my life, for it showed me the mockery of our so-called civilization. Here we are, riddled with guilt and dread and nervous indigestion in the midst of our clutter of spindryers, off-white telephones, double-action corn-flakes, electronic computers and quick-frozen chips: and all the time the Mugu are squatting in their impregnable valley, crudely fashioning axes and not even caring a hoot what day of the week it is, unless they happen to be next on the list for sacrifice to Ko, the volcano goddess. For they are essentially a happy people, if slightly stupid. The sound of their merry laughter comes back to me now[5] as I think of them hitting one another on the head with slabs of alabaster in the midsummer mating game, or lying in hot cinders to cure their dandruff, or kicking their spare wives into the river in an intriguing ceremony of great antiquity (the ones that float are taken out and put up for auction), or chewing the traditional live fresh-water fish on someone's birthday, or gathering poisonous berries in the woods in the cool of the morning, or shredding them into a friend's midday stew to settle a difference of opinion. No worries here about super-

[5]It is really a sort of uncontrollable giggle.

tax or corked claret, no frustrations about parking, no dissatisfaction with the quality of the caviar on long-distance flights, no fear of your ball-point pen leaking all over your drip-dry shirt, no sleepless nights over stocks and shares or what to wear if it happens to rain in Venice. How I envied them! Here at last, I thought, was the idyllic, uncomplicated life for which all men had yearned for years in secret, and these delightful Mugu took it all for granted!

We played their simple games.[6] We ate their parboiled mice, cold insect soup, braised fillets of wolf, sea-gulls' eyes in batter, and other homely dishes. (The Mugu didn't like any of them much, which seems strange.) We fought alongside them at their weddings, coming-out parties and propitiation ceremonies. With the exception of Mr. Rossiter, who said it wasn't his department, we attended several orgies, sitting in a kind of minstrels' gallery as honoured guests and helping to bury the dead the next morning. We studied their typically uncomplicated national ailments, such as asthma, dropsy, eye-sores, hereditary deafness, alcoholism, trench mouth, colour-blindness, epilepsy, myopia, eczema, premature senility and a tendency to shrink in hot water. (I should point out that, at any given time, one Mugu in thirty is not attending the witch-doctor. Average expectation of life is seven years. The only thing they have a cure for is measles, and hardly any of them get it.) We studied their demonstrations of religious fervour, those who worship the volcano chasing those who worship the haunted mountain up trees and chopping off their arms with hatchets. We noted that they have no proper clothes, no industries, no sense of moral values, no future, no democracy, no potatoes, no stamina, no fuel, no shame, and no hope. They are there, and that is all, and they sing some very peculiar songs.

I could not but wonder on the last day of our visit, as we crawled painfully aboard the landing-craft and set our course for home, whether the time will ever come when the rest of the world manages to catch up with the Mugu. I remember I asked one of the native bearers, and he said "Brother, I shouldn't worry one bit if I were you. The way you're going you'll equal them in no time at all."

---

[6]One consisted in running about swinging half a hundred-weight of granite on the end of a piece of crude rope until you broke somebody's leg.

The concept
of
culture

*E*very discipline has its key terms and concepts and cultural anthropology is no exception. The key term and concept is "culture." As in other disciplines, there is in cultural anthropology considerable disagreement as to precisely what the key term means. One approach, not a recent one, to the definition of culture is through recourse to a minimal unit called a culture trait. A culture trait, unfortunately itself vaguely defined, could be anything from a fishhook to a hair style. According to the culture trait approach, an individual culture consists of the sum of all of its culture traits. This overly atomistic view of culture is no longer widely held and, in fact, it is the relationships between traits, the *patterns* of trait organization, that are of more interest to the contemporary anthropologist.

One of the burning issues with respect to defining culture has to do with whether or not culture includes concrete behavior. Generally speaking, there is a tendency to consider culture as the patterns of behavior, rather than the behavior itself. Culture in this sense is not the physical act of doing things but the way of doing them. Thus the proverb "Every man his way" would mean "Every man his culture." Anthropologists would readily admit that without concrete, actual behavior, there would obviously be no patterns of behavior, but nevertheless the majority do persist in distinguishing "culture" from "behavior."

There is agreement, however, that culture is acquired and learned (through communication by symbols, such as language). This distinguishes it from innate, instinctive, or genetically determined behavioral patterns. In terms of the familiar "nature-nurture" dichotomy, culture is nurture. Another characteristic of culture is that it may be unconscious or, to put it another way, that man is not conscious of all aspects of his culture. Individuals can use language (at an early age) without consciously understanding its grammatical and syntactic patterning. This is one of the most amazing things about culture. It is all around us; it shapes our lives and thought; yet we know relatively little about it.

One reason for studying culture is to make the unconscious conscious. By making the unconscious content of culture conscious, we may, at least in theory, be better able to do something about controlling or changing it. This brings us to the fundamental question of whether culture makes man or man makes culture. (The answer, of course, is neither or both!) Those who argue that culture constitutes a level of reality unto itself, that is, those who advocate what is called a superorganic conception of culture, are convinced that man is a helpless victim of cultural forces. The reasoning is along the following lines. Although the organic (e.g., man) is composed of inorganic elements (e.g., chemicals), the organic is more than the sum of its inorganic constituents. In other words, if you put all the chemical constituents of man together, you don't get man. Man, the organic, depends upon the inorganic, but he is not completely reducible to inorganic principles. By analogy, superorganicists argue that culture (the superorganic) is more than simply a sum total of men (organic constituents). It depends upon men—it could not exist without them—but it is allegedly not reducible to a purely organic basis. Culture as a level of reality operates in accordance with its own rules. For example, a superorganicist would probably contend that history makes men great rather than that great men make history. According to this view, it is the combination of historical factors and forces that causes inventions to be invented and political crises to be solved. It is only the merest historical accident—the right person being in the right place at the right time—that leads to any one individual's achieving fame. One clue which gives away a superorganic position (and there are obviously many analogous intellectual positions in almost all academic disciplines) is when issues are discussed in terms of "isms" rather than people. When someone says that democracy is or does this, when someone says that communism is or does that, when one speaks of this ideology fighting with that ideology, he is probably a superorganicist, that is, a man who holds a superorganic concept of culture. (It is interesting that superorganicists invariably anthropomorphize their concepts to the point that the reified concepts have a "life" of their own.)

The superorganic view continues to be important in cultural anthropology. One can easily see, for example, why a superorganic concept of culture would tend to exclude concrete behavior. Concrete behavior by human beings is organic or at least organically based. In contrast, according to this view the abstract patterns or "laws" governing concrete behavior are a different order of phenomena.

One other consequence of the superorganic concept of culture and the definition of culture as behavior patterns rather than behavior is the lack of interest in individuals. It is the shared, acquired human characteristics which concern cultural anthropologists. Thus in the anthropological study of personality, it has been largely social rather than individual psychology that has been investigated. It is the basic or modal personality of all those sharing the same culture which is of interest. Although it is individuals serving as informants who are interviewed, these individuals are traditionally lost when the generalizing anthropologist writes up his data. An individual Kiowa Indian says X to the ethnographer and in the final published monograph it is reported as "The Kiowa say X."

The emphasis upon what is shared rather than upon what is idiosyncratic (i.e., not shared) is a critical bias in cultural anthropology. In a way, it is the issue of whether one chooses to search for similarities or delve for differences. The cultural anthropologist with his concept of culture knows that all men are not exactly alike and it is culture, according to the cultural anthropologist, which makes some men different from some other men. But from the worldwide perspective, the men in the same culture have similar differences, that is, they are similarly different from men in other cultures. This may be seen in the context of the historical development of anthropology.

The reaction of Boas and his students to the sweeping nineteenth-century unilinear evolutionary schemes, which studied all cultures at once and which emphasized similarities, has been to study one culture at a time in depth and to concentrate upon the differences between one culture and another. Cultural relativists insist that patterns of human behavior are relative to individual cultures. Yet within any one individual culture, the anthropologist has tended to emphasize similarities rather than differences. Perhaps this is why the discipline is called *cultural* anthropology. But there are significant individual differences. There is "individual relativism" as well as "cultural relativism." Maybe there will have to be a separate though related discipline called "Individual Anthropology" as opposed to "Cultural Anthropology" in order to study intra-cultural as opposed to inter-cultural differences. The whole issue may be clarified by referring to a pseudo-proverbial distinction appearing in Kluckhohn's writings: Every man is, in certain respects, (a) like all other men, (b) like some other men, and (c) like no other men. The nineteenth-century concern with universals, that would be (a), has yielded to the study of shared, learned behavioral patterns (i.e., similarities) communicated by symbols, which is (b). The intensive study of individuals (c) and individual *differences* should be the next step.

George Peter Murdock

AN OUTLINE OF CULTURAL MATERIALS

When a cultural anthropologist says that he studies culture, what does that mean? What in fact do cultural anthropologists study? One possible way of learning part of the answer to this question is by reading the *Outline of Cultural Materials* from cover to cover. In this work, one will find listed most of the topics investigated by cultural anthropologists.

The *Outline* was originally intended to be an aid for cross-cultural comparative studies. It was first drafted in 1937 as a cooperative project by a number of staff members of the Institute of Human Relations at Yale University. The immediate purpose of the classification scheme was to facilitate the standard organization of ethnographic data in a set of files. Since in theory the *Outline* classification system provided each ethnographic detail with an identifying number (e.g., divorce is 586 and suicide is 762), excerpters could be set to work breaking ethnographies down so that their contents could be placed on appropriate cards for filing. Ethnographic information for several hundred different cultures has been excerpted in this way. The advantages should be obvious. If someone wanted to undertake a cross-cultural survey of suicide, he would normally have to spend days or months of hunting through ethnographies, government publications, and unpublished manuscripts searching for references to suicide. If, however, he used the Cross-Cultural Survey file, he could pull all the "762" cards from each of the separate cultures abstracted and in a matter of moments he would have considerable relevant data. It is also possible to undertake cross-

Reprinted from George P. Murdock, *et al., Outline of Cultural Materials,* 4th revised ed., second printing with modifications. (New Haven, 1965), by permission of George P. Murdock and the Human Relations Area Files, Inc.

cultural correlation studies and this, in fact, is one of the most exciting aspects of cross-cultural research. For example, if one wanted to check a hypothesis concerning a possible relationship between divorce and suicide, one could pull all the "586" and "762" cards in a relatively short time.

There are, to be sure, weaknesses of both the classification system and the files. For one thing, not all the peoples of the world are represented in the files. Only about 10 per cent of the world's cultures have been excerpted. On the other hand, this is not an insignificant amount of material and care has been taken to include cultures from Asia, Africa, South America, and so on. Another problem is that not all the ethnographic sources are equally comprehensive. If there were no discussion of suicide reported for a given culture, then there could be no information on card 762 for that culture. Still another difficulty is that one does an injustice to data when one wrenches bits of it out of context and forces them into narrow classificatory categories (using a classification scheme, which is, after all, part of *our* culture, not the culture being excerpted). However, despite these and other weaknesses, the files have led to productive cross-cultural research.

Up until 1949, the only set of files was located at Yale University in New Haven, Connecticut. In that year, an inter-university organization called the Human Relations Area Files, Inc., commonly referred to as HRAF, was established. Member institutions of HRAF were permitted to duplicate the Yale file so that similar cross-cultural research projects could be conducted at these institutions. Although additional universities have joined HRAF over the years, there are still many major universities without a set of the HRAF files.

An important fringe benefit of the classification scheme has been its use as a field manual. Although it was not designed for this purpose, some ethnographers have found it valuable in the field. Ethnographers have become increasingly specialized and, for this reason, an ethnographer going into the field to study modern local political organization might well consult the *Outline* for reminders in subject areas outside his particular research project in order to obtain data in these areas. As a means of acquainting the reader with the *Outline,* the table of contents plus several representative sections, specifically those dealing with marriage, death, and ideas about nature and man, are presented. Those interested in other topics might wish to consult the *Outline* itself.

There is a considerable body of research that is based upon the HRAF files. Samples of this research would include Murdock's own *Social Structure* (New York, 1949), John W. M. Whiting and Irvin L. Child, *Child Training and Personality: A Cross-Cultural Study* (New Haven, 1953), and William N.

Stephens, *The Oedipus Complex: Cross-Cultural Evidence* (New York, 1962). See also Frank W. Moore, *Readings in Cross-Cultural Methodology* (New Haven, 1961).

10 ORIENTATION
  101 Identification
  102 Maps
  103 Place Names
  104 Glossary
  105 Cultural Summary
11 BIBLIOGRAPHY
  111 Sources Processed
  112 Sources Consulted
  113 Additional References
  114 Comments
  115 Informants
  116 Texts
  117 Field Data
12 METHODOLOGY
  121 Theoretical Orientation
  122 Practical Preparations
  123 Observational Role
  124 Interviewing
  125 Tests and Schedules
  126 Recording and Collecting
  127 Historical Research
  128 Organization of Results
13 GEOGRAPHY
  131 Location
  132 Climate
  133 Topography and Geology
  134 Soil
  135 Mineral Resources
  136 Fauna
  137 Flora
14 HUMAN BIOLOGY
  141 Anthropometry
  142 Descriptive Somatology
  143 Genetics
  144 Racial Affinities
  145 Ontogenetic Data
  146 Nutrition
  147 Physiological Data
15 BEHAVIOR PROCESSES
  AND PERSONALITY
  151 Sensation and Perception
  152 Drives and Emotions

153 Modification of Behavior
154 Adjustment Processes
155 Personality Development
156 Social Personality
157 Personality Traits
158 Personality Disorders
159 Life History Materials
16 DEMOGRAPHY
  161 Population
  162 Composition of Population
  163 Birth Statistics
  164 Morbidity
  165 Mortality
  166 Internal Migration
  167 Immigration and Emigration
  168 Population Policy
17 HISTORY AND CULTURE
  CHANGE
  171 Distributional Evidence
  172 Archeology
  173 Traditional History
  174 Historical Reconstruction
  175 Recorded History
  176 Innovation
  177 Acculturation and Culture Contact
  178 Socio-Cultural Trends
18 TOTAL CULTURE
  181 Ethos
  182 Function
  183 Norms
  184 Cultural Participation
  185 Cultural Goals
  186 Ethnocentrism
19 LANGUAGE
  191 Speech
  192 Vocabulary
  193 Grammar
  194 Phonology
  195 Stylistics
  196 Semantics
  197 Linguistic Identification

564 Castes
565 Classes
566 Serfdom and Peonage
567 Slavery

57 INTERPERSONAL RELA-
TIONS
571 Social Relationships and
Groups
572 Friendships
573 Cliques
574 Visiting and Hospitality
575 Sodalities
576 Etiquette
577 Ethics
578 Ingroup Antagonisms
579 Brawls, Riots, and
Banditry

58 MARRIAGE
581 Basis of Marriage
582 Regulation of Marriage
583 Mode of Marriage
584 Arranging a Marriage
585 Nuptials
586 Termination of Marriage
587 Secondary Marriages
588 Irregular Unions
589 Celibacy

59 FAMILY
591 Residence
592 Household
593 Family Relationships
594 Nuclear Family
595 Polygamy
596 Extended Families
597 Adoption

60 KINSHIP
601 Kinship Terminology
602 Kin Relationships
603 Grandparents and
Grandchildren
604 Avuncular and Nepotic
Relatives
605 Cousins
606 Parents-in-Law and
Children-in-Law
607 Siblings-in-Law
608 Artificial Kin Relationships

609 Behavior toward Non-
relatives

61 KIN GROUPS
611 Rule of Descent
612 Kindreds and Ramages
613 Lineages
614 Sibs
615 Phratries
616 Moieties
617 Bilinear Kin Groups
618 Clans
619 Tribe and Nation

62 COMMUNITY
621 Community Structure
622 Headmen
623 Councils
624 Local Officials
625 Police
626 Social Control
627 Informal Ingroup Justice
628 Inter-community Rela-
tions

63 TERRITORIAL ORGANIZA-
TION
631 Territorial Hierarchy
632 Towns
633 Cities
634 Districts
635 Provinces
636 Dependencies

64 STATE
641 Citizenship
642 Constitution
643 Chief Executive
644 Executive Household
645 Cabinet
646 Parliament
647 Administrative Agencies
648 International Relations

65 GOVERNMENT ACTIVI-
TIES
651 Taxation and Public Income
652 Public Finance
653 Public Works
654 Research and Develop-
ment
655 Government Enterprises

746 Public Assistance
747 Private Welfare Agencies
748 Social Work

75 SICKNESS

751 Preventive Medicine
752 Bodily Injuries
753 Theory of Disease
754 Sorcery
755 Magical and Mental Therapy
756 Psychotherapists
757 Medical Therapy
758 Medical Care
759 Medical Personnel

76 DEATH

761 Life and Death
762 Suicide
763 Dying
764 Funeral
765 Mourning
766 Deviant Mortuary Practices
767 Mortuary Specialists
768 Social Readjustments to Death
769 Cult of the Dead

77 RELIGIOUS BELIEFS

771 General Character of Religion
772 Cosmology
773 Mythology
774 Animism
775 Eschatology
776 Spirits and Gods
777 Luck and Chance
778 Sacred Objects and Places
779 Theological Systems

78 RELIGIOUS PRACTICES

781 Religious Experience
782 Propitiation
783 Purification and Expiation
784 Avoidance and Taboo
785 Asceticism
786 Orgies
787 Revelation and Divination

788 Ritual
789 Magic

79 ECCLESIASTICAL ORGANIZATION

791 Magicians and Diviners
792 Holy Men
793 Priesthood
794 Congregations
795 Sects
796 Organized Ceremonial
797 Missions
798 Religious Intolerance

80 NUMBERS AND MEASURES

801 Numerology
802 Numeration
803 Mathematics
804 Weights and Measures
805 Ordering of Time

81 EXACT KNOWLEDGE

811 Logic
812 Philosophy
813 Scientific Method
814 Humanistic Studies
815 Pure Science
816 Applied Science

82 IDEAS ABOUT NATURE AND MAN

821 Ethnometeorology
822 Ethnophysics
823 Ethnogeography
824 Ethnobotany
825 Ethnozoology
826 Ethnoanatomy
827 Ethnophysiology
828 Ethnopsychology
829 Ethnosociology

83 SEX

831 Sexuality
832 Sexual Stimulation
833 Sexual Intercourse
834 General Sex Restrictions
835 Kinship Regulation of Sex
836 Premarital Sex Relations
837 Extramarital Sex Relations
838 Homosexuality
839 Miscellaneous Sex

58 Marriage

Marriage is a socially sanctioned relationship between a man and a woman involving economic cooperation and residential and sexual cohabitation. The culturally patterned norms of this relationship regularly specify who may and may not enter into it, how it may be established and terminated, and what each partner may and may not do within it. As a relationship, marriage is to be distinguished sharply from the family, the social group within which it is typically embedded.

581 Basis of Marriage

Theories of the origin, purpose, sanctity, and permanency of marriage; conception of the marriage bond and of the status of matrimony; economic, sexual, and romantic factors in marriage; incentives to marriage; qualities desired in a spouse (e.g., beauty, wealth, industry, skill); relation of marriage to the family; etc. See also:

582 Regulation of Marriage

Minimum and average age at marriage for each sex; postponement of marriage (e.g., for economic reasons, to enable an elder sibling to marry first) ; physical and mental bars to marriage; endogamous and exogamous restrictions; preferred primary marriages (e.g., with a cross-cousin) ; explanations and rationalizations of marriage restrictions; tests of marriageability (e.g., of skill, prowess, fertility) ; trial marriage; etc. See also:

583 Mode of Marriage

Wife-capture (e.g., actual, ceremonial) ; marriage by exchange (e.g., of sisters) ; wife-purchase; marriage by payment of consideration (e.g., substantial bride-price, token bride-price, dowry) ; bride-service (e.g., premarital, postmarital) ; marriage by gift exchange; marriage by formal or informal initiation of common residence; elopement (e.g., motives, subsequent adjustments) ; prevalence and prestige of each mode; relation to rules of residence; conceptualization of bride-price or dowry (e.g., as purchase price, as compensation for loss of services, as guarantee of marriage stability) ; content and mode of payment of consideration; contributors and recipients, etc. See also:

584 Arranging a Marriage

Marriage preliminaries; courtship (e.g., opportunities, methods) ; initiation of negotiations (e.g., by youth, by girl, by parents of either) ; conduct of negotiations (e.g., by parents, through a go-between) ; marriage brokers; proposal of marriage; methods and consequences of rejection; requirement of consent (e.g., of youth, of girl, of parents, of chief) ; betrothal (e.g., conceptualization, announcement, ceremonial, symbols, duration) ; status and behavior of betrothed persons; infant betrothal (e.g., prevalence, procedure, nullification) ; breaking an engagement (e.g., reasons, procedure, consequences) ; adjustment to death of betrothed (e.g., substitution of a sibling) ; etc. See also:

585 Nuptials

Wedding (e.g., preferred time and place, ceremonial, persons attending and officiating); symbolic rites; means of assuring publicity and legality (e.g., banns, licenses); civil and ecclesiastical weddings; variations dependent upon status; associated property transactions (e.g., transfer of gifts, of bride-price); homecoming of bridal couple; consummation (e.g., immediate or deferred, private or public); defloration rites (e.g., jus primae noctis); concern for virginity of bride (e.g., exhibiting tokens); postwedding events (e.g., honeymoon, exchange of visits); status and activities of newly married persons; etc. See also:

586 Termination of Marriage

Methods (e.g., desertion, separation, annulment, divorce); prevalence of each; reasons (e.g., cruelty, infidelity, laziness, sterility); initiative and rights of each sex; procedure; residence readjustments; allocation of children (e.g., to mother, to father, to parent least at fault, division by age or sex); property arrangements (e.g., return of bride-price, alimony), subsequent relations of divorced spouses; social attitudes toward separation and divorce; etc. See also:

587 Secondary Marriages

Remarriage of widowed and divorced persons; differential rules governing secondary marriages (e.g., preference for relative of first spouse, reduction in bride-price, curtailing of ceremonial); levirate and sororate unions (e.g., prevalence, preferences, procedure); etc. See also:

588 Irregular Unions

Marriages in violation of incest taboos, exogamous rules, caste restrictions, or prohibitions of bigamy; common-law marriages; marriages to gods, to deceased persons, to trees, to persons of the same sex; frequency of irregular unions; social reactions; etc. See also:

589 Celibacy

Prevalence of bachelors and spinsters; reasons for celibacy; status and activities of unmarried, widowed, and divorced celibates; etc. See also:

Religious celibates 79
Care of widows 736
Mourning 765
Chastity 831
Premarital adulthood 883

76 Death

This section deals with ideas about death and with practices which accompany and follow the occurrence of death. For beliefs concerning a life after death see 775.

761 Life and Death

Theories about life and death; notion of a life force; conception of death (e.g., as natural, as unnatural); beliefs about the causes of death; attitude toward death (e.g., confidence, fear, fatalism); etc. See also:

Theories of health and
disease 75
Conception of fate, animistic
beliefs, eschatology, and
myths about origin of
death 77
Mortality statistics 165
Prescriptions for longevity. . 886

762 Suicide

Incidence of suicide; motives (e.g., humiliation, thwarted love); common methods (e.g., jumping, drowning, shooting, poison); stereotyped methods (e.g., hara-kiri); justifications; attitude toward suicides; etc. See also:

Personality disorders 158
Punishment of attempted
suicide 682

763 Dying

Omens and predictions of death; notions about dying; recognizing the approach of death; settlement of affairs; assembling of relatives; attempts to postpone death; preparing the patient for death (e.g., removal from dwelling, dressing in mortuary garments, last rites); preparing the funeral equipment (e.g., shroud, coffin); last words and last favors; criteria of death (e.g., coma, cessation of breath or heart action); attempts at revival; reaction to the impact of death (e.g., wailing, flight, self-mutilation); announcement of death; postmortem examinations; etc. See also:

Deathbed testaments 428
Capital punishment 681
Omens 787

764 Funeral

Attitude toward the corpse; mortuary toilet (e.g., dressing and decorating the body); laying out in state, preservative techniques (e.g., embalming, desiccation, mummification); determination of time, place, and mode of burial; interval between death and burial (e.g., duration, measures to prevent further deaths, manifestations of grief); vigils and wakes; place of disposal of corpse (e.g., cemetery, ossuary); receptacles (e.g., coffin, canoe, urn, tomb); method of disposal (e.g., abandonment, inhumation, cremation, sea burial, cave burial, tree or scaffold burial); preparation of grave, pyre, or scaffold; transport of corpse to place of disposal; procession to grave; disposition of corpse (e.g., posture, orientation); funerary mounds, monuments, and memorials; burial rites; mortuary sacrifices; disposition of grave goods; roles of relatives at funerals; precautions against return of the soul (e.g., silence, disguise, doors of the dead); return from the funeral; purification of participants; etc. See also:

765 Mourning

Duration of the mourning period; behavior of spouse and other relatives after the funeral (e.g., seclusion, mourning garb, observance of taboos, sacrifices); treatment of relics (e.g., preservation of skull or head, wearing of bones, use of hair for artifacts); visits to the grave; mortuary feasts; exhumation, second funeral, and reburial; ceremonies terminating mourning; etc. See also:

766 Deviant Mortuary Practices

Abbreviated and extended funerals; distinctive mortuary rites in special cases of death (e.g., for an enemy, stranger, executed criminal, pauper, slave, child, woman dying in childbirth, chief, shaman, warrior, person dying abroad, victim of accidental death, suicide, homicide, victim of epidemic or loathsome disease); ceremonies at the death of animals; etc. See also:

767 Mortuary Specialists

Burial associations; gravediggers; cemetery guards and caretakers; hired mourners; embalmers and undertakers; funeral parlors; status and remuneration of mortuary specialists; etc. See also:

768 Social Readjustments to Death

Disposition of the possessions of the deceased (e.g., abandonment or relocation of dwelling, destruction or mutilation of movable possessions, redistribution of property); provision for support of spouse and children; residence changes of survivors; etc. See also:

769 Cult of the Dead

Avoidance of graves and cemeteries; propitiation of ghosts and ancestors; recurrent feasts of the dead; maintaining relations with the long dead; ancestor worship; household cults; hero worship; etc. See also:

82 Ideas About Nature and Man

This section is designed to cover speculative and popular notions concerning phenomena of the external world and of the human organism.

821 Ethnometeorology

Ideas about night and day, dawn and twilight, rising and setting of the sun, phases of the moon, eclipses, solstices and equinoxes, and the succession of seasons; notions about heavenly bodies (e.g., sun, moon, stars, constellations, planets, comets, meteorites); ideas about meteorological phenomena (e.g., clouds and fog, frosts and drought, rain and snow, hail and sleet, winds and whirlwinds, storms, thunder and lightning, rainbow, parhelion and aurora); associated behavior patterns (e.g., greeting the dawn, dispelling an eclipse); etc. See also:

822 Ethnophysics

Popular conceptions of matter, energy, and their properties; notions about space, time, and gravitation; ideas about form, color, and sound (e.g., color symbolism); beliefs about shadows, reflections, and echoes; notions about electricity and magnetism; pre-scientific theoretical systems (e.g., alchemy); etc. See also:

823 Ethnogeography

Notions about water; ideas about hydrographic phenomena (e.g., oceans and seas, waves and tides, currents and whirlpools, rivers and streams, lakes and springs, floods); ideas about topographic phenomena (e.g., hills and mountains, canyons and valleys, caves and grottoes, striking natural formations, volcanoes and earthquakes); notions about minerals, metals, and precious stones; geographical and geological lore; directions (e.g., upstream and downstream, cardinal points); ideas about the beauty of nature; associated behavior patterns (e.g., attempts to quell earthquakes); etc. See also:

824 Ethnobotany

Notions about plants in general; ideas about particular plants (e.g., mistletoe); cultural uses of plants; native terms for plants; knowledge of poisonous plants; associated behavior patterns; etc.

See also:

825 Ethnozoology

Notions about animals (e.g., mammals, birds, reptiles, fish, crustaceans, insects) ; ideas about particular animals (e.g., snakes, fireflies) ; technological and other cultural uses of wild animals and their products; native terms for animals; associated behavior patterns (e.g., avoidance of snakes) ; etc. See also:

826 Ethnoanatomy

Conception of ideal bodily proportions; ideas about the torso and its parts (e.g., belly, breasts, buttocks, navel, neck, spine), skin and pigmentation, hair (e.g., axial, body, facial, head, pubic), head and its parts (e.g., brain, ears, eyes, lips, mouth, nose, teeth, tongue), limbs (e.g., arms, legs, hands, feet, fingers, toes, nails), blood, veins and arteries, bones, fat and muscles, nerves and sinews, internal organs (e.g., heart, intestines, kidneys, liver, lungs, stomach) ; interpretations of physical abnormalities (e.g., albinism, clubfoot, cretinism, dwarfism, harelip, hermaphroditism, hunchback) ; associated behavior patterns; etc. See also:

827 Ethnophysiology

Ideas about anal reactions (e.g., urination, defecation, farting), circulatory reactions (e.g., heartbeat, pulse), dermal reactions (e.g., flushing, fever and temperature, perspiring, shivering, itching and twitching, sloughing of skin and hair), facial reactions (e.g., laughing, smiling, grinning, sneering, frowning), nasal and respiratory reactions (e.g., breathing, panting, sneezing, running of nose), ocular and auricular reactions (e.g., weeping, blinking, dilation of pupils, ringing of ears, secretion of wax), oral reactions (e.g., salivation, spitting, swallowing, vomiting, coughing, hiccoughing, yawning); ideas about digestion and respiration; notions about heredity; associated behavior patterns (e.g., scratching, congratulations upon sneezing); etc. See also:

828 Ethnopsychology

Ideas about impulses or drives; conceptualization of sensation, perception, and emotions; standards of sensory pleasantness and unpleasantness; ideas about conscious and unconscious mental processes; notions about abnormal mental states (e.g., aphasia, catalepsy, coma, delirium, hallucination, hypnosis, hysteria, swoon); interpretations and explanations of neuroses and psychoses; ideas about habits, attitudes, and the learning process; concepts of the self, of human nature, of motivation, of personality, of character; associated cultural behavior; etc. See also:

829 Ethnosociology

Social philosophy; interpretations of the society's charter; native ideas about social relationships and social structure; concepts of society (e.g., social contract); notions about culture and cultural change; economics and political behavior (e.g., mercantilism), racial inequality; etc. See also:

Ruth Benedict

THE SCIENCE OF CUSTOM

Anthropology has been fortunate in having had its fair share of articulate spokesmen, and of these spokesmen none have been more eloquent than Ruth Benedict. "The Science of Custom" is probably one of the most clearly written essays of all those that have attempted to define the nature of culture. This brilliant, brief, but remarkably comprehensive essay, published in 1929, later became the basis of the first chapter of Ruth Benedict's internationally famous *Patterns of Culture,* which appeared in 1934. In this exceptionally lucid exposition, Ruth Benedict touches upon almost all of the central issues surrounding the meaning and use of the anthropologist's concept of culture.

For a short sketch of Ruth Benedict, see Abram Kardiner and Edward Preble, *They Studied Man* (New York, 1963), pp. 178–86. For more detail, see Margaret Mead, *An Anthropologist at Work: Writings of Ruth Benedict* (Boston, 1959).

Anthropology is the study of primitive peoples[1]—a statement which helps us to understand its bearing on contemporary thought as little as if, in the time of Copernicus, we had defined astronomy as the study of the stars, or biology, in the time of Darwin, as the science of bugs. It was not facts about stars that made astronomy suddenly of first-class importance, but that—quite casually, as it were—the Copernican scheme placed the earth, this planetary scene of human life, in a perspective of such infinitesimal insignificance. In much the same way the significance of anthropology to modern thought does not lie in any secrets that the primitive has saved for us from a simpler world, with which to solve the perplexities of this existence. Anthropology is not a search for the philosopher's stone in a vanished and golden age. What anthropologists find in the study of primitive people is a natural and well-nigh inexhaustible laboratory of custom, a great workshop in which to explore the major rôle it has played in the life-history of the world.

Reprinted from *The Century Magazine,* 117 (1929), 641–49.

[1][It is interesting to note that the first sentence in *Patterns of Culture* defines anthropology as the study of human beings as creatures of society. It is significant that at one time anthropologists themselves limited their attention to the so-called primitive peoples. They can therefore scarcely blame the general public for thinking that anthropologists study only primitive peoples. Anthropologists study man, not just some men, but all men. One of the newest areas of cultural anthropology research is "urban anthropology." The effect of city environment upon peoples all over the world needs to be investigated, especially as formerly rural, agriculturally oriented peoples become citified.—*Ed. Note.*]

Now custom has not been commonly regarded as a subject of any great moment. It is not like the inner workings of our own brains, which we feel to be uniquely worthy of investigation. Custom, we have a way of thinking, is behavior at its most commonplace. As a matter of fact, it is the other way around. Traditional custom, taken the world over, is a mass of detailed behavior more astonishing than any one person can ever evolve in personal acts no matter how aberrant. Yet that is a rather trivial aspect of the matter. The fact of first-rate importance is the predominant rôle that custom plays in experience and in belief. No man ever looks at the world with pristine eyes. He sees it edited by a definite set of customs and institutions and ways of thinking. Even in his philosophical probings he cannot go behind these stereotypes; his very concepts of the true and the false will still have reference to the structure of his particular traditional customs. John Dewey has said in all seriousness that the part played by custom in shaping the behavior of the individual as over against any way in which he can affect traditional custom, is as the proportion of the total vocabulary of his mother tongue over against those words of his own baby talk that are taken up into the vernacular of his family. There is no social problem it is more incumbent upon us to understand than that of the rôle of custom in our total life. Until we are intelligent as to the laws and the varieties of customs, the main complicating facts of human life will remain to us an unintelligible book.

The first concern of the anthropologist is always for an understanding of this affair of custom: how each society comes to be possessed of whole systems of it, how it is stabilized, cross-fertilized, how it is inculcated into all the members of the group among whom it flourishes. In other words, the business of the anthropologist is with the great ideational systems of language, social organization and religion of which every people on earth finds itself possessed, and which are passed on to every child as it is born into the group, but of which no child born in any other territory could ever achieve the thousandth part.

This matter of culture, to give it its anthropological term—that complex whole which includes all the habits acquired by man as a member of society—has been late in claiming scientific attention. There are excellent reasons for this. Any scientific study requires first of all that there be no preferential weighting of one or another of the items in the series it selects for its consideration. Anthropology was therefore by definition impossible as long as those old distinctions between ourselves and the barbarian, ourselves and the pagan, held sway over people's minds. It was necessary first to arrive at that degree of sophistication where one no longer set his belief over against his neighbor's superstition, and it is worth considering that it is barely one hundred years ago that any one took his superstitious neighbors seriously enough to include them in any general purview of serious belief.

In the second place, custom did not challenge the attention of social theorists, because it was the very stuff of their own thinking. We do not see the lens through which we look. Precisely in proportion as it was fundamental, it was automatic, and had its existence outside the field of conscious attention. The custom of greeting a guest by an array of weeping women who sit in his lap and embrace him, may not need more or less psychological elucidation than the handshake, but it communicates the necessary shock, and the subject of the handshake will remain unexplored long after we have mustered our efforts toward the understanding of the tears-greeting. We have only to admit alien customs to the same rank in regulating human nature that ours have for us, and we are perpetually galvanized into attention.

It is not fair to lay our blindness to custom wholly to the fact that it is closer to us than breathing. Primitive people are sometimes far more conscious of the rôle of cultural traits than we are, and for good reason. They have had intimate experience of different cultures, and we have not. White civilization has standardized itself over most of the globe. We have never seen an outsider unless he is already Europeanized. The uniformity of customs, of outlook, seems convincing enough, and conceals from us the fact that it is after all an historical accident. All our observation reinforces the testimony of our easy assent to the familiar, and we accept without any ado the equivalence of human nature and of our own cultural standards. But many primitives have a different experience. They have seen their religion go down before the white man's, their economic system, their marriage prohibitions. They have laid down the one and taken up the other, and are quite clear and sophisticated about variant arrangements of human life. If they talk about human nature, they do it in plurals, not in the absolute singular, and they will derive dominant characteristics of the white man from his commercial institutions, or from his conventions of warfare, very much after the fashion of the anthropologist. If civilized Europeans have been especially dense to the scientific implications of custom, it has been not only because their own customs were too familiar to be discernible, and because they resisted the implication that their culture belonged to a series that included the customs of lesser people, but also because the standardization of their own culture over the globe has given an illusion of a world-wide uniform human behavior.

What is it that anthropologists have to say about this matter of custom? In the first place, it is man's distinguishing mark in the animal kingdom. Man is the culture-making animal.[2] It is not that insects, for instance, do

2[This is a moot point. Thinking that only men can have culture may be part of the same anthropocentric worldview which at various stages of human history insisted that the earth was the center of the universe or denied that man was an animal. The list of features peculiar to man keeps diminishing. For example, until recently, man was defined as the tool-making animal to differentiate him from other forms of animal life. Then it was discovered that some primates devised and used elemental objects which functionally speaking had to be termed tools. Similarly, linguists have held the line, contending that only humans have language. Animals, they argue, have communication, but not language, which is a special kind of communication! Rather than playing semantic hair-splitting games, it might be more accurate to say that there is a continuum and that many if not most human characteristics have close parallels or analogs in primate and other animal life. The difference, if any, would thus be more of degree than kind. With this perspective, one could perfectly well speak of monkey culture or more specifically of baboon social organization. It is true that insect culture is largely predetermined, as Benedict observes, but not have complex cultural traits like the domestication of plants and animals, political organization, division of labor. But the mechanism of transmission makes them contrast sharply with man's particular contribution of traditionally *learned* behavior. Insect society takes no chances; the pattern of the entire social structure is carried in the cell structure of each individual ant, so that one isolated individual can automatically reproduce the entire social order of its own colony just as it reproduces the shape of antennæ or of abdomen. For better or worse, man's solution has been at the opposite pole. Not one item of his tribal social organization, of language, of his local religion, is carried in his germcell. His whole centuries-evolved civilization is at the mercy of any accident of time and space. If he is taken at birth to another continent, it will be the entire set of cultural traits of the adoptive society that he will learn, and the set that was his by heredity will play no part. More than this, whole peoples in one generation have shaken off their patterns, retaining hardly a residual vestige, and have put on the customs of an alien group.

What is lost in nature's guarantee of safety, is made up in the advantage of greater plasticity. The human animal does not, like the bear have to wait to grow himself a polar coat before he can adapt himself to the arctic; he learns to sew himself a coat and put up a snow house. It is a direct corollary of this difference in the mechanism of human culture that ant societies have been stable for sixty-five million years, and human societies are never to-morrow what they are to-day.

Anthropology has no encouragement to offer to those who would trust our spiritual achievements to the automatic perpetuation of any selected hereditary germ-plasms. Culture, it insists, is not carried in that fashion for the human race. We cannot trust any program of racial purity. It is a significant fact that no anthropologist has ever taught, along with so many popular theorists, that high civilization is bound up with the biological homogeneity of its carriers. Race is a classification based on bodily form, and the particular cultural behavior of any group is strikingly independent of its racial affiliations. We must accept all the implications of our human inheritance, one of the most important of which is the small scope of biologically transmitted behavior, and the enormous rôle of the cultural process of the transmission of tradition.

There is another analogy with the animal world which has to be laid aside in the study of culture: no less than the idea of evolution. The modern anthropologist at this point is only throwing in his lot with the psychologist and the historian, emphasizing the fact that the order of events in which they all deal in common is best studied without the complications of any attempted evolutionary arrangement. The psychologist is not able to

---

mammals other than man are capable of learning behavioral patterns, of responding to symbols, and even of producing creative solutions to problems. For further information bearing on this definitional controversy, see Weston La Barre, *The Human Animal* (Chicago, 1954), S. L. Washburn, ed., *Social Life of Early Man* (New York, 1961), and Irven DeVore, ed., *Primate Behavior: Field Studies of Monkeys and Apes* (New York, 1965).—*Ed. Note.*]

demonstrate any evolutionary series in the sensory or emotional reactions of the individuals he studies, and the historian is not helped in the reconstruction of Plantagenet England by any concept of the evolution of government; just as superfluous for him also, the anthropologist insists, is any scheme of cultures arranged according to an ascending scale of evolution.

Since the science of anthropology took shape in the years when the "Origin of Species" was still new, it was inevitable that there should have been this attempt to arrange human societies from this point of view. It was simplicity itself. At the summit of the ascent was placed our own culture, to give meaning and plan to all that had preceded; to the lowest rungs was relegated by hypothesis all that was most different from this consummation; and the intermediate steps were arranged as these two fixed points suggested. It is important to insist that there was never any argument from actual chronology; even in cases where it could have been ascertained, it was not considered of such importance that it could compete with the *a priori* hypothesis. In this way the development of art, religion and marriage institutions was classically charted. It is a monument to the force of a theory that asked no proof other than its own conviction.

Now if there is no positive correlation between culture and an evolutionary scheme, is there any order and arrangement of any kind in the diversity of human customs? To answer this question it is necessary to go back to fundamentals, to man's equipment of basic responses to environment. These responses, as anthropologists see them, are mere rough sketches, a list of bare facts; but they are hints that may be illimitably fertile. They are focal centers which any peoples may ignore, or which they may make the starting point of their most elaborated concepts. Let us take, for instance, the example of adolescence. Adolescence is a necessary biological fact for man and for his animal forebears, but man has used it as a springboard. It may be made the occasion for the major part of the ritual the group practices; it may be ignored as completely as Margaret Mead has recently shown that it is in Samoa. It may be seen, as among the African Masai, as one item of an elaborate crisis ceremonialism that institutionalizes not only adolescence but provides, for instance, a ceremony for putting the father on the shelf after his son has attained young manhood. It may be, on the other hand, a magic occasion that will, in after life, give back as from a mirror every technique that is practiced at this time. So a girl will pick each needle carefully from a pine-tree that she may be industrious, or a boy will race a stone down the mountain that he may be swift of foot. The rites may be limited to the young girls, or, it may be, to the boys; the period may be marked with horror and with torture, it may be a consecration to the gods. It is obvious that the physical fact of adolescence is only the touch to the ball of custom, which then follows grooves of thought not implied in the original impetus.

What these grooves are we can sometimes account for out of the cultural history of a people; more often we can only record the facts. We know that traits that have once found themselves in company are likely to maintain that association quite apart from any intrinsic fitness in their nature. So bone head-scratchers and the pursuit of a supernatural vision may go hand in hand over a continent, and the absence of foot-gear may coincide with carved door-posts.

What we do know is that there is no one of the bare reactions of the human animal that may not be selected by some people for a position in the very forefront of its attention and be elaborated past belief. It may be that the economic facts of life, as for instance the buffalo herds of the Todas of India, may be singled out, and the whole life of the people may turn on the ritual, of perpetuating and renewing the sacred *pep,* the soured milk saved by the Todas from day to day as the continuum of their culture, and used to hasten the next day's souring. The dairymen are the priests, anointed and sacrosanct, the holy of holies is the sacred cow bell. Most of the taboos of the people have to do with the infinite sacredness of the milk.

Or a culture may, instead, elaborate an item of the social organization. All people over the earth recognize some forbidden degrees within which marriage may not take place. These are alike only in the common idea of incest; the degrees themselves differ entirely. In a large part of the world you may marry only one variety of own cousin, say your mother's brother's daughter, and it is incest to marry the other variety, say your father's sister's daughter. But however unreasonable the distinctions may seem from our point of view, some concept of forbidden degrees all men have, and animals, it seems, have not. Now this idea has been taken up by the aborigines of Australia and made the basis of a social system that knows no restraint in the elaboration of its favorite pattern. Not satisfied with stipulating one cousin group within which, and no other, one must find a mate, certain of these tribes have heaped the incest taboos on lineages, on local groups, on all who participate with them in certain ceremonies, until even in the specified cousin group there is no one who is not touched by some one of the taboos. Quite in keeping with the violence of their obsession with this detail of social organization, they are accustomed to visit death upon any one who transgresses the fantastic rules. Do they pull themselves together before they have reached the point of tribal suicide and reject their overgrown anti-social rulings? No, they get by with a subterfuge. Young men and women may escape together to an island which is regarded as asylum. If they succeed in remaining in seclusion until the birth of a child, they may return with no more than a formalized drubbing. So the tribe is enabled to maintain its ethics without acknowledged revision, and still avoid extinction.

But it need not be incest that has run away with itself in the culture of a group; it may be some trick of ritualism, or love of display, or passion of acquisitiveness. It may be fish-hooks. In a certain island of Oceania fish-hooks are currency, and to have large fish-hooks came gradually to be the outward sign of the possession of great wealth. Fish-hooks therefore are made very nearly as large as a man. They will no longer catch fish, of course. In proportion as they have lost their usefulness they are supremely coveted.

After a long experience of such cultural facts anthropologists have made up their minds on two points. In the first place, it is usually beside the point to argue, from its important place in behavior, the social usefulness of a custom. Man can get by with a mammoth load of useless lumber, and he has a passion for extremes. Once his attention is engaged upon one trait of behavior, he will juggle his customs till they perforce accommodate themselves to the outward manifestations of his obsession. After all, man has a fairly wide margin of safety, and he will not be forced to the wall even with a pitiful handicap. Our own civilization carries its burden of warfare, of the dissatisfaction and frustration of wage-earners, of the overdevelopment of acquisitiveness. It will continue to bear them. The point is that it is more in line with the evidence to regard them as our equivalents of the fish-hooks or of the Australian marriage rules, and to give over the effort to prove their natural social utility.

For every people will always justify their own folkways. Warfare, as long as we have it, will be for our moralists the essential school in which justice and valor are to be learned; the desire for possession similarly will be the one motive power to which it is safe to trust the progress of the world. In the same way, China relied upon reverence for one's ancestors. There are too many of these folkways. They cannot all be the *sine qua non* of existence, and we shall do better to concentrate our attention upon an objective appreciation of different schemes, and to give our enthusiasms to those special values we can always discern in the most diverse civilizations.

The second point on which anthropologists have made up their minds in this connection—and this holds true for all customs whether or not they have been carried to extremes—is that in any study of behavior it is these cultural patternings that turn out to be compulsive, not any original instincts with which we are born equipped. Even the basic emotions of fear and love and rage by the time they have been shaped over the different cultural lasts are well-nigh unrecognizable. Is there a jealousy of the mate innate in our sexual organization? Perhaps, but it will not dictate behavior except according to a cultural permit. Over a large part of the world, the woman is aggrieved if her husband does not take other wives—it may be to aid her in the duties of the household, or to relieve her of child-bearing, or to make plain her husband's social importance. And in other parts of the world, the male's virtues of generosity and of dignity are chiefly summed up in his practice of sharing his wife, and his calm acceptance of her desertion. Is there a maternal instinct? It will always be operative according to the conventions of the group. If there is great emphasis upon rank, women may voluntarily kill their children to raise their own status, as among the Natchez, or the Polynesian Tonga. If there is a pattern of seemingly meaningless adoption, most families will place their infants in other households, sometimes assigning them before birth. And how often have different apologists tried to give reasons for infanticide, when all the reasons they list are just as operative outside as within the region where this cultural compulsion rests upon the women.

Man evolves always elaborate traditional ways of doing things, great superstructures of the most varying design, and without very striking correlations with the underpinnings on which they must each and all eventually rest. It is only in a fundamental and non-spectacular sense that these superstructures are conditioned by their foundation in man's original endowment. And it is the superstructure in which man lives, not the foundation. The compulsion of folkways in a well-knit culture is just as strong as the compulsion of a style in architecture, Gothic, or Renaissance, or Egyptian. It fashions as it will the instincts of the people who live within it, remaking them in conformity with its own requirements. So it is that the cultural patterns are themselves creative; they take the raw material of experience and mold it into fifty different shapes among fifty different peoples. The traditional patterns of behavior set the mold and human nature flows into it.

It follows that man's established folkways are also his morals. Judgments of right and wrong and of the glory of God grow up within the field of group behavior and attach themselves to those traits that have become automatic in the group. Interference with automatic behavior is always unpleasant, and it is rationalized as evil. No people have any truly empirical ethics; they uphold what they find themselves practicing. Even our own literature of ethics is far from being a detached survey of different possible solutions; it is a system of apologetics for the well-known scheme of our own culture. It is not that the anthropologist would subtract a jot or tittle from this preference for one's own customs; there are values in any way of living that can be plumbed only by those who have been born and bred in them, and in an ideal world every man would love best his own culture. What the anthropologist would have us add to our understanding is that all cultures have alike grown up blindly, the useful and cumbersome together, and not one of them is so good that it needs no revision, and not one is so bad that it cannot serve, just as ours can, the ideal ends of society and of the individual.

And how is it with regard to religion? All peoples have been religious; it is only what constituted religion that has varied. There is no item of experience, from the orientation of a house, to sleight of hand or foretelling the future, that has not been somewhere, it seems, the distinguishing matter of religion. Surely it is not this heterogeneous content of religion that is its essence. The rôle of religion is its slow and halting exploration of the spiritual life. Often it has wedged itself into blind alleys and wasted generations of experiment. It made a mistake and included within its scope not only its proper field, but also all that area of existence that is better handled in secular fashion. Its special field of the spiritual life is still in the process of delimitation. In that field it shares with art and with abstract thought and with all enthusiastic dedications of the self, the spiritual rewards of life. What the future holds we do not know, but it is not too much to hope that it will include a reinstating and reshaping of the spiritual values of existence that will balance the present immense unfolding of the material values.

What is the upshot of this analysis of custom for our contemporary thinking? Is it subversive? Certainly not, except in the sense in which Copernicus's demonstration of the stellar series to which this earth belonged, was subversive. The culture we are born into, according to anthropology, is also—as the earth is in the solar scheme—one of a series of similar phenomena all driven by the same compulsions. What we give up, in accepting this view, is a dogged attachment to absolutes; what we gain is a sense of the intriguing variety of possible forms of behavior, and of the social function that is served by these communal patternings. We become culture-conscious.

We perceive with new force the ties that bind us to those who share our culture. Ways of thinking, ways of acting, goals of effort, that we tend so easily to accept as the order of the universe, become rather the precious and special symbols we share together. Institutions that were massive Juggernauts demanding their toll become instead a world of the imagination to which all those of common culture have common access. For the social function of custom is that it makes our acts intelligible to our neighbors. It binds us together with a common symbolism, a common religion, a common set of values to pursue. In the past these groups have been geographical, and there has been little individual difference of choice among the members of a group. In the future there will be less geographical differentiation, more differentiation perhaps of voluntary groups. But though it will change the picture of civilization, it will not change the necessity in every sort of complicated human behavior of the cultural symbol, the framework within which alone our acts have meaning. The most individualistic rebel of us all would play a foolish rôle stripped of the conventions of his culture. Why should he make wholesale attack upon its institutions? They are the epic of his own people, written not in rime but in stone and currency and merchant marines and city colleges. They are the massive creation of the imaginations of generations, given a local habitation and a name.

We do not stand to lose by this tolerant and objective view of man's institutions and morals and ways of thought. On the one hand, we shall value the bold imagination that is written in all great systems of behavior; on the other, we shall not fear for the future of the world because some item in that system is undergoing contemporary change. We know all culture changes. It is one of its claims upon our interest. We hope, a little, that whereas change has hitherto been blind, at the mercy of unconscious patternings, it will be possible gradually, in so far as we become genuinely culture-conscious, that it shall be guided by intelligence.

For what is the meaning of life except that by the discipline of thought and emotion, by living life to its fullest, we shall make of it always a more flexible instrument, accepting new relativities, divesting ourselves of traditional absolutes? To this end we need for our scientific equipment something of the anthropologist's way of looking at human behavior, something of respect for the epic of our own culture, something of fine tolerance for the values that have been elaborated in other cultures than our own.

Clyde Kluckhohn and William H. Kelly

THE CONCEPT OF CULTURE

One of the most enjoyable ways of learning about what anthropologists say culture is and isn't is reading Clyde Kluckhohn and

Reprinted from *The Science of Man in the World Crisis*, ed. Ralph Linton (New York, 1945), pp. 78–105, by permission of Florence Kluckhohn, William H. Kelly, and Columbia University Press.

William H. Kelly's dramatized symposium on the subject. Here many misconceptions are analyzed and some of the diversity of opinion within anthropology is displayed. Those who prefer a more conventional treatment should consult A. L. Kroeber and Clyde Kluckhohn, *Culture: A Critical Review of Concepts and Definitions* (New York, 1963). For the view that the concept of culture is so important that it should be studied as a separate discipline, "culturology," the study of culture as opposed to anthropology which is the study of man, see Leslie A. White, *The Science of Culture* (New York, 1949), paperback edition (New York, 1958), or his excellent polemic paper "The Concept of Culture," *American Anthropologist,* **61** (1959), 227–51. For some of the theoretical problems involved in the concept of culture, see David Bidney, *Theoretical Anthropology* (New York, 1953), pp. 23–53. Also recommended is Edmund R. Leach, "Culture and Social Cohesion: An Anthropologist's View," *Daedalus: Journal of the American Academy of Arts and Sciences,* **94** (1965), 24–38.

The Lawyer: At the last meeting of this little discussion group of ours, we got into quite an argument about "culture" as a technical term in anthropology—exactly what anthropologists mean by it and whether it is any use or not.[1] The big dictionaries and even the anthropological books here in the club library didn't help us out very much. We did gather that the anthropological conception, like all the other scientific and popular usages, carries with it an implication of human interference, of something being added to, or altered from, a state of nature. But we found ourselves wishing that we could ask questions which might clear up points which were sidestepped or simply not discussed by these formal statements. We therefore prevailed upon you gentlemen to come here and let us put you on the spot.

The Historian: Was I right in insisting last time that the anthropologist's conception of culture is much more inclusive than the historian's?

First Anthropologist: Yes, to anthropologists a humble cooking pot is as much a cultural product as is a Beethoven sonata.

The Businessman: I am relieved to hear that. For my wife a person who has culture is a person who can talk about Debussy, T. S. Eliot, Picasso, and those people.

The Lawyer: Do anthropologists apply the term "culture" to our civilization? Isn't there a difference between "culture" and "civilization"?

Second Anthropologist: To most anthropologists, a civilization is simply a special type of a culture, namely, a complex or "high" culture. More specifically, a civilization is—as the derivation of the word itself suggests— the culture of a people who live in cities. People who have lived in cities

[1]We are grateful to Dr. Florence Kluckhohn for critical suggestions and other help.

have invariably possessed a somewhat complex way of life, and have almost always had a written language.

Third Anthropologist: Perhaps it would also be well to state for the record that anthropologists have never followed another distinction which certain sociologists have made between culture and civilization. This usage discriminates between "civilization" as comprising the sum total of human "means" and "culture" as constituting the collectivity of human "ends."

First Anthropologist: Many educated people seem to have the notion that "culture" applies only to exotic ways of life or to societies where relative simplicity and relative homogeneity prevail. Some sophisticated missionaries, for example, will use the anthropological conception in discussing the special modes of living of South Sea Islanders, but seem amazed at the idea that it could be applied equally to the inhabitants of New York City. And social workers in New York City will talk about the "culture" of a colorful and well-knit immigrant group, but boggle at utilizing the concept toward understanding the behavior of staff members in the social service agency itself.

The Economist: A moment ago you used the term "society." This brings me to a point which I have found confusing in certain recent more or less popular writings of anthropologists. Sometimes the terms "culture" and "society" seem to have been used almost as synonyms.

First Anthropologist: There would be fairly general agreement in our profession that this is undesirable. The usage which has attained almost complete acceptance among us can be put simply, though not altogether precisely, as follows: A "society" refers to a group of people who have learned to work together; a "culture" refers to the distinctive ways of life of such a group of people.

The Philosopher: In my language, then, "a culture" is an abstraction, whereas "a society" is not?

Third Anthropologist: That is certainly correct in the sense that you can see the individuals who make up a society, while you never see "culture." However, the statement must not be made to imply that the processes of inference and abstraction are not involved in many of the specific problems of deciding where one society leaves off and another begins. Some anthropologists assert that such problems can always be resolved by sufficiently detailed observation of the frequencies with which human beings in a defined territory interact. This is doubtless a valid operation by which to decide what individuals constitute "a society," but we should be deluding ourselves if we pretended that reasoning were not as necessary as observation to the delimitation of a society.

Second Anthropologist: I can't agree with your first statement that culture is never observed directly. What does an anthropologist actually do when he is working in the field? Yes, he sees the human organisms who make up a society. He sees not only them, but also their behavior. He likewise sees the objects they have made and all of the alterations which they produced in their natural environment. What the anthropologist does is to record the distinctive ways of behaving which he sees and those results of behavior which are also characteristic. These constitute the culture of the group.

Third Anthropologist: There is no doubt that you have rightly described what anthropologists actually do in the field. But those recordings which you have mentioned I would prefer to consider as the anthropologist's raw data. Both "society" and "culture" are conceptual constructs. In each case, although in importantly different ways, the anthropologist has added to or subtracted from what he actually saw. Both the society and the culture which he portrays are conceptual models—not firsthand recordings of all he observed.

The Psychologist: Let me see if I can translate into my own lingo. Culture means the totality of social habits.

First Anthropologist: "Habit" is too neutral a term. It would be more exact to say "socially valued habits," for a group is never affectively indifferent to its culture.

The Psychologist: I suppose that branch of psychology which is most intimately related to "culture" is what we today call "learning theory." Wouldn't you agree that the transmission of culture can be understood only in so far as learning and teaching are understood?

First Anthropologist: Yes, inasmuch as all human beings of whatever "races" seem to have about the same nervous systems and biological equipment generally, we would anticipate that the basic processes of learning are very similar if not identical among all groups. We therefore look to the psychologist to inform us about the laws of learning. On the other hand, we can show that *what* is learned, from whom learning takes place, and when the learning of certain skills usually occurs, varies according to culture. Also, I should like to point out that there is one danger in speaking of culture as being "taught." "Teaching" is not limited, as in the popular sense, to conscious instruction. Individuals learn—"absorb" more nearly suggests, in nontechnical language, the process—much of their culture through imitation of both the "matched-dependent" and "copying" types. Take, for example, those gestures and expressive movements ("motor habits") which are observed as characteristic of certain groups. Every anthropologist regards these as cultural phenomena, and yet only in dancing schools, armies, and the like is explicit instruction as to posture, and so forth, given.

The Psychologist: If I am not mistaken, C. S. Ford has defined culture as consisting of "traditional ways of solving problems" or "learned problem solutions."

Third Anthropologist: It is true that any culture is, among other things, a set of techniques for adjusting both to the external environment and to other men. In so far as Ford's statement points to this fact, it is helpful, but it will not do as a synoptic definition. For cultures create problems as well as solving them. If the lore of a people states that frogs are dangerous creatures, or that it is not safe to go about at night because of were-animals or ghosts, threats are posed which do not arise out of the inexorable facts of the external world. This is why all "functional" definitions of culture tend to be unsatisfactory: they disregard the fact that cultures create needs as well as provide a means of fulfilling them.

The Psychiatrist: In fact, my profession has always tended to think of culture as something which was repressive to the "natural" nature of man, as something which produced needless neuroses by demands and thwartings during the process of molding individuals into shapes uncongenial to their native temperament.

Third Anthropologist: This seems to us to be another half-truth. Culture is *both* fulfilling and frustrating.

Fourth Anthropologist: I have held my peace, but at this point I really must protest. Where is the "culture" which you talk about as doing this and that? If anthropology is to become a natural science, it must deal only in empirical and observable entities. In spite of the fact that most archeologists, ethnologists, and social anthropologists still feel that "culture" is their master concept, I maintain we would get further if we stuck to human interaction with other humans and with the natural environment. You can see those things, but has any of you ever seen "culture"?

First Anthropologist: I freely admit that to say "culture" does something is an inexact or metaphorical way of speaking. But this is merely a convenient shorthand expression in place of the long-winded though admittedly more precise "the human representatives of the group which share this culture do thus and so." As for "seeing": your admired natural scientists have never seen "gravity" or "evolution." And yet they find the introduction of these concepts indispensable for making the facts intelligible and for predicting them. "Culture" is an abstract generalizing concept, as essential to the understanding and prediction of events in the human world as is gravity to the understanding and prediction of events in the physical world.

Second Anthropologist: I accept and use the concept "culture," but I shy away from these high abstractions. I think it is better to stick to a more traditional definition, such as: "Culture is that complex whole which includes artifacts, beliefs, art, all the other habits acquired by man as a member of society, and all products of human activity as determined by these habits."

First Anthropologist: That is all right as a descriptive statement of what students of culture investigate. But as a definition I find it awkward. The enumeration is incomplete, and experience shows that in definitions by enumeration those elements which are not explicity stated tend to be forgotten even though they be implied. You, for example, have not even mentioned language.

Third Anthropologist: I would file two other objections. First, the definition is too intellectualistic. One gets no hint that people are other than affectively neutral toward their culture. This is just a list of culture content. Except, possibly, for the single word "whole," there is no indication that culture has organization as well as content.

The Economist: How about "social heredity" as a brief abstract definition of culture?

Third Anthropologist: This definition has been widely current and has been of much utility in drawing attention to the fact that human beings have a social as well as a biological heritage. The principal drawbacks to this conception of culture are that it implies too great stability of culture and too passive a role on the part of man. It suggests that man gets his culture as he gets his genes—without effort and without resistance. It tends too much to make us think of the human being as what Dollard has called "the passive porter of a cultural tradition." Men are, as Simmons has recently reminded us, not only the carriers and the creatures of culture—they are also creators and manipulators of culture. "Social heredity" suggests too much of the dead weight of tradition.

The Psychiatrist: Yes, culture is not merely a "given." Really, in a strictly literal sense, it is not a "given" at all—it is only available. Indeed, Ortega y Gasset has defined culture as "that which is sought." The phrase "social legacy" perhaps avoids some of these difficulties, but even this is hardly satisfactory. One wants a definition which points to the fact that the irreducible datum of the social scientist is the individual and his behavior. From the angle of individual psychology, no definition of culture is adequate which does not make us aware of the active role of the individual as regards his culture and of the fact that he has an impulse life.

The Businessman: Much of what has been said was mildly diverting as an exhibition in logical adroitness, but frankly I still don't altogether see why anybody bothers about "culture" at all.

First Anthropologist: Well, one of the interesting things about human beings is that they try to understand themselves and their own behavior. While this has been particularly true of Europeans in recent times, there is no group which has not developed a scheme or schemes to explain man's actions. I would claim that the concept of culture is essential to such understanding.

Second Anthropologist: I would phrase the case a little differently. Science is concerned with all observable phenomena, including man himself and his behavior. "Culture" is a convenient descriptive category for organizing our objective reports on human behavior.

The Philosopher: It strikes me that the last two statements contain the key to much of our apparent disagreement. For some anthropolgists "culture" is primarily a descriptive concept; for others it is primarily an explanatory concept. So-called "definitions" are always constructed from a point of view—which is all too often left unstated. Not all definitions are substantive (that is, "descriptive"). Nor is "explanatory" the only other alternative. Some of the definitions which have been partially stated or implied have been "functional"; others may be characterized as epistemological—that is, they have been intended to point toward the type of phenomena from which we gain our knowledge of "culture." There is also the point that some definitions look toward the actions of the individual as the starting point of all assertions, whereas others, while perhaps admitting these as ultimate referents, depart from abstractions attributable to groups. However, the distinction between "explanatory" and "descriptive" seems to be most central.

"Culture" as an Explanatory Concept

Third Anthropologist: By *"culture" we mean those historically created selective processes which channel men's reactions both to internal and to external stimuli.*

Second Anthropologist: That is certainly an "analytical abstraction" all right.

Third Anthropologist: That is precisely the idea: that with this concept certain aspects of the concrete phenomena may be analyzed out, and thus whole events may be better "explained" and predicted.

First Anthropologist: Very neat. And it seems to me to cover the ground. It avoids the difficulty lurking in those many definitions of culture which employ the phrase "acquired by man as a member of society." That phrase seems to suggest that "culture" as an explanatory concept refers *only* to dimensions of the behavior of individuals resultant upon their membership in a particular society (either through birth or through later affiliation). But "culture" also helps us to understand such processes as "diffusion," "culture contact," "acculturation."

Third Anthropologist: Yes, culture as an explanatory concept is useful alike in analyzing actions of individuals (whether treated as individuals or as groups) and in elucidating geographical distributions of artifacts or forms of behavior and historical sequences.

First Anthropologist: One could perhaps rephrase your definition along substantive lines by saying that by culture we mean those historically created definitions of the situation which individuals tend to acquire by virtue of participation in or contact with groups which tend to share ways of life which are in some respects distinctive.

Fourth Anthropologist: Even I find some merit in the explanatory definition proposed. You at least make some concession to a behavioristic approach when you speak of "reactions" and "stimuli."

Third Anthropologist: Naturally I would agree that any concept or proposition in social science must be ultimately referable back to human behavior. Even when we deal with distribution of "culture traits," we must not forget that we are dealing with products of human hands, with traces left by human activity.

Fourth Anthropologist: But why did you find it necessary to include *"internal* stimuli"?

Third Anthropologist: When a man eats, he is reacting to an internal "drive," namely, hunger contractions consequent upon the lowering of blood sugar and so forth, but his precise reaction to these internal stimuli cannot be predicted by physiological knowledge alone. Whether a healthy adult tends to "feel hungry" twice, three times, or four times a day and the hours at which these "feelings" tend to recur is a question of culture. *What* he eats is of course limited by sheer objective availability, but is also partly regulated by culture. It is a biological fact that some types of berries are poisonous, but it is a cultural fact that, a few generations ago, most Americans considered tomatoes to be poisonous and refused to eat them. On the other hand, milk, which we regard as a healthful and pleasing food, is regarded by certain peoples of the earth as either dangerous or disgusting. Such selective, discriminative use of the environment is characteristically cultural. In a still more general sense, too, the process of eating is channeled by culture. Whether a man eats to live, lives to eat, or eats and lives is partly individual idiosyncrasy, but there are also marked correlations of individual tendencies along these lines with cultural groups.

Second Anthropologist: Why do you use the word "reaction" instead of more straightforward "action"?

Third Anthropologist: Because "reaction" comes nearer to conveying the feeling tone which is associated with all selective designs for living.

Fourth Anthropologist: I am partially convinced, but I must once more come back to my question: Why did you introduce this unseen "culture"?

Third Anthropologist: There is no human being, if he be even a few weeks old, who reacts completely freshly to any stimulus situation. Very few human responses indeed can be explained entirely through even the most complete knowledge of the individual biological equipment, private experience up to that point, and the objective facts of the given situation.

Fourth Anthropologist: But where does "culture" come from? You seem to invoke it as a kind of *deus ex machina.*

Third Anthropologist: Culture is, as it were, the precipitate of history. It includes those aspects of the past which, usually in altered form, live on in the present. In more than one sense "history is a sieve."

Biologist: Do you mean that culture consists of those ways of meeting situations which prove to have survival value?

Third Anthropologist: This is a large and important part of the truth. The process of culture may well be regarded as something added to man's innate biological capacities; it provides instruments which enlarge or may even substitute for biological functions and which to a limited degree compensate for biological limitations—as in insuring that the biological fact of death does not always mean that what the dead individual has learned is lost to humanity.

Nevertheless, I believe this to be a dangerously misleading formulation unless it is properly explained and qualified. In the first place, as Linton and others have documented, it is an observed fact that most groups elaborate certain aspects of their culture far beyond maximal relative utility or survival value. In other words, not all culture is adaptive—in the sense of promoting sheer physical survival. At times indeed it does exactly the opposite. We must bring in the concept of adjustment (that is, lowering of tension) as well as that of adaptation. In the second place, aspects of culture which once directly promoted survival may persist even after they have ceased to have survival value. An analysis of contemporary Navaho culture will disclose many features which cannot possibly be construed as adaptations to the total environment in which Navahos now find themselves. However, it is altogether likely that these represent survivals, with modifications which have occurred during the centuries, of cultural forms which were adaptive in one or another environment in which certain ancestors of the contemporary Navaho lived prior to entering the Southwest.

First Anthropologist: In other words, you are saying that no way of reacting is taken over by the group unless it has direct adaptive or adjustive value for individuals as such (or as constituting a group) at the time the design for living becomes cultural.

Third Anthropologist: Right. The main point is that, as Boas so often insisted, we cannot account for complex historical changes by any simple formula. While many patterned ways of reacting unquestionably represent almost inevitable responses to an external environment in which the group lives or once lived, there are certainly also many cases where the inexorable conditions of action merely limit the possibility of response rather than eventually compelling one and only one mode of adaptation. These "choices" are probably themselves determined—if we make our theoretical system wide enough to encompass all possible types of factors. But, within the more usual frame of reference, they are the "accidents of history."

Let me give an example or two. In a society where the chief really has great power, one particular chief happens to be born with an endocrine imbalance which brings about certain (to that group) unusual idiosyncrasies in personality. By virtue of his position, he is able to bring about certain modifications in the way of life of his group (say, in religion) which are congenial to his "temperament." It may be argued, and it may be true, that no amount of authority could insure the persistence of such alterations unless they somehow had adjustive or adaptive value for more than a single individual. I do not believe that the empirical evidence bearing on this problem has been sufficiently analyzed to permit a definite answer to the question. But what is certain is that such a circumstance has been known to be followed by relatively temporary or relatively enduring changes in group designs for living—sometimes primarily in the form of strong "reaction formations." The fact of the chief's position and all that was consequent upon it is not an accident from the point of view of the theoretical systems usually employed in analyzing such steps. The unusual temperament is, however, due to an "accident of the genetic process."

Or, suppose that in the same group a chief dies as a relatively young man, leaving an infant as his heir. This has been observed to result in a marked crystallization of two factions around two rival older relatives, each of whom has about an equally valid claim to act as "regent." Through these circumstances a complete and lasting splitting off of two groups has been observed to take place. Each group thereafter has pursued its own separate destiny, and the end result is the formation of two distinguishable variants of what was at one time a more or less homogeneous culture. Now, to be sure, it is likely that the original factional lines had their bases in "economic," demographic, or other "external" conditions. Yet, had it not been for the "accidental" death of the one chief in his early maturity, the society might have indefinitely continued intact as an equilibrium of opposed tendencies. In short, the form and the mesh of the "sieve which is history" must be seen and shaped not only by the total "environment" at any given point in time but also by individual "psychological" and "accidental" factors.

First Anthropologist: Could we then say that culture includes all those ways of feeling, thinking, and acting which are not inevitable as a result of human biological equipment and process and (or) objective external situations?

Third Anthropologist: My objection to that definition would be: first, that this defines culture as a "residual category"—which is logically undesirable; second, I believe it is better to mention explicitly the time dimension as indicated by the phrase "historically created."

First Anthropologist: This suggests also the cumulative nature of culture.

Third Anthropologist: Yes, provided we remember that in another sense culture is not exactly "cumulative." Culture at any given timepoint has likewise the property of uniqueness. That is why it is absolutely essential to include the word "selective" in any definition.

The Lawyer: I can see that there has been a selection of possible modes of behavior and that these selections then may become established in a group, but aren't you overemphasizing this aspect? It seems to me that in common sense terms if we understand human nature, and if we then make our interpretation in the light of the concrete situation at hand, we get along very well.

First Anthropologist: No, if you will look beyond the records of our own time and place you will find that the matter is not so simple. There are certain recurrent and inevitable human problems, and the ways in which man can meet them are limited by his biological equipment and by certain facts of the external world. Anthropologists have perhaps in recent years been too much preoccupied with the diversity found upon the earth and have neglected the basic similarities. But apart from these important but very general resemblances, the conception of one single, unchanging "human nature" is a reassuring fiction of folklore. When it comes to details, there are "human natures." For example, old age is a situation to which all human beings who live long enough must adjust. But we find that in some human societies the old, regardless of their particular achievements, are entitled to respect and even to authority. In other societies, we find that the old, again regardless of individual differences, are ordinarily treated with relative indifference or active contempt. In still other societies, whether or not an aged person is treated with deference or with neglect seems to depend on his own past history rather than upon his period of life. Thus we see that though age is a biological fact it is always culturally defined. This fact of the plasticity of "human nature" is the widest and the most certain induction which anthropologists can derive from the cross-cultural record.

The precise *forms* which biological and social processes take are myriad, and these *forms* are cultural. Let us take an instance where, as so often, biological and social facts are intertwined. In many human groups which have been described, the physically weak have been, almost without qualification, at a disadvantage. In some groups, however, it has been observed that there have been effective deterrents against the strong taking advantage of the weak. Bullying has been punished by social disapproval and hence has actually been relatively rare. In a few societies, there is a tendency to give privileged positions to the physically weak or to certain types of the physically weak.

Just as sociobiological situations or purely social situations can be stylized, so also some purely biological situations may be stylized. Take vomiting, for example. Vomiting is a biological event and it can be produced by causes which are solely biological. But in other cases, although individual differences in neurological equipment and in previous experience play their part, the event sequence which would lead up to vomiting could never be predicted purely on the basis of biological knowledge. For instance, Americans who have eaten rattlesnake have been known to vomit upon being told what they had been fed. Since rattlesnake meat is perfectly nutritious, the vomiting is produced by some extrabiological factor.

Similar illustrations could be given for other biological processes, such as weeping and fainting. These biological processes are also caught in a cultural web, as it were. Here is a particularly telling example. The newborn infant excretes whenever tensions in bladder and colon reach a certain level of intensity. Before long, however, biological rhythms have surrendered to superimposed designs which are not directly derived from the facts of biology. Most adult human beings in normal health defecate only once or at most twice during a day. This tends to occur within rather fixed hours and, in many human groups, only at certain designated places and under defined conditions as to who else may (should) or may (should) not be present. So interesting and so vital is the interrelation of the biological and the cultural dimensions of human behavior that some anthropologists feel the study of these connections to be the differential feature of anthropology.

The Psychologist: Isn't this just a kind of "conditioning"?

The Biologist: Yes, couldn't we call it simply "environmental conditioning"?

First Anthropologist: A very special sort of conditioning. No group deliberately sets out to train its children to vomit under certain circumstances. This result, rather, is a kind of incidental by-product of a style of life or of some aspect of such a style of life.

Third Anthropologist: The naïve—and very powerful—view is that we have individual organisms (they can be seen) and that they exist in an external world (which can also be seen and described). This is the view which "common-sense" takes, and it is very hard to shake oneself out of this apparently sensible formula. But it simply won't cover the facts, the awareness of the external environment is too highly selective for that. Put down various groups of adults who have been trained in different social traditions in the same desert island. What they see in their surroundings will not be identical at all. Nor will, of course, the techniques by which they endeavor to adjust themselves to the surroundings. Between culturalized men and their environment there exists, as it were, a screen which is intangible and invisible but none the less real. This screen is "culture."

The Psychologist: In trying to understand a single concrete act on the part of an individual I have found it helpful to ask these questions:

1. What are the innate endowments and limitations of the individual?
2. What has his total experience been prior to the act we are studying?
3. What is his immediate situation?

First Anthropologist: No one of these variables can be elucidated in a completely satisfactory manner without introducing the concept "culture."

1. Except in the case of newborn babies and of individuals born with clear-cut structural or functional abnormalities we can observe "innate endowments" only as modified by cultural training. In a hospital in New Mexico where Zuni Indian, Navaho Indian, and white American babies are born it is possible to classify the newly arrived infants as hyperactive, average, and hypoactive. Some babies from each "racial" group will fall into each category, though a higher proportion of the white babies will fall into the hyperactive class. But if a Navaho baby, a Zuni baby, and a

white baby—all classified as about equally hyperactive at birth—are again observed at the age of two years, the Zuni baby—*as compared with the white child*—will no longer seem given to quick and restless activity, though he may seem so as compared with other Zunis of the same age. The Navaho child is likely to fall in between as contrasted with the Zuni and the white though he will probably still seem hyperactive if seen against the standard of a series of Navaho youngsters.

2. The sheer factual description of the individual's experience doesn't get us very far. His interpretation of these events is indispensable, and this will be made, at least in part, in terms of norms current in his group. Losing a mother tends to mean one thing in one society, quite a different thing in another society.

3. Naturally, the immediate situation as well as past experience is reacted to, not in purely rational or objective fashion but in terms of the situation as meaningfully defined by the participant. Almost no human situations are viewed in ways which are altogether a consequence of the individual's experience. Culture is—among other things—a set of ready-made definitions of the situation which each participant only slightly retailors in his own idiomatic way.

The Biologist: May we get back to some examples?

Third Anthropologist: If we are to begin at the beginning we start off, I suppose, with the basic observation of the diversity of human behavior.

A few years ago a young man of American parentage but who had been reared in a Chinese family from infancy on, paid his first visit to America. Reporters commented not only upon his apparently complete bewilderment in the American way of life, but also upon the fact that his walk, arm and hand movements, and facial expression were "Chinese—not American." They insisted that one had to fix one's attention upon his blond hair and blue eyes to convince oneself that he was of white stock at all. Here the point is that an individual's acts and attitudes not only failed to resemble those of his own close relatives in this country but that they resembled those of all members of an alien physical group and contrasted with those of all members of his own physical group.

To take a less dramatic but better-known illustration, a third generation Italian, unless he has been reared in the Italian colony of a large American city, shows "social habits" which resemble those of "Old Americans" much more closely than they do those of residents of Italy. The influence of the various domestic and geographical environments in which these Italian-Americans grew up was not so powerful but that we can recognize common tendencies in all of them which ally them to other "Americans."

The variations and similarities which obtain between groups of human beings must also both be clarified. Groups of the same strain of physical heredity show great differences in behavioral norms and groups of unquestionably different strains show great similarities. It has been remarked by many observers in the Japanese relocation centers that Japanese who have been born and brought up in this country, especially those who were reared apart from any large colony of Japanese, resemble their white neighbors in all behavioral characteristics much more closely than they do their own

Japanese relatives who had been educated in Japan and then immigrated to this country.

The Psychologist: This proves that human beings can learn from each other—and we knew that already. What proof is there that if all white Americans were wiped out the Japanese-American wouldn't eventually revert to designs for living highly similar to those characteristic of the Japanese of Japan?

Third Anthropologist: Obviously, there can be no certain answer to such a hypothetical question. But note carefully that the concept of culture as I have phrased it in no way denies the possible importance of innate factors. It does not assert the patent absurdity that the behavior of all Japanese (of Japan) or the behavior of all white Americans is minutely identical. It says merely that the behavior of each group though showing much individual variation still shows certain common tendencies within the one group which contrast sharply with those within the other group. Since the common tendencies of the American group are also to a perceptible degree exhibited by large numbers of individuals of Japanese racial stock—although it is not claimed that their behavior shows precisely the same modalities as the white Americans—it is argued that these shared trends may be attributed to the presence and influence of communicable designs for living.

The Economist: Perhaps if Japan were depopulated and colonized by white Americans these would, within a certain number of generations, develop social definitions of the situation which would hardly be distinguishable from those characteristic of the Japanese today.

Third Anthropologist: The natural environments of the United States are very various, and yet the Americans of the arid Southwest and of rainy Oregon still behave in ways which are easily distinguishable from inhabitants of the Australian desert on the one hand and from those of verdant England on the other.

Tribes like the Pueblo and Navaho, living in substantially identical natural and biological environments, still manifest very different ways of life. The English who live in the Hudson Bay region and those who live in British Somaliland still share common designs for living. It is true, of course, that the different natural environments are responsible for observable alterations. But the striking fact is that, in spite of the tremendous environmental differences, shared designs for living still persist.

The inhabitants of two not widely separated villages in New Mexico, Ramah and Fence Lake, are both of the so-called "Old American" physical stock. Almost certainly a physical anthropologist would say they represented random samples from the same physical population. The rocky tablelands, the annual rainfall and its distribution, the flora and fauna surrounding the two villages hardly show perceptible variations. The density of population and the distance from a main highway is almost exactly the same in the two cases. Nevertheless, even the casual visitor immediately notices distinctions. There are characteristic differences in dress; the style of the houses is different; there is a saloon in one town and not in the other. A completion of this catalog would conclusively demonstrate that very different patterns of life prevail in the two settlements. Why? Primarily because the two villages represent variants of the general Anglo-American social traditions. They have slightly different cultures.

The Philosopher: There are two questions upon which I must pin you down. The first is: where is the locus of culture—in society or in the individual?

Third Anthropologist: Asking the question that way poses a false dilemma. Remember that "culture" is an abstraction. Hence culture as a concrete, observable entity does not exist anywhere—unless you wish to say that it exists in the "minds" of the men who make the abstractions. The objects and events from which we make our abstractions do have an observable existence. But culture is like a map. Just as a map isn't the territory but an abstract representation of the territory so also a culture is an abstract description of trends toward uniformity in the words, acts, and artifacts of human groups. The data, then, from which we come to know culture are not derived from an abstraction such as "society" but from direct observable behavior and behavioral products. Note, however, that "culture" may be said to be "supra-individual" in at least two nonmystical, perfectly empirical senses:

1. Objects as well as individuals manifest culture.
2. The continuity of culture never depends upon the continued existence of any particular individuals.

The Philosopher: Very good. Now my second question: Can "culture" ever be said to be the cause of anything?

Third Anthropologist: Not in any very strict or exact way of speaking. In the first place, I would always question the advisability of using the term "cause" in any social science theory. Too much of a unidirectional force is implied. Rather I should use "determinant" with its connotation of interdependence of the relevant forces. But even to say "culture determines" is a very inexact and elliptical way of speaking, justified perhaps in certain circumstances by the convenience of brevity. Inexact, however, it is, because no concrete phenomenon is ever completely and solely determined by culture. Sometimes, to be sure, culture may be the "strategic factor"—that is, the crucial element that determines that a given act tends to be differently carried out in one group than in another or that the act is somehow not what we would anticipate from a knowledge of the physical and biological forces operative. But "cultural determinism" in any simple or literal sense is as objectionable as any other class of unilateral determinism such as "geographical determinism" or "economic determinism."

Although, in the concrete, the influence of culture is always mediated by men or artifacts, one is nevertheless justified in speaking of culture as *a* determinant of events when a discussion is being carried on at a high level of abstraction—provided the degree of abstraction is not lost sight of. The point may become clearer from an analogy—though all analogies (including this one!) are dangerous. Suppose a man who has a plague which is thought to be due to a postulated but unseen virus enters a city and infects the population. What "causes" the epidemic—the man or the virus?

Clearly, either answer is equally correct depending upon the conceptual system within which one is working. We should be too close to reifying an abstraction if we said that, in similar fashion, either men or things can become "hosts" to culture. Also, this metaphor, like the definition of culture as "social heredity" implies too passive a relationship between men and culture—as if culture were a bacteria acquired entirely casually and unknowingly by contact. And yet the simile remains tantalizing. One may even point out that it is less misleading than "social heredity," for genes are acquired in fixed and immutable form—once and for all—at birth, whereas bacteria change with the host and in time, though a given species remains recognizable in spite of this variation according to different hosts.

The Philosopher: Could you relate what you have just said to the arguments over the proposition of Spengler, Sorokin, and others that cultures have their own independent laws of growth and decay?

Third Anthropologist: If what I have said is correct, anthropologists have probably been too hasty in their rejections of these theories. The theories you mention have, to greater or lesser degree, been phrased unfortunately so that condemnations of them as "mystical" or "metaphysical" can be given superficial plausibility. But an anthropologist who really wishes to understand these interpretations can "translate" them into his own conceptual scheme so that, if the levels of abstraction be kept straight, they seem to merit partial acceptance or at least careful reëxamination.

For, while no culture is "superorganic" in the sense that it would continue to "exist" after all the human beings who shared it had died and all the nonhuman manifestations of that culture had been destroyed, still a culture that is a going concern has properties which exhibit some independence from the other forces with which the culture is in interaction. One of the diagnostic features of a culture is its selectivity. Most specific needs can be satisfied in a wide variety of ways but "the culture selects" only one or a very few of the organically and physically possible modes. "The culture selects" is, to be sure, a metaphorical way of speaking. The *original* choice was necessarily made by an individual and then followed by other individuals (or it wouldn't have become culture). But from the angle of those individuals who later learn this bit of culture the existence of this element in a design for living has the *effect* of a selection which was not made by these human beings as a reaction to their own particular situation but was rather a choice made by individuals long gone but which still tends to bind our contemporary actors.

Such a selective awareness of the natural environment, such a stereotyped interpretation of man's place in the world is not merely inclusive; by implication it also excludes other possible alternatives. Because of the "strain toward consistency" in cultures such inclusions and exclusions are meaningful far beyond the specific activity which is overtly involved. Just as the "choice" of an individual at a crucial epoch commits him in certain directions for the rest of his life, so the original bents, trends, "interests" which become established in the designs for living of a newly formed society tend to channel a culture in some directions as opposed to others. Subsequent variations in the culture—both those which arise internally and those which are a response to contact with other cultures or to changes in the natural environment—are not random. In some sense, at least, there is probably "cultural orthogenesis" as well as biological orthogenesis.

The Lawyer: Now I only wonder how you are going to make the transition from "culture" to "a culture." No physicist speaks of "a gravity."

First Anthropologist: Surely when the physicist "explains" the falling of certain concrete bodies at a given time and place he must—if he is to be precise as to details—get beyond the general principle of "gravity." He must describe the particular field of gravity which affected those bodies at just that time. Similarly "a culture" is just a convenient short expression for "a special field of that force known as culture."

"Culture" as a Descriptive Concept

The Physician: Can we say that culture in general as a descriptive concept means the accumulated treasury of human creation: books, paintings, buildings, and the like; the knowledge of ways of adjusting to our surroundings, both human and physical; language, customs, and systems of etiquette, ethics, religion, and morals that have been built up through the ages?

First Anthropologist: In referring to culture as "a storehouse of adjustive responses" and as a human creation you strike notes upon which we would all now agree. But the objections to an enumerative definition and to a definition which lists, in part, concrete phenomena are serious.

Second Anthropologist: Yes, I also now fully share the view that, even at a descriptive level, culture must be considered as an abstraction. Even a "culture trait" is, in a sense, an "ideal type." Take, for instance, the alarm clock. No two are ever exactly alike: some are large, some are small; some work perfectly and others don't; some are shiny and some are painted in soft colors. If we examine minutely enough several which have just been produced by the same factory, we should find that even these show small differences.

The Businessman: Let me take this idea a little further. A bank is a general term applying to all the specific institutions that conduct certain types of financial transactions. Doesn't culture, then, as a descriptive concept mean the sum of all such generalizations?

First Anthropologist: I would prefer to say "a summation of all the ideas for standardized types of behavior."

Third Anthropologist: The notion of defining culture, in a descriptive sense, as a set of blueprints for action in the widest sense (including feeling, of course) is very attractive. And it is probably perfectly sound, provided that it is clearly realized that such a statement is made from the standpoint of the observer, the student of culture, rather than from that of the participant in culture. For the participant much of culture is unverbalized and probably in a still wider sense implicit.

The Psychiatrist: I agree. I have always protested against such statements as "culture consists of ideas" because we know well from comparative psychiatry that there is also such a thing as "culturally standardized unreason."

First Anthropologist: Yes, while a great deal of culture is cognitive and is cognitively transmitted, the place of feeling bulks enormously.

The Economist: Perhaps we need three categories: rational, irrational, and nonrational.

Third Anthropologist: Quite. In Pareto's jargon, some of culture is "logical," some is "illogical," but probably the highest proportion is "nonlogical."

Fourth Anthropologist: May we then give the following substantive definition: *By culture we mean all those historically created designs for living, explicit and implicit, rational, irrational, and nonrational, which exist at any given time as potential guides for the behavior of men.*

The Lawyer: I have only one question: Why is it necessary to say "at any given time"?

Fourth Anthropologist: Because culture is constantly being created and lost. No definition must suggest that culture is static or completely stable.

Second Anthropologist: Does "designs for living" mean that you intend the concept to include only "theory"—that is, the ways in which things ought to be done or felt?

Fourth Anthropologist: No, "design" denotes both "theory" and "practice." In our own professional jargon "design" is meant to designate both "behavioral patterns" and "ideal patterns." Remember that culture is always a conceptual construct. The anthropologist not only observes that people say (or otherwise indicate) that they have certain standards for behavior, violations of which are punished by great or small sanctions; he equally notes that even disapproved behavior systems tend to fall into certain modalities. From the observer's standpoint it is as if people were unconsciously adhering to certain "blueprints" or "designs" also for conduct which is prohibited or indifferent from the standpoint of shared "moral" norms.

The Lawyer: May we have a definition of "a culture," in the descriptive sense?

First Anthropologist: *A culture is a historically derived system of explicit and implicit designs for living, which tends to be shared by all or specially designated members of a group.*

Third Anthropologist: That satisfies me. The word "system" does a lot of work in that definition. It suggests abstraction. It directly implies that a culture is organized, that it is selective.

The Psychologist: I like the word "tends." Some of us have in the past felt cheated because we have been assured that studying a culture would give us the common ground against which various personality figures emerged. Our own investigations along this line seem to indicate that it was misleading to depict any single background as being in any literal sense "common" to all members of any group.

First Anthropologist: Yes, just as "tends" reminds us that no individual thinks, feels, or acts precisely as the "design" indicates that he will or should, so also "specially designated" is a reminder that not all of the "blueprints" which constitute a culture are meant to apply to each and every individual. There are sex differentials, age differentials, class differentials, prestige differentials, and so on.

Third Anthropologist: It seems to me that you have enunciated two related but separate propositions. It is important that we should not mix them. First, there is the proposition that the sharing is tendency rather than fact. As L. K. Frank puts it, what we can actually observe is the "idiomatic version of each personality's utilization of cultural patterns." And he goes on to make a useful analogy something along these lines:

> We can abstract the regularities and uniformities and likewise observe the personality distortions and skewings, as we have learned to observe the statistical regularities of a gas but also recognize and acknowledge the irregular and nonconforming behavior of individual molecules of that gas.

Second, there is the proposition of the compartmentalization and segmentation of a culture. While each individual's utilization of pattern is idiomatic, some sets of patterns are always felt as appropriate for certain categories of individuals. A background of culture is to be regarded as approximately constant—not for every individual in all groups which have some continuity and functional wholeness, but rather for those who occupy the same set of statuses or perform about the same roles within the total group.

First Anthropologist: Correct. But this important fact must not obscure another fact of equal or greater significance. At least in those groups which have some historical continuity and which are generally designated as "societies," all individuals tend to share common interpretations of the external world and man's place in it. To some degree every individual is affected by this common "view of life." A culture is made up of overt patterned ways of behaving, feeling, and reacting. But it also includes a characteristic set of unstated premises or hypotheses which vary greatly in different societies. Thus one group unconsciously assumes that every chain of actions has a goal and that when this goal is reached tension will be reduced or disappear. To another group, thinking based upon this assumption is meaningless: they see life not as a series of purposive sequences but as made up of experiences which are satisfying in and of themselves, rather than as means to ends.

The Philosopher: Are you saying that each culture is integrated about certain dominant interests and in accord with certain postulates and assumptions?

Third Anthropologist: Probably very few cultures indeed can be regarded as completely integrated systems. Most cultures, like most personalities, can be regarded as equilibria of opposed tendencies. But even in cultures which do not approach complete integration one may detect certain recurrent themes in a variety of specific contexts.

The Psychologist: Are you talking about what some anthropologists have called the "absolute logics," of a people or about what others refer to as "the logic of the sentiments."

Third Anthropologist: Both. Every people not only has a sentiment structure which is to some degree unique but also a more or less coherent body of distinctive presuppositions about the world. This last is really a borderland between reason and feeling. Perhaps in a certain ultimate sense the "logic" of all peoples is the same. But their premises are certainly different.

The Philosopher: Do you mean the conscious, the stated premises—what a logician would call the "postulates"—or the unstated premises or "assumptions"?

Third Anthropologist: Both. Certainly some of the most critical premises of any culture are often unstated, even by the intellectuals of the group. Likewise the basic categories of "thinking" are implicit, save, perhaps, to a tiny minority in rationally sophisticated societies like our own.

Fourth Anthropologist: If the premises and the system of categories are unconscious, how are they transmitted?

First Anthropologist: Mainly, probably, through the language. Especially the morphology of a language preserves the unformulated philosophy of the group. For example, Dorothy Lee has shown that among the Trobriand Islanders "the sequence of events does not automatically fall into the mold of causal or telic relationship." Because of the mold which grammar imposes upon their "thinking" these people find certain types of communication with Europeans difficult since Europeans almost inevitably talk in causal terms.

The very morphology of any language inevitably begs far-reaching questions of metaphysics and of values. A language is not merely an instrument for communication and for rousing the emotions. Every language is also a device for categorizing experience. The continuum of experience can be sliced very differently. We tend all too easily to assume that the distinctions which Indo-European languages (or our own particular language) force us to make are given by the world of nature. As a matter of fact, comparative linguistics shows very plainly that any speech demands unconscious conceptual selection on the part of its speaker. No human organism can respond to all the kaleidoscopic stimuli which impinge upon it from the external world. What we notice, what we talk about, what we feel as important is in some part a function of our linguistic patterns. Because these linguistic habits tend to remain as unquestioned "background phenomena," each people tends to take its fundamental categories, its unstated basic premises for granted. It is assumed that others will "think the same way," for "it's only human nature." When others face the same body of data but come to different conclusions, it is seldom thought that they might be proceeding from different premises. Rather, it is inferred that they are "stupid" or "illogical" or "obstinate."

Fourth Anthropologist: How does it happen that different people have different systems of categories?

First Anthropologist: A language is one aspect of a culture. Therefore, we must refer to the "accidents of history" and to all the other forces which we mentioned as producing the forms of culture. Each individual tends to classify his experiences along the lines laid down by the grammar to which he is habituated, but the grammar itself is a cultural product. Dorothy Lee has made this point very well:

> True enough, the thought of the individual must run along its grooves; but these grooves, themselves, are a heritage from individuals who laid them down in an unconscious effort to express their attitudes toward the world. Grammar contains in crystalized form the accumulated and accumulating experience, the Weltanschauung of a people.

Third Anthropologist: There is perhaps also another angle to the perpetuation of cultural organization, particularly at the implicit level. This is the culturally prescribed system of child training. If all adults have been subjected to about the same deprivations and frustrations during socialization, they tend to see life in somewhat the same terms. Roheim says, "The dominant idea of a culture may be an addiction but it is always a system formation that can be explained on the basis of the infantile situation." Margaret Mead deals with the relation of "infantile traumas" to the one or more focal points in each culture under the conception of "plot in culture."

Fourth Anthropologist: Although partially won over, I am still unhappy about this term "implicit culture."

Third Anthropologist: A conception of this order is made necessary by certain eminently practical considerations. It is well documented that programs of the British Colonial services or of our own Indian service which have been carefully thought through for their continuity with the cultural inventory and with the overt cultural patterns, nevertheless fail to work out. Intensive investigation also does not reveal any flaws in the set-up at the technological level. The program is sabotaged by resistance which must be imputed to the manner in which the members of the group have been conditioned by *implicit* designs for living to think and feel in ways which were unexpected to the administrator.

First Anthropologist: Students of culture change are also agreed that the way in which a group accepts, rejects, or readapts borrowed elements cannot be fully understood in terms of direct and explicit functions. The process is also related to the cultural structure, including those portions of it which are implicit. Even after the content of the culture of a group of American Indians has become completely European, its way of life still somehow retains a distinctive flavor, as if the "container" remained "aboriginal."

Third Anthropologist: We would freely admit that conceptual instruments which are objective enough and precise enough to deal with the patterning of implicit culture are only beginning to be evolved. The importance of tacit cultural premises and categories is probably obvious enough. But the sheer statement of the presence and absence of these (and of all other features of culture, whether implicit or explicit) is not enough. The full significance of any single element in a cultural design will be seen only when that element is viewed in the total matrix of its relationship to other elements and indeed to other designs. Naturally, this includes accent or emphasis, as well as position. Accent is manifested sometimes through frequency, sometimes through intensity. The indispensable importance of these questions of arrangement and emphasis may be driven home by an analogy. Take a musical chord made up of three notes. If we are told that the three notes in question are A, B, and G, we receive information which is fundamental. But it alone will not enable us to predict the type of sensation which the playing of this chord is likely to evoke in us or in other specified visitors. We need many different sorts of relationship data. Are the notes to be played in that or some other order? What duration will each receive? How will the emphasis, if any, be distributed? We also need, of course, to know whether the chord will be played in the key of C or in the key of B-flat minor, and whether the instrument is to be a piano or an accordion.[2]

The Utility of the Concept "Culture" in Its Various Senses

The Businessman. I'd like to interject a practical question: What good is this concept so far as the contemporary world is concerned? What can you do with it?

First Anthropologist: First and foremost I would insist that its use lies in the aid the concept gives to man's endless quest to understand himself and his own behavior. For example, this relatively new idea makes some of the questions which trouble one of the most learned and acute thinkers of our age, Reinhold Niebuhr, seem pseudo-problems. In his recent book *The Nature and Destiny of Man* he argues that the universally human sense of guilt or shame and man's capacity for self-judgment necessitates the assumption of supernatural forces. But these facts are susceptible of self-consistent and relatively simple "explanation" in purely naturalistic terms through the concept of culture. Social life among humans never occurs without a system of "conventional understandings" which are transmitted more or less intact from generation to generation. Any individual is familiar with some of these and they constitute a set of standards against which he judges himself. To the extent that he fails to conform he experiences discomfort, because the intimate conditioning of infancy and childhood put great pressure on him to internalize these norms, and his unconscious tendency is to associate withdrawal of love and protection or active punishment with deviation.

This and other issues which have puzzled philosophers and scientists for countless generations become fully or partially understandable by means of

[2]Limitations of space necessitated shortening the final typescript draft of this paper by one third. In addition to the elimination of certain technical refinements, the authors were obliged to omit two topics which they consider essential to a complete treatment of the subject: The distinction between the "social" and the "cultural" and the place of symbols in a consideration of culture theory. [For a complete and revised version of this paper, see *Culture and Behavior: The Collected Essays of Clyde Kluckhohn,* ed. Richard Kluckhohn (New York, 1962), pp. 19–73.—*Ed. Note.*]

this fresh conceptual instrument. But if your interest is in action rather than thought, the principal claim which can be made for culture is that it helps us enormously toward predicting human behavior. One of the reasons that such prediction has not been very successful thus far has been that it has been carried out, for the most part, on the naïve assumption of a minutely homogeneous "human nature." In the framework of this assumption all human thinking proceeds from the same premises; all human beings are motivated by the same needs and goals. But in the cultural framework we see that, while the ultimate logic of all peoples may be the same (and thus communication and understanding are possible), the thought processes depart from radically different premises—especially unconscious or unstated premises. But those who have the cultural outlook are more likely to look beneath the surface and bring the culturally determined premises to the light of day. This may well not bring about immediate agreement and harmony, but it will at least facilitate a more rational approach to the problem of "international understanding" and to diminishing friction between groups within a nation.

The conception of culture also encourages paying attention to the more concrete aspects of ways of life other than our own. It suggests, for example, the usefulness of knowledge of alien "customs" if we wish to predict how a foreign people will behave in a certain situation and of respect for these same customs if we wish to get along with that foreign people.

A culture is not only a reticulum of patterned means for satisfying needs but equally a network of stylized goals for individual and group achievement. If we need to predict human action we must not assume that the effective motivations in all human groups are the same. Even the primary drives, like hunger and sex, though biological "givens," are subtly modified and channeled by culture. What kind of food, what type of sexual experience will be most striven after cannot be predicted through biological knowledge alone. There exists for every human group "secondary drives." Among us, for example, the "need" for cars or radios often goads individuals even harder than that for sexual satisfaction.

Every culture is also a structure of expectancies. If we know a culture, we know what various classes of individuals within it expect from each other—and from outsiders of various categories. We know what types of activity are held to be inherently gratifying.

Second Anthropologist: One great contribution is that of providing some persons with some detachment from the conscious and unconscious emotional values of their own culture. The phrase "some detachment" must be emphasized. An individual who viewed the designs for living of his group with complete detachment would almost certainly be disoriented and unhappy. But I can prefer (that is, feel affectively attached to) American manners while at the same time perceiving certain graces in English manners which are lacking or more grossly expressed in ours. Thus while unwilling to forget that I am an American and hence with no desire to ape English drawing room behaviors, I can still derive a lively pleasure from association with English people on "social" occasions. Whereas if I have no detachment, if I am utterly provincial, I am likely to regard English manners as utterly ridiculous, uncouth, perhaps even immoral. With that attitude I shall certainly not get on well with the English and I am likely to resent bitterly any modification of our manners in the English or any other direction. Such attitudes clearly do not make for international understanding, friendship, and cooperation. They equally make for a too rigid social structure. Anthropological documents and anthropological teachings are valuable, therefore, in that they tend to emancipate individuals from a too perfervid allegiance to every item in the cultural inventory. The person who has been exposed to the anthropological perspective by incongruity is more likely, on the one hand, to "live and let live" both within his own society and in his dealings with members of other societies; on the other hand, he will probably be more flexible in regard to needful changes in social organization to meet changed technological structure and changed economies.

Third Anthropologist: In a way, I would say that the most important implication of "culture" for action is the profound truth (so frequently overlooked by every sort of "social planners") that you can never start with a clean slate so far as human beings are concerned. No human being or group of human beings can ever freshly see the world in which they move. Every human is born into a world defined by already existing cultural patterns. Just as an individual who has lost his memory is no longer "normal," so the idea that at any point in its history a society can become completely emancipated from its past culture is inconceivable. This is the source of the tragic failure of the Weimar constitution in Germany. Seen in detached context, it was an admirable document. But it failed miserably in actual life, partly because it provided for no continuity with existent designs for acting, feeling, and thinking.

Finally, as the word "design" in our definitions implies, every culture has organization as well as content. This fact carries with it the highly practical warning to administrators and lawmakers that a "custom" which it is desired to abolish or modify cannot be isolated. Any change may have repercussions in areas of behavior where they are least expected.

While serious anthropologists disavow all messianic pretensions and make no claim that "culture" is any "philosopher's stone" which will end all problems, nevertheless the explanatory concept does carry an overtone of legitimate hope to troubled men. If the Germans and the Japanese are as they have been mainly because of their genes, the outlook is an almost hopeless one, but if their propensities for cruelty and aggrandizement are primarily the result of situational factors ("economic" pressures and so on) and their cultures, then something can be done about it.

BIBLIOGRAPHIC NOTE

We have thought it inappropriate to burden this paper with detailed documentation. But the principal sources which have directly influenced our thinking follow.

Bidney, David, "On the Philosophy of Culture in the Social Sciences," *Journal of Philosophy*, XXXIX (1942), 449–57; "On the Concept of Culture and Some Cultural Fallacies," *American Anthropologist*, XLVI (1944), 30–45.

Blumenthal, Albert, "A New Definition of Culture," *American Anthropologist*, XLII (1940), 571–86.

Dollard, John, "Culture, Society, Impulse and Socialization," *American Journal of Sociology*, XLV (1939), 50–63.

Ford, C. S., "Culture and Human Behavior," *Scientific Monthly*, LV (1942), 546–57.

Frank, L. K., "Man's Multidimensional Environment," *Scientific Monthly*, LVI (1943), 344–57.

Lee, Dorothy, "Conceptual Implications of an Indian Language," *Philosophy of Science*, V, No. 1 (Jan., 1938); "A Primitive System of Values," *Philosophy of Science*, VII, No. 3 (July, 1940).

Linton, Ralph, *The Study of Man* (New York, 1936); "Culture, Society and the Individual," *Journal of Abnormal and Social Psychology*, XXXV (1938), 425–36; *Acculturation in Seven American Indian Tribes* (New York, 1940).

Malinowski, B., "Culture," *Encyclopedia of the Social Sciences*, IV (1931), 621–45; "Man's Culture and Man's Behavior," *Sigma Xi Quarterly*, XXIX (1941), 182–96; XXX (1942), 66-78.

Miller, Neal E., and John Dollard, *Social Learning and Imitation* (New Haven, Conn., 1941).

Murdock, G. P., "The Science of Culture," *American Anthropologist*, XXXIV (1932), 200–215.

Redfield, Robert, *The Folk Culture of Yucatan* (Chicago, 1941).

Roheim, Geza, *The Origin and Function of Culture* (Nervous and Mental Disease Monograph Series, No. 69, New York, 1943).

Sapir, Edward. "Culture, Genuine and Spurious," *American Journal of Sociology*, XXIX (1924), 401–29.

Simmons, Leo, *Sun Chief* (New Haven, Conn , 1942).

Selected studies in cultural anthropology

A cultural anthropologist normally specializes in a geographical or a cultural area. He might, for example, specialize in North American Indian cultures and, within that area, perhaps California Indians or Indians of the Plains. He may also specialize in topic. For example, his research may center around economic anthropology or the study of language. When cultural anthropologists teach, they frequently offer both area courses, e.g., Peoples of the Pacific, and topic courses, e.g., Primitive Religion. Sometimes geographical, cultural, and topic specialties are combined so that a cultural anthropologist elects to concentrate upon law in Africa or music in Southeast Asia. Bearing this in mind, one can see that it is clearly impossible for one book, much less one section in one book, to cover all the geographical and cultural areas of the world, all of the specialized subdisciplinary topics of cultural anthropology, and even a fraction of the various combinations of areal and topical specialties.

The following samples of anthropological scholarship represent some, though by no means all, of the principal topical spe-

213

cialties in cultural anthropology. Whole books have been or could be written about some of the subjects included—social organization, economics, law, medicine, philosophy, culture and personality (psychological anthropology), language and culture (linguistic anthropology), folklore, ethnomusicology, and primitive art. It is therefore obviously not realistic to expect to read one paper on any one topic that will adequately discuss the entire range of phenomena studied by experts on that general topic. The papers presented here are intended only to illustrate one or more aspects of a particular subdisciplinary research area. At the same time, the papers clearly demonstrate the fallacy of subdisciplinary compartmentation. One cannot consider religion without also considering values. Values in turn may entail an analysis of linguistic data, and so it goes. No topic is an island! One could very easily combine any two or more topics in a single research problem (e.g., art and religion; social organization and law). It is well to remember then that the subdisciplinary subdivisions of cultural anthropology (like academic disciplines in general) are strictly part of our own cultural scheme of categories. They are arbitrary and artifical, though nonetheless influential in our own culture. Culture is a whole and anthropologists only divide it the better to study it.

Melville J. Herskovits and Frances S. Herskovits

PARENTS AND CHILDREN

The study of social structure and kinship systems has continued to fascinate each new generation of anthropologists. And as each anthropologist goes into the field, one of the first aspects of culture he investigates is the kinship system and terminology. The confusing nature of a classificatory kinship terminology— that is, confusing to a member of our culture—is entertainingly demonstrated by a number of graphic illustrations provided by Melville and Frances Herskovits. The Herskovitses, especially interested in African peoples, conducted fieldwork among New World as well as African Negroes. In 1928 and 1929 they visited one of several tribal groups making up the Bush Negro population living in relative isolation in the interior of Dutch Guiana. This group, the Saramacca tribe, lived along the upper portion of the Suriname River. Despite the South American setting, many of the cultural features have remained strongly West African.

Reprinted from Melville J. Herskovits and Frances S. Herskovits, *Rebel Destiny: Among the Bush Negroes of Dutch Guiana* (New York, 1934), pp. 125–30, by permission of Frances S. Herskovits and McGraw-Hill Book Company.

Those interested in learning more about this group should read the Herskovitses' *Suriname Folklore* (New York, 1936). Those who wish to investigate some of the extensive anthropological literature on social organization and kinship systems should consult George Peter Murdock, *Social Structure* (New York, 1949) and Elman R. Service, *Primitive Social Organizaiton* (New York, 1962).

With Angita was a man we had not seen before, holding a small child by the hand.

"This is Awingu, my brother-in-law," said Angita in explanation. "His eyes trouble him. I brought him to you for medicine."

After the exchange of courtesies demanded by the visit, we turned to the child.

"Is this your child, Awingu?" we asked.

His answer came promptly. "No, he is not my child. He is my wife's child. I made him."

Here was a fine distinction. He made him, but the child was not his.

Just then our cook came up with a small present for the child, but, since he would not take it from his hands or ours, Angita gave it to him.

"Thank you, father," he said to Angita.

Angita looked down affectionately at the youngster. "Two, three years more, Awingu, and he will be ready to go and live with his father at Gankwe. Do you remember your father at Gankwe? It was he who showed you how to make a gun from a reed. And you made it well. . . ."

There appeared, then, to be yet another father, for it was clear that Angita was not speaking of himself when he referred to the Gankwe father who had showed the child how to make a play gun.

All this, in itself, however confusing to a visitor, is by no means an unusual phenomenon. Different peoples have their own sanctions for establishing kinship and their own designations for relationships. In the city we had been told many tales of the manner of life of these Negroes of the bush. And the "matriarchate," as the custom of counting descent through the mother was termed, had often come up when these people were being discussed.

"Among them only the mothers count, because among savages, who can tell who the real father is? That is why a child calls many men 'father,' " we had heard variously explained and elaborated.

Yet here was a man who said without hesitation, "No, he is not my child. He is my wife's child. I made him." And the very next instant the child called Angita father, and Angita referred to still another man as the father who would in a few years take the child with him to live and train him for manhood.

Any number of questions came to our minds, but at daybreak a stranger coming to the planting ground of a village not his own is the least willing of talkers.

"This is not your child, Awingu," we took the occasion to remark when we were saying goodbye, "yet he seems to like you very much."

"*Ma, tye! Ma Neng'e!*—Mother of all Negroes! What would you have? I am his father!"

The man showed by his amused expression that this was a story to carry back to his village. Only the politeness due a stranger kept Awingu and Angita from laughing aloud at this strange question. But Awingu was a thoughtful fellow. "Tell me," he said, after a while, "in your white man's country, don't children care for their fathers?"

But there were not only multiple fathers, as the story told in the city ran. The matter was not disposed of so simply as that. In point of fact, each person seemed to have several mothers as well. Take the case of Angita himself, whose brother-in-law we met at dawn in the provision ground. Angita was first pointed out to us by Tita, who, behind her back, was called Mother Snake. It was at Gankwe when we came to see the dancing for the dead Zimbi.

"Look," she had said, as she indicated one of the principal dancers who wore seed rattles at his ankles. "This is Angita. He dances well. He is my son." And she had showed her pleasure at our appreciation of his excellent dancing.

The following day Angita came to our camp, bringing with him Kutai, a woman of about Tita's age. He left to go farther upstream for a time, but she remained with us and sat and talked with the others who were standing about, as they discussed the wood carvings we were in the act of buying.

"Have you seen Angita's carvings?" she asked us. "He is one of the best young carvers at Gankwe. When he is older, he will be one of the best on the Saramacca."

An old man standing by said drily, "Chicken says, 'You can lie about an egg, but you can't lie about a chicken.'"

"That's right," commented another. "We know Angita's carving. It is good, but..."

But Kutai would not be contradicted. She interrupted the speaker with a gesture. "I am his mother, and a mother knows her son. You can say what you like."

About the fifth day after we had started up the river for the country of the Granman, we came to a village where Angita stopped to supplement his food for the journey. When he returned, his arms were filled with the large cassava cakes. Behind him came a young girl with a bottle of palm oil, and some rice in an open calabash, and she was followed by the people of the village who came to see the Bakra. A woman of middle age, whom both the young girl and Angita resembled, took the rice from the girl and, wading into the shallow water, came up to our boat and gave it to us. "This is rice for you. I am Angita's mother. Angita is strong. You will walk well with him."

Later that day, when our boat found itself abreast of the dugout which Angita was poling, we lost no time in questioning him.

"Angita," we called, "is the woman who gave us the rice your mother?"

He nodded.

"But what of Tita, who said she was your mother, too?"

He was a quick-witted lad, and he saw at once what we had in mind. He said with a laugh, "You are asking about my true, true mother, the one who made me? It is not this one, and it is not Tita, who made me. It is Kutai."

"But who are the other two?"

"They are her sisters."

Yet the family life of the Bush Negro does not differ in any essential respect from that of any other group of individuals, who, related by close ties of blood, live their lives together. Men and women marry and beget children, and their children in turn marry and beget others. In reality, but for the fact that a man or a woman claimed more than one father and mother, and a great number of brothers and sisters, of uncles and aunts, there was little to indicate the existence of conventions of family life which differed radically from those we ourselves know.

None the less, there were differences, and, once we were permitted to see beneath the surface, a slight incident here, another hint there, threw into relief the life of these people, and their own attitudes toward their actual and spiritual relationships.

Let us take the instance of Misomba and his son. Misomba was a man of middle age, and the incident we tell occurred as we were sitting in his house in a village above the Mamadam. He was speaking of the wood he had cut and of his plans to take it to the city to sell. With him in the house were his wife and a young lad, perhaps fifteen or sixteen years old, and, besides ourselves, our paddler Kasanya, who was Misomba's wife's elder brother.

"I need someone to take the rafts down the river. There are none in my family who are free, and I need help. But Adyabu here," he said, indicating his son, "knows about taking down rafts, and it will be good for him to learn more of the river leading to the white man's city. I am glad you came, brother-in-law. Now I can ask you if he may go with me. Is it your wish that he go?"

Kasanya glanced at the boy, who showed by his manner his eagerness to accompany his father, and then at his sister. "How will it be with you, sister, if Adyabu goes? Do you want him to go with Misomba?"

"Yes," she replied. "Misomba will care for him. Let him go."

The three older people talked over the details of the trip down the river, until it was made clear to all that Adyabu would share whatever money his father might receive for the lumber.

"You will treat him well, brother-in-law," said Kasanya, with a smile, "for in a few years his girl will be ripe for marrying, and he will need money for a fine wedding."

That night we talked this over with Kasanya.

"Why must a man ask another if he may take his own son with him on a journey? Is a man not to be trusted to take care of a boy he himself has made?"

"You do not understand, Bak'a. It is not that we don't trust Misomba," he replied. "He has lived with my sister for many years. She is his first wife, and my family have always liked him. When my sister's eldest daughter was asked in marriage by a man of this village, and our great family came together here to consider whether we should promise her to him or not, we asked Misomba to give us his advice. Misomba does not have a bold face. He did not speak until after much urging. To ask a man's advice about what does not concern his own family is a great honor. But we did this, and when he spoke, we found that what he said was good. So, you see, it is not that we do not trust Misomba."

We encouraged him to explain further.

"Adyabu is not his heir. He is the child of my sister and belongs to my family. I am the one to say what he is to do and what he is not to do, because I am the oldest living brother. Adyabu does not belong to Misomba's family. He is of my blood. When I die, he will inherit my possessions. When Misomba dies, his possessions will go to his own brothers and to his sisters' children. That is how we live here in the bush. That is how we do."

Alfred L. Kroeber

CLASSIFICATORY
SYSTEMS OF RELATIONSHIP

The following essay is a classic analysis of some of the principles underlying kinship terminological systems. Kroeber's initial point of departure is a dichotomy suggested by the early American anthropologist Lewis Henry Morgan. Morgan, in a chapter of his *Systems of Consanguinity and Affinity of the Human Family* (published in 1871), suggested that in Indo-European kinship the primary terms (e.g., father, mother, son, daughter) were descriptive and, further, that these *lineal* kin (i.e., kin in one's own immediate line such as one's father, grandfather, great-grandfather or one's son, grandson, or great-grandson) had designating kinship terms separate and distinct from the terms used to denote one's collateral relatives (such as one's mother's brother, mother's brother's son, father's sister, father's sister's daughter, etc.). Morgan realized that the terms for some of the collateral relatives were not terribly specific or descriptive. For example, "uncle" could refer to either one's mother's brother or one's father's brother (not to mention "uncles" by marriage, that is, affinal rather than blood or consanguineal relatives). The important point, in Morgan's view, was that the term father (lineal) was distinct from the term(s) uncle used for collaterals.

In contrast to descriptive systems, Morgan defined what he labeled classificatory systems in which some of one's collateral

Reprinted from the *Journal of the Royal Anthropological Institute,* **39** (1909), 77–84, by permission of the Royal Anthropological Institute and Mrs. Theodora Kroeber.

relatives were called by the same terms as some of his lineal relatives. For example, one's father's brother and one's father might be called by the same term, or one's mother and one's mother's sister might be called by the same term. It should be noted that there is an implicit hint of ethnocentrism in Morgan's formulation. Our own system, which keeps linear relatives separate from collaterals, is descriptive whereas the "primitive" classificatory systems tend to merge (=confuse?) collateral and lineal relatives. Kroeber's paper reveals the weakness of the descriptive-classificatory dichotomy. No kinship system provides a separate term for every single theoretically possible kinship relation. Most systems contain both descriptive and classificatory features, as Kroeber shows.

Another important issue in kinship studies raised by Kroeber is whether there are historical behavioral correlates to kinship terminological distinctions. Reacting in part to the attempt of nineteenth-century anthropologists to reconstruct the evolution of family types on the basis of kinship terminology, Kroeber tended to minimize the social or sociological significance of the terms. The causes which determine the formation, choice, and similarities of terms of relationship, he argues, are primarily linguistic. However, it seems clear that there are in fact behavioral correlates to kinship terms and that if two individuals in a society are addressed by a third by means of an identical term, then to some extent the roles of these two with respect to the third person will share some similarities. In any case, Kroeber's cogent analysis still stands as a major contribution to the study of kinship.

Suggested additional readings in the analysis of kinship terminology include the second chapter, "General Observations Upon Systems of Relationships," in Lewis Henry Morgan, *Systems of Consanguinity and Affinity of the Human Family,* Smithsonian Contributions to Knowledge 218 (Washington, 1871), pp. 10–15; Robert H. Lowie, "Relationship Terms," *Encyclopaedia Britannica,* 14th ed., 19 (1929), 84–89; George Peter Murdock, *Social Structure* (New York, 1949); and E. L. Schusky, *Manual for Kinship Analysis* (New York, 1965). For American kinship terminology, see the article by Schneider and Homans in this volume.

The distinction between classificatory and descriptive systems of relationship has been widely accepted, and has found its way into handbooks and general literature. According to the prevalent belief the systems of certain nations or languages group together distinct relationships and call them by one name, and are therefore classifying. Other systems of consanguinity are said to indicate secondary differences of relationship by descriptive epithets added to their primary terms and to be therefore descriptive.

Nothing can be more fallacious than this common view. A moment's reflection is sufficient to show that every language groups together under single designations many distinct degrees and kinds of relationship. Our word brother includes both the older and the younger brother and the brother of a man and of a woman. It therefore embraces or classifies four relationships. The English word cousin denotes both men and women cousins; cousins on the father's or on the mother's side; cousins descended from the parent's brother or the parent's sister; cousins respectively older or younger than one's self, or whose parents are respectively older or younger than the speaker's parents; and cousins of men or women. Thirty-two different relationships are therefore denoted by this one English word. If the term is not strictly limited to the significance of first cousin, the number of distinct ideas that it is capable of expressing is many times thirty-two. Since then it is not only primitive people that classify or fail to distinguish relationships, the suspicion is justified that the current distinction between the two classes or systems of indicating relationship is subjective, and has its origin in the point of view of investigators, who, on approaching foreign languages, have been impressed with their failure to discriminate certain relationships between which the languages of civilized Europe distinguish, and who, in the enthusiasm of formulating general theories from such facts, have forgotten that their own languages are filled with entirely analogous groupings or classifications which custom has made so familiar and natural that they are not felt as such.

The total number of different relationships which can be distinguished is very large, and reaches at least many hundred. No language possesses different terms for all of these or even for any considerable proportion of them. In one sense it is obvious that a language must be more classificatory as the number of its terms of relationship is smaller. The number of theoretically possible relationships remaining constant, there must be more ideas grouped under one term in proportion as the number of terms is less. Following the accepted understanding of what constitutes classificatory consanguinity, English, with its twenty terms of relationship, must be not less but more classificatory than the languages of all primitive people who happen to possess twenty-five, thirty, or more terms.

It is clear that if the phrase classificatory consanguinity is to have any meaning it must be sought in some more discriminating way. The single fact that another people group together various relationships which our language distinguishes does not make their system classificatory. If there is a general and fundamental difference between the systems of relationship of civilized and uncivilized people, its basis must be looked for in something more exact than the rough and ready expressions of subjective point of view that have been customary.

It is apparent that what we should try to deal with is not the hundreds or thousands of slightly varying relationships that are expressed or can be expressed by the various languages of man, but the principles or categories of relationship which underlie these. Eight such categories are discernible.

1. *The difference between persons of the same and of separate genera-tions.*—The distinctions between father and grandfather, between uncle and cousin, and between a person and his father, involve the recognition of this category.

2. *The difference between lineal and collateral relationship.*—When the father and the father's brother are distinguished, this category is operative. When only one term is employed for brother and cousin, it is inoperative.

3. *Difference of age within one generation.*—The frequent distinction between the older and the younger brother is an instance. In English this category is not operative.

4. *The sex of the relative.*—This distinction is carried out so consistently by English, the one exception being the foreign word cousin, that the discrimination is likely to appear self-evident. By many people, however, many relationships are not distinguished for sex. Grandfather and grand-mother, brother-in-law and sister-in-law, father-in-law and mother-in-law, and even such close relationships are son and daughter, are expressed respec-tively by single words.

5. *The sex of the speaker.*—Unrepresented in English and most European languages, this category is well known to be of importance in many other languages. The father, mother, brother, sister, and more distant relatives may receive one designation from a man and another from his sister.

6. *The sex of the person through whom relationship exists.*—English does not express this category. In consequence we frequently find it necessary to explain whether an uncle is a father's or a mother's brother, and whether a grandmother is paternal or maternal.

7. *The distinction of blood relatives from connections by marriage.*—While this distinction is commonly expressed by most languages, there are occasional lapses; just as in familiar English speech the father-in-law is often spoken of as father. Not strictly within the domain of relationship, but analogous to the occasional failure to express this category, is the frequent ignoring on the part of primitive people of the difference between actual relatives and fictitious clan or tribal relatives.

8. *The condition of life of the person through whom relationship exists.*—The relationship may be either of blood or by marriage; the person serving as the bond of relationship may be alive or dead, married or no longer married. Many North American Indians refrain from using such terms as father-in-law and mother-in-law after the wife's death or separation. Some go so far as to possess terms restricted to such severed relationship. It is natural that the uncle's relation to his orphaned nephew should tend to be somewhat different from his relation to the same boy while his natural protector, his father, was living. Distinct terms are therefore sometimes found for relatives of the uncle and aunt group after the death of a parent.

The subjoined table indicates the representation of the eight categories, and the degree to which they find expression, respectively in English and in several of the Indian languages of North America.

It appears that English gives expression to only four categories. With the exception, however, of the one and foreign word cousin, every term in

	English	Arapaho	Dakota	Pawnee	Skokomish	Chinook	Yuki	Pomo	Washo	Miwok	Yokuts	Luiseño	Mohave
			N. A. Indian						**California Indian**				
No. of terms	21*	20	31	19	18	28	24	27	28	24	28	34	35
Generation	21	20	31	11	13	23	24	21	27	24	22	30	26
Blood of marriage	21	19	31	17	18	26	24	27	28	24	28	32	34
Lineal or collateral	21	10	20	5	11	25	24	21	28	18	26	34	28
Sex of relative	20	18	29	17	2	12	16	21	20	20	17	18	22
Sex of connecting relative	0	6	6	2	0	20	13	13	14	10	14	19	21
Sex of speaker	0	3	18	4	0	15	3	3	10	2	12	10	14
Age in generation	0	3	7	2	2	2	3	4	4	4	4	12	8
Condition of connecting relative	0	0	0	0	8	1	0	0	0	0	†	0	1

*All terms are omitted, such as great grandfather, great-uncle, and second-cousin, which are not generally used in ordinary speech and exist principally as a reserve available for specific discrimination on occasion.
†Terms denoting relatives by marriage undergo a vocalic change to indicate the death of the connecting relative.

English involves the recognition of each of these four categories. All the Indian languages express from six to eight categories. Almost all of them recognize seven. But in all the Indian languages the majority of the categories occurring are expressed in only part of the terms of relationship found in the language. There are even Indian languages, such as Pawnee and Mohave, in which not a single one of the seven or eight categories finds expression in every term. While in English the degree of recognition which is accorded the represented categories is indicable by a percentage of 100 in all cases but one, when it is 95, in Pawnee corresponding percentages range variously from about 10 to 90, and in Mohave from 5 to 95. All the other Indian languages, as compared with English, closely approach the condition of Pawnee and Mohave.

It is clear that this difference is real and fundamental. English is simple, consistent, and, so far as it goes, complete. The Indian systems of relationship all start from a more elaborate basis, but carry out their scheme less completely. This is inevitable from the fact that the total number of terms of relationship employed by them is approximately the same as in English. The addition of only one category to those found in English normally doubles the number of terms required to give full expression to the system; and the presence of three additional categories multiplies the possible total by about eight. As the number of terms occurring in any of the Indian languages under consideration is not much more than half greater than in English, and sometimes is not greater at all, it is clear that at least some of their categories must find only very partial expression.

In short, as far as the expression of possible categories is concerned, English is less complete than any of the Indian languages; but as regards the giving of expression to the categories which it recognizes, English is more complete. In potentiality, the English scheme is poorer and simpler; but from its own point of view it is both more complete and more consistent. As English may evidently be taken as representative of European languages, it is in this point that the real difference is to be found between the systems that have been called classificatory and those that have been called descriptive.

The so-called descriptive systems express a small number of categories of relationship completely; the wrongly-named classificatory systems express a larger number of categories with less regularity. Judged from its own point of view, English is the less classificatory; looked at from the Indian point of view it is the more classificatory, inasmuch as in every one of its terms it fails to recognize certain distinctions often made in other languages; regarded from a general and comparative point of view, neither system is more or less classificatory.

In short, the prevalent idea of the classificatory system breaks down entirely under analysis. And in so far as there is a fundamental difference between the languages of European and of less civilized peoples in the method of denoting relationship, the difference can be determined only on the basis of the categories described and can be best expressed in terms of the categories.[1]

The categories serve also to indicate the leading characteristics of systems of the same general order. It is obvious, for instance, that the most important difference between Dakota and Arapaho is the strong tendency of the former to recognize the sex of the speaker. Chinook is notable for laying more stress on the sex of the speaker and of the connecting relation than on the sex of the relative.[2] General differences such as naturally occur between the languages of one region and of another can also be expressed in terms of the

[1] A tendency toward reciprocal expression is sometimes of importance and may influence the degree to which categories are given expression. Reciprocal terms are such that all the persons included in the relationship expressed by one term call by one name all the persons who apply this term to them. In the most extreme form of reciprocity the two groups of relatives use the same term. The paternal grandparents call their sons' children, whether boys or girls, by the same term which these children, both boys and girls, apply to their fathers' parents. Nevertheless, the reciprocal relation is just as clear, though less strikingly expressed, when each of the groups uses a different term for the other. Our English words father and child, or brother and sister, are not reciprocal, for the term child is employed also by the mother, and brother is used by the brother as well as by the sister. In fact the only reciprocal term in English is cousin. The tendency toward reciprocal expression is developed in many Indian languages. It is particularly strong in California. In some languages this tendency has brought it about that different categories are involved in the terms applied to a pair of mutual relationships. The term father's sister indicates the sex of the relative but not of the speaker. The exact reciprocal of father's sister is woman's brother's child. This term, however, does not recognize the sex of the relative indicated, but does imply the sex of the speaker. The two reciprocal terms therefore each involve a category which the other does not express. If the same categories were represented in the two terms, brother's daughter would correspond to father's sister and exact reciprocity would be impossible. When, therefore, the terms found are father's sister and woman's brother's child, it is clear that the tendency toward the establishment of exactly reciprocal terms has been stronger than the feeling favoring the consistent use or neglect of certain categories; in other words, the extent to which certain categories are expressed has been determined by the vigor of the reciprocal tendency.

[2] No doubt, as has been pointed out, owing to the fact that the sex of the relative is indicatable by purely grammatical means in this and certain other languages.

categories. All the California systems, for instance, lay much more stress upon the sex of the connecting relative than do any of the Plains languages examined. The Plains systems are conspicuous for their weak development of the distinction between lineal and collateral relationship, this finding expression in two-thirds of all cases in Dakota, half in Arapaho, one-fourth in Pawnee. In seven California languages the corresponding values lie between three-fourths and complete expression. The method can be applied successfully even in the case of smaller and contiguous geographical areas. Of the seven California languages Luiseño and Mohave are spoken in southern California. Their systems show a unity as compared with the systems of the five languages from northern and central California. Both the southern California languages have a greater number of terms; both are stronger in the expression of the categories of the sex of the connecting relative and of age within the same generation; and both are weaker in the category of sex of the relative, than the others. Again, Chinook and Skokomish, both of the North Pacific Coast, are alike in indicating the condition of the connecting relative and in failing, on account of the possession of grammatical sex gender, to distinguish the sex of relatives themselves in many terms of relationship. There is a very deep-going difference between them, however, in the fact that Skokomish is as free as English from recognizing the sex of the speaker and of connecting relatives, while Chinook generally expresses both categories. In short, the categories present a means of comparing systems of terms of relationship along the basic lines of their structure and of expressing their similarities and differences without reference to individual terms or details.

The reason why the vague and unsatisfactory idea of a classificatory system of consanguinity has found such wide acceptance is not to be sought in any primary interest in designations of relationship as such, but in the fact that terms of relationship have usually been regarded principally as material from which conclusions as to the organization of society and conditions of marriage could be inferred. If it had been more clearly recognized that terms of relationship are determined primarily by linguistic factors, and are only occasionally, and then indirectly, affected by social circumstances, it would probably long ago have been generally realized that the difference between descriptive and classificatory systems is subjective and superficial. Nothing is more precarious than the common method of deducing the recent existence of social or marital institutions from a designation of relationship. Even when the social condition agrees perfectly with expressions of relationship, it is unsafe to conclude without corroborative evidence that these expressions are a direct reflection or result of the condition.

In the Dakota language, according to Riggs, there is only one word for grandfather and father-in-law. Following the mode of reasoning sometimes employed, it might be deduced from this that these two relationships were once identical. Worked out to its implications, the absurd conclusion would be that marriage with the mother was once customary among the Sioux.

In the same language the words for woman's male cousin and for woman's brother-in-law have the same radical, differing only in a suffix. Similar reasoning would induce in this case that marriage of cousins was or had been the rule among the Sioux, a social condition utterly opposed to the basic principles of almost all Indian society.

The use of such identical or similar terms for distinct relationships is due to a considerable similarity between the relationships. A woman's male cousin and her brother-in-law are alike in sex, are both of opposite sex from the speaker, are of the same generation as herself, and are both collateral, so that they are similar under four categories. In view of the comparative paucity of terms as compared with possible relationships, it is entirely natural that the same word, or the same stem, should at times be used to denote two relationships having as much in common as these two.

No one would assume that the colloquial habit in modern English of speaking of the brother-in-law as brother implies anything as to form of marriage, for logically the use of the term could only be an indication of sister marriage. It is easily conceivable that in the future development of English the more cumbersome of these two terms might come into complete disuse in daily life and the shorter take its place, withthout the least change in social or marital conditions.

The causes which determine the formation, choice, and similarities of terms of relationship are primarily linguistic. Whenever it is desired to regard terms of relationship as due to sociological causes and as indicative of social conditions, the burden of proof must be entirely with the propounder of such views.

Even the circumstance that the father's brother is frequently called father is not necessarily due to or connected with the custom of the Levirate; nor can group marriage be inferred from the circumstance that there is frequently no other term for mother's sister than mother. A woman and her sister are more alike than a woman and her brother, but the difference is conceptual, in other words linguistic, as well as sociological. It is true that a woman's sister can take her place in innumerable functions and relations in which a brother cannot; and yet a woman and her sister, being of the same sex, agree in one more category of relationship than the same woman and her brother, and are therefore more similar in relationship and more naturally denoted by the same term. There are so many cases where the expression of relationship cannot have been determined by sociological factors and must be purely psychological, as in the instances just discussed, that it is fair to require that the preference be given to the psychological cause, or that this be admitted as of at least equal probability, even in cases where either explanation is theoretically possible and supporting evidence is absent.

On the whole it is inherently very unlikely in any particular case that the use of identical terms for similar relationships can ever be connected with such special customs as the Levirate or group marriage. It is a much more conservative view to hold that such forms of linguistic expression and such conditions are both the outcome of the unalterable fact that certain relationships are more similar to one another than others. On the one hand this fact has led to certain sociological institutions; on the other hand, to psychological recognitions and their expression in language. To connect the institutions and the terms causally can rarely be anything but hazardous. It has been an unfortunate characteristic of the anthropology of recent years to seek in a great measure specific causes for specific events, connection between which can be established only through evidence that is subjectively selected. On wider knowledge and freedom from motive it is becoming increasingly apparent that causal explanations of detached anthropological phenomena can be but rarely found in other detached phenomena, and that it is even difficult to specify the most general tendencies that actuate the forms taken by culture, as the immediate causes of particular phenomena.

The following conclusions may be drawn:—

1. The generally accepted distinction between descriptive and classificatory systems of terms of relationship cannot be supported.

2. Systems of terms of relationship can be properly compared through an examination of the categories of relationship which they involve and of the degree to which they give expression to these categories.

3. The fundamental difference between systems of terms of relationship of Europeans and of American Indians is that the former express a smaller numbers of categories of relationship than the latter and express them more completely.

4. Terms of relationship reflect psychology, not sociology. They are determined primarily by language and can be utilized for sociological inferences only with extreme caution.

Janheinz Jahn

A YORUBA
MARKET-WOMAN'S LIFE

One topic that must be considered in the study of any society is the definition of the family unit. Does the family consist of a man and his wife and their children—sometimes called the nuclear family? Does the family consist of a nuclear family plus the parents of the husband or wife? In such an extended family, as it is called, a man might bring his bride to his home to live. This new nuclear family would then be a part of a larger family unit. Probably the most striking form of family unit to members of our culture is the polygamous family, in which one or more nuclear families are linked by one common spouse. Two varieties of polygamy are *polyandry*, where one woman is married to two or more men, and *polygyny*, where one man is married to two or more wives. Polyandry is quite rare (one example is the Toda of India), but polygyny is quite common. In fact polygyny is found all over the world. Our form of exclusively monogamous

Reprinted from Janheinz Jahn, *Through African Doors: Experiences and Encounters in West Africa,* trans. Oliver Coburn (London, 1962), pp. 84–98. Reprinted by permission of Grove Press, Inc., and Faber & Faber, Ltd. Copyright © 1962 by Faber & Faber, Ltd.

marriage is, in contrast, found in a minority of the world's cultures. (Some observers have facetiously suggested that with our divorce and remarriage procedures we in fact practice "serial" polygamy.) Not only are simultaneous plural marriages common, but the women involved are quite happy with the system. With our monogamous bias, it is difficult for us to envision a woman's content under such circumstances. For this reason, the following sketch of a Yoruba woman should prove of special interest.

One relatively new technique in gathering ethnographic data is the presentation of a life history of a particular individual in a society. Too often one reads monographs which tell how "the Yoruba" do this or "the Ibo" do that. One can read an entire book without ever coming upon a flesh and blood individual. Life histories, to be sure, cannot be used in place of standard ethnographic techniques. Often important aspects of culture, e.g., religion, are only briefly mentioned by an informant, and thus the ethnographer's information on a certain point might be badly incomplete if he had to rely solely upon what was serendipitously collected in a life history. On the other hand, an informant in a life history may give important emotional attitudinal information about various aspects of his culture, information which the ethnographer might never have thought of eliciting or might never have obtained even if he had attempted to elicit it. The following life history is well written, and it was written by a literary man, not an anthropologist. (The author shows his amateur standing when he indicates that much of his information came from European friends rather than from the subject herself.)

For further discussion of life histories, see Clyde Kluckhohn, "The Personal Document in Anthropological Science," in Louis Gottschalk, Clyde Kluckhohn, and Robert Angell, eds., *The Use of Personal Documents in History, Anthropology, and Sociology,* Social Science Research Council Bulletin 53 (New York, 1945), pp. 78–173, and L. L. Langness, *The Life History in Anthropological Science* (New York, 1965). For an excellent paperback anthology of life histories, see Joseph B. Casagrande, ed., *In the Company of Man: Twenty Portraits of Anthropological Informants* (New York, 1964). For more information about the six million Yoruba of Nigeria, see P. C. Lloyd, "The Yoruba of Nigeria," in James L. Gibbs, Jr., ed., *Peoples of Africa* (New York, 1965), pp. 549–82, or the references in the standard bibliographical aid, Ruth Jones, comp., *Africa Bibliography Series: West Africa* (London, 1958), pp. 38–42.

Anyone who tours West Africa with a camera will first seek out the markets in all the places he goes to: for the striking contrasts in colour between all the fruits in their bright yellows and greens and reds; the shapes of the chicken-baskets, the pots, bowls and calabashes; and above all for the women in their cotton, velvet and tulle dresses, with gay and often daring patterns which emphasize the silky blackness of bare arms and shoulders; for the bold twisting of the headscarves and the immense numbers of elaborate 'hair-dos' in which the fuzzy hair is parted, tied up or plaited; for the dignified gait of the housewives as they carry home their purchases in calabashes filled to overflowing; for the lofty patience with which the market-women squat behind their wares, the tender grace and the lack of embarrassment with which they give their breasts to their babies, the flashing smile with which they coax likely customers, the beauty of the young women and the characterful faces of the old; for their quiet gestures and gliding steps, and the play of light and shade on the matte gloss of dark skin. At the markets Africa reveals itself as a continent of human beauty.

All West African markets are gay with colour and vitality, but there are fine distinctions between different regions. The European manufacturers in Manchester, Birmingham, Rotterdam and Lyons, who produce the cheaper materials and print them with bright colours, cannot simply sell the same patterns and colour combinations to Abidjan on the Ivory Coast and Ibadan in Nigeria. Every region has its stylistic traditions, which decide the local fashions; the manufacturer has the pattern for each market designed and tried out in the place where he hopes to sell it. Dakar is attuned to a medley of pastel shades, glittering with incrustations of polished bronze and bright silver tones. Freetown likes straight-line patterns and lines of dots in deeper colours, Abidjan goes in for harmonies of three colours with one dominant, such as green-yellow-white, white-yellow-brown, blue-black-white. Accra prefers earthy shades ranging from yellow to dark brown by way of ochre and red. In the markets of the Niger Delta, at Sapele and Warri, yellow and red check is worn, combined with violet, and with gay embroidered birds and elephants on it. Yoruba markets, on the other hand, have an overall blue appearance from the varied shades of blue in the women's dresses, combining materials of natural indigo batik with symbolical patterns or their commercial imitations.

The camera may capture the colours, the gestures, the shadows, the robes, the wares. It may carry the pictures across the oceans, turning them into exotic and erotic dreams. But for the women the markets are part of everyday life, the rhythms and conditions of which are more concealed than revealed by the whirl of surface gaiety. Consequently the life of the women receives strangely little attention in travellers' accounts. It is not easy to probe into, of course, and discloses itself to a foreigner only if he adds up his separate observations and connects them into a single whole. If he does this, a pattern emerges by which all these women live, women who cannot read or write and are therefore summarily dismissed by many European authors. Rolf Italiaander, for instance, in a book published in 1954, says they '...can neither read nor write, so they are not even half civilized, but are at a most primitive stage of development.'[1]

[1]Rolf Italiaander, *Wann reist du ab, weisser Mann?* (Hamburg, 1954), p. 25.

Just how 'primitive' these women are or are not, I hope to show by a particular example, a woman whom I will call Ewumi, born twenty-seven years ago in the town of Ede, which may be regarded as fairly typical of Nigeria. It is in Yoruba country, 150 miles from the coast and thus not directly exposed to the commercial influences of the ports. It is not too deep in the bush either, but on the main railway line from Lagos to Kano; and it has a good asphalt road leading to it. It is of medium size, with about 70,000 inhabitants; much of my information on 'Ewumi' comes from European friends who live there.

Ewumi, then, was born in 1933. Her father, a respectable citizen of Ede, was like most other citizens a farmer, his land being a day's walk away from the town. He would be away from home for days, planting the yams, hoeing the round hillocks, weeding his land, tying up the beans, harvesting the maize, digging up the yams, and so on. With uncles, cousins and neighbours he marched out into the bush, where amidst much singing and also encouragement from the drummers[2] they would lend each other a hand in tilling their fields. Sometimes, but not often, baby Ewumi was there too, on the back of her mother, who might be helping to hoe, should there ever be a shortage of hands. But Ewumi's mother had her own field between her family's estates, which was usually looked after by her brothers.

In her first years Ewumi seldom saw her father, and he played no part in her life. Only the mother was ever present: Ewumi was strapped to her back, and it was from there that by degrees the girl came to take in her own little world. This included her brother, three years old, and her sister, six years older, who was already helping mother and was sometimes allowed to carry her little sister on her own back. Then there were the grandmother and aunts and their children. Ever since she could think, Ewumi's family provided a solid framework within which she could feel secure; but she was never away from her mother.

Her mother slept near Ewumi. She took Ewumi to market on her back (with the purchases stacked on her head) and to the seasonal dances of town or clan.[3] Ewumi would go to sleep there whenever she felt like it, whether her mother was going out to the fields, sitting at the market or dancing through the night at one of the religious festivals: practically before she could stand, Ewumi learnt the rhythms of the music for these. She sucked at her mother's breasts whenever she wanted, she never had to cry in hunger or lie alone in the dark. 'Timetable-feeding is unheard of and self-regulation of the child is the absolute rule,' writes Beier. 'Moreover the child can get as much erotic pleasure from its mother's breast as it likes, as it will be allowed to play with the breast at any time. Weaning too is done most gently and carefully. In some cases, where a child is extremely difficult, it may even be allowed to come to its mother's breast (very occasionally) after the new child is born.'[4]

When Ewumi was three, her mother gave birth again, and this time it

2Cf. Janheinz Jahn, *Muntu* (London, 1961), pp. 124ff.
3Cf. Ulli Beier, *A Year of Sacred Festivals in One Yoruba Town* (Lagos, 1959).
4Ulli Beier, "The Position of Yoruba Women," *Présence Africaine*, I–II (1955), p. 45.

was a boy. By now Ewumi had grasped something of life, she was weaned and no longer so completely dependent on her mother. But so that she should not feel neglected, she was now treated by her mother with extra tenderness, a cock was sacrificed for her, and she was bathed in the same water as her baby brother to develop feelings of kinship with him. Three years later, when Ewumi was six, her mother had another baby, and now it was the three-year-old brother who was bathed with the baby.

It is no matter of chance that the mother has a child every three years, and there would be great disapproval in her family if things were any different. For as soon as a woman finds herself pregnant, she may not have any more intercourse with her husband until the child is weaned. Most mothers leave their husbands for quite a long time and return to their own mothers, so as to devote themselves wholly to the children. 'All this is only possible,' Beier remarks, 'in a society where men have many wives, because otherwise they would have to remain celibate for stretches of nearly three years.'[5]

The three-year rhythm of births has many advantages for the child. In a European family the father may often feel the accidentally-born child as an intruder robbing him of his wife's attention, and conversely the child may feel neglected because of his father, which sometimes leads to an Oedipus complex; whereas here the father does not figure in the small child's existence at all. Moreover the baby's feeding is ensured in a country where the protective bodies contained in the mother's milk are essential defences against a whole series of dangerous diseases; cow's milk would provide no adequate substitute, even if cattle-breeding were possible in these areas infested by the tsetse fly. But there is of course no cow's milk, except for European tinned milk or milk powder, which is both far too expensive and also very hard to obtain, especially in the quantities that would be necessary if the native population were to depart from the three-year rhythm of births. Finally this also stops an elder child feeling too jealous on the birth of the next baby. It is natural for a child of less than two to feel neglected when the new baby arrives; a three-year-old is already more sensible and beginning to discover a world of his own. 'All these things may account for the balance and harmony we find in Yoruba children.'[6]

While her brother came under his father's care at seven, Ewumi, being a girl, stayed on with her mother, learning housework and having her own household duties, going to fetch water from the well in a calabash, which she had learnt to carry on her head, helping look after her small brother, now four, and minding him when her mother went to market; for her mother had grown older too and did not find it so easy now to have the four-year-old strapped to her hips, as well as the market goods on her head and the baby on her back. Yet Ewumi was by no means alone with her little brother, she was in the midst of her elder sisters and cousins, a whole troop of children going about their games and duties under the surveillance of relatives and neighbours.

[5]*Ibid.*
[6]Beier, "The Position of Yoruba Women," p. 45.

She learnt to cook, and wash clothes, to grind pepper, and pound maize and dried yam slices in the mortar. On Sundays she went with her mother and sisters and brothers to the Baptist Mission church, and eagerly joined in the hymns she had learnt there. That did not stop her taking part in the town's old religious festivals,[7] especially in the four-day festival of the new yams in July in honour of the *Orishas*[8] (the gods) and the seven-day festival in honour of the god Shango at the end of the rainy season. Ewumi was an intelligent girl, and the Baptist minister thought she ought to go to the mission school; but since her parents couldn't afford to pay school fees for all the children, they decided to send only the two boys, who might thereby get an office job later on.

Ewumi grew up into a fine girl. At fifteen she was going to market on her own, her wares being matches, razor-blades and cigarettes; and this gave her a chance to talk to and flirt with young men while selling. When her mother had reached marriageable age, *her* parents had long chosen their daughter a mate, who had as little choice in the matter as the girl. Ewumi, however, could herself choose—of course within limits. She was shrewd enough to consider only the young men of whom her clan would approve; it would have been foolish for a young woman to throw away light-heartedly the support she needed from her family when married. Partly with her knowledge and partly without, contacts were made between families: a few young men were tipped off by their relatives to buy razor-blades or cigarettes from her, and between the three or four proposed candidates she could exercise a free choice.

The one she liked best was Dele from the Olabisi family, a merry fellow and a hard-working farmer, who besides the traditional crops grew cocoa on his land—the fashionable new crop from which you were supposed to get rich quick. When both were sure that their families approved the connection, Ewumi received expensive bridal gifts from her suitor, worth the equivalent of about £25. These belonged to her, they were the basic capital for her subsequent trading, and had nothing to do with the bride-price, which at Ede is fixed at £12. Dele found no difficulty in paying this price, for a marriage here is not so much a contract between two individuals as the symbol of two families being joined together. Every member of Dele's family contributed something to the sum needed, and Ewumi's father, who received the bride-price, had to distribute it among all the members of the family.[9]

So the day came when amidst the customary ceremonies and festivities she entered her husband's household. The young couple lived in an annex, a mud hut with a corrugated-iron roof and room for further expansion. At first she had much to order and arrange before she could settle down in the new clan. Being a true Yoruba woman, she could not let her husband keep her, and with the price of her bridal gifts she bought wares for sale; she set them out on a rough-hewn table outside the hut at a corner of the road, where there would be a lot of people passing. She offered sugar, tinned milk,

---

[7]Cf. Beier, *A Year of Sacred Festivals.* . . .
[8]Cf. Jahn, *Muntu*, pp. 65ff.
[9]Cf. Beier, "The Position of Yoruba Women," p. 40.

tinned sardines, soap, matches, kerosene for lamps and refrigerators—all European articles which did not spoil.

When she became pregnant, the marriage had so far fulfilled its purpose, for marriage is not consummated by two people living together but by the begetting of children. Ewumi was proud of her fertility, and as she loved her husband, she brought him her friend Toro, who with Ewumi had for years excelled in the Baptist Church choir, as second wife—after thorough consultation with all the families concerned. Dele's hut got an extension, and Ewumi carried out her duties at the wedding of Dele and Toro, thereby showing herself a true '*iyali*'—mother of the house—as she could now call herself. Having welcomed her husband's guests in the prescribed way, and initiated Toro into her duties, she now returned with all her belongings into her parents' family.

She was now free to concentrate on her business. She got rid of the European wares, which were likely to bring only a small profit, and transferred her activity to the market. She was very good at making *ogi*, a maize-meal dish. Since both her own family and her husband's grew maize, she bought the raw material cheap direct from the producer. She had only to take the maize to the miller to be ground into meal, and then make *ogi* with it. So her profit came from the difference between the retail and wholesale price as well as from the work she put in. These profits were 'ploughed back' into wares that would not spoil.

Her confinement was properly celebrated: Dele was proud of Ewumi and buried the after-birth, the ceremony required to make him the legal father, the 'owner' of the child. It was a girl, and was given the name of Gbemi after a dead great-grandmother. Ewumi carried her baby daughter on her back, went to the market every day with fresh *ogi*, and increased her prosperity. The only snag was the miller's price for grinding, which was gradually going up.

Communication with her husband and Toro was confined to periodical friendly visits, going to church with them on Sundays, and taking part in the festivals of town and clan. Little Gbemi on her back grew bigger, and when she was beginning to wean her daughter, many a man at the market made her friendly offers—for she was beautiful, had shown she could bear healthy children and had enough milk for them. She was now nineteen.

But she only laughed at her suitors' advances; as soon as Gbemi was weaned, she returned to her husband's house. Toro had still not become pregnant, and Ewumi told her of all sorts of effective 'medicines' (charms), recommended prayers and sacrifices to Shango, the *Orisha* embodying reproduction powers, and to *Egungun* (the ancestors). As 'mother of the house' she organized communal living according to the prevailing custom: for five days she cooked the food for her husband and slept with him; then Toro cooked for him and slept with him for the next five days. Ewumi as '*iyale*' had to welcome guests when they came, but this is the only privilege she had. For a few months the two wives looked after their husband in turn, till Ewumi was sure she was pregnant again and returned once more to her family's farm.

At the market she had long had her fixed place among other women who also sold *ogi*; her two neighbours were old, and their *ogi* was not so good, but their clans saw to it that they also had their turnover. Their children were already grown up, so they no longer needed to earn such large amounts.

When Ewumi was delivered again, it was a boy, and they called him Adebayo. But great as was their joy, it was mixed with anxiety, for Adebayo was rather delicate, and also prone to fits. And when the worried parents brought him to the *Ifa* oracle,[10] it transpired that he was an *abiku,* a spirit-child, who only comes on earth to leave it again soon. Ewumi would have to make all possible efforts to see the child stayed on the earth and did not go back again to his spirit companions. An *abiku* has wonderful dreams, he has visions of his spirit companions and plays wonderful imaginary games with them.[11] And when his time comes, some time between the ages of four and ten, the spirits demand that the child returns to them. However attached he may be to his mother, if he is not strong enough, he must obey them. The mother will then pray that the child be restored to her, and there are women who maintain that they have given birth to the same child seven times. If the child is reborn, it can easily be recognized by a small mark which is scratched on a dead child's face or body; the scar will then appear on the new-born baby in the same place. Many grown-ups show such 'identification marks'; in one confirmed case, Beier notes, 'the parents expected a certain mark to appear, and described it before the baby was born. The mark appeared as expected, and I saw it myself.'[12]

Ewumi would treat Adebayo with the greatest care, would never let him out of her sight, would satisfy his every want, put up with all his moods. If he was called away even so, she could be sure he would be born to her again and again, until one day he would stay alive and with her. But if her care for him never let up for a moment, the *abiku* might even stay with her the first time, and she would be able to have more children than if she had to give birth to the same one several times.

'The *abiku* is often a problem child,' says Beier. 'Many of those I have known are very temperamental and make great demands on their parents. If a wish is not fulfilled at once, they will threaten to die. The terrified parents will then all too often put up no resistance to the child and suffer its tyranny in the hope that it may be persuaded to live. The *abiku* is nearly always the unusual one, the out-of-the-ordinary child, in many cases it is the exceptionally brilliant child. Therefore the *abiku* is given exceptional treatment. But this does not offend the other children, who are treated much more sternly. Because after all, they know that these are not ordinary children like themselves. Thus Yoruba society has solved the educational problem of how to give the exceptional child the freedom it requires to develop its personality, while at the same time supplying the more rigid discipline which the average child must have to feel secure.'[13]

[10]Cf. Ulli Beier, *Sacred Wood Carvings from One Small Yoruba Town* (Lagos, 1957), p. 9. [For further discussion of the Ifa oracle, see William Bascom, "The Sanctions of Ifa Divination," *Journal of the Royal Anthropological Institute* 71 (1941), 43–54.—Ed. Note.]
[11]Cf. Beier, *A Year of Sacred Festivals...*, p. 26.
[12]Beier, *A Year of Sacred Festivals...*, p. 92.
[13]Beier, *A Year of Sacred Festivals...*, p. 64.

So Ewumi had given birth to a spirit-child, a problem child; but soon other worries were added. The price the miller demanded for grinding the maize had gone up so much that the women who sold *ogi* found their earnings seriously reduced. Ewumi discussed the matter with the other women at the main market, and they all agreed not to accept the price any longer; so Ewumi appealed to the *iyalode,* the woman chief of the town, who looked after the women's interests in their dealings with the men and the king: every town in Yoruba country has such a woman chief.

Ewumi was one of the delegation which conducted negotiations with the millers for the *iyalode.* But millers are men: they were adamant and refused to lower the grinding price. The *iyalode* began to threaten, and after a few days the millers said they were ready to come to terms; yet the negotiations trailed on, and the *iyalode* had the impression that the millers were dragging them out till the *ogi*-sellers' stores were used up and one or other of them would be forced to have more maize ground and pay the price demanded. Then the *iyalode* called all the *ogi*-sellers out on strike. She sent her messengers—and on the same day all the *ogi*-sellers began to grind their maize by hand. After a week the millers yielded and accepted unconditionally the price fixed by the *iyalode* according to the women's wishes.[14]

The *iyalode* and the *ogi*-sellers would scarcely have heard of such a thing as a trade union. Their strike was no imitation of European methods, no transference of modern European processes into Yoruba life; it was simply the way such conflicts were traditionally settled. As every clan has its chief and every professional group its spokesman, so the women too have their independence and their own organizations, which owe their impact above all to the traditional religious cults. In the Shango cult, which is the most important one at Ede, the high priest is a women, the *Iya Shango* (Mother of Shango), and it gives her tremendous influence. There are two male secret societies, the *egungun* (ancestors) society, which makes the bond between the living and the dead,[15] and the *oro* society, which has a secret executive power.[16] But the *ogboni* society, which controls both these and is a check on the king's power—it consists of all important tribal chiefs and priests— contains women members as well as men. Unlike Christian social life, that of the Yorubas has never been patriarchal; so the women have long been able to secure special economic monopolies for themselves. Pottery, dyeing, spinning and the batik process are exclusively women's business; no man may practise these trades. At the market women have a monopoly in most of the goods for sale. Men may sell meat and leather goods there, but almost everything else is in the hands of the women: yams and cassava, tomatoes and other vegetables, cola nuts, palm oil, cooked dishes, mats, baskets, skins, necklaces, jewellery, native 'medicines',[17] and materials.

Ewumi was now earning well again at the market. Her attention to customers was often distracted, of course, by Adebayo, her spirit-child, but

14Cf. Beier, "The Position of Yoruba Women, p. 40.
15Cf. Beier, *A Year of Sacred Festivals...*, p. 26.
16Cf. Geoffrey Parrinder, *West African Religion* (London, 1949), pp. 141ff., and Olumide Lucas, *The Religion of the Yoruba* (Lagos, 1948), pp. 120ff.
17Cf. Beier, "The Position of Yoruba Women," p. 41.

the customers were patient and understanding, for they knew the duties of a mother to an *abiku*. Dele often came to visit her either in the market of in her house, not only to see how Adebayo was going on. He was worried about Toro, who had still not conceived, was unhappy over it and moody, now imploring Ewumi and Dele for new counsels and 'medicines', now accusing people of making her barren by witchcraft. Ewumi advised Dele to take a third wife, particularly as she herself had given birth to an *abiku,* did not know if he would stay in this world and how often she might have to bring him into it again. Dele had for some time been toying with the idea, and had already picked out a woman called Efuneye, a blacksmith's second wife, who had already born her husband two healthy children and who sold cola nuts a few market alleys away. Dele had now and then bought cola nuts from her for years, but in the last weeks his need for them seemed to have increased enormously, and Efuneye had shown that she did not object to his wooing—Dele being ten years younger than her husband. So a meeting was arranged between Efuneye and Ewumi, the two women liked each other, and the rest was only a financial matter.

Since Efuneye had lived with her husband for over five years, she had to return only half the bride-price on divorce, and could keep the bridal gifts. Dele readily gave her further bridal gifts, and his family readily found the bride-price. The blacksmith was not exactly pleased, but had to admit that he sometimes beat Efuneye, so that grounds had been given for the divorce. After the usual formalities Efuneye entered Dele's household with her two children, a six-year-old boy and a three-year-old girl.

The coming of a new wife already blessed with children made Toro even more painfully aware of her failure. Her depressions alternated with fits of temper, and Dele's aunts and grandmother had to intervene to see that order was kept in his house. Efuneye, however, was very popular with all, which incensed Toro all the more. Ewumi watched the situation with distress; Efuneye often came and asked her to come home soon, as with two of them there Toro's tempers would be more easily controlled. Dele would have been glad to get rid of Toro, he beat her to give her grounds for divorce, dropped hints to friends about her beauty—she was certainly the most beautiful and also the youngest of his wives—yet no suitor would turn up. Dele had even got his family's permission to do without the return of the bride-price if need be, but Toro wanted to stay, so he just had to put up with her.

The nearer the time came when Ewumi had to wean her problem child, the more worried she became. She went on feeding him longer than usual, which in itself was good for an *akibu,* but because of this child she was afraid of going back into her husband's house. With a directness that was almost unseemly she pointed out to the men who flirted with her at the market that there was a fine shapely girl to be had in Dele's house; but they only laughed, they knew the situation and paid all the more compliments to Ewumi herself. She entreated Dele either to bring Toro somehow to her senses or else get rid of her. But neither the sacrifices to Shango and other *Orishas* nor prayers in the churches seemed to help. Even Toro's mother couldn't cope with her.

Ewumi began to listen more attentively to the friendly things said to her, and in particular she could not help thinking about the advances of a rich elderly merchant. He already had eight wives and a lot of children, all of whom lived together in harmony and comfort; and he offered most attractive bridal gifts.

When Dele learnt that the merchant's hopes were well founded, Ewumi and he had a long discussion. Dele would like to have kept her, but for the sake of her little *akibu* she refused to return into a house of strife. The air the child breathed there was poison, she said: a spirit-child had to have happiness round him and peace; if he saw Torơ in one of her rages, he would die. Dele admitted she was right. He loved Ewumi, and she loved him, yet the child's welfare was decisive as ever. 'The child is the cornerstone of African society.'[18]

She gave him and his family half the bride-money back, neglect on the part of the husband was given as grounds for the divorce, and both wept on parting. The merchant was received formally but very politely by Ewumi's family; his gifts to the bride were in keeping with his wealth, but Ewumi did not seem particularly impressed and kept them with her own savings.

The *iyale* of her new home was an elderly, wise and kindly woman, who took great care over household arrangements and saw to it that the rota of wifely duties did not get out of hand. Some of the wives were already quite old, and only two were suckling children. Ewumi had to prepare her husband's food only five days every month. In such a well-off household there was no lack of assistance or space; she found the peace she had longed for in order to devote herself entirely to her little *abiku*. After she had carried out her wifely duties three times—she had to be passed over at her first turn because of menstruation—it transpired that she was again pregnant. But as she had learnt to appreciate the household's cheerful and harmonious atmosphere, she did not go back to her own family. Adebayo was thriving, and it really seemed as if he meant to stay with her; while Gbemi, now five, romped about with the other children as if they were her brothers and sisters.

With Dele, meanwhile, things were much less peaceful. When Efuneye became pregnant, Toro almost went out of her mind, and the two women came to blows. The relatives had to intervene, and Toro was sternly rebuked, but she only worked everybody up the more with her poisonous talk; and when Dele came home from his fields two days later, he beat her harder than ever. She cried the whole night, but next morning immediately started a new row. Dele's clan conferred, after which a delegation was sent off to Toro's clan, earnestly requesting them to take the misguided creature back. But she would not even listen to the remonstrances of her own relatives, and abused the clan elder so violently that they formally renounced her: the elder said that never in human memory had such a thing occurred in his clan. So Dele had to take her back home again. Divorce is easy for a woman, almost impossible for a man. For morals in Yoruba society, and the rules

[18]Georges Balandier, *Zwielichtiges Afrika* (Stuttgart, 1959), p. 38.

derived therefrom, are based on a simple but good principle: any arrangement which tends to ensure the production of many children and which guarantees that no women will be left to die as spinsters, is moral in this society.[19] Since nobody now wanted to have Toro, Dele was obliged to go to the last resort.

Having donned his ceremonial robes and taken some money, he seized Toro's hand, pulled her crying out of the house, and went with her into the palace of the king, the *Timi* of Ede. There he threw himself down before the king, gave him the money, and pointing to Toro said: 'Timi, I present her to you.' Then he told the king how things had come to this pass. The king could not refuse the present, but had to take her.

A 'town king' among the Yorubas has some privileges, of course, in the choice of wives: for instance, if a woman kneels on his carpet by mistake, he may claim her as his wife. But he has more duties than rights, he must marry the crippled and sick girls, all those who normally would have no chance of finding a husband, and must take the women nobody wants.[20]

When she heard what Dele had done, Ewumi did not stay much longer in the merchant's house. She discussed things with Dele and her family, gave the merchant the full bride-money back and all the rich personal gifts, for she had been with him less than a year. In order to marry her again, Dele had to make good half the bride-money which she returned. It was his right to hold it back three months, to make sure of her faithfulness and constancy; but he paid it at once, being sure of his Ewumi.

The celebrations for her re-entry into his house coincided with a farewell party; for Efuneye's eldest son was now seven and returned to his real father, the blacksmith, according to custom. Since both wives, Ewumi and Efuneye, were now pregnant again, they together looked for a third wife for Dele; their choice fell on Ewumi's youngest sister, with whom Ewumi had always got on extremely well.

Since then another three years have passed, Ewumi and Efuneye have had their babies, and their entire offspring, including the 'problem child', Adebayo, have stayed alive. Ewumi's sister has also had a baby, but it died soon after it was born—infant mortality is still high. Ewumi and Efuneye have remained close friends, they mind the children alternately and also swap stalls at the market. Efuneye too now sells *ogi*, but Ewumi has spent her savings on hardware: lamps, bicycle-chains, clothes-hangers, alarm-clocks, aluminium pots and buckets. Her youngest brother, a lanky lad of seventeen, still single, who lives with a great-uncle, looks after her stall in the covered market at Onitsha. He is a reliable boy and hands over his profits every month, which she puts back into goods. If her businesses go on flourishing like this, she will soon have her own lorry (as her aunt has), will engage a good driver, and earn still more with haulage deals, which bring in good money. Adebayo will then one day be able to study in Europe.

[19]Cf. Beier, "The Position of Yoruba Women," p. 44.
[20]Cf. *Ibid.*, p. 43.

Raymond W. Firth

WORK AND WEALTH
OF PRIMITIVE COMMUNITIES

One of the principal criticisms anthropologists make of their colleagues in other academic disciplines is that although these colleagues speak of man in general, their data comes from Euro-American (and occasionally Asian) cultures only. A psychologist conducts an experiment using American university undergraduates as subjects and presents his findings as evidence of human learning, not *American* human learning. Sociologists interview American men on the subject of sexual practices and then title their findings as *Sexual Behavior in the Human Male*. Philosophers speculate on the nature of man but they consider no data from the peoples of New Guinea or aboriginal Australia. And so one could comment in similar fashion on a great many academic disciplines. In a sense it is analogous to the ethnocentric hubris which makes Americans call the playoff series of baseball games between the champions of the National and American League teams the *World* Series.

Students of economics are unfortunately guilty of the same kind of parochial ethnocentric thinking. By defining economics in terms of their own society, they are forced to conclude that societies without capital or markets are essentially societies without sophisticated economic principles. As Professor Firth of the London School of Economics clearly shows, nothing could be further from the truth.

For further reading in the anthropological study of economics, see such works as Melville J. Herskovits, *Economic Anthropology* (New York, 1952), available since 1965 in paperback; Karl Polanyi, Conrad M. Arensberg, and Harry W. Pearson, eds., *Trade and Market in the Early Empires: Economies in History and Theory* (Glencoe, N. Y., 1957); Cyril S. Belshaw, *Traditional Exchange and Modern Markets* (Englewood Cliffs, N. J., 1965); or Manning Nash, *Primitive and Peasant Economic Systems* (San Francisco, 1966). There are, of course, more specialized studies dealing with the economics of single cultures, e.g., Raymond Firth, *Primitive Polynesian Economy* (London, 1939), or Bronislaw Malinowski's classic account of the *kula* exchange cycle, *Argonauts of the Pacific* (New York, 1922), which has been available in paperback since 1961.

Reprinted from Raymond W. Firth, *Human Types* (New York, 1938), pp. 71–97, by permission of the author and Thomas Nelson and Sons, Ltd.

The eager extension of our Western industrial system over the world, with its desire for raw materials, for new markets, and for fresh sources of labour supply, has brought us into contact with the economic attitudes of primitive peoples. The white man in the tropics often finds these difficult to understand. He encounters resistance to his plans for economic expansion and social betterment from what he often thinks are inadequate and irrational native ideas. In the Trobriand Islands native men may refuse to dive for pearl-shell for a trader and will go out on a tribal fishing expedition instead, even though they can earn ten or twenty times more from the first than from the second. In the Solomon Islands, where a native can buy three sticks of tobacco for a shilling, he may prefer those three sticks in exchange for his wares to two shillings in money. In New Guinea and elsewhere the wages earned by months of labour may be dissipated in a few days by gifts to kinsfolk and the purchase of paltry trinkets. In East and South Africa, where cattle-keeping is an important part of tribal life, the native will hang on to the most decrepit beasts and overstock his pastures to the peril of their fertility in an obviously uneconomic way. How can these facts be explained? Have we to do with people who have no sense of value and of economic principles? Observations such as these, which could be paralleled from almost any part of the British Empire, and from other colonial empires as well, have led to a number of popular misconceptions about native behaviour and the fundamental motives which govern it.

It should be the function of the anthropologist, whose business is the systematic study of primitive communities, to throw light on these problems. Unfortunately, however, many anthropological observations on primitive economics have been studies of technology and arts and crafts, rather than of the basic principles which control the work and wealth of native societies.

Economics is the study of that broad aspect of human activity which is concerned with resources, their limitations and uses, and the organization whereby they are brought into relation with human wants. In modern industrial societies economists have worked out an elaborate technique for the study of this organization, and have produced a body of generalizations upon it. It is still a matter of argument as to how far this technique and these generalizations can be applied in the study of primitive communities. These communities have a comparatively simple material equipment which has not been integrated into an industrial organization. They are frequently small in size, and they lack any system of wide inter-communication with each other—they are not part of a world market. Moreover, apart from their contact with European civilization, they lack that price system which can act, however imperfectly, as a measure of wants and energies. The economist, again, assumes in his analysis certain basic human attitudes which he refers ultimately to his experience of what people do in our society. It is possible that these attitudes are not present with the same force in primitive people, and that other attitudes may take their place as the prime regulators of human behaviour. For all these reasons some of the terms which the modern economist uses—such as capital, saving, and interest—cannot be applied directly to primitive economics.

Certain broad principles, however, do seem to emerge from our studies. It has been said by an earlier German economist that some primitive peoples are in a kind of pre-economic stage in which an individual search for food is the characteristic feature. Nowadays this would not be admitted. In every primitive group there is a problem of food supply in relation to population, and this problem is not one realized by single individuals in isolation, but is dealt with as a collective question by some planned system of production and distribution. It is important for us to understand from the outset that family ties, wider obligations to kinsfolk and to neighbours, loyalty to chiefs and elders, respect for clan taboos and beliefs in control of food and other things by spirits, ancestors, and gods can all play their part in this system.

How do natives work in their own tribal life when they are not subject to the regulations of a European employer? They do not have a wage system, in which so much reward is given for so much labour. Participation in work is often undertaken as a duty towards the person who wants the work done, rather than for the material gain which can be expected from him. But work for its own sake is not regarded as a duty. There are no sayings like, "Satan finds mischief for idle hands to do," or moral ideas about the "dignity of labour." And time is not such an important element in the economic process as it is with us. The calculation of payment for work is not made on the basis of the units of time spent by the different persons engaged, and if there is a pause between two steps of the task—as in waiting for a metal or a liquid to heat up, or cloth to dry, or shoots to sprout—there is no feeling that the time taken is "lost" or "wasted," just because of this. It is perhaps difficult for the European reader to understand just how much moral value he himself unconsciously gives to the passing of time, and how little the native attaches to it. This does not mean that natives are normally idle, or slack at what they are supposed to be doing. When the work itself calls for industry, or even haste, they respond, but this response is always within the sphere of the needs of the task; again, they frequently find other occupations for their spare time. But a general responsibility to be busy does not lie on them.

It is sometimes imagined that the main drive to the economic activity of a primitive people is their immediate desire to satisfy their material wants. Certainly it is obvious that this is an important factor in their life. But it would be untrue to interpret their economic organization as a simple response to their requirements of food, clothing, shelter, and the like. In the first place, it is a socialized and not an individual response. The values which they put upon their food do not consist simply in its capacity to satisfy hunger, but in the use they can make of it to express their obligations to their relatives-in-law, their chiefs, their ancestors; to show their hospitality; to display their wealth; to initiate or marry off their sons. The value that is put on a canoe is not to be measured only in terms of the capacity of the vessel to carry goods and passengers, and of the fish that are caught from it, but also by the way in which it is a symbol of craftsmanship in wood, an object of artistic carving and decoration, a reminder of traditional voyages, and even the resting-place or embodiment of a god. The value of a cow does not simply consist in its yield of milk, and the uses to which its flesh, hide, and horns can be put, or in what it will fetch at a sale, but also in its rôle as part of a marriage portion, as a ritual sacrifice, and as a token of social status. The whole economic system of the people is run with this complex set of values in mind. From this it is seen, then, in the second place, that many of the wants upon which their economic life is based are of an immaterial kind. And the desire to build up a reputation may lead a man to accumulate more food, or cows, or canoes; but in some cases it leads him to reject mere accumulation—deliberately to give more than he receives in an exchange; or to expend his resources in marrying off his son, or burying his father; or, in the extreme case of the potlatch of the American Indian of the north-west coast, in destroying his most valued property in order to outface a rival in public esteem. This is all economic behaviour, in that it involves his making a choice as to what he will do with his wealth. But it is not covered by the idea that the maximization of *material* satisfactions is the economic goal.

Again, it is not an immediate return that is always sought. As Malinowski and Thurnwald have shown, the principle of reciprocity seems to be fundamental to most human relationships. When, as often happens in primitive society, a present is made or a service given without any payment handed over on the spot, what has been given is mentally "chalked up" by both parties, and ultimately a return is made. It may be of the same type, or of a different type; it may take the form of material goods or labour, or of some action such as wailing at a funeral, or a public recital in praise of the donor. Sometimes there is an immediate response. In Tikopia, when one man at a dance festival chants a song in honour of another man's god, the latter at once trails out before the assembly a length of bark-cloth and presents it to him to "cover" the song. But for a funeral there is an element of delayed response. A kinsman of the dead person is not supposed to prepare his own food, since his heart is heavy with mourning; he is accordingly fed by some one else who comes in from outside for the purpose, moved by "sympathy," as the natives say. At the end of three days the mourner hands over to this "feeder" a wooden bowl, some sinnet cord, and some fish-hooks as payment. But when next there is a funeral in the family of the other, he himself returns the service, going along with his basket of food, and receiving similar property in return. The two sets of acts thus cancel each other out. This example illustrates other points: how closely the preparation and eating of food is connected with sentiments of sympathy and family affection; and how the principle of reciprocity demands not merely that property should be handed over in return for food, but that the service of sympathy should itself receive acknowledgment and return.

To what is all this complex behaviour due? Alfred Marshall has said that "in the ruder stages of human life many of the services rendered by the individual to others are nearly as much due to hereditary habit and unreasoning impulse, as are those of the bees and ants."[1] It is true that he goes on at once to qualify this by saying that a deliberate sense of self-sacrifice and tribal duty soon make their appearance. But it is important to

[1]*Principles of Economics*, p. 243. (8th ed., 1922.)

realize that the habit is not hereditary, nor the impulse unreasoning, but the result of training in the social values of the particular community; and, as we have just seen, that self-sacrifice and duty are not intelligible until they are considered in relation to the demand for reciprocity.

Continuing our summary observations on the primitive economic system, we see that it is not characterized by any permanent specialization of individuals or groups in different tasks. Sometimes, as with the metal-workers of Africa, a man or a family will devote their major interest to a specific task, but even here they have, as a rule, some subsidiary source of income. In an Oceanic island every man is normally a cultivator and a fisherman, and has some competence in woodworking, manufacture of thatch and cordage, and all the other crafts practised in the community. There is division of labour, particularly between the sexes, but no one is expected to gain his livelihood by the exercise of one special skill alone. An obvious result of this is the absence of seasonal unemployment, and of a floating labour supply which depends upon capitalist initiative for its subsistence.

Work in co-operation is a frequent aspect of primitive economic life. The stimuli which keep the working group together may be different from those we use. The responsibility of employed to employer and the fear of loss of pay or job are not the prime forces which keep them at work. More important are the conventions about industry, the reproof which laziness is likely to draw from a man's fellows,[2] and the stimulus given by work in company with songs and jokes which lightens drudgery and gives it some tinge of recreation. It is significant, too, that for really heavy work such as dragging a log or a canoe primitive peoples have adopted rhythm as a guide and lightener of the labour. Not only does a working song like a sailor's shanty give the time for pulling together, but it also distracts the mind from the dullness of the task.

Another common feature of primitive industry is the close association between technical and ritual activities. In theory it is easy to draw the distinction between these, but in practice the acts which produce the result desired are interwoven with a set of performances directed towards the promotion of fertility; the control of what we would regard as the incalculable factors of chance and of Nature; and the intervention of ancestors or gods on behalf of human effort. It has been pointed out by Malinowski and other anthropologists that this ritual is not a mere drag upon the economic activity but plays an important part in integrating the efforts of the workers and in giving confidence in the face of what might be the inhibiting fear of the unknown. On the other hand, these ritual performances, and the beliefs which they express, do appear at times to operate against the efficiency of the economic process, by leading to the retention of traditional technique of a less efficient kind than might be discovered by freer experimental methods. They also absorb time which might be devoted to the increase of wealth in other directions. Still, it must be remembered

[2]The Maori people formerly used proverbs a great deal to spur on laggards or to praise the industrious man. See my "Proverbs in Native Life," *Folk-Lore*, xxxvii., 1926, pp. 135–53, 245–70.

that considering the native attitude to time already mentioned, the discarding of magical or ritual accompaniments to work might not increase the efficiency of the productive process. It has been shown that the abandonment of the ritual of agriculture in communities under European influence, such as the Maori, has reacted unfavourably upon the quality of the work performed.

It is difficult to speak of capital in a primitive economy in a way which makes it comparable with the idea in our own society. Primitive peoples do devote certain types of goods to facilitating production, and from time to time accumulate them in advance for this specific purpose. Thus, before starting to have a canoe built, a Tikopia man may plant extra areas of food and see that the women of his household get in stock a quantity of bark-cloth and pandanus mats additional to normal requirements. But this capital is fluid in its nature, and the objects so used can be at once turned to a variety of other purposes if the need arises. Thus should a person die in the man's family before he starts his canoe-building, or even during the process of his work, the goods accumulated will be turned into material for a series of funeral exchanges. The mobility of "capital" is high in such primitive societies; diversion to other uses without loss is usually possible. The investment of capital with the definite idea of getting a return from it in the form of interest is, however, not at all common in primitive economics. Where goods are contributed by others to assist a man in productive enterprise, these are usually given either in accordance with kinship obligations or as part of a general scheme of reciprocal arrangements, and are transferred back again with no additional increment.

This last point brings up the problem of primitive exchange. Prior to contact with Europeans most primitive communities had no objects which could properly be called "money," and, therefore, no price system. Such communities are commonly spoken of as practising barter. But as an equivalent of buying and selling on a non-price level, barter implies the idea of haggling, in the attempt by each party to secure the highest return for what he hands over. Now this is by no means always the case in a primitive transaction. Not only are customary rates of exchange common, but the traditional factor which guides these rates is not mere inertia, but a complex set of ideas about liberality, respect for the personality of the other party, and for the act of exchange as one of social linkage wider than the purely material transaction. This reaches its highest form in what has been termed the "gift exchange." Here a recognized rate is observed, and the principle of reciprocity operates, but the form of the transaction is that of a gift and a counter-gift—between gentlemen, so to speak, avoiding the notion of haggling as being derogatory to the social position of both. At times, in fact, the recipient of the first gift deliberately makes his return gift higher in value in order to maintain his social standing. Another feature of such primitive transactions is the existence of what may be termed "spheres of exchange." There are various groups of goods and services, and exchange of one item can only take place with another item in the same group. In south-eastern New Guinea, for instance, a very important series of exchanges takes place between the possessors of shell arm-rings and of necklaces of shell discs, while other important exchanges are of fish for vegetables. But the food items can only be exchanged against each other, and so also the shell valuables. It would be unthinkable for a man who wished a shell valuable to offer in return yams or fish or other property not of a shell kind. There is no free market, no final measure of the value of individual things, and no common medium whereby every type of goods and services can be translated into terms of every other. A primitive economy thus presents a strong contrast to our money economy.

A primitive distributive system, therefore, does not consist of finding exact equivalents for the services rendered by the different factors of production. It tends rather to follow the conception of reward for the social advantages conferred by participation in production, instead of a quantitative return for the material advantage obtained. The categories of wages, interest, and profit cannot easily be isolated in such a system. Moreover, the needs of the component members of the society are taken directly into account, so that the system is governed by principles of welfare and justice which vary according to the particular community. But primitive communities cannot be classed as communistic in any exact sense of the term. There are concepts of property-holding, and the means of production are held in ownership by individuals as well as by groups. Frequently these individual property rights are of a very complicated character. They may be based upon ties with father's and with mother's kin, and involve the rights of women in the family goods, and of chiefs in the goods of the people of their clan. At the same time the theory of corporate responsibility is usually well developed, restraining individuals from the exploitation of their fellows by moral codes of considerable force.

Some of the complexities of primitive economics should now be obvious. After this general sketch it is advisable to examine in more detail some aspects of a primitive economy. It is impossible to give detailed consideration to every point that has been mentioned. But one cardinal feature of a primitive economic system is clearly the absence of money, of a price mechanism, and in many cases of a formal market. We may take this as symptomatic of the economy as a whole. Because of this situation it may be thought that the economy operates without clear principle, that transactions take place either in a kind of individual anarchy, or, as Marshall put it, "by hereditary habit."

In our own economic system money gives a universal measure of values, a convenient medium of exchange through which we can buy or sell almost anything, and also a standard by which payments at one time can be expressed as commitments for the future. In a wider sense it allows for the measurement of services against things, and promotes the flow of the economic process. In a primitive society without money we might expect all this to be absent, yet the economic process goes on. There is a recognition of services, and payment is made for them; there are means of absorbing people into the productive process, and values are expressed in quantitative terms, measured by traditional standards.

Let us examine, to begin with, a situation of simple distribution such as occurs when an animal is killed in a hunt. Do the hunters fall on the carcass and cut it to pieces, the largest piece to the strongest man? This is hardly ever the case. The beast is normally divided according to recognized principles. Since the killing of an animal is usually a co-operative activity one might expect to find it portioned out according to the amount of work done by each hunter to obtain it. To some extent this principle is followed, but other people have their rights as well. In many parts of Australia each person in the camp gets a share depending upon his or her relation to the hunters. The worst parts may even be kept by the hunters themselves. In former times, at Alice Springs, according to Palmer, when a kangaroo was killed the hunter had to give the left hind leg to his brother, the tail to his father's brother's son, the loins and fat to his father-in-law, the ribs to his mother-in-law, the forelegs to his father's younger sister, the head to his wife, and he kept for himself the entrails and the blood. In different areas the portions assigned to such kinsfolk differ. When grumbles and fights occur, as they often do, it is not because the basic principles of distribution are questioned, but because it is thought they are not being properly followed. Though the hunter, his wife, and children seem to fare badly, this inequality is corrected by their getting in their turn better portions from kills by other people. The result is a criss-cross set of exchanges always in progress. The net result in the long run is substantially the same to each person, but through this system the principles of kinship obligation and the morality of sharing foods have been emphasized.

We see from this that though the principle that a person should get a reward for his labour is not ignored, this principle is caught up into a wider set of codes which recognize that kinship ties, positions, or privilege, and ritual ideas should be supported on an economic basis. As compared with our own society, primitive societies make direct allowance for the dependents upon producers as well as for the immediate producers themselves.

These same principles come out in an even more striking way in the feasts which are such an important part of much primitive life. The people who produce the food, or who own it, deliberately often hand over the best portions to others.

A feast may be the means of repaying the labour of others; of setting the seal on an important event, such as initiation or marriage; or of cementing an alliance between groups. Prestige is usually gained by the giver of the feast, but where personal credit and renown are linked most closely with the expenditure of wealth, the giving of a feast is a step upon the ladder of social status. In the Banks Islands and other parts of Melanesia such feasts are part of the ceremonial of attaining the various ranks of the men's society, which is an important feature of native life. In Polynesia these graded feasts do not normally occur, but in Tikopia a chief is expected to mark the progress of his reign by a feast every decade or so. The "feasts of merit" of the Nagas of Assam are not so much assertion against social competitors as means of gaining certain recognized ranks in the society.

Let us take as an example the feast of *Khuang tsawi*, the greatest feast of all among the Zahau Chins of Burma, which has been described by H. N. C. Stevenson. A most important feature of this feast is the killing and division of the meat of three of the curious kind of cattle known as *mithan*. The flesh of the animal is not cut up at random, but is divided into a series of recognized joints, each of which has its own name. Moreover, each type of joint must be handed over to a particular class of people. The figure on page 247 shows the way in which the animal is cut up. The following table gives the distribution of the various joints. It will be remembered that three of the animals are killed; the numbers given after each joint indicate the total number of pieces available for distribution:

Joint	Number	Recipients
a	3	Divided between father, brother, and father's brothers' sons. After the meat is taken off the skulls are returned to the feast-giver, who hangs them up in front of his house as a sign of his wealth.
b	6	1 to feast-giver; 1 to a scape-goat (an idiot on whom ill-luck should fall); 1 to supplier of bamboo for a chair for the feast-giver's wife; 1 to an assistant; 2 to former feast-givers.
c	6	6 to former feast-givers.
d	3	1 to headman; 2 to bond-friends.
e	3	Divided between father, brother, and father's brothers' sons.
f	6	3 to former feast-givers; 3 to sisters or close female cousins.
g	6	6 to assistants.
h	3	3 to "working-sisters" that is to female relatives, not very closely related, who help in the work.
i	6	1 to headman; 2 to former feast-givers; others not mentioned.

In addition to this, three portions of flesh beneath the breast-bone are given to the blacksmith; the entrails to a wife's brother and a mother's brother of the feast-giver; blood in sausages warmed with slivers of meat and some small portions of flesh to widows and the destitute.

In this complicated scheme of distribution we see that three main sets of people receive meat. One set are kinsfolk of the feast-giver; another set are people who have performed services for him (including his two friends the blacksmith and the headman); and the third set are the givers of former feasts. The deference shown to this last set of people is a token of how in this community a man builds up his social position by a free use of his wealth. When he himself has given a feast, then he gets more meat and better beer at future feasts given by other people; he gets a higher bride price for his daughters when they marry; he becomes eligible for membership of the village council; and, if he goes on with his feast-giving, he earns the right to make windows in his house, and to build a little summer-house on the platform of his courtyard. And finally, by the *Khuang tsawi* feast he becomes eligible to enter at his death the highest heaven of the Chin people. Among the Chin, as among many other primitive people, it is more blessed to give than to receive, but only because the act of giving entitles one to receive more at a future date.

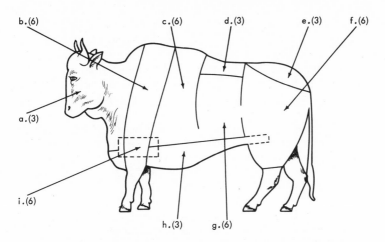

Division of Meat at a Chin Feast. (After H. N. C. Stevenson.)

This ceremonial division of animals at a feast is a common feature. Peter Buck has described the division of pigs, bonito, and shark in Samoa. A pig is divided up into ten portions, each of which has its name, and is appropriate to people of a certain rank or status. So important is the ceremonial division of a Samoan pig that the quality of the food becomes a secondary affair. If the pig is too well cooked, then the flesh is likely to tear when cut, and the exact boundaries of the ceremonial division cannot be kept. Then the hosts are ashamed and the people who get the joints are critical. The result is that the pig is often served nearly raw. Not that the Samoans like raw pork to eat. The guest is not expected to consume his share immediately; he satisfies himself with the fish and vegetables which go with it. The important thing is not for him to eat the pork, but for him to have been *given* it. So highly have the Samoans developed their system of etiquette and of social precedence that our rules of behaviour, even on formal occasions, seem crude and unorganized beside theirs.

We may now consider how inequalities in possession of resources between different people are met, in the absence of a monetary commercial system. The absence of money does not mean that there is no exchange. Even among very primitive peoples there is usually some contact with other tribes and some exchange of things between them. Sometimes there are regular markets, as used to occur in Malaita in the Solomon Islands, and still do in many parts of Africa; often exchange takes place as the result of expeditions sent out for the purpose.

Trading expeditions of a dramatic kind have been recorded among the tribes of the New Guinea coast. The *hiri* of the Motu, described by Seligman and Barton, and the *kula* of the Trobriand Islands, described by Malinowski, have in fact, become classical accounts of seafaring among native people.

The Motu, who live in a dry belt of Papua, and whose women are potters, set out each year at the end of the south-east trade wind with a cargo of pots on a 200-mile voyage. They return six months later, before the end of the north-west monsoon, with a raft of new dug-out canoes and tons of sago in their holds. Each voyage is an adventure with risk, so it is not surprising to find that taboos are laid in plenty both on the sailors and on their wives at home, and that magic is performed to promote the sailing powers of the canoe and avert shipwreck. The Trobrianders, who participate in the famous *kula,* carry on two types of exchange, the one of useful articles such as pots, the other of necklaces of red shell and bracelets of white shell, which though ornaments, are hardly ever worn. The necklaces are exchanged between partners in the various island groups through a circle of several hundred miles, and move in the direction of the hands of a clock. The arm-shells move likewise, but in the opposite direction, and are exchanged for the neck-laces as they meet them. These exchanges, which are of a complicated kind, take place mostly by means of special expeditions in canoes, and like the canoes of the *hiri* those of the *kula* are built and sailed in the midst of a cloud of magic. This *kula* institution draws our attention to one feature of primitive exchange which is extremely important, namely, that this exchange often reaches its highest peak, not with objects of ordinary domestic use, but with things which may be of little or no practical use. They have their value, as it were, through their elevation in exchange, and not for any outside reason. In a sense the exchange itself is the thing of value, and not the object.

There are regions, however, where ceremonial exchange is carried on without regular expeditions. The opportunity for exchange is given by large inter-tribal gatherings for initiation or other ceremonials. Such is the case of the Mulluk Mulluk and Madngella of the Daly River in Northern Australia, as described by W. E. H. Stanner. The native system is termed *merbok.* A great variety of articles travel along the *merbok* paths. They include iron oxides, pipe-clay, hair belts, spears, boomerangs, beeswax, pearl-shell orna-ments, stone axes, and knives. Some of these articles are not actually used by certain of the tribes who exchange them; they merely pass the things on to their partners in the opposite direction. Many of these articles go immense distances; pearl-shell from the west coast has been found hundreds of miles inland, and a type of boomerang characteristic of tribes around Wave Hill has been seen among tribes of the Finniss and Daly rivers over 200 miles to the north.[3] Nowadays many European articles pass along the *merbok* paths in this way.

The *merbok* exchange, like those of New Guinea, is carried on between definite partners, all of whom in this case are kinsfolk of one kind or another. The transactions take place with little fuss. But they have a cere-monial side, since they do not serve merely utilitarian ends, and the posses-sion of a partner is in itself a mark of social maturity. The transient possession of a store of objects, even though he himself does not use them, gives a man a satisfaction, especially when he can hand them on to others and receive a return. Moreover, the gift of an object is a mark of friend-ship, and serves to strengthen social bonds which are of value in other

[3]For the benefit of those who think that every Australian aborigine uses a boomerang, it may be noted that boomerangs are one type of object which are taken in exchange by the Daly River tribes, but are not used by them.

directions. But the position of a *merbok* partner is not always an easy one. He often has to decide whether, for instance, he will divert an object from one of his partners to meet a claim raised by marriage or the initiation of his sister's son. If he does so, then he will have to find an equivalent object soon or risk his partner's anger, detrimental gossip, possible attempt at sorcery, or even a challenge to fight.

Among many primitive peoples occasions of human rejoicing or sadness are treated as an opportunity for complicated exchanges of goods, and from their point of view the expression of the appropriate emotions would not be fully possible without such exchanges. Vast quantities of goods may then change hands. At one betrothal in Ontong Java in the Solomon Islands Hogbin records that 16,000 coconuts and ten large baskets of dried fish were given to the parents of the girl by the boy's father. This gift increased the respect in which the donor was generally held. But a few weeks later, when another man gave 17,000 coconuts as a betrothal present for his son, he was criticized as a vulgar boaster, and felt himself to be so unpopular that he retired to an island out of public view for some months. Frequently custom prescribes that the goods from the bridegroom's and the bride's family should be of different types. In Samoa, for instance, the relatives of the bridegroom gave the *oloa* of canoes, pigs, and other food, while the relatives of the bride presented in return the *tonga* of beautiful fine mats of native cloth. When a marriage took place between Maori people of rank, heirlooms were exchanged and served future generations as a token of the union between the noble families. Such an heirloom as a valued neck ornament might be handed back to the original donors many years later at a death in their family. It was then described as *roimata*, "tears," a description which indicates the imagery of the Maori. Sometimes such exchanges serve utilitarian purposes by providing the other party with goods not previously in their possession. More often the gain is not so much in terms of useful objects as in the social value of the exchange itself.

We have already stated that money is not a characteristic feature of primitive economic systems. Yet the terms "native currency" and "native money" are commonly used. They have been applied to a wide variety of objects of value: coconuts in the Nicobar Islands; cowrie shells, hoes, and spear-heads in Africa; pigs and strings of shell discs in the New Hebrides, the Solomon Islands, and New Guinea; shields in Guadalcanal; coils of red feathers in Santa Cruz; whale's teeth in Fiji; beeswax in Borneo; and glass jars in Burma. How far are these terms accurate? We have already described the function of money as giving a medium of exchange between other objects and a measure of their value. From this point of view some of the items mentioned seem to be fairly described. Coconuts in the Nicobar Islands do appear to fulfil the functions of money. Thus, needles are exchanged at 12 coconuts per dozen, matches at 24 nuts per dozen boxes, and red cloth at 1,600 coconuts per piece. Moreover, though payment need not be made in nuts, they serve as a measure of values. A racing canoe was bought for 35,000 coconuts. But this was simply a measure of its value. The payment was made in cloth, beads, and implements which themselves were valued in terms of nuts. The money of India, too, has its value in terms of Nicobar coconuts. A two-anna bit is worth 16 nuts, a rupee, 100 nuts. Since a two-anna bit is one-eighth of a rupee it seems as if the multiplication of the Nicobar people is at fault. But the two coins are used for ornament as well as for exchange, and a rupee as a single coin is less prized for personal adornment than eight of the two-anna pieces. Here, then, coins are not simply money, but objects depending for their value upon other considerations, and the real objective standard is provided by coconuts. In many parts of Africa cowrie shells appear to perform the same function of currency or money.

On the other hand, items such as feather coils, shields, mats, and whales' teeth do not seem to be properly classified as primitive money. They are important items of exchange, but their transfer does not facilitate the exchange of other things, and they do not serve as a standard to which the values of other things can be referred. Even pigs, which are exchanged very freely, and the possession of which is a measure of a man's wealth in many of the South Sea islands, can hardly be called money. In Malekula, for instance, pigs are treasured for their tusks, and quality is much more important than quantity. Sows are of no social importance and are regarded as food fit only for women and children. With boars the two upper canine teeth are knocked out while the animal is young, with the result that the lower teeth grow longer and longer, curving round till they pierce the lower jaw and sometimes even grow out again in more than a complete circle. There are many grades of value of these boars, the index being their tusk development. Each grade has its name and special function. For the higher grades special gong signals are sounded when at a feast the animal is presented or killed. All important ceremonies are bound up with pig-killing, and the borrowing, lending, and transfer of these animals. As many as a hundred or a hundred and fifty pigs may be distributed at one of these ceremonies. The social importance of these animals, their graded values, and the credit transactions that take place with them still do not entitle them to be termed money in the strict economic sense. But what is important to observe is that without a money system as ordinarily defined, these natives manage an economic scheme of considerable complexity, have standards of value, and exchange freely large quantities of goods.

The classification of strings of shell discs which are used freely in the western Pacific is more difficult. Malinowski has shown the need for scepticism about the classing of an object as "native money" unless it can be shown that the mechanism of exchange among a native people requires the existence of an article to be used as a common medium of exchange and measure of value. He has rightly pointed out that the valued shell ornaments exchanged in the *kula* ring are never used in this way. They are condensed wealth, to which is attached a complex sentiment aroused by competitive desire and by the ritual use of these objects, but they are not money.

It does seem, though, that in the Solomon Islands and the Banks Islands strings of shell discs do at times play this rôle. In Buin, Thurnwald has described the use of fathoms of shell discs, one fathom now being valued at a shilling. In olden times spears arrows, bows, stone axe-blades, and clam shell arm-rings were sometimes traded for these shell strings; and nowadays fishing nets, bags, painted hats, combs, bamboo cases for lime, native tobacco, and European products are freely bought and sold with them. There are no markets, but bargains are made between individuals at casual meetings. Pigs, too, which are very important as an index of a man's wealth and the chief item in feasts, are exchanged for these shell strings—from 10 or 20 up to 100 fathoms. Thurnwald speaks, in fact, of a "pig standard of currency," since the value of the shell strings lies largely in their ability to be converted into pigs, which are in turn the fundamental element in a feast, which itself is the pivot on which the social and economic life turns.

Another interesting system has been recorded by Armstrong from Rossel Island. Here there are two types of shell discs, one called *dap* and the other *kö*. Of *dap* there are 22 classes, each with a name and comprising a number of single reddish triangular pieces of shell. In classes 15 to 22 each coin has an individual name; there are 81 of them in all, and each is known individually to natives with financial interests. *Kö* is a unit of ten discs of clam shell, and there are 16 classes of it. The first is equivalent in name to the seventh class of *dap,* so that No. 16 *kö* equals No. 22 *dap* in name. There is no real equivalence of value between them; they are not exchanged for each other. In each of the two groups the value of an item in one class is proportionate to that of an item in a class below it, according to the amount of time taken before the latter must be repaid by the former. Thus, if a No. 7 *dap* is lent for a few days a No. 8 *dap* must be given in return for it; if for some weeks, then a No. 9 or 10 must be returned. These objects circulate a great deal. They are used to buy other articles, and are borrowed for the purpose, being repaid after some time by the appropriate piece that the borrower possesses. There are brokers, too, who lend these objects and get those of higher value in return.

But though these shell strings are very freely used, and the values of many other objects can be expressed in terms of them, they still do not appear to have that universal applicability which money has attained in our own society. Coins of the highest value have to be handled with much ceremonial. When one of No. 18 *dap* is handed over from one person to another both parties crouch down out of respect to it. Nos. 19 to 22 *dap* are so sacred that they are not supposed to see the light of day, and are always kept enclosed. They are owned only by chiefs, and function only as security for loans. Of No. 22 there are only seven coins, inherited in the male line, and the chiefs who own them are apparently the most important in the island. Again, *dap* and *kö* cannot be expressed in terms of each other as our coins of different metal can. *Kö* is to some extent women's money. And items of higher value are individualized and have personal names. Armstrong maintains that these shell articles are really money in the strict sense. Not only do they serve as a medium of exchange and as a standard of value, he says, but they are not desired for their utility for other purposes, even for ornament or display. But it is not clear that his classification can be accepted. In their use for special ritual purposes, those of the highest value at least seem to be objects of wealth in themselves, and something more than money.

In a community without true money, how are the values of goods determined, and indeed have they any value at all? The answer to this question depends upon the meaning we attach to "value." We can perhaps agree that things have no intrinsic value in themselves apart from their relation to people and people's wants. If, in the first place, we think that value is "price," then value obviously cannot be measured in a community without money. If, then, by value we mean the cost of making a thing, we cannot measure primitive values in this sense either, because relative costs can be measured only in the vaguest way. The labour-cost theory of value, which has sometimes been put forward, has very little meaning because of the absence of any exact calculation of time spent, or of any final distinction between work and recreation, and because the relation between skilled and unskilled labour is not clearly defined. In any case, cost alone cannot be a clue to primitive values because the reasons which lead people to want things are often independent of the difficulties of producing them. By value in our buying-and-selling society we usually mean exchange-value. But in many primitive societies, as we have seen, there is no attempt to exchange each kind of object against another, and no medium which can express their comparative worth for exchange purposes. A purist might then argue that *economic values* do not exist in many primitive societies. Every primitive society does, however, appear to have some rating of the worth of different kinds of things outside the sphere of their immediate practical use. Some kind of comparison between them usually takes place as by the limited exchanges of trade or ceremony which we have already described. And the preferences shown seem to have a more general application than those of simple individual taste. Thus an Australian aborigine may be expected always to prefer a shell pubic pendant to a hair belt; a Polynesian, a canoe to a piece of plain bark-cloth; an African, a cow to a goat. There is, then, some sort of scale of comparative utilities or wants, though, especially in the most primitive cultures, the scale is not finely adjusted, and there is no exact expression of the worth of one object in terms of another.

REFERENCES

Firth, R., *Primitive Economics of the New Zealand Maori* (Routledge, 1929).
Thurnwald, R., *Economics of Primitive Communities* (Oxford, 1932).
Deacon, B., *Malekula*, ed. C. H. Wedgwood (Routledge, 1934).
Armstrong, E. W., *Rossel Island* (Cambridge, 1928).
Mauss, M., "Essai sur le Don," *L' Année Sociologique* (Paris, 1925).
Seligman, C. G., *The Melanesians of British New Guinea* (Cambridge, 1910).

Max Gluckman

THE REASONABLE MAN
IN BAROTSE LAW

The anthropological study of law is one of the most fascinating subdisciplines of cultural anthropology. The early investigators,

Reprinted from Max Gluckman, *Order and Rebellion in Tribal Africa* (London, 1963), pp. 178–206, by permission of the author, Cohen and West, Publishers, and The Macmillan Company. © 1963 by Max Gluckman.

not finding written codified law or courts constituted as we know them, tended to brand primitive societies as lawless. With such a view, the imposition of rule by law was regarded as a hallmark of civilization. Anthropological fieldwork has revealed the error of assuming that the categories and concepts of law in Western civilization are universals. Law may be universal, but our categories of it are not. All societies have behavioral norms, some of which if violated bring about socially sanctioned judgment and punishment. The means of identifying rule violations and of deciding appropriate action to be taken against the violator vary from culture to culture. The cultural relativity of legal systems is nowhere more apparent than when two cultures are in contact. For example, a Florida Seminole kills one of his fellows and, according to Seminole law, the oldest member of the victim's family is supposed to take revenge by killing the murderer. In one case, an old Seminole of more than ninety years had to be propped up with a gun and told to pull the trigger. The state of Florida, of course, has its own law and in accordance with this law the old man was arrested and brought to trial. The point is that by acting in accordance with his own law, the Seminole violated the law of the white man. Another obvious example of the relativity of law concerns the definition of international waters. If an American fisherman fishes outside the three-mile limit, he is in international waters. However, some countries have decided that international waters begin outside a fifteen-mile limit. An American fisherman fishing five miles off the coast of such a country would be arrested by the police of that country for trespassing or fishing without a license. He may not be guilty in terms of his own law, but he may be in terms of the law of another country. Such instances should clearly demonstrate the need for rigorous research on the nature of law in different societies. As the world shrinks, different legal systems come increasingly into contact. The establishment of canons of international law is one attempt to substitute one aspect of a consciously designed international culture for analogous elements in many individual cultures. Unfortunately, one difficulty is that much of international law grew out of the law of Western civilization and there is some doubt that emergent African nations, among others, will readily be able to abide by all of it.

The following essay by Max Gluckman, Professor of Anthropology at the University of Manchester, shows the necessity of collecting concrete cases. It is difficult, if not impossible, to elicit abstract principles of law in the field. However, if one records disputes and their settlement, one has the raw material from which one can induce the local definition of law. Whether one accepts Gluckman's hypothesis about the importance of what he calls the "reasonable" man or not, one can appreciate the excellent detail of the reports he gives of actual cases he observed among the Barotse, a Bantu people living in Rhodesia.

For further discussion of Barotse law, see the various writings of Professor Gluckman, e.g., *The Judicial Process Among the Barotse of Northern Rhodesia* (Glencoe, Illinois, 1955), and *The Ideas in Barotse Jurisprudence* (New Haven, 1965). For the anthropological study of law in general, see E. A. Hoebel, *The Law of Primitive Man* (Cambridge, 1954), and Laura Nader, ed., *The Ethnography of Law,* Special Publication of *American Anthropologist,* **67,** No. 6, Part 2 (1965), and an excellent anthology of articles of law and anthropology, Paul Bohannan, ed., *Law and Warfare: Studies in the Anthropology of Conflict* (Garden City, 1967). For a useful annotated bibliography, see Laura Nader, Klaus F. Koch, and Bruce Cox, "The Ethnography of Law: A Bibliographic Survey," *Current Anthropology,* **7** (1966), 267–94.

1. The Case of the Violent Councillor

I come from a family of lawyers, and through my childhood I constantly heard my father and his colleagues discussing their cases at the family-table. Later I intended to go to the South African Bar, and besides reading Law at the University I worked in my father's office in Johannesburg and attended on him in court. Therefore when, diverted by a desire for the exotic, I became an anthrolopogist and began to study African social life, I hoped I might make some contribution on the problems of African law. But I found that, though the setting of this law might be exotic, its problems were those which are common to all systems of jurisprudence. I can still recall vividly how I was sitting in my

This essay consists of four talks delivered on the Third Programme of the B.B.C. in August 1954. They abstract a part of the argument of my book, *The Judicial Process among the Barotse,* published in 1955; I reduced certain important parts of the argument there set out in 367 pages, to 11,000 words. The talks were successful: indeed, they got an appreciation index equivalent to that of the star comedy feature on the Light Programme, 'Take It From Here'—I mean an appreciation index as Third Programme talks. When I told an American friend this, he replied: 'You have reached the top now. All that is left is a long, slow, coast downhill.' Higher praise still came from a B.B.C. producer who told an anthropological colleague that the talks 'were almost good enough for the Home Programme.' When I heard the late Sir Arthur Grimble broadcast his *Pattern of Islands,* I realized how right she was: mine were not good enough for the Home. Still, they were sufficiently good for the Colonial Overseas Service to ask me to produce a shorter version of the whole argument in only 1,350 words. Doubtless the argument could be reduced yet further. The talks were printed in the *Journal of African Administration.* (vii, 1955, and viii, 1956).

While my own book was in press, I read a newly published book, *It's Your Law,* by Mr. Charles P. Curtis of Boston. Mr. Curtis argues about American legal terminology in much the way that I argue about Barotse legal terminology. But he put in five words, as a sub-title to a section, what I had striven to say through many pages. Legal terms, he said, had 'a precise degree of imprecision'.

deckchair one day listening to a trial in a Barotse Court, when I recognized an old friend. He is inscribed in huge letters on the blank page opposite my notebook's record of the process of cross-examination: 'Hullo, the reasonable man!'

This was not the first Barotse trial I had attended, and in an earlier piece of research in Zululand I had also listened to cases. So I share with many colleagues a long blindness to the existence of this basic figure of jurisprudence in African law. Indeed, it was the facts of the case, rather than my own perception, which made me aware of his existence in Barotse law. But once I had observed him, I was able to reconsider all the cases I had heard as exhibitions of his dominant rôle in the judicial process. I came to appreciate that he was the means by which the judges applied the fixed rules of general law and morality to the varied circumstances of Barotse life. Above all, he was the means by which they adjusted these fixed rules to cope with the great changes which the Barotse's life is undergoing as they are absorbed in the modern world.

This is the general problem I am going to talk about. Obviously, it is a problem which is fundamental to our own jurisprudence, where the reasonable man is an equally important figure. The phrases, 'reasonable man', 'reasonable behaviour', 'reasonable care', 'reasonable precautions', and the like, crop up in every judgment and every chapter of a textbook of law. Indeed, in the very first of his *Misleading Cases at Common Law,* Sir Alan Herbert—in a case in which the judges hold that there is no such thing as a reasonable woman in English law—comes to the following conclusion:

> There has never been a problem, however difficult, which His Majesty's judges have not in the end been able to resolve by asking themselves the simple question, 'Was this or was it not the conduct of a reasonable man?', and leaving that question to be answered by the jury.

It seems to me that in this misleading case Sir Alan puts the reasonable man into his proper position, at the centre of the law. The reasonable man occupies this central position because he is the means by which abstract legal rules are focused on to the varied circumstances of life. In textbooks of law he is cut up according to the technical divisions of jurisprudence—he comes in under many separate heads, such as reasonable care and guilty beyond reasonable doubt. In this process of dissection he loses his integrated character. And it is this integrated character which interests me as an anthropologist. I am going to exhibit his dominance in Barotse lawsuits, and to suggest that this exhibition may help to solve certain long-standing controversies in our own jurisprudence. For as Barotse judges define the reasonable man, they bring into their definitions many facets of Barotse life which are not ostensibly part of the law. These facets include a variety of social and personal prejudices. I believe the same process can be detected in the decisions of our own judges and juries.

Let me describe the exotic setting in which I first met this familiar figure. From its source in the Belgian Congo, the Zambezi flows southwards towards the Kalahari Desert, before it bends east towards the Indian Ocean. About half-way down its north to south course the river has carved out a great plain in the woodlands which cover North-Western Rhodesia. This plain is 120 miles long and about thirty-five miles wide, and it is the homeland of the tribe who rule over the vast region marked as Barotseland on maps. Each year the summer rains flood the plain, so that it becomes a great lake. The Barotse therefore build their villages on mounds in the plain, which are islands in the flood-season; though as snakes and rodents and insects seek sanctuary in the villages, life in the flood is so uncomfortable that the Barotse move for these months to dwell in other villages on the margins of the plain. From their plain-villages the Barotse work rich pockets of alluvial soil, pasture their cattle, and trap fish in many ways. These villages, on the only building land available, are of strategic importance in Barotse life. Rights to work land and to fish in certain trap-sites and pools depend on membership of a village.

The Barotse have a Paramount Chief who has two capitals, one in the heart of the plain, the other at the margin, to which he moves for the flood-season. The chief rules through an elaborately organized council, which is a court of law, a cabinet, a parliament, a civil service, an ecclesiastical chapter, and, in the old days, was a military headquarters. Now war is a thing of the past, for under a treaty signed in 1900 the Barotse accepted British protection. Under the Treaty the Barotse Chief's rights to punish his subjects were defined by British law, but his council still tries civil and some criminal cases. It does so by old procedures. The plaintiff states his case in full detail to the numerous judges, and the defendant replies. The judges themselves cross-examine the parties and witnesses, and when they are satisfied that they have heard all the evidence, give judgment. There are no lawyers to assist the parties, and their rôle is played by the judges. The chief himself does not listen to lawsuits, but the judgments are referred to him in his Palace for the final verdict.

It was at Lialui, the flood-season capital, that I recognized the reasonable man during a trial which I call 'The Case of the Violent Councillor'. Most Barotse villages are inhabited by a grouping of kinsfolk, but some are attached to members of the royal family and are inhabited by several families, all of which are ruled by a councillor. A quarrel had broken out in the village which was destined to be the burial-village of the then reigning chief. Hot words had passed between the son of the councillor and a young villager. The villager had gone to the councillor's house to complain about the son's behaviour, and he alleged that he was attacked there by three of the councillor's children who flung him to the ground. The councillor seized his wrist and dragged him along the ground, with the three youngsters clinging to his waist. He screamed: 'The councillor is breaking me, the councillor is breaking me.' His wife came in and accused the councillor of fighting: this is a heinous offence for a councillor, since a councillor is not a policeman, and must never take violent action. The councillor released him and got one of the stamping-poles with which the women pound grain. It was taken away by another man. The councillor seized a whip which was also taken away. The plaintiff was then released by the councillor's children and carried away, fainting. He sued the councillor and children in a subordinate court which fined the councillor £1, of which it said ten shillings were to go to the plaintiff, and ten shillings as a fine to the Barotse Treasury. The plaintiff said he would appeal for the latter ten shillings to the court at the capital, and persisted in this appeal even when he was offered fifteen shillings, with five shillings only to the Treasury.

This was the story which the plaintiff told the appeal court where I was listening in, since Barotse appeal courts hear all the evidence anew. He had independent witnesses for most of the incidents. But the councillor's defence was as follows. He said that the plaintiff had come to his house spoiling for a fight with his son. His children had attacked the plaintiff who was thrown to the ground. He had seized the plaintiff's arm in an attempt to raise him and stop the fight. Then he had taken the stamping-pole to put it out of the way in case someone seized it as a weapon. Finally he had taken the whip to frighten the fighters into their senses, but had not intended to use it.

The serious aspect of this case was that the councillor had taken violent action—had fought. Barotse gave me several precedents in which councillors, who are supposed to be restrained, grave, controlled, and so forth, had been discharged for taking action against wrongdoers with their own hands. The violent councillor was afraid that this would happen to him, and he therefore cast his story so that his witnessed actions would appear to conform to Barotse ideas of right conduct—so that he would appear to have acted reasonably. It seems probable that he was lying, but it is very important to notice that he lied in such a way that he accepted the rules for rightdoing. In almost every case which I heard in Barotseland litigants and witnesses, whether they lied or were mistaken, worked with the same moral and legal rules as the judges did. This is the mark of a homogeneous society; and it alone allows a satisfactory process of law. If the litigants have rules of rightdoing different from those of the judges, the judges can punish them, but not convict them.

Since the violent councillor accepted the standard rules of how a councillor should behave, he lied in terms of these rules, and this enabled the judges to attack him. A prince asked him: 'When the plaintiff came to your house, why did you not tell him to sit down, and then summon your children, so that you could enquire into the dispute between them?' The councillor hedged and replied, 'They are binding me with lies'. The head of the court pressed him: 'Why did you not make them sit down so that you could judge between them?' The councillor did not reply. The head of the court, who is noted for his gentleness but was enraged by the offence, went on angrily: 'You should have seated the plaintiff, called your son, and summoned all the men of the village to hear their quarrel.' The councillor said, 'I did not do this.' The head of the court commented: 'This is councillorship—this is ruling!' The councillor made an attempt to defend himself: 'It was night, I could not.' The head of the court pursued his point:

If an affair comes here to the capital at night to me, I go to the prime minister, I call the senior councillors. If it is a thief, we put him in gaol for the District Commissioner. Also, you say you tried to raise the plaintiff, that you did not drag him along the ground. What manner of arbitrating in a fight is this, to seize the one who is on the ground, who is being overwhelmed, not to seize those who are fighting him?

Here the judges have set up two standards by which they can break the councillor's ingenious defence of his witnessed actions. First, he did not behave as a reasonable man would do in intervening in a fight; second, he behaved quite unlike a reasonable councillor, acting by the customs of a good councillor, in handling the quarrel when it was brought to him. It was at this point that I realized how the Barotse had elaborated the concept of the reasonable man.

The court was aware that the councillor feared discharge, but did not mind paying a fine for his children's assault. This is implicit in the next question put to him, though it seems also to stem only from the concept of a reasonable man. For the court knew the councillor did not want it to become aware of his offence. A prince challenged him: 'You deny that you were at fault. Why then when the subordinate court penalized you £1, did you not appeal?' The councillor replied: 'If a man is penalized, what can he do?' The prince insisted: 'He can appeal.' The councillor hedged: 'I would have appealed if the plaintiff had not done so.' The prince crushed him: 'But you did not protest in the lower court. This boy complained that the court was taking ten shillings of his money for the Treasury, you did not protest that you should pay nothing. . . . Your fault was that you, a councillor, entered into a fight.'

With this question the bias of the trial shifted from the assault to whether the defendant was fit to be a councillor. Another judge asked him: 'Why when the plaintiff's wife cried, "The councillor is fighting", did you release him, if you were trying to raise him? You knew you were wrong, as a councillor, to fight.' And another prince concluded the cross-examination: 'You say you came with the whip to frighten them. Is it your custom to threaten with a whip?' The councillor was caught in a cleft stick, because only a policeman and not a councillor should threaten with violent action. He had to answer, 'No'. The prince asked: 'Did you shout as you came with the whip, to show that you wanted to beat them, but did not mean to beat them?' Here the councillor perforce answered, 'Yes'. The prince concluded: 'Then why has not one witness of all who heard the plaintiff cry, "The councillor is breaking me", said that he heard you shout?'

All the judges held he was guilty. Some wished to raise the payment, but the final judgment held that he should pay £1 and it should all go to the plaintiff. He and his children were warned that if they did not behave properly he would be discharged from his post and they might be expelled from the chief's village.

There are many implications in this brilliant cross-examination. I can discuss only a few. First, we see that an African court decides on the facts of a lawsuit by listening to and sifting evidence, and weighing it by cogency and corroboration, just as an English court does. The judges also insisted on direct as against hearsay evidence: a witness was told, 'What you heard with your ears, what you saw with your eyes, tell us. Hearing and seeing the quarrel are good. Do not tell us everything you have been told about the fight.' This has always been the procedure of Barotse courts: ordeals and magical oracles were only resorted to in accusations of sorcery, which cannot be demonstrated by ordinary evidence, and in criminal cases where the verdict on the evidence was, 'almost certainly guilty, but not proven.'

But the truth is arrived at mainly by contrasting the behaviour of the parties, as witnesses report it and as the parties themselves describe it, against the standards of how a reasonable man would behave. Both the parties and the judges erect common standards of reasonable behaviour, and this makes possible judicial cross-examination. But the standards in this case are two-fold. First there is the standard of a generally reasonable man—a man who arbitrates in a fight by helping the person who is overwhelmed and intervening with the attackers, i.e. a reasonable peacemaker; a man who appeals against an unjust conviction, i.e. a reasonable innocent man. Second, there is the standard of a reasonable councillor, who when people are quarrelling makes them sit down and tell their stories so that he can judge between them, who summons the public to assist in this process, who is firm and authoritative but not violent, who is impartial and not biased in favour of his own children. After this case gave me the clue, I found this two-fold character present in every lawsuit—the generally reasonable person, and what I call 'the reasonable incumbent of a particular social position', be it councillor, husband or wife, father or son. And as these characters were held up as standards before litigants, as when the head of the court described how he handled an affair coming to him at night, I saw how important the reasonable man is during that part of a lawsuit when the raw facts given in evidence are assessed, and become facts-in-law for the purpose of judgment. This process is barely handled in orthodox legal studies. But it is here, in defining the reasonable standards which are the yardstick in cross-examination, that many things creep into the law which are not part of its rules. No Barotse law says that an innocent man must appeal against conviction: but, with other circumstances, if he does not, he is held guilty. No law says a councillor must summon and seat people who quarrel: but if he does not, with other facts, he may be convicted of bias. I suggest that an analysis of trials in English courts would show that there too all sorts or presumptions, customs, standards and ideas about how persons of different types should behave, enter into cross-examination and influence the process of litigation. They enter through the definition of the reasonable man, because 'reasonable' is a flexible concept which can cover many different things and ways of behaviour. This is its strength for it enables rules of wide moral validity to be accommodated to quite new situations. The duty of 'reasonable care', formulated in ancient Roman times, can cope with the accidents of the machine-age. In Barotseland, a traveller recorded in 1896 a case involving 'the reasonable councillor'; this character can be re-defined by the judges to meet the conditions of modern life.

2. The Case of the Eloping Wife

Our textbooks of law take as their units of analysis a series of abstract concepts like right and duty, marriage, property, care and negligence, guilt, contract, crime; and they analyse legal rules grouped under these concepts. The anthropologist's units of investigation are social positions—such as husband and wife, owner, thief, councillor, king and so forth. These social positions are linked together by rights which the incumbents of the positions can claim and by duties they should fulfill. The anthropologist studies how rights are claimed and duties fulfilled, and how breaches of their rules are enforced in relation to all the social positions in a community. So that he regards the same facts from a viewpoint which differs from that of the lawyer.

Now every one of these social positions carries with it certain ideals—a councillor is grave and impartial, a king is brave and just, there are the perfect husband and the perfect wife. Human frailty, alas, acting in the vicissitudes of life, is such that few people can live up to the ideals of the positions they occupy. But fortunately the law, both in England and in Barotseland, only demands that we attain these ideals up to a reasonable standard, so that most of us, despite our deserts, escape whipping. Therefore, trials often reduce to the question, was the defendant a reasonable councillor? a reasonable husband? or wife? or father? Even before that stage of the trial is reached, the judges in their cross-examination begin to assess litigants' behaviour against these standards. And because as an anthropologist I am dominantly interested in social positions, I came to concentrate in my study of Barotse law on the problem of the reasonable incumbent of a position, and to pull legal rules together about this problem. I began also to look anew, in these terms, at problems of English jurisprudence.

Every individual occupies several positions in society—as father, workman, citizen, and so forth. In Barotseland, because commercial life is little developed in a small-scale community, people act in all their capacities with the same lot of their fellows. Hence in any trial all of a person's actions, in his several rôles, are considered by the judges in assessing the evidence against him. Let me illustrate this with a trial which I call 'The Case of the Eloping Wife'.

A Barotse woman married a foreign immigrant. They had a quarrel and the wife left home. Shortly afterwards her husband visited a nearby white township where he found his wife living with another man. He reported this to his wife's father, and sued the abductor for damages. The abductor and the woman pleaded in defence first, that the husband had divorced his wife by driving her away, and secondly that when the abductor went to the woman's father, the father demanded 30s. as marriage payment. Therefore, they argued, if the husband had not divorced his wife and he had a case for damages, it lay against the father who had married off his daughter before she'd been divorced from her husband. In the course of their statements the two defendants abused the husband as a foreigner.

It quickly became clear that the husband had a claim for damages against someone, since his wife could not prove that he had sent her away (as a man is entitled to do), nor had she obtained a divorce in court (which a woman must do). But was he to be recompensed for the loss of his wife by her abductor or by her father? The father admitted he had taken 30s. from the abductor, but he said he took the money as a fine for the abduction, and not as a marriage-payment to validate the new marriage.

The court satisfied itself that the father was telling the truth by the following cross-examination. Under questioning by the court, the woman said that after the quarrel she left her husband and stayed for two days in her father's home, from which he was absent, for two days. On the third day she married the defendant. As she put it, 'I thought I would take my husband to court to get a divorce, then this man came to marry me and I saw time was passing, so I married him.' The judges burst into laughter and exclaimed: 'Time was passing, to wait two days!' That is, the judges have an idea of 'reasonable time' which reasonable people ought to take over certain social actions, and this involves that they conform with various customs and rules. Similarly, the abductor was forced to admit that the first night he slept with the woman they were fornicating, because it was only on the next day that he made payment to the woman's father. Again, this was not a reasonable and customary order of actions in time. The father argued that he could not have taken the money as a marriage-payment, since, in his words: 'How can you come to ask for a girl in marriage when you come from the bed on which you have slept with her?'

On this evidence the court had no hesitation in making the abductor pay the damages. The judges argued as follows: No father would accept marriage-payment for his daughter from a man who came to him from a bed shared with his daughter. That is, no reasonable father would do this. But they rebuked the father for taking the 30s. as a fine on abduction, since his daughter was stolen not as an unmarried ward of his, but as a married ward of her husband. The father must return the money to the abductor to give to the husband. Please note that this argument involves a judicial presumption about how fathers—reasonable fathers—behave. Secondly, no good woman, or reasonable woman, would in three days move from one marriage to another. And, as they showed the woman in another piece of cross-examination, no good woman goes by herself to her husband *before* arrangements are made with her father. She should be escorted to the husband's hut by a party of her friends and his. So too no reasonable would-be son-in-law would approach his sweetheart's father to seek her in marriage *after* sleeping with her. The time periods involved here were patently unreasonable: in some cases they involve complex calculations of gestation for women and cows, or the cycle of growing crops. Thirdly, the two defendants were bad citizens, not *reasonable* citizens: they had not waited for a court to adjudicate on the woman's quarrel with her husband, and they had abused the husband because he was a foreigner. On this the senior judge, in a speech which reminded me of Shylock's, said:

About his being a foreigner. All the different tribes—they are all people under our one great king. . . . There is no such thing as a foreigner. We are one thing, with two eyes and two ears, and our children marry them. They feel hunger like us and ask us for land which we give to them.

Over all, in every one of their positions, the defendants had behaved unreasonably: the woman as wife, daughter, woman, and citizen: the man, as son-in-law, husband, and citizen. Hence their stories could be totally discredited. Thus there are implicit in the judges' views of the evidence a series of presumptions: that fathers will not take marriage-payments from seducers of their daughters; that reasonable and good daughters consult their fathers before marriage; that reasonable citizens seek the protection of the court and don't abuse foreign immigrants. These presumptions about how reasonable people behave flow into judgment but are not always formulated. They arise from the judges' views of morality, and of custom, and from their personal experience in society. Nor are all the presumptions rules of law. But they control the vital process of forming judgment on evidence. Some presumptions about witnesses' demeanour influence the value judges attach to the evidence of different people. By these presumptions about 'reasonable behaviour' the judges perform their vital task of assessing circumstantial evidence, which is what produces chanciness in litigation. Now the judges can state any presumption of this kind with the *ex cathedra* authority of a legal rule, since it can be absorbed in the meaning of '*reasonable* behaviour'. I do not mean to suggest that the judgments are entirely subjective, since there is continuous social control of the presumptions, and an accepted logic in the way judges have to expound their decisions: the logic of how reasonable fathers act, with its implied science of psychology, the logic that reasonable women seek divorce in courts, that reasonable women wait a reasonable time before remarrying, that reasonable suitors consult their sweetheart's parents and marry them usually with ceremonies.

But the presumptions can vary, and can be based on mistaken ideas, or rumours, or even personal prejudices. This is not a process confined to African judges. A learned but naïve South African judge is reputed to have once refused to grant a divorce although a detective proved the wife had spent an afternoon in a hotel with a man. The judge stated baldly that he did not believe people had sexual relations in the daylight: hence the alleged lovers would not have committed adultery even if they spent an afternoon in a bedroom.

Similar personal prejudices are exhibited in another Barotse case. A husband returned home from a visit to find his wife absent, and their children crying hungrily, unfed, and not sent back to school. He fed them. When his wife returned home she said she had been hoeing in her garden. This happened again the next day, and the wife made the same excuse. On the third day, when his wife was again late, the husband went to the garden and failed to find his wife. He therefore challenged her excuse and she admitted she had been lying in the bush with the defendant, a young teacher. The teacher denied the charge, and said when the husband sued him that the woman was using him to conceal her true lover. He alleged that she had a grudge against him because he had refused to accept her invitation, conveyed to him by letter, to become her lover. He asked the judges if a woman would thus admit who was her lover, just on her husband's challenge. The first judge accepted this argument on the grounds (which may or may not be true— I don't know) that a girl at her puberty ceremony is taught by the older women to conceal her true lover. This judge had a man's prejudice about women, whom—like all Barotse men—he holds responsible for all sexual lapses; hence this would be for him the behaviour of a reasonable woman— but not an upright woman. But the second judge smashed this argument: 'I've been caught that way myself!' He had committed adultery and been exposed in this way. Hence his personal experience overcame the belief held by men about how women act. Some judges held that the evidence was not strong enough to convict; but most considered that if the teacher was innocent he would, like a reasonable man, have shown the women's letter tempting him to adultery, to her kinsmen, or to her husband immediately the husband returned. He would have done this especially as the woman had a bad reputation. Moreover, while the husband was away, he had sat at her hut and accepted food from her; and since there is a presumption in Barotse- land that unrelated men and women do not have platonic relations, only a lover of the woman would act in this way. Hence, reasonably, he was guilty.

This last case suggests that the Barotse have a picture not only of reason- able and customary right ways of behaving, but also a picture of the reason- able wrongdoer—the reasonable thief, adulterer, slanderer, and so forth. By this paradox,—the reasonable wrongdoer—I sum up the fact that wrong- doers in any society also behave in customary ways which are socially stereo- typed—there are the criminal slouch as against the scholarly stoop, the spiv's clothes and hairstyle, the whole manner of loitering with intent to commit a criminal action. When there is only circumstantial evidence, these sorts of actions build up before the judges till they conclude that, as in the Case of the Eloping Wife, the total picture is that of a reasonable wrongdoer —as we say, a person guilty beyond reasonable doubt. And I have heard cases which indicate that these customary ways of doing wrong in fact influ- ence adulterers and thieves, so that they give themselves away in circum- stances in which they could have acted so as to cover up their misdeeds.

Barotse judges have no police or detectives, no expertise of fingerprinting, no lawyers, to help them in collecting and sifting evidence. Therefore they have to depend almost entirely on their cross-examination of evidence to arrive at the truth. And for these reasons they must rely on testing the credibility of a story told by any person against the flexible standards of reasonable behaviour for the incumbent of the social position involved. This is largely true of our own courts, though our lawyers and not our judges conduct the cross-examination. But this point is not always appreciated in the academic view of law. Nor do all lawyers see how these flexible standards enable the raw facts of a case to be fitted into the fixed and abstract rules of law. When I once lectured on this theme to an audience of Scottish lawyers, one of them protested on behalf of the poor Barotse that they should be so subjected to the control of the vague, ill-defined, litigation- breeding reasonable man. He asked if a code of the reasonable man could not be promulgated each year to protect them. This view fails to see the value of the concept. Many rules of law in Barotseland are necessarily general principles such as, 'a councillor must not be partial', or 'a husband must care well for his wife'. Beyond these are more general principles like, anyone who injures another shall make recompense. This principle exists in all systems of law. But in litigation these general rules have to cover a great variety of actual situations in life. They can only do so if the general moral ideas involved can be brought to bear on the particularities of a perhaps unique situation. This is the function of reasonable standards, and, despite aberrations of particular judges as in the cases of adultery I have just narrated, the standards are defined by the objective tests of traditional and developing customs and morals. For these general rules of law last through the life of a society despite great social changes. The development of 'reason-ableness' for such positions as the reasonable husband, the reasonable wife, the reasonable landlord and tenant and king and subject, enables the law to cope with all changes. Without this the law would ossify.

This is well illustrated by a Barotse divorce suit—'The Case of the Prudish Wife'. Here the wife sued for divorce on several grounds. First she complained that when she was ill her husband did not treat her at his home, as required by law, but took her to her parents. The husband replied that he obtained to treat her a medicine which had to be inserted in cuts on her body; but he could not give her the medicine himself as she would not let him see her naked (astonishment in court). Then drums had to be beaten for her treatment and this could not be done in his village which was inhabited by converts to Jehovah's Witnesses who do not allow drumming. So he took her to her mother. The judges held that in the circumstances of the wife's unique prudery, and in the new situation created by the coming of the Jehovah's Witnesses Christian sect, a reasonable husband could only take her to her mother. She claimed divorce secondly because her husband before going to work at a distant place took from her some blankets, which he then used with a new wife—thus breaking the law which forbids a Barotse to confuse his relations with two wives. The court found that her husband had given her eight blankets (a new form of goods), that this was wealth by the standards of Barotse poverty, and that he could therefore *reasonably* take back two blankets for himself on a new type of journey—and then use them with a new wife. He was a reasonable husband and her plea for divorce was rejected. Thus in fact many cases are decisions about whether a person has been a reasonable husband, or other incumbent of a particular social position.

In this way Barotse judges are constantly re-defining the scope of 'reason-able' standards for spouses, kinsfolk, lords and underlings, so as to handle new conditions of life. Judicial decision supplements legislation. Through the 'reasonable standards' they maintain their traditional laws and traditional morals, and yet cope with the effects of the introduction of Christianity and schools, labour for whites and money and trade-goods, new skills, changes in every aspect of Barotse life. Hence it seems to me that it is in the study of the reasonable man, in every society, that anthropologists and lawyers can meet. In him social principles and prejudices, customs and habits, group interests and individual experiences, are absorbed, to relate the fixed rules of law to the changing variety of life. But the law aims at justice, and the idea of a reasonable man implies an upright man. I shall next describe what the Barotse think about the upright man.

3. The Case of the 'Dog-in-the-Manger' Headman

Generally, Barotse law demands from people only reasonable exercise of rights, and correspondingly only reasonable fulfilment of duties. This is all the judges will enforce. But in practice Barotse judges tend to erect higher standards—those of the upright man, or woman—the upright husband, wife, lord or underling. In this way they bring into the trial the ultimate standards of Barotse ethics, which lie beyond those of the law. The law demands right and reasonable action: morality asks for right and generous action. A man should not insist on the letter of his rights, and he should be prodigal in meeting his obligations.

This does not mean that the judges can enforce these very high ethical standards, but only that they set upright behaviour as the goal of all good men and women. They can only *order* men to meet the demands of the law. For example, under Barotse law a man can divorce his wife by sending her home to her parents. If he does this, the court will compel him to give her half of the crops she planted in his land, and also half of the goods in their house—dresses, pots, blankets and so forth. A woman must sue in court for a divorce and has to establish that her husband has not been a reasonable husband. If she gets her divorce, she obtains half the crops grown by *her* labour, but on *his* land. However, as she rejects the marriage, she also rejects all the goods which his earnings have bought for her own needs and for her domestic tasks. I once heard a case tried in which the woman thus established her claim to be divorced. Listen to the senior judge's decision: 'The woman is freed, and she will take home with her half of the crops which she planted. There has been so much ill-feeling in this case that we will send a judge to see that it is fairly done'. Turning to the husband he went on: 'Now what else, my kinsman, will you give her of the goods of the marriage to take with her?'

The husband objected: 'I will give her nothing; she has infected me with disease, and bound me here with lies'. The judge admonished him:

> Come, my kinsman, you cannot do this. When you married her, taking her from her parents, you all rejoiced together. You hoped that you would have a strong marriage, with children to bind you together. It has not worked out thus, but you cannot send a woman home to her parents, naked like a dog. We beg you, give her a blanket and a dress and some plates.

But the husband persisted in his meanness: 'I will give her nothing, not even a shawl.'

The judge had to resign himself to this: 'Very well; we have power to make you divide the crops, and we will send someone to see this is done. But we have not power to make you behave like an upright man. Go.'

Later that day the husband craved permission to speak again to the court. He said he had been reflecting on the judge's words, and saw that he was wrong. He would give his wife a dress, a shawl, a blanket, a hoe, a pot and a plate.

The judge approved: 'We thank you, my child. This is behaving like a decent upright man.' And he called on the other judges to salute this generosity.

This case shows that the law limits the extent to which judges can enforce morality. Judges on occasion, in Barotseland as in England, cannot enforce upright behaviour, and may even have to find for the person who has behaved wrongfully by moral standards, but who is supported by the law. The judges find for the wrongdoer in the interests of certainty of law: our maxim states, 'Hard cases make bad law.' The Barotse say, 'It is hard, but it is the law.' Sometimes an English judge feels compelled to say something after this form to a wrongful litigant: 'Fortunately for you this is a court of law, and not a court of justice or morals.' And he then proceeds to upbraid in round terms the litigant who is successful in law but morally in the wrong. Conversely, a judge may openly state his reluctance to convict a person who is legally a wrongdoer, but morally justified. I do not believe that these situations arise because a court is only a forum of law, and not a source of justice and morality. I myself consider that these situations demonstrate that courts of law are in fact courts of morality: for the judge uses his high office publicly to state what morality demands and to upbraid the person who has departed from it and kept within the law, or to justify the person who is trapped by a technical law or driven by altruistic motives to commit an offence. This is certainly the way in which Barotse regard their judges and their courts.

Let me quote another divorce case to emphasize the point. The Barotse believe that it is natural to help one's blood relatives, and that the true test of the upright man is how he behaves to his relatives-in-law. In this case the wife made various allegations about her husband's neglect of herself and her relatives, but the court accepted his evidence, backed by her own parents, that he had behaved more than punctiliously. The senior judge rejected the plea for divorce thus:

> You, woman, have astonished us by your suit. You thought you would shame your husband before the country, which we represent. But you have instead brought honour to him, for we have never heard of so good a son-in-law. Your father told us the overcoat he wears is a present from your husband; see how your husband sits himself in a ragged jacket. He is not a rich man, but when he brought an overcoat for his father, he brought one for your father; when he brought a dress for his mother, he brought one for your mother. He gave shawls to your unmarried sisters, and he built granaries for them and moved their crops on the flood, not in the dugout of your village, but in his own dugout. And so forth. You have not disgraced your husband here before the judges of the land, but you have brought fame to him, for none of us is as good a son-in-law as he.

You, my son, we admire what you have done, and we thank you. Do not cease to behave thus because your wife has brought you to court; continue to look after your relatives-in-law as you have done in the past. We thank you.

He then instructed his fellow-judges, and all in court, to join him in saluting the husband.

I mention these two cases because they show the judges upholding, to a mean husband and to a generous husband, the ideal of the man who is upright beyond the demands of reasonable standards. Their standards are similar in cases of property-holding and of contract, but to describe these would involve me in the intricacies of the Barotse environmental situation. Marital relations are familiar to us from our own life—they are the same the whole world over. But these cases did not catch the judges between the law and morality. Here is a case—'The Case of the Dog-in-the-Manger Headman'—which did this. It led to divergent judgments.

The Barotse dwell in higher pieces of land in the great Zambezi flood-plain which is their habitat. From these islands—as they are during the flood—the Barotse cultivate pockets of alluvial soil and use sites for fish-traps. I was told again and again that in Barotse law a man has to dwell in a village if he wishes to work any of the resources which belong to the village. If he leaves the village, he loses his rights in its land. This land is vested in the title of the village-headman.

A certain village-headman, named Mahalihali, was very quarrelsome, and his bad temper drove many people out of the village. He personally expelled one of his daughters whom he accused of sorcery. Eventually he died and his son inherited his position, and took his title as Mahalihali the Second. He found himself with a village, but few villagers. His nephew, son of the sister expelled from the village, was using some of its trap-sites in a fish-dam, but was living with his widowed mother in her mother's village. Another sister of the new headman had married into a nearby village and her sons were using a fish-dam which her father had let her have. The new headman brought a suit that his sisters and their sons must stop using the fish-dams unless they moved into his village. The judges satisfied themselves that the one sister, accused of sorcery, had been badly wronged when she was driven out of the village. Since then she and her son, and the married sister married nearby and her sons—that is, all the defendants—had behaved with proper respect to the headman. Hence arose the judges' dilemma. The law, I repeat, is clear: if you do not live in my village, you lose your rights in its land. By this rule the headman was upheld in his claim that the others join his village or cease to use its fish-dams. But the defendants had not done him any wrong, and the headman was behaving unjustly—like the dog-in-the-manger in our fable. How did the judges solve this dilemma.

In Barotse courts when the judges come to give their decision, the most junior judge speaks first, and then his seniors in turn, until the head of the court gives judgment. This is the binding decision, even if it contradicts the verdicts of all other judges, though it is referred to the king in his palace for confirmation. Well, the first three judges felt themselves bound by the basic premiss of their land-tenure law: the dog-in-the-manger headman was entitled to expel his sisters and their sons from the dams unless they moved into his village. *But* they all stressed that he ought not to treat his relatives in this niggardly way since there was more land than his villagers could use; being rich, he ought to help his relatives. Nevertheless, the dams were his. The next set of judges were reluctant to apply the letter of the law in favour of the dog-in-the-manger headman, against people who, in their words, had 'done nothing wrong'. Many judges told the headman, 'If they had done wrong, you would have a case.' Most judges therefore contented themselves with stating the moral issue, that he ought to let his relatives fish. One said the fish-dams had passed out of his control, though this was upsetting the basic law of Barotse land-holding. But the senior judge sitting in court returned to this basic law: the dams were the headman Mahalihali's. But, the judge added, he ought to let his kin fish them. As it happens, the head of the court was busy on administrative business elsewhere. Next day he came to deliver his decision on the basis of reports of evidence and judg-ments made to him by other judges. He found the headman still insisting on his rights to take the dams unless the others moved to join him, as laid down in the last decision. So the head of the court found a brilliant solution to the judicial dilemma. The dams clearly belonged to the title Mahalihali; but if the present incumbent of that title was not upright—generous to his kin who did not live with him—the court would discharge him from his headmanship and appoint a more generous successor.

What happened here was that the judge achieved a just and equitable solution by stressing a new kind of sanction. He invoked the administrative powers of the court to discharge unsatisfactory headmen, in order to compel a headman to be generous in exercising his rights. In this way, the judge enforced the standards of the upright headman in favour of the defendants who had done no wrong, while he maintained the basic law of land tenure. For the fish-dams remained vested in the headman's title.

This case shows strikingly that Barotse courts are dominated by ideas of justice and equity. These ideas influence their total evaluation of evidence; and on occasion spur them to apply particular equities, as against the dog-in-the-manger headman. The Barotse believe that justice in this sense is self-evident to all men, and they call their principles within this justice, laws of God, or laws of humankind. That is, the Barotse have a clear idea of natural justice, which they constantly apply. They apply natural justice, of course, within particular economic and social conditions: for they have set ideas on the relations of men and women, lords and underlings, and so forth. But it is natural justice. And natural justice involves for them, as for us, certain ultimate principles of law, as that a man who injures another shall make recompense; no man should be judge in his own suit; a judge should not come to a decision before hearing both sides; a man should be generous and not mean. These and other moral rules they share with us; and the rules are axiomatic, they cannot be demonstrated. An example of such a rule is equivalent to the Roman Law maxim, *volenti non fit injuria*: a man who willingly exposes himself to injury, cannot sue for damages if he is then injured. The Barotse maxim is, 'If you are invited to a meal and a fish-bone sticks in your throat, you cannot sue your host.' Under this rule (which they say is patently fair), they will not allow damages to a man who is injured in a fishing-party when men enter a pool at the dry season, and blindly hurl bundles of spears to get catfish buried in the mud. Nor will they allow damages to a man injured on a hunt. Nor did they allow damages to a woman who became pregnant, or contracted venereal disease, in illicit inter-course—though they have now, by statute, imposed penalties on the man who infects a woman thus.

These general moral rules, and a host of particular rules defining Barotse personal relations, property-holding, contracts, and so forth, constitute the total body of Barotse law. Besides moral rules, the body of law embraces customary ways and relations, statutes of their king and of the British Government, judicial precedents. Their law includes the ordered regularities of the environment, of organic life, and of human psychology—what we call scientific laws. The judges draw on all these sources to make their decisions. But the different rules of this body of law are not entirely depend-ent on one another. And the judges therefore can achieve justice by apply-ing different rules in different situations, according to how they see the moral deserts of the parties. In contrast to the case of the dog-in-the-manger headman, I heard several cases in which the judges insisted on the rule that if a man leaves a village, he loses his rights to land in it; but these were cases where the underlings were in the wrong. Where it was the dog-in-the-manger headman who was in the wrong, the judges did not want to support him. Some judges felt compelled to do so, against their view of the moral merits of the case, in order to meet the demand for certainty of law. Others tried to vary the law to meet those moral merits. The final decision seized on a different rule—the power of the court to discharge unsatisfactory head-men—to achieve justice, while maintaining the law of land-tenure itself.

This decision illustrates one important way in which judicial discretion can operate in the interests of justice. The body of Barotse law consists of a large number of different kinds of rules. These rules may be consistent with one another, but they do not depend on one another. There is no essential logical interdependence between the rule that a man loses his rights in land belonging to a village if he leaves the village, and the rule that the court can discharge an unsatisfactory headman. The judges can often, as in this case, decide to apply one rule rather than another, out of the whole body of law, to achieve justice. In doing so, they—so to speak—*manipulate* the inde-pendence of the rules. This gives great scope to intelligent judicial discretion.

But the judges' main power to manipulate legal rules during a trial arises from the nature of the words which compose the rules. A law such as that if a man leaves a village he loses his rights in its land is a general statement; in particular disputes the judges have to apply it to very different circum-stances. Do these actions amount to 'leaving' the village? In the case of the dog-in-the-manger headman, for instance, one woman did not 'leave' the village; on the contrary, she was driven out of it. If a simple word like 'leaves' requires this kind of interpretation the problem becomes more complex and uncertain with the abstract ideas of law. But there is an inherent uncertainty of this kind in all legal words, which enables them to cover a great variety of actual events. And application of these uncertain concepts to actual events is the major part of the judges' task. In the case I have been describing, what is an 'unsatisfactory' headman? He is, by prevailing standards, not a 'reasonable' headman. We are back with the 'reasonable' man; and I have already shown that this valuable uncertainty is a prime characteristic of 'the reasonable man'.

4. The Case of the Unfaithful Councillor

The divorce rate in Barotseland is very high. Men can divorce their wives simply by sending them home; women have to go to a Barotse court and establish a case for their release from marriage. They can do so successfully on many grounds. In fact a woman has only to show that her husband has not behaved as a reasonable husband to her in order to obtain a divorce.

What then, for the Barotse, is a reasonable husband? He is one who cares properly for his wife, sleeps with her adequately so that she has children, does not discriminate between her and his other wives, and does not drive her out of his home. These are old rules of Barotse law which date from the days before the British protectorate was established. And Barotse life has altered considerably since those day. Women who previously wore one skin-skirt and had a skin-rug, now want dresses, petticoats, shawls and blankets. They need kerosene lamps, iron pots, plates and cups and cutlery, and many other of the goods of our civilization. Some men can earn the money to purchase these things by selling fish, cattle or crops; but most Barotse men have to go out for long periods to earn wages at distant European settlements. And it is therefore in a radically different situation that Barotse judges now apply their ancient rules about the duties of husbands and the rights of wives. The judges have continually to decide what amount of goods a husband must nowadays give his wife if he is to be a reasonable husband. To do this they interpret what is the meaning of 'care for a wife' by reasonable modern standards.

One element in the modern situation produces a radical conflict to prevent a husband fulfilling two of his conjugal duties. He has to buy European goods for his wife, and to do this he must go away to work: then he cannot sleep with her and be a companion to her. The Barotse have therefore by legislation fixed a maximum period for which a husband can be away. If a husband is away for longer than this period his wife is entitled to a divorce. And while he is away, he must send goods or money to her. These statutes aim to bring the nation's men home and to maintain contented marriages. But a difficult legal problem arose even out of the apparently simple judicial task of deciding whether a husband has been absent for the set period. A woman brought suit for divorce on grounds that her husband had been away for longer than the period allowed: his kinsmen opposed the suit, pleading that he had sent her money, blankets, and so forth. The court held, 'This woman did not marry a blanket', and granted the divorce. Within a few days the husband arrived: he had been on the journey home when the divorce was granted. His wife wished to return to him, but her father demanded a new marriage-payment for what, under the court's decision for divorce, was a new marriage. The court held that had it known the husband was on his way home, it would not have granted a divorce. The court thus interpreted 'return home' to mean 'leave place of employment', because the purpose of the statute is to maintain marriages. The judges thus upheld what they believed to be good morals and public policy.

This case seems simple enough, but it illustrates a crucial task which Barotse judges have to perform if they are to help their people adjust to the new situation in which they are living. The judges have constantly to reinterpret their definitions of what are reasonable husbands and wives, reasonable councillors and headmen, and so forth. This process of defining how a reasonable incumbent of some social position should behave, lies at the core of the way in which judges nowadays define what is reasonable companionship of husband and wife, in terms of modern conditions. These new conditions and the standards they contain according to modern public opinion, are brought into the law through the elasticity of the concept 'reasonableness'. And meanwhile the basic law remains unchanged from the very different past—a husband must be a reasonable husband.

Here is a case in a different kind of relationship to illustrate the elasticity of legal concepts, and to show how this elasticity enables the law to cope with new sitautions. I call it 'The Case of the Unfaithful Councillor'. Some villages in the Barotse plain on the Upper Zambezi belong to members of the royal family. These princes and princesses may not actually reside in their villages, which they leave in charge of a headman. Under Barotse law a man holds land first by being a citizen; and he is entitled to keep that land as long as he is a faithful subject of the king. Secondly, he must be a member of a village, and he must be a faithful underling of the owner of the village, respectful and helpful. In 1945 a certain princess had as headman of one of her villages a councillor holding the title Indiye. She sued to have him dismissed from the title, and from its rights in village and land, on the grounds that he did not work for her. He pleaded in defence that he worked as overseer of a barge carrying goods down the 300 miles of the Zambezi from Barotseland to Livingstone. He had no time to work for her or attend on her. The court held that this plea indeed absolved him, since men nowadays earn their living by working for Europeans, and not for their Barotse overlords. But he did not go to say farewell to the princess before he started on a journey, or to greet her when he returned. This he could easily do. Hence, he did not respect the princess, and was not faithful to her, and so he merited dismissal from her village. The court thus defined 'faithful'—and incidentally a reasonably faithful councillor—to accommodate modern conditions. But the law remains that a man must be faithful to his overlord.

These judicial problems are common to all countries. Judges have to apply certain well-known rules to the great variety of circumstances which occur in social life, and which may well be changing, as they are in modern Barotseland. Judges must maintain the law, in the sense of abiding by its rules, and yet they must serve justice in every case if possible. I am suggesting that they do so by manipulating the uncertainty which resides in all words when these are applied to the facts of life. Is this 'two years' absence? Is this 'caring for a wife'? Is this 'fidelity to an overlord'? The judges make these definitions in terms of 'reasonableness' for a particular kind of reasonable man—husband or councillor or citizen or son. And because 'reasonableness' itself is flexible, they can adapt a persisting body of legal rules to quite new conditions and standards. Therefore the law remains certain, since Barotse judges state their decisions in terms of old well-established rules. But my examples show that judicial decisions, and hence litigation, are often uncertain.

So that when judges are interpreting words by applying them to external facts, they do so by the flexible test of 'reasonableness'. This allows them great play, and it means that they can introduce into their decisions a whole variety of social presumptions, and indeed of prejudices personal to them, or peculiar to the group they represent. But on the whole the standard of 'reasonableness' is drawn from the Barotse community as a whole—Barotse public opinion, and customs, and standards. And all these change as Barotse life changes, and the law develops to accommodate new facts. In short, changing Barotse life itself controls the way in which Barotse judges reinterpret legal concepts.

Barotse judges have had to reinterpret sharply the implications of many of their legal concepts to meet this abruptly changed situation. Hence we can see clearly in their judicial process a problem which is present in our own. Let me illustrate this. Section 154 of our Public Health Act of 1936 lays down that a rag-and-bone merchant shall not give children under 14 'any article whatsoever'. In 1952 a rag-and-bone merchant gave a child a goldfish, and a stipendiary magistrate held that the goldfish was not 'an article' in the meaning of this section. About a year later a bench of justice held that a live chick was an article for purposes of the statute, and another bench held again that a goldfish was *not* an article. This last case went on appeal to a court of three judges who dismissed the appeal and upheld the view that a goldfish is not an article—though it was said that if the goldfish were in a bowl, that bowl would be an article. The word 'article' was here being defined for purposes of a statute which aimed to prevent the spread of disease: under another statute, 'article' might cover goldfish; and the court followed the rule that where a penalty is imposed, it applies the narrow interpretation in favour of the accused. As the judges put it, 'Would anyone in common parlance talk about a goldfish as an article? I do not think they would. . . . I think that it is a straining of language to say a goldfish is an article.'

I do not believe there is any way in which we can establish by objective evidence, so to speak, that a chicken or a goldfish is or is not an article. But I have already said that the process of decision is not entirely subjective. In English law the process is controlled by written rules, judicial precedents, and textbooks of law. But something else is left—the question which is so often framed, 'Would a reasonable man call a goldfish an article?' This passes the uncertainty to, what is a reasonable man? And here I have suggested that defining the reasonable man—which is indirectly defining an 'article'—may give room for judges to introduce not only social ideas, but also individual prejudices, into their decisions. I take the goldfish case as an entirely hypothetical example—I feel safer that way. I can imagine a judge who feels that there is too much statutory interference in our lives interpreting the word 'article' as narrowly as possible; while a judge who favours benevolent government control would interpret it widely. This is a possibility only; and I use it just to illustrate that the uncertainty which resides in all words, allows judges to manipulate the words in the interests of what they believe to be justice. In doing so, they accommodate into their decisions changes in public opinion and in morals.

It is obvious that this flexibility of words is a great source of strength in judicial logic. Without it, judges could not apply the general rules of law to actual disputes. Despite this, many academic lawyers have attacked it as a source of uncertainty in law, and have therefore regarded it as a weakness. Even judges have done so. But judges are more aware of the value of this characteristic of words. This is clearly exhibited in the words of Lord Chief Justice Coleridge: 'The Attorney-General has asked us where we are to draw the line. The answer is that it is not necessary to draw it at any precise point. It is enough for us to say that the present case is on the right side of any reasonable line that could be drawn.' This judicial statement seems to me to sum up admirably the judicial value of uncertainty in reference of legal terms. Every case is in a sense unique. How is a unique case to be settled? It may have to be covered by legal rules which are stated in very abstract terms, such as that any man who injures another shall make recompense. Even if the rule contains as specific a term as 'article', some judicial decision on the application of the terms to the facts of the situation must be made. What test can there be except that of 'reasonableness'?

But "reasonableness" itself has a great deal of uncertainty. The line may be drawn differently by different judges. More importantly, it will be drawn differently by judges in new centuries, in accordance with new standards and problems and with advancing knowledge. There may be aberrant decisions: most societies have foolish, ignorant, and perhaps even unjust, judges. But generally the judges will be influenced by changing public opinion in their community, or at least that section of the community from which they are drawn.

Imprecision is thus an inherent attribute of legal concepts. Yet a few years ago a Professor of Jurisprudence complained that, 'Philosophy stands out as a striking example of the flatulencies that may gather round the unacknowledged puns of language. On the whole, lawyers have appreciated the danger, and have been at pains to construct and preserve a moderately precise technical language. Oddly enough, it is least precise in its most fundamental parts. We use the word "right" in some half-dozen different senses and often pass insensibly from one to the other, of course with disastrous results upon our reasoning.' Thus the jurist. As an anthropologist I would suggest that the results may have been disastrous for the reasoning of formal logic; but they may well have resulted, in judicial logic, in a number of very just decisions. Judicial logic has rules of its own: by formal logic alone a judge could not fit the raw facts of evidence into legal categories. Nor could he get justice. For example, this word 'right' that has some half-dozen meanings. I heard Barotse judges in many cases listen to evidence on a whole series of actions by the litigants: then come to the conclusion that, say, defendant had done 'right'. From this they made a jump to saying he was in the 'right', therefore that he had 'a right' to the piece of land in dispute. Then they manipulated the rules of law to defend that right. Here are three different meanings of 'right'—Barotse also have one word for all three, and this word also means 'duty'. So they can make a 'right' into a 'duty'. It is, formally, bad logic: but it may be brilliant judicial logic.

I think myself that it is not at all odd that lawyers' language should be least precise in its most fundamental parts—terms like law, right and duty, crime and injury, property, and so forth. For clearly these are the words which have to serve the most manifold functions in a legal system. They have to cover the greatest number of types of legal situations, and within each type, the greatest variety of actual situations. Hence I would expect them to have the greatest imprecision; and therefore to be capable of the greatest judicial manipulation.

Since Barotse law is unwritten I was made vividly aware of how important is this judicial manipulation. It convinced me that while it is obviously necessary for jurists to dispute this manipulation, they might also accept imprecision as an attribute—and clearly a valuable attribute—of legal concepts. Once one makes this acceptance, one can begin to study how and why judges operate the imprecision of their verbal apparatus. And there are different kinds of imprecision. The Barotse word *swanelo* covers 'right' and 'duty', and as a 'right' or 'duty' it refers to many different kinds of actions and claims. Most fundamental concepts—like 'law' and 'injury' and 'property'—have this kind of imprecision. Other concepts are elastic in that they can be stretched to cover different kinds of action—and frequently they form pairs which can only be defined in terms of one another, such as 'guilt' and 'innocence', or 'negligence' and 'due care'. They form two poles at each end of an elastic line along which litigants' behaviour can be measured. But it is a reasonably elastic line. Barotse judges listen to the evidence, stretch the elastic concepts to decide which man is 'guilty' and which is 'innocent', and then cover these decisions by applying to them the concepts of right and duty which can refer to many things.

In doing this the judges have to make words like 'guilt', or 'negligence', or 'right', cover a great variety of facts. Therefore I call the concepts 'absorbent', for they absorb into their abstract categories the raw material of life. And they have another important attribute. A survey of the law of all societies shows that they have the same fundamental conceptions—law itself, right, duty, property, guilt, innocence—and, in addition, these conceptions are built into similar principles. But they operate in quite different social conditions. Therefore I call them 'permeable'—they are permeated by their social background. A husband must everywhere be reasonable: but the demands on a reasonable husband vary from country to country and at different periods in the same country.

Acceptance of this inherent imprecision of words immediately disposes of certain long-standing controversies in jurisprudence. What is 'law'? Many volumes have been written proffering various definitions. But 'law', which has to cover every kind of regularity in social and physical and organic life, the whole process of social control, and so forth, cannot be restricted within a single definition. The *Concise Oxford Dictionary* gives thirteen definitions: obviously then for every definition advanced by one scholar, another definition can be advanced by another scholar. This breeds only fruitless controversy. The Barotse word *mulao,* which can be translated—reasonably translated—as 'law', means a body of rules accepted by the community as binding, a particular decision of a court, the existence of courts, a personal habit, the regularities of the natural world and of human physiology and psychology and so forth. It is all regularity and order, and all control. Hence it has to be accepted as having many definitions.

At the moment, in particular, controversy rages between orthodox jurists who hold that law is certain, and a so-called sceptical or realist school of American lawyers, who hold that law is uncertain. If we examine their arguments, it is obvious that they are talking about law in two different kinds of senses. Those who insist on law's certainty are examining law in the sense of a body of rules, which judges use and in terms of which they state their decisions. The sceptical lawyers who consider the certainty of law to be a myth are speaking of judges' decisions, and guesses as to future probable decisions. Only those who know nothing of litigation can doubt that law in this sense is uncertain and chancy. But law in this sense—going to law—is litigation. And it results in adjudication. Law in the orthodox sense is a known code of moral principles and legal rules many of which have endured for centuries and are known in most countires—in Ancient Rome, in France and England, and in Barotseland. The body of rules is fairly certain; judges' decisions, in terms of those rules, on various disputes may be uncertain. But the decisions are given in those rules. They can be given thus because the rules are composed of flexible concepts which can be permeated by changing social presumptions and which can absorb the variety of life itself. The 'certainty' of law depends on the 'uncertainty' of its basic concepts. I have punned on the word 'certainty': but I hope this does not negate the value of my paradox.

Paul Fejos

MAGIC, WITCHCRAFT, AND MEDICAL THEORY IN PRIMITIVE CULTURES

The anthropological study of medicine has been impeded in part by the fact that not enough anthropologists have competence in medicine and not enough medical missionaries have training in anthropology. One notable exception was Paul Fejos, who was a physician and an anthropologist. In this clearly written exposi-

Reprinted from Iago Gladstone, ed., *Man's Image in Medicine and Anthropology* (New York, 1963), pp. 43–61, by permission of the New York Academy of Medicine, International Universities Press, Inc., and Lita Fejos Osmundsen, widow of the author.

tory essay, Dr. Fejos discusses some of the central issues and concepts in medical anthropology and he draws upon his own fieldwork experiences to illustrate some of them.

For further discussion of medical anthropology, the reader should consult the various writings of Edwin H. Ackerknecht, who is one of the leading authorities on primitive medicine. Some of his works are: "Problems of Primitive Medicine," *Bulletin of the History of Medicine,* **11** (1942), 503–21; "Psychopathology, Primitive Medicine and Primitive Culture," *Bulletin of the History of Medicine,* **14** (1943), 30–67; "Natural Diseases and Rational Treatment in Primitive Medicine," *Bulletin of the History of Medicine,* **19** (1946), 467–97; and "Primitive Surgery," *American Anthropologist,* **49** (1947), 25–45.

Today, our culture in Western society is incredibly complex. Compared to non-literate, primitive cultures, our socially transmissible body of knowledge, particularly in the field of natural science, is staggering to the imagination. It also shows, by contrast, the kind of culture man has had for perhaps a million years. Some people call that the period of man's "animal-like" existence. I believe this to be a misnomer, because our ancestors—let's say in Europe's paleontological period—had brains as good as our own; they differed very much from animals through their possession of *Culture*. Thereby, they knew and were conscious of the precariousness of life and the inescapable fact of death. They knew the worst of all constants, that all living organisms are sentenced to death when they are born. This must have made man's life bitterly harsh—a life constantly charged with the fear of disease and death.

Thus primitive man, ever since the earliest period of history, when face to face with bodily pain or mental anguish, or in danger of losing his life, must have sought salvation from some power *outside* of himself.

This brings us to the word I propose to define in its anthropological sense: *magic*. Contrary to its general use, the word magic does not denote trickery, prestidigitation or pulling a white rabbit out of a hat. Webster's dictionary defines magic as

The art, or body of arts, which claims or is believed to be able to compel a deity or supernatural power to do or refrain from doing some act or to change temporarily the order of natural events, or which claims or is believed to produce effects by the assistance of supernatural beings, as angels, demons, or departed spirits, or by a mastery of secret forces in nature. Magic is not clearly differentiated from science by primitive peoples. It is a part of most primitive religions. With the rise of Christianity to power many magical practices were banned; the Church condemned resort to spirits and demons for knowledge or assistance (as in witchcraft, sorcery, diabolism) not as false, but as evil or *black magic.* Magic which aims to produce death or injury is also called *black magic.* On *white or natural magic* no ban was placed, and largely from this, which also survives in legerdemain, was developed modern natural science....[1]

Magic means all the formulas for doing things which are beyond one's personal powers. It is not, however, a complicated proposition like nuclear chemistry. It makes use of fairly simple things: *medicines,* which are the proper things to use, and *spells,* which are the proper things to say. Magic is world-wide. It is the property of *all* the genus *Homo.* It is a fallacy to believe that magic exists only for the primitive. It exists for us as it existed for our ancestors; I hope to illustrate and prove this contention a bit later.

In Western society, magic is quite disreputable, but it has no bad reputation among primitive peoples. It is not a superstition or stupid belief for them, but is considered simply the right way of doing something. It is hardly possible for a primitive to define magic at all, or to see it as something by itself. For Westerners, this is possible, because we have developed the concept of science.

Curiously enough, there is a similarity between magic and science, in that people use science and magic to reach the same goals. However, their basic philosophical assumptions are different. Science accepts no compromises, contradictions, or beliefs. Science wants to know *if* a thing or method will work, and *why*. Magic also wants to know whether a thing or method will work, and is also much interested in the why; but it is willing to *believe* why, and does not look for physical reasons or causes. Its causes, therefore, are based upon faith and the supernatural.

Black magic is the most well-known. Fear of black magic may be responsible for this. Black magic is the evil magic, the one used to kill, maim or render people impotent or sterile. *White* magic, on the other hand, always combats black magic, counteracts it, defends against it and neutralizes it. Among primitive people much more white magic is performed than black.

Magical practices can somewhat arbitrarily be classified into four types: (1) *sympathetic magic,*[2] which is based upon the principle that like effects produce like results, or that a desired result may be brought to pass by mimicking it, or naming it in spells, etc., and on the belief that things once in contact continue to act upon each other after being separated; (2) *divination,* which includes the various means of gaining hidden knowledge, such as augury, clairvoyance, necromancy and astrology; (3) *thaumaturgy,* or wonder-working, which includes alchemy and trickery ascribed to demons; and (4) *incantation,* the recital of magical formulas, pronouncement of a word or words of magical power or the performance of a magical ritual procedure.

Black magic is universally feared, not only in primitive societies but in

[1]*Webster's New International Dictionary* (unabridged, 2nd ed.). Springfield, Massachusetts: Merriam, 1943.
[2][Under "sympathetic magic" Dr. Fejos includes both of Frazer's principles: homeopathic magic and contagious magic. For further explanation of these principles with numerous illustrations, see Frazer's "The Roots of Magic," in this volume.—*Ed. Note.*]

our own Western societies. Knocking on wood, not walking under a ladder, not seating thirteen at the dinner table—all such practices, which we call *superstitions,* are magic.

Magic is honest; that is to say, those who practice it believe in it. It is fully and unquestionably valid for them. Here lies, I believe, the basic obstacle to the average Westerner seeing magic in its proper sense. For a Westerner, to knock on wood is a superstition, but to see a vaudeville performer saw a woman in half is magic! The opposite is the truth! For in sawing a woman in half, the magician knowingly, and with intent, practices deception; he *tricks* his audience. The intentions of primitive magic, on the other hand, are never deception or trickery, but, rather, are based upon fully honest, dogmatic belief and faith.

Protective, white magic is used to insure us against black magic.[3] The origins of many—but not all—of these practices go back into the early history of man. White magic is frequently born in modern societies; for instance, the belief that it is bad luck for three men to light their cigarettes from the same match, which arose during World War I, for magically logical reasons.

Possibly, the ingroup-outgroup behavior pattern has its origin in the fear of black magic. Black magic, as a rule, can be practiced only extra-clanwise, the shaman of a clan usually being able to provide only white—protective—magic within his own group. His ability to do bad, black magic, is a potential only toward the outgroup. Much of this belief still exists in our present-day society.

How is black magic practiced? The methods are astronomical in number. Libraries have been written about it. Basically, the method seems to be to do things the "wrong" way, that is to speak backwards, in the wrong order, the "bad" way, at the wrong time, with bad or malicious intent, and for evil purpose. For example, in medieval times, the ill-famed "Black" Mass was a mass said backwards. It was said at night, and the consecrated host was black, not white. It was not round, but angular, with three or seven points. It was not wine, but water, which the priest used for transubstantiation, and the water had to have had a bad history, such as water taken from a polluted well into which a newborn, unbaptized, infant had been thrown to drown.

In most primitive societies, anything connected with the person against whom black magic is to be practiced can be used to make an effigy. This is the so-called "image" magic. Nail cuttings, hair, spittle or menstrual blood of a person are the best materials, but even belongings, such as wearing apparel, bedding, tools or weapons can be used. One method of using them is for the sorcerer to fashion a figure representing the victim, using his saliva, mixed with clay. If a lock of the victim's hair is available, it is attached to the figurine's head, if nail parings, they are attached to its hand, and so on. Once the figure is finished, pins or thorns are stuck into it, periodically. This process is accompanied by incantations of a definite traditional form. The incantations may be partly mumbo-jumbo, but will usually contain words denoting the intent of the sorcerer. As the pins or thorns are stuck into the

[3][For further discussion of black versus white magic, see C. Grant Loomis, *White Magic: An Introduction to the Folklore of Christian Legend* (Cambridge, 1948).— Ed. Note.]

body of the figurine, the victim sickens. Sometimes, when the victim is aware that sorcery is being practiced against him, the corresponding parts of his body sicken or become paralyzed.[4] Then, the victim becomes even more sick, and when, after several days or weeks, the sorcerer pierces the figurine's heart, the victim dies.

You will notice the qualification: when the victim is aware that black magic is practiced against him. It is rarely the case that the victim does not know of the process. People love to talk and gossip in primitive societies, just as much as in our own. The sorcerer will very likely visit the victim, or at least visit his dwelling, and may loiter about in the vicinity. In most instances, it is the sorcerer himself who announces that he is doing the evil magic, as a public relations measure to increase his social status in the community. There are records in Papua of a number of instances in which a sorcerer, though actually innocent, confessed to the killing of victims in order to gain reputation. The sorcerer, in most cases, risks little in his own society, for to kill the sorcerer would be to no avail: one cannot kill magic. The fluid magic, the *mana,* will proceed swiftly from the dead body into another chosen one, and the danger of evil magic will still be over the head of the victim. One can combat, counteract, or neutralize magic; one cannot kill it.

Mana[5] is a Polynesian word denoting "fluid, transmissible magic." It means a kind of force or power which can be present in anything or anybody, and by its very presence, can endow that person or thing with supernatural qualities. Mana is not, however, a spirit; it has no will or purpose of its own. Mana can be supplied by various sources: It may come from gods or spirits, it may exist naturally, or it may be instilled by a correct ritual. It may be transmitted by the laying of a hand of a person possessing it onto the body of a novice, or it can be simply "willed" into another body.

A native on the Papuan coast may find a stone or a shell which is peculiarly shaped, or has an unusual color, or it may come his way under circumstances, he deems peculiar, magical or supernatural. He will take his find home and, possibly, will bury it in his garden, because he will believe it has mana. If he now gets an unusually good harvest, he will know he was right: the stone *does* have mana. Or, he may bring it into contact with his spear, and if the spear proves afterwards to be extraordinarily speedy and exact in finding the target, he will decide it has mana. It is not the workmanship, niceness of balance or straightness of the spear that count. If a spearmaker turns out consistently superior spears, spears which seem to find their way to the target with unfailing accuracy, then it is the maker of the tool that has the mana. There is no difference in the mana which is in the spear, its maker or its owner. Mana is simply the endowment of each with magical excellence.

Though the real home of the mana is the Pacific Ocean area, it is also

[4][For a consideration of this phenomenon, which is the opposite of faith healing (we might call it "faith killing"), and a possible physiological explanation, see Walter B. Cannon, " 'Voodoo' Death," *American Anthropologist,* 44 (1942), 169–81.— *Ed. Note.*]

[5][The term 'mana' was first reported by Bishop R. H. Codrington, who was a missionary in Melanesia from 1863–1887. See Codrington, *The Melanesians: Studies in Their Anthropology and Folklore* (Oxford, 1891), pp. 118–20.—*Ed. Note.*]

found elsewhere, all over the globe. We, in Western society, have a good share of it, though, as with magic, we hate to acknowledge it by its name. Instead we might call its vehicle a keepsake, memento, or, simply, our "pet" gun or tennis racquet.

I have encountered, in numerous homes in the United States, shiny silver dimes mounted in elaborate frames; always, they were hung in a conspicuous place on the parlor wall. These were dimes received from John D. Rockefeller, Sr. by the father or the grandfather in the household: it seems Mr. Rockefeller frequently gave away dimes to policemen, conductors and attendants. Most of these dimes were never spent, but were kept, and were highly treasured by the families of the recipients—they had the "Midas touch". Many of the owners told me that since the Rockefeller dime was in their possession, their families' material well-being had improved miraculously. I must add that none of the owners of Rockefeller dimes whom I met seemed to be ashamed of harboring a "superstition", and most of them genuinely believed in its magical properties, for it had Mr. Rockefeller's magical touch.

The possession of mana has its disadvantages, however. Chiefs, having close kinship with the gods, are usually endowed with much powerful mana. This can constitute an involuntary menace to others. Chiefs, kings and priests may have such powerful mana that they endow with fluid magic everything that comes into contact with their bodies. It is easy to see what can happen to a small kingdom—let's say an island in the Pacific—when a few generations of kings have walked it. The land touched by the king's feet becomes dangerously potent with magic, by that touch. In no time, this can render an island sterile, because it becomes untouchable for an ordinary mortal. The carrying of kings and chiefs on ceremonial chairs and sedans may have its origin as a protective measure against this. In primitive Polynesian philosophy, mana must exist in a proper state of balance. Too much *or* too little portends disaster. Such upset in the equilibrium of mana is denoted by the Polynesian word taboo.[6]

Taboo is something to be avoided as an unlimited danger for the transgressor. As with the word "culture", the anthropologist's meaning of taboo is different from that of common usage. In common usage, it is "taboo" to eat baked beans with one's fingers, or to be guilty of any other breach of etiquette. I have even heard it said that it is taboo to park an auto on the west side of Fifth Avenue in New York. These are improper or unlawful acts, but not taboo, for the supernatural is missing from them. One can park on Fifth Avenue and get away with it, as the police may not come around. Breaking a taboo, however, will inevitably bring a horrible supernatural punishment down upon the head of the transgressor, and in some instances, upon his family, clan, and sometimes even upon his community. Such

[6][There is considerable scholarship devoted to the concept of taboo. For examples of taboo from all over the world, see James George Frazer, *The Golden Bough*. For a psychoanalytic treatment of the concept, see the second chapter of Sigmund Freud's *Totem and Taboo* (New York, 1918). For additional references, see Franz Steiner, *Taboo* (London, 1956).—*Ed. Note.*]

punishment is inescapable and inevitable. It may be impotence, sterility, failure of crop, disappearance of game, famine or death. Transgression of taboo makes a person unclean and ritually bad—it exposes him to every kind of worldly or supernatural evil. Any and all transgressors of taboo are punished. One will bear the consequences if he breaks a taboo voluntarily or involuntarily. There is no recognition of mistake, accident or lack of malice. A transgressor is a terrible danger to his community. He is a supreme carrier of potential catastrophe—a veritable and deadly Typhoid Mary.

All this should not suggest, however, that native peoples live a dire existence, in eternal dread because of taboo. Rather, taboo should be viewed as an excellent system of signposts, showing the correct roads to take through all the phases of life from the cradle to the grave. The mere observance of a few limitations in diet, dress, work, or behavior, insures the native the ability to look forward with confidence and tranquility to his future. It supplies a system of values for him to live by.

To man, be he Western or primitive, disease is a terrifying and abnormal state. It is potent with the ultimate of all disasters—death. To be able to return to a normal state we usually need help—help from someone who knows *what* our ailment is and *how* to combat it. That someone is the healer. In Western society he is called the physician, the doctor, the M.D., or frequently that affectionate abbreviation, "Doc".

In primitive societies also, the healer has many names. We in Western culture call him witchdoctor, medicine man, sorcerer, magician or devil doctor. The anthropologist prefers the collective term: *shaman*. Shaman is a Siberian word meaning one who is endowed with supernatural potentialities and abilities. Sometimes the shaman is "possessed" by spirits.

Both the physician and the shaman are learned men. Both are subjected to rigid discipline and a prodigious amount of education, during many years. Both are under the rules of strict professional ethics, both are usually respected members or leaders of their communities. In many primitive societies the shaman is also the priest. It is logical that he should be that, because of the primitive native concept of disease.

The rational, scientific concept of disease is a comparatively recent development in man's history. In immensely large areas of our world today, for many millions of people, there is no such concept as "disease", in our sense of the word. Consequently there is no such thing as *natural* disease-caused death. For the primitive, natural death is one caused by warfare, violence or accident—it is to be struck by lightning, to drown or to fall from a coconut tree. All other deaths are due to supernatural causes—magic. No matter how inconsequent, unreasonable or childish it may sound to the Westerner, this is for them truth, gospel and dogma. It is not unreasonable to them, because their *reasoning* is different from ours.

There is no difference between the civilized, scientific physician and the shaman, insofar as their work or duties are concerned. They both will first endeavor to find the cause for the onset of the disease. They both take a history of the case; a shaman taking a case history frequently spends hours and even days or weeks longer at it than his scientific colleague. They both conduct and perform routine examinations of the patient's body. They both make a diagnosis and prescribe therapy. Frequently, too, they make a prognosis, an estimation of the future outcome of the ailment. Moreover, if the diagnosis is uncertain and "specialist" help is available, the shaman may call for consultation, just as does his colleague in London, Paris or New York.

There is, however, a tremendous fundamental difference between the shaman and the physician in their conceptions of disease. The native shaman is no trickster. He is just as honest and sure in his knowledge of causes of illness as his scientific colleague. But, while the province of the physician is anatomy, physiology and pathology—the natural sciences—the shaman's is magic, the supernatural. Thus, while the physician has his chemotherapy, his *materia medica,* his primitive confrere has his *materia magica.* The physician cures the patient through knowledge and understanding of the mechanism and functioning of the human body. The shaman works his therapy through the understanding of a supernatural world, existent and real, but invisible, behind the immediate worldly scene.

The understanding of the supernatural world is the shaman's "scientific" knowledge. It was transmitted to him by his teachers, much as our knowledge was instilled in us by our venerated professors in medical schools. Furthermore, the truth of the supernatural was proved to him countless times during his apprentice years. He has seen for himself that the patients of his teachers were cured by them, were made healthy again. He has had "experimental" proof that the theories taught to him are solid. The reasoning that the patients were cured is based on fact, which no one would deny. What we Westerners object to is the assertion that they were cured by the supernatural means used by the shaman.

How does the shaman cure an illness? The methods used all over the world would fill libraries, and would be impossible to even survey here.[7] One can, however, group them into three categories, according to the etiology of the disease.

1. *Disease by intrusion of foreign objects.* Under this category fall all beliefs that a foreign object of evil power has entered the body of the patient, causing his illness. Such objects can be magical pebbles, small stones, thorns, arrows, miniature blowgun darts or even small living animals.

The therapy is obviously the removal of the object. This can be accomplished by the shaman's sucking the object out, squeezing it out with his fingers, forcing it out with tobacco smoke, with poultices or irritants, etc., or even enticing it out by petting, stroking, tickling or fondling the diseased body.

2. *Intrusion by spirits or demons.* The patient's body has been entered into by an evil spirit or demon. These demons waste away his body because they eat up all the food he takes in. The spirit or demon, however, sometimes

[7][One of the best surveys of primitive disease theories is F. E. Clements, "Primitive Concepts of Disease," *University of California Publications in American Archaeology and Ethnology,* 32 (1932), 181–254. For a thorough investigation of the object intrusion theory, see L. Honko, *Krankheitsprojektile. Untersuchung über eine urtümliche Krankheitserklärung,* Folklore Fellows Communications 178 (Helsinki, 1959).—Ed. Note.]

may not act as a true parasite, and may not need any nourishment. In this case, the ailment may be diagnosed—if the symptoms recur periodically—as the demon's "kicking up", or making a row, in the patient's body. The treatment then will be the expulsion of the intruding spirit—exorcism. This can be accomplished by ceremony, incantations, commands, or polite requests adjuring the spirit to depart and not return. If the spirit does not respond, its temporary abode can be made unpleasant for it. This can be accomplished by making it "hot" for the spirit by sweat bath, or freezing it out by the application of cold. Some spirits will need to be starved out by a restricted diet or vigorous fasting. Demons sometimes depart if the diet is loathsome and disgusting. In such cases, they can be expelled in a vomitus. A spirit can also be gotten rid of by cathartics. In some cultures, demons can be extracted by surgery, such as punctures or trepanations.

3. *Incidents of "soul capture", or "straying soul".*   The patient's illness is caused by the absence of his soul. It is an *AWOL* proposition, in which the soul leaves the body without the owner's permission, and enters into another realm, or body, leaving the patient's body in distress, because its "chief" or "governor" is absent.

The therapy here is to recapture the soul, by ceremonial means, and by making the patient's body attractive to it. The ceremonial means are usually incantations and the "locating of the soul". The latter is frequently a complex procedure of deductive reasoning, taking days or even weeks. The shaman, or his soul, becomes a sort of private eye for shadowing the straying soul. Dietary and hygienic measures are also ordered to make the body a desirable, comfortable home for the straying soul. If the patient's soul is captured with malicious intent by a sorcerer, then the power of that sorcerer needs to be fought to make him give up the captive. This, again, is usually a long procedure, sometimes involving public duels between shaman and sorcerer.

The immediate causes for the onset of these magical ailments can be: (a) Sorcery or black magic, when a magic arrow is shot into the victim or a magic stone is thrown into his body with malicious intent; when image magic is being practiced against him. (b) Sleep and dreams, which are dangerous states, for in them one is not in possession of all one's faculties. This is the most frequent onset for soul-straying. Particularly dangerous are dreams about illness, or anything related to it. Most dangerous are dreams in which one violates a taboo. In such cases one may come under the next category, that of (c) a ritually bad state, or moral delinquency. Here belong not only actual transgressions of taboos, but also the careless execution of rituals or ceremonies. Diseases of such origin are always serious, and the prognosis is at best uncertain. Patients afflicted with such ailments are usually on the shaman's critical list.

I have stated that primitive societies, where the disease concept is magical, have no *materia medica,* only *materia magica.* However, a number of important drugs and herbs, such as quinine, ephedrine and, recently, the Rauwolfia alkaloid, were gotten by Western medicine from primitive societies. Thus, my statement may seem paradoxical. An explanation may clear this up. If you visit a rubber plantation in Malaya, you find that the coolies of the plantation are paid a fee twice weekly to take the necessary pro-phylactic dose of anti-malarial medicine. It usually amazes the visiting West-ern tourist to find that the workers are paid for swallowing, for their own good, a medicament costing the plantation annually a large sum of money. But, from the coolies' viewpoint the atabrine or plasmochin is not a remedy. To them, malaria is caused not by the presence of parasite *Plasmodium vivax* in the blood, but by magical causes. Hence, the white man makes the coolies swallow a bitter pill for no rational reason, but for his amusement or peculiar pleasure. It is right, proper and just therefore that the coolies should receive payment for doing his bidding.

At the same time, if you would travel northward and visit a camp of the Bombay-Burma Teak Company in northern Siam, you would find native workers readily begging for anti-malarial medicines consisting of the same atabrine[R] tablets, but given to them in conjunction with a complicated ceremony following a purification ritual and numerous dietary restrictions, certain clothing prohibitions, and so on. Here, the atabrine ceases to be a useless whim of the white man, but becomes a part of *materia magica*. It is therefore a logical therapeutic material to use.

In much the same manner, most primitive medical practices contain med-ically proven ingredients. In the Mentawei Islands, southwest of Sumatra, the standard therapy for diarrhea is to send the patient at sundown to a certain point of the seashore, where he must lie down on the edge of a white cliff and lie there on his stomach flat and motionless for a definite period of time, and periodically lick the earth. The therapy is magical, but it has a scientific rationale nevertheless. The cliffs are of kaolin—a refined kind of clay—an absorbent, which we frequently prescribe under the Latin name of *bolus alba*. It is an effective medicine for diarrhea. The warm, sunbaked surface of the cliff acts as a hot water bottle or electric heating pad; thus, the psychosomatic effects of the shaman's mana frequently effect a cure.

Many other facets of primitive medicine have a detectable scientific basis. Modern science, as a matter of fact, has some of its origins in it. For example, the Indians of New England inserted a fish into each hill of corn they planted. They taught this "magic" to the Pilgrim Fathers. They certainly could not have given any scientific explanation of enriching the soil with nitrogen. The Pilgrim Fathers, too, were ignorant of scientific theories of organic chemistry, but they followed the example of the Indians because they found it effective. Remember, magic is the formula of doing the right thing at the right time, using the proper thing and saying the proper words. Some of the things or some of the words become proper, in time, from experience with them. Thus, many magical practices are based by the native peoples on empirical observations. Once a thing consistently proves its superior excellence, it becomes endowed with mana.

On Soembawa Island, lives a shaman in the village of Do Dongo. Across his chest is tattooed a large circle with an ornamental capital letter *B*. The story of his tattoo is a case in point: He was my principal informant, in 1937, when I was doing field work on the ethnology of his tribe. Through close association, we became fast friends. He taught me native medicine, and I occasionally helped out with his cases when he asked for my assistance or wanted me in consultation. All my drugs originated from the German Bayer

Company, and on the packing cases was painted their trademark, an ornamented *B* in a circle. As I had taken all my "magical" supplies from such cases, my friend came to associate the power of my magic with the design of the trademark. After several months, he very formally asked my permission to use my magical symbol.

As I have mentioned before, shamans are usually governed by very strict ethics. Less ethically, and without the permission of the Bayer Company, I released the copyright, and the letter *B* within the circle was emblazoned on my friend's chest. It gave him a tremendous additional amount of mana, and *de facto* increased his curative powers.

I am not being facetious about all this, and I ask you to realize that for the primitive concept of medicine these things are just as real and valid as our most cherished theories in serology or in the chemistry of the endocrine glands.

As a matter of fact, as mentioned above, magic is not the monopoly of the primitive people. We Westerners, too, have our magical practices in medicine, though we label them as traditions or superstitions. When next you look at a prescription remember that the Rx on the top left corner is really an invocation to a deity for effective work of that prescription.[8] I trust you will remember also that our theories and knowledge are not based on magical theories, but on scientific facts. Nevertheless—though fast disappearing— magic is still present in modern medicine. This is not "bad". It is an important adjunct and adjuvant to our chemotherapy, our surgery and our science, and, above all, to the art of medical practice. It is not trickery; it is not malicious intent to deceive.

In an issue of *Time* magazine, in the section on medicine, there appeared an article entitled "A Cure for Curanderismo." This dealt with a survey by the University of Texas, in which it was found that the some 2,000,000 United States citizens of Mexican origin in Texas "still reject the germ theory of disease and infection: to them, a raw egg has more healing power than an antibiotic, and a hospital is a place to go to die." According to Study Director William Madsen, a University of Texas anthropologist, "it is useless for M.D.'s to assail this quackery. To the Mexican-American, *the gringo doctor is the quack*".[9] These 2,000,000 people are not in a far away tropical land in the Pacific Ocean, but right here in the United States, and their faith in *Curanderismo* flourishes throughout the Rio Grande Valley.[10]

---

[8][Rx is an abbreviation of the Latin word *recipe,* referring in this case not to cooking formula, but medical formula. It derives from the imperative form of the verb *recipere,* to take. According to some authorities, the abbreviation is based upon ♃ the sign of Jupiter, and is used to propitiate the god in writing a prescription.— *Ed. Note.*]

[9]*Time,* August 25, 1961, p. 44.

[10][For further details on Mexican-American folk medicine and other aspects of culture, see William Madsen, *Mexican-Americans of South Texas* (New York, 1964). Additional relevant materials include Lyle Saunders, *Cultural Differences and Medical Care: The Case of the Spanish-Speaking People of the Southwest* (New York, 1954); Margaret Clark, *Health in the Mexican-American Culture: A Community Study* (Berkeley, 1959); Arthur J. Rubel, "Concepts of Disease in Mexican-American Culture," *American Anthropologist,* **62** (1960), 795–814; and William Madsen, *Society and Health in the Lower Rio Grande Valley* (Austin, 1961).—*Ed. Note.*]

Our earth is shrinking in size with tremendous speed. Modern methods of transportation and communication are the reason. If the map of the world just before the travels of Columbus were represented as the size of a stage, that map has now shrunk to the size of a lectern. The steamship, the railway and now aerial transport by jet aircraft have made this so. The process we call civilization has made enormous, unbelievable inroads on primitive societies. Incredibly large segments of populations are subjected to civilizing processes by numerous methods of varying political and economic propaganda. Among these, public health reforms, based upon modern, scientific medicine, loom large. It is of course well and proper for such reforms to be effected, for they are an important and organic part of the programs of betterment for the backward areas.

The question uppermost in my mind is: how far and by what means shall we effect the change? How much understanding and patience will need to be exercised?

To illustrate my point: during World War II, I lectured to officers and officer candidates of the U.S. Army and Navy who were being trained to act as liaison officers between the armed forces and primitive natives in the Pacific. The purpose was to prepare them for the eventuality that their arrival on a primitive island might coincide with the outbreak of a disease epidemic. Such an occurrence is a great misfortune indeed, as the native population is likely to blame the newly arrived Western people for the outbreak, logically believing them to be evil magicians.

In my lecture I offered the suggestion to my students that if they should be confronted with such a situation, they should attempt to shift the blame away from themselves. As an expedient, I suggested that they put the blame on an animal, preferably a malformed one, or one of strange coloring, or on a plant or a tree which had a strange appearance or location, and advised them to devise a ceremony for removing that animal or object from the island and purifying the area where it was located. I gave prodigious numbers of suggestions as to how to make the ceremony properly complicated and impressive.

At the end of the lecture, a young officer candidate, a Western-educated Korean, rose and in sharp words questioned the honesty of my suggestions. He pointed out that, instead of educating the natives, I was, with pernicious intent, fostering their stupid and barbarous beliefs, thereby leaving them in a dark state of ignorance, instead of enlightening them. I asked this student what suggestion he would volunteer in such a case. Very matter-of-factly he told me that the natives should be told the truth, that the causative agent of cholera is the cholera *Vibrio koch*.

I accepted his offer and asked him to use me as a native informant and give me the literal text he would deliver to a native. He launched into an explanation on the theory of micro-organisms, then abruptly stopped and said that he could not go any further without demonstrating the theory with a microscope. I then obtained a microscope from the biology department, together with a cholera slide, which he put under the microscope and then asked me to view so that I could see the bacteria. Acting out the native's role, I told him that I could see nothing, as of course no primitive native

would be able to see through such a solid object as the ocular of a microscope, much less be able to recognize stained bacteria on a slide. About half
an hour sufficed to convince my young Korean friend that it would indeed
take months or possibly years to train a primitive native to use a complicated
optical instrument, let alone to use it with understanding.

This may illustrate what difficulties a scientifically trained physician may
encounter in a *magical* society. To inculcate concepts of bacteriology,
pathology or physiology into the primitive mind will take time. Education
is a very slow process, even under ideal circumstances, and impatience and
contempt for the natives' "stupidity" is not education—it is folly which will
result in tragedy for educator and student alike. The process will need to be
slow, a slow transition rather than a fast change. We will need to adopt,
temporarily, some of the natives' primitive concepts in order to be able to
educate them.

How can such things be done? As in the case of the Bombay-Burma
Company's anti-malarial campaign, magic will need to be part of the arma-
mentarium of modern medicine in such areas.

Some 20 years ago, I was doing ethnological field work among the Yagua,
a little-known tribe located between the Amazon and the Putumayo Rivers
in South America. My main informant was Unchi, the shaman, the most
erudite and learned primitive physician I encountered in my years of field
work around the world. We became very good friends during my stay with
the Ant Clan, and I felt a deep sense of gratitude for the enormous amount
of information he gave me, not only in the art of medicine among the Yagua,
but also on the customs and philosophy of his people. Occasionally he
requested me to act as consultant on one of his cases. Mostly, he wanted my
aid whenever it was necessary to remove some of his patients' teeth.

Naturally I did the extractions under local anesthesia. For Unchi, my
ability to remove teeth painlessly was a highly impressive ceremony, and I
believe he considered me and my instruments endowed with powerful mana.
He also came to know that the magic of painlessness rested not in my forceps
but in the dental syringe used for administering the anesthesia. It was logical
for him to come to this conclusion, for the syringe received special ceremonial attention. It was taken apart, put into my portable sterilizer and
vigorously boiled for a considerable time. Furthermore, my hands had been
carefully washed and scrubbed before the components of the syringe were
lifted from the boiling water. Unchi very quickly observed that once the
syringe came out of the boiling water, it was handled with meticulous care.
He came to know that once the instrument was sterile, it could not be
touched and could not touch anything. The novocain[R] cartridges too were
handled with a method which for him represented high magical ceremony,
as they were carefully washed with alcohol, and the solution gingerly
extracted from them, into the syringe. Unchi witnessed these "ceremonies"
possibly a dozen times. His eyes never left my hands, even for a fraction of a
second, and he always was in rapt attention throughout the process.

When the time came for me to leave the Yagua, I conducted the procedure, customary for ethnologists, of rewarding all my informants, and
distributing among the other members of the clan all the tools, wearing

apparel and materials we could leave behind. Partly in deference to Unchi's exalted position, and also out of gratitude and friendship, I asked him before any one else to select whatever he wanted from my belongings as a keepsake and reward for himself. I was almost sure that he would want one of the *escopetas*—we had several of these muzzle-loading shotguns, which were very much admired and desired by the Yagua. Though they had splendid blow-guns and curare-tipped darts, the range and effect of a shotgun meant much for Indians whose economy consists solely of hunting. Unchi, however, asked that I part with my upper and lower root forceps, and my syringe. Without hesitation I handed over to him the two forceps, but—I am now ashamed to say—I did not give him my syringe and store of novocain. My refusal stemmed, almost automatically, from the belief that I could not put into the hands of an illiterate Indian an instrument for parenteral administration. I was afraid that possible lack of sterility, and ignorance in anatomical topography, might make the instrument a potential danger in his hands.

After my departure, I had time to reflect, and I wished that my decision in not giving Unchi the syringe had been better considered. I could have, in a little time, taught Unchi how to sterilize the syringe, where to insert the needle and in what direction—all, of course, not on a scientific basis of germ theory and regional anatomy, but simply as a highly potent magical procedure. Unchi would have learned fast, and would have been more than qualified to execute the "ceremonies" with an unheard-of meticulousness and without error.

Any physician will bear me out that it is a difficult educational process to teach a student in a nursing school the importance of sterility in parenteral administration. Though the concept of micro-organisms is well inculcated in the student's mind, he or she is liable to slip, or forget, when under pressure or tired. The sterility of a hypodermic needle thus may be questioned in the hand of a novice, though, fortunately, I believe rarely. It would never need to be questioned in the hands of my friend Unchi. His very life, his existence, his salvation, even his community's, would be at stake—not only his job or the welfare of a single patient.

Thus, magic can be a potent ally of the scientific physician. Used with full understanding, it can become one of his important tools, not only in education of primitives but also in the art of his practice, not as unethical trickery, not as malicious aid, but as a fully proper, rational, scientific adjunct for healing the sick.

John M. Cooper

THE CREE WITIKO PSYCHOSIS

The *witiko* or *windigo* psychosis is a form of mental disorder found among the Ojibwa, Cree, and several other American

Reprinted from *Primitive Man*, 6 (1933), 20–24, by permission of The Catholic University of America Press.

Indian groups in Canada. It is one of a number of classic examples of culturally patterned forms of mental illness reported in the anthropological literature. Some of the important theoretical issues involved in studying mental illness in other cultures include the difficulty of defining what is or what is not normal *in the culture under study*. Behavior which is deemed abnormal in our culture may be regarded as perfectly normal in another cultural context. Another problem is relating the possible disorder to other aspects of culture. For example, this brief account of the *witiko* by Reverend Cooper shows the intimate connection between folklore and mental illness. It would be difficult for a member of our society to think he had become a *witiko*; on the other hand, it might be equally difficult for a Cree who was not a Christian to think that he was Jesus Christ!

For a survey of some of the *witiko* literature, see Victor Barnouw, *Culture and Personality* (Homewood, Illinois, 1963), pp. 366–68. For the general problem of mental illness in other cultures, see Ralph Linton, *Culture and Mental Disorders* (Springfield, Ill., 1956); Marvin K. Opler, ed., *Culture and Mental Health* (New York, 1959); Paul K. Benedict and Irving Jacks, "Mental Illness in Primitive Societies," *Psychiatry,* **17** (1954), 377–89, P. M. Yap, "Mental Diseases Peculiar to Certain Cultures," *Journal of Mental Science,* **97** (1951), 313–27, Donald A. Kennedy, "Key Issues in the Cross-Cultural Study of Mental Disorders," in Bert Kaplan, ed., *Studying Personality Cross-Culturally* (Evanston, Ill., 1961), pp. 405–25, and Barnouw's chapter "Culture and Mental Disorders," in his *Culture and Personality* (Homewood, Ill., 1963), pp. 361–85. For references on Cree culture, see George Peter Murdock, *Ethnographic Bibliography of North America,* 3rd ed. (New Haven, 1960), pp. 198–202.

A very typical psychosis occurring among the eastern Cree and some other northern Canadian tribes is the "Witiko malady". This peculiar form of mental disturbance is characterized by (1) a craving for human flesh, and (2) a delusion of transformation into a Witiko who has a heart of ice or who vomits ice.[1]

This short paper gives some details on the psychosis itself and offers a hypothesis regarding the factors responsible for the two above-mentioned characteristics of the psychosis. The factual data here given are, except where otherwise stated, from the present writer's field notes taken among the eastern and western Cree and other Algonquian-speaking peoples.

[1]This form of "hysteria" appears to be absent from northern Asia. In fact, the so-called "arctic hysteria" of Siberia seems to be in the main fundamentally different in pattern from the Algonquian. Cf. M. A. Czaplicka, *Aboriginal Siberia*, Oxford, 1914, 308–25.

1. The Craving for Human Flesh

Among the eastern Cree, as among other Algonquian-speaking Indians of northeastern Canada, the Athapascans of the Mackenzie, and some of the Eskimo, scattered instances of cannibalism during famine are recorded in our published sources, and, among the Cree at least, are still remembered by the older natives or else are a common theme of folk-lore and semi-historical tradition. There is among the eastern Cree no ceremonial or magical cannibalism, although magical cannibalism existed among some of the Ojibwa and St. Lawrence Algonquians who were in contact with the Iroquoian tribes. Nor is there any trace of socially approved eating of human flesh for the taste or pleasure of it. The eastern Cree, and most of the other northern Algonquians, had and have just as profound aversion to and horror of cannibalism in any form as we have.

Cannibalism was resorted to by the Cree only in cases where actual starvation threatened. Driven to desperation by prolonged famine and often suffering from mental breakdown as a result thereof, the Cree would sometimes eat the bodies of those who had perished, or, more rarely, would even kill the living and partake of the flesh. This solution, however, of the conflict between hunger and the rigid tribal taboo often left, as its aftermath, an "unnatural" craving for human flesh, or a psychosis that took the form of such craving. More rarely such a psychosis developed in men or women who had not themselves previously passed through famine experience.

It seems fairly clear that this particular craving in the psychosis is directly traceable to prevalent environmental and cultural conditions in the northeastern Canadian woodlands, where death by starvation has been relatively very common, perhaps more common than in any other part of the world, and where the native culture includes both a rigid taboo on and a profound horror of cannibalism.

2. The Transformation into a Witiko

Cannibalistic giants are familiar figures in the folk-lore of many peoples, particularly in the folk-lore of the North American aborigines. In Cree folk-lore and traditions the cannibal giant—or giants, for they may be more than one, and of either sex—plays a prominent rôle under the name of *Wī'tikō, Atcen,* or *Kōkōdjē'o.* He is greatly dreaded by the Cree, even today and among those who are in other respects much Europeanized.

The Cree man or woman who under stress of famine had eaten human flesh was afterwards shunned and feared. He or she was not only commonly called a Witiko, but also was considered as having become a Witiko while yet alive on earth, and often so considered himself or herself. He was further believed to have, like the superhuman Witiko, a heart of ice, or to have ice inside him,—a point to which we shall return in a moment. Human Witikos were dangerous, as they were apt to kill or to be suspected of desiring to kill living adults or children in order to satisfy their psychotic craving for human flesh. Hence, human man-eaters who had become Witikos were often put to death.

That the belief in identification with or metamorphosis into a Witiko is genetically related to the folk-lore belief in cannibal giants with hearts of ice seems clear enough. A further question may, however, be raised: "Why has the superhuman Witiko himself a heart of ice?"

Many stories are told by the Cree and other Algonquians of the slaying of superhuman Witikos by Indians or by other Witikos. A common theme is that, after the killing, the Witiko's body is thrown into the fire and consumed, all except the heart which turns out to be of hard ice. This icy heart is then taken out of the fire, pounded to bits, and so destroyed or else the bits are thrown back into the fire and melted.[2]

Many stories containing the same theme are related of human Witikos among the Crees and other Algonquian groups. One story was told me about an aged Waswanipi Indian whom I met several years ago but who has since died. He had in earlier life trespassed on another man's hunting ground. The other man conjured him and he began to eat uncooked rabbit flesh. At last he nearly turned into a Witiko. In the nick of time, his old grandfather sang and drummed to cure him, and gave him a little hot bear-grease. A short while after swallowing the grease, the conjured man vomited a lot of clear ice which was then thrown into the fire. This marked the turning point and the victim escaped becoming a Witiko. A similar belief is found among the western Cree of Montana. They say that a human Witiko has a piece of ice inside him. To cure him, give him a bit of grease, which will melt this ice.[3]

Cree children are forbidden by their elders to eat ice. Their elders say to them: "Do not eat ice; you will turn into a Witiko". This custom is found among the Alberta and Montana Cree as well as among the eastern Cree as far as the Tête de Boule. The Montagnais-speaking Waswanipi, to express the above admonition to their children, use the formula: *Ekàwi'yà mu misku'mi; tcī kà wītikō'win.*

The icy heart would of itself suggest a folk-lore reflection of winter-time, the time of ice, the time when famine and cannibalism usually occur. There are, however, two further correlations that seem to corroborate this inference.

The Micmac Chenoo is obviously identical with the Cree Witiko. Both have the same characteristics, including the icy heart. The very name Chenoo seems to be identical with the Montagnais and Tête-de-Boule (Cree) name, *Atcen,* for the Witiko. The Micmac Chenoo, according to Rand, comes from the cold north. In one legend as spring advanced and he traveled south he grew weaker day by day.[4]

The Tête-de-Boule Witiko "used to rub himself, like the animals, against the fir, spruce, and other resinous trees. When he was thus covered with gum or resin, he would go and roll in the sand, so that one would have thought that, after many operations of this kind, he was made of stone." A similar

---

[2]Cf. similar Micmac and Passamaquoddy folk tales: S. T. Rand, *Legends of the Micmacs,* N. Y., 1894, 196–97; C. G. Leland, *Algonquin Legends of New England,* Boston, 1885, 241–42, 246–48.

[3]Cf. similar Micmac and Nipigon beliefs: Rand, 1. c., 248; Leland, 1. c., 253; D. Cameron, in Masson, *Les bourgeois de la Compagnie du Nord-ouest,* Quebec, 1890, ii, 250.

[4]Rand, 1. c., 190, 194, 197–98; cf. Leland, 1. c., 233, 247.

habit is ascribed to the Passamaquoddy Chenoo who used to rub themselves all over with fir balsam and then roll themselves on the ground so that everything adhered to the body.[5]

This habit is highly suggestive of the Iroquoian Stone Coats, the blood-thirsty cannibal giants, who used to cover their bodies carefully with pitch and then roll and wallow in sand and down sand banks. The etymological connection (stone, flint = ice) and the constant tradition that the homeland of the Stone Coats is in the region of the north, where Iroquoian tradition placed the burial place of the Winter God, indicate, Hewitt believes, that the Winter God, the Great Frost Giant of the common Iroquois genesis myth, was the source of the Iroquoian concept of the Stone Coats.[6] As there seems to be a fairly clear relation between Witiko and the Stone Coats, this would suggest Witiko's affinity in certain important respects with winter-time, the time of ice and famine.

We seem, therefore, to have probable grounds for inferring that the Witiko's heart of ice symbolizes an environmental condition, namely, the icy winter of the north, and that this note has become associated with the giant-cannibal conception because winter time is the time of famine and of famine-cannibalism.

To sum up. A common psychosis among the eastern Cree and some kindred tribes shows two peculiar characteristics: the victim develops an "unnatural" craving for human flesh; he turns into an ice-hearted Witiko. The craving for human flesh appears pretty clearly to be derived *directly* from prevalent environmental and cultural conditions. The transformation into an ice-hearted Witiko seems to be derived *indirectly*, through the Witiko folk-lore concept, from the same conditions.

Ruth Benedict

CHILD REARING IN CERTAIN EUROPEAN COUNTRIES

In the nineteenth century those making ethnographic inquiries rarely recorded information about child rearing. The child was not utilized as an informant and relatively little data about childhood was elicited from adults. This was, in part, a reflection of the ethnographers' culture, insofar as children were ideally to be infrequently seen and certainly never heard. With the impact

[5]J. E. Guinard, in Primitive Man, 1930, iii, 69; Leland, l. c., 247.
[6]J. N. B. Hewitt, in BAE-R 32, 1918, 64; cf. Hewitt, "Tawiskaron," BAE-R 30, ii, 707–11, and W. E. Connelley, *Wyandot Folk-lore*, Topeka, 1899, 92.

Reprinted from the *American Journal of Orthopsychiatry*, Vol. XIX, No. 2 (1949), 342–48. Copyright, the American Orthopsychiatric Association, Inc. Reproduced by permission.

of Freud's discovery that infancy and childhood conditioning had enormous significance for the development of adult personality, there began to be increasing interest in childhood patterns. However, anthropologists committed to cultural relativism could hardly accept Freud's and his followers' sweeping generalizations about the specific nature of the infantile determination of adult character. It was Abram Kardiner, a psychiatrist who gave a joint seminar at Columbia University with anthropologist Ralph Linton, who helped reconcile cultural relativism with Freudian psychodynamics. If the infant's experience is crucial with respect to adult personality formation, Kardiner argued, one would expect adult personalities in different cultures to vary in accordance with the kind of child care in these cultures. Adding the factor of cultural relativism to Freudian concepts made Freudian psychology much more acceptable to cultural anthropologists. However, there are still some extreme forms of Freudian inspired analysis which have not been widely accepted by anthropologists despite the fact that cultural relativistic details have been taken into account.

One of the most extreme forms of Freudian analysis in anthropology is the so-called "swaddling hypothesis." It was developed primarily by Geoffrey Gorer, who was working on a project initiated by Ruth Benedict and later directed by Margaret Mead. Gorer published his controversial paper, "Some Aspects of the Psychology of the People of Great Russia," in 1949 and the same year he and John Rickman issued their book *The People of Great Russia: A Psychological Study*. Although Gorer was careful to state (in a footnote) that he was not arguing that all of Russian national character could be explained as a consequence of the length and degree of the swaddling of Russian infants, but rather that it was only one of several possible characterological antecedents, most of Gorer's critics pounced on his emphasis upon the alleged importance of swaddling.

In Ruth Benedict's brief but perceptive comparison of the swaddling techniques found in several different cultures, one can see that there are diverse ways in which parents may regard children and, further, that such attitudes may indeed be implicit in the mechanical details of early infant care. Whether or not the swaddling hypothesis or modifications thereof are ever satisfactorily validated, there can be no question of the importance of the initial parental response to neonates in the development of the world view and personality of those infants when they become adults.

For Freud's views of infantile determinism, see any of his major works, e.g., any of those contained in *The Basic Writings of Sigmund Freud* (New York, 1938). For example, Freud's suggestion that religious systems are projections of parent-child relationships may be found in his *The Future of an Illusion*

(Garden City, 1957). A Freudian might argue in the case of Euro-American culture that the Oedipus Complex (in which a boy rejects his father and loves his mother) would be reflected in the Christian religious family. A virgin birth is the ultimate repudiation of the father. If one is the result of a virgin birth, then there need never have been sexual intercourse between one's father and mother. Further, if it were believed that the father and son were the same person, then the son would be the husband of his own mother, that is, he would succeed in the Oedipal ideal of replacing his father. In addition, a Freudian might argue that the Electra Complex (in which a daughter rejects her mother and loves her father) would also be found in the religious social structure. A virgin who is miraculously impregnated by a heavenly father would represent this supposed childhood female wish. For an excellent discussion of the impact of Freud's ideas on cultural anthropology, see Weston LaBarre, "The Influence of Freud on Anthropology," *American Imago,* 15 (1958), 275–328. For Kardiner's modification of Freudian theory, see *The Individual and His Society* (New York, 1939), and *The Psychological Frontiers of Society* (New York, 1945). For Gorer's article, see "Some Aspects of the Psychology of the People of Great Russia," *The American Slavic and East European Review,* 8 (1949), 155–66. For some of the responses, see Margaret Mead, "The Swaddling Hypothesis: Its Reception," *American Anthropologist,* 56 (1954), 395–409, and Clyde Kluckhohn, "Recent Studies of the 'National Character' of Great Russians," in Richard Kluckhohn, ed., *Culture and Behavior: Collected Essays of Clyde Kluckhohn* (New York, 1962), pp. 210–43. For an introduction to national character studies, see Alex Inkeles and Daniel J. Levinson, "National Character: The Study of Modal Personality and Socio-Cultural Systems," in Gardner Lindsey, ed., *Handbook of Social Psychology,* II (Cambridge, 1954), 977–1020. For some evidence of the interest in studying childhood, see Erik H. Erikson, *Childhood and Society* (New York, 1950); John W. M. Whiting and Irving L. Child, *Child Training and Personality* (New Haven, 1953); Margaret Mead and Martha Wolfenstein, eds., *Childhood in Contemporary Cultures* (Chicago, 1955); and Sister M. Inez Hilger, *Field Guide to the Ethnological Study of Child Life* (New Haven, 1960). For the general area of psychological anthropology, or as it is usually termed "culture and personality," see such works as Anthony F. C. Wallace, *Culture and Personality* (New York, 1961); Francis L. K. Hsu, ed., *Psychological Anthropology: Approaches to Culture and Personality* (Homewood, Ill., 1961); Bert Kaplan, ed., *Studying Personality Cross-Culturally* (Evanston, Ill., 1961); and Victor Barnouw, *Culture and Personality* (Homewood, Ill., 1963).

Systematic study of national character is an investigation into a special and paradoxical situation. It must identify and analyze continuities in attitudes and behaviors yet the personnel which exhibits these traits changes completely with each generation. A whole nation of babies have to be brought up to replace their elders. The situations two different generations have to meet—war or peace, prosperity or depression—may change drastically, but Americans, for instance, will handle them in one set of terms, Italians in another. Even when a nation carries through a revolution or reverses fundamental state policies, Frenchmen do not cease to be recognizable as Frenchmen or Russians as Russians.

The cultural study of certain European nations on which I am reporting[1] has taken as one of its basic problems the ways in which children are brought up to carry on in their turn their parents' manner of life. It accepts as its theoretical premise that identifications, securities, and frustrations are built up in the child by the way in which he is traditionally handled, the early disciplines he receives, and the sanctions used by his parents. The study has been carried on in New York City by a staff of interviewers who have supplemented their work with historical, literary, journalistic and economic materials. The aims of the research have been to isolate exceedingly fundamental patterns and themes which can then be tested and refined by study of local, class, and religious differences. It is believed that such preliminary hypotheses will make future field work in the home countries more rewarding, and such field work in the Old World is already being carried out under other auspices by students who have taken part in this research.

The Project has necessarily seen its work as a comparative study of cultures. It has blocked out large culture areas and their constituent subcultures. When a great area shares a generalized trait, the particular slants each subarea has given to these customs is diagnostic of its special values and the range of variation gives insight which could not be obtained from the study of one nation in isolation. This culture area approach commits the student, moreover, when he is working outside his own cultural area, to a detailed study of behaviors which, since they are not present in his own experience, have not been incorporated into his own theoretical apparatus. It is therefore a testing ground for theoretical assumptions and often involves a rephrasing of them.

The custom of swaddling the baby during its first months of life in Central and Eastern Europe illustrates well, in the field of child rearing, the methodological value of a culture area approach. It illustrates how the comparison of attitudes and practices in different areas can illuminate the

[1]Research in Contemporary Cultures, government-aided Columbia University Research Project sponsored by the Psychological Branch of the Medical Sciences Division of the Office of Naval Research. The Russian material was collected and organized under the leadership of Geoffrey Gorer and Margaret Mead, and I am especially indebted to Mr. Gorer's skill and insights; Prof. Conrad M. Arensberg directed the group gathering Jewish material, and Dr. Sula Benet organized the information on Poland. Thanks are due to these leaders and to all their co-workers.

characteristics of any one region that is being intensively studied, and the kind of inquiry which is fruitful. Specifically I shall try to show that any such student of comparative cultures must press his investigation to the point where he can describe *what is communicated* by the particular variety of the widespread technique he is studying. In the case of swaddling, the object of investigation is the kind of communication which in different regions is set up between adults and the child by the procedures and sanctions used.

Because of our Western emphasis on the importance of the infant's bodily movement, students of child care who discuss swaddling in our literature often warn that it produces tics. Or with our stress on prohibition of infant genitality, it is subsumed under prevention of infant masturbation. Any assumption that swaddling produces adults with tics ignores the contradictory evidence in the great areal laboratory where swaddling occurs, and the assumption that it is simply a first technique to prevent a child from finding pleasure in its own body is an oversimplified projection of our Western concern with this taboo. Any systematic study of the dynamics of character development in the swaddling area is crippled by these assumptions. Infant swaddling has permitted a great range of communication.

Careful studies of mother-child relations in this country have abundantly shown the infant's sensitivity to, the mother's tenseness or permissiveness, her pleasure or disgust, whether these are expressed in her elbows, her tone of voice or her facial expression. Communications of these sorts take place from birth on, and when a particular form of parental handling is standardized as "good" and "necessary" in any community, the infant has a greatly multiplied opportunity to learn to react to the traditional patterns. Local premises, too, about how to prepare a child for life will be expressed in modification of procedure in swaddling, and these detailed differences are means of communication to the child, no less than his mother's tone of voice. Any fruitful research in national character must base its work upon such premises and utilize them as basic principles in comparative study.

Swaddling is tightest and is kept up longest in Great Russia. The baby's arms are wrapped close to its sides and only the face emerges. After tight wrapping in the blanket, the bundle is taped with criss-cross lashings till it is, as Russians say, "like a log of wood for the fireplace." Babies are sometimes lashed so tight that they cannot breathe, and are saved from strangling only by loosening the bindings. The bundle is as rigid as if the babies were bound to a cradleboard, and this affects carrying habits and the way a baby is soothed in an adult's arms. It is not rocked in the arms in the fashion familiar to us, but is moved horizontally from right to left and left to right.

The swaddling in Russia is explicitly justified as necessary for the safety of an infant who is regarded as being in danger of destroying itself. In the words of informants, "It would tear its ears off. It would break its legs." It must be confined for its own sake and for its mother's. In the '30's the Soviet regime made a determined effort to adopt Western customs of child rearing and to do away with swaddling. Young women were trained to instruct mothers that a baby's limbs should left free for better muscular development and exhibitions of pictures of unswaddled baby care were distributed widely. But swaddling persisted. Informants who have recently lived in Russia say constantly "You couldn't carry an unswaddled baby." "Mothers were so busy they had to make the child secure." Several hundreds of pictures of babies available at the Sovfoto Agency shows the prevalence of swaddling; photographs taken in 1946 and 1947 still show the completely bunted baby with only the face exposed. This physical restriction of the baby is traditionally continued for nine months or longer. It is not accompanied by social isolation. Babies are kept where adults are congregated, and their little sisters and grandmothers act as nurses; they are talked to and their needs are attended to.

In many ways the infant apparently learns that only its physical movement is restricted, not its emotions.[2] The Russian emphasis upon the child's inherent violence appears to preclude any belief among adults that its emotions could be curbed. The baby's one means of grasping the outside world is through its eyes, and it is significant that in all Russian speech and literature the eyes are stressed as the "mirrors of the soul." Russians greatly value "looking one in the eyes," for through the eyes, not through gestures or through words, a person's inmost feelings are shown. A person who does not look one in the eyes has something to conceal. A "look" also is regarded as being able to convey disapproval more shattering than physical punishment. Throughout life the eyes remain an organ which maintains strong and immediate contact with the outside world.

The baby's physical isolation within its bindings appears to be related to the kind of personal inviolability Russians maintain in adulthood. It is difficult for foreigners to appreciate the essential privacy accorded the individual in Russian folk life, for their pattern of "pouring out the soul" would be in most cultures a bid for intimacy, and their expressive proverb, "It is well even to die if there are plenty of people around," seems a vivid statement of dislike of isolation. These traits, however, coexist in Russia with a great allowance for a personal world which others do not, and need not, share. "Every man," they say, "has his own anger," and the greatest respect is given to one who has taken his own private vow—either in connection with a love affair or with a mission in life. Whatever an individual must do in order to carry out this personal vow, even if the acts would in other contexts be antisocial, is accepted. He must be true to himself; it is his *pravda*.

The Russian version of swaddling can also be profitably related to the traditional Russian attitude that strong feeling has positive value. Personal outbreaks, with or without intoxication, are traditionally ascribed to the merchant class and to peasants, but they were characteristic of all classes. Official pressure at present attempts to channel this strong feeling toward foreign enemies, but the uses of violence to the individual psyche seem to be stressed in traditional fashion in this modern propaganda.

Not only is violence in itself a means to attain order, but it is also relatively divorced from aggression against a particular enemy. In Czarist days "burning up the town," breaking all the mirrors, smashing the furniture on

[2]In this entire section I am indebted to Mr. Gorer's analysis.

a psychic binge were not means of "getting even" or of avenging one's honor; they were "in general." Even the peasants characteristically fired the home of a landowner other than the one on whom they were dependent. This trait is prepared for in the first years of life by the relative impersonality of the swaddling. Even in the villages of Great Russia, moreover, there is constant use of wet nurses and *nyanyas,* older women who are engaged to care for the baby; there is consequently a much more diffuse relationship during the first year of life than in societies where the child's contact is more limited to that with its own mother. It is characteristic of Russia, also, that poems and folk songs with the theme of mother love are practically nonexistent. The Great Russian mother is not specifically a maternal figure; she is quite sure of her sex without having to produce children to prove that she is female—as the man also is sure of his sex.

The Polish version of swaddling is quite different from the Russian. The infant is regarded not as violent, but as exceedingly fragile. It will break in two without the support given by the bindings. Sometimes it is emphasized that it would be otherwise too fragile to be safely entrusted to its siblings as child nurses; sometimes that the swaddling straightens its bent and fragile legs. Swaddling is conceived as a first step in a long process of "hardening" a child. "Hardening" is valued in Poland, and since one is hardened by suffering, suffering is also valued. A man does not demean himself by retailing his hardships and the impositions put upon him. Whereas an Italian, for instance, will minimize his dissatisfactions and discouragements and respect himself the more for so doing, Poles characteristically tend to prove their own worth by their sufferings. A usual peasant greeting is a list of his most recent miseries, and Polish patriots have exalted Poland as "the crucified Christ of the Nations." From infancy the importance of "hardening" is stressed. In peasant villages it is good for a baby to cry without attention, for it strengthens the lungs; beating the child is good because it is hardening; and mothers will even deny that they punish children by depriving them of dessert and tidbits, because "food is for strengthening; it would be no punishment to deprive them of any food."

Another theme in Polish swaddling has reference to the great gulf fixed between clean and dirty parts of the body. The binding prevents the infant from putting its toes into its mouth—the feet are practically as shame-ridden as the genitals in Poland—or from touching its face with its fingers which may just before have touched its crotch or its toes. When the baby is unswaddled for changing or for bathing, the mother must prevent such shameless acts. Whereas the Russian baby is quite free during the occasional halfhours when it is unswaddled, the Polish baby must be only the more carefully watched and prevented. Polish decency is heavily associated with keeping apart the various zones of the body.

Although it was possible to sketch Russian infancy without describing details of nursing and toilet training, which are there warm and permissive, in Poland this is impossible. The high point of contrast is perhaps the weaning. In Russia supplementary food is given early; a very small swaddled baby has a rag filled with chewed bread tied around its neck; this is pushed down on its mouth as a "comforter" by anyone present. The baby is eating many foods long before it is weaned. In Poland, however, weaning is sudden.

It is believed that a child will die if it is nursed beyond two St. John's Days of its life—or the day of some other saint—and therefore, when the child is on the average eighteen months old, the mother chooses a day for weaning. The child is not given an opportunity beforehand to accustom itself to eating solid food; the sudden transition is good because it is "hardening." It is further believed that a twice-weaned child will die and though many mothers relent because of the child's difficulties, it is necessarily with guilt.

Another contrast with Russia is a consequence of the strong feeling about the evil eye in Poland. Only the mother can touch the baby without running the danger of harming it; in the villages even the baby's aunts and cousins fall under this suspicion. Certainly no woman except the mother can feed the baby at the breast. During the spring and summer months the babies are left behind at home with three and four-year-olds since all older children go to help their parents in the fields. In house after house neglected children are crying and women incapacitated for the fields might advantageously care for them. But this is regarded as impossible.

The Polish child gets nothing from crying. He is hurried toward adulthood, and the steps which reach it are always ones which "harden" him; they are not pleasant in themselves. As a child he has tantrums, but the word for tantrums means literally "being stuck," "deadlocked." He does not cry or throw himself about as the Jewish child in Poland does; he sits for hours with rigid body, his hands and his mouth clenched. He gets beaten but he takes it without outcry or unbending. He knows his mother will not attempt to appease him. His defense of his honor in his later life is the great approved means of unburdening himself of resentments and turning them into personal glory. There are many Polish proverbs which say idiomatically and with great affect: Defend your honor though you die. The long process of childhood "hardening" lies back of their insult contest and their spirited struggles in lost causes.

The swaddling of the Jewish baby, whether in Poland or the Ukraine, has characteristics of its own. The baby is swaddled on a soft pillow and in most areas the bindings are wrapped relatively loosely around the baby and his little featherbed. The mother sings to the baby as she swaddles it. The specific stress is upon warmth and comfort, and the incidental confinement of the baby's limbs is regarded with pity and commiseration. People say in describing swaddling, "Poor baby, he looks just like a little mummy," or "He lies there nice and warm, but, poor baby, he can't move." Swaddling is also good, especially for boys, because it insures straight legs. There is no suggestion that it is the beginning of a process of "hardening" or that it is necessary because the baby is inherently violent. Rather, it is the baby's first experience of the warmth of life in his own home—a warmth which at three or four he will contrast with the lack of comfort, the hard benches, the long hours of immobility and the beatings at the *cheder,* the elementary Jewish school where he is taught Hebrew.[3] In strongest contrast to the experience of

[3][For a fascinating, detailed account of the early school experience among Eastern European Jews, see "From the Kheyder to the Grave," a chapter in a book which grew directly out of Ruth Benedict's research project, Mark Zborowski and Elizabeth Herzog, *Life Is with People: The Jewish Little-Town of Eastern Europe* (New York, 1952), pp. 88–104.—*Ed. Note.*]

the Gentile child, swaddling is part of the child's induction into the closest kind of physical intimacy; within the family the mother will expect to know every physical detail of her children's lives and treats any attempts at privacy as a lack of love and gratitude. The pillowed warmth of his swaddling period apparently becomes a prototype of what home represents, an image which he will have plenty of opportunity to contrast with the world outside, the world of the *goy*.

It is profitable also to relate Jewish swaddling to another pattern of Eastern European Jewish life: its particular version of complementary interpersonal relations. I am using "complementary" in a technical sense as a designation of those interpersonal relations where the response of a person or group to its vis-a-vis is in terms of an opposite or different behavior from that of the original actors. Such paired actions as dominance-submission, nurturance-dependence, and command-obedience are complementary responses. The Jewish complementary system might be called nurturance-deference. Nurturance is the good deed—*mitzvah*—of all parents, elders, wealthy, wise and learned men toward the children, the younger generation, the poor, and the still unschooled. In interpersonal relations these latter respond to the former with deference, "respect," but not with *mitzvah*. One never is rewarded in a coin of the same currency by one's vis-a-vis, either concurrently with the act or in the future. Parents provide for all their children's needs, but the obligation of the child to the parent does not include support of his aged parents when he is grown, and the saying is: "Better to beg one's bread from door to door than to be dependent on one's son." The aged parent feels this dependence to be humiliating, and this is in strongest contrast to the non-Jews of Poland, for instance, among whom parents can publicly humiliate their children by complaining of nonsupport. Among the Jews, a child's obligation to his parents is discharged by acting toward his own children, when he is grown, as his parents acted toward him. His aged parents are cared for, not by a son in his role as a son, but in his role as a wealthy man, contributing to the poor. Such impersonal benefactions are not humilitating to either party.

The swaddling situation is easily drawn into this Jewish system of complementary relations. The personnel involved in swaddling is necessarily complementary; it includes the binder and the bound. The bound will never reciprocate by binding the binder, and the Jewish binder conceives herself as performing a necessary act of nurturance out of which she expects the child to experience primarily warmth and comfort; she is rather sorry for the accompanying confinement but she regards random mobility as a sign of the baby's being uncomfortable. She is not, like the Polish mother, "hardening" the baby or preventing indecencies, or like the Russian mother, taking precautions against its destroying itself. She is starting the baby in a way of life where there is a lack of guilt and aggression in being the active partner in all complementary relationships and security in being the passive partner.

In swaddling situations the communication which is then established between mother and infant is continued in similar terms after swaddling is discontinued. Diapering of older babies is understood by Jewish mothers as contributing to the baby's comfort, and by Polish non-Jewish mothers as preventing indecencies by insuring that the baby's hands do not come in successive contact with "good" and "bad" parts of his body. In Rumania, where all informants from cities and towns stressed first, last and always that swaddling was necessary to prevent masturbation, the infant's hands, when he is too old to be swaddled, are tied to his crib, incased in clumsy mittens and immobilized by special clothing. His nurse or mother spies on him and punishes any slip.

The different kinds of swaddling communication which are localized in Central and Eastern Europe make it clear that the practice has been revamped to conform to the values of the several cultural groups. As in any culture area study, investigation discloses the patterning of behavior in each culture. The diversities do not confuse the picture; they enrich it. And the detailed study of this one widespread trait, like any other, throws light on the individuality of each cultural group, while at the same time it emphasizes the kinship among them.

Clifford Geertz

ETHOS, WORLD-VIEW AND THE ANALYSIS OF SACRED SYMBOLS

Despite an immense amount of anthropological research on the study of religion, our knowledge of ethical and philosophical systems found among many peoples of the world is very limited. The formal features of religions, e.g., the techniques of worship or the names and hierarchal ordering of the principal deities, have been dutifully recorded, but too often the underlying or implicit attitudes toward fellow men, toward life, or toward nature in general have not been rigorously investigated. Yet it is essential to know the values of a society if one has any aspirations to understanding that society. It is one thing to record every single kinship term and it is another to discover which relatives are favored or favorite; it is one thing to record a large corpus of songs and it is another to learn whether some songs are better than others and if "better," in what sense they are better. (Do some singers sing better than others? What, in fact, are the relevant aesthetic criteria?) In other words, the crucial question is not what is the culture of such and such a people, but how does this people (or how do different individuals among the people) interpret the various elements of their culture?

In this brilliant paper, Clifford Geertz, Professor of Anthro-

Reprinted from *The Antioch Review*, **17** (1957), 421–37, by permission of the author and *The Antioch Review*.

pology at the University of Chicago, investigates some of the basic value premises of Javanese culture. Of special significance is Geertz's discussion of the Javanese shadow-puppet play and its relevance to important Javanese philosophical and metaphysical constructs. The reader should imagine seeing a shadow-puppet play *without* a thorough knowledge of Javanese culture. Unfortunately, this is precisely the way most of the peoples of the world see elements from cultures other than their own. If we enjoy a piece of African sculpture or a carved mask from a Northwest Pacific Coast Indian tribe, we do so in the light of our own culture. There is nothing wrong with this, but we should realize that behind that art object from another culture lies a whole system of ethos and world view. And, if we wish to approach more complete understanding of other peoples' points of view, then we must make an effort to explore these ill defined but terribly important aspects of culture.

For references to the anthropological study of religion, see William A. Lessa and Evon Z. Vogt, eds., *Reader in Comparative Religion: An Anthropological Approach,* 2nd ed. (New York, 1965). For Java in particular, see Clifford Geertz, *The Religion of Java* (New York, 1960). The world-view literature is not as bountiful. There is Lucien Lévy-Bruhl, *Primitive Mentality* (Boston, 1966), a translation of the earlier French work, and Paul Radin's *Primitive Man as Philosopher* (New York, 1957). More recent studies include Clyde Kluckhohn, "The Philosophy of the Navaho Indians," in F. S. C. Northrop, ed., *Ideological Differences and World Order* (New Haven, 1949), pp. 356–84, Daryll Forde, ed., *African Worlds: Studies in the Cosmological Ideas and Social Values of African Peoples* (London, 1954), and Claude Lévi-Strauss, *The Savage Mind* (London, 1966). For an extraordinary anthropological study of the relationship between architecture and world view, see Clark E. Cunningham, "Order in the Atoni House," *Bijdragen Tot de Taal-, Land- En Volkenkunde,* **120** (1946), 34–68. A useful bibliographical aid is Ethel M. Albert and Clyde Kluckhohn, *A Selected Bibliography on Values, Ethics, and Esthetics in the Behavioral Sciences and Philosophy, 1920–1958* (Glencoe, Illinois, 1959).

Religion is never merely metaphysics. For all peoples the forms, vehicles, and objects of worship are suffused with an aura of deep moral seriousness. The holy bears within it everywhere a sense of intrinsic obligation: it not only encourages devotion, it demands it; it not only induces intellectual assent, it enforces emotional commitment. Whether it be formulated as *mana*, as *Brahma*, or as the Holy Trinity, that which is set apart as more than mundane is inevitably considered to have far-reaching implications for the direction of human conduct. Never merely metaphysics, religion is never merely ethics either. The source of its moral vitality is conceived to lie in the fidelity with which it expresses the fundamental nature of reality. The powerfully coercive "ought" is felt to grow out of a comprehensive factual "is," and in such a way religion grounds the most specific requirements of human action in the most general contexts of human existence.

In recent anthropological discussion, the moral (and aesthetic) aspects of a given culture, the evaluative elements, have commonly been summed up in the term "ethos," while the cognitive, existential aspects have been designated by the term "world-view." A people's ethos is the tone, character, and quality of their life, its moral and aesthetic style and mood; it is the underlying attitude toward themselves and their world that life reflects. Their world-view is their picture of the way things, in sheer actuality are, their concept of nature, of self, of society. It contains their most comprehensive ideas of order. Religious belief and ritual confront and mutually confirm one another; the ethos is made intellectually reasonable by being shown to represent a way of life implied by the actual state of affairs which the world-view describes, and the world-view is made emotionally acceptable by being presented as an image of an actual state of affairs of which such a way of life is an authentic expression. This demonstration of a meaningful relation between the values a people holds and the general order of existence within which it finds itself is an essential element in all religions, however those values or that order be conceived. Whatever else religion may be, it is in part an attempt (of an implicit and directly felt rather than explicit and consciously thought-about sort) to conserve the fund of general meanings in terms of which each individual interprets his experience and organizes his conduct.

But meanings can only be "stored" in symbols: a cross, a crescent, or a feathered serpent. Such religious symbols, dramatized in rituals or related in myths, are felt somehow to sum up, for those for whom they are resonant, what is known about the way the world is, the quality of the emotional life it supports, and the way one ought to behave while in it. Sacred symbols thus relate an ontology and a cosmology to an aesthetics and a morality: their peculiar power comes from their presumed ability to identify fact with value at the most fundamental level, to give to what is otherwise merely actual, a comprehensive normative import. The number of such synthesizing symbols is limited in any culture, and though in theory we might think that a people could construct a wholly autonomous value system independent of any metaphysical referent, an ethics without ontology, we do not in fact seem to have found such a people. The tendency to synthesize world-view and ethos at some level, if not logically necessary, is at least empirically coercive; if it is not philosophically justified, it is at least pragmatically universal.

Let me give as an example of this fusion of the existential and the normative a quotation from one of James Walker's Oglala (Sioux) informants, which I find in Paul Radin's neglected classic, *Primitive Man as a Philosopher:*

> The Oglala believe the circle to be sacred because the great spirit caused everything in nature to be round except stone. Stone is the implement of destruction. The sun and the sky, the earth and the moon are round like a shield, though the sky is deep like a bowl. Everything that breathes is round like the stem of a plant. Since the great spirit has caused everything to be round mankind should look upon the circle as sacred, for it is the symbol of all things in nature except stone. It is also the symbol of the circle that makes the edge of the world and therefore of the four winds that travel there. Consequently it is also the symbol of the year. The day, the night, and the moon go in a circle above the sky. Therefore the circle is a symbol of these divisions of time and hence the symbol of all time.
>
> For these reasons the Oglala make their *tipis* circular, their camp-circle circular, and sit in a circle at the ceremonies. The circle is also the symbol of the *tipi* and of shelter. If one makes a circle for an ornament and it is not divided in any way, it should be understood as the symbol of the world and of time.

Here is a subtle formulation of the relation between good and evil, and of their grounding in the very nature of reality. Circle and eccentric form, sun and stone, shelter and war are segregated into pairs of disjunct classes whose significance is aesthetic, moral and ontological. The reasoned articulateness of this statement is atypical: for most Oglala the circle, whether found in nature, painted on a buffalo skin, or enacted in a sun dance, is but an unexamined luminous symbol whose meaning is intuitively sensed, not consciously interpreted. But the power of the symbol, analyzed or not, clearly rests on its comprehensiveness, on its fruitfulness in ordering experience. Again and again the idea of a sacred circle, a natural form with a moral import, yields, when applied to the world within which the Oglala lives, new meanings; continually it connects together elements within their experience which would otherwise seem wholly disparate and, wholly disparate, incomprehensible.

The common roundness of a human body and a plant stem, of a moon and a shield, of a *tipi* and a camp-circle gives them a vaguely conceived but intensely felt significance. And this meaningful common element, once abstracted, can then be employed for ritual purposes—as when in a peace ceremony the pipe, the symbol of social solidarity, moves deliberately in a perfect circle from one smoker to the next, the purity of the form evoking the beneficence of the spirits—or to construe mythologically the peculiar paradoxes and anomalies of moral experience, as when one sees in a round stone the shaping power of good over evil.

II

It is a cluster of sacred symbols, woven into some sort of ordered whole, which makes up a religious system. For those who are committed to it, such a religious system seems to mediate genuine knowledge, knowledge of the essential conditions in terms of which life must, of necessity, be lived. Particularly where these symbols are uncriticized, historically or philosophically, as they are in most of the world's cultures, individuals who ignore the moral-aesthetic norms the symbols formulate, who follow a discordant style of life, are regarded not so much as evil as stupid, insensitive, unlearned, or in the case of extreme dereliction, mad. In Java, where I have done field work, small children, simpletons, boors, the insane, and the flagrantly immoral are all said to be "not yet Javanese," and, not yet Javanese, not yet human. Unethical behavior is referred to as "uncustomary," the more serious crimes (incest, sorcery, murder) are commonly accounted for by an assumed lapse of reason, the less serious ones by a comment that the culprit "does not know order," and the word for "religion" and that for "science" are the same. Morality has thus the air of simple realism, of practical wisdom; religion supports proper conduct by picturing a world in which such conduct is only common sense.

It is only common sense because between ethos and world-view, between the approved style of life and the assumed structure of reality, there is conceived to be a simple and fundamental congruence such that they complete one another and lend one another meaning. In Java, for example, this view is summed up in a concept one hears continually invoked, that of *tjotjog*. *Tjotjog* means to fit, as a key does in a lock, as an efficacious medicine does to a disease, as a solution does to an arithmetic problem, as a man does with the woman he marries (if he does not, they will divorce). If your opinion agrees with mine we *tjotjog*; if the meaning of my name fits my character (and if it brings me luck) it is said to be *tjotjog*. Tasty food, correct theories, good manners, comfortable surroundings, gratifying outcomes are all *tjotjog*. In the broadest and most abstract sense, two items *tjotjog* when their coincidence forms a coherent pattern which gives to each significance and a value it does not in itself have. There is implied here a contrapuntal view of the universe in which that which is important is what natural relationship the separate elements have to one another, how they must be arranged to strike a chord and to avoid a dissonance. And, as in harmony the ultimately correct relationships are fixed, determinate, and knowable, so religion, like harmony, is ultimately a kind of practical science, producing value out of fact as music is produced out of sound. In its specificity, *tjotjog* is a peculiarly Javanese idea, but the notion that life takes on its true import when human actions are tuned to cosmic conditions is widespread.

The sort of counterpoint between style of life and fundamental reality which the sacred symbols formulate varies from culture to culture. For the Navaho, an ethic prizing calm deliberateness, untiring persistence, and dignified caution complements an image of nature as tremendously powerful, mechanically regular, and highly dangerous. For the French, a logical legalism is a response to the notion that reality is rationally structured, that first principles are clear, precise, and unalterable and so need only be discerned, memorized, and deductively applied to concrete cases. For the Hindus, a transcendental moral determinism in which one's social and spiritual status in a future incarnation is an automatic outcome of the nature of one's action in the present, is completed by a ritualistic duty-ethic bound to caste. In itself, either side, the normative or the metaphysical, is arbitrary, but taken together they form a gestalt with a peculiar kind of inevitability; a French ethic in a Navaho world, or a Hindu one in a French world would seem only quixotic, for it would lack the air of naturalness and simple factuality which it has in its own context. It is this air of the factual, of describing, after all, the genuinely reasonable way to live which, given the facts of life, is the primary source of such an ethic's authoritativeness. What all sacred symbols assert is that the good for man is to live realistically; where they differ is in the vision of reality they construct.

However, it is not only positive values that sacred symbols dramatize, but negative ones as well. They point not only toward the existence of good but also of evil, and toward the conflict between them. The so-called "problem of evil" is a matter of formulating in world-view terms the actual nature of the destructive forces within the self and outside of it, of interpreting murder, crop failure, sickness, earthquakes, poverty, and oppression in such a way that it is possible to come to some sort of terms with them. Declaring evil fundamentally unreal—as in Indian religions and some versions of Christianity—is but one rather uncommon solution to the problem; more often, the reality of evil is accepted and characterized positively, and an attitude toward it—resignation, active opposition, hedonistic escape, self-recrimination and repentance, or a humble plea for mercy—is enjoined as reasonable and proper, given its nature. Among the African Azande, where all natural misfortune (death, illness, crop failure) is seen as caused by the hatred of one man for another acting mechanically through witchcraft, the attitude toward evil is a straightforward and practical one: it is to be dealt with by means of reliably established divination in order to discover the witch, and proven methods of social pressure to force him to abandon his attack, or failing this, by effective vengeance-magic to kill him. Among the Melanesian Manus, the conception that illness, death, or financial failure are the result of a secret sin (adultery, stealing, lying) which has offended the moral sensibilities of the household spirit is coupled with an emphasis on public confession and repentance as the rational way to cope with evil. For the Javanese, evil results from unregulated passion and is resisted by detachment and self-control. Thus, both what a people prizes and what it fears and hates are depicted in its world-view, symbolized in its religion, and in turn expressed in the whole quality of its life. Its ethos is distinctive not merely in terms of the sort of nobility it celebrates, but also in terms of the sort of baseness it condemns; its vices are as stylized as its virtues.

The force of a religion in supporting social values rests, then, on the ability of its symbols to formulate a world in which those values, as well as the forces opposing their realization, are fundamental ingredients. It represents the power of the human imagination to construct an image of reality in which, to quote Max Weber, "events are not just there and happen, but they have a meaning and happen because of that meaning." The need for such a metaphysical grounding for values seems to vary quite widely in intensity from culture to culture and from individual to individual, but the tendency to desire some sort of factual basis for one's commitments seems practically universal; mere conventionalism satisfies few people in any culture. However its role may differ at various times, for various individuals, and in various cultures, religion, by fusing ethos and world-view, gives to a set of social values what they perhaps most need to be coercive: an appearance of objectivity. In sacred rituals and myths values are portrayed not as subjective human preferences but as the imposed conditions for life implicit in a world with a particular structure.

III

The sort of symbols (or symbol complexes) regarded by a people as sacred varies very widely. Elaborate initiation rites, as among the Australians; complex philosophical tales, as among the Maori; dramatic shamanistic exhibitions, as among the Eskimo; cruel human sacrifice rites, as among the Aztecs; obsessive curing ceremonies, as among the Navaho; large communal feasts, as among various Polynesian groups—all these patterns and many more seem to one people or another to sum up most powerfully what it knows about living. Nor is there commonly but one such complex: Malinowski's famous Trobrianders seem equally concerned with the rituals of gardening and those of trade. In a complex civilization such as that of the Javanese—in which Hinduistic, Islamic, and pagan influences all remain very strong—one could choose any of several symbol complexes as revealing one or another aspect of the integration of ethos and world-view. But perhaps the clearest and most direct insight into the relation between Javanese values and Javanese metaphysics can be gained through a brief analysis of one of the most deeply rooted and highly developed of their art forms which is at the same time a religious rite: the shadow-puppet play, or *wajang*.

The shadow play is called so because the puppets, which are flat cutouts of leather, painted in golds, reds, blues, and blacks, are made to cast large shadows on a white screen. The *dalang*, as the puppeteer is called, sits on a mat in front of the screen, with a *gamelan* percussion orchestra behind him, an oil lamp hanging over his head. A banana tree-trunk lies horizontally in front of him into which the puppets, each of them fastened to a tortoise-shell handle, are stuck. A performance lasts a whole night. As the play progresses, the *dalang* takes and replaces characters from the tree-trunk as he needs them, holding them up in either hand over his head and interposing them between the light and the screen. From the *dalang's* side of the screen—where traditionally only the men were permitted to sit—one sees the puppets themselves, their shadows rising up dominant on the screen behind them; from the reverse side of the screen—where the women and children sit—one sees their shadows only.

The stories dramatized are mostly episodes taken from the Indian epic Mahabarata, somewhat adapted and placed in a Javanese setting. (Stories from the Ramayana are sometimes dramatized, but they are less popular.) In this cycle there are three major groups of characters. First, there are the gods and goddesses, headed by Siva and his wife Durga. As in the Greek epics, the gods are far from uniformly righteous, are marked by human frailties and human passions, and seem peculiarly interested in the things of this world. Second, there are the kings and nobles, who are, in theory, the ancestors of the present-day Javanese. The two most important groups of these nobles are the Pendawas and the Korawas. The Pendawas are the famous five hero brothers—Yudistira, Bima, Arjuna, and the identical twins, Nakula and Sadéwa—who are usually accompanied, as a general advisor and protector, by Krisna, an incarnation of Visnu. The Korawas, of whom there are a hundred, are cousins of the Pendawa. They have usurped the kingdom of Ngastina from them, and it is the struggle over this disputed country which provides the major theme of the *wajang;* a struggle which culminates in the great Bratajuda war of kinsmen, as related in the Bhagavad Gita, in which the Korawas are defeated by the Pendawas. And, third, there are those Javanese additions to the original Hindu cast of characters, the great low clowns—Semar, Petruk, and Garèng, constant companions of the Pendawas, at once their servants and their protectors. Semar, the father of the other two, is actually a god in all-too-human form, a brother to Siva, king of the gods. The guardian spirit of all Javanese from their first appearance until the end of time, this gross and clumsy fool is perhaps the most important figure in the whole *wajang* mythology.

The types of action characteristic of the *wajang* also are three: there are the "talking" episodes in which two groups of opposed nobles confront one another and discuss (the *dalang* imitates all the voices) the issues between them; there are the fighting episodes, in which diplomacy having failed, the two groups of nobles fight (the *dalang* knocks the puppets together and kicks a clapper with his foot to symbolize the sounds of war); and there are the slapstick comic scenes, in which the clowns mock the nobles, each other, and, if the *dalang* is clever, members of the audience or the local powers-that-be. Generally, the three sorts of episodes are differentially distributed over the course of the evening. The declamatory scenes are mostly toward the beginning, the comic ones toward the middle, and the war toward the end. From nine until midnight, the political leaders of the various kingdoms confront one another and state the framework of the story—a *wajang* hero wishes to marry the daughter of a neighboring king, a subjugated country wants its freedom, or whatever. From midnight until three o'clock or so difficulties of some sort set in—someone else is bidding for the daughter's hand, the imperialist country refuses freedom to its colony. And, finally, these difficulties are resolved in the last section, ending at dawn, inevitably, by a war in which the heroes triumph—an action followed by a brief celebration of the accomplished marriage or the achieved freedom. Western-educated Javanese intellectuals often compare the *wajang* to a sonata; it opens with an exposition of a theme, follows with a development and complication of it, and ends with its resolution and recapitulation.

Another comparison which, offhand, strikes the Western observer is with Shakespeare's chronicle plays. The long formal scenes in the courts with the messengers coming and going, interspersed with short, breathless transitional scenes in the woods or along the road, the double plot, the clowns speaking a rough common language full of worldly-wise ethics, caricaturing the forms of action of the great nobles, who speak an elevated language full of apostrophes to honor, justice, and duty, the final war, which, like those at Shrewsbury and Agincourt, leaves the vanquished beaten but still noble—all these suggest Shakespeare's historical dramas. But the world-view the *wajang* expresses, despite the surface similarities in the two feudal codes, is hardly Elizabethan at base. It is not the external world of princi-palities and powers which provides the main setting for human action, but the internal one of sentiments and desires. Reality is looked for not outside the self, but within it, and consequently what the *wajang* dramatizes is not a philosophical politics but a metaphysical psychology.

For the Javanese (or at least for those of them in whose thought the influence of Java's Hindu-Buddhist period from the second to the fifteenth centuries still is dominant), the flow of subjective experience, taken in all its phenomenological immediacy, presents a microcosm of the universe generally; in the depths of the fluid interior world of thought-and-emotion they see reflected ultimate reality itself. This inward-looking sort of world-view is best expressed in a concept the Javanese have also borrowed from India and also peculiarly reinterpreted: *rasa. Rasa* has two primary mean-ings: "feeling" and "meaning." As "feeling" it is one of the traditional Javanese five senses—seeing, hearing, talking, smelling, and feeling, and it includes within itself three aspects of "feeling" that our view of the five senses separates: taste on the tongue, touch on the body, and emotional "feeling" within the "heart" like sadness and happiness. The taste of a banana is its *rasa*; a hunch is a *rasa*; a pain is a *rasa*; and so is a passion. As "meaning," *rasa* is applied to the words in a letter, in a poem, or even in common speech to indicate the between-the-lines type of indirection and allusive suggestion that is so important in Javanese communication and social intercourse. And it is given the same application to behavioral acts generally: to indicate the implicit import, the connotative "feeling" of dance movements, polite gestures, and so forth. But in this second, semantic sense, it also means "ultimate significance"—the deepest meaning at which one arrives by dint of mystical effort and whose clarification resolves all the ambiguities of mundane existence. *Rasa,* said one of my most articulate informants, is the same as life; whatever lives has *rasa* and whatever has *rasa* lives. To translate such a sentence one could only render it twice: whatever lives feels and whatever feels lives; or: whatever lives has meaning and whatever has meaning lives.

By taking rasa to mean both "feeling" and "meaning," the more speculatively inclined among the Javanese have been able to develop a highly sophisticated phenomenological analysis of subjective experience to which everything else can be tied. Because fundamentally "feeling" and "meaning" are one, and therefore the ultimate religious experience taken *subjectively* is also the ultimate religious truth taken *objectively,* an empirical analysis of inward perception yields at the same time a metaphysical analysis of outward reality. This being granted—and the actual discrimina-tions, categorizations and connections made are often both subtle and detailed—then the characteristic way in which human action comes to be considered, from either a moral or an aesthetic point of view, is in terms of the emotional life of the individual who experiences it. This is true whether this action is seen from within as one's own behavior or from without as that of someone else: the more refined one's feelings, then the more profound one's understanding, the more elevated one's moral character, and the more beautiful one's external aspect, in clothes, movements, speech, and so on. The management of the individual's emotional economy becomes, therefore, his primary concern, in terms of which all else is ultimately rationalized. The spiritually enlightened man guards well his psychological equilibrium and makes a constant effort to maintain its placid stability. His inner life must be, in a simile repeatedly employed, like a still pool of clear water to the bottom of which one can easily see. The individual's proximate aim is, thus, emotional quiescence, for passion is crude feeling, fit for children, animals, madmen, primitives and foreigners. But his ultimate aim, which this quiescence makes possible, is gnosis—the direct comprehension of the ultimate *rasa*.

Javanese religion (or at least this variant of it) is consequently mystical: God is found by means of spiritual discipline, in the depths of the self as pure *rasa*. And Javanese ethics (and aesthetics) are, correspondingly, affect-centered without being hedonistic: emotional equanimity, a certain flatness of affect, a strange inner stillness, is the prized psychological state, the mark of a truly noble character. One must attempt to get beyond the emotions of everyday life to the genuine feeling-meaning which lies within us all. Happiness and unhappiness are, after all, just the same. You shed tears when you laugh and also when you cry. And, besides, they imply one another: happy now, unhappy later; unhappy now, happy later. The reasonable, prudent, "wise" man strives not for happiness, but for a tranquil detachment which frees him from this endless oscillation between gratification and frustration. Similarly, Javanese etiquette, which comprises almost the whole of this morality, focuses around the injunction not to disturb the equilibrium of another by sudden gestures, loud speech, or startling, erratic actions of any sort, mainly because so doing will cause the other in turn to act erratically and so upset one's own balance. On the world-view side, there are yoga-like mystical techniques (meditation, staring at candles, repeating set words or phrases) and highly involved speculative theories of the emotions and their relations to sickness, natural objects, social institutions, and so on. On the ethos side, there is a moral stress on subdued dress, speech and gesture, on refined sensitivity to small changes in the emotional state both of oneself and of others, and on a stable, highly regularized predictability of behavior. "If you start off north, go north," a Javanese proverb says, "don't turn east, west, or south." Both religion and ethics, both mysticism and politesse, thus point to the same end: a detached tranquility which is proof against disturbance from either within or without.

But, unlike India, this tranquility is not to be gained by a retreat from the world and from society, but must be achieved while in it. It is a this-worldly, even practical mysticism, as expressed in the following composite quotation from two Javanese petty traders who are members of a mystical society:

> He said that the society was concerned with teaching you not to pay too much attention to worldly things, not to care too much about the things of everyday life. He said this is very difficult to do. His wife, he said, was not yet able to do it much, and she agreed with him, e.g., she still likes to ride in motorcars while he doesn't care; he can take them or leave them alone. It takes much long study and meditation. For example, you have to get so that if someone comes to buy cloth you don't care if he buys it or not...and you don't get your emotions really involved in the problems of commerce, but just think of God. The society wants to turn people toward God and avoids any strong attachments to everyday life.
>
> ...Why did he meditate? He said it was only to make the heart peaceful, to make you calm inside, so you will not be easily upset. For example, if you're selling cloth and are upset you may sell a piece of cloth for forty rupiah when it cost you sixty. If a person comes here and my mind is not calm, well then I can't sell him anything....I said, well, why do you have a meeting, why not meditate at home? And he said, well, in the first place you are not supposed to achieve peace by withdrawing from society; you are supposed to stay in society and mix with people, only with peace in your heart.

This fusion between a mystical-phenomenological world-view and an etiquette-centered ethos is expressed in the *wajang* in various ways. First, it appears most directly in terms of an explicit iconography. The five *pendawas* are commonly interpreted as standing for the five senses which the individual must unite into one undivided psychological force in order to achieve gnosis. Meditation demands a "cooperation" among the senses as close as that among the hero brothers, who act as one in all they do. Or the shadows of the puppets are identified with the outward behavior of man, the puppets themselves with his inward self, so that in him as in them the visible pattern of conduct is a direct outcome of an underlying psychological reality. The very design of the puppets has explicit symbolic significance: in Bima's red, white and black sarong, the red is usually taken to indicate courage, the white purity, the black fixity of will. The various tunes played on the accompanying *gamelan* orchestra each symbolize a certain emotion; similarly with the poems the *dalang* sings at various points in the play, and so on. Second, the fusion often appears as parable, as in the story of Bima's quest for the "clear water." After slaying many monsters in his wanderings in search of this water which he has been told will make him invulnerable, he meets a god as big as his little finger who is an exact replica of himself. Entering through the mouth of this mirror-image midget, he sees inside the god's body the whole world, complete in every detail, and upon emerging he is told by the god that there is no "clear water" as such, that the source of his own strength is within himself, after which he goes off to meditate. And third, the moral content of the play is sometimes interpreted analogically: the *dalang's* absolute control over the puppets is said to parallel God's over men; or the alternation of polite speeches and violent wars is said to parallel modern international relationships, where so long as diplomats continue talking peace prevails, but when talks break down war follows.

But neither icons, parables, nor moral analogies are the main means by which the Javanese synthesis is expressed in the *wajang;* for the play as a whole is commonly perceived to be but a dramatization of individual subjective experience in terms at once moral and factual:

> He [an elementary school-teacher] said that the main purpose of the *wajang* was to draw a picture of inner thought and feeling, to give an external form to internal feeling. He said that more specifically it pictured the eternal conflict in the individual between what he wanted to do and what he felt he ought to do. Suppose you want to steal something. Well, at the same time something inside you tells you not to do it, restrains you, controls you. That which wants to do it is called the will; that which restrains is called the ego. All such tendencies threaten every day to ruin the individual, to destroy his thought and upset his behavior. These tendencies are called *goda,* which means something which plagues or teases someone or something. For example, you go to a coffee-shop where people are eating. They invite you to join them, and so you have a struggle within—should I eat with them...no, I've already eaten and I will be over full...but the food looks good...etc....etc.
>
> Well, in the *wajang* the various plagues, wishes, etc.—the *godas*—are represented by the hundred Korawas, and the ability to control oneself is represented by their cousins, the five Pendawas and by Krisna. The stories are ostensibly about a struggle over land. The reason for this is so the stories will seem real to the onlookers, so the abstract elements in the *rasa* can be represented in concrete external elements which will attract the audience and seem real to them and still communicate its inner message. For example, the *wajang* is full of war and this war, which occurs and reoccurs, is really supposed to represent the inner war which goes on continually in every person's subjective life between his base and his refined impulses.

Once again, this formulation is more self-conscious than most; the average man "enjoys" the *wajang* without explicitly interpreting its meaning. Yet, in the same way as the circle organizes Oglala experience, whether the individual Sioux is able to explicate its significance, or indeed has any interest in doing so, so the sacred symbols of the *wajang*—the music, characters, the action itself—give form to the ordinary Javanese experience.

For example, each of the three older Pendawas are commonly held to display a different sort of emotional-moral dilemma, centering around one or another of the central Javanese virtues. Yudistira, the eldest, is too compassionate. He is unable to rule his country effectively because when someone asks him for his land, his wealth, his food, he simply gives it out of pity, leaving himself powerless, poor or starving. His enemies continually take advantage of his mercifulness to deceive him and to escape his justice. Bima, on the other hand, is single-minded, steadfast. Once he forms an intention, he follows it out straight to its conclusion; he doesn't look aside, doesn't turn off or idle along the way—he "goes north." As a result, he is often rash, and blunders into difficulties he could as well have avoided. Arjuna, the third brother, is perfectly just. His goodness comes from the fact that he opposes evil, that he shelters people from injustice, that he is coolly courageous in fighting for the right. But he lacks a sense of mercy, of sympathy for wrongdoers. He applies a divine moral code to human activity and so he is often cold, cruel or brutal in the name of justice. The resolution of these three dilemmas of virtue is the same: mystical insight. With a genuine comprehension of the realities of the human situation, a true perception of the ultimate *rasa,* comes the ability to combine Yudistra's compassion, Bima's will to action, and Arjuna's sense of justice into a truly moral outlook, an outlook which brings an emotional detachment and an inner peace in the midst of the world of flux, yet permits and demands a struggle for order and justice within such a world. And it is such a unification that the unshakable solidarity among the Pendawas in the play, continually rescuing one another from the defects of their virtues, clearly demonstrates.

But what, finally, of Semar, in whom so many oppositions seem to meet —the figure who is both god and clown, man's guardian spirit and his servant, the most spiritually refined inwardly and the most rough-looking outwardly? Again one thinks of the chronicle plays and of, in this case, Falstaff. Like Falstaff, Semar is a symbolic father to the play's heroes. Like Falstaff, he is fat, funny, and worldly-wise; and, like Falstaff, he seems to provide in his vigorous amoralism a general criticism of the very values the drama affirms. Both figures, perhaps, provide a reminder that, despite over-proud assertions to the contrary by religious fanatics and moral absolutists, no completely adequate and comprehensive human world-view is possible, and behind all the pretense to absolute and ultimate knowledge, the sense for the irrationality of human life, for the fact that it is unlimitable, remains. Semar reminds the noble and refined Pendawas of their own humble, animal origins. He resists any attempt to turn human beings into gods and to end the world of natural contingency by a flight to the divine world of absolute order, a final stilling of the eternal psychological-metaphysical struggle.

In one *wajang* story, Siva comes down to earth incarnated as a mystical teacher in an attempt to bring the Pendawas and Karawas together, to arrange a negotiated peace between them. He is succeeding quite well, opposed only by Semar. Arjuna is therefore instructed by Siva to kill Semar so that the Pendawas and Korawas will be able to get together and end their eternal struggle. Arjuna does not want to kill Semar whom he loves, but he wishes a just solution to the differences between the two groups of cousins and so goes to Semar to murder him. Semar says: so this is how you treat me after I have followed you everywhere, served you loyally, and loved you. This is the most poignant point in the play and Arjuna is deeply ashamed; but true to his idea of justice, he persists in his duty. Semar says: all right, I will burn myself. He builds a bonfire and stands in it. But instead of dying, he is transformed into his godly form and defeats Siva in combat. Then the war between the Korawas and the Pendawas begins again.

Not all people have, perhaps, so well developed a sense for the necessary note of irrationality in any world-view, and thus for the essential insolubility of the problem of evil. But whether in the form of a trickster, a clown, a belief in witchcraft, or a concept of original sin, the presence of such a symbolic reminder of the hollowness of human pretensions to religious or moral infallibility is perhaps the surest sign of spiritual maturity.

IV

The view of man as a symbolizing, conceptualizing, meaning-seeking animal which has become increasingly popular both in the social sciences and in philosophy over the past several years, opens up a whole new approach not only to the analysis of religion as such, but to the understanding of the relations between religion and values. The drive to make sense out of experience, to give it form and order, is evidently as real and as pressing as the more familiar biological needs. And, this being so, it seems unnecessary to continue to interpret symbolic activities—religion, art, ideology—as nothing but thinly disguised expressions of something other than what they seem to be: attempts to provide orientation for an organism which cannot live in a world it is unable to understand. If symbols, to adapt a phrase of Kenneth Burke's, are strategies for encompassing situations, then we need to give more attention to how people define situations and how they go about coming to terms with them. Such a stress does not imply a removal of beliefs and values from their psychobiological and social contexts into a realm of "pure meaning," but it does imply a greater emphasis on the analysis of such beliefs and values in terms of concepts explicitly designed to deal with symbolic material.

The concepts used in this paper, ethos and world-view, are vague and imprecise; they are a kind of proto-theory, forerunners, it is to be hoped, of a more adequate analytical framework. But even with them, anthropologists are beginning to develop an approach to the study of values which can clarify rather than obscure the essential processes involved in the normative regulation of behavior. One almost certain result of such an empirically oriented, theoretically sophisticated, symbol-stressing approach to the study of values is the decline of analyses which attempt to describe moral, aesthetic and other normative activities in terms of theories based not on the observation of such activities but on logical considerations alone. Like bees who fly despite theories of aeronautics which deny them the right to do so, probably the overwhelming majority of mankind is continually drawing normative conclusions from factual premises (and factual conclusions from normative premises, for the relation between ethos and world-view is circular) despite refined, and in their own terms impeccable, reflections by professional philosophers on the "naturalistic fallacy." An approach to a theory of value which looks toward the behavior of actual people in actual societies living in terms of actual cultures for both its stimulus and its validation will turn us away from abstract and rather scholastic arguments in which a limited number of classical positions are stated again and again with little that is new to recommend them, to a process of ever increasing insight into both what values are and how they work. Once this enterprise in the scientific analysis of values is well launched, the philosophical discussions of ethics are likely to take on more point. The process is not that of replacing moral philosophy by descriptive ethics, but of providing moral philosophy with an empirical base and a conceptual framework which is somewhat advanced over that available to Aristotle, Spinoza, or G. E. Moore. The role of such a special science as anthropology in the analysis of values is not to replace philosophical investigation, but to make it relevant.

Kenelm O. L. Burridge

A TANGU GAME

To most of us, folklore means myths, folktales, folk songs, and proverbs. Yet one of the most interesting forms of folklore includes traditional games. Games may be considered to be structural models of the adult world in a given culture. In such microcosms of play, the principal problems of reality as they are perceived in the culture are posed. In American culture, for example, many, if not most, of our games are competitive. There is a winner and there is a loser. Indeed, there are even special provisions for "overtime" periods in the event that normal play results in a tie or draw. The "sudden death" overtime period is designed to break the tie and to ensure there being a winner. This competition ethic so clearly etched in American games is found throughout the fabric of American culture. For this reason an account of a game from another culture, in which the participants do not play to win, but to draw, should be particularly striking.

The Tangu are a fairly remote people living fifteen miles inland from Bogia Bay on the north coast of New Guinea in the Madang District. In this brief consideration by Dr. Kenelm O. L. Burridge, Lecturer at the Pitt Rivers Museum in Oxford, of one of the traditional games played by the Tangu, one can see how folklore provides behavioral models.

For further information on folklore, see Alan Dundes, "The American Concept of Folklore," *Journal of the Folklore Institute,* 3 (1966), 226–49, and J. L. Fischer, "The Sociopsychological Analysis of Folktales," *Current Anthropology,* 4 (1963), 235–95. For representative scholarship in this area, see Alan Dundes, ed., *The Study of Folklore* (Englewood Cliffs, N. J., 1965). For the notion of games and other folklore as models, see John M.

Reprinted from *Man,* 57 (1957), 88–89, by permission of the author and the Royal Anthropological Institute.

Roberts, Brian Sutton-Smith, and Adam Kendon, "Strategy in Games and Folk Tales," *Journal of Social Psychology*, **61** (1963), 185–99, and T. O. Beidelman, "Hyena and Rabbit: A Kaguru Representation of Matrilineal Relations," *Africa*, **31** (1961), 61–74. For more on Tangu folklore, see Kenelm O. L. Burridge, "Social Implications of Some Tangu Myths," *Southwestern Journal of Anthropology*, **12** (1956), 415–31.

One of the ideas dominating Tangu relationships and activities is equivalence: a notion of moral equality between persons which receives primary expression in the attempt to exchange equivalent amounts of foodstuffs—a task entailing almost insuperable practical difficulties and rarely explicitly attained except by mutual consent and agreement.[1] The same idea of equivalence is expressed in a game, popular with Tangu, which is played mostly by children but which is also a pastime of adults and youths.

The game, known as *taketak*, takes its name from the word for the hard spines of coconut palm fronds. Before play the spines are stripped and stuck in the ground about six inches apart so that they form two lots of massed spines standing rather less than three feet in height. Each lot would contain about 30 spines and is separated from the other by approximately five yards. Care is taken to plant the *taketak* so that there are no empty corridors, and so that the *taketak* do not form parallel or diagonal lines. Tops—hollow hemispheres about two inches in diameter, made from a dried rind, the half of a wild jungle fruit, with a spindle forced through the apex of the hemisphere—are also required.

The two teams that form up are usually roughly equivalent as regards numbers of persons, but what is important is that the number of tops used by each team should be the same. A player spins a top in the palms of his hands, and, in one movement, throws it into one lot of spines with the object of striking as many as possible—either during the flight of the top or whilst it is spinning on the ground. Those *taketak* which have been touched by the top are pulled out and laid aside. When the first team have completed their play into one lot of *taketak*, the second take up their tops and play into the other. Supposing the first team to have struck three *taketak*, and the second two, two *taketak* are replaced in the lot into which the first team is spinning. If, with their second turn, the first team hit one *taketak*, it is removed— leaving both teams with two *taketak* out of each lot. Both teams are now equivalent as to the number of *taketak* removed, but the second team owe their series of spins: their object is to throw their

---

[1]A situation known as *mngwotngwotiki*, precise equivalence. Pairs who are *mngwotngwotiki* do not exchange, nor are they allowed to co-operate—since the latter means management of one by the other. An oppositional or co-operative relationship may be revived later either by agreement or by some personal irritant which may throw doubt on the reality of the equivalence agreed to.

tops into the *taketak* without hitting one. Should they succeed in *not* hitting any *taketak*—and the top has to be thrown fairly into the middle of the lot—the game is over and both teams are equivalent. If, on the other hand, the second team should strike one *taketak*, two are replaced. The game goes on in this wise until either the players tire of the game—when equivalence is reached by mutual consent—or until all the *taketak* are replaced in both lots.

Another and significantly different version of the game came into vogue in a particular settlement which, incidentally, had had most to do with Tangu Cargo cult activities.[2] In this version the two teams spin their tops into the lots of *taketak* without any replacements. The game continues until one team has struck and extracted all the *taketak* belonging to the other. The first round is then over and the winning team are described as *gtangi*—strong, obdurate, not susceptible to persuasion. Another round follows. Should the losers of the first round win the second, the teams are regarded as equivalent and only rarely is a third and decisive round embarked upon. If the winners of the first round also win the second they are described as emphatically *gtangi,* and no third round is initiated.

In the second version the Pidgin term 'gol,' derived from our own 'goal' in its context in Association Football, is used to acclaim the striking of a *taketak*. Much simpler to play than the original game, the later version—both in its form and in the spirit in which it is played—is biased towards selecting a 'stronger' or winning team. Yet no team that loses is content to leave it at that. A return match is arranged in which every effort is made by *both* sides to come out equivalent in the series. To remain *gtangi* at the

---

[2]*Cf*. my 'Cargo Cult Activity in Tangu,' *Oceania,* Vol. XXIV, No. 4, June 1954. [Cargo cults are Melanesian examples of modern native religious movements that have arisen to protest some of the results of acculturation. In acculturation, two or more distinct cultures come into contact. Most studies of acculturation have dealt with what are in fact colonial situations, that is, a native culture invaded and dominated by a Euro-American culture. In one form of what amounts to an almost predictable religious movement, one finds collective wishful thinking in that the overbearing white man is neatly eliminated but his desirable manufactured goods are happily retained. In Melanesia the natives had never seen factories and without knowledge of the manufacturing process they fell back upon what they knew to be the origin of these goods. The goods arrived by ship. Thus in the ideal world that was to come, ships would come bearing precious cargo, but the cargo would be for the natives, not for the overlord whites. To ensure this, sometimes the self-proclaimed messiahs in these so-called messianic movements would set specific preconditions for the arrival of the cargo. For example, in the John Frum movement in New Hebrides, the people were told that before their wishes could be realized they had to kill all the Europeans in the area, get rid of all their European money, and return to the various old customs and ways which had been forbidden by the missionaries. For a consideration of the cargo cult and allied phenomena, see William A. Lessa and Evon Z. Vogt, eds., *Reader in Comparative Religion: An Anthropological Approach.* 2nd ed. (New York, 1965), pp. 499–541. For specific studies in Melanesia, see Peter Worsley, *The Trumpet Shall Sound: A Study of "Cargo" Cults in Melanesia* (London, 1957), or some of the references in Ida Leeson, *Bibliography of Cargo Cults and Other Nativistic Movements in the South Pacific,* South Pacific Commission, Technical Paper No. 30 (Sydney, 1952). For an extended analysis of the Tangu cargo cult in particular, see Kenelm Burridge, *Mambu, A Melanesian Millennium* (London, 1960).—*Ed. Note.*].

expense of others in the community may, today, give a pinch of self-satisfaction to the winners—but they also feel anxious about the ill-feeling it generates. The older version of the game, which may be taken to be relatively unaffected by European contacts, has much the same competitive spirit during play as the other and it is also more subtle. It does not require perfecting a single skill in order to strike down more *taketak* more rapidly: it requires the ability to hit *taketak* when necessary, and to miss them if it is expedient. Finishing the game by consent and agreement is not only in itself a mutual recognition of parity, but it is also an acknowledgment that the game can end in no other way.

Food exchanges and the rivalries that go with them can also be ended by mutual consent. Theoretically at least, though not often in practice, the game can be completed.[3] But there is no third factor to pronounce on equivalence in food exchanges: failing the mutual consent they go on until death or retirement.[4]

Benjamin Lee Whorf

SCIENCE AND LINGUISTICS

There are two aspects of culture in which patterning is especially obvious: kinship and language. The patterning present in many other aspects of culture, e.g., art or economics, is not as easily discerned and placed into elegant paradigms as are the materials of kinship and linguistic systems. For this reason, among cultural anthropologists, it is the students of social organization and language who have made some of the most striking discoveries of cultural patterning.

In all of the vast literature on language in general and on

[3]But I have never seen a game ended other than by mutual consent. 'Missing' requires an almost impossible combination of skill and fortune.

[4][The Tangu penchant for establishing equilibrium appears to have parallels in other New Guinea cultures. For example, virtually the same phenomenon has been reported among the Gahuku-Gama, a people of the Eastern Highlands of New Guinea. It is interesting to see what happened when a Euro-American competitive game was introduced to this equivalence oriented group. In the Gahuka-Gama adaptation of soccer (termed "football" in Europe), the "rules" were altered so that the object of the game was for each team to equal the goals scored by the other. Games apparently went on for days until the scores were deemed equivalent. This shows not only that games are microcosmic models of social reality but that each culture in almost predictable fashion molds borrowings from other cultures to fit culturally preferred patterns. For a discussion of Gahuku-Gama soccer and the cultural pattern to which it seems to conform, see K. E. Read, "Leadership and Consensus in a New Guinea Society," *American Anthropologist*, 61 (1959), 425–36.—*Ed. Note.*]

anthropological linguistics in particular, one of the most imaginative thinkers was a chemical engineer who worked for a fire insurance company in Hartford, Connecticut. Benjamin Lee Whorf, a graduate of Massachusetts Institute of Technology, became interested in American Indian languages as a hobby. Later he went to Yale University to study with the brilliant linguist Edward Sapir, who inspired him to investigate the relationship between patterns of language and patterns of thought. Whorf wrote a paper in 1939, "The Relation of Habitual Thought and Behavior to Language," which stated his idea that cognitive categories (of space, time, etc.) were largely linguistically determined.

Whorf was not interested merely in demonstrating linguistic relativity, but rather in showing that there was a correlation between the relativistic perception and behavior in a culture and the language of that culture. That the structure of a given language influences the categories of perception and thought of speakers of that language cannot be doubted, but the extent of the influence continues to be debated. Whorf, as a linguist, perhaps tended to overemphasize the importance of language in the determination of cognitive categories, for the categories might have influenced the development of the language. The relationship between language and thought may well be a "Which came first, the chicken or the egg?" type of proposition. In any case, there is the question of why the patterning of one aspect of culture should necessarily be given logical priority over the patterning of another. On the other hand, the built-in bias of linguistic structures, if Whorf is right, certainly could be a significant factor in shaping the modes of reasoning and understanding in a society, and this would make the study of language absolutely essential if we wished to see the relativity of our own thought patterns and if we wished to communicate more effectively with the inhabitants of other linguistic "prisons." Hopefully, by realizing that there is a linguistic determinant and by eventually understanding its nature man could free himself somewhat from the bonds of cultural determinism.

For "The Relation of Habitual Thought and Behavior to Language," and other essays by Whorf, see *Language, Thought and Reality, Selected Writings of Benjamin Lee Whorf,* ed. John B. Carroll (Cambridge, 1956). The introduction by Carroll gives some details of Whorf's life and scholarship. For discussion of the controversial Whorf hypothesis (or as it is sometimes called, the "Sapir-Whorf" hypothesis), see Harry Hoijer, ed., *Language in Culture: Conference on the Interrelations of Language and Other Aspects of Culture* (Chicago, 1954), and such representative articles as Max Black, "Linguistic Relativity: The Views of Benjamin Lee Whorf," *Philosophical Review,* **68** (1959), 228–38; Joshua Fishman, "A Systematization of the

Whorfian Hypothesis," *Behavioral Science,* **5** (1960), 232–39; and G. A. Brutyan, "A Marxist Evaluation of the Whorf Hypothesis," *ETC.: A Review of General Semantics,* **19** (1962), 199–220. For additional references, see Dell Hymes, *Language in Culture and Society: A Reader in Linguistics and Anthropology* (New York, 1964), p. 150. For general introductions to language (from a linguistics point of view) see the older classics: Edward Sapir, *Language* (New York, 1921), and Leonard Bloomfield, *Language* (New York, 1933). For further readings in the field of language and culture, including the less controversial and more conventional types of linguistic research (e.g., involving phonological, morphological, and syntactic analysis) see the articles in Hymes' reader or those mentioned in his various voluminous bibliographical reference notes.

Every normal person in the world, past infancy in years, can and does talk. By virtue of that fact, every person —civilized or uncivilized—carries through life certain naïve but deeply rooted ideas about talking and its relation to thinking. Because of their firm connection with speech habits that have become unconscious and automatic, these notions tend to be rather intolerant of opposition. They are by no means entirely personal and haphazard; their basis is definitely systematic, so that we are justified in calling them a system of natural logic—a term that seems to me preferable to the term common sense, often used for the same thing.

According to natural logic, the fact that every person has talked fluently since infancy makes every man his own authority on the process by which he formulates and communicates. He has merely to consult a common substratum of logic or reason which he and everyone else are supposed to possess. Natural logic says that talking is merely an incidental process concerned strictly with communication, not with formulation of ideas. Talking, or the use of language, is supposed only to "express" what is essentially already formulated nonlinguistically. Formulation is an independent process, called thought or thinking, and is supposed to be largely indifferent to the nature of particular languages. Languages have grammars, which are assumed to be merely norms of conventional and social correctness, but the use of language is supposed to be guided not so much by them as by correct, rational, or intelligent *thinking.*

Thought, in this view, does not depend on grammar but on laws of logic or reason which are supposed to be the same for all observers of the universe —to represent a rationale in the universe that can be "found" independently by all intelligent observers, whether they speak Chinese or Choctaw. In our own culture, the formulations of mathematics and of formal logic have acquired the reputation of dealing with this order of things: i.e., with the realm and laws of pure thought. Natural logic holds that different languages

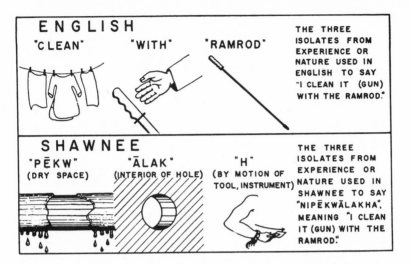

Figure 1. Languages dissect nature differently. The different isolates of meaning (thoughts) used by English and Shawnee in reporting the same experience, that of cleaning a gun by running the ramrod through it. The pronouns "I" and "it" are not shown by symbols, as they have the same meaning in each language. In Shawnee ni- equals "I"; -a equals "it."

are essentially parallel methods for expressing this one-and-the-same rationale of thought and, hence, differ really in but minor ways which may seem important only because they are seen at close range. It holds that mathematics, symbolic logic, philosophy, and so on are systems contrasted with language which deal directly with this realm of thought, not that they are themselves specialized extensions of language. The attitude of natural logic is well shown in an old quip about a German grammarian who devoted his whole life to the study of the dative case. From the point of view of natural logic, the dative case and grammar in general are an extremely minor issue. A different attitude is said to have been held by the ancient Arabians: Two princes, so the story goes, quarreled over the honor of putting on the shoes of the most learned grammarian of the realm; whereupon their father, the caliph, is said to have remarked that it was the glory of his kingdom that great grammarians were honored even above kings.

The familiar saying that the exception proves the rule contains a good deal of wisdom, though from the standpoint of formal logic it became an absurdity as soon as "prove" no longer meant "put on trial." The old saw began to be profound psychology from the time it ceased to have standing in logic. What it might well suggest to us today is that, if a rule has absolutely no exceptions, it is not recognized as a rule or as anything else; it is then part of the background of experience of which we tend to remain unconscious. Never having experienced anything in contrast to it, we cannot isolate it and formulate it as a rule until we so enlarge our experience and expand our base of reference that we encounter an interruption of its regularity. The situation is somewhat analogous to that of not missing the water till the well runs dry, or not realizing that we need air till we are choking.

For instance, if a race of people had the physiological defect of being able to see only the color blue, they would hardly be able to formulate the rule that they saw only blue. The term blue would convey no meaning to them, their language would lack color terms, and their words denoting their various sensations of blue would answer to, and translate, our words "light, dark, white, black," and so on, not our word "blue." In order to formulate the rule or norm of seeing only blue, they would need exceptional moments in which they saw other colors. The phenomenon of gravitation forms a rule without exceptions; needless to say, the untutored person is utterly unaware of any law of gravitation, for it would never enter his head to conceive of a universe in which bodies behaved otherwise than they do at the earth's surface. Like the color blue with our hypothetical race, the law of gravitation is a part of the untutored individual's background, not something he isolates from that background. The law could not be formulated until bodies that always fell were seen in terms of a wider astronomical world in which bodies moved in orbits or went this way and that.

Similarly, whenever we turn our heads, the image of the scene passes across our retinas exactly as it would if the scene turned around us. But this effect is background, and we do not recognize it; we do not see a room turn around us but are conscious only of having turned our heads in a stationary room. If we observe critically while turning the head or eyes quickly, we shall see, no motion it is true, yet a blurring of the scene between two clear views. Normally we are quite unconscious of this continual blurring but seem to be looking about in an unblurred world. Whenever we walk past a tree or house, its image on the retina changes just as if the tree or house were turning on an axis; yet we do not see trees or houses turn as we travel about at ordinary speeds. Sometimes ill-fitting glasses will reveal queer movements in the scene as we look about, but normally we do not see the relative motion of the environment when we move; our psychic makeup is somehow adjusted to disregard whole realms of phenomena that are so all-pervasive as to be irrelevant to our daily lives and needs.

Natural logic contains two fallacies: First, it does not see that the phenomena of a language are to its own speakers largely of a background character and so are outside the critical consciousness and control of the speaker who is expounding natural logic. Hence, when anyone, as a natural logician, is talking about reason, logic, and the laws of correct thinking, he is apt to be simply marching in step with purely grammatical facts that have somewhat of a background character in his own language or family of languages but are by no means universal in all languages and in no sense a common substratum of reason. Second, natural logic confuses agreement about subject matter, attained through use of language, with knowledge of the linguistic process by which agreement is attained: i.e., with the province of the despised (and to its notion superfluous) grammarian. Two fluent speakers, of English let us say, quickly reach a point of assent about the

Figure 2. Languages classify items of experience differently. The class corresponding to one word and one thought in language A may be regarded by language B as two or more classes corresponding to two or more words and thoughts.

subject matter of their speech; they agree about what their language refers to. One of them, *A*, can give directions that will be carried out by the other, *B*, to *A*'s complete satisfaction. Because they thus understand each other so perfectly, *A* and *B*, as natural logicians, suppose they must of course know how it is all done. They think, e.g., that it is simply a matter of choosing words to express throughts. If you ask *A* to explain how he got *B*'s agreement so readily, he will simply repeat to you, with more or less elaboration or abbreviation, what he said to *B*. He has no notion of the process involved. The amazingly complex system of linguistic patterns and classifications, which *A* and *B* must have in common before they can adjust to each other at all, is all background to *A* and *B*.

These background phenomena are the province of the grammarian— or of the linguist, to give him his more modern name as a scientist. The word linguist in common, and especially newspaper, parlance means something entirely different, namely, a person who can quickly attain agreement about subject matter with different people speaking a number of different languages. Such a person is better termed a polyglot or a multilingual. Scientific linguists have long understood that ability to speak a language fluently does not necessarily confer a linguistic knowledge of it, i.e., understanding of its background phenomena and its systematic processes and structure, any more than ability to play a good game of billiards confers or requires any knowledge of the laws of mechanics that operate upon the billiard table.

The situation here is not unlike that in any other field of science. All real scientists have their eyes primarily on background phenomena that cut very little ice, as such, in our daily lives; and yet their studies have a way of bringing out a close relation between these unsuspected realms of fact and such decidedly foreground activities as transporting goods, preparing food, treating the sick, or growing potatoes, which in time may become very much modified, simply because of pure scientific investigation in no way concerned with these brute matters themselves. Linguistics presents a quite similar case; the background phenomena with which it deals are involved in all our foreground activities of talking and of reaching agreement, in all reasoning and arguing of cases, in all law, arbitration, conciliation, contracts, treaties, public opinion, weighing of scientific theories, formulation of scientific results. Whenever agreement or assent is arrived at in human affairs, and whether or not mathematics or other specialized symbolisms are made part of the procedure, *this agreement is reached by linguistic processes, or else it is not reached.*

As we have seen, an overt knowledge of the linguistic processes by which agreement is attained is not necessary to reaching some sort of agreement, but it is certainly no bar thereto; the more complicated and difficult the matter, the more such knowledge is a distinct aid, till the point may be reached—I suspect the modern world has about arrived at it—when the knowledge becomes not only an aid but a necessity. The situation may be likened to that of navigation. Every boat that sails is in the lap of planetary forces; yet a boy can pilot his small craft around a harbor without benefit of geography, astronomy, mathematics, or international politics. To the captain of an ocean liner, however, some knowledge of all these subjects is essential.

When linguists became able to examine critically and scientifically a large number of languages of widely different patterns, their base of reference was expanded; they experienced an interruption of phenomena hitherto held universal, and a whole new order of significances came into their ken. It was found that the background linguistic system (in other words, the grammar) of each language is not merely a reproducing instrument for voicing ideas but rather is itself the shaper of ideas, the program and guide for the individual's mental activity, for his analysis of impressions, for his synthesis of his mental stock in trade. Formulation of ideas is not an independent process, strictly rational in the old sense, but is part of a particular grammar, and differs, from slightly to greatly, between different grammars. We dissect nature along lines laid down by our native languages. The categories and types that we isolate from the world of phenomena we do not find there because they stare every observer in the face; on the contrary, the world is presented in a kaleidoscopic flux of impressions which has to be organized by our minds—and this means largely by the linguistic systems in our minds. We cut nature up, organize it into concepts, and ascribe significances as we do, largely because we are parties to an agreement to organize it in this way—an agreement that holds throughout our speech

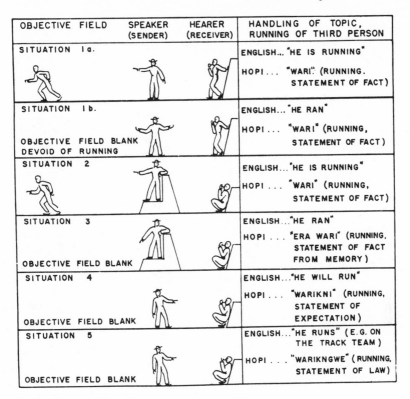

OBJECTIVE FIELD	SPEAKER (SENDER)	HEARER (RECEIVER)	HANDLING OF TOPIC, RUNNING OF THIRD PERSON
SITUATION I a.			ENGLISH... "HE IS RUNNING" HOPI... "WARI" (RUNNING. STATEMENT OF FACT)
SITUATION I b. OBJECTIVE FIELD BLANK DEVOID OF RUNNING			ENGLISH... "HE RAN" HOPI... "WARI" (RUNNING, STATEMENT OF FACT)
SITUATION 2			ENGLISH... "HE IS RUNNING" HOPI... "WARI" (RUNNING, STATEMENT OF FACT)
SITUATION 3 OBJECTIVE FIELD BLANK			ENGLISH... "HE RAN" HOPI... "ERA WARI" (RUNNING. STATEMENT OF FACT FROM MEMORY)
SITUATION 4 OBJECTIVE FIELD BLANK			ENGLISH... "HE WILL RUN" HOPI... "WARIKNI" (RUNNING, STATEMENT OF EXPECTATION)
SITUATION 5 OBJECTIVE FIELD BLANK			ENGLISH... "HE RUNS" (E.G. ON THE TRACK TEAM) HOPI... "WARIKNGWE" (RUNNING, STATEMENT OF LAW)

Figure 3. Contrast between a "temporal" language (English) and a "timeless" language (Hopi). What are to English differences of time are to Hopi differences in the kind of validity.

community and is codified in the patterns of our language. The agreement is, of course, an implicit and unstated one, *but its terms are absolutely obligatory;* we cannot talk at all except by subscribing to the organization and classification of data which the agreement decrees.

This fact is very significant for modern science, for it means that no individual is free to describe nature with absolute impartiality but is constrained to certain modes of interpretation even while he thinks himself most free. The person most nearly free in such respects would be a linguist familiar with very many widely different linguistic systems. As yet no linguist is in any such position. We are thus introduced to a new principle of relativity, which holds that all observers are not led by the same physical evidence to the same picture of the universe, unless their linguistic backgrounds are similar, or can in some way be calibrated.

This rather startling conclusion is not so apparent if we compare only our modern European languages, with perhaps Latin and Greek thrown in for good measure. Among these tongues there is an unanimity of major pattern which at first seems to bear out natural logic. But this unanimity exists only because these tongues are all Indo-European dialects cut to the same basic plan, being historically transmitted from what was long ago one speech community; because the modern dialects have long shared in building up a common culture; and because much of this culture, on the more intellectual side, is derived from the linguistic backgrounds of Latin and Greek. Thus this group of languages satisfies the special case of the clause beginning "unless" in the statement of the linguistic relativity principle at the end of the preceding paragraph. From this condition follows the unanimity of description of the world in the community of modern scientists. But it must be emphasized that "all modern Indo-European-speaking observers" is not the same thing as "all observers." That modern Chinese or Turkish scientists describe the world in the same terms as Western scientists means, of course, only that they have taken over bodily the entire Western system of rationalizations, not that they have corroborated that system from their native posts of observation.

When Semitic, Chinese, Tibetan, or African languages are contrasted with our own, the divergence in analysis of the world becomes more apparent; and, when we bring in the native languages of the Americas, where speech communities for many millenniums have gone their ways independently of each other and of the Old World, the fact that languages dissect nature in many different ways becomes patent. The relativity of all conceptual systems, ours included, and their dependence upon language stand revealed. That American Indians speaking only their native tongues are never called upon to act as scientific observers is in no wise to the point. To exclude the evidence which their languages offer as to what the human mind can do is like expecting botanists to study nothing but food plants and hothouse roses and then tell us what the plant world is like!

Let us consider a few examples. In English we divide most of our words into two classes, which have different grammatical and logical properties. Class 1 we call nouns, e.g., 'house, man'; class 2, verbs, e.g., 'hit, run.' Many words of one class can act secondarily as of the other class, e.g., 'a hit, a run,' or 'to man (the boat),' but, on the primary level, the division between the classes is absolute. Our language thus gives us a bipolar division of nature. But nature herself is not thus polarized. If it be said that 'strike, turn, run,' are verbs because they denote temporary or short-lasting events, i.e., actions, why then is 'fist' a noun? It also is a temporary event. Why are 'lightning, spark, wave, eddy, pulsation, flame, storm, phase, cycle, spasm, noise, emotion' nouns? They are temporary events. If 'man' and 'house' are nouns because they are long-lasting and stable events, i.e., things, what then are 'keep, adhere, extend, project, continue, persist, grow, dwell,' and so on doing among the verbs? If it be objected that 'possess, adhere' are verbs because they are stable relationships rather than stable percepts, why then should 'equilibrium, pressure, current, peace, group, nation, society, tribe, sister,' or any kinship term be among the nouns? It will be found that an "event" to us means "what our language classes as a verb" or something analogized therefrom. And it will be found that it is not possible to define 'event, thing, object, relationship,' and so on, from nature, but that to define them always involves a circuitous return to the grammatical categories of the definer's language.

In the Hopi language, 'lightning, wave, flame, meteor, puff of smoke, pulsation' are verbs—events of necessarily brief duration cannot be anything but verbs. 'Cloud' and 'storm' are at about the lower limit of duration for nouns. Hopi, you see, actually has a classification of events (or linguistic isolates) by duration type, something strange to our modes of thought. On the other hand, in Nootka, a language of Vancouver Island, all words seem to us to be verbs, but really there are no classes 1 and 2; we have, as it were, a monistic view of nature that gives us only one class of word for all kinds of events. 'A house occurs' or 'it houses' is the way of saying 'house,' exactly like 'a flame occurs' or 'it burns.' These terms seem to us like verbs because they are inflected for durational and temporal nuances, so that the suffixes of the word for house event make it mean long-lasting house, temporary house, future house, house that used to be, what started out to be a house, and so on.

Hopi has one noun that covers every thing or being that flies, with the exception of birds, which class is denoted by another noun. The former noun may be said to denote the class $(FC - B)$—flying class minus bird. The Hopi actually call insect, airplane, and aviator all by the same word, and feel no difficulty about it. The situation, of course, decides any possible confusion among very disparate members of a broad linguistic class, such as this class $(FC - B)$. This class seems to us too large and inclusive, but so would our class 'snow' to an Eskimo. We have the same word for falling snow, snow on the the ground, snow packed hard like ice, slushy snow, wind-driven flying snow—whatever the situation may be. To an Eskimo, this all-inclusive word would be almost unthinkable; he would say that falling snow, slushy snow, and so on, are sensuously and operationally different, different things to contend with; he uses different words for them and for other kinds of snow. The Aztecs go even farther than we in the opposite direction, with 'cold,' 'ice,' and 'snow' all represented by the same basic word with different terminations; 'ice' is the noun form; 'cold,' the adjectival form; and for 'snow,' "ice mist."

What surprises most is to find that various grand generalizations of the Western world, such as time, velocity, and matter, are not essential to the construction of a consistent picture of the universe. The psychic experiences that we class under these headings are, of course, not destroyed; rather, categories derived from other kinds of experiences take over the rulership of the cosmology and seem to function just as well. Hopi may be called a timeless language. It recognizes psychological time, which is much like Bergson's "duration," but this "time" is quite unlike the mathematical time, T, used by our physicists. Among the peculiar properties of Hopi time are that it varies with each observer, does not permit of simultaneity, and has zero dimensions; i.e., it cannot be given a number greater than one. The Hopi do not say, "I stayed five days," but "I left on the fifth day." A word referring to this kind of time, like the word day, can have no plural. The puzzle picture (Fig. 3) will give mental exercise to anyone who would like to figure out how the Hopi verb gets along without tenses. Actually, the only practical use of our tenses, in one-verb sentences, is to distinguish among five typical situations, which are symbolized in the picture. The timeless Hopi verb does not distinguish between the present, past, and future of the event itself but must always indicate what type of validity the *speaker* intends the statement to have: (a) report of an event (situations 1, 2, 3 in the picture); (b) expectation of an event (situation 4); (c) generalization or law about events (situation 5). Situation 1, where the speaker and listener are in contact with the same objective field, is divided by our language into the two conditions, 1*a*, and 1*b*, which it calls present and past, respectively. This division is unnecessary for a language which assures one that the statement is a report.

Hopi grammar, by means of its forms called aspects and modes, also makes it easy to distinguish among momentary, continued, and repeated occurrences, and to indicate the actual sequence of reported events. Thus the universe can be described without recourse to a concept of dimensional time. How would a physics constructed along these lines work, with no T (time) in its equations? Perfectly, as far as I can see, though of course it would require different ideology and perhaps different mathematics. Of course V (velocity) would have to go too. The Hopi language has no word really equivalent to our 'speed' or 'rapid.' What translates these terms is usually a word meaning intense or very, accompanying any verb of motion. Here is a clue to the nature of our new physics. We may have to introduce a new term I, intensity. Every thing and event will have an I, whether we regard the thing or event as moving or as just enduring or being. Perhaps the I of an electric charge will turn out to be its voltage, or potential. We shall use clocks to measure some intensities, or, rather, some *relative* intensities, for the absolute intensity of anything will be meaningless. Our old friend acceleration will still be there but doubtless under a new name. We shall perhaps call it V, meaning not velocity but variation. Perhaps all growths and accumulations will be regarded as V's. We should not have the concept of rate in the temporal sense, since, like velocity, rate introduces a mathematical and linguistic time. Of course we know that all measurements are ratios, but the measurements of intensities made by comparison with the standard intensity of a clock or a planet we do not treat as ratios, any more than we so treat a distance made by comparison with a yardstick.

A scientist from another culture that used time and velocity would have great difficulty in getting us to understand these concepts. We should talk about the intensity of a chemical reaction; he would speak of its velocity or its rate, which words we should at first think were simply words for intensity in his language. Likewise, he at first would think that intensity was simply our own word for velocity. At first we should agree, later we should begin to disagree, and it might dawn upon both sides that different systems of rationalization were being used. He would find it very hard to make us understand what he really meant by velocity of a chemical reaction. We should have no words that would fit. He would try to explain it by likening it to a running horse, to the difference between a good horse and a lazy horse. We should try to show him, with a superior laugh, that his analogy also was a matter of different intensities, aside from which there was little similarity between a horse and a chemical reaction in a beaker. We should point out that a running horse is moving relative to the ground, whereas the material in the beaker is at rest.

One significant contribution to science from the linguistic point of view may be the greater development of our sense of perspective. We shall no longer be able to see a few recent dialects of the Indo-European family, and the rationalizing techniques elaborated from their patterns as the apex of the evolution of the human mind, nor their present wide spread as due to any survival from fitness or to anything but a few events of history— events that could be called fortunate only from the parochial point of view of the favored parties. They, and our own thought processes with them, can no longer be envisioned as spanning the gamut of reason and knowledge but only as one constellation in a galactic expanse. A fair realization of the incredible degree of diversity of linguistic system that ranges over the globe leaves one with an inescapable feeling that the human spirit is inconceivably old; that the few thousand years of history covered by our written records are no more than the thickness of a pencil mark on the scale that measures our past experience on this planet; that the events of these recent millenniums spell nothing in any evolutionary wise, that the race has taken no sudden spurt, achieved no commanding synthesis during recent millenniums, but has only played a little with a few of the linguistic formulations and views of nature bequeathed from an inexpressibly longer past. Yet neither this feeling nor the sense of precarious dependence of all we know upon linguistic tools which themselves are largely unknown need be discouraging to science but should, rather, foster that humility which accompanies the true scientific spirit, and thus forbid that arrogance of the mind which hinders real scientific curiosity and detachment.

Dorothy Lee

CODIFICATIONS OF REALITY:
LINEAL AND NONLINEAL

Here is a classic essay in comparative cognition. The perception and classification of "objective reality" is not culture-free, no matter how ardently a scientist wishes it were. However, by studying the nature of individual cultural cognitive systems, we may be able to see the arbitrariness and the normally unperceived biases of such systems, including our own.

In this paper, Dorothy Lee analyzes some of the field data obtained by Bronislaw Malinowski in the Trobriand Isles. If her analysis is correct (and she does argue very convincingly), then she sees things in Malinowski's data which Malinowski himself did not. And even if her analysis is not correct, there are at least two important theoretical lessons to be learned. First of all, an ethnographer in the field cannot escape the biases of his own culture. In fact, often what an ethnographer

Reprinted from *Psychosomatic Medicine,* 12 (1950), 89–97, by permission of the author and the Hoeber Medical Division of Harper and Row, Publishers, Inc.

chooses to study is a reflection of his own personality and culture; the choice is not necessarily dictated by the culture under study. Thus a French ethnographer and a Chinese ethnographer both studying the same African culture might write very different ethnographies. On the other hand, and this is the second lesson, if an ethnographer is careful to separate his raw data from his interpretation of that data, then other investigators will be able to reevaluate this raw data. Thus even though Malinowski may not have realized his "lineal" bias, it is greatly to his credit that the accuracy of his field data permitted Dorothy Lee to make her study.

For a Chinese anthropologist's comments on how views of Zuni culture (one of the Pueblo peoples of the Southwest United States) have been influenced by the fact that those who have conducted the fieldwork have been Americans, see An-Che Li, "Zuni: Some Observations and Queries," *American Anthropologist*, 39 (1937), 62–76. For another study of divergent views of the same culture, see John W. Bennett, "The Interpretation of Pueblo Culture: A Question of Values," *Southwestern Journal of Anthropology*, 2 (1946), 361–74. For those who would like to read more of Dorothy Lee's fascinating philosophical and speculative essays, see her *Freedom and Culture* (Englewood Cliffs, N. J., 1959).

The people of the Trobriand Islands codify, and probably apprehend reality, nonlineally in contrast to our own lineal phrasing. Basic to my investigation of the codification of reality in these two societies, is the assumption that a member of a given society not only codifies experienced reality through the use of the specific language and other patterned behavior characteristics of his culture, but that he actually grasps reality only as it is presented to him in this code. The assumption is not that reality itself is relative; rather, that it is differently punctuated and categorized, or that different aspects of it are noticed by, or presented to the participants of different cultures. If reality itself were not absolute, then true communication of course would be impossible. My own position is that there is an absolute reality, and that communication is possible. If, then, that which the different codes refer to is ultimately the same, a careful study and analysis of a different code and of the culture to which it belongs, should lead us to concepts which are ultimately comprehensible, when translated into our own code. It may even, eventually, lead us to aspects of reality from which our own code excludes us.

It is a corollary of this assumption that the specific phrasing of reality can be discovered through intensive and detailed analysis of any aspect of culture. My own study was begun with an analysis of linguistic formulation, only because it is in language that I happen to be best able to discover my clues. To show how these clues can be discovered and used as guides to the apprehension of reality, as well as to show what I mean by codification, I shall present at first concrete material from the field of language.

That a word is not the reality, not the thing which it represents, has long been a commonplace to all of us. The thing which I hold in my hand as I write, *is* not a pencil; I *call* it a pencil. And it remains the same whether I call it *pencil, molyvi, Bleistift,* or *siwiqoq.* These words are different sound-complexes applied to the same reality; but is the difference merely one of sound-complex? Do they refer to the same *perceived* reality? *Pencil* originally meant little tail; it delimited and named the reality according to form. *Molyvi* means lead and refers to the writing element. *Bleistift* refers both to the form and to the writing-element. *Siwiqoq* means painting-stick and refers to observed function and form. Each culture has phrased the reality differently. To say that *pencil,* for example, applies primarily to form is no idle etymologic statement. When we use this word metaphorically, we refer neither to writing element nor to function, but to form alone; we speak of a pencil of light, or a styptic pencil.

When I used the four words for this object, we all knew what reality was referred to; we knew the meaning of the word. We could visualize the object in my hand, and the words all delimited it in the same way; for example, none of them implied that it was a continuation of my fist. But the student of ethnography often has to deal with words which punctuate reality into different phrasings from the ones with which he is familiar. Let us take, for instance, the words for "brother" and "sister." We go to the islands of Ontong Java to study the kinship system. We ask our informant what he calls his sister and he says *ave;* he calls his brother *kainga.* So we equate *ave* with "sister" and *kainga* with "brother." By way of checking our information we ask the sister what she calls her brother; it turns out that for her, *ave* is "brother," not "sister" as we were led to expect; and that it is her sister whom she calls *kainga.*

The same reality, the same actual kinship is present there as with us; but we have chosen a different aspect for naming. We are prepared to account for this; we say that both cultures name according to what we would call a certain type of blood relationship; but whereas we make reference to absolute sex, they refer to relative sex. Further inquiry, however, discloses that in this, also, we are wrong. Because in our own culture we name relatives according to formal definition and biologic relationship, we have thought that this formulation represents reality; and we have tried to understand the Ontong Javanese relationship terms according to these distinctions which, we believe, are given in nature. But the Ontong Javanese classifies relatives according to a different aspect of reality, differently punctuated. And because of this, he applies *kainga* as well to a wife's sister and a husband's brother; to a man's brother's wife and a woman's sister's husband, as well as to a number of other individuals.

Neither sex nor blood relationship, then, can be basic to this term. The Ontong Javanese name according to their everyday behavior and experience, not according to formal definition. A man shares the ordinary details of his living with his brothers and their wives for a large part of the year; he sleeps in the same large room, he eats with them, he jokes and works around the house with them; the rest of the year he spends with his wife's sisters and their husbands, in the same easy companionship. All these individuals are *kainga* to one another. The *ave,* on the other hand, names a behavior of great strain and propriety; it is based originally upon the relative sex of siblings, yes, but it does not signify biologic fact alone. It names a social relationship, a behavior, an emotional tone. *Ave* can never spend their adult life together, except on rare and temporary occasions. They can never be under the same roof alone together, cannot chat at ease together, cannot refer even distantly to sex in the presence of each other, not even to one's sweetheart or spouse; more than that, everyone else must be circumspect when the *ave* of someone of the group is present. The *ave* relationship also carries special obligations toward a female *ave* and her children. *Kainga* means a relationship of ease, full of shared living, of informality, gaiety; *ave* names one of formality, prohibition, strain.

These two cultures, theirs and our own, have phrased and formulated social reality in completely different ways, and have given their formulation different names. The word is merely the name of this specific cultural phrasing. From this one instance we might formulate the hypothesis—a very tentative one—that among the Ontong Javanese names describe emotive experiences, not observed forms or functions. But we cannot accept this as fact, unless further investigation shows it to be implicit in the rest of their patterned behavior, in their vocabulary and the morphology of their language, in their ritual and their other organized activity.

One more instance, this time from the language of the Wintu Indians of California, will deal with the varying aspect or segmentation of experience which is used as a basis of classification. To begin with, we take the stem *muk.* On the basis of this stem we form the word *mukeda,* which means: "I turned the basket bottom up"; we form *mukuhara,* which means: "The turtle is moving along"; and we form *mukurumas,* which means: "automobile." Upon what conceivable principle can an automobile be put in the same category as a turtle and a basket? There is such a principle, however, and it operates also when the Wintu calls the activity of laundering, *to make foam continuously.* According to this principle, he uses only one stem, (puq or poq) to form words for all of the following:

puqeda: I just pushed a peg into the ground.
olpuqal: He is sitting on one haunch.
poqorahara: Birds are hopping along.
olpoqoyabe: There are mushrooms growing.
tunpoqoypoqoya: You walk shortskirted, stifflegged ahead of me.

It is difficult for us to discover the common denominator in the different formations from this one stem, or even to believe that there can be one. Yet, when we discover the principle underlying the classification, the categories themselves are understandable. Basic to the classification is the Wintu view of himself as observer; he stays outside the event. He passes no judgment on essence, and where we would have used kinesthetic or participatory experience as the basis of naming, he names as an observer only, for the shape of the activity or the object. The turtle and the automobile can thus naturally be grouped together with the inverted baskets. The mushroom standing on its stem, the fist grasping a peg against the ground, the stiff leg topped by a short skirt or by the body of a bird or of a man resting on a haunch, obviously all belong together in one category. But the progress of a grasshopper cannot be categorized with that of a hopping bird. We, who classify on a different basis, apprehend the hop of the two kinesthetically and see it as basically the same in both cases; but the Wintu see the difference in recurrent shape, which is all-important to them, and so name the two by means of completely different stems. Again, when we discover this principle, it is easy to see that from the observer's point of view laundering is the making of a lot of foam; and to see why, when beer was introduced to the Wintu, it was named *laundry*.

I have discussed at length the diversity of codification of reality in general, because it is the foundation of the specific study which I am about to present. I shall speak of the formulation of experienced reality among the Trobriand Islanders in comparison to our own; I shall speak of the nature of expectancy, of motivation, of satisfaction, as based upon a reality which is differently apprehended and experienced in two different societies; which is, in fact, for each, a different reality. The Trobriand Islanders were studied by the late Bronislaw Malinowski, who has given us the rich and circumstantial material about them which has made this study possible. I have given a detailed presentation of some implications of their language elsewhere; but since it was in their language that I first noticed the absence of lineality, which led me to this study, I shall give here a summary of the implications of the language.

A Trobriand word refers to a self-contained concept. What we consider an attribute of a predicate, is to the Trobriander an ingredient. Where I would say, for example, "A good gardener," or "The gardener is good," the Trobriand word would include both "gardener" and "goodness"; if the gardener loses the goodness, he has lost a defining ingredient, he is something else, and he is named by means of a completely different word. A *taytu* (a species of yam) contains a certain degree of ripeness, bigness, roundedness, etc.; without one of these defining ingredients, it is something else, perhaps a *bwanawa* or a *yowana*. There are no adjectives in the language; the rare words dealing with qualities are substantivized. The term *to be* does not occur; it is used neither attributively nor existentially, since existence itself is contained; it is an ingredient of being.

Events and objects are self-contained points in another respect; there is a series of beings, but no becoming. There is no temporal connection between objects. The taytu always remains itself; it does not *become* over-ripe; over-ripeness is an ingredient of another, a different being. At some point, the taytu *turns into a yowana,* which contains over-ripeness. And the yowana, over-ripe as it is, does not put forth shoots, does not *become* a sprouting yowana. When sprouts appear, it ceases to be itself; in its place appears a *silasata*. Neither is there a temporal connection made—or, according to our own premises, perceived—between events; in fact, temporality is meaningless. There are no tenses, no linguistic distinction between past or present. There is no arrangement of activities or events into means and ends, no causal or teleologic relationships. What we consider a causal relationship in a sequence of connected events, is to the Trobriander an ingredient of a patterned whole. He names this ingredient *u'ula*.

There is no automatic relating of any kind in the language. Except for the rarely used verbal it-differents and it-sames, there are no terms of comparison whatever. And we find in an analysis of behavior that the standard for behavior and of evaluation is non-comparative.

These implications of the linguistic material suggest to my mind an absence of axiomatic lineal connection between events or objects in the Trobriand apprehension of reality, and this implication, as I shall attempt to show below, is reinforced in their definition of activity. In our own culture, the line is so basic, that we take it for granted, as given in reality. We see it in visible nature, between material points, and we see it between metaphorical points such as days or acts. It underlies not only our thinking, but also our aesthetic apprehension of the given; it is basic to the emotional climax which has so much value for us, and, in fact, to the meaning of life itself. In our thinking about personality and character, we have taken for granted the presence of the line.

In our academic work, we are constantly acting in terms of an implied line. When we speak of *ap*plying an *at*tribute, for example, we visualize the process as lineal, coming from the outside. If I make a picture of an apple on the board, and want to show that one side is green and the other red I connect these attributes with the pictured apple by means of lines, as a matter of course; how else would I do it? When I organize my data, I *draw* conclusions *from* them. I *trace* a relationship between my facts. I describe a pattern as a *web* of relationships. Look at a lecturer who makes use of gestures; he is constantly making lineal connections in the air. And a teacher with chalk in hand will be drawing lines on the board whether he be a psychologist, a historian, or paleontologist.

Preoccupation with social facts merely as self-contained facts is mere antiquarianism. In my field, a student of this sort would be an amateur or a dilettante, not an anthropologist. To be an anthropologist, he can arrange his facts in an upward slanting line, in a *unilinear* or *multilinear course* of development; or in *parallel lines* or *converging lines*. Or he may arrange them geographically, with *lines* of diffusion connecting them; or schematically, using *concentric circles*. Or at least, he must indicate what his study *leads to,* what new insights we can *draw from* it. To be accorded status, he must use the guiding line as basic.

The line is found or presupposed in most of our scientific work. It is present in the *induction* and the *deduction* of science and logic. It is present in the philosopher's phrasing of means and ends as lineally connected. Our statistical facts are presented lineally as a *graph* or reduced to a normal *curve*. And all of us, I think, would be lost without our *diagrams*. We *trace* a historical devolopment; we *follow the course* of history and evolution *down* to the present and *up from* the ape; and it is interesting to note, in passing, that whereas both evolution and history are lineal, the first goes up the blackboard, the second goes down.

Our psychologists picture motivation as external, connected with the act through a line, or more recently, entering the organism through a lineal channel and emerging transformed, again lineally, as response. I have seen lineal pictures of nervous impulses and heartbeats, and with them I have seen pictured lineally a second of time. These were photographs, you will say, of existing fact, of reality; a proof that the line is present in reality. But I am not convinced, perhaps due to my ignorance of mechanics, that we have not created our recording instruments in such a way that they have to picture time and motion, light and sound, heartbeats and nerve impulses lineally, on the unquestioned assumption of the line as axiomatic. The line is omnipresent and inescapable, and so we are incapable of questioning the reality of its presence.

When we see a *line* of trees, or a *circle* of stones, we assume the presence of a connecting line which is not actually visible. And we assume it metaphorically when we follow a *line* of thought, a *course* of action or the *direction* of an argument; when we *bridge* a gap in the conversation, or speak of the *span* of life or of teaching a *course,* or lament our *interrupted career.* We make children's embroidery cards and puzzle cards on this assumption; our performance tests and even our tests for sanity often assume that the line is present in nature and, at most, to be discovered or given visual existence.

But is the line present in reality? Malinowski, writing for members of our culture and using idiom which would be comprehensible to them, described the Trobriand village as follows: "Concentrically with the circular row of yam houses there runs a ring of dwelling huts." He saw, or at any rate, he represented the village as two circles. But in the texts which he recorded, we find that the Trobrianders at no time mention circles or rings or even rows when they refer to their villages. Any word which they use to refer to a village, such as *a* or *this,* is prefixed by the substantival element *kway* which means *bump* or *aggregate of bumps.* This is the element which they use when they refer to a pimple or a bulky rash; or to canoes loaded with yams. In their terms, a village is an aggregate of bumps; are they blind to the circles? Or did Malinowski create the circles himself, out of his cultural axiom?

Again, for us as well as in Malinowski's description of the Trobrianders, which was written necessarily in terms meaningful to us, all effective activity is certainly not a haphazard aggregate of acts, but a lineally planned series of acts leading to an envisioned end. Their gardening with all its specialized activities, both technical and magical, leading to a rich harvest; their *kula* involving the cutting down of trees, the communal dragging of the tree to the beach, the rebuilding or building of large sea-worthy canoes, the provisioning, the magical and ceremonial activities involved—surely all these can be carried through only if they are lineally conceived.

But the Trobrianders do not describe their activity lineally; they do no dynamic relating of acts; they do not use even so innocuous a connective as *and.* Here is part of a description of the planting of coconut: "Thou-approach-there coconut thou-bring-here-we-plant-coconut thou-go thou-plant our coconut. This-here it-emerge sprout. We-push-away this we-push-away this-other coconut-husk-fiber together sprout it-sit together root." We who are accustomed to seek lineal continuity, cannot help supplying it as we read this; but the continuity is not given in the Trobriand text; and all Trobriand speech, according to Malinowski, is "jerky," given in points, not in connecting lines. The only connective I know of in Trobriand is the *pela* which I mentioned above; a kind of preposition which also means "to jump."

I am not maintaining here that the Trobrianders cannot see continuity; rather that lineal connection is not automatically made by them, as a matter of course. At Malinowski's persistent questioning, for example, they did attempt to explain their activities in terms of cause or motivation, by stating possible "results" of uncooperative action. But Malinowski found their answers confused, self-contradictory, inconsistent; their preferred answer was, "It was ordained of old"—pointing to an ingredient value of the act instead of giving an explanation based on lineal connection.

And when they were not trying to find answers to leading questions, the Trobrianders made no such connection in their speech. They assumed, for example, that the validity of a magical spell lay, not in its results, not in proof, but in its very being; in the appropriateness of its inheritance, in its place within the patterned activity, in its being performed by the appropriate person, in its realization of its mythical basis. To seek validity through proof was foreign to their thinking, yet they attempted to do so at the ethnographer's request. I should add here that their names for constellations imply that here they do see lineal figures; I cannot investigate the significance of this, as I have no contextual material. At any rate, I would like to emphasize that, even if the Trobriander does occasionally supply connecting lines between points, his perception and experience do not automatically fall into a lineal framework.

The fact remains that Trobrianders embark on, what is certainly for us, a series of acts which "must require" planning and purposiveness. They engage in acts of gift-giving and gift-receiving which we can certainly see as an exchange of gifts if we want to. When we plot their journeys, we find that they do go from point to point, they do navigate a course, whether they say so or not. Do they merely refrain from giving linguistic expression to something which they actually recognize in nature? On the nonlinguistic level, do they act on an assumption of a lineality which is given no place in their linguistic formulation?

I believe that, where valued activity is concerned, the Trobrianders do not act on an assumption of lineality at any level. There is organization or rather coherence in their acts because Trobriand activity is patterned activity. One act within this pattern brings into existence a pre-ordained cluster of acts. Perhaps one might find a parallel in our culture in the making of a sweater. When I embark on knitting one, the ribbing at the bottom does not *cause* the making of the neckline, nor of the sleeves or the armholes; and it is not part of a lineal series of acts. Rather it is an indispensable part of a patterned activity which includes all these other acts. Again, when I choose a dress pattern, the acts involved in the making of the dress are already present for me. They are embedded in the pattern which I have chosen.

In this same way, I believe, can be seen the Trobriand insistence that though intercourse is a necessary preliminary to conception, it is not the cause of conception. There are a number of acts in the pattern of procreating; one is intercourse, another the entrance of the spirit of a dead Trobriander into the womb. However, there is a further point here. The Trobrianders, when pressed by the ethnographer or teased by the neighboring Dobuans, showed signs of intense embarrassment, giving the impression that they were trying to maintain unquestioningly a stand in which they had to believe. This, I think, is because pattern is truth and value for them; in fact, acts and being derive value from the embedding pattern.

So the question of the perception of a line remains. It is because they find value in pattern that the Trobrianders act according to nonlineal pattern; not because they cannot perceive lineality.

But all Trobriand activity does not contain value; and when it does not, it assumes lineality, and is utterly despicable. For example, the pattern of sexual intercourse includes the giving of a gift from the boy to the girl; but if a boy gives a gift so as to win the girl's favor, he is despised. Again, the kula pattern includes the eventual reception of a gift from the original recipient; the pattern is such that it keeps the acts physically and temporally completely disparate. In spite of this, however, some men are accused of giving gifts as an inducement to their kula partner to give them a specially good kula gift. Such men are labeled with the vile phrase: he barters. But this means that, unvalued and despised, lineal behavior does exist. In fact, there are villages in the interior whose inhabitants live mainly by bartering manufactured articles for yams. The inhabitants of Omarakana, about whom Malinowski's work and this study are mainly concerned, will barter with them, but consider them pariahs.

This is to say that it is probable that the Trobrianders experience reality in nonlineal pattern because this is the valued reality; and that they are capable of experiencing lineally, when value is absent or destroyed. It is not to say, however, that this in itself means that lineality is given, is present in nature, and that pattern is not. Our own insistence on the line, such as lineal causality, for example, is also often based on unquestioned belief or value. To return to the subject of procreation, the husband in our culture, who has long hoped, and tried in vain, to beget children, will nevertheless maintain that intercourse causes conception; perhaps with the same stubbornness and embarrassment which the Trobrianders exhibited when maintaining the opposite.

The line in our culture not only connects, but it moves. And as we think of a line as moving from point to point, connecting one to the other, so we conceive of roads as *running from* locality to locality. A Trobriander does not speak of roads either as connecting two points, or as *running from* point *to* point. His paths are self-contained, named as independent units;

they are not *to* and *from* they are *at*. And he himself is *at;* he has no equivalent for our *to* or *from*. There is, for instance, the myth of Tudava, who goes—in our view—from village to village and from island to island planting and offering yams. The Trobriand text puts it this way: "Kitava it-shine village already (i.e., completed) he-is-over. 'I-said I-go Iwa'; Iwa he-anchor he-go ashore...He-sail Digumenu...They-drive (him off)... he-go Kwaywata." Point after point is enumerated, but his sailing from and to is given as a discrete event. In our view, he is actually following a southeasterly course, more or less; but this is not given as course or line, and no directions are even mentioned. In fact, in the several texts referring to journeyings in the Archipelago, no words occur for the cardinal directions. In sailing, the "following" winds are named according to where° they are *at,* the place where they strike the canoe, such as wind-striking-the-outrigger-beam; not according to where they *come from*. Otherwise, we find names for the southwest wind (youyo), and the northwest wind (bombatu), but these are merely substantival names which have nothing to do with direction; names for kinds of wind.

When a member of our society gives an unemotional description of a person, he follows an imaginary line, usually downward; from head to foot, from tip to toe, from hair to chin. The Navaho do the opposite, following a line upward. The Trobriander follows no line, at least none that I can see. "My head boils," says a kula spell; and it goes on to enumerate the parts of the head as follows: nose, occiput, tongue, larynx, speech, mouth. Another spell casting a protective fog, runs as follows: "I befog the hand, I befog the foot, I befog the head, I befog the shoulders..." There is a magic formula where we do recognize a line, but it is one which Malinowski did not record verbatim at the time, but which he put down later from memory; and it is not improbable that his memory edited the formula according to the lineality of his culture.

When the Trobriander enumerates the parts of a canoe, he does not follow any recognizable lineal order: "Mist...surround me my mast... the nose of my canoe...my sail...my steering oar...my canoe-gunwale ...my canoe-bottom...my prow...my rib...my threading stick...my prow-board...my transverse stick...my canoe-side."

Malinowski diagrams the garden site as a square piece of land subdivided into squares; the Trobrianders refer to it in the same terms as those which they use in referring to a village—a bulky object or an aggregate of bumps. When the plots in the garden site are apportioned to the gardeners, the named plots are assigned by name, the others by location along each named side of the graden. After this, the inner plots, the "belly" of the garden, are apportioned. Following along a physical rim is a procedure we find elsewhere also. In a spell naming villages on the main island there is a long list of villages which lie along the coast northward, then westward around the island, then south. To us, of course, this is lineal order. But we have no indication that the Trobrianders see other than geographical location, point after point, as they move over a physically continuous area; the line as a guide to procedure is not necessarily implied.

No terms are used here which might be taken as an implication of continuity; no "along the coast" or "around" or "northward."

When we in our culture deal with events or experiences of the self, we use the line as guide for various reasons, two of which I shall take up here. First, we feel we must arrange events chronologically in a lineal order; how else could our historians discover the causes of a war or a revolution or a defeat? Among the Trobrianders, what corresponds to our history is an aggregate of anecdotes, that is, unconnected points, told without respect to chronological sequence, or development, or causal relationship; with no grammatical distinction made between words referring to past events, or to present or contemplated ones. And in telling an anecdote, they take no care that a temporal sequence should be followed. For instance, they said to Malinowski, "They-eat-taro, they-spew-taro, they-disgusted-taro"; but if time, as we believe, is a moving line, then the revulsion came first in time, the vomiting was the result, coming afterward. Again, they say, "This-here...ripes...falls-down truly gives-birth...sits seed in belly-his"; but certainly the seed is there first, and the birth follows in time, if time is lineal.

Secondly, we arrange events and objects in a sequence which is climactic, in size and intensity, in emotional meaning, or according to some other principle. We often arrange events from earlier to later, not because we are interested in historical causation, but because the present is the climax of our history. But when the Trobriander relates happenings, there is no developmental arrangement, no building up of emotional tone. His stories have no plot, no lineal development, no climax. And when he repeats his garden spell, his list is neither climactic, nor anticlimactic; it sounds merely untidy to us:

The belly of my garden lifts
The belly of my garden rises
The belly of my garden reclines
The belly of my garden is-a-bushhen's-nest-in-lifting
The belly of my garden is-an-anthill
The belly of my garden lifts-bends
The belly of my garden is-an-ironwood-tree-in-lifting
The belly of my garden lies-down
The belly of my garden burgeons.

When the Trobrianders set out on their great ceremonial kula expedition, they follow a pre-established order. First comes the canoe of the Tolabwaga, an obscure subclan. Next come the canoes of the great chiefs. But this is not climactic; after the great chiefs come the commoners. The order derives meaning not from lineal sequence, but from correspondence with a present, experienced, meaningful pattern, which is the recreation or realization of the mythical pattern; that which has been ordained of old and is forever. Its meaning does not lie in an item-to-item relationship, but in fitness, in the repetition of an established unit.

An ordering of this sort gives members of our society a certain esthetic dysphoria except when, through deliberate training, we learn to go beyond our cultural expectation; or, when we are too young to have taken on the phrasings of our culture. When we manipulate objects naively, we arrange them on some climactic lineal principle. Think of a college commencement, with the faculty arranged in order of rank or length of tenure or other mark of importance; with the students arranged according to increasing physical height, from shortest to tallest, actually the one absolutely irrelevant principle as regards the completion of their college education, which is the occasion for the celebration. Even when the sophisticated avoid this principle, they are not unconscious of it; they are deliberately avoiding something which is there.

And our arrangement of history when we ourselves are personally involved, is mainly climactic. My great grandmother sewed by candle light, my grandmother used a kerosene lamp, my mother did her studying by gaslight, I did it by a naked electric ceiling light, and my children have diffused fluorescent lighting. This is progress; this is the meaningful sequence. To the Trobriander, climax in history is abominable, a denial of all good, since it would imply not only the presence of change, but also that change increases the good; but to him value lies in sameness, in repeated pattern, in the incorporation of all time within the same point. What is good in life is exact identity with all past Trobriand experience, and all mythical experience.

There is no boundary between past Trobriand existence and the present; he can indicate that an action is completed, but this does not mean that the action is past; it may be completed and present or timeless. Where we would say "Many years ago" and use the past tense, the Trobriander will say, "In my father's childhood" and use non-temporal verbs; he places the event situationally, not temporally. Past, present, and future are presented linguistically as the same, are present in his existence, and sameness with what we call the past and with myth, represents value to the Trobriander. Where we see a developmental line, the Trobriander sees a point, at most a swelling in value. Where we find pleasure and satisfaction in moving away from the point, in change as variety or progress, the Trobriander finds it in the repetition of the known, in maintaining the point; that is, in what we call monotony.

Esthetic validity, dignity, and value come to the Trobriander not through arrangement into a climactic line, but rather in the undisturbed incorporation of the events within their original, nonlineal order. The only history which has meaning for him is that which evokes the value of the point, or which, in the repetition, swells the value of the point. For example, every occasion in which a kula object participates becomes an ingredient of its being and swells its value; all these occasions are enumerated with great satisfaction, but the lineal course of the traveling kula object is not important.

As we see our history climactically, so do we plan future experiences climatically, leading up to future satisfaction or meaning. Who but a very young child would think of starting a meal with strawberry shortcake and ending it with spinach? We have come to identify the end of the meal with the height of satisfaction, and we identify semantically the words dessert and reward, only because of the similarity of their position in a climactic line. The Trobriand meal has no dessert, no line, no climax. The special bit, the relish, is eaten *with* the staple food; it is not something to "look *forward to*," while disposing of a meaningless staple.

None of the Trobriand activities is fitted into a climactic line. There is no job, no labor, no drudgery which finds its reward outside the act. All work contains its own satisfaction. We cannot speak of S—R here, as all action contains its own immanent "stimulus." The present is not a means to future satisfaction, but good in itself, as the future is also good in itself; neither better nor worse, neither climactic nor anticlimactic, in fact, not lineally connected nor removed.

It follows that the present is not evaluated in terms of its place within a course of action leading upward to a worthy end. In our culture, we can rarely evaluate the present in itself. I tell you that Sally is selling notions at Woolworth's, but this in itself means nothing. It acquires some meaning when I add that she has recently graduated from Vassar. However, I go on to tell you that she has been assistant editor of *Vogue,* next a nursemaid, a charwoman, a public school teacher. But this is a mere jumble; it makes no sense and has no meaning, because the series leads to nothing. You cannot relate one job to another, and you are unable to see them discretely simply as part of her being. However, I now add that she is gathering material for a book on the working mother. Now all this falls in line, it makes sense in terms of a career. Now her job is good and it makes her happy, because it is part of a planned climactic line leading to more pay, increased recognition, higher rank. There was a story in a magazine about the college girl who fell in love with the milkman one summer; the reader felt tense until it was discovered that this was just a summer job, that it was only a means for the continuation of the man's education in the Columbia Law School. Our evaluation of happiness and unhappiness is bound with this motion along an envisioned line leading to a desired end. In the fulfillment of this course or career—not in the fulfillment of the self as point—do we find value. Our conception of freedom rests on the principle of non-interference with this moving line, non-interruption of the intended course of action.

It is difficult to tell whether climax is given in experience at all, or whether it is always imposed on the given. At a time when progress and evolution were assumed to be implicit in nature, our musicians and writers gave us climactic works. Nowadays, our more reflective art does not present experience climactically. Then, is emotion itself climactic? Climax, for us, evokes "thrill" or "drama." But we have cultures, like the Tikopia, where life is lived, to our perception, on an even emotive plane without thrill or climax. Experiences which "we know to be" climactic, are described without climax by them. For example, they, as well as the Trobrianders, described intercourse as an aggregate of pleasurable experiences. But Malinowski is disturbed by this; he cannot place the erotic kiss in Trobriand experience, since it has no climatic function.

In our culture, childbearing is climactic. Pregnancy is represented by the usual obstetrician as an uncomfortable means to a dramatic end. For most women, all intensity of natural physical experience is nowadays removed from the actual birth itself; but the approach of birth nevertheless is a period of mounting tension, and drama is supplied by the intensive social recognition of the event, the dramatic accumulation of gifts, flowers, telegrams. A pregnancy is not formally announced since, if it does not eventuate in birth, it has failed to achieve its end; and failure to reach the climax brings shame. In its later stages it may be marked with a shower; but the shower looks forward to the birth, it does not celebrate the pregnancy itself. Among the Trobrianders, pregnancy has meaning in itself, as a state of being. At a first pregnancy, there is a long ceremonial involving "preparatory" work on the part of many people, which merely celebrates the pregnancy. It does not anchor the baby, it does not *have as its purpose* a more comfortable time during the pregnancy, it does not *lead to* an easier birth or a healthy baby. It makes the woman's skin white, and makes her be at her most beautiful; yet this leads to nothing, since she must not attract men, not even her own husband.

Are we then right in accepting without question the presence of a line in reality? Are we in a position to say with assurance that the Trobrianders are wrong and we are right? Much of our present-day thinking, and much of our evaluation, are based on the premise of the line and of the line as good. Students have been refused admittance to college because the autobiographic sketch accompanying their application showed absence of the line; they lacked purposefulness and ability to plan; they were inadequate as to character as well as intellectually. Our conception of personality formation, our stress on the significance of success and failure and of frustration in general, is based on the axiomatically postulated line. Yet can there be blocking without presupposed lineal motion or effort? If I walk along a path because I like the country, or if it is not important to get to a particular point at a particular time, then the insuperable puddle from the morning's shower is not frustrating; I throw stones into it and watch the ripples, and then choose another path. If the undertaking is of value in itself, a point good in itself, and not because it leads to something, then failure has no symbolic meaning; it merely results in no cake for supper, or less money in the family budget; it is not personally destructive. But failure is devastating in our culture, because it is not failure of the undertaking alone; it is the moving, becoming, lineally conceived self which has failed.

Ethnographers have occasionally remarked that the people whom they studied showed no annoyance when interrupted. Is this an indication of mild temper, or might it be the case that they were not interrupted at all, as there was no expectation of lineal continuity? Such questions are new in anthropology and most ethnographers therefore never thought of recording material which would answer them. However, we do have enough material to make us question the line as basic to all experience;

whether it is actually present in given reality or not, it is not always present in experienced reality. We cannot even take it for granted as existing among those members of our society who are not completely or naively steeped in their culture, such as many of our artists, for example. And we should be very careful, in studying other cultures, to avoid the unexamined assumption that their actions are based on the predication of a lineal reality.

BIBLIOGRAPHY

Lee, Dorothy, "A Primitive System of Values," *Philosophy of Science*, **7** (1940), 355–78.
Lee, Dorothy, "Being and Value in a Primitive Culture," *Journal of Philosophy*, **46** (1949), 401–15.
Malinowski, Bronislaw, *Argonauts of the Western Pacific*. London, 1922.
Malinowski, Bronislaw, *The Sexual Life of Savages*. New York, 1929.
Malinowski, Bronislaw, *Coral Gardens and Their Magic*. New York, 1935.

Alan Merriam

PURPOSES OF ETHNOMUSICOLOGY: AN ANTHROPOLOGICAL VIEW

The anthropological study of music is called ethnomusicology. Unfortunately, ethnomusicology tends to fall between the disciplines of anthropology and music. Too few colleges and universities offer instruction in this fascinating interdisciplinary field. Partly as a result of its ties with two academic disciplines, ethnomusicology is studied from at least two major points of view. One approach is musicological insofar as the emphasis is upon the construction of the musical composition. The concern is with the form of the music and such formal features as rhythm, scale types, melody shapes or contours, and the like. The other approach is anthropological in that the meaning of the music to the performer and to his audience is the intellectual point of departure. The anthropological approach is more concerned with the uses of the music than with the formal analyses of the music itself.

The distinction between form and function is an important one in anthropology generally. In folklore research there are those who analyze the text apart from its context, that is, who study the lore rather than the folk. In contrast, there are

Reprinted in slightly abridged form from *Ethnomusicology,* 7 (1963), 206–13, by permission of the author and the Society for Ethnomusicology.

anthropological folklorists who are primarily interested in the relationship between lore and folk. Similarly, in the anthropological study of language, one finds formalist linguists who analyze the language as a code. Attempts are made to isolate sound (phonological) patterns and syntactic patterns. On the other hand, there are anthropological linguists who are more concerned with the use of the code than with formal features of the code itself. And so the dichotomy may be found in most of the subdisciplines of cultural anthropology. It is, of course, a false dichotomy in that one needs both types of studies; one needs to study both the form of music *and* the functions of music.

For further discussion of the "musicological" approach to ethnomusicology, see Bruno Nettl, *Theory and Method in Ethnomusicology* (New York, 1964), or Nettl's *Folk and Traditional Music of the Western Continents* (Englewood Cliffs, N.J., 1965). For the "anthropological" approach, see Alan P. Merriam, *The Anthropology of Music* (Evanston, Ill., 1964). A useful bibliographical aid is Jaap Kunst, *Ethnomusicology*, 3rd ed. (The Hague, 1959). For some exciting though highly speculative attempts to relate formal features to social context and personality factors, see Alan Lomax, "Folk Song Style," *American Anthropologist,* **61** (1959), 927–54, or Lomax, "Song Structure and Social Structure," *Ethnology,* **1** (1962), 425–51. For examples of the shift in anthropological linguistics from "language as code" to "language as behavior," see John J. Gumperz and Dell Hymes, eds., *The Ethnography of Communication,* Special Publication of the *American Anthropologist,* **66**, No. 6, part II (1964).

It is important first, I think, to distinguish briefly among three kinds of problems which emerge when we talk about a discipline. First, we can use definition; that is, what is the thing with which we deal, and what are its characteristics? Second, we can use description; that is, what does it do and how does it do it? These questions have been discussed at some length by Willard Rhodes (1956), M. Kolinski (1957), Mantle Hood (1957), Gilbert Chase (1958), myself (Merriam, 1960), and J. H. Kwabena Nketia (1962), but these two problems of definition and description can be distinguished from the purpose of what we do; that is, why do we do what we do, what is it for, and perhaps most important, what should we do? The distinctions among these kinds of problems are not always easy to make, but I shall attempt in the following discussion to exclude the first two and to concentrate upon the third—the purposes of ethnomusicology.

I

In looking through the literature of ethnomusicology, it is remarkable to see how little attention has been paid to this problem, but among those approaches which have been mentioned, mostly in passing, it is possible to discern perhaps four major points of view, each of which I should like to discuss briefly.

The first of these I think is common to us all, and with tongue in cheek and with no malice intended, I should like to label it the White Knight Concept.[1] This is the point of view that the music of other peoples of the world is much abused and maligned, that such music is, in fact, fine and worthy both of study and appreciation, that most Westerners do not give it its due, and that therefore it is up to those of us who know better to protect it from the scorn of others and to explain and champion it wherever possible. At one time or another, this point of view has appeared in a great variety of writings by a great number of scholars, among them for example, Jaap Kunst, who calls attention to the fact that most Westerners think of the music of other peoples "as nothing more than either expressions of inferior, more primitive civilizations, or as a kind of musical perversion" (Kunst 1959: 1), and who goes on to debate the point with intensity. This kind of argument implies that the purpose of ethnomusicology is to disabuse Westerners of their distorted notions; in other words, we function here as knights in shining armor riding to the defense of non-Western music. Even those of us who are not Westerners often take this point of view, and of course this is not surprising, for it is truly one of our functions, one of our legitimate purposes, and we would be derelict if we did not attack ethnocentrism where we find it. But our purpose, I hope, is wider and more substantial than this, although I am perfectly happy to accept it as a smaller subdivision of what it is that we should do.

A second approach to the problem of our purpose is one which is again widespread among ethnomusicologists, but at the same time one which involves fears that I find I cannot fully accept. I shall call this, with similar facetiousness I fear, the Duty of Preservation Concept, and this has to do with the oft-expressed fear that the music of the folk is fast disappearing and that it must be recorded and studied before it is gone. Curt Sachs has expressed this concept in terms most analogous to what I have said here; in writing about tribal, folk and Oriental music, he has noted:

> Such music cannot be bought in stores, but comes from faithful tradition or
> from personal contributions of tribesmen. It is never soulless or thoughtless,

---

[1][This paper was presented in a Plenary Session of the Seventh Annual Meeting of the Society for Ethnomusicology, held at Indiana University, Bloomington, Indiana, November 29–December 2, 1962. The paper has been published as it was given and for this reason it has some characteristics of oral rather than written prose. Prof. Merriam noted in a footnote that the labels attached to the various approaches taken by his friends and colleagues were given in a humorous vein and that he would not like to see them taken seriously.—Ed. Note.]

never passive, but always vital, organic, and functional; indeed, it is always dignified. This is more than we can say of music in the West.

As an indispensable and precious part of culture, it commands respect. And respect implies the duty to help in preserving it. (Sachs, 1962:3)

There is, of course, something of the White Knight approach involved here, but what is specifically important is the idea that the music of non-literate peoples is dying out and that it is our duty to preserve it. Erich M. von Hornbostel wrote to the same point as early as 1905, and in his first full-fledged Editorial in the *African Music Society Newsletter*, Hugh Tracey commented on the problems of "... working against time in studying the receding natural art forms of [Africa's] people," a theme which he has since consistently followed (Hornbostel 1905; Tracey 1949: 2).

Again, I should like to make it clear that this seems to me to be a legitimate aim or purpose in our studies, but I do not feel that it is of exclusive importance. I cannot help but observe that on the one hand music has extraordinary tenacity, and on the other, that change is a constant in human experience. In respect to the former, one need only draw attention to the Negro in the New World; in Brazil, for example, where the first African slaves were imported about 1525, African music still flourishes and indeed does so in urban areas where we would expect the greatest accultura-tive impact to be present. In respect to the latter, change *is* a constant in human experience, and there is very little we can do about it. Africans in Johannesburg adopt jazz and the pennywhistle; American Indians compart-mentalize their own and Western music and in some cases forget the former and adopt the latter.

This is not an argument, of course, that we should neglect the recording and study of any music simply because change is inevitable; I hold quite the contrary point of view. But change does occur and there is no reason to suppose either that it will not do so in the future or that we can stem the process. By all means let us be aware of the problems of changing music systems, but certainly preservation of the present so that it will, hopefully, not become the past, is not our major purpose.

A third approach to the problem of the purpose of ethnomusicology can perhaps best be called the Communication Concept. This idea has been most widely advanced by Mantle Hood, at least in recent years, and it involves the viewpoint that music is a means of communication which can thus be used in certain ways to further world understanding. I find this concept somewhat difficult to understand precisely, because it seems to me that it has been approached in at least three different ways. In the Preface to the brochure concerning the UCLA Institute of Ethnomusicology, Hood writes as follows:

In the latter half of the Twentieth Century it may well be that the very existence of man depends on the accuracy of his communications. Communica-tion among peoples is a two-way street: speaking and listening, informing and being informed, constructively evaluating and welcoming constructive criticism.

> Communication is accurate to the extent that it is founded on a sure knowledge
> of the man with whom we would hold intercourse. (Hood 1961:n.p.)

He then continues to point out that music is one means of communication
which has been neglected, and indicates that it is a fruitful means of
communication between and among the world's people.

There is, of course, a sharp difference between regarding music as a
communicative device on the one hand and as a so-called "universal language" on the other. In the past there has been considerable espousal of the
latter view, but ethnomusicologists have consistently rejected it; George
Herzog in 1946 noted:

> We indulge in a surprising number of beliefs that are fittingly called popular
> myths. One of them is the notion that music is a 'universal language.'...[But]
> our music...consists of a number of dialects, some of them as mutually unintel-
> ligible as are found in language. (Herzog 1946:11)

Even earlier, in 1941, Charles Seeger took an almost identical point of view:

> We must, of course, be careful to avoid the fallacy that music is a 'universal
> language.' There are many music-communities in the world, though not,
> probably, as many as there are speech-communities. Many of them are mutually
> unintelligible. (Seeger 1941:122)

I think we can accept without further discussion the idea that music is
not a universal language, but that it is, clearly, a mechanism of communication between and among human beings. However, it is not precisely clear
how and why music is communication. On a simple level we can say that
music communicates within a given music community; we may further extend this to say that the very fact that people sing may communicate certain
limited things to members of markedly different music communities, but
certainly, to the best of my knowledge, we know little about such problems.
If it is questions of this sort that Mantle Hood intends to raise in speaking
of communication as a world problem, and the study of music in that
context, then it is indeed important that the question be considered.

In another context, Hood has emphasized the importance of music in
fostering international understanding:

> Today, as never before, governmental agencies of the nations of the world
> are recognizing the fact that the international understanding and goodwill is
> possible only when the cultural expressions of the peoples involved are com-
> prehended. To this end the ethnomusicologist must set for himself exacting
> standards worthy of his responsibility. (Hood 1957:8)

This would seem to imply, at least, that ethnomusicology ought to function
primarily to smooth international tension; if this is indeed the meaning of
this paragraph, I find myself sympathetic with the proposition and supportive
of it, but to a limited extent.

Finally, in an address at the 1958 meetings of the Society for Ethno-musicology in Berkeley, Hood expressed himself as follows:

> These cultural expressions, representing the heart and soul of a people, can serve as a kind of camera obscura reducing the vast and complex panorama of their multifarious activities to a sharp image in miniature. Through language and literature, through. music, dance and theater, through the graphic and plastic arts can be revealed in natural color and living images all of those essential attributes which go to make up the very identity of a people. (Hood, 1958:19)

With this point of view, I find myself in almost complete accord.

The Communication Concept, then, seems to me to be divided into three possible approaches: first, music as communication between and among peoples; second, ethnomusicology as an agency of international understanding; and third, music as a reflection and condensation, as it were, of the values, goals, and attitudes of peoples. The purpose of ethnomusicology, in this case, is apparently to understand people through music, and to apply the result toward lessening international tension.

A fourth approach to this problem of the purposes of ethnomusicology falls under the rubric of the Shotgun Concept. That is, we have sometimes tended to throw all possible reasons for studying ethnomusicology into the common pot, apparently in the hope that nothing, or very little, will be forgotten. This is not necessarily bad, but it results in an approach which is primarily unstructured and in which catholicity is substituted for direction. In the Introduction to *Music in Primitive Culture,* Bruno Nettl takes something of this approach, listing at least nine different reasons for studying, not ethnomusicology as we have come to define it, but rather what he calls "primitive music." Such music, he says, "is a new, rich source of experience for Western musicians," and composers. It "widens and enriches the experience of the listener as well as the composer." "Used as an educational medium, primitive music tends to make a student more tolerant of diverse styles and idioms." "The music historian may use it in his efforts to determine the origin of music." "A knowledge of primitive musical styles is...helpful to the psychologist of music." "The anthropologist and the historian of culture may find through examination of primitive music a substantiation of their theories; the folklorist may see its relationship to the music of rural European populations and be able to trace the latter to its origins; the historian of musical instruments often finds prototypes of European forms in some of the simpler ones in primitive cultures. And the linguist uncovers ethno-linguistic materials." (Nettl 1956:2–3).

Although my emphases would not tend to fall in the. same places, each of these may be one legitimate purpose for studying ethnomusicology, but the problem is that a broad listing of this sort leads to no real conclusion. Nettl adds:

> In summary, then, to all people interested in music and to all interested in

primitive culture, the study of this music offers new fields for exploration and a wider range for reflection. (*ibid.*:3)

This is, of course, perfectly true, but it is also almost totally bland; surely in studying ethnomusicology we are searching for more than broader horizons.

These four approaches are those which have characterized most of what little effort we have made in the past to describe the purposes of our study. I should like to reemphasize two things: first, I find little with which I flatly disagree in these approaches, save for the fact that each seems to me to be too narrow in scope, emphasizing one thing over another to the exclusion of our wider purpose; and second, given the tiny amount of space devoted to this general question of purpose in the vast amount of ethnomusicological writing, I can only express my thanks to those students I have cited, for they are the very few who have come to grips with the problem. Each has contributed in his own way, and I am grateful to them.

II

I am sure that no one here will be surprised to learn that I have my own ideas on this subject; indeed, having noted the ideas of others and commented upon them, it would be unfair and even unwise of me to attempt to get away scot free. I should like, then, to put forward these ideas for your consideration and discussion, for I hope, at least, that they represent both a fusion of the concepts that have already been expressed and a consolidation of them into a reasonably precisely honed point of view.

Without further ado, then, there are but two major reasons for studying ethnomusicology, two purposes of our study. These are not vastly complex or difficult to understand, though in their ramifications they become, of course, more involved than might appear at first blush.

First, music is a universal human phenomenon and, as such, it deserves study in its own right. The ultimate interest of man is man himself, and thus music, produced and nurtured by man, is part of what he does and part of what he studies about himself. This study, further, can in my opinion be carried on for either of two reasons with equal legitimacy. First, it can be done for the aesthetic pleasure it gives us. There is nothing wrong with this; men everywhere are concerned in one way or another with the pleasures of life, and if listening to and studying music are pleasurable activities, we may as well take advantage of it. I well recall talking as a graduate student with the British anthropologist E. E. Evans-Pritchard; the conversation turned to his own reasons for being an anthropologist, and his answer to the direct question was simply, "Why, I like it." But we may also study this human phenomenon on the scientific basis that in studying any and all phenomena we increase our knowledge of ourselves. This knowledge may or may not be immediately useful, it may or may not apply to other problems quite unexpectedly, and it may or may not turn out to be vastly important in connection with other pieces of information. I think this is a simple fact we must consider; man studies himself and he does so in the hope that what he learns may lighten his lot. If it does, well and good; if it does not—well, our culture places a premium upon learning, and the history of our learning indicates clearly that there has indeed been little, if any product of our learning that has turned out to be useless. I do not really believe, you see, that ethnomusicology is useless; we have too much evidence to the contrary already. But even if it were, while I would not myself pursue it further I think I would defend the right of others to do so.

My second reason for studying ethnomusicology is equally important, but perhaps more precise and more immediately "scientific." I have expressed these ideas once before in print, but not in the same context, and I hope that you will bear with me if I repeat myself to some small extent (Merriam 1962). It seems to me that in the history of ethnomusicology we have given undue importance and stress to musical sounds as a thing in themselves. That is, we have taken the sounds produced by any particular group of people as a phenomenon made up of interrelated parts which behave according to certain principles and regularities inherent in themselves. We have looked at musical sound as a structural system, i.e., in static, synchronic terms, and we have tended to make our analyses without reference to the human behavior out of which the sound system arises.

For music is, after all, human behavior. No musical sounds, with the debatable exception of the wind in the trees or the singing of birds, can exist, without, first, the production of that sound by a human being, and second, the reception of that sound by another human being. Music does not exist unless some individual or group of individuals produces it.

But in order to produce music, the human being must behave in certain ways. In order to produce a sound the individual must indulge in physiological behavior; he must tense the vocal cords, expel air, and so forth, and if he wishes the sound to concur with what is considered to be music in his particular society, he must learn to do these things in patterned ways. No musical performer, on no matter what level his performance is couched, can escape the cultural conditioning which shapes music as inevitably as it does other aspects of behavior. But second, the behavior of the individual making music is conditioned in other, outward ways simply by the fact that he is indulging in music behavior. His motor behavior is a part of this, and so is his social behavior: a person singing a funeral song does not behave in the same way as when he is singing as accompaniment to drinking beer. And further, if he is a recognized musician, his behavior is different again, for what we require of musicians is an almost total way of life. This, too, is behaving, and it is learned; without it, we cannot perform music according to the tenets of our particular society. So music cannot exist unless there is human behavior, for music is but a product of that behavior.

But the behavior itself is always underlain by a deeper level, and this concerns the concepts that men have of what proper musical behavior is and should be. Thus before the behavior comes the concepts; we think about what we do and shape our behavior accordingly, and thus produce musical sound.

Finally, the sound we produce, which comes through behavior, which in turn is shaped by concept, is judged both by the individual and by other members of his society in terms of its success in meeting musical criteria according to the principles accepted by that society. If the sound product is judged successful, then the concept is reinforced and the behavior repeated as nearly as possible; if the sound product is unsuccessful, then the concept must be changed which in turn alters the behavior, resulting in a changed sound product which more closely approximates the standards for music in the society at hand.

Looked at from this point of view, then, music is a product of human behavior; behavior depends upon concept; and concept is, in turn, shaped by a feedback from the product in which the latter is judged by the society at large in its own musical terms. It thus seems extremely important to me to realize that music sound is but a product of human behavior; that it is not a phenomenon by and of itself, operating according to its own inherent structural principles; and that an understanding of it depends upon an understanding of behavior, concept, and feedback upon concept. This is why I have previously defined ethnomusicology as the study of music in culture (Merriam, 1960), and it is also why I think ethnomusicology should be studied.[2] We share both with social science and with the humanities the extremely important task of studying human behavior, for we seek—through music in this case—an understanding of why men behave as they do.

REFERENCES CITED

Chase, Gilbert
    1958 "A dialectical approach to music history," Ethnomusicology 2 : 1–9.
Herzog, George
    1946 "Comparative musicology," The Music Journal 4 (Nov.-Dec.) : 11 et seq.
Hood, Mantle
    1957 "Training and research methods in ethnomusicology," Ethnomusicology
          Newsletter No. 11 : 2–8
    1958 The ugly American in music. MS
    1961 Institute of ethnomusicology, Los Angeles : University of California.
Hornbostel, Erich M. von
    1905 "Die probleme der vergleichende musikwissenschaft," Zeitschrift der
          Internationale musikgesellschaft 7 : 85–97.
Kolinski, Mieczyslaw
    1957 "Ethnomusicology, its problems and methods," Ethnomusicology Newsletter
          No. 10 : 1–7.
Kunst, Jaap
    1959 Ethnomusicology. The Hague: Martinus Nijhoff, Third Edition.
Merriam, Alan P.

[2][Hopefully the perceptive reader has realized that most of the arguments adduced by Merriam for the study of ethnomusicology could be equally well applied to the study of other aspects of culture. One could easily substitute art, language, or folk-lore in place of music and the force of Merriam's arguments would not be diminished in any way.—*Ed. Note*.]

1960 "Ethnomusicology: discussion and definition of the field," Ethnomusicology 4:107–14.

1962 A prologue to the study of the African arts. Yellow Springs: Antioch Press.

Nettl, Bruno

1956 Music in primitive culture. Cambridge: Harvard University Press.

Nketia, J. H. Kwabena

1962 "The problem of meaning in African music," Ethnomusicology 6:1–7.

Rhodes, Willard

1956 "On the subject of ethnomusicology," Ethnomusicology Newsletter No. 7: 1–9.

Sachs, Curt

1962 The Wellsprings of music. The Hague: Martinus Nijhoff.

Seeger, Charles

1941 "Music and culture," in Theodore M. Finney (Ed). Proceedings of the Music Teachers National Association. Pittsburg, 64:112–22.

Tracey, Hugh

1949 "Editorial," African Music Society Newsletter 1 (March):2–3.

Ralph Linton

PRIMITIVE ART

Because of the great interest in so-called primitive art by artists of our own society, and the undoubted influence of this material upon our artists, there is more general knowledge of the art of the peoples of the world than of other creative forms, for example, music. Another reason is that it is far easier to take a photograph of an art object than to tape-record a musical performance and, more importantly, it is easier to publish photographs than to transcribe and publish the contents of musical tapes. Yet despite the general interest in primitive art, there are, as former Sterling Professor of Anthropology at Yale University Ralph Linton points out, a great many popular misconceptions about the nature and origin of it. Rightfully attacking the traditional but false child-savage equation and several other similar fallacies, Professor Linton spells out some of the principal theoretical and methodological problems arising from the study of art in culture.

For further readings in this area, see Hjalmar Stolpe, *Collected Essays in Ornamental Art* (Stockholm, 1927); Franz Boas, *Primitive Art* (Oslo, 1927; paperback, New York, 1955); Paul S. Wingert, *Primitive Art, Its Traditions and Styles* (New York, 1962); and Douglas Fraser, ed., *The Many Faces of*

Reprinted from *The Kenyon Review*, 3 (1941), 34–51, by permission of Kenyon College and *The Kenyon Review*.

Primitive Art (Englewood Cliffs, N. J., 1966). A survey with some bibliography may be found in Herta Haselberger, "Method of Studying Ethnological Art," *Current Anthropology,* **2** (1961), 341–84. For studies of individual artists, see Raymond W. Firth, "The Maori Carver," *Journal of the Polynesian Society,* **34** (1925), 277–91, and Ruth L. Bunzel's classic *The Pueblo Potter: A Study of Creative Imagination in Primitive Art* (New York, 1929).

In its current application to art the term primitive is as vague and unspecific as the term heathen in its application to religion. A heathen sect is simply one which is not affiliated with one or another of three of four organized systems of theology. Similarly, a primitive art is any one which flourishes outside a small number of cultures which we have chosen to designate as civilizations. Such arts differ vastly more among themselves than do those of the civilizations in question and it is correspondingly difficult to generalize with respect to them. Any statements which will hold true for such diverse aesthetic expressions as the pictographs of the Australians, the woven designs of the Peruvians and the abstract sculptures of African Negroes must be of the broadest and simplest sort. Moreover, the problem is complicated by the meaning attached to the term primitive in its other usages. It stands for something simple, undeveloped and, by implication, ancestral to more evolved forms. Its application to arts and cultures other than our own is an unfortunate heritage from the ethnocentrism of the 19th Century European scientists who laid the foundations of anthropology. Elated by the newly enunciated doctrines of evolution, these students saw all culture as stages in a single line of development and assigned them to places in this series on the simple basis of the degree to which they differed from the European culture which was blandly assumed to be the final and perfect flower of the evolutionary process. This idea has long since been abandoned by anthropologists, but before its demise it diffused to other social sciences and became a part of the general body of popular misinformation. It still tinges a great deal of the thought and writing about the arts of non-European peoples and has been responsible for many misunderstandings.

Actually, there is no culture extant today to which the term primitive can be applied legitimately. There are cultures of greater or less complexity and cultures which have many or few features in common with our culture, but every one of them is a product of its own evolutionary sequence. The culture of an American Indian tribe, or of a Polynesian island, does not represent a stage in the development of our civilization any more than a modern dog represents a stage in the evolution of the elephant. This is as true for the arts of such groups as for any other aspect of their activities. Primitive stages in the development of particular arts have been preserved here and there. Thus it is quite legitimate to speak of Italian primitives in the light of the general development of Italian painting. However, no art can rightly be termed primitive with respect to the development of art as a whole. There are merely arts of greater or less complexity or sophistication. Even the much advertised pictures of animals left by the European cave men of thirty thousand years ago cannot be considered primitive in the popular usage of the term. They show a sophistication scarcely inferior to the modern Japanese drawings in which the essential qualities of an animal are caught in half a dozen lines. Moreover, this art seems to have been a local flowering which had no parallels except, perhaps, in parts of Africa. Elsewhere in the world there were innumerable groups living at the same time, or at the same general level of technological advancement, whose arts developed along different lines. It is even impossible to show that the art of the caves contributed anything to subsequent developments in Europe. The later neolithic peoples of that continent have left nothing which in any way resembles it and if any influences from it reached the historic arts of the area these influences came in a back wash by way of later steppe nomads and the Near East.

The student of "primitive" art is confronted, therefore, with a wide range of arts which have little in common beyond the fact that they are all expressions of a deep seated and seemingly universal urge toward the creation of beauty. The forms which these expressions take are controlled in each case by the culture of the groups and, more remotely, by the series of historic events which have been responsible for giving this culture its particular form. However, the human beings who have and express the urge seem to be very much the same everywhere. Whether there are racial differences in intelligence, or in that imponderable thing which we call temperament, is a problem which we still cannot answer by scientific methods. However, I have never met an anthropologist who was willing to admit that the members of any "primitive" group with which he himself had lived and worked were inferior in intelligence to Europeans. And the better one comes to know individuals in such a group the more they seem to resemble particular people you know in your own society. The gross range of individual differences in a native village seems to be about as great as that in the average European community of the same size and this applies to ability as well as personality. The primitive artist, like the civilized one, may be a genius, a clever and industrious mediocrity or quite devoid of talents. Even if he is a genius, he will have his good and bad times, his successes and his failures. Masterpieces are as rare in primitive art as in our own and, talks with native artists lead me to believe, as difficult for even their creators to predict. There is bad primitive art just as there is bad civilized art and the indiscriminate admiration of primitive work which has been a recent fad certainly does not aid the cause of aesthetics.

If there are inherent psychological differences between "primitives" as a group and Europeans as a group, they are certainly of a very minor sort. Nothing could be more fallacious than to regard the primitive artist as a retarded individual whose work can be treated on a par with that of the civilized child. He is an adult and frequently an exceedingly intelligent one. He has laboriously acquired skills, extensive technical knowledge and clearly defined aesthetic standards. His work is not a simple, spontaneous outpouring of his desire for beauty. It is, in most cases, controlled by conventions considerably more rigid than those of our own art. If his work sometimes appears naive, it is because of these conventions and the systems of interests and values which they reflect. If he ignores certain aspects of his subject, it is because, to his society, these aspects are either unimportant or taboo. Victorian art also treated certain aspects of human anatomy with a reticence incomprehensible to a Melanesian or African. To blame the primitive artist for such omissions is quite on a par with blaming a modernistic painter for not reproducing the individual leaves on a tree or the weave of his subjects' clothing. The similarities which have been pointed out between certain examples of primitive art and the efforts of children in our own society are purely fortuitous and depend upon a very careful selection of the primitive examples. In the first place, no European child reared in a home with books and pictures can be considered uninfluenced by European art. In the second, no child, civilized or otherwise, ever produced anything remotely resembling the intricate grotesques of the New Zealand Maori or the abstract sculpture of West Africa. To find parallels for the former one has to go to Gothic art in its most virile period; for the latter, to the work of advanced modernists who have, confessedly, been influenced by Negro sculpture.

Similar objections hold, in even larger measure, for attempts to equate primitive art with that of the insane in our own culture. A particular schizophrenic may develop a configuration of associated ideas and symbols which happens to resemble a configuration present in some non-European culture. If the insane individual has sufficient technical skill and works in the same medium as an artist reared in this particular culture, the products of the two may be quite similar. However, this does not indicate that the primitive artist is a schizophrenic. Every culture includes seemingly irrational configurations of ideas and symbols. Our own association of lambs, doves, crosses, and ideas of immortality would appear the purest schizophrenia to an intelligent Eskimo.

A word should also be said about the attitudes and supernatural beliefs attributed to primitive artists in much of the current literature. There are many primitive groups in which the artist's attitude toward his work and its finished product are as practical as they are in our own. However, when the artist is a devout animist, his relations with his tools and materials may assume a mystic quality. If he regards these as animate, intelligent beings, he must also regard them as conscious collaborators in the act of artistic creation. The rituals by which their willing cooperation is assured then become as important for the success of his work as the technical processes involved. Moreover, to the animist his own artistic product has, or at least should have, a life of its own and a place in the universe. Without this it remains incomplete and his work unfinished. Thus the Iroquois mask-maker carved his masks from the trunks of living trees so that life would be transferred to them. In the Marquesas Islands, the maker of images accompanied his work by chants in which the genealogies of his tools and materials were traced from the beginning of the world so that their offspring, the image, would have its proper place in the scheme of things. His own act of artistic creation was equated with that of physical procreation and this equation was more than a figure of speech. While the work was in progress his procreative powers were protected and strengthened by strict taboos on sexual intercourse. Practices of this sort must be considered a rare and extreme development of animistic tendencies. They pass by imperceptible degrees into rituals and taboos designed to shield the work in progress from evil influences or to further it by magical means. Many of these rituals provide excellent illustrations of the interweaving of magical and practical considerations which is characteristic of many primitive activities. They are spells, but they are also shop formulae, keeping in mind the various things to be done and the order in which they must be done to get the best results.

In spite of the frequent presence of magical practices in connection with the primitive artist's work, his motives seem to be much like those of his civilized confrere. He may work because of an inner drive toward the creation of beauty or for profit or prestige or through any combination of these factors. He may also work simply because aesthetic activities are expected of persons in his position. There are tribes in which woodcarving is as regular for men as fancywork was for English ladies in the early 19th Century. It is true that, in many primitive arts, there is an element of magical utility, but this is by no means universal. Thus I never found that any magical significance was attached to the elaborate and beautiful designs which many Madagascar tribes weave into their mats or to the carvings with which they decorate their houses. This in spite of the fact that these people are strong believers in both benevolent and malevolent magic and have a great variety of magical formulae and charms. Even when a magical element does enter into primitive art it is inextricably interwoven with aesthetic elements and it is often impossible to say which dominates. Perhaps the only test is the degree to which the artist has gone on working after the magical purpose has been fulfilled. The problem is, after all, quite on a par with that presented by European sacred art. A Renaissance madonna was painted for a sacred purpose and according to certain conventions which this purpose imposed, but these requirements could have been met by the crudest daub. Other motives lay behind its perfection of color and line. Similarly, a design carved on an arrow to increase its efficacy was amplified and improved to satisfy the aesthetic needs of the savage who carved it. Hand in hand with man's search for supernatural aid goes his search for beauty and which urge is stronger depends upon the time and place.

Among uncivilized peoples this search for beauty is not intellectualized or even verbalized. The primitive artist is, almost without exception, unable to describe his process of artistic creation or to define the aesthetic canons which he recognizes. Even when all allowances have been made for the difficulties of a European in a native language or vice versa there seem to be no terms for these things. They are felt but they are not talked about. During a year's sojourn in the Marquesas Islands it was my good fortune to work with the best man among the native wood carvers. He was not only an artist of the first rank but also a highly intelligent individual with a philosophic and introspective turn of mind. Nevertheless, he was never able to explain to me the way in which he conceived his designs or why he felt that certain examples of his work were good or mediocre. The nearest I have ever come to getting a coherent statement about the process of creation from a primitive artist was when an Indian woman told me that she dreamed her beadwork designs. Similarly, the most that can be obtained in the way of artistic criticism is the bald statement that such a piece is good, bad or indifferent. The uniformity of the judgments given by different individuals in such cases proves that aesthetic canons exist in any primitive culture but leaves it an open question in how far these canons are conscious. It is plain that the processes of both creation and appreciation go on among primitive peoples with little or no manipulation of verbal symbols. However, this is far from uncommon even among ourselves. Many of our best and most productive artists seem to be unfamiliar with formulated rules of aesthetics and as incoherent as any native when it comes to discussion of their own work. The facts of artistic creation and appreciation seem to be much the same for primitive and civilized but the primitives have never felt the needs for verbalization and for rationalization after the fact which have given us our conscious aesthetic philosophy.

In the absence of such a philosophy, the only possible approach to primitive art is an objective one. The primitive artist can describe his work in terms of the techniques involved and of his practical aims, the uses to which the finished product will be put. He can also describe what he is trying to make, but he cannot tell why he finds one form more satisfying than another. The aesthetic principles involved must be deduced from the work itself. It seems probable that there are, at the foundations of all successful art, certain general principles of harmony in line, color and composition, but these must hold for primitive and civilized work in equal degree. In the more superficial matters of preferred colors, designs and types of symmetry the variations from one primitive art to another are so great that valid generalizations become impossible. Thus within even such a restricted area as the Plains the work of several tribes can be identified in collections simple by their varying choice of colors. The factors which are common to all primitive arts and at the same time lacking in our own are not, strictly speaking, aesthetic ones. They are matters of technique and immediate aim and their universality is due to certain similarities in the social and cultural milieus in which primitive artists must function.

In the first place, the primitive artist is normally a member of a small closely knit community. Here and there, as in certain parts of Africa, this community may belong to a much larger social unit, but even so its members have few outside contacts. They are not completely cut off from new ideas, but novelties come to them infrequently and tend to be regarded with suspicion. Interests and loyalties center in the immediate group and the only response which the artist can hope for is that of his neighbors. The situation is not unlike that in European peasant communities prior to the 19th Century. However, primitive art differs from peasant art in certain respects. Peasant art filled a particular niche in a larger artistic configuration, with the professionally executed fine arts standing above and distinct from it. Even the most isolated peasant artist knew something of the work of the professionals and derived from this a certain sense of inferiorty. He limited the scope of his endeavors and thought of his work as common art for common things. Moreover, really talented individuals were likely to attract the attention of the Church or the nobility and to be drawn away into the professional field. The primitive artist has no such feeling of inferiority. There is no distinction in his thinking between fine and common art, except possibly in a recognition of the skill required. Talented individuals are not drawn away from the community, for the professional artist is a phenomenon of complex culture and economic surplus. Like the peasant artist, the primitive one practices his work as a spare time occupation and his gains from it come in terms of prestige, not wealth.

Like the peasant artist also, the primitive one has an intelligent, participant audience. If one man in a primitive community carves or paints, most of the other men will usually do so. The genius rises from a plateau of fellow workers who may be less gifted but who have an intimate knowledge of his aims and of the techniques available for their fulfillment. Under these conditions technical virtuosity acquires a new aspect. The skill displayed with brush or chisel becomes, in itself, a source of aesthetic satisfaction to those accustomed to handle the brush and chisel. I have seen native carvers make unconscious movements while studying the work of another carver which indicated clearly that they were participating at a kinesthetic level and deriving pleasure from this. Problems of organization, design and color arrangement are similarly familiar and the skill shown in solving them a source of intellectual delight. The primitive artist really works for other artists, and communication with his audience is far simpler for him than it is for the artist in our own society. I have often thought that the extreme stress on naturalism which characterized European professional art during much of its history was, in part, a by-product of professionalism. When the man in the street no longer had first-hand knowledge of the artist's problems and techniques, only the visual image remained as a common field of experience and discourse. The better the artist reproduced this the more intelligible he became.

In spite of these advantages, the primitive artist is subject to certain limitations which do not exist at the civilized level. Most important of these is the rigid division of labor and the assignment of particular crafts, or of work with particular materials, to certain groups within the society. Primitive art is inseparably linked with the production of utilitarian objects. Thus, with very few exceptions, work with wood, stone and metal falls in the men's province, weaving and the making of baskets and pottery in that of the women. In most primitive societies it would be quite impossible for a woman, no matter what her ability, to become a carver of wood or stone while, conversely, a man who sought aesthetic expression in one of the women's crafts would find his masculinity suspect. Some groups carry this division even farther, reserving certain arts to certain castes. Thus among the Imerina of Madagascar the weaving of warp-dyed fabrics was orginally limited to women of the noble caste while in Dahomey, in Africa, the casting of brass figures was the hereditary privilege of a single clan.

It is this rigid ascription of occupations which is responsible for the not infrequent phenomenon of two or more totally different art styles coexisting in a single primitive society with little or no influence on each other. Thus the tribes of the Northwest Coast of America had a curvilinear art style in which men and animals were represented according to elaborate conventions. The most familiar examples of this age are the totem poles, but it was also applied to all the various objects made by men. Side by side with this there was an only slightly less elaborate angular geometric art practiced by the women in their basketry. These geometric designs were interpreted as representing plants and inanimate objects. The two arts differed so completely that, if the actual situation was not known, they would be assigned to different design areas of North America. The women's designs never appeared on men's work while the men's designs appeared on women's work at only one point, in the so-called Chilkat blankets. Men painted the patterns for these on boards and women copied the patterns in their weaving. The male designer had a proprietary right in the pattern and the painted board had to be returned to him as soon as the weaving was finished. These blanket patterns made no allowance for the limitations ordinarily imposed on textile designs by the medium and their execution called for extreme technical skill. The whole arrangement seems to have been a very late development and must be classed as a bit of virtuosity in no way characteristic of primitive conditions.

A somewhat similar situation was present in Plains Indian art where angular geometric designs and a vigorous naturalistic representation of men and animals flourished side by side. Here again the geometric art was the work of women, the naturalistic art that of men. Many other examples of such plurality of art styles could be cited and the idea is not entirely foreign to us, although the lines are drawn with less rigidity. Thus certain of our own textile designs rarely appear in carving or painting. However, we lack the sex division in the use of designs which is important in most primitive groups. It is a curious fact that where a free, naturalistic style and an angular geometric one coexist in the same culture, the former is practically always executed by men, the latter by women. The explanation may be partly technological since the media in which men work usually permit of freer execution, as in carving versus weaving, but the situation would seem to require further study.

Because of this rigid division of activities the primitive artist normally works in only a few media and with a limited number of art forms. However, his technical control of these is usually excellent. The effectiveness of primitive tools is constantly underrated by those who have not seen them in action. Much of the apparent clumsiness of these tools is due to the fact that Europeans have not developed the muscular habits that go with their use. Thus in Madagascar I was much puzzled by the long handles of certain knives used in carving small objects until I discovered that these knives were held in the arm pit and the object to be carved pressed and turned against the cutting edge. In Africa, where iron has been in use for thousands of years, the equipment of the native sculptor is quite on a par with that of European sculptors of the classical and even Gothic periods. Even when metal is lacking, surprisingly good work can be done with stone, bone and animal teeth, and the tools made from these are often highly specialized. The main difference between such implements and those made from metal lies in the time, effort and manual skill involved. Since the primitive artist is rarely interested in mass production, these factors do not loom very large in his mind. At most, they are an encouragement to simplification of his work. Thus the Marquesans were able to cut the hardest volcanic rock with rats' teeth and actually carved small images and decorated the tops of their food pounders by this method. I was told that to make even a rigidly stylized image required all a man's spare time for six months. To have made a naturalistic one would have taken a year or more and the aesthetic gain did not seem worth the effort. That they had the necessary skill for naturalistic work was shown by the ease with which they turned to it in response to European demands.

Very little information is available about the training of artists in primitive societies. Apprenticeships are not unknown but are probably limited to those groups in which art training has an economic value. Except in the Marquesas Islands, no native artists to whom I talked could give any coherent account of how they learned their craft. They seemed to have picked it up by watching and working with older people. In the Marquesas, where skill in carving was an economic as well as a social asset, most men learned it in this informal way but ambitious ones received regular instructions from one of the master carvers. The training given by these men was as functional as anything ever envisaged by Frank Lloyd Wright. It began with learning how to make one's tools and gather one's raw materials, with great attention to the potentialities of these materials and their appropriateness for various uses. This was followed by training in techniques of carving, in the use and organization of designs, again with much attention to their appropriateness, and in the magical chants which were here an accompaniment of all the more important work. Sculpture was very definitely regarded as a craft, comparable to canoe-making or carpentry, and a similar attitude seems to be characteristic of all primitive societies.

Actually, there is no distinction in the simpler cultures between the artist and the artisan. With very few exceptions, such as that of the blankets previously noted, the same individual both designs and executes, and he takes an equal pride in both. I believe that most of the native artists I have known would have regarded with extreme disfavor the common European practice of creating a design in an easily worked medium and then turning it over to someone else to be executed in a difficult and laborious one. As has been said, native audiences are as sensitive to skill in execution as to excellence of design and a man who did not carry his own work through to completion would be subject to censure.

As a rule, the primitive artist does not even transfer his designs from one medium to another. He works without preliminary sketches and, if he has achieved a mastery of his craft, rarely makes even guide marks upon his material. Thus if it is wood that he is handling, he thinks and works in terms of wood from the start. The functional quality of much primitive sculpture and the excellence of its design when seen from any angle derive very largely from this lack of transfer of design from one medium to another. A primitive statue is not a series of sketches put together at various angles and then connected by chisel work. It is a coherent whole which the artist has already seen, in his mind's eye, from every possible direction. It may take him longer to do this and to memorize the results than it will take him to carve the statue, but once the conception is clear, the task of execution requires no guide marks. It is on a par with Michelangelo's "freeing the statue from the marble."

This ability for abstract conceptualization is not limited to primitives, but the necessity for it is stressed in many primitive arts much more than it is in our own. Thus the Marquesan carver was required to give tangible proof that he had his design in mind down to the last detail before he began work. If he was carving a bowl, the bowl was shaped and highly polished before the carving began so that any deviation from the original plan, as well as any slip of the chisel was immediately evident. Both the Marquesans and the related New Zealanders developed the ability to conceive and organize designs without the aid of preliminary sketches to a point almost incredible to Europeans. In New Zealand, in particular, it was not uncommon for the artist deliberately to plan his design for a field larger than that offered by the object to be decorated and then reproduce on the object only those elements of the total design which fell within the part of the imaginary field which the object would cover if superimposed upon it. It is safe to say that few European artists would be capable of such a *tour de force*. The not uncommon European system of letting a design grow under the hand, changing and expanding as the work goes on, appears to such artists as something "primitive" and juvenile. A master craftsman does all that in his mind before the mechanical work begins.

It is clear such introspective conceptualization is quite incompatible with the use of models. However, they are very rarely used by primitive artists even in those groups where such conceptualization is poorly developed. Exact reproductions of subjects as seen are quite outside the intent of most primitive art. A beginner may copy directly from a better artist's work until he has learned his craft, but when he launches out on original work he ceases to imitate even life forms. The reason for this may be party technical. In the absence of the technique of making preliminary sketches and then transferring, the use of living models becomes impossible for work in many media. Even the most obliging subject could hardly be expected to pose while his portrait was carved from a tree trunk with a stone chisel. However, this certainly is not the whole explanation. Except for a very limited development of human portraiture in a few groups which have developed great technical skill in their arts, primitive peoples make no attempt to reproduce their visual image of the thing they are trying to represent. The aim of the primitive artist is to present his subject as he and his society think of it, not as he sees it. The development of conventions for this not only saves labor but also facilitates communication between the artist and his audience.

This indifference to naturalism opens the way to a subtle type of conventionalization which is foreign to our own artistic concepts but which finds some parallel in the arts of Asiatic civilizations. When one attempts to make an accurate copy of almost any primitive art work he discovers that, in addition to the conventionalization of form and design, there is a rigid conventionalization in the quality of the lines and curves used in presenting these. These conventions unquestionably depend upon the development of certain muscular habits and are comparable with those developed in connection with various styles of writing, as Latin, Arabic or Chinese. They are also comparable with the individual tricks of brush or chisel work which aid in identifying the products of our own masters, but in primitive art they are characteristic of a tribe or area rather than an individual. Their influence is so strong that even when the native artist attempts to copy European designs the native conventions survive and give his work a recognizable quality. The development of this type of conventionalization is quite impossible as long as the artist aims at exact reproduction of what he sees since no two irregular curves present in nature are ever exactly the same. Its presence in nearly all primitive arts is an additional proof of the degree to which these arts are consciously divorced from naturalism.

It has already been said that the aim of the primitive artist is to present his subject as he and his society think of it, not as he sees it. This mental image includes not only a memory of how the thing looks but also all sorts of evaluations based on the relations of the thing to the artist's society and culture. Thus his mental image of a bear can scarcely fail to give added importance to the animal's teeth and claws, the most significant thing about it from the point of view of one likely to be attacked by it. The mental image may even include details of the animal's anatomy which are quite invisible while it is alive. Thus in both the Plains and Southwest, pictures of game animals nearly always show not only the external contours of the animal but also the heart and aorta; the seat of its life and, for the hunter, the bull's eye of his living target. What the primitive artist draws is, therefore, an abstraction based on nature but never intended to correspond to nature. It is thus comparable to the work of some of our own modern artists except at one very important point. Modern abstractions tend to be based upon the artist's personal reactions to his subject and, as a result, are often quite unintelligible to the greater part of his audience. The primitive artist's abstractions are based upon the reactions common to members of his society and are thus entirely intelligible to his audience.

Practically all primitive art is conventionalized, but the forms of conventionalization differ enormously in different groups and tend to reflect, in each case, the value system of the society. Most striking, to a European, is the freedom which many primitive peoples show in the treatment of the human body. They exaggerate certain parts of it and suppress others or reduce its surfaces to a few essential angles and planes. Thus masks from the Sepik River, in New Guinea, usually show tremendous exaggeration of the nose. This is comprehensible when one learns that among these tribes a big nose is considered an indication of virility. In the Marquesas, the heads and faces of images were worked out according to elaborate conventions while the rest of the body was treated in rather summary fashion. This was because, to these people, the head was the seat of the *mana* or spiritual power of the individual while the eyes, ears, nose and mouth symbolized the four senses of sight, hearing, smell and taste. The conventional representations of these organs conveyed the idea perfectly to a native audience and also had a decorative quality lacking in the natural arrangement. When I showed one of the best native artists there pictures of European statuary he was not impressed. He considered that the European naturalism was a trick in which the artist had used his technical skill to avoid meeting the authentic artistic problems of abstraction and composition. What, he asked, was the point of laboring to make something that would look exactly like a man when it would not feel like one or smell like one?

The conventionalization of primitive art does not reflect naïveté or even, in many cases, a lack of ability to do naturalistic work. It reflects a different set of artistic aims and is thus no more truly primitive in relation to our own than was the conventionalized art of the Byzantines in relation to the naturalism of Hellenistic sculpture. It is even questionable whether such conventionalization detracts from the aesthetic quality of the work or the artist's facilities for self-expression. Certainly it limits him in certain directions, but it also serves to focus his forces on problems of pure form, design and organization. He may be permitted to use only a limited number of motifs, but, freed from the demands of naturalism, he can treat these with intellectual clarity. The symbolism of the forms which he employs is so familiar both to him and to his audience that he can convey emotional effects without detracting from the purely aesthetic value of his work. I once obtained a pair of Arapaho Indian moccasins whose decoration conformed to the ordinary pattern of that worn by men at all except one point. Across the white band running from ankle to toe, which symbolized the wearer's path of life, there was an oblong figure in red and brown which was so placed that it harmonized perfectly with the rest of the design. The owner explained that in his youth he had been a great warrior and a man of pride and furious temper but he had now become so gentle that he would not injure even a worm. The red and brown figure symbolized the worm in his path.

The aims of the primitive artist are not very different, at bottom, from those of the civilized one. Superficial differences are his lack of intent for naturalistic representation and his greater attention to technical virtuosity, rendered important by his audience's understanding of the problems and techniques involved in his work. However, his work is not lacking in either emotional or narrative qualities. It appears so to the European because the latter does not understand native symbolism. Thus to a white man the moccasin design just noted would be only a bit of beadwork to be evaluated in terms of pattern and color. To an Arapaho it would convey the poignancy of old age. Again, the arrangement of figures on a carving from the Northwest Coast would convey no more to a European than a group made up of three pigs and a highly conventionalized wolf, cast in bisque, would convey to a Hindu. To the instructed, each brings to mind a legend and evokes certain emotions. Purely aesthetic problems of design and color harmony are the same for the civilized and the primitive artist, modified only by their difference in technical resources, and the results can be judged by the same standards. Success in these fields is something easier to recognize than to analyse, but I believe that comparative studies of primitive and civilized art will throw more light on the basic principles of aesthetics than any study of civilized art alone.

Regina G. Twala

BEADS AS REGULATING
THE SOCIAL LIFE
OF THE ZULU AND SWAZI

If an anthropologist were to tell a nonanthropologist friend that he was conducting research on the wearing of beads by an African people, no doubt he would hear hoots of derision in reply. On the surface, such a research project would appear to be the ultimate in the study of trivia. Yet there is no aspect of culture so trival that its study would not result in some increase of knowledge of that culture. In fact, often it is precisely what is apparently trivial and mundane which yields the most important insights. For it is what the members of a culture take for granted that is often what the ethnographer needs to know in order to understand more fully the behavior of the people under observation.

This unusual essay on the social significance of beads also reveals the weaknesses of subdisciplinary distinctions in cultural anthropology. Is this a study of art? Is this a study of communication? Is this a study of ritual? The answer, of course, is that it is all of these and more. The point is that once you have asked so much as one question, you cannot answer it completely until you have described the entire culture. Culture is holistic; it is the ethnographer who insists upon the specialized compartmentation of the study of culture.

This analysis of bead symbolism also reveals the fallacy of thinking that mere empirical observation is all there is to fieldwork. An ethnographer could stare at a Swazi bead pattern all of his life (and this is too often what happens when we visit museums of primitive art—we stare admiringly but uncomprehendingly at a particular object) and he still could not decipher the message contained therein. One must obtain the

Reprinted from *African Studies,* **10** (1951), 113–23, by permission of the author and the Witwatersrand University Press, Johannesburg.

natives' own art, music, and literary criticism and interpretations.

For further references on Zulu culture, see E. J. Krige, *The Social System of the Zulus* (London, 1936), and I. Schapera, *Select Bibliography of South African Native Life and Problems* (London, 1941), pp. 97–102. For references to Swazi culture, see Hilda Kuper, *The Swazi, A South African Kingdom* (New York, 1963), or her "The Swazi of Swaziland," in James L. Gibbs, Jr., ed., *Peoples of Africa* (New York, 1965), pp. 497–511.

Very little has been written on the subject of beads among the Bantu. The following information has been collected from the Swazi of Swaziland Protectorate, and Zulu of eMangwaneni, Bergville, Natal. All facts are from personal observation and conversation with the people of these tribes, in their own environment. Regulating the social life of the Zulu and Swazi, beads are here treated as social sanctions of social codes; as tokens of love between young people in different tribes. The literature of beads with vocabulary is given, and colours and designs explained. Beads as decorations for status, and rank are discussed. Finally how to decipher bead patterns is explained.

Beads are an ancient commodity. They have been found in the ruins of ancient cities of Nineveh, Greece, Rome and Britain. Glass beads have been found buried with Egyptian mummies. They are made of various seeds, stone, bone, metal, glass and from ostrich egg shells such as were made by the Bushmen in South Africa. There are also certain types of ornaments made of wood, shaped into round pegs and pierced across; although these may be given a different name by the tribes using them, one would also class them as a type of bead, since they are perforated and are strung like beads.

Uses of Beads

The Southern Bantu tribes all use beads both for ornamental reasons and for other purposes as well. Importance is attached to both colour and design. The Zulu have taken to beads more than any other Southern Bantu tribe; then come the Amandebele or Mapoko tribes as they are usually called. The Xosa, Sotho and Swazi make little use of beads in comparison with the Zulu, who wear much finery. A young man of Zulu origin will wear string upon string of beads in various designs and colours, sometimes covering the whole thorax region with bead work. Because these men get their beads from their sweethearts, the more girls a man has, the more beads he will wear. A family man will sometimes wear beads to signify the number of wives he has.

Social Obligations Supported by Sanctions

Every society has its sanctions, so that the individual will be guided in his behaviour by following certain prescribed obligations. From childhood therefore the individual is trained to fit into the social scheme by means of a body of observances and traditions. Because primitive people cannot put their codes of conduct in writing as the more civilized races do, some invent a system by which the individual will be guided indirectly. Among the Bantu beads have been used as a regulating agent in the social life affecting the young people—in matters of sex relations in particular.

Writers on the social problems of detribalized natives in urban areas repeatedly mention the fact that there is no longer any effective public opinion among town dwellers; that Africans have no longer those sanctions which controlled their form of society; that delinquency is appalling because of the lack of parental control over juveniles. This article aims at explaining one item out of many which were used as methods of controlling youth in Bantu society.

Among the Zulu and Swazi beads mark certain stages in the development of both a young girl and a young boy. Beads further mark the various stages in the development of love, from what we may call calf love to romantic love and finally terminating in marriage. Love making has never been a private affair amongst these tribes; everyone in the village knows who is already mature for marriage. Beads were some of the outward signs which showed every one in that society the exact position of feminine affairs. Just as much as it was once compulsory among members of the western culture for a girl who is engaged to wear her engagement ring in public, so also these Bantu had a number of distinguishing objects of various designs in bead work showing the young wooer how far to go.

Beads in the Regulation of Sexual Intercourse

Among the Swazi when a child is born it wears no beads or clothing. At this stage the mother and child are still impure and have to keep away from the public; the husband is not supposed to go where the child is. Marwick in his book *The Swazi* mentions the fact that the child may not be seen by its father before it has been *lalatelwa* because it might get very thin and probably die. The word *ukulalatela* means to sing a lullaby. When a child is born into a Swazi kraal, it must be initiated into the family so as to be recognized as a human being, *umuntfu*. It takes four months for a baby to start moving in the uterus and proving that it has life, and after it is born it takes another four months for the mother to be purified from the impurities connected with child-birth. It is only then that the child must be shown to the new moon to start the real life of human beings and be given a proper lullaby *ukulalatela*. Before this ceremony the *lalala* sound is not used.

In reality when the Swazi say that the child must not be seen by the father, all that they mean is that the father may not go in unto the mother. When a man talks about his children he means his wife—it is *ukuhlonipha* —decency. A man will say: *"Ngikhanuka aɓantaɓami"*—"I long for my children," when he means that he longs for his wife. For a first-born child the mother waits for four months before the custom of *ukulalatela* takes place, and for the following babies only two months.

After the baby has been shown to the moon, the mother must make a string of white beads for the baby to wear round the waist, the wrists and ankles. Then can the father go into the mother's hut. This action is called *kufumbatisa umntwana ligadze*. He takes a piece of earth and hands it to the child and he can then have sexual intercourse with the mother. At this time they say that the baby will benefit by gaining more strength and vigour, and if a baby is a weakling they will say that it is because the father went in unto the mother before it had worn the white beads. The baby wears them until weaned. Then it can wear a different colour.

Little Zulu girls wear only one string of beads round the waist, ankles and wrists until they have reached maturity. As soon as a girl falls in love, she must make a simple string of beads all one colour. This is called *ucu lokuqoma,* a string for falling in love. This she gives to her first lover to wear round the neck; then she makes a similar one for herself for the waist, wrist and ankles. If one met a group of young girls one could tell immediately which of the group had recently fallen in love, and which were too young for love affairs. Until now the girl had been called *litshitshi,* then *lijongosi* when her breasts are full; but as soon as she falls in love and wears the special beads, she is called *iqhikiza*. After this she will be permitted to wear any kind of bead, and to beautify herself for young men to admire her.

Love Letters

Since people of primitive culture were illiterate[1] and could not read and write, some devised ways and means of communication. Courting letters are expressed in bead-work. It is the women who send bead letters to their

[1][Most anthropologists would use the term "nonliterate" rather than "illiterate." Illiterate refers to people who can't read or write *in a society which has a written language.* In a society that has no written language, it seems a bit arbitrary to call the entire society "uneducated." Illiteracy is a negative term which has meaning only if literacy, the positive term, is also present. Anthropologists used to call primitive peoples "preliterate" peoples. However, this term smacked of invidious ethnocentric bias insofar as it implied that in a grand scheme of evolutionary progress, preliterate peoples had not yet arrived at a state or stage where writing was found. For this reason, semantically sensitive anthropologists elected to substitute the term "nonliterate," which had no such evolutionary value judgment bias built in. However, this allegedly more neutral euphemism for "primitive" does have a bias. For why should the peoples of the world be classified (divided) on the basis of one single culture trait, namely, the presence or absence of writing? No one disputes the importance of this one trait, but it does seem to be ethnocentric bias on our part to arbitrarily choose one aspect of *our culture* to classify the majority of the other cultures of the world.—*Ed. Note.*]

lovers, therefore communication was one sided, unless young men asked their sisters to make bead letters for them.

Once a girl was fully grown and had fallen in love, she would set herself the task of sewing bead designs for her sweetheart expressing her desires, aspirations, conflicts; in brief her joys and sorrows. The young man would cherish such a letter and he would never part with it even for money because it became part of himself; he would wear the beads whenever there was a gathering and he was well dressed, it was a symbol of his conquest, therefore it could not be classed with those things that are of commercial value.

Whenever I go to Swaziland many of my European friends always ask me to bring back some bead-work from the people and if I tell these people that one cannot buy these things they do not understand the reason. It would be as if you went up to a European lady wearing a ring and asked her to sell it to you. Such things are not bought and sold because they are part of the culture of the people; they help in the formation of the general set up of society. Perhaps a man could be persuaded to sell some of the beads if his young woman has rejected him, but even that is very rare because these beads form part of what we would call documentary evidence. Even if a young girl does reject a man by sending a bead-letter, later on it may be necessary to prove that certain relations once existed. If for instance a girl, after rejecting a young man, finds that she is pregnant, and she accuses her late lover, the man in trying to escape a fine may produce the rejection bead-letter as evidence against the charge.

Every district had its own cipher for bead love letters, and if a young man found it difficult to decipher a message he would ask his sisters to help him in solving the problem. All girls are good in deciphering messages because when they sew these beads they are always in groups consulting one another. It is interesting to note that whereas an ordinary letter is a private thing, a bead love letter is open for inspection by anyone who knows the cue. The system of reading these love letters was based on the principle that symbols represent words, and words ideas. Sometimes beads stand for letters, threads of beads for words, then the pattern would stand for a sentence, a complete thought. The sentence may have a double meaning. The article itself usually stands for a complete message. In reading a message therefore one takes note of the meaning of the colour of the bead, its position in the pattern, the background on which it is fitted, and the sex of the person to whom the message is addressed or her social status.

The colours that are used to-day by both the Zulu and the Swazi are not the exact shades that existed in olden times. Beads, like dyed wool, may not keep to the same strength of dye for several years; there are always slight variations. The principal colours are white, red, blue, green, yellow, pink and black. Then there may be different shades of the same colour and also shades between two main colours. The meaning also depends on whether the colour is transparent or opaque. White beads of various sizes, opaque white, not glass, are called *uɓuhlalu oɓumhlophe* or *ithambo*. Such stand for all that is good, and have cleansing and purifying powers called *inkanyiso*. They appease ancestors, bring luck, and represent the heart, love itself, and all light coloured objects. Such beads are likened to the purity of the sea sand and are sometimes referred to as *isihlaßathi solwandle*—sea sand.

BLUE is divided into the following shades:
Azure—*isibakabaka* (sky); *ulwandle* (sea). Navy—*ufefefe,* stands for talkativeness, gossip. Dark—*ijußa lehlathi,* forest-pigeon. Greyish—*isende lenkawu,* the testicles of a monkey. Light *ijußa lentaßa,* a mountain-pigeon.

RED, two types, opaque red, *ußuhlalu oßußomvu.* It stands for blood, tears. Then there is glass red, transparent, this stands for fire, *umlilwana,* anger, a red heart.

GREEN—*uhlaza,* it stands for grass, implying cattle, the veldt.

BLACK—For a kaross, a symbol of marriage; it also stands for evil, disappointment, misfortune.

YELLOW—*iphuzi,* a pumpkin, also signifying a garden.

BLUE AND WHITE band, *intothoviyane,* a type of greenish spotted locust whose habit is to hop in pairs one resting on the back of the other in mating.

SHELL PINK—I am told this is a new type of bead, *ußuhlalu ßesilungu,* but it resembles a bead that was used long ago called *imfißinga* mostly used by courtiers. During the days of Mpande the Zulu used to *swear* by this type of bead saying: *"Ngiyihulule imfißinga"* meaning that, if what they said was not true, they would rather enter the palace, which act in those days meant death. This bead if used by commoners signifies poverty.

Bead Messages

In writing out a message the key word is the "heart" always in the first person, the designer, with a message addressed to the second person, the lover. Messages centre around the following leading words; love, marriage, kraal, family, cattle for *lobolo,* happiness, sadness, good and evil. There are about twenty or more different designs worn on the head, across the shoulders, round the neck, wrists, ankles and waist. The most popular are the following:

1. *Ucu olumhlophe lokuqoma*—a single white thread.
2. *Ingusha*—worn round the neck with a little flap in front.
3. *Ingcagcane*—neck wear.
4. *Iqaßane*—another neck wear.
5. *Ixhuße*—Mixed colours which are made into sentences and sewn in various ways.

These are some of the messages:

Pattern A

o-o-o-o-o–O–O–O–o-o-o-o-o–O–O–O–o-o-o-o-o–O–O–O–o-o-o-o-o
   (a)   (b)   (c)   (d)   (e)   (f)   (a)
                                          repeat twice.

(a) WHITE: *Ngisho ngenhliziyo yami emhlophe əthe qwa.* I say this with an open white heart.

(b) BLUE: *Ngithi kudela ijuɓa lona lidle.* I say, Oh for the dove that picks food.

(c) WHITE: *Eɓaleni kwenu.* In the yard at your kraal.

(d) RED: *Uyadela nowotha umlilo eziko lakwenu.* I envy also the one who enjoys your fire place.

(e) WHITE: *Noma imhlophe inhliziyo kepha.* Although my heart may be pure.

(f) PINK: *Wena umpofu.* You are poor.

Pattern B

o-o-o-o-o–O–O–O–o-o-o-o-o–O–O–O
       (a)   (b)   (c)   (d)

(a) WHITE: *Inhliziyo yami.* My heart.

(b) BLUE: *Iluhlaza njengolwandle.* Is as blue as the sea.

(c) DEEP BLUE: *Ungafefezi ngami eɓantwini, nami negeke ngifefeze.* Do not gossip and back-bite me, I shall also do likewise.

(d) PINK: *Noma simpofu njalo.* Although we be so poor.

Pattern C

In this design white forms the whole background and signifies a whole situation, then bits of white in between are an emphasis on the central theme.

o-o-o-o-o–O–O–O–o-o-o-o-o–O–O–O–o-o-o-o-o
  (a)   (b)   (a)   (c)   (a)
–O–O–O–o-o-o-o-o–O–O–O–
    (d)   (a)   (e)
o-o-o-o-o–O–O–O–o-o-o-o-o–O–O–O
    (f)   (a)   (g)

(a) WHITE:

Ugcala ɓagcove, ɓafana ɓasemzini,
Akukho-muzi ongakhulumi,
Nakwandlwana kuyakhulunywa,
Nasemanxuluɓeni kuyakhulunywa.

The one who frowns at you, you strange boys,
There is no kraal that remains silent,
All kraals must eventually speak,
Even in a one-kraaled village they speak,
Just as in a big kraal they speak.

(b) BLUE AND WHITE: *Ziyadela izintothoviyane ezifa ziɓelethene.* The spotted locusts rejoice for in their death they cling to one another.

(c) GREEN: *Ziyajaɓula izinkomo ezidla utshani emasangweni akini.* Lucky are the cattle that eat in the green pastures passing through the gates of your kraal.

(d) YELLOW: *Sengathi ngingazopheka lawo-maphuzi alapho kini.* Oh, if I could come and pick those pumpkins from your garden.

(e) BLACK: *Ngisho ngesidwaɓa sami esimnyama.* I would then be wearing my black kaross (skin skirt).

(f) RED: *Inhliziyo yami iɓomvu.* Yet my heart is red (sore).

(g) YELLOW: *Ngoɓa nakhu umpofu ngasezinkomeni.* Because you are poor and have no cattle.

This is a message from a girl who has long been in love with a certain young man who feels that they cannot go on loving indefinitely; she feels that she is now grown up. The white expresses that she has been bound to speak openly because there comes a time in every kraal when decisions have to be made, be it in a small kraal of a poor man or in a big kraal of a rich man. She expresses her desire of wishing to remain with this man for life till death just like the locusts. The time has come for her to wear a kaross which is a bridal dress and is only for married women. She says I want a kaross, I am grown up, I want to enter through the gates. Cipher and colours as used by the Emangwaneni tribes, Bergville District, Natal.

1. OPAQUE WHITE: *Uɓisi,* milk. *Ithambo,* bone.
2. BLACK: *Isitimane.*
3. OPAQUE GRASS GREEN: *Umamlambo,* green snake.
4. OPAQUE RED: *Umgazi,* blood.
5. TRANSPARENT RED: *Umlilwana,* fire.
6. OPAQUE DEEP YELLOW: *Uthuvi ɓenkonyane,* calf excreta.
7. OPAQUE PINK: *Imfiɓinga,* at times it means beer.
8. PALE BLUE: *Inkosazana,* a young girl, daughter.
9. DEEP BLUE: *Ijuɓa lasendle,* forest or mountain dove.
10. GREYISH BLUE: *Ijuɓa lasekhaya,* common dove.
11. ROYAL BLUE: *Inkankane,* a species of a noisy bird of migration.
12. TRANSPARENT GREEN: *Amehlo ekati,* cat's eyes, for wealth.
13. PALE YELLOW: *Incombo,* for married women.
14. DARK GREEN: *Ibuma,* river grass.
15. WHITE WITH BLACK OR BLUE STRIPES: *Intothoviyane,* type of locust.

The article in Fig. 1 with three flaps is a necklet which was worn by a married woman who has been widowed. She is from *Emangwaneni,* Bergville, Natal.

This particular neckwear contains the life story of a widow who has no desire of marrying again. The necklet is called *uMaphapheni* derived from *phapha* to flap or fly. It gets its name from the three flappers that hang in front, *amagceɓetsha.* The colours used are:

1. WHITE: *Ithambo,* bone.
2. BLACK: *Isitimane.*
3. TRANSPARENT RED: *Umlilwana.*
4. LAVENDER BLUE: *Inkosazana.*
5. LEAF GREEN: *Umamlambo.*

6. PINK: *Imfiɓinga.*
7. OPAQUE YELLOW: *Uthuvi ɓenkonyane.*

You begin reading from the centre front at *B*, and you proceed anti-clockwise, that is from left to right and round ending up with the small flap. The white forms the background. Reading from *B* you get the following story:

BLACK means: "I am a widow."

RED: I did kindle a fire, so I have had a home of my own.

Ngawuɓasa umlilo

Note that when the young man's people negotiate marriage for their son they will address the bride's people by saying: *"Sizocela umlilo"* or *"Sizokokha umlilo."* We have come to ask for a fire-brand.

GREEN: My husband was rather treacherous.

CENTRE WHITE: o°o I am the fourth child in the family.

LAVENDER BLUE: °o I am one of the three daughters.

Design C

The key line is black, so the story begins by saying: "In my widowhood ..." Here the same story is repeated but in contrast there is more black appearing with lines of pink, *imfiɓinga.* Many black beads signify that the father of this widow was a well to do man with herds of cattle and besides there was always beer in the home as a symbol of affluence. The last line in the design is blue for *inkosazana.*

Design D

This is the belt that goes round the neck, the background is white, and it has three distinct patterns which are repeated.

Design E

Colours follow one another in this order: pink, black, yellow, black, pink. This means that I (the widow) would have had cattle and beer in my own kraal were it not for the disgraceful treatment shown by the presence of the yellow in between these colours.

Design F

The order of colours is: black, blue, red, blue, black. The key word is *umlilwana*—red, which divides black and blue. The meaning is that the young woman though widowed has no desire to be asked to make fire again once more in this kraal. Here, lighting a fire for the second time would mean *ukungenwa*, to be taken by her husband's brother in order to raise seed. If the brothers of the deceased man visit the widow she wears a necklet of this particular design to scare them away and saves face if she feels she does not care for *ukungenwa. Umlilwana phakathi kwenkosazana kanye nokumnyama emacaleni.*

Design G

Order of colours; yellow, black, pink, lavender blue, pink black, yellow. *Inkosazana phakathi kwemfiɓinga.*

This reads: "The man no longer loved me. When he died he had already

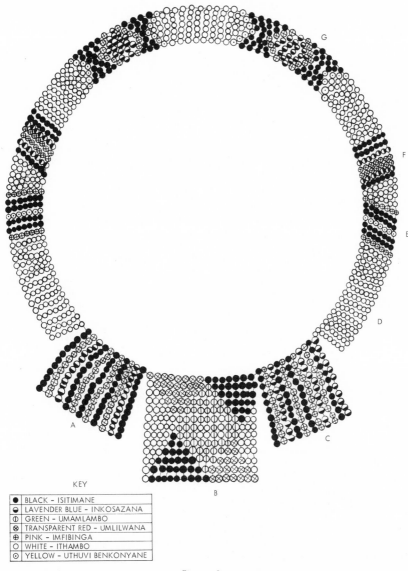

KEY

●	BLACK - ISITIMANE
◒	LAVENDER BLUE - INKOSAZANA
⦶	GREEN - UMAMLAMBO
⊗	TRANSPARENT RED - UMLILWANA
⊕	PINK - IMFIBINGA
○	WHITE - ITHAMBO
⊙	YELLOW - UTHUVI BENKONYANE

Figure 1.

rejected me." The reversal of the order of these colours would give a different interpretation altogether. If the colours were in this order: yellow, black, lavender blue, pink, lavender blue, yellow. This would mean that when he died I had already rejected him, which is centre pink surrounded by blue. *Imfiɓinga izungelezwe inkosazana.*

Design A

This is almost the same as *C* except that *C* has a border of black on one side and another of blue on the other side. This last flap has a black border on both sides which signifies that the woman wishes to remain a widow: the path of another marriage is closed.

Beads as Conveying Evil Messages

Black Beads

These beads are never used by themselves except when a young girl has been rejected by her lover. If the girl goes to a man's home to *ukugana* prepare for marriage, and the young man has changed his mind and objects to such advances, the girl goes to other maidens of her *intanga* "age-group" and tells them, because every young girl in matters of love was responsible not to her parents but to the girls of her own age-group. She dares not go home in this dark cloud but must go through a purifying ceremony with the other maidens. They all get black beads and they march with them to the young fellow's hut and there scatter them in the yard, after which they seize a goat belonging to this kraal and drag it to the river. They kill it with their hands only, skin it, remove the contents of the stomach and cleanse themselves with this preparation. They then eat the goat which is called *isahhukulu*. The girl will then pass on to another kraal to try her luck. The rejection of a girl was considered a very serious matter. It was said to be immoral because if a man was not pleased with the girl there was always an open gate to taking another wife and so avoiding a surplus of unwanted women. If the girl herself felt that she had changed her mind about a man she would make a necklet of the pink beads for poverty. This would be carelessly sewn and would be left unfinished with no buttoning loops to show that the connection had been severed and the heart had been rendered poor. Then it would be sent to him.

Inkankane—Royal Blue

A young man disappointed about the character of his sweetheart may ask his sister to make a necklet for him so as to present it to the girl just a day before an important tribal ceremony. The rule is that if beads are sent by a sweetheart they must be worn in a public gathering of young people.

A pattern which means: "You are a woman of an immoral character" is designed in the following fashion. The colours used are:

1. WHITE: This forms the background but is dotted all over with the other colours.
2. DEEP BLUE: *Ijuɓa lasendle,* mountain or forest dove.
3. ROYAL BLUE: *Inkankane,* a wandering noisy bird.
4. TRANSPARENT RED: *Umlilwana,* fire.
5. YELLOW OPAQUE: *Uthuvi ɓenkonyane,* calf's excreta.
6. PALE YELLOW: *Incombo,* not worn by unmarried women.

The pattern begins with yellow instead of white.

YELLOW: *Wena uʃana nothuvi ɓenkonyane.* You are like the excreta of a calf.

WHITE: *Isimilo soɓuntombi ɓakho simaɓalaɓala.* Your purity is full of smudges, spots.

RED: *Endaweni yoɓa ngaɓe uhleli kahle wotha umlilo.* Instead of settling down and basking by the fire.

DEEP BLUE: *Ujaɓule njengejuɓa.* And be happy as a dove.

ROYAL BLUE: *Kodwa uyandinda unomsindo njengenkankane.* You are as restless and as noisy as the *inkankane* bird.

PALE YELLOW: *Kwenza umuntu aɓusole uɓuntombi ɓakho.* Therefore one doubts your virginity.

RED: Appearing several times in the pattern means that the girl delights in kindling fires all over the place.

YELLOW: This is one thread forming the border of the necklet and worn on the neck side right round the neck.

Beads and Magic

Emadloti, the spirits of ancestors delight in beads; if they are to be appeased beads must be used. White beads play a prominent part; they stand for all that is best and pure. The supernatural beings may be harmful to society at different times and therefore white beads are used at such times. Those who use the white beads a great deal are the *isanusi,* diviners. The *isanusi* call white beads *ithambo,* bones, meaning the bones of the dead; they represent the ancestors who are bones. A full-fledged *isanusi* covers himself with opaque white beads, some are worn on the head and they hang in veil-like fashion over the region of the eyes right round the head. Some beads are worn round the waist, arms, wrists, ankles and as sashes over both shoulders. These beads fortify the man against the apparitions that are said to possess him. An *isanusi* gets his wisdom from the *emadloti.* They speak through him. He is their agent, therefore in their presence he must appear in white beads. When the *isanusi* is first initiated into this new life he is given a short single string of white beads to fasten on the hair at the back for the purpose of *ukukhanyisa amadloti*—to pacify the ancestral spirits.

With the *isanusi* who throws bones one finds that two of the bones are tied up with two strings of white beads. These bones are representatives of ancestral spirits male and female, that is, those of the father's clan and those of the mother's clan. Before the *isanusi* reads one's fortune, he asks for *inkanyiso,* that is something white to make the path clear. In the olden days the *inkanyiso* used to be white beads or a white goat; nowadays it is silver coin.

In doctoring a patient suffering from an incurable disease a white bead is often added to the medicine and remains in the calabash at the bottom as the patient drinks the medicine. This is a prayer to the spirits to add healing powers to the medicine. There is a particular type of medicine which must be bought from the ancestors before it can be dug up. The plant grows on the mountain-side and a white bead is placed on the plant first. The bead is then removed and the plant dug out and in its place the bead is buried. A female *isanusi* if compelled to go and dig medicine roots at a time when she is menstruating, removes the white beads from her hair and holds them in her hand until she has finished digging. She drops a white bead in the hole to maintain the purity of the medicine.

Beads in the Marriage Ceremony

Marwick gives in his book *The Swazi* an account of a marriage ceremony and he mentions certain stages where beads play a part. When the bride arrives in the evening to *gana,* be officially betrothed in the kraal, she is met at the cattle kraal gate by her in-laws. Then she goes to an old woman of the kraal who usually sits in a convenient place to be seen. To her the bride says: *"Ngite kukhonta"* (I have come to pay allegiance) so saying she drops a string of white beads in the old lady's hands. The old lady will ask her if she comes legally and she will reply that she has come with the full consent of her parents. The old woman is, a link between the dead and the living so she takes the beads on behalf of the ancestors because the bride has come to *konta* not to her husband but to the clan as a whole, past and present.

At another stage of the ceremony just before the consummation of the marriage, the bride performs a ceremony of rolling white beads very fast in her hollow hand, and the groom is supposed to pick one out neatly without letting it fall. Each time he fails to pick the bead the young girls deride him for they say that he will also fail to consummate the marriage. They say: "Look at him, the fool, he has been so anxious to have it and now that it is freely given to him he fails to take it." This shows clearly that the beads are identified with the woman's purity in this case. For every mistake the groom will pay a fine not to the parents of the girl but to the maidens, as I have explained before that young persons are responsible to their age-groups. Sometimes there is a variation in this ceremony and the bridegroom's sister is sent to pick the beads to save the man the embarrassment of being the laughing stock of girls.

Beads are used at a latter stage in the day when the bridegroom's people come to slaughter the *ulugege* beast, which is identified with the bride herself and her sexual life. The gall-bladder, *inyongo* from this beast is first handed from one group to the other; the bride's people now disown the woman so they can no longer keep her *inyongo;* the young man's people send it back to them with the hope of getting another bride; finally the game ends in the appeasing of the ancestors by dedicating white beads instead of the *inyongo.* This is called *ukuβekela inyongo.*

The Royal Beads

I had been to Swaziland several times and had spoken to various people about beads, but no one ever mentioned to me that there were special beads that could only be worn by those who were so permitted by the Paramount Chief. It was not until one day I decided to dress myself up in tribal fashion that I learnt about these beads. I had on an *ilihhiya* (cloth) I had borrowed and I went into a fowl run and there got myself white feathers and arranged them in the hair as the Swazi do, I then realised that I was not properly dressed unless I had beads on so I went to a group of young men having a beer drink and I asked one of them who had been with me at a wedding to lend me his beads for the day.

At the mention of this the whole group rose in disgust and said: "You cannot have those beads." Then I pointed out that I had seen many people wearing beads and I saw no reason why I could not wear beads. Then the Swazi who never let out a secret unnecessarily subsided and one man said: "Oh yes, you can wear them as long as you have a beast to pay." After this interview I decided to find out more about these beads.

I was told that these beads are called *usimohlwane,* royal beads, and anyone wearing such beads is fined a beast by the king. In the old days one would actually be killed and people would say *uyahlola,* he is planning evil.

Simohlwane is a pinkish bead of almost the same colour as the *imfiβinga* of Mpande which I described earlier. It is not perfectly round and it measures one eighth of an inch. It is worn as a single string and is wound several times to the length required. Young men wear it suspended on the right shoulder and hanging as a sash under the left arm. The second lot is worn round the neck and the ankles—a single thread usually although others may add a few lines. The Swazi are very simple in their taste and they will never be seen with several layers of beads all over their person.

A third lot of beads is made into a bracelet about two inches broad and finished off with a fringe of small beads of the same colour or any other colour. For the long threads the colours that go with *usimohlwane* are red, white, blue and black repeated after each bead right through. Even the Paramount Chief wears the same beads in the same pattern.

The beads are restricted to the following people: all the princes and princesses, and members of the royal family wear them. Their strings are much more in number in comparison with the commoners. The royal wives use these beads as necklets and bracelets. As soon as a girl falls in love with one of the princes *umntanenkosi,* she must buy this type of bead and wear it so that other young men who meet her and wish to make love will refrain from doing so because it is a crime to compete with royalty.

The beads are also worn by all heralds, page boys, and everyone who comes within reach of any of the prominent royal persons. These beads are a protection and a badge so that the ordinary people may know that they cannot insult or fight the wearers, for if they do, they would be insulting royalty itself. If a messenger is sent to deliver a message and wears the type of bead mentioned, one will ask him if he has been sent by royalty or not, *ukutsi uthunywe yiɓukhosi na?* If he has, one must by custom salute him saying *ɓayete* and thank him for his message as though one were in the presence of the king himself.

All warriors who have been recruited to occupy the barracks guarding the royal kraal wear *usimohlwane* besides any other beads they may choose as ornaments. It is a sign of *umɓutho,* that a man is the king's warrior. Young girls take it as an honour to fall in love with one of the warriors who wears these beads for they know that he is a man indeed. He has been through proper discipline and can show stamina in any hardship. Even the commoners claim a certain prestige once they have been allowed to wear these beads. Shops are not restricted in the sale of these beads, but every Swazi knows that no matter how he may envy the colour, he cannot wear it without permission, because these are the king's colours.

The *aɓelwandle,* medicine men who doctor the king during the *incwala* ceremony, although belonging to the Ndwandwe clan have a hereditary right to wear these beads and also the red feathers of the *igwalagwala* bird. When they travel across the country in search of the prescribed medicines for the *incwala,* they are protected by this badge. They may not be molested and are given the best hospitality. On their way back from collecting the sea-water, in every kraal where they are put up, they must be given a beast to slaughter. During the December 1950 *incwala* it was reported that one man had fought with these people and had injured one with a spear. Everyone was surprised at this, and they said that the fine for this act would be very high since this was a serious matter, and there was no excuse for not knowing who the herald was because he wore the royal badge.

It would be interesting to find out if the *usimohlwane* beads were one and the same thing as the *imfiɓinga* of the Zulu royal family, and also if one could get the exact replica of the ancient beads, because the beads that are being used now are of recent manufacture.

The Ematinta Beads

Of importance too are the *ematinta* which are not real beads but are cylinders made out of wood and threaded to form a sort of neck-wear. The Queen-mother of the Swazi wears *ematinta* round her waist, neck, wrists and ankles. She also wears them as a crown holding the mysterious red feather and lucky seed charms which stand out over the forehead. The *ematinta* I am told represent first, *ilive lika-Ngwane,* the Swazi nation itself.

The Swazi say that she holds together the Swazi people and their country, so she must always wear these day and night. Should one of the strings be broken she remains out of the public eye until it has been fixed. She cannot have any conference with anybody without them because she is considered naked.

Ematinta are a prerogative of all royal women and are worn by all mothers who are suckling royal infants. Be they born in wedlock or not the mother must wear them throughout the nursing stage. These *ematinta* are not all made out of the same species of tree. They differ according to the ranks of individuals concerned, according to the position of the mother in the harem.

Here are the various ways in which beads help to keep each person's behaviour within the prescribed sanctions of the group. Beads are signposts which show a young individual exactly where danger lies, and by them he is constantly reminded of his duty of society. It is interesting to note that the young people were only indirectly responsible to their parents. It was the age-group that had a say in many of the matters referring to sex. Note the case of the young woman who was disgraced by her sweetheart. She did not appeal either to her parents or to the law, but to her other companions who took it upon themselves to put right the wrong.

The anthropologist looks at his own culture

*M*ost individuals (anthropologists included) come to know only one culture well: their own. Every time he uses informants, the anthropologist recognizes the fact that members of a culture can provide information about their culture. Yet surprisingly enough, the anthropologist has had a block against analyzing *his* own culture. One reason for this block may be the traditional notion that anthropologists study "other" people. Probably most anthropologists would admit, somewhat reluctantly, that an anthropologist from another culture could come to study their culture, e.g., a Japanese ethnographer could come to the United States to study American kinship, but like the rules of exogamy, which require that an individual marry outside of his own family, it would somehow be tantamount to incest for the anthropologist to study his own culture.

The distinction is clear in German. The two relevant terms are *Volkskunde,* folklore, which is the study of one's own folk or any folk living in a civilized country (in German and European tradition, the folk are defined essentially as peasants, the illiterate in a literate society), and *Völkerkunde,* ethnology or cultural anthropology, which is the study of other peoples (in German and European tradition this would mean primitive or nonliterate peoples). In Germany, then, a man studying German *Volkskunde* would be studying German folklife or German peasant culture. It is basically ethnography and in fact some Europeans call it "regional ethnology" instead of *Volkskunde* or folklore. In this type of field research, the investigator and his informants are from the same culture. In contrast, a man studying *Völkerkunde* at a university in Germany would be studying the life and culture of primitive peoples. It should be noted that both parts of the *Volkskunde/Völkerkunde* dichotomy reflect an obsolete survival of a long-standing tradition of ethnocentric snobbery based upon unilinear evolutionary reasoning in which "we," the civilized, study "them," the savages (the study of which is anthropology) and the peasants (the study of which is folklore). The modern notion is that anthropology is the study of *all* men including the anthropologists doing the studying and their culture. Folklore, similarly, should not be limited to any particular segment of society. Any group of people formed for any reason whatsoever (common religion, common occupation, common ethnicity, etc.) is a folk which has its own in-group traditions (slang, proverbs, songs, etc.), that is to say, its folklore.

In the United States, anthropologists sometimes defend their policy of studying primarily primitive peoples by arguing that it is sociologists who study our society. It is true that sociologists study civilized societies, including their own, but sociologists are concerned with society, not culture. This is not semantic nit-picking. The point is that sociologists do not always ask the same questions that anthropologists ask, although there is certainly some overlap between the two disciplines.

If it is true that one is bound to know his own culture better than any other culture, and if it is true that anthropologists are genuinely interested in understanding some of the nuances and subtleties of the nature of culture, then it seems clear that anthropologists should study their own cultures in addition to the other cultures they have always studied. For one thing, the language barrier problem would be minimized. The anthropologist studying his own culture would not have to rely upon either a bilingual interpreter or his own partial understanding of the interview language. The rapport problem would be similarly eased. Admittedly, the thrill of the exotic and the romance of remoteness (from "civilization") might be absent, but if the goal of anthropologists is truly the proper study of mankind then "know thyself" really should become part of the anthropologists' credo.

Although the papers presented here are for the most part

American anthropologists' analyses of American culture, the issues of whether or not and how an anthropologist should study his own culture should be seen in a larger framework. The question is: should anthropology, like charity, begin at home?

Ralph Linton

ONE HUNDRED PERCENT AMERICAN

One of the most fascinating types of studies in cultural anthropological research concerns the diffusion of culture traits from one culture to another. The constant borrowing and lending of traits, sometimes consciously, more often unconsciously, goes on continually. Tracking the path(s) of diffusion of even a single culture trait can take years of effort. One must first ascertain where in the world the particular trait is found. Then one may attempt to reconstruct the possible or probable direction of diffusion. It is one thing to say that culture X and culture Y both have trait A; it is quite another to say that culture X borrowed the trait from culture Y, or that culture Y borrowed the trait from culture X. Of course, the people living in these cultures may care little about origins. It normally does not matter to them who borrowed what from whom. What is important is that they have the trait. (There are, to be sure, sometimes a few ardent "nationalists" who attempt to prove that the trait originally sprang from their native soil.) Typically, people in a culture automatically tend to regard the trait as characteristic of their culture, and they would be very surprised if they were to learn that it originated elsewhere. American readers of the following short essay by Ralph Linton may see for themselves how many artifacts and mentifacts involved in their everyday life are cultural borrowings.

For samples of the huge diffusionist literature, see G. Elliot Smith, Bronislaw Malinowski, Herbert J. Spinden, and Alexander Goldenweiser, *Culture: The Diffusion Controversy* (New York, 1927). For elaborate theories of diffusion, see G. Elliot Smith, *The Diffusion of Culture* (London, 1933), and Wilhelm Schmidt, *The Culture Historical Method of Ethnology* (New York, 1939). For a convenient summary, see Robert H. Lowie, *The History of Ethnological Theory* (New York, 1937), pp. 156–95.

1937—"One Hundred Percent American" by Ralph Linton. Reprinted from *The American Mercury*, 40 (1937), 427–29, by permission of *The American Mercury*, P.O. Box 1306, Torrance, California 90505.

There can be no question about the average American's Americanism or his desire to preserve this precious heritage at all costs. Nevertheless, some insidious foreign ideas have already wormed their way into his civilization without his realizing what was going on. Thus dawn finds the unsuspecting patriot garbed in pajamas, a garment of East Indian origin; and lying in a bed built on a pattern which originated in either Persia or Asia Minor. He is muffled to the ears in un-American materials: cotton, first domesticated in India; linen, domesticated in the Near East; wool from an animal native to Asia Minor; or silk whose uses were first discovered by the Chinese. All these substances have been transformed into cloth by methods invented in Southwestern Asia. If the weather is cold enough he may even be sleeping under an eiderdown quilt invented in Scandinavia.

On awakening he glances at the clock, a medieval European invention, uses one potent Latin word in abbreviated form, rises in haste, and goes to the bathroom. Here, if he stops to think about it, he must feel himself in the presence of a great American institution; he will have heard stories of both the quality and frequency of foreign plumbing and will know that in no other country does the average man perform his ablutions in the midst of such splendor. But the insidious foreign influence pursues him even here. Glass was invented by the ancient Egyptians, the use of glazed tiles for floors and walls in the Near East, porcelain in China, and the art of enameling on metal by Mediterranean artisans of the Bronze Age. Even his bathtub and toilet are but slightly modified copies of Roman originals. The only purely American contribution to the ensemble is the steam radiator, against which our patriot very briefly and unintentionally places his posterior.

In this bathroom the American washes with soap invented by the ancient Gauls. Next he cleans his teeth, a subversive European practice which did not invade America until the latter part of the eighteenth century. He then shaves, a masochistic rite first developed by the heathen priests of ancient Egypt and Sumer. The process is made less of a penance by the fact that his razor is of steel, an iron-carbon alloy discovered in either India or Turkestan. Lastly, he dries himself on a Turkish towel.

Returning to the bedroom, the unconscious victim of un-American practices removes his clothes from a chair, invented in the Near East, and proceeds to dress. He puts on close-fitting tailored garments whose form derives from the skin clothing of the ancient nomads of the Asiatic steppes and fastens them with buttons whose prototypes appeared in Europe at the close of the Stone Age. This costume is appropriate enough for outdoor exercise in a cold climate, but is quite unsuited to American summers, steam-heated houses, and Pullmans. Nevertheless, foreign ideas and habits hold the unfortunate man in thrall even when common sense tells him that the authentically American costume of gee string and moccasins would be far more comfortable. He puts on his feet stiff coverings made from hide prepared by a process invented in ancient Egypt and cut to a pattern which can be traced back to ancient Greece, and makes sure that they are properly polished, also a Greek idea. Lastly, he ties about his neck a strip of bright-colored cloth which is a vestigial survival of the shoulder shawls worn by seventeenth-century Croats. He gives himself a final appraisal in the mirror, an old Mediterranean invention, and goes downstairs to breakfast.

Here a whole new series of foreign things confronts him. His food and drink are placed before him in pottery vessels, the popular name of which —china—is sufficient evidence of their origin. His fork is a medieval Italian invention and his spoon a copy of a Roman original. He will usually begin the meal with coffee, an Abyssinian plant first discovered by the Arabs. The American is quite likely to need it to dispel the morning-after effects of over-indulgence in fermented drinks, invented in the Near East; or distilled ones, invented by the alchemists of medieval Europe. Whereas the Arabs took their coffee straight, he will probably sweeten it with sugar, discovered in India; and dilute it with cream, both the domestication of cattle and the technique of milking having originated in Asia Minor.

If our patriot is old-fashioned enough to adhere to the so-called American breakfast, his coffee will be accompanied by an orange, domesticated in the Mediterranean region, a cantaloupe domesticated in Persia, or grapes domes-ticated in Asia Minor. He will follow this with a bowl of cereal made from grain domesticated in the Near East and prepared by methods also invented there. From this he will go on to waffles, a Scandinavian invention, with plenty of butter, originally a Near-Eastern cosmetic. As a side dish he may have the egg of a bird domesticated in Southeastern Asia or strips of the flesh of an animal domesticated in the same region, which have been salted and smoked by a process invented in Northern Europe.

Breakfast over, he places upon his head a molded piece of felt, invented by the nomads of Eastern Asia, and, if it looks like rain, puts on outer shoes of rubber, discovered by the ancient Mexicans, and takes an umbrella, invented in India. He then sprints for his train—the train, not the sprinting, being an English invention. At the station he pauses for moment to buy a newspaper, paying for it with coins invented in ancient Lydia. Once on board he settles back to inhale the fumes of a cigarette invented in Mexico, or a cigar invented in Brazil. Meanwhile, he reads the news of the day, imprinted in characters invented by the ancient Semites by a process invented in Germany upon a material invented in China. As he scans the latest editorial pointing out the dire results to our institutions of accepting foreign ideas, he will not fail to thank a Hebrew God in an Indo-European language that he is a one hundred per cent (decimal system invented by the Greeks) American (from Americus Vespucci, Italian geographer).

David M. Schneider and George C. Homans

KINSHIP TERMINOLOGY
AND THE AMERICAN KINSHIP SYSTEM

If anthropologists are right about the importance of kinship in the various societies of the world, then the study of American kinship should also provide valuable insights into the nature

Reprinted from *American Anthropologist,* 57 (December, 1955), 1194–1208, by per-mission of the authors and the American Anthropological Association.

of American culture. Of great interest in this excellent study by Professors Schneider and Homans are the social and interpersonal ramifications of the use of one rather than another kinship term for a specific relative. The weakness of the traditional dichotomy of terms of reference (how *A* refers to *B* when talking to *C*) and terms of address (how *A* addresses *B*) is all too apparent. It is the social situation including the presence of third parties that determines in large measure what term will be used. If I am speaking to my three-year-old daughter and referring to my wife, I might say, "Go ask mommy for a glass of water." If I am speaking to my maid, I might say, "Go ask Mrs. Dundes for a glass of water." If I am speaking to my daughter's playmate from across the street, I might say, "Go ask Alison's mother for a glass of water." If I am speaking to that playmate's mother, who is a close friend of my wife, I might say, "Go ask Carolyn for a glass of water." If I am speaking to a door-to-door salesman, whom I have never seen before, I might say, "Go ask my wife for a glass of water." How then would I reply to an anthropologist interviewing me when he asked me how I referred to my wife? The point is that the term of reference depends upon the identity of the person to whom I am speaking and perhaps what I think that person's term of reference ought to be. The term wife, for example, would be used to complete strangers. One wonders, in view of the fact that anthropologists are usually strangers in the societies they visit, whether they have elicited mostly the formal reference kinship terms rather than the actual terms used by members of the family. In any case, as the following study shows in detail, a kinship terminology system is hardly a static set of terms which accommodate reference and address. Rather, there is a wide variety of terms for any one individual, and the nuances and implications of the use of one term rather than another may be of great significance to those interested in understanding interpersonal relationships.

For other studies of American kinship, see Talcott Parsons, "The Kinship System of the Contemporary United States," *American Anthropologist,* **45** (1943), 22–38, and Helen Codere, "A Genealogical Study of Kinship in the United States," *Psychiatry,* **18** (1955), 65–79. For numerous references to studies of address terms and cultural context, see Dell Hymes, *Language in Culture and Society* (New York, 1964), p. 225.

Introduction

The American kinship system is marked by bilateral descent, and the nuclear family and the kindred are the basic kin groups. Marriage is monogamous, residence neolocal, and inheritance by testamentary disposition. Succession is absent; a man gets no political or other office simply through kinship ties. The range of kinship is narrow, and kinship tends to be sharply divorced from other institutions such as the occupational system, the effect being to make kinship appear small beside such complex and ramifying institutions as economics and technology. The American kinship system appears to be "pushed to the wall" by other institutions, and much of its coloring derives from this.

For the light it may throw on the American kinship system we shall describe here a study of American kinship terminology. We believe it may also illuminate certain problems of kinship terminology in general.

It appears at first glance, and many commentators have remarked, that the formal terms of American kinship are "Eskimo" in type.[1] Fa is terminologically distinguished from FaBr, Mo from MoSi, while parents' siblings are grouped in categories distinguished from one another by sex but not collaterality.[2] Cross and parallel cousins are grouped together and distinguished from siblings, while own children are differentiated from the children of siblings, who are differentiated from each other only on the basis of sex. Of this much, there seems little doubt.

These rather broad generalizations are clear enough, but at the time we began our study we were not sure what they implied or how far they held. Further investigation, we felt, might be useful. To this end we decided to

[1][Anthropologists have decided upon various labels to be used in describing kinship systems. One typology or classification scheme is based upon the terms for siblings and cousins. The designation "Eskimo" refers to one type in a classification devised by anthropologists, a classification which distinguishes the different patterns of grouping, or not grouping, siblings with cousins. Two categories of cousins one must remember are cross cousins and parallel cousins. Cross cousins are the children of siblings of opposite sex. Note that it is the sex, the opposite sex, of the sibling parents, not the sex of the cousins, which determines the designation of cross cousins. Thus my father's sisters' children are my cross cousins and my mother's brothers' children are my cross cousins. (This is true regardless of my sex and regardless of the sex of the cousins.) In contrast, parallel cousins are children of siblings of the same sex. My father's brothers' children are my parallel cousins and my mother's sisters' children are my parallel cousins. As far as kinship terminology is concerned, there are a limited number of possibilities of grouping siblings and cousins. One could have, for example, just one term to refer to one's siblings, one's cross cousins, and one's parallel cousins. This system is called Hawaiian by anthropologists because this is one culture where this arrangement is found. Another system is the Iroquois type in which there is one term for cross cousins (on both the father's and mother's side) and commonly another term which refers to *both* parallel cousins and siblings. Eskimo terminology refers to a system in which there is one term for siblings and usually another term for both cross and parallel cousins. This is the case in American kinship terminology because there are the terms for siblings which are distinct from the general term cousin which lumps together cross and parallel cousins. For further information about these and the other types of kinship terminology based upon sibling and cousin groupings, see George Peter Murdock, *Social Structure* (New York, 1949), pp. 223–24.—*Ed. Note.*]

[2][To facilitate the description of various relatives in a kinship system, anthropologists customarily use abbreviations. Father is "Fa," mother is "Mo," son is "So," daughter is "Da," brother is "Br," sister is "Si," husband is "Hu," wife is "Wi," and child is "Ch."—*Ed. Note.*]

collect some information on the terms Americans actually use for their kinsmen.[3]

Obviously we could not sample, exhaustively and systematically, all age, sex, class, regional, and other groupings in America; indeed, we were not at all sure at the outset whether a genealogical, interview, or questionnaire method, or some combination of these, was the most fruitful approach. We therefore set up a pilot study, using a variety of techniques to assemble data on kinship usages, with students and faculty in the Department of Social Relations at Harvard as informants, but supplementing these with data from certain similar sources.

Our informants were 209 in number, of whom 154 were male and 55 female. We carried out intensive interviews from one to four hours in length, including, with 37 of the informants, 21 male and 16 female, the collection of full genealogies with the terms used for every kinsman. For the rest, we got completed forms for one version of a simplified questionnaire on terminology from 76 persons and, for another version, from 78.

Although the size of the sample is in one sense 209 persons, it is in another sense much larger. For example, data on terms used for uncles and aunts exist for 419 different persons: our 209 respondents had 419 different uncles and aunts.

Although we achieved a fair spread among age and sex groups and a thin coverage of most of the major regions of the United States, this was clearly no sample from which generalizations applicable to the whole American population might be derived with precisely stipulated probability values. It is our conviction that a fair picture of some of the major processes in American usage emerges, but this is a conviction, not a proved finding.

Certain Characteristics of the American Terminological System

Perhaps the fundamental characteristic of the American system of terms for kinsmen is the presence of a wide variety of alternate terms. Mother may be called "mother," "mom," "ma," "mummy," "mama," by her first name, nickname, diminutive, "old woman," and a variety of other less commonly used designations.

Father may be called "father," "pop," "pa," "dad," "daddy," by his first name, nickname, diminutive, "old man," "boss," and a variety of less commonly used designations. Uncles may be addressed or referred to as uncle-plus-first-name, first name alone, or uncle alone. Similarly for aunts.

The variety of alternate terms is increased by two other devices: the use of possessive pronouns—mother, for instance, may be "my mother" or just "mother"—and variations in specifying whom the relationship is *to*. We believe the latter mechanism has not been given enough attention in the

---

[3]We wish to acknowledge the assistance of the Laboratory of Social Relations, which made this collection of data possible, and the skillful assistance of Mrs. Hope Leichter in the collection and subsequent analysis of these data. Mr. Nathan Altschuler gave valuable assistance in the early stages of the study.

literature on terminology. There are always at least three persons involved in the use of a term of reference: the speaker, the person spoken to, and the person referred to. In the United States, one may refer to a third person by his relationship to the speaker or to the person spoken to or even, as in teknonymy, to someone not necessarily present. Thus when speaking to mother's sister's son about mother's sister, the term of reference may be "your mother" or "Aunt Sally."

Closely related to the wide variety of alternate terms is the fact, which we documented far more fully than can be reported here, that forms of reference as well as address vary with situational context. In fact, it is not possible to give a single form of reference or a single form of address for a given class of kinsmen that is used in all contexts of address or reference. To put this in another way, the classic distinction between terms of address and terms of reference is not of much help in dealing with the American system. It tends to obscure certain important processes, partly, at least, because it presumes that there is a single term used in all referential contexts.

It is, of course, true that certain forms are never used in address and occur only in referential contexts. The term "second cousin" is one such term. But its use is confined to only one out of the total range of referential contexts. The term "second cousin" is confined to that situation in which the question is explicitly or implicitly, "Who is he to you?" or "How are you related?" But a variety of other referential contexts occurs in which the term "second cousin" is rarely, if ever, used. Ego, addressing his own mother or father, asks, "How is cousin John these days?" or "How is John these days?" He does not say, "And how is second cousin John these days?"

It is almost unnecessary to note the interdependence of alternate terms and the use of different forms in different contexts. If there were but one form available, this one form would have to be used in all contexts. If there are two forms, one for address and one for reference, then two general categories of context alone can be differentiated. In the contemporary American system the wide variety of alternate forms allows them to differentiate a variety of different contexts.

Perhaps an example or two will make clear what we are describing. One informant would refer to his mother as "mother" when speaking with his father, as "ma" or "mom" when speaking to his brother, and as "my mother" when speaking with an uncle. Another informant, who usually calls his mother-in-law "mom" when speaking with his wife about her, conscientiously avoids calling her anything when his own mother and his mother-in-law are both present. Another informant calls his father's brother "Uncle Bill' when speaking with his father, "Bill" when speaking with the father's brother directly, and "my uncle" when telling stories about him to some friend who does not know him.

The distinction we found most useful in dealing with this efflorescence of terminology is one we believe to be universal for kinship terms. Each term has two aspects or functions: first, an *ordering* or *classifying* aspect and, second, a *role* or *relationship*-designating aspect. By "ordering" aspect we mean the class to which the various genealogically distinct categories of kinsmen are assigned. By "role-designating" aspect we mean the pattern of behavior or relationship that the term symbolizes. A term like "father" thus does two things: it defines a class of kinsmen—in this case there is but a single genealogical category to the class—and it symbolizes the role which the person so classed is expected to play—in this case a relatively formal and authoritarian one.

The first question that arises in the light of this distinction is whether the various alternate terms are alternates in their role-designating or in their ordering aspects or in both. Put more simply, are the alternate terms mere synonyms for one another or do they have some perceptible and significant differences in meaning? If there are differences of meaning, do these differences center on the mode of classifying kinsmen or on the roles they play or on both these dimensions?

In the series "father," "papa," "pa," "pop," "dad," "daddy," we find that the ordering aspects of all these terms is identical; they refer to ego's presumed genitor. In the "mother," "ma," "mom," "mummy," "mama" series the same is true; each refers, in its classifying aspect, to the same class of kinsmen, in this case the single category of own mother.

If we go on to inspect the alternates that occur throughout the system, we discover that they never transgress the basic scheme of Eskimo-type classification. Fa is never classed with FaBr or MoBr; Mo is never classed with MoSi or FaSi; Br and Si are never classed with parallel or cross-cousins; So and Da are never classed with BrCh or SiCh. Some of the alternates do cross certain of the lines of classification. Thus the term *parents* classes Mo with Fa, *children* classes So with Da, and the newly invented and rapidly spreading *sibling* classes Br with Si, overriding in every case the criterion of sex but not disturbing the basic criteria for Eskimo systems. Certain other alternates, like first names, nicknames, and diminutives, leave the field of kinship entirely. We shall soon return to instances of these last two sorts.

On the other hand, what about the role-designating aspects of these terms? It is precisely here that the differences lie. The different alternates designate different roles or relationships or, more precisely in some cases, differently emphasized aspects of a given relationship.

Space limitations preclude a full inventory of the evidence we have collected on this point. Nor will it be possible to explore all the implications of the differences of role designation from term to term. We shall therefore confine ourselves to illustrations that we feel have particular interest.

Terms for father and mother have already been mentioned. One interesting feature is that only rarely did an informant confine himself to the use of a single term. More usually informants reported that they used a "principal" term and one or more "variant" terms. The principal term most frequently reported was "dad" by males, "daddy" by females. The most frequent variant term reported by males was "father"; by females, "dad." But, further investigation indicated that, if an informant used "father" as either a principal or variant term, he would never use "pop" or "pa" as an alternate. Conversely, those who used "pop" or "pa" as either a principal or variant term would never use "father" as an alternate. Both groups would use dad"; the one used "father" and would not use "pop" or "pa," the other used "pop" or "pa" but would not use "father." Those who used "father" explained that they would not use "pop" or "pa" because it was too familiar, too egalitarian, and would verge on disrespect. They sometimes added that, "Father is no authority figure or stern old patriarch, but it just wouldn't seem right to call him 'Pop'." On the other hand, those who used "pop" or "pa" invoked the same problem, but in reverse, explaining that they could not use "father" because their father was "not that sort of person; he is not a stern authority figure, he's much too friendly." The term "father" connotes formality and some qualified implications of authority and its attendant variety of respect; "pop" or "pa" connotes informality and familiarity, and, although authority and respect are by no means absent, they are not the primary implications. "Dad" seems to indicate an area where the formal and the friendly roles overlap.

The situation seemed to be different with mother terms. Here, no informant said that he would not use one of the alternates, and we got the impression that the roles designated by these terms were so close as to be seen by most informants as almost interchangeable. That is, while "pop" and "father" implied mutually incompatible roles—ego picks one or the other but cannot play both—no such sharp line divided the mother terms. Nonetheless, perceptible differences among mother terms are brought out when informants are divided by sex of speaker. Female speakers use "mother" predominantly; the term "ma" is reported by our female informants only rarely. Male speakers, on the other hand, use "mom" most frequently, and "mother" and "ma" occur much less frequently.

The formal term "father" is used far less frequently than the formal term "mother," and the evidence suggests that there is no simple symmetry between the terms "father" and "mother." "Father" has formality and respect implications which are lacking in the term "mother." For instance, some male informants reported that when they would argue with their fathers they would avoid any form of address, and one informant reported that if, during an argument with his father, he used the term, he would feel forced to abandon the argument: "You shouldn't argue with your father." By avoiding the use of the term, he was not forced to face the transgression of the norm.

On the other hand, male informants who reported that they would avoid any form of address while arguing with father readily stated that an argument with mother included such exclamations as, "Oh, mother" and, "But mom, how can you say such a thing," etc. That is, there was no such inhibition on the use of the mother term as there was on the use of the father term.

One implication of these data is that there is a kind of homogeneity among the alternate mother roles which is not entirely present with the father roles. There is instead a kind of split in the father roles, starting with the term "dad," which everyone either employed or said he would see no reason not to employ, and dividing either toward formality, respect, and authority or away from this toward familiarity, companionship, and a more egalitarian relationship. These two directions of variation are in some degree seen as "either-or" choices.

If in one respect our informants used father-terms very differently from mother-terms, in another respect they used them the same way. Among our other questions, we asked about changes over time in the use of kinship terms. We found that, as small children, both males and females reported using "daddy" and "mommy" or "mummy"—that is, fairly "informal" or diminutive terms. But the men reported changing, as they grew up, to "dad" for father and "mom" or "ma" for mother, and the women reported keeping "daddy" for father but shifting to "mother" for mother. That is, if we consider "dad" and "mother" more formal than "daddy" and "ma," our informants tended, with time, to become relatively more formal with the parent of the same sex as their own and remained relatively less formal with the parent of different sex. Have we to do here with the Oedipus complex, with the possibility that father is more apt to exert authority over son, mother over daughter, or that as the children grow up they become increasingly rivals with the parent of the same sex?

One rather interesting process emerged from a study of terms for aunts and uncles. Although the combination of aunt- or uncle-plus-first-name is the most frequently employed term, many informants reported the use of first name alone. In working over particular genealogies with informants we encountered a sizable group which did not apply any particular term consistently for all aunts or for all uncles. That is, one informant called his mother's elder brother "Uncle Jim" and his mother's younger brother "Bill." Another reported that he called his mother's sister "Aunt Jane" and his mother's sister's husband "John."

We spent some time trying to determine when the aunt or uncle term plus-first-name would be used as against the use of the first name alone, and a few interesting facts emerged.

First, there was a tendency for more first-name-alone designations to be applied to aunts and uncles on the mother's side than on the father's. About as many uncles as aunts were called by first names, and about as many affinal uncles and aunts as consanguineal ones. The only apparently significant difference was the side of the family they happened to be on. Does this represent a patrilateral tendency, in a society with a patripotestal bias, for ego's close and warm ties to be with his mother's kin?

Second, there was a slight tendency for male speakers to use the first name alone more often than female speakers. This may mean that women are more concerned with and perceptive of kinship obligations and relations than men, or that women still think of themselves as being of somewhat lower status than men and so are less willing to assert the equality implied by the use of the first name, or, finally, that women are less inclined to allow themselves the display of affect that is also, as we shall see, implied by the first name alone.

Third, some informants reported that they dropped aunt and uncle terms and used first names alone after they started going to college. Here, far more surely, the use of the first name implies a role of equality with uncle and aunt. The formal term is dropped when children view themselves, and are viewed, as being grown-up and so almost on the same plane as uncle and aunt.

Fourth, we ran across a number of situations of the following sort. An informant with three uncles would call one "John," one "Uncle Bill," and the other "Jim." When pressed to explain why he called the first uncle just plain "John," he would reply by saying that the person was a dirty so-and-so and that he would not dignify the man by calling him uncle. (This, by the way, was never said of mother or father.) The next question would be, "Well, how about your other uncle, Jim? Why don't you call him Uncle Jim?" And the explanation would be, "Jim is a wonderful guy! He and I have always been the closest friends. When I was a kid we would…" and out would come a picture of an idyllic relationship. The final question, of course, would be, "What about Uncle Bill?" And Uncle Bill would usually prove to be liked—a nice guy—"He's o.k.," or some such mildly positive or mildly negative sentiment.

The pattern seemed to be that wherever there was strong affect, either positive *or* negative, the "uncle" form would be dropped and the first name alone used. Alternatively, if we think of these terms as status designators, the first name may imply either the equality of the speaker with the person referred to *or* the inferiority of the latter. Where the affect was mild, one way or the other and the relative statuses were simply those expected in the kinship norms, the uncle term was used.

It is, of course, a statement of some significance about the nature of the American kinship system that there can be three broad possibilities in the relationship between ego and uncles or aunts; the relationship may be intensely close, warm and intimate with egalitarian overtones; or it may be intensely hostile with or without the prominent display of this affect; or it can be mildly positive, mildly negative, or, to put it in another way, the affect can be subordinate to other, primarily kinship, considerations. Not all bilateral systems or even Eskimo-type systems permit ego to say quite bluntly: "I wouldn't dignify that S.O.B. by the use of a kinship term"; or even, conversely, "We are the closest of friends and always have been."

The use of first names as an alternate form of designation raises some more general problems. Let us look at the data. First, we found that first names occurred as alternate terms for all classes of kinsmen except grandparents. Our informants with but one exception never called their grandparents by first name. Second, they did call members of the parental generation by first name but not very often, whereas the first name was the dominant designation for kinsmen of ego's own or lower generations. That is, where some informants reported that they used father's first name as their primary designation, there were very few such informants. On the other hand, almost all informants reported that the principal term employed for them by their parents was first name, nickname, or diminutive. Third, as we have already seen, the use of first name as the principal term for uncle or aunt occurs where there is strong affect, either positive or negative.

If we review the actual cases in which strong affect occurs, it turns out that it is not the mere presence of the affect which is important but that the strong affect implies a relationship which is basically different from the general conception of what uncle (aunt)-nephew (niece) should be. Where strong positive affect was indicated, the relationship seemed far more a relationship of friendship than of kinship. Uncles were described as being "pals," "close friends all my life"; "I'd go talk over all my troubles with him, and we'd figure them out together." On the other hand, many informants reported real affection for an aunt or an uncle but this was seen as a special attribute of the particular kinship relation, of the relationship which normally *should* obtain between uncle and nephew rather than of a fundamentally different sort, as in the case of friendship.

Where uncles or aunts were designated by their first names alone, the relationship seemed to be predominantly a person-to-person relationship, and whatever elements of kinship were implicit in it were kept at an implicit level. Its primary tone was of person to person; ego was either very close to or very hostile to him or her, as a person. Asked to describe why a particular uncle was not called "uncle," an informant would dwell on the particular person's personal qualities; he was mean, unpleasant, untrustworthy, etc. These are not the usual components of kinship relations. Similarly, on the other side, it was the personal qualities of, "We get along well" or, "We like the same things" that were cited in the cases where the affect was positive.

Our impression is that the use of first names designates relationships which have as their *dominant quality* considerations of a personal sort. When fathers address sons by their first names, this does not imply that the relationship is free from considerations of kinship, from the obligations that the son has to his father or the father to the son. What it does imply is that, from the point of view of the father, it is the personal qualities of his son which are of particular importance to him. How the son fulfills his kinship obligations are seen as particular qualities of the particular son. How the son behaves toward his mother are seen as qualities of the son as a person, and it is these that are the *emphasized* concerns of the father. Although there is clearly a kinship tie between them, with obligations and privileges based on their kinship, the aspect of the relationship that the parent stresses is the qualities of the child as a person, and his performance of his kinship role is seen not as the end, or even the primary concern, but only as one among a series of standards in terms of which the quality of the persons may be judged, guided, socialized.

If we make this interpretation of the use of personal names for members of the contemporary generation or below, are we justified in making the other obvious interpretation of the relatively greater use of formal kinship terms for members of older generations? Is it perhaps true that we Americans look on our contemporaries and descendants as individuals and our elders as representatives of the system? That we and our children are responsible to the self, our parents to society—that is, to us? At any rate, there is a thoroughgoing generational asymmetry in our kinship terminology.

It is worth noting the obvious point that in uncle and aunt designations the dominant tendency is neither toward the use of first name alone nor toward the use of the kinship term alone. Indeed, among our informants first name alone was the more frequent designation than kinship term alone for uncles and aunts. Instead the dominant tendency is toward a combination of first name and kinship term. In a very important sense the American system classes all uncles together and then subdivides members of the class. That is, within the category of uncle, designations are practically descriptive since, even where two uncles have the same first name, they are almost always distinguished. The tendency, thus, is to particularize uncles and aunts and, in effect, to differentiate individuals within each class. This is clearly in line with the tendency to treat kinsmen as particular people with particular and unique qualities of a personal nature. Uncles, for instance, might be distinguished as elder, second, third, or younger and yield the same differentiation. But there the stress would be on the ranking among uncles and not, as in the American system, the stress on the person as such within the kinship setting.

In our study of the use of personal names for kin, especially for uncles and aunts, we have found reason to recur again to our fundamental point—that the nature of the relationship between the speaker and the person referred to is an important determinant of the term used. But in the uncle-aunt case, there are really only two available terms—"Jim" or "Uncle Jim"—yet the elements that enter the relationship are many: status similarities or differences, affect or lack of it, kinship or personal interest. The disproportion between the number of terms and the number of elements in the relationship means that, though the terms do reflect the relationship, they often do so crudely and sometimes ambiguously.

There can be no such complaint about the terms for husband and wife. Here the elaboration of alternate terms goes much further than it does anywhere else in the American system.

The terms fall into three rough categories: kinship terms, variants on given name (first name, diminutives, nicknames, etc.), and a group that might be given dignity by being labeled "terms of endearment." Kinship terms break down into two subcategories: first, terms used to indicate the order of kin, i.e., terms of reference mainly explaining who he or she is, such as "my wife," "my husband," "Mrs. X," "Mr. X"; second, parent terms, i.e., wife is called "mother," "mom," or "my old woman"; husband, "father," "dad," "papa," etc., or "my old man." "Terms of endearment" fall into a series of classes: saccharine terms (honey, sugar, sweet, cookie, etc.), affection terms (love, beloved, lover, etc.), animal and vegetable terms (kitten, bear-cat, pumpkin, etc.), and a large and varied collection of miscellaneous and idiosyncratic terms, some of them nonsense syllables (baby, pookums, etc.). We all are familiar with at least some of these terms. There is probably a greater variety of terms for wife than there is for husband.

Without going deeply into the wealth of detail here, we can make a few interesting inferences from the terminology. In the first place, the marital relationship seems either to center on a highly individual definition of a presumedly perpetual love affair, which is outside the realm of kinship altogether and has as its dominant element the particular harmony of the two unique persons involved, or it is a relationship defined by the presumption of children, so that the roles of husband and wife are predominantly the by-products of their roles as parents. Remember that we are not speaking here of the total relationship but of the elements in the total relationship which are stressed. That is, no matter how much saccharine terminology is employed, there is a relationship in which the law limits how far one or the other party may go in ignoring kinship rights and obligations. But it is not the rights and obligations that are stressed in terminology as predominant concerns; it is either the personal qualities of the pair or their common concerns as parents. In a very important sense, there is no clear-cut kinship relationship in marriage itself; there is either love or parenthood.

Yet another characteristic of the terminological system that reflects the stress on the individual as such is the importance placed on real genealogical position, especially in the nuclear family. Only those who truly occupy the particular genealogical positions are seen as the proper persons to play the roles and receive the designations associated with those positions. Americans distinguish "father" from "stepfather," "mother" from "step-mother," real sibling from half-sibling and stepsibling, and so on. It is true that courtesy aunts and uncles occur, but there is never any doubt about their status as courtesy kin and not "real" kin. Further, the occupation of a structurally identical position and the playing of an identical role is not enough to warrant the use of the kinship term appropriate to that position and role. Thus, when a child is reared from infancy by its aunt or grandparent, the aunt playing a maternal role toward the child, she is still not called "mother." Informants will state that, "She was just like a mother to me" and mean just that: she was *just like,* but she was still not the mother. The term "mother" is reserved for the person who occupies the correct genealogical category. This practice is very different from, for instance, the Zuni one, where a term is applied when it designates the role-relationship regardless of the appropriateness of the genealogical positions occupied by the persons concerned.

The manner of using personal pronouns may serve as our last bit of evidence that the great concern of the language of American kinship is individual persons. The possessive pronoun which is usually used by ego for any of his kinsmen is "my": "my father," "my uncle," "my mother," and so forth. The form "our father," our mother," or "our brother" is only occasionally heard, though it is not uncommon in England. If the form "my" is inappropriate, as when one brother speaks to another brother about their father, then the kinship term is used without any qualifying possessive pronoun. Brothers seldom say to each other "our father"; they say "father" or "pop" or "dad."

Terminology, the Kinship System, and American Culture

We have suggested that the use of alternate terms for kinsmen in the American terminological system might vary with their classifying aspects or their role-designating aspects or both. What in fact happens is that variation is greatest along the dimension of role designation and least with respect to classification. Further, in the few places where there are alternate modes of classification, the basic scheme of Eskimo type is almost never transgressed.

One important implication of these data is that there is a single, basic pattern of kinship structure *within* which, but not across which, wide degrees of latitude for variation occur. That is, the American people do not show a wide variety of descent systems, a wide variety of kin group types or a wide variety of terminological types, but a single, basic form—bilateral descent, strongly emphasized nuclear family, and a distinct but secondarily important kindred. But within this framework there is considerable latitude for variation, and the variation is in terms of roles and relationships, not in terms of the basic kin group affiliations or contrasting commitments to divergent kin groups or kinsmen.

To make this point in another way, it might be said that the American ideal of "unity in diversity" might better be phrased, in the kinship system at least, as "diversity centering on a basic unity."

A second implication of these data is further specification of what is already well known and widely commented on, and that is the central importance of the nuclear family in the kinship system. It is, after all, one of only two kin groups in the system, and the evidence suggests that the other, the loose, amorphous kindred, tends to vary in importance from time to time in the life-history of any given nuclear family, from region to region, from class to class, and from ethnic group to ethnic group. In some groups it looms large; in others it is held to a bare minimum. Upward mobile persons keep only shallow ties with members of their kindred, if they keep them at all; downward mobile persons may be neglected by their kindred; members of spatially static occupation groups can but need not, and so on.

The features reflecting the central importance of the nuclear family as against the kindred are many. First, there is elaborate role-differentiation within the nuclear families of orientation and procreation and a much lower level of differentiation outside these groups. This situation is comparable to the high degree of internal differentiation found in lineage systems in the "own lineage" group as against the minimal differentiation within more distant groups such as, in matrilineal systems, father's matrilineage and mother's father's matrilineage. Second, there are those few alternate terms that present alternate modes of classification.

With only one exception, those alternate terms which vary in their classifying aspect occur either *within* the nuclear family or *outside* it, but the nuclear family line is never crossed. Thus the term "parents" and its reciprocal "the children" or "the kids" makes a unit of Mo and Fa vis-à-vis the internally undifferentiated unit of So and Da. Here, in addition to the alternates for Fa and Mo, there is the additional alternate which groups them together into one unit. Similarly, and of more than passing interest, are the terms "old man" and "old woman" applied to Hu and Fa, Wi and Mo, respectively, and the term "father" or "dad" for both Hu and Fa, the term "mother" or "mom" for both Mo and Wi. It is our impression that the classes and the regions where "old man" and "old woman" refer to Hu-Fa and Wi-Mo, respectively, are not the same as the class or regions where "father" or "dad" and "mother" or "mom" group Hu-Fa and Wi-Mo, respectively. The fact that these occur in very different subgroups of the populations suggests that a very general and basic process is at work and not merely class or regional styling. But the point of primary concern here is that this alternate mode of classification again is confined within the nuclear family and does not cut across that line.

It should be noted that, in the group we interviewed, neither of these two patterns for the grouping of Fa-Hu and Mo-Wi was at all common. Informants suggested that spouse is only called by a parental term in the presence of children, or at least after children come on the scene. We have too few cases of this sort to provide anything like a secure ground for generalization, but our impression is that in some cases the designation of the spouse by a parental term preceded the presence of children, and in some cases occurred among couples of sufficiently advanced age so that the prospect of children might be taken as unlikely and among couples whose children were full grown and far away.

It is interesting, too, that when one spouse uses a parental term for the other, the other does not reciprocate with a child term; that is, when husband is called "father," wife is not called "daughter"—this despite the frequent comment that one of the classic reefs on which marital relations may founder or, conversely, thrive is the psychological identification of the spouse with the parent of opposite sex. It is noteworthy that we did not discover a single terminological symbol of this psychological relationship, unless it be argued that, when husband calls wife "mother," she acts as mother to him, and he reciprocates by alternating his roles between father and son. We did not delve deeply enough to discover evidence either for or against this view.

Outside the nuclear family, the alternates are of a somewhat different sort. Where "parents," "the children," "old man," "old woman," "dad," and "mom" combine two otherwise differentiated genealogical categories, the alternate modes of classification outside the nuclear family tend toward what might be called "gross grouping," taking in a wide swath of genealogically distinct categories. The term "cousin" applied to cousins of each and every remove is one such term. Another is the appearance of such designations as "the Ohio Browns," "the bunch from Maine," "the Joneses," "the drunken Smiths." The one possible exception to the generalization that alternate modes of classification do not cut across the nuclear family is the designation "father's family" or "mother's side." Some informants were concerned to point out that, when they said "father's family" or "mother's family," they did not include father or mother but only their relatives. But other informants either implied or stipulated that father along with all his kinsmen were or were not held in high esteem, low esteem, or at any rate lumped together in some fashion by such terms.

We may now return to the problem of variation within the framework of bilateral kinship and emphasized nuclear family. The question is whether the variation is random or determinate.

The variation occurs along two distinct dimensions. One is variation from subgroup to subgroup within the American population, the subgroups being regional, ethnic, class, age-group, sex group, etc. Our sample was too small and unsystematically selected to show what we suspect to be the case—that this kind of variation is associated with what Florence Kluckhohn has called "variant value patterns."

The other kind of variation is in the forms any individual employs within a given relationship—what we call the use of alternate terms. As one informant said, "I usually call my father 'pop,' but if I want something from him I say, 'Dad, may I take the car tonight?'"

One of the determinants of the latter form of variation is the degree to which personal qualities or individualistic values are emphasized. We have already noted that the use of personal names reflects the value of personal qualities or the special value of the individual. We now want to say something about the over-all social arrangements within which this value may be more or less stressed.

Generally speaking, kinship terms are employed primarily when the person spoken to is senior in age or generation, but first names are employed between age and generation equals or when the speaker is senior in age or generation to the person addressed or referred to. Thus Fa calls So by the latter's first name, but the So usually uses some kinship term for Fa. Br calls Br or Si by first name, but BrCh usually calls FaBr by a designation involving a kinship term—"Uncle Bill," for instance.

As Linton noted, American culture is oriented about achieved rather than ascribed status, and parents are concerned that their children achieve some appropriate status.[4] Ascribed status as a family member is insufficient to carry most people through life. If status is to be achieved, it has to be achieved, according to American values, on the merits of the person, his qualities and accomplishments as a person that meet value standards that Parsons has called "universalistic." Hence to go out and do the things that need to be done to achieve something, he must be relatively free of any encumbering bonds of kinship, and he must be motivated to do so. It is as part of this wider context, we suspect, that the older generation uses personal names rather than kinship terms toward the younger generation. Again, we repeat, this does not mean that the young person is freed from all kinship obligations. It only stresses personal qualities within the definition of his kinship role. It stresses the unique qualities of a person as he himself will have to stress his own initiative, his own inventiveness, if he is to achieve anything on his own.

On the other hand, there are two problems from the point of view of the younger generation. On the one hand, their view of the older generation is in part that the latter have achieved; they have arrived, so to speak. This is seen especially clearly in the usages of preschool children. In their view, almost all adults are mothers or fathers, depending on sex, if they are not otherwise designated as aunts, uncles, or grandparents. In a suburban housing project with the high birthrate characteristic of such units, where practically every family has at least one and usually more children, it was

4[Linton's important distinction between ascribed and achieved statuses is somewhat analogous to the distinction between biological and cultural reality. The biological or given would be the analogue of ascribed status. Ascribed status refers to status assigned to individuals automatically, that is, without regard to their native abilities. It could be status built-in by birth such as being born the son of a king. In contrast is achieved status which normally accrues through the demonstration of special qualities and talents. Achieved status is thus acquired by an individual through time just as culture in general is. For further discussion, see Ralph Linton, *The Study of Man* (New York, 1936), pp. 113–31.—*Ed. Note.*]

customary for all adults to be known teknonymously as "Johnny's daddy" or "Margaret's mother," etc. Here, one of the authors encountered a young man of about four engaged in a hopeless struggle with a knotted shoelace. The author did not know this child, and the child did not know the author. The child looked up and called out, "Somebody's daddy! Please fix my shoelace." Similarly, children of this age have difficulty comprehending the possibility that a woman might have any other status than mother. In this same housing project it was repeatedly noted that small children would ask adult men to, "Go ask your mother if you can come out and make a snowman with us." For the younger generation, there is an entirely imaginary quality of stability to the older generation: they are set, while the young are to make their way onward, upward, around, and past their elders. Hence their designation by kinship terms, that is, by terms that stress their status and their apparently eternal roles, is entirely appropriate.

On the other hand, the tasks of socialization and the responsibilities of parents all too often require that they act according to the long view of "what we want our child to be." They must exercise some discipline, however much or little they like, and this exercise must be stated in moral and rational terms and not as the product of transient states of mood or momentary emotions. In the nature of the case it is impossible to discipline an equal. The asymmetrical distribution of authority and the knowledge of right and wrong must be made clear as part of the institutionalized definitions of the respective roles. There is thus a problem, for the older generation, of maintaining the generational stratification or, as adults sometimes put it, of "keeping children in their place." When parent and child each uses first name, they tend to view one another as equals. Informants whose children used first names for them and informants who themselves used their parents' first names constantly indicated that the problem of maintaining the separation of status and blocking the tendency toward treating each other as equals was especially prominent. Parents always have the problem of dealing with children who, at certain ages, insist that, "If you can do it, why can't I?" But where first names are used reciprocally, we find that this problem is especially acute and especially difficult to handle. This is not to imply that *only because* first names are used is the relationship difficult; rather, the self-reciprocal use of first names reflects the definition of the relationship as one which tends toward equality.

The use of kinship terms from junior to senior is thus an affirmation of the authority and superordination of the elder and, equally, of the junior's view of the static position of the elder, which the junior is to equal or surpass. The use of first name from senior to junior thus affirms the elder's view of the junior as "up and coming" and emphasizes the qualities of junior as a unique person, an individual in his own right.

It is worth noting, in this connection, the very narrow range of kinship in America and the very narrow limits within which it is extended. In part this is probably connected with the high value placed on the individual. But in part it is probably tied equally closely to the fact that the dominant social values center on achievement and not on ascription. The wider the range of extensions, the narrower the possibilities for achievement.

We have heard the view expressed that American kinship is "pushed to the wall" and "distorted by nonkinship considerations and values from outside the kinship system." By this is meant, of course, that kinship has a narrow range not only in the sense that there are only a few kinsmen compared with an enormous number of nonkinsmen with whom ego interacts but also in the sense that considerations of kinship are confined to only a small portion of the total activities which ego enters into. Occupational achievement is supposed to be outside the realm of kinship, and, where other societies view nepotism as an ideal, we treat it under certain circumstances as a crime.

We have no basic quarrel with this view, except that it is not the most useful formulation from which to work. The kinship system occupies a unique place in any culture, since it is almost always the context within which most socialization takes place. If the dominant values of a culture are to be transmitted and if the culture is to continue beyond the lifespan of any individual, then new recruits to the society must be taught that culture. The dominant values of the total culture must find expression in the kinship system, and they must be so expressed that they can be conveyed to children. This means, for one thing, that those values must be distilled and simplified. The first social system in which an individual acts is the reduced system of kinship. If he learns the lessons of kinship, he can go on. Kinship must therefore teach him more than the limited scope of pure kinship; *it must teach him the fundamentals of his whole culture.*

In a sense the whole complex of kinship relations is informed by the system of which those relations are a part. The kinship system as a whole is therefore a socialization device, a "child-training practice," if you will, which looms considerably larger than any given child-training practice like weaning or toilet training or aggression control. Weaning and toilet training, to use two well-worn examples, are aspects of the kinship relation between mother and child, take their shape from this larger context, and therefore may be treated as expressions of it. Where it may be difficult to place an exact socialization value on weaning as such, it is much less difficult to discover the socialization values of a whole kinship system.

Far from being "pushed to the wall" and "distorted by values from outside kinship," the American kinship system embodies in clear and communicable form the essence of the dominant values of the whole culture even while it manages to discharge those functions universal to kinship systems, those social functions which are prerequisite to the maintenance of any social and cultural system.

Alan Dundes

THE NUMBER THREE
IN AMERICAN CULTURE

Students undertaking professional training in anthropology are rarely, if ever, required to formally study their own cultures.

They must demonstrate competence in various topics and areas, but these do not normally include materials from their own cultures. They may be told that the identification and careful delineation of native categories may be crucial to a fuller understanding of that culture which they investigate, but their own native categories, the identification of which is equally important for an understanding of *another* culture, may not be considered at all. With our present knowledge of the cultural relativity of perception and cognition, it seems clear that students of anthropology should be encouraged to analyze their own native categories with the same care and methodological rigor that is demanded of them in their fieldwork in other cultures. If the reduction of ethnocentric bias is truly an ideal of anthropological scholarship, then anthropologists should go into the field armed with as comprehensive an understanding of the nature of their own culture as possible.

This essay, appearing for the first time in this volume, is an attempt to describe just one native category in American culture. The category concerns the number three in various forms: tripartition, trebling, and others. It will be shown that this folk cognitive category pervades not only virtually every aspect of American life, but also a good many of the supposedly objectively and empirically derived analytical categories. In other words, some of our allegedly scientific categories turn out to be nothing but culturally relative folk categories in disguise.

"Nothing is as difficult to see as the obvious." Bronislaw Malinowski, *A Scientific Theory of Culture.*

Ever since the publication of H. Usener's monograph in 1903, no one has questioned the importance of the number three in Greek and Roman culture. Subsequent investigations of classical literature, law, and medicine (Göbel, Goudy, Tavenner) have served only to confirm the pattern. More recent scholarship (Deonna, Dumézil) has demonstrated the existence of the pattern in most of Western civilization and has suggested it may be a characteristic of Indo-European culture. Some of the more convincing evidence is provided by mythology and, more specifically, by the widespread occurrence of triads of deities. Typical examples would be the Babylonian Ea, Anu, and Enlil, and the Hindu Brahma, Vishnu, and Shiva. Also pertinent is the widespread distribution of single gods with three heads (Kirfel). However, relatively few of the numerous studies of the number three have concerned themselves with the "three-determinism" of contemporary thought.

In a valuable study which appeared polygenetically the same year as Usener's, Raimund Müller suggests that modern European culture is just as three-oriented as classical culture was. Unfortunately, because Müller's essay was published in a somewhat obscure graduate exercise program, it has had little influence. As for American culture in particular, only one of the studies made by classicists and Indo-Europeanists (Lease) and some of the latest of a long line of overtly Christian treatises seeking to reveal the presence of the Trinity in nature (e.g., Strand) have documented in any detail that the number three is of ritual importance in the United States.

One should realize that three is not a universal pattern number. There are several pattern numbers, each with its own distribution. The majority of American Indian cultures have four as their ritual or sacred number. Sometimes a member of Euro-American culture is surprised or amused at the American Indian's obvious cultural insistence upon fourfold repetition. Parsons (1916:596) remarked on the "obsessive character" of the Zuni use of four. Earlier, Buckland (1895:96) had mistakenly thought that all American Indians had four as their ritual number, but he was unaware of the ritual five among numerous tribes in western North America (Jacobs, 1959:224–28; Lowie, 1925:578). The occurrence of five in South America and in China (Geil) suggests that the ritual use of five may be of considerable antiquity. Of course, American Indians are not particularly bothered by what appears to us as an exaggerated use of four or five repetitions, just as we are not irritated by our own equally persistent use of threefold repetitions.

It should also be noted that three is not the only pattern number in American culture. In fact, there is clearly a plurality of pattern numbers —two, seven, and twelve are three obvious examples. Certainly, philosophical dualism is very much a part of American culture and individuals do dichotomize. Common polarities include: life/death, body/soul, and male/female. Indeed, although Lease (1919:72, n.2) suggests that the primary divisions of the human arm and leg, not to mention the finger, tend to support trichotomic thinking, the anatomical datum would appear to reinforce "two" rather than "three." There are two sexes, two ears, eyes, nostrils, arms, legs, and so forth. These universally recognized pairs would help to explain why dualism is probably worldwide. Whether one uses such criteria as dual social organization (e.g., in moiety systems) or some variation of a "self-other" or "us-them" dichotomy (e.g., as in exogamy), there seems little doubt that "two" is more widely distributed in the world than "three." In American culture one finds quite frequently that there are alternative classification schemes: one binary and one trinary. The present thesis is not that the number three is the only numerical native category in American culture, but rather that it is the predominant one.

The following general statements about the nature of trichotomy may be of interest. (1) Often three appears to be an absolute limit; there are three terms or three categories and no more. In folk speech one can give three cheers for someone, but not two or four. (And each cheer may consist of "Hip, Hip, Hooray.") The starter for a race will say "One, two, three, go." He will not count to two or four. (Cf. the three commands "On your mark, get set, go.) The alphabet is referred to as the ABC's and in the common folk simile, something is as easy as ABC; one does not speak of learning his AB's or his ABCD's. (2) If there are more than three terms, the additional ones will not infrequently be defined primarily in terms of one of the three basic terms, usually one of the extremes. For example, in shirt sizes, one finds small, medium, and large. The size "extra-large" is certainly linguistically and very probably conceptually derived from "large," rather than possessing separate individual status. (3) One source of trichotomies consists of positions located in reference to some initial point. In golf one tries to shoot par for the course. He may, however, shoot "under" par or "over" par. In music, the point of reference may be "middle C," which serves, for example, as a midpoint between the base and treble clefs in addition to functioning as a point of reference from which to describe voice ranges (e.g., "two octaves above middle C"). (4) On the other hand, a third term may be the result of splitting a polarity. If A and B represent two extremes, then a trichotomy may be achieved by establishing their average, median, or mean as a midpoint. Or if "early" and "late" represented extremes in describing arrivals and departures, then "on time" would presumably be the midpoint. Obviously, in some instances, it is difficult to say whether the midpoint or the extremes came first. (5) Another common means of trichotomy formation is the merging or combining of two terms such that one has $A, B,$ and AB. In Robert's *Rules of Order* it is started that "an amendment may be in any of the following forms: (a) to insert or add, (b) to strike out, or (c) to strike out and insert." In theory, any polarity can be converted to a trichotomy by this or the immediately preceding principle. Moreover, it is decidedly easier to move from two to three (cf. Usener, 1903:323) than from three to two. The majority of the most common trichotomic schemes in American culture could not easily be put into a dichotomic mold. (6) The strength of the trichotomic tendency is indicated in part by its "repetition compulsion." In a considerable number of tripartite schemes, each of the three units in question may itself be divided into three parts. Each of these parts may in turn be broken down into three subdivisions and so on almost ad infinitum. (7) A final generalization concerns the special case of the triune or the three-in-one. In some trichotomies the three subdivisions are not separate and independent; instead they are part of a whole. The doctrine of the Trinity as opposed to a doctrine of tritheism illustrates this form of trichotomy.

We may now turn to specific examples of trichotomy in American culture. One of the very best sources for the study of native categories is folklore. Folklore, consisting as it does of native documents or autobiographical ethnography, is prime data for investigations of cognitive patterning. A number of scholarly studies have described the frequent occurrence of "three" in European folklore (e.g., Lehmann, Müller) and indeed the overwhelming consistency of trifold repetition in both classical and modern European folklore led the distinguished Danish folklorist Axel Olrik to claim that the "law of three" was one of the fundamental epic laws governing the composition of folk narrative. There has also been a Christian-anthropological treatise (Seifert) that has sought to demonstrate threeness as a manifestation of the trinity in the myths of primitive peoples. This is questionable, but certainly in Euro-American folktales there are three brothers, three wishes, three magic objects, and often a three-day interval of waiting or fighting. In jokes, which are the modern equivalents of *märchen* (fairy tales), there are commonly three principals: an Englishman, an Irishman, and a Scotchman; a minister, a priest, and a rabbi; or a blonde, a brunette, and a redhead. Structurally, there are usually three action sequences in such jokes. Three is equally popular in other genres of American folklore.

In American folksongs there are numerous examples of trebling and it is doubtful whether many singers are fully conscious of it. For example, in many songs the verse consists of a line which is repeated three times before being followed by a final line. Typical illustrations include: "John Brown's body lies a moulderin' in the grave...but his soul goes marching on"; "John Brown had a little Indian...one little Indian boy"; "Polly put the kettle on...we'll all have tea"; "Go tell Aunt Rhody (Nancy)...her old grey goose is dead"; "Lost my partner, what'll I do?...skip to my Lou, my darlin' "; etc. In other instances, a word or phrase is thrice repeated: "Row, row, row your boat," "Mary had a little lamb, little lamb, little lamb," "Do you know the muffin man, the muffin man, the muffin man?" "Did you ever see a lassie, a lassie, a lassie?" and such other favorites as "Buffalo gals, won't you come out tonight?" "Joshua fit the battle of Jericho," "Here we go round the mulberry bush," and "London Bridge is falling down," to list just a few.

The number three also figures prominently in American superstitions. Sometimes, it signifies luck: "Third time's a charm." Sometimes it is the opposite: "Three times a bridesmaid, never a bride," "Three on a match is bad luck," and "Going down for the third time" (i.e., drowning). Riddles as well as superstitions may reflect triadic form. The celebrated riddle of the Sphinx, which is very old and very widely distributed, is a particularly noteworthy example, especially if one considers that, in a way, the riddle constitutes a folk definition of man: "It first walks on four legs, then on two, then on three legs." In many versions the "morning, noon, and night" time trichotomy is used as a metaphor for the "three" ages of man, "Four legs in the morning, two legs at noon, three legs at night"—making the tripartite categorization even more explicit.

The pattern is also found in traditional games. In the popular parlor game of Tick-Tack-Toe, whose title itself is trinary, the object of the game is to get three *x*'s or ciphers in a row. In card games, three of a kind or sequential runs of at least three cards may be important. In games such as "Hearts," where each individual passes cards to his neighbor, the number passed is three. The playing cards themselves are of interest. While there are four suits (possibly a reflection of a Chinese origin), there are but three face cards in American decks of cards. When it is realized that some European sets have four face cards, and further that the particular face cards in American culture are a King, Queen, and Jack, a secular trio of father, mother, and son, the three penchant becomes more apparent.

Threeness also occurs in team games or sports. In the "national pastime" threes abound. In baseball there are nine players; nine innings; three outs; three strikes; first, second, and third base; left, center, and right field; and often three umpires. Moreover, the fact that in professional baseball both batting and fielding averages are calculated to three places, pitching "earned run averages" (ERA) consist of three digits, and box scores commonly list "runs, hits, and errors" does tend to suggest a ternary pattern. While the patterning is not perfect (a walk is earned by four balls), three does seem to be the prevailing number. Batters are measured in part by the number of RBI's (runs batted in) and whether or not they hit over .300. (Is it just a coincidence that this particular percentage is singled out?)

Other sports in the United States reveal similar patterning. In football, the "line" consists of seven men (another magic number), but is divided into a left side, center, and right side in common parlance. The left and right sides consist of three slots: guard, tackle, and end. The backfield has four men, but only three linguistic slots: quarterback, halfback and fullback. (This is analogous to the front, side, and back yards of a house, in that four areas are labeled with just three basic designatory terms, and perhaps analogous also to the three instruments found in the normal form of the string quartet: violins, viola, and cello.) Obviously, there are other number patterns present in football. Ten yards is the immediate objective and there are four attempts (downs) permitted to attain this goal. However, a field goal is three points and a touchdown is six points.

In professional boxing, bouts take place in a "ring" which is surrounded by three strands of rope. Rounds consist of three minutes of fighting. A comparison of American and European practices once again reveals the American bias. Whereas fights in Great Britain and most of continental Europe are judged by the referee alone, in the United States the winner is determined by a referee and two judges, i.e., by three votes.

One could find many additional examples from other American sports, but perhaps most striking are the following points. In many instances, only the first three participants to finish a race receive official recognition. Similarly, in horseracing the three possibilities are win, place, and show. Noteworthy also is the fact that in many American games there is more than the binary possibility of winning or losing. The third alternative, that is, drawing or tying, allows the choices "win, lose, or draw," which is consistent with trichotomic patterning. Even the partisan cheers at athletic events often consist of three words, e.g., fight team fight, hold that line, get that ball.

Another form of spectacle, the circus, though not strictly speaking a game, provides a rather striking example of trichotomy. Besides the obvious difference between a one-ring show and a three-ring circus, the latter being an excellent example of the "three-in-one" type of trichotomy, among American circus performers there has historically been a burning desire to do things in triplicate. Specifically, there were attempts to "turn a triple somersault from a trapeze bar to a catcher's hands as a grand finale of the flying return act" and to "do a triple from a springboard" (E. C. May, 1932:249). The goal, though culturally appealing, was extremely difficult physically and a host of would-be triplers actually broke their necks in attempting this feat (E. C. May, 1932:255). The existence of trebling in circus acts and of the "three-in-one" tent show may serve to illustrate how a particular widespread pattern of culture can be manifested in a single aspect of culture, an aspect which might easily be overlooked.

Another revealing aspect of folk culture concerns naming conventions. Perhaps the trichotomy here is attributable in part to the theory and methodology of logical definition itself. In formal definitions, the trinary criteria are term, genus, and differentia. In any event, scientific names for plants and animals are often in trinomial form, giving genus, species, and variety. In American culture most individuals have three names, any of which may be converted into initials: John Fitzgerald Kennedy to JFK. Most formal documents have space for three names and individuals with only two names may be obliged to indicate "none" or n.m.i. (no middle initial) in the middle name slot. Significantly, it is the last or third name which is the principal identifier. The clumsiness of this system has led to the practice on many forms of requesting that the last name be given first. Organizations as well as individuals have three word names. Typical American organizations' titles include: American Anthropological Association (AAA), American Medical Association (AMA), and Ku Klux Klan (KKK). In some instances, the organization's title has more than three words, but there are still only three initials: Daughters of the American Revolution (DAR), Parents and Teachers Association (PTA), and Congress of Industrial Organizations (CIO). In addition to individuals and organizations, there are the names of projects: Tennessee Valley Authority (TVA), of chemical products: trinitrotoluene (TNT), and of tests: Thematic Apperception Test (TAT). The names of the *three* major television networks are: ABC, CBS, and NBC. In fact, often the set of three initials has virtually replaced the words for which they stand: COD, DNA, DOA, FBI, FOB, GOP, LSD, MGM, RIP, rpm, TKO, USO, and VIP. The item may be considered a local family expression such as FHB (family hold back), a command directing family members to refrain from taking too much food so that guests will have enough. However, most of the items are national in scope, as in the case of the common abbreviation for the whole country: USA. The preeminence of the three letter gestalt is also suggested by SOS, in which the Morse Code signals consist of three dots, three dashes, and three dots.

A final bit of folkloristic evidence for the existence of a trichotomic pattern in American culture is provided by folk speech. The model for America's rhetorical heritage includes such triple constructions as *veni, vidi, vici* (and it was surely no accident that all Gaul was divided into three parts) or *liberté, égalité, fraternité*. Small wonder that American political style favors: life, liberty, and the pursuit of happiness; a government of the people, by the people, and for the people. Political slogans likewise may consist of three words: I Like Ike; We Shall Overcome. But nonpolitical folk expressions are equally three-structured: beg, borrow, or steal; bell, book, and candle; blood, sweat, and tears; cool, calm, and collected; fat, dumb, and happy; hither, thither, and yon; hook, line, and sinker; hop, skip, and jump; lock, stock, and barrel; me, myself, and I; men, women, and children; ready, willing, and able; signed, sealed, and delivered; tall, dark, and handsome; Tom, Dick, and Harry; and wine, women, and song. Railroad crossing signs warn motorists to "stop, look, and listen." Advertising clichés manifest the same structure. A skin cream advertisement maintains: "she's lovely, she's engaged, she uses Pond's"; the breakfast cereal Rice Krispies is represented by "Snap, Crackle, and Pop." Commercial products such as SOS scouring pads and 3-in-1 Oil use three in their names, while others claim to have an essential three-initial ingredient (Shell gasoline has TCP) or to operate on three levels (such as fighting headaches three ways). Superman, a mass media folk hero for American children, is introduced in threes: "Faster than a speeding bullet, more powerful than a locomotive, able to leap tall buildings at a single bound. It's a bird! It's a plane! It's Superman!" Superman's own formula is "Up, up, and away."

Many American verbal rituals are in the same tradition. The various countdowns prior to the starting point of events may be in threes: ready, set, go; or ready, aim, fire. The auctioneering phrase—going once, going twice, sold; or going, going, gone—is an example. There is also the barker's cry: "Hurry, hurry, hurry," often followed by "Step right up." American judicial rituals also provide illustrations. The cry of "hearye" or "oyez" repeated three times is one, while the oath sworn by a witness is another. A witness is sworn by asking him to repeat "truth" three times, as he must do when he swears to "tell the truth, the whole truth, and nothing but the truth." Similarly, in wedding ritual, there is the promise to "love, honor, and obey."

There are many more examples from American folk speech. Some are in rhyme: "First is worst, second the same, but third is best of all the game." Some are not: "A minute in your mouth, an hour in your stomach, a lifetime on your hips"; or the Army credo, one version of which directs, "If it moves, salute it! If it doesn't move, pick it up! If you can't pick it up, paint it!" Even more interesting is the American tendency to build triple constructions from original single ones. Thus starting from "Those who can, do" one moves to add, "Those who can't, teach." In final form, one has "Those who can, do; those who can't, teach; and those who can't teach, teach teachers!" The same pattern is reflected in a popular American leave-taking formula: "be good." The second stage: "If you can't be good, be careful" is followed by the third: "If you can't be careful, have fun" (or "name it after me").

It is not just in American folklore that the trichotomic and trebling tendency is found. Almost every aspect of American culture is similarly three-patterned. One may examine food, clothing, education, social organization, religion, time, or any other aspect of American culture and one will find abundant examples of trichotomy. Yet, most Americans are unaware of the pervasiveness of this pattern. It might therefore be worthwhile to observe a small portion of this patterning.

Americans customarily eat three meals a day (at morning, noon, and night). One must remember that three meals a day is by no means a universal custom. Moreover, while the actual number of artifacts employed to move the food from a container to the mouth may vary with the type of meal and its formality, there are only three basic implements: knife, fork, and spoon. With respect to silverware, it is of interest that Emily Post, an authority on American etiquette, states that one of the important differences

between place settings in formal and informal dining concerns the number
of forks. On formal occasions, there should be no more than three forks (and
three knives), whereas in informal dining, the three fork limit is absent.
In many American homes the sets of china include three plate sizes: bread
and butter, luncheon, and dinner. While the number of courses served at
a meal is, like the number of eating implements, determined in part by
the occasion and place, one might conceivably consider that dinners served
in average restaurants consist of three parts: soup or appetizer; entree with
vegetable or salad; and dessert with coffee. (One might define the segments
of the continuum of a meal served in a restaurant on the basis of the
number of times the waiter or waitress removes dishes or brings a new
set of food items to the table.) In any event, while the number of courses
is admittedly open to question, it is true that entrees are commonly divided
on menus into meat, poultry, and fish. And it is equally true that patrons
order their steak to be cooked: rare, medium, or well-done. The beverage
choice may be "coffee, tea, or milk." If an alcoholic beverage were desired,
the choice might be beer, wine, or whiskey. Noteworthy is one dessert
commonly served in restaurants, Neapolitan ice cream with its three flavor
layers: chocolate, strawberry, and vanilla.

Of theoretical interest is the fact that the smallest detail may reveal
the same patterning present in larger aspects of culture. Such a detail is
the cutting of sandwiches. While it is true that the cutting of sandwiches is
almost always binary, the way in which sandwiches are cut in half may be
significant. In restaurants sandwiches are usually halved with a diagonal
cut so that the patron is presented with two triangular halves. At home,
however, sandwiches are often cut to form two rectangles. The point is
that when the sandwiches are cut into rectangles, there is no opposition to
the basic binary division, but rather a reinforcement of this pattern. The
rectangle has four sides which consist of *two* pairs of parallel lines, i.e.,
its length and its width. In contrast, when the sandwiches are cut into two
triangular sections, the resultant three-sided figures represent trinary, not
pure binary division. Note also that on the rarer occasions when sandwiches
are divided into four rather than two sections, the same kind of 'restaurant-
home' patterning prevails. In a restaurant the sandwich is normally divided
by means of two diagonal cuts into four *triangular* sections:

At home, the mother making smaller sandwich sections for her younger
children is more likely to divide the sandwich into four square sections:

From this, one might be led to hypothesize a possible association of "two" with informal occasions as opposed to the association of "three" with more formal occasions. In any case, sandwiches, surely a very popular item on the American menu, consist of two bread covers and a "middle." Sometimes the "middle" consists of three components, such as bacon, lettuce, and tomato (the BLT sandwich). The popularity of the club sandwich or triple decker, in which three slices of bread are used, is also worth noting.

Clothing is as rewarding a subject as food for the study of cultural patterns. As noted earlier, many articles of clothing come in three sizes: small, medium, and large. Moreover, generally speaking, American clothing is worn in three layers. Beneath the layer visible to one's fellows lie *under*garments (e.g., underwear). For outside wear and for warmth, one may don such outergarments as an *over*coat. Thus with respect to any one part of the body, for example, the feet, one might find socks, shoes, and overshoes. That this is a manifestation of culture patterning is suggested by the fact that not all cultures prescribe three layers of clothing. Socks and underwear are not universal. One is tempted to suggest that the body is divided into three basic parts for clothing purposes. In terms of standard indoor apparel, one ordinarily covers the feet, the lower torso up to the waist, and the upper torso above the waist. In men's clothing, for example, these three parts are dressed separately. Shoes and socks are put on after shorts and trousers. Undershirt and shirt clothe the third unit of the body. Although stylistic features do vary, men's sport jackets more often than not have three buttons down the front and often, though not always, there are three buttons sewn on the cuffs of the jacket. The usual number of outside pockets on such jackets is three and in the upper one of these pockets, one may place a handkerchief. The handkerchief may be folded into a triangle so that one point protrudes or, in a fancy dress variant, the handkerchief may be folded such that three points protrude.

The subject of folding is a most fascinating microcultural detail. It appears, for example, that a binary versus trinary distinction occurs with respect to folding letters. Personal or social letter paper should be folded once, thus forming two parts. In contrast, business letter paper is ordinarily folded twice, thus "dividing" one letter into three parts (Post, 1960:503). Note that the two-part letter is informal and the three-part letter is formal, a distinction paralleling one made previously in connection with alternative ways of cutting sandwiches. (The association of tripartite division with formality is also manifested in the ritual folding of the American flag into triangles on ceremonial occasions.) The outside of the envelope provides further data. On the front of the envelope, one writes the address of the person to whom the letter is to be sent and this address is frequently divided into three parts. On the first of the three lines, one puts the addressee's name, usually preceded by one of three titles: Mr., Mrs., or Miss, e.g., Mr. Alan Dundes. The second line typically has a number, a street name, and the word street or its equivalent, e.g., 985 Regal Road. The third line consists of city, state, and ZIP code (or zone number), e.g., Berkeley, California 94708. The two versus three distinction occurs on the first line. The use of two names may indicate a close and personal relationship between the sender and addressee, while the use of three names or two names plus the middle initial very probably indicates that there is some social distance and a certain amount of formality in the relationship. (The most intimate relationship, that signaled by a reciprocal "first name" arrangement, is of course not feasible in written as opposed to spoken tradition.) The formalizing effect of the presence of a third party upon a previous two-party group is also relevant (Simmel). (Cf. the folk judgment: two's company, three's a crowd!)

Some examples of American material culture have already been discussed, but there are many more. Traffic lights are usually divided into three parts: red/stop, yellow/caution, and green/go. Superhighways commonly have three lanes (the middle one of which contributes to a metaphor for American political positions: left, right, and middle of the road). Freeway signs often list the next three exits. Standard gear shifts in automobiles have traditionally been divided into forward, neutral and reverse. While this might appear to be necessary, the further division of forward into first, second, and third gears is not. Even the modern automatic shift systems have a low gear and two drive positions. Some makes of cars come in three degrees of quality, although obviously the idea of first-rate, second-rate, and third-rate is disguised.

Moving away from automobiles, we may note some other examples of American technological culture. Until recently most record players and tape recorders had three speeds; there are three major types of motion picture film (8, 16, and 35 millimeter); stoves and window fans may have settings of low, medium, and high; toasters frequently have settings for light, medium, and dark; modern light bulbs have three settings for three degrees of brightness; and typewriters have single, double, and triple spacing. Cold drink vending machines usually offer three choices and one may make a choice by depositing a nickel, dime, or quarter. In slot machine gambling, the winning combination may be three of a kind, e.g., three lemons.

The pattern is also found in the telephone. On modern telephones, one finds that on the dials there are groups of three letters which correspond to one finger slot. Moreover, the United States and Canada have recently been divided into more than one hundred telephone areas, each of which is identified by a three-digit area code. By means of this system, DDD (Direct Distance Dialing) has been established. Other three-centered features include the three-digit numbers for information (411) or repair (611), not to mention the standard basic time unit of telephone calls: three minutes. While the telephone is not as obvious an example as the three-color American flag, it is influenced by the same general culture pattern.

The American educational system reflects the pattern too, with its breakdown into primary, secondary, and higher education. It is in primary or elementary school that the three R's (Reading, 'Riting, and 'Rithmetic) are taught. Higher education consists of three degrees: bachelor's, master's, and doctoral. In colleges where a credit system is employed, the usual number of credits needed to be promoted is thirty, a multiple of three. Most college courses are worth three credits and they ordinarily meet three times or three hours a week. The college school year is divided into two semesters, Fall and Spring, plus a summer session. (A trimester scheme, in which the three school year units are equal, is in effect at a few colleges.) Frequently, a "social organizational" distinction is made between freshmen and upperclassmen, with the latter consisting of three classes: sophomore, junior, and senior. (The alternate distinction of lower division versus upper division is in the binary cultural category and provides an illustration of the dichotomy-trichotomy choice.) Interestingly enough, this scheme parallels the professorial rankings in which at least linguistically there is a distinction between "instructor" and the upper three ranks: assistant professor, associate professor, and (full) professor. While at college, a student may specialize in the humanities, the social sciences, or the natural sciences. If he distinguishes himself, he may receive his bachelor's degree *cum laude, magna cum laude,* or *summa cum laude.* In graduate schools, doctoral candidates may be examined in three major fields of specialization and their thesis committees consist of at least three members. Even educational philosophy and methodology is three-bound. One teaching technique consists of "Preview, Teach, and Review," which keeps its tripartite form in an analogous folk pedagogical principle: tell 'em what you're going to tell 'em; tell 'em; and tell 'em what you told 'em.

American social organization, like American education, is under the influence of the pattern. The continuum of the American population is divided into upper, middle, and lower classes. These distinctions have even been further refined so that the upper class yields upper upper, middle upper, and lower upper. In the same way, American intellectual levels are high brow, middle brow, and low brow. American government is divided into three branches: executive, legislative, and judiciary. While the legislative branch is bicameral, it is of interest that senators are elected for six year terms with a stagger system such that only one third can be changed at one time. In terms of sociopolitical geographical units, most Americans feel loyalty to their community, their state, and their country.

Perhaps the best example of trinary social organization is found in the American military system, which consists of the Army, Navy, and Air Force. With a supreme Secretary of Defense, one has a prime illustration of the division of a unity into three parts, a secular parallel to the sacred Trinity. Each of the services has a system of rank based in part upon three. In the Navy, for example, the three initial grades are: Seaman Recruit (one stripe), Seaman Apprentice (two stripes), and Seaman (three stripes). The sequence of unrated men, that is, SR, SA, and SN, does not continue; instead a new sequence begins: Third Class Petty Officer (one chevron), Second Class Petty Officer (two chevrons), and First Class Petty Officer (three chevrons). Although there is a Chief Petty Officer grade, his uniform and status are quite different from PO3, PO2, and PO1, different enough so that the apparent binary split between "officers" and "men" is in fact trinary: officers, chiefs, and men. This trichotomy is even more obvious when the criteria of separate messing and berthing and the extension of privileges (e.g., the time of the expiration of liberty or shore leave) are taken into account. A threefold division of officers is less obvious (and there is, of course, a system of four stripes rather than three) but junior officers include: Ensigns, Lieutenants Junior Grade, and Lieutenants. Senior officers include Lieutenant Commanders, Commanders, and Captains. Flag officers include Rear, Vice, and Full Admirals.

Army social organization is similar, although triangular infantry organization was replaced in 1957 by a pentomic plan. However, historically, Army units have been based on a three-in-one breakdown (Lease, 1919:67). A battalion consisted of three rifle companies, a rifle company of three rifle platoons, and a rifle platoon of three squads. A strong survival of triangular organization is found in the Boy Scouts, the American analog of primitive puberty initiation societies. The ranks include tenderfoot, second class, and first class scouts. Thereafter, the accumulation of merit badges and the satisfaction of various requirements permit a scout to attain the ranks of Star, Life, and Eagle Scout. An Eagle Scout may, upon the earning of additional merit badges, be awarded Eagle Palms: a Bronze Palm (5 badges), a Gold Palm (10 badges), or a Silver Palm (15 badges). The ritual use of three is also explicit in such items as: a triangular neckerchief; a Scout badge whose design is the *fleur-de-lis;* the Scout sign, a gesture whose most salient characteristic is three upstretched fingers; the Scout handclasp, accomplished by extending the left hand with the three middle fingers outstretched; and the Scout Oath, which consists of three parts.

Military material culture, so to speak, and military ritual demonstrate the identical pattern. Whether it be ship division into Forward, Amidships, and Aft or the color of anchor chain paint markings (to indicate how much chain is out) into red, white, and blue fifteen fathom lengths, the trichotomic principle prevails. Military music, that is to say, bugle calls, is based upon three notes, the triad. Noteworthy also is the use of fanfares on ritual or formal occasions. There are either three trumpets playing the tones of the triad in unison or playing three part harmony. Moreover, it may not be amiss to point out that in terms of bugle playing technique, the most frequently used method of increasing tonguing speed is known as triple-tonguing. Even more pertinent to the present inquiry is occurrence of triple meter. Ternary time is not common in primitive music, and thus its presence in Western and American music is all the more striking. Besides the glaring example of waltz time, there is the rhythm employed in military ritual drumming. For instance, one pattern is based upon a series of three beats.

This may be contrasted with typical ritual drumming patterns of American Indian culture in which the pattern number is most often four. One such is four beats with the first beat heavily accented. Note well that the concept of the triplet itself is quite a remarkable example of trichotomy. It is in essence the substitution of three notes in place of one. Although 3/8 does not equal 1/4, culturally sanctioned and conditioned aesthetics permit, if not encourage, the substitution of three eighth notes in place of one quarter note beat.

Nonmusical examples of military ritual include the sentry's challenge

"Halt, who goes there?" "Advance and be recognized," and "Pass." At Officer's Candidate School (OCS) officer trainees during their three months sojourn (= "ninety day wonders") learn of the three types of court martial: summary, special, and general. They may also learn that the final act of military funerals is the firing of three volleys. (One wonders if the act of an assassin in firing three shots at the President is purely fortuitous and one wonders further about the statement of the assassin of the assassin that he meant to fire three shots instead of one!) The twenty-one gun salute for the President appears to be a combination of two sacred numbers—twenty-one is thrice seven.

The occurrence of three-symbolism in American religion is almost too obvious to require mention. In American culture, three major faiths are distinguished: Catholicism, Protestantism, and Judaism. Judaism can be broken down into three types. Orthodox, Conservative, and Reform. Of course, the Old and the New Testaments provide numerous examples. Noah who had three sons sent the dove out of the three-storied ark three times. (See Lehmann, 1914:18; and Lease, 1919: 66 for other Old Testament examples.) Christian examples include the three Magi, Satan's three temptations of Christ, Peter's three denials of Christ, the three crucifixions at Calvary, the three Marys, the three nails, the three days intervening between the burial and the resurrection, and Christ's age of thirty-three. After the resurrection, Christ showed himself three times to his disciples (John 21:14) and asked Peter three times "Lovest thou me?" (John 21:17). Of course, the ultimate charter for belief in three is the concept of the Trinity, with its sacred confirmation of the notion of three-in-one. Christian culture includes the triptych, such mottoes as "faith, hope and charity," and a three-movement ritual gesture starting at the forehead to make the sign of the cross. As for American religions, one can see that the Mormons' reverence of the three Nephites is just as patterned as the addition of the concept of Purgatory in Catholicism to form a third alternative to the previously binary Heaven and Hell.

The nature of culture is such that if one finds a pattern in social organization and religion, one is likely to find that pattern manifested in time and language (or vice versa, of course). Whorf, in his celebrated analysis of the relation of thought and behavior to language, made special mention of the cultural relativity of time concepts. While his statement "The three-tense system of SAE (Standard Average European) verbs colors all our thinking about time" (1964:143) does lean perhaps a little too far in the direction of linguistic determinism, the keen insight is a valid one. It is of considerable historical interest that Brinton made the following statement in 1894: "The two universal categories of the understanding (or modes of perception), Space and Time, invariably present themselves in a threefold aspect: Time as the Past, the Present, the Future, *as expressed in the grammar of every language;* Space, as Length, Breadth, and Thickness; or, with reference to position, Above, Beneath, and Here." (1894:169, emphasis added). Brinton saw the relationship between grammatical categories and concepts of time. His error lay in assuming the universality of his own particular native categories. Certainly in American culture, the continuum of time (and admittedly the concept of continuum is itself culturally relative) is segmented into past, present, and future. The day may be divided binarily into night and day, but dawn and twilight provide middle terms at the two junctures. Day is also divided into morning, noon, and night. Moreover, the twenty-four hour day is also subject to tripartition. In certain types of work, e.g., in hospitals, there are commonly three eight-hour work shifts. Noteworthy also is the formal way of referring to a particular day. The reference consists of three parts: month, day, and year, e.g., January 1, 1968, or 1/1/68. The principal time indicators, the watch and the calendar, refer to three units. The average watch has three hands: hour, minute, and second. Calendars indicate day, month, and year. It is of interest that many calendars, in addition to displaying the current month on any one page, also provide small displays of the month immediately preceding and the month which is to follow. This symbolizes a concern with both past and future while living in the present.

The past, present, and future trichotomy remains constant no matter what the time unit is. Whether one is concerned with day, week, month, or year, there is yesterday, today, and tomorrow. The limiting nature of three is demonstrated by the fact that if one wishes to refer to, let us say, days other than those three, one must do so in reference to the two extremes, e.g., the day before yesterday, the day after tomorrow. There is no independent term available for measures outside of the basic three. In some instances, even dependent terms outside of the limiting three are lacking. Thus one can say last night, tonight, and tomorrow night, but while one can refer easily to the night before last, one cannot with equal idiomatic facility speak of the night after tomorrow night. With weeks, months, or years, one can employ "last, this, and next," and thus weeks falling outside the extremes are the week before last and the week after next. Curiously enough, the same type of structure found in time applies to trinary linear kinship terminology. Ego has parents (= yesterday) and he has children (= tomorrow). Linear relatives beyond these two extremes must be named in reference to one of the two extremes, e.g., grand*parents* or grand*children*. Moreover, in either direction, there is something of a trinary terminological limit. Ego has parents, grandparents, and great-grandparents, generational distinctions being signaled by a distinct prefix. Additional distinctions can be made only by successive repetition of the last prefix, e.g., great-great-grandparents. The same holds for ego's children, grandchildren, and great-grandchildren. Note also the incremental repetition of one to three words in parent (1), grandparent (2), and great-grandparent (3). The time-kinship parallel is also obvious in American values. In a scheme like past, present, and future (or man, woman, and child), it is the third and last term which is valued most. Americans are future-oriented and to the amazement of their enemies, they tend to forget about the past. Similarly, they are child-oriented and they tend to forget about their elders, banishing them to old age homes or communities.

Still another time trichotomy stems from regarding noon as a midpoint. Time is denoted in reference to noon inasmuch as A.M. and P.M. are before and after noon respectively. In the same fashion, historical time in American

culture is measured with respect to the birth of Christ. Years are either
B.C. or A.D. However, the initial points of reference are separate from the
periods of "before" and "after," just as the present is in theory distinct
from the past and the future. Thus noon is neither A.M. nor P.M. Twelve
o'clock is ambiguous and one is required to say twelve midnight or twelve
noon. It should be noted that in Europe generally, an unambiguous *four-
digit* time indicator system is employed. The practical advantages of a four-
digit symbol such as 1530 over a three-digit 3:30 are obvious—there are
two three-thirties daily—and this is probably why the American military
has adopted the more efficient four-digit system. Incidentally, a possible
mathematical-logical analogue for the "before" and "after" terms in reference to an initial point is provided by the usual ways of relating one term
to another. Either a equals b; a is less than b, or a is greater than b.
Distinctions such as a is slightly less than b or a is much less than b are not
culturally defined as relevant or significant. There are only the three possibilities. Similarly we have three ways of relating man to nature, man
subjugated to nature (less than); man in nature (equal); and man over
nature (greater than); in interpersonal relations, an individual is inferior
(or subordinate), equal, or superior (or superordinate) to another.

The discussion of time is in part a discussion of the terminology of time
and is thus a discussion of language. In any case, the very nature of the
Sapir-Whorf hypothesis would make one suspect that if trichotomy were
a pattern of American culture, it would also be found in American English.
However, the greater part of Whorf's own consideration of English suggests
that English has primarily binary features. Whorf emphasizes that there
are basically nouns and verbs (1964:215), with the nouns of two sorts:
individual nouns and mass nouns (1964:140). Whorf also draws attention
to the fundamental categorical distinction between singular and plural. All
this leads him to see some of the linguistic correlates of the strong tradition
of philosophical dualism in Western civilization and he cites the example
of the dichotomy of form and substance (1964:141). (He might also have
cited active/passive, mind/body, spirit/flesh, and many other polarities.)
While Whorf is undoubtedly correct in his fundamentally binary analysis,
there are some trinary features besides the three-tense system which he
might have mentioned. The pronouns are first person, second person, and
third person. (The names of these distinctions are themselves part of the
pattern.) In modern English there are no more than three distinct forms
of any one pronoun, e.g., he, his, him. Third person nominative singular
is divided into he, she, and it, corresponding to the genders masculine,
feminine, and neuter. Hoijer's argument (1954:97) that this is strictly
a grammatical survival with no semantic correlate is somewhat beside the
point, even assuming he is correct. Whether it is actually part of linguistic
structure or whether it is simply part of what traditional grammarians say
is linguistic structure, the fact remains that in our educational system, the
distinction between the three genders is made. What members of a culture
think about their language (i.e., folk linguistics) can influence other aspects
of culture probably almost as much as the actual linguistic patterning.
Linguists with their concern for the latter have tended to ignore folk

linguistics, that is, folk analytical categories. Brown (1960:342) has put the matter well in her proposition that "many of the perceptions we derive from language do not arise from anything inherent in the structure of the language itself, but as the result of what we have been *taught* about it." That American grammarians analyze English sentences into actor/action/goal or subject/predicate/object is important culturally, regardless of whether or not this is in fact an accurate delineation of English structure. Grammarians also distinguish simple, compound, and complex sentences. In punctuation rules, one finds three major medial marks: comma, semicolon, and colon, whose orthographic symbolism itself reflects trichotomic structuring (*a, ab,* and *b*). There are also three principal terminal marks: period, question mark, and exclamation point. The latter marks are allegedly indicators of the three major sentence types: declarative, interrogative, and exclamatory. In another instance of orthographic symbolism, one finds that ellipsis, an indefinite quantity, is signaled by the definite convention of using three periods or asterisks.

Of course, there are actual trinary structural features of English. One of the most important of these is the number of degrees employed with modifiers—specifically, the comparative and superlative. One might even go so far as to conjecture that it is the "good, better, best" paradigm, perhaps more than any other single factor, which has encouraged the concept formation of three classes or three types of merchandise sizes, quality, etc. In a recent study, Deonna has brilliantly pointed out (1954:415) that three is in part a semantic derivative of the superlative degree and cites the roots "ter," "tri," and "tre" as evidence. In French, for example, "très" is a superlative. (In English, one might think of *ter*rific and *tre*mendous. Moreover, etymologies of triumph—and trump in the game of bridge—might show that three was all-powerful, just as the origins of terminus, in the sense of limit and eternity—ternity is an obsolete form of trinity—in the sense of time without limit, or past plus present plus future, or as a synonym for the deity—who is tripartite—may stem from an archaic ur-three root.) In any event, Whorf's distinction between nouns and verbs notwithstanding, tripartition in English is an important structural feature. The division of time and history into threes would appear to be influenced by verb action tense (past, present, future), while the division of objects or object qualities into three would seem to be related to the degrees of comparison (correct, more correct, most correct). Whether the relationship of linguistic feature to other aspects of culture is causal or only correlative, the fact that there are trichotomies of verb tense, modifier degree, pronoun category, and gender tends to support the notion that patterning underlying a culture generally will be evident in language.

That trichotomy is a cognitive category in the sense that individuals tend to perceive in threes is suggested by the results of experiments in gestalt psychology. Continua involving both sight and sound were segmented into groups of three (Köhler, 1959:83, 89). However, experiments such as the classic pioneering ones made by Wertheimer (1923) did not take the pattern number three into account. Subjects did tend to see things in threes, but Wertheimer attributed his results to such factors as organization (in terms of proximity) and the grouping of similar forms (such as three dots opposed to three circles). The results might be more a matter of "three" gestalt, an explanation which would no doubt have delighted Wertheimer. Subjects might, for example, see threes even in a continuous line of dots. In any case, it is difficult to isolate such variables as proximity and form similarity when *three* figures are used in the experiment.

This brings us to an important theoretical point and one of the primary purposes of the present paper. Thus far, an attempt has been made to show that the pattern of trichotomy does in fact exist as a native category in Western and, more specifically, American culture. What remains to be seen, however, is how such a native category can unconsciously affect the formation of supposedly objective analytical categories. This is the really insidious part of cultural patterning. No individual can escape his culture and its built-in cultural cognitive categories. Yet many individuals think they have escaped, and they claim to have described the nature of objective reality in culture-free terms. But often what scientists and scholars present as bona fide analytical categories are in fact ethnocentric extensions of their own native categories. While a few analysts specify that their trichotomic models are solely for heuristic purposes (and certainly a tripartite scheme would have both mnemonic and aesthetic value in American culture), many do not do so, and the reader is led to believe that the trichotomic model comes from the data, not from the analyst. Having identified a folk pattern of trichotomy in a variety of aspects of American culture, one is in an excellent position to perceive the arbitrary and culturally determined nature of many of our accepted "objective" analytic schemes.

No doubt there will be those who will be offended by the implication that their analytical categories are but folk or native categories in disguise. They may claim that the analytical categories in question really do correspond to objective reality. (This would also be the argument of those defending the notion of the Trinity.) Others, with a penchant for nit-picking, will be quick to point out that some of the analytical schemes here presented have long been discarded. The point is that all of the following analytical schemes did or do have some standing in American culture. Not just Gaul, but the whole world is divided into three parts. There is animal, vegetable, and mineral. (These and other categories are so deeply embedded in our culture that it may be difficult for some to see their arbitrariness.) Yet is there an absolute difference between plant and animal life or is there a continuum? Similar examples may be taken from almost any discipline. Entomologists define insects as those members of the phylum Arthropoda in which the body is divided into three parts: head, thorax, and abdomen. The question is: are insects truly morphologically tripartite or do we simply see them as tripartite? And what of the trichotomy explicit in the metamorphic continuum of some insects into larva, pupa, and adult? Are the three stages simply a reflection of the same cultural convention which suggests that literature has a beginning, a middle, and an end or that plays commonly be written in three acts?

At least we are consistent, for all the world is conceived and perceived in tripartite terms—*by us*. The continuum of states of matter is neatly divided into solid, liquid, and gas. The projection of this scheme to the entire earth results in distinguishing land (solid), sea (liquid), and air (gas). These in turn are subdivided. The air or atmosphere may be broken down into troposphere, stratosphere, and ionosphere, while the earth may be divided into three types of climate zones: frigid, temperate, and torrid. (Cf. the spacial-geographical divisions such as North, Central (or Middle), and South America or the East, the Middle West, and the West.) As the world is divided, so is man. The human ear is divided into the outer, middle, and inner ear, the brain into cerebrum, cerebellum, and medulla, the small intestine into the duodenum, the jejunum, and the ileum. Are these divisions any less arbitrary than the segmentation of human voice range continuum into soprano, mezzo-soprano, and alto (female), and tenor, baritone, and bass (male)? But the issue is not just taxonomic or classificatory. When physicians prescribe dosages in threes, e.g., one pill every three hours or three pills a day, or when infants are given a three-in-one DPT (diphtheria toxoid, pertussis vaccine, and tetanus toxoid) shot or a series of three polio shots, the question is whether this is the most efficacious procedure, medically speaking, or not. Perhaps the ritual element is in fact an additional beneficial feature.

One can pick up an elementary textbook in any discipline and find numerous instances of three-determined thinking. It is really astonishing to realize that anthropologists, students of cultural conditioning, have been so culture-bound in their theoretical formulations. Among the numerous versions of a three stages of man theory (cf. Comte, Hegel, and Vico), one thinks of Morgan's savagery, barbarism (which was subdivided into Opening, Middle, and Closing periods), and civilization, and Frazer's stages of magic, religion, and science. Other obvious examples of tripartition include Van Gennep's classic analysis of rites of passage in which he distinguishes rites of separation, transition, and incorporation.

There is just as much three-conditioning evident in the other branches of anthropology. In physical anthropology, the traditional conventional number of races is three: Caucasoid, Mongoloid, and Negroid, although the inadequacy of the classification is well known. Similarly, European peoples are divided into northern, central, and southern, that is, Nordic, Alpine, and Mediterranean. In the study of body measurement and typology, tripartition is also found. (The folk system of measuring females in terms of bust, waist, and hips is in the same pattern.) In craniology, for example, the measurements of the various craniometric indices fall invariably into one of three categories (cf. Comas, 1960:406–12). Archaeology is even more three-ridden. The three-age system of Stone, Bronze, and Iron is still in vogue (Heizer), but more important are the subdivisions of time periods. Ages are divided into three. Thus the Stone Age is commonly divided into Old, Middle, and New, i.e., Paleolithic, Mesolithic, and Neolithic. The Paleolithic can then be subdivided into Lower, Middle, and Upper Paleolithic. The Upper Paleolithic can then be broken down into Aurignacian, Solutrean, Magdalenian. If this weren't enough evidence to indicate that archaeologists are culture-bound, one should consult V. Gordon Childe's argument that tripartition is a necessary means of establishing chronological sequences in archaeology (1956:66) and that this is true, not because of any Hegelian metaphysics or trinitarian mysticism, but because of the very nature of the material to be seriated. The question is, of course, whether the method of tripartition is really dictated by the nature of the material or is it rather dictated by the nature of the culture of the archaeologist? If human history is a continuum, then the segmentation of a portion of that continuum into ages, stages, or levels is arbitrary.

Anthropology is typical insofar as the three-patterning of its scholarship is concerned. It would be easy to cite hundreds of examples from other disciplines. Yet anthropologists do not seem to have been aware of the pattern. Whorf, one of the pioneers in the study of the cultural conditioning of thought patterns, failed to see the influence of tripartition on his own work. His coinage of the three-word phrase "Standard Average European" is an example. His decision to compare *three* isolates of English—"clean," "with," "ramrod"—with *three* isolates from Shawnee would be another. (Note also his three-part figure in which he shows how one Hopi word equals three English words and how one English word equals three Eskimo words.) Another indication that anthropologists are not aware of their cultural propensity for tripartition is found in Edward Hall's *The Silent Language*. Hall, in collaboration with George L. Trager, developed an elaborate tripartite scheme which distinguished what was termed formal, informal, and technical levels. However, Hall, an expert on the implicit assumptions of various cultures, claimed that Americans had a bipolar way of analyzing data and that "The ease with which Americans tend to polarize their thoughts about events may make it difficult for them to embrace an approach which employs three categories rather than two" (1959:66).

Having demonstrated that the number three is a folk category in American culture, a folk category which has made inroads into the various analytic categories of academic disciplines, it remains to be seen what the meaning, if any, of the category is. It is one thing to describe a cultural category; it is another to speculate about its origin and meaning. Does the category stem from the family group of father, mother, and child? Is it a reflection of the divine nature of the universe as defined by trinitarian Christian doctrine? A Whorfian would no doubt place language rather than social organization or religion at the source. Thus a Whorfian might claim that the tense system, the first, second, third person distinctions, and the "good, better, best" paradigm were the roots of the pattern. A Freudian would argue along different lines (Glenn). Freud suggested that the number three was a masculine symbol, the *phallus cum testiculis*.[1] This is most inter-

---

[1]Freud was by no means the first to suggest that the number three might be related to phallic symbolism. See, for example, Thomas Inman, *Ancient Faiths Embodied in Ancient Names*, I (London, 1868), 76, n. 1, 89. As a matter of fact, the folk had also interpreted the number three in phallic terms long before Freud. For an example from modern Greek folklore, see Curt Wachsmuth, *Das alte Griechenland im neuen* (Bonn, 1864), p. 80, n. 24. Since anthropologists frequently "discover" data which is already known (to the people in the culture under study), they can understand how a modern student of symbols could "discover" an interpretation which was in some sense already known to the people who use these symbols.

esting in the light of Freud's own work: e.g., *Three Contributions to the Theory of Sex,* or the id, ego, superego classification. Incidentally, the standard kinship notation employed by anthropologists would tend to support Freud's view. The triangle represents a male while a circle represents a female. However, the convention of three as a masculine symbol is more probably a manifestation of the traditional symbolism of Western civilization than a cause or origin of trichotomy. Only if one were to argue that male as opposed to female thought was trichotomized and that male thought was a compensatory activity for not being able to give birth to children as females do could one make a case for a most hypothetical origin theory. The only child a man produces is a brainchild. His intellectual project serves as his "baby." His products bear his stamp, the number three, the mark of masculinity. Since the majority of Western constructs and classification schemes have been devised by men rather than women, this could account for the preoccupation with three.[2] This type of explanation would also make clear why aspects of American culture which are exclusively masculine, e.g., the military, the Boy Scouts, baseball, are especially three-ridden. (Note also that the Christian Trinity is all masculine. This would be further evidence that three is male creativity denying or replacing female creativity.) However, like most psychological explanations, this one is highly speculative. One must conclude that it is difficult if not impossible to state with any degree of certainty what the ultimate origins of trichotomy might be.

One thing is certain though, and that is that trichotomy is a pattern of American culture. Whether it is related to masculinity or male mental creativity or not, it is, and will probably continue to be, an important cognitive category in American (and Old World) culture. As for how individuals learn about the pattern, there are probably many sources. Three dimensions of space, the three tenses of time, and the good-better-best paradigm all exert some influence. But an American three-year-old has already been exposed to the category in folkloristic form, perhaps before he realizes the space, time, and linguistic features. For are there not three men in a tub? three bags of Baa Baa Black Sheep's wool? three little kittens who lost their mittens? three little pigs? Is not the third item called for by Old King Cole his fiddlers three? Is there an American child who has not heard the story of the three bears? This latter story is a narrative listing of trichotomies in which the mediating third term is invariably "just right." (Note that the third term is associated with the child bear rather than the mother and father bears.) The child is conditioned by his folklore to expect three and his culture does not disappoint him. Language, social organization, religion, and almost all other aspects of American culture confirm the pattern.

Trichotomy exists but it is not part of the nature of nature. It is part

[2]One small bit of personal biographical data does support this thesis. The author first began to jot down examples of "threes" while awaiting the arrival of his third child. However, it was not until some time after the child's birth that it occurred to the author that his mentally straining to produce examples of threes might be a curious idiosyncratic form of intellectual couvade!

of the nature of culture. At this point, if anyone is sceptical about there being a three-pattern in American culture, let him give at least three good reasons why.

REFERENCES

Abbot, A. E.
    1962 *The Number Three: Its Occult Significance in Human Life.* London: Emerson Press.
Ben Cheneb, Mohammed
    1926 "Du nombre Trois chez les Arabes." *Revue Africaine* **67** : 105–78.
Brinton, Daniel G.
    1894 "The origin of sacred numbers." *American Anthropologist* **7** : 168–73.
Brough, J.
    1959 "The tripartite ideology of the Indo-Europeans: an experiment in method." *Bulletin of the School of Oriental and African Studies* **22** : 69–95.
Brown, Dora Worrall
    1960 "Does language structure influence thought?" *ETC.: A Review of General Semantics* **17** : 339–45.
Buckland, A. W.
    1895 "Four, as a sacred number." *Journal of the Anthropological Institute* **25** : 96–102.
Childe, V. Gordon
    1956 *Piecing Together the Past,* New York: Frederick A. Praeger.
Comas, Juan
    1960 *Manual of Physical Anthropology.* Springfield: Charles C. Thomas.
Crawley, E. S.
    1897 "The origin and development of number symbolism." *Popular Science Monthly* **51** : 524–34.
Deonna, W.
    1954 "Trois, superlatif absolu." *L'Antiquité Classique* **23** : 403–28.
Dumézil, Georges
    1958 *L'idéologie tripartite des Indo-Européens.* Brussels: Collection Latomus 31.
Erben, Karel Jaromir
    1857 "O dvojici a o trojici v bájesloví slovanském" ("About the number two and the number three in Slavic mythology"), *Časopis Musea Království Českého* **31** : 268–86; 390–415.
Freud, Sigmund
    1953 *A General Introduction to Psychoanalysis.* Garden City: Permabooks.
Geil, William Edgar
    1926 *The Sacred 5 of China.* Boston and New York: Houghton and Mifflin.
Glenn, Jules
    1965 "Sensory determinants of the symbol three." *Journal of the American Psychoanalytic Association* **13:** 422–434.
Göbel, Fritz
    1935 *Formen und Formeln der epischen Dreiheit in der griechischen Dichtung.* Stuttgart: W. Kohlhammer.
Goudy, Henry
    1910 *Trichotomy in Roman Law.* Oxford: Clarendon Press.

Günther, R. F.
1912 "Worauf beruht die Vorherrschaft der Drei im Menschen?" *Nord und Süd* **142** : 313–325.

Hall, Edward T.
1959 *The Silent Language*. New York: Fawcett Publications.

Heizer, Robert F.
1962 "The background of Thomsen's three-age system." *Technology and Culture* **3** : 259–66.

Hoijer, Harry
1954 *Language in Culture*. Chicago : University of Chicago Press.

Kirfel, Willibald
1948 *Die dreiköpfige Gottheit*. Bonn : Ferd. Dümmlers Verlag.

Köhler, Wolfgang
1959 *Gestalt Psychology*. New York: Mentor Books.

La Sorsa, Saverio
1963 "Il numero 3 nella terapia popolare." *Annali di Medicina Navale* **68:** 171–74.

Lease, Emory B.
1919 "The number three, mysterious, mystic, magic." *Classical Philology* **14 :** 56–73.

Lehmann, Alfred
1914 *Dreiheit und dreifache Wiederholung im deutschen Volksmärchen*. Leipzig : Buchdruckerei Robert Noske.

Littleton, C. Scott
1967 "Toward a genetic model for the analysis of ideology: the Indo-European case." *Western Folklore* **26 :** 37–47.

Lowie, Robert H.
1925 "Five as a mystic number." *American Anthropologist* **27 :** 578.

May, Earl Chapin
1932 *The Circus from Rome to Ringling*. New York: Duffield and Green.

Morgan, Lewis H.
1876 "Ethnical periods." *Proceedings of the American Association for the Advancement of Science* **24 :** 266–74.

Müller, Raimund
1903 "Die zahl 3 in sage, dichtung und kunst." in *XXX Jahresbericht der K. K. Staats-Oberrealschule in Teschen am Schlusse des Schuljahres 1902–1903*, pp. 1–23. Teschen: K. und K. Hofbuchdruckerei Karl Prochaska.

Olrik, Axel
1909 "Epische Gesetze der Volksdichtung." *Zeitschrift für Deutsches Altertum* **51 :** 1–12. Reprinted in translation in Alan Dundes, ed., *The Study of Folklore*, pp. 129–41. Englewood Cliffs, N. J. : Prentice-Hall, 1965.

Paine, Levi Leonard
1901 *The Ethnic Trinities and Their Relations to the Christian Trinity*. Boston and New York: Houghton, Mifflin and Company.

Parsons, Elsie Clews
1916 "The favorite number of the Zuni." *Scientific Monthly* **3 :** 596–600.

Post, Emily
1960 *Etiquette*, 10th ed. New York : Funk and Wagnalls.

Seifert, Josef Leo
    1954 *Sinndeutung des Mythos: Die Trinität in den Mythen der Urvölker.* Wien, München: Verlag Herold.

Simmel, Georg
    1902 "The number of members as determining the sociological form of the group." *American Journal of Sociology* **8**: 1–46, 158–96.

Strand, T. A.
    1958 *Tri-Ism: The Theory of the Trinity in Nature, Man and His Works.* New York: Exposition Press.

Tavenner, Eugene
    1916 "Three as a magic number in Latin literature." *Transactions of the American Philological Association* **47**: 117–43.

Usener, H.
    1903 "Dreiheit." *Rheinisches Museum für Philologie* **58**: 1–47, 161–208, 321–62.

Wertheimer, Max
    1923 "Untersuchungen zur lehre von der gestalt." *Psychologische Forschung* **4**: 301–50

Whorf, Benjamin L.
    1964 *Language, Thought and Reality.* Cambridge, Mass.: The MIT Press.

Ruth Benedict

CONTINUITIES AND DISCONTINUITIES IN CULTURAL CONDITIONING

Here is a brilliant analysis of some critical characteristics of American culture. They are seen all the more clearly for their being contrasted with appropriate data from other cultures. While in theory one would have to admit that it is possible to see the webbing of one's own culture and the probable consequences of that particular pattern of webbing *without* ever examining the webbing of other cultures, in practice one can rarely do so. It is difficult to see one's culture objectively because the very act of seeing is itself conditioned by that same culture. In this important paper, Ruth Benedict points out some remarkable discontinuities in our system of education. Despite the fact that the bulk of the paper is devoted to examples from other cultures, her principal aim was to illuminate some of our cultural conditioning, which makes it difficult rather than easy for a child to become an adult. If her insights are valid ones, and they appear to be, then one has an indisputable argument for the

Reprinted from *Psychiatry*, 1 (1938), 161–67, by special permission of The William Alanson White Psychiatric Foundation, Inc. Copyright 1938 by The William Alanson White Psychiatric Foundation, Inc.

conduct of anthropological research. For even if all the data gathered from other cultures were useful only in seeing our own culture more clearly (and seeing is the first step if one wishes to improve one's culture), it would still be more than worth the effort.

All cultures must deal in one way or another with the cycle of growth from infancy to adulthood. Nature has posed the situation dramatically: on the one hand, the new born baby, physiologically vulnerable, unable to fend for itself, or to participate of its own initiative in the life of the group, and, on the other, the adult man or woman. Every man who rounds out his human potentialities must have been a son first and a father later and the two roles are physiologically in great contrast; he must first have been dependent upon others for his very existence and later he must provide such security for others. This discontinuity in the life cycle is a fact of nature and is inescapable. Facts of nature, however, in any discussion of human problems, are ordinarily read off not at their bare minimal but surrounded by all the local accretions of behavior to which the student of human affairs has become accustomed in his own culture. For that reason it is illuminating to examine comparative material from other societies in order to get a wider perspective on our own special accretions. The anthropologist's role is not to question the facts of nature, but to insist upon the interposition of a middle term between "nature" and "human behavior"; his role is to analyse that term, to document local man-made doctorings of nature and to insist that these doctorings should not be read off in any one culture as nature itself. Although it is a fact of nature that the child becomes a man, the way in which this transition is effected varies from one society to another, and no one of these particular cultural bridges should be regarded as the "natural" path to maturity.

From a comparative point of view our culture goes to great extremes in emphasizing contrasts between the child and the adult. The child is sexless, the adult estimates his virility by his sexual activities; the child must be protected from the ugly facts of life, the adult must meet them without psychic catastrophe; the child must obey, the adult must command this obedience. These are all dogmas of our culture, dogmas which in spite of the facts of nature, other cultures commonly do not share. In spite of the physiological contrasts between child and adult these are cultural accretions.

It will make the point clearer if we consider one habit in our own culture in regard to which there is not this discontinuity of conditioning. With the greatest clarity of purpose and economy of training, we achieve our goal of conditioning everyone to eat three meals a day. The baby's training in regular food periods begins at birth and no crying of the child and no inconvenience to the mother is allowed to interfere. We gauge the child's physiological make-up and at first allow it food oftener than adults, but, because our goal is firmly set and our training consistent, before the child is two years old it has achieved the adult schedule. From the point of view of other cultures this is as startling as the fact of three-year old babies perfectly at home in deep water is to us. Modesty is another sphere in which our child training is consistent and economical; we waste no time in clothing the baby and in contrast to many societies where the child runs naked till it is ceremonially given its skirt or its pubic sheath at adolescence, the child's training fits it precisely for adult conventions.

In neither of these aspects of behavior is there need for an individual in our culture to embark before puberty, at puberty or at some later date upon a course of action which all his previous training has tabued. He is spared the unsureness inevitable in such a transition.

The illustration I have chosen may appear trivial, but in larger and more important aspects of behavior, our methods are obviously different. Because of the great variety of child training in different families in our society, I might illustrate continuity of conditioning from individual life histories in our culture, but even these, from a comparative point of view, stop far short of consistency and I shall therefore confine myself to describing arrangements in other cultures in which training, which with us is idiosyncratic, is accepted and traditional and does not therefore involve the same possibility of conflict. I shall choose childhood rather than infant and nursing situations not because the latter do not vary strikingly in different cultures but because they are nevertheless more circumscribed by the baby's physiological needs than is its later training. Childhood situations provide an excellent field in which to illustrate the range of cultural adjustments which are possible within a universally given, but not so drastic, set of physiological facts.

The major discontinuity in the life cycle is of course that the child who is at one point a son must later be a father. These roles in our society are strongly differentiated; a good son is tractable, and does not assume adult responsibilities; a good father provides for his children and should not allow his authority to be flouted. In addition the child must be sexless so far as his family is concerned, whereas the father's sexual role is primary in the family. The individual in one role must revise his behavior from almost all points of view when he assumes the second role.

I shall select for discussion three such contrasts that occur in our culture between the individual's role as child and as father: 1. responsible—non-responsible status role. 2. dominance—submission. 3. contrasted sexual role. It is largely upon our cultural commitments to these three contrasts that the discontinuity in the life cycle of an individual in our culture depends.

1. Responsible—Non-Responsible Status Role

The techniques adopted by societies which achieve continuity during the life cycle in this sphere in no way differ from those we employ in our uniform conditioning to three meals a day. They are merely applied to other areas of life. We think of the child as wanting to play and the adult as having to work, but in many societies the mother takes the baby daily in her shawl or carrying net to the garden or to gather roots, and adult labor is seen even in infancy from the pleasant security of its position in close contact with its mother. When the child can run about it accompanies its parents still, doing tasks which are essential and yet suited to its powers, and its dichotomy between work and play is not different from that its parents recognize, namely the distinction between the busy day and the free evening. The tasks it is asked to perform are graded to its powers and its elders wait quietly by, not offering to do the task in the child's place. Everyone who is familiar with such societies has been struck by the contrast with our child training. Dr. Ruth Underhill tells me of sitting with a group of Papago elders in Arizona when the man of the house turned to his little three-year old granddaughter and asked her to close the door. The door was heavy and hard to shut. The child tried, but it did not move. Several times the grandfather repeated, "Yes, close the door." No one jumped to the child's assistance. No one took the responsibility away from her. On the other hand there was no impatience, for after all the child was small. They sat gravely waiting till the child succeeded and her grandfather gravely thanked her. It was assumed that the task would not be asked of her unless she could perform it, and having been asked the responsibility was hers alone just as if she were a grown woman.

The essential point of such child training is that the child is from infancy continuously conditioned to responsible social participation while at the same time the tasks that are expected of it are adapted to its capacity. The contrast with our society is very great. A child does not make any labor contribution to our industrial society except as it competes with an adult; its work is not measured against its own strength and skill but against high-geared industrial requirements. Even when we praise a child's achievement in the home we are outraged if such praise is interpreted as being of the same order as praise of adults. The child is praised because the parent feels well disposed, regardless of whether the task is well done by adult standards, and the child acquires no sensible standard by which to measure its achievement. The gravity of a Cheyenne Indian family ceremoniously making a feast out of the little boy's first snowbird is at the furthest remove from our behavior. At birth the little boy was presented with a toy bow, and from the time he could run about serviceable bows suited to his stature were specially made for him by the man of the family. Animals and birds were taught him in a graded series beginning with those most easily taken, and as he brought in his first of each species his family duly made a feast of it, accepting his contribution as gravely as the buffalo his father brought. When he finally killed a buffalo, it was only the final step of his childhood conditioning, not a new adult role with which his childhood experience had been at variance.

The Canadian Ojibwa show clearly what results can be achieved. This tribe gains its livelihood by winter trapping and the small family of father, mother and children live during the long winter alone on their great frozen hunting grounds. The boy accompanies his father and brings in his catch to his sister as his father does to his mother; the girl prepares the meat and skins for him just as his mother does for her husband. By the time the boy is 12, he may have set his own line of traps on a hunting territory of his own and return to his parent's house only once in several months—still bringing the meat and skins to his sister. The young child is taught consistently that it has only itself to rely upon in life, and this is as true in the dealings it will have with the supernatural as in the business of getting a livelihood. This attitude he will accept as a successful adult just as he accepted it as a child.[1]

2. Dominance—Submission

Dominance—submission is the most striking of those categories of behavior where like does not respond to like but where one type of behavior stimulates the opposite response. It is one of the most prominent ways in which behavior is patterned in our culture. When it obtains between classes, it may be nourished by continuous experience; the difficulty in its use between children and adults lies in the fact that an individual conditioned to one set of behavior in childhood must adopt the opposite as an adult. Its opposite is a pattern of approximately identical reciprocal behavior, and societies which rely upon continuous conditioning characteristically invoke this pattern. In some primitive cultures the very terminology of address between father and son, and more commonly, between grandchild and grandson or uncle and nephew, reflects this attitude. In such kinship terminologies one reciprocal expresses each of these relationships so that son and father, for instance, exchange the same term with one another, just as we exchange the same term with a cousin. The child later will exchange it with his son. "Father—son," therefore, is a continuous relationship he enjoys throughout life. The same continuity, backed up by verbal reciprocity, occurs far oftener in the grandchild—grandson relationship or that of mother's brother —sister's son. When these are "joking" relationships, as they often are, travellers report wonderingly upon the liberties and pretensions of tiny toddlers in their dealings with these family elders. In place of our dogma of respect to elders such societies employ in these cases a reciprocity as nearly identical as may be. The teasing and practical joking the grandfather visits upon his grandchild, the grandchild returns in like coin; he would be led to believe that he failed in propriety if he did not give like for like. If the sister's son has right of access without leave to his mother's brother's possessions, the mother's brother has such rights also to the child's possessions. They share reciprocal privileges and obligations which in our society can develop only between age mates.

From the point of view of our present discussion, such kinship conventions allow the child to put in practice from infancy the same forms of behavior which it will rely upon as an adult; behavior is not polarized into

[1]Landes, Ruth, *The Ojibwa Woman*, Part 1, Youth—Columbia University Contributions to Anthropology, Volume XXXI.

a general requirement of submission for the child and dominance for the adult.

It is clear from the techniques described above by which the child is conditioned to a responsible status role that these depend chiefly upon arousing in the child the desire to share responsibility in adult life. To achieve this little stress is laid upon obedience but much stress upon approval and praise. Punishment is very commonly regarded as quite outside the realm of possibility, and natives in many parts of the world have drawn the conclusion from our usual disciplinary methods that white parents do not love their children. If the child is not required to be submissive however, many occasions for punishment melt away; a variety of situations which call for it do not occur. Many American Indian tribes are especially explicit in rejecting the ideal of a child's submissive or obedient behavior. Prince Maximilian von Wied who visited the Crow Indians over a hundred years ago describes a father's boasting about his young son's intractibility even when it was the father himself who was flouted; "He will be a man," his father said. He would have been baffled at the idea that his child should show behavior which would obviously make him appear a poor creature in the eyes of his fellows if he used it as an adult. Dr. George Devereux tells me of a special case of such an attitude among the Mohave at the present time. The child's mother was white and protested to its father that he must take action when the child disobeyed and struck him. "But why?" the father said, "he is little. He cannot possibly injure me." He did not know of any dichotomy according to which an adult expects obedience and a child must accord it. If his child had been docile he would simply have judged that it would become a docile adult—an eventuality of which he would not have approved.

Child training which brings about the same result is common also in other areas of life than that of reciprocal kinship obligations between child and adult. There is a tendency in our culture to regard every situation as having in it the seeds of a dominance-submission relationship. Even where dominance-submission is patently irrelevant we read in the dichotomy, assuming that in every situation there must be one person dominating another. On the other hand some cultures, even when the situation calls for leadership do not see it in terms of dominance-submission. To do justice to this attitude it would be necessary to describe their political and especially their economic arrangements, for such an attitude to persist must certainly be supported by economic mechanisms that are congruent with it. But it must also be supported by—or what comes to the same thing, express itself in—child training and familial situations.

3. Contrasted Sexual Role

Continuity of conditioning in training the child to assume responsibility and to behave no more submissively than adults is quite possible in terms of the child's physiological endowment if his participation is suited to his strength. Because of the late development of the child's reproductive organs continuity of conditioning in sex experience presents a difficult problem. So far as their belief that the child is anything but a sexless being is concerned, they are probably more nearly right than we are with an opposite dogma. But the great break is presented by the universally sterile unions before puberty and the presumably fertile ones after maturation. This physiological fact no amount of cultural manipulation can minimize or alter, and societies therefore which stress continuous conditioning most strongly sometimes do not expect children to be interested in sex experience until they have matured physically. This is striking among American Indian tribes like the Dakota; adults observe great privacy in sex acts and in no way stimulate children's sexual activity. There need be no discontinuity, in the sense in which I have used the term, in such a program if the child is taught nothing it does not have to unlearn later. In such cultures adults view children's experimentation as in no way wicked or dangerous but merely as innocuous play which can have no serious consequences. In some societies such play is minimal and the children manifest little interest in it. But the same attitude may be taken by adults in societies where such play is encouraged and forms a major activity among small children. This is true among most of the Melanesian cultures of Southeast New Guinea; adults go as far as to laugh off sexual affairs within the prohibited class if the children are not mature, saying that since they cannot marry there can be no harm done.

It is this physiological fact of the difference between children's sterile unions and adults' presumably fertile sex relations which must be kept in mind in order to understand the different mores which almost always govern sex expression in children and in adults in the same culture. A great many cultures with preadolescent sexual license require marital fidelity and a great many which value pre-marital virginity in either male or female arrange their marital life with great license. Continuity in sex experience is complicated by factors which it was unnecessary to consider in the problems previously discussed. The essential problem is not whether or not the child's sexuality is consistently exploited—for even where such exploitation is favored in the majority of cases the child must seriously modify his behavior at puberty or at marriage. Continuity in sex expression means rather that the child is taught nothing it must unlearn later. If the cultural emphasis is upon sexual pleasure the child who is continuously conditioned will be encouraged to experiment freely and pleasurably, as among the Marquesans;[2] if emphasis is upon reproduction, as among the Zuni of New Mexico, childish sex proclivities will not be exploited for the only important use which sex is thought to serve in his culture is not yet possible to him. The important contrast with our child training is that although a Zuni child is impressed with the wickedness of premature sex experimentation he does not run the risk as in our culture of associating this wickedness with sex itself rather than with sex at his age. The adult in our culture has often failed to unlearn the wickedness or the dangerousness of sex, a lesson which was impressed upon him strongly in his most formative years.

[2]Ralph Linton, class notes on the Marquesans.

Discontinuity in Conditioning

Even from this very summary statement of continuous conditioning the economy of such mores is evident. In spite of the obvious advantages, however, there are difficulties in its way. Many primitive societies expect as different behavior from an individual as child and as adult as we do, and such discontinuity involves a presumption of strain.

Many societies of this type however minimize strain by the techniques they employ, and some techniques are more successful than others in ensuring the individual's functioning without conflict. It is from this point of view that age-grade societies reveal their fundamental significance. Age-graded cultures characteristically demand different behavior of the individual at different times of his life and persons of a like age-grade are grouped into a society whose activities are all oriented toward the behavior desired at that age. Individuals "graduate" publicly and with honor from one of these groups to another. Where age society members are enjoined to loyalty and mutual support, and are drawn not only from the local group but from the whole tribe as among the Arapaho, or even from other tribes as among the Wagawaga of Southeast New Guinea, such an institution has many advantages in eliminating conflicts among local groups and fostering intratribal peace. This seems to be also a factor in the tribal military solidarity of the similarly organized Masai of East Africa. The point that is of chief interest for our present discussion however is that by this means an individual who at any time takes on a new set of duties and virtues is supported not only by a solid phalanx of age mates but by the traditional prestige of the organized "secret" society into which he has now graduated. Fortified in this way, individuals in such cultures often swing between remarkable extremes of opposite behavior without apparent psychic threat. For example, the great majority exhibit prideful and non-conflicted behavior at each stage in the life cycle even when a prime of life devoted to passionate and aggressive head hunting must be followed by a later life dedicated to ritual and to mild and peaceable civic virtues.[3]

Our chief interest here, however, is in discontinuity which primarily affects the child. In many primitive societies such discontinuity has been fostered not because of economic or political necessity or because such discontinuity provides for a socially valuable division of labor, but because of some conceptual dogma. The most striking of these are the Australian and Papuan cultures where the ceremony of the "Making of Man" flourishes. In such societies it is believed that men and women have opposite and conflicting powers, and male children, who are of undefined status, must be initiated into the male role. In Central Australia the boy child is of the woman's side and women are tabu in the final adult stages or tribal ritual. The elaborate and protracted initiation ceremonies of the Arunta therefore snatch the boy from the mother, and dramatize his gradual repudiation of her. In a final ceremony he is reborn as a man out of the men's ceremonial "baby pouch." The men's ceremonies are ritual statements of a masculine

[3]Henry Elkin, manuscript on the Arapaho.

solidarity, carried out by fondling one another's *churingas,* the material symbol of each man's life, and by letting out over one another blood drawn from their veins. After this warm bond among men has been established through the ceremonies, the boy joins the men in the men's house and participates in tribal rites.[4] The enjoined discontinuity has been tribally bridged.

West of the Fly River in southern New Guinea there is a striking development of this Making of Men cult which involves a childhood period of passive homosexuality. Among the Keraki[5] it is thought that no boy can grow to full stature without playing the role for some years. Men slightly older take the active role, and the older man is a jealous partner. The life cycle of the Keraki Indians includes, therefore, in succession, passive homosexuality, active homosexuality and heterosexuality. The Keraki believe that pregnancy will result from post-pubertal passive homosexuality and see evidences of such practices in any fat man whom, even as an old man, they may kill or drive out of the tribe because of their fear. The ceremony that is of interest in connection with the present discussion takes place at the end of the period of passive homosexuality. This ceremony consists in burning out the possibility of pregnancy from the boy by pouring lye down his throat, after which he has no further protection if he gives way to the practice. There is no technique for ending active homosexuality, but this is not explicitly tabu for older men; heterosexuality and children however are highly valued. Unlike the neighboring Marindanim who share their homosexual practices, Keraki husband and wife share the same house and work together in the gardens.

I have chosen illustrations of discontinuous conditioning where it is not too much to say that the cultural institutions furnish adequate support to the individual as he progresses from role to role or interdicts the previous behavior in a summary fashion. The contrast with arrangements in our culture is very striking, and against this background of social arrangements in other cultures the adolescent period of *Sturm und Drang* with which we are so familiar becomes intelligible in terms of our discontinuous cultural institutions and dogmas rather than in terms of physiological necessity. It is even more pertinent to consider these comparative facts in relation to maladjusted persons in our culture who are said to be fixated at one or another pre-adult level. It is clear that if we were to look at our social arrangements as an outsider, we should infer directly from our family institutions and habits of child training that many individuals would not "put off childish things"; we should have to say that our adult activity demands traits that are interdicted in children, and that far from redoubling efforts to help children bridge this gap, adults in our culture put all the blame on the child when he fails to manifest spontaneously the new behavior or, overstepping the mark, manifests it with untoward belligerence. It is not surprising that in such a society many individuals fear to use behavior which has up to that

[4]Spencer, B., and Gillen, F. J., *The Arunta;* N. Y., Macmillan, 1927 (2 vols.). Róheim, Géza, Psycho-Analysis of Primitive Cultural Types. *Internat. J. Psychoanal.* (1932) **13**:1–224—in particular, Chapter III, on the Aranda, The Children of the Desert.

[5]Williams, Francis E., *Papuans of the Trans-Fly;* Oxford, 1936.

time been under a ban and trust instead, though at great psychic cost, to attitudes that have been exercised with approval during their formative years. Insofar as we invoke a physiological scheme to account for these neurotic adjustments we are led to overlook the possibility of developing social institutions which would lessen the social cost we now pay; instead we elaborate a set of dogmas which prove inapplicable under other social conditions.

Horace Miner

BODY RITUAL
AMONG THE NACIREMA

This delightful classic, written by Professor Horace Miner of the University of Michigan, shows in parody form how an anthropological perspective can help us see ourselves in a new light. Many disciplines study man, but it is anthropology in particular in which most commonly one begins by studying others and ends by understanding oneself. Numerous ethnographers have indicated in their fieldwork reports specific instances when they were struck with *how like us the people being studied were.* In the following essay, the point is *how much we are like the peoples we study.* After reading about the Nacirema, perhaps one can see the absurdity of segmenting the continuum of homo sapiens into such name-calling categories as "civilized" and "primitive" peoples.

For other parodies of anthropological techniques, see Robert Nathan, *The Weans* (New York, 1960), which is a pretended archaeological reconstruction made in the 79th century of American culture, satirizing archaeological techniques and guesswork, or William Henry Scott, "Sagada Legends," *Journal of American Folklore,* **74** (1961), 57–62, in which fake myths of a fake primitive people are given fake analyses with fake footnotes. For a charming fictional account of the trials and tribulations of a graduate student doing his fieldwork in anthropology, see the title short story in George P. Elliott, *Among the Dangs* (New York, 1961).

The anthropologist has become so familiar with the diversity of ways in which different peoples behave in similar situations that he is not apt to be surprised by even the most exotic

Reprinted from *American Anthropologist,* **58** (June, 1956), 503—07, by permission of the author and the American Anthropological Association.

customs. In fact, if all of the logically possible combinations of behavior have not been found somewhere in the world, he is apt to suspect that they must be present in some yet undescribed tribe. This point has, in fact, been expressed with respect to clan organization by Murdock (1949:71). In this light, the magical beliefs and practices of the Nacirema present such unusual aspects that it seems desirable to describe them as an example of the extremes to which human behavior can go.

Professor Linton first brought the ritual of the Nacirema to the attention of anthropologists twenty years ago (1936:326), but the culture of this people is still very poorly understood. They are a North American group living in the territory between the Canadian Cree, the Yaqui and Tara-humare of Mexico, and the Carib and Arawak of the Antilles. Little is known of their origin, although tradition states that they came from the east. According to Nacirema mythology, their nation was originated by a culture hero, Notgnihsaw, who is otherwise known for two great feats of strength—the throwing of a piece of wampum across the river Pa-To-Mac and the chopping down of a cherry tree in which the Spirit of Truth resided.

Nacirema culture is characterized by a highly developed market economy which has evolved in a rich natural habitat. While much of the people's time is devoted to economic pursuits, a large part of the fruits of these labors and a considerable portion of the day are spent in ritual activity. The focus of this activity is the human body, the appearance and health of which loom as a dominant concern in the ethos of the people. While such a concern is certainly not unusual, its ceremonial aspects and associated philosophy are unique.

The fundamental belief underlying the whole system appears to be that the human body is ugly and that its natural tendency is to debility and disease. Incarcerated in such a body, man's only hope is to avert these characteristics through the use of the powerful influences of ritual and ceremony. Every household has one or more shrines devoted to this purpose. The more powerful individuals in the society have several shrines in their houses and, in fact, the opulence of a house is often referred to in terms of the number of such ritual centers it possesses. Most houses are of wattle and daub construction, but the shrine rooms of the more wealthy are walled with stone. Poorer families imitate the rich by applying pottery plaques to their shrine walls.

While each family has at least one such shrine, the rituals associated with it are not family ceremonies but are private and secret. The rites are normally only discussed with children, and then only during the period when they are being initiated into these mysteries. I was able, however, to establish sufficient rapport with the natives to examine these shrines and to have the rituals described to me.

The focal point of the shrine is a box or chest which is built into the wall. In this chest are kept the many charms and magical potions without which no native believes he could live. These preparations are secured from a variety of specialized practitioners. The most powerful of these are medicine men, whose assistance must be rewarded with substantial gifts. However, the medicine men do not provide the curative potions for their clients, but decide what the ingredients should be and then write them down in an ancient and secret language. This writing is understood only by the medicine men and by the herbalists who, for another gift, provide the required charm.

The charm is not disposed of after it has served its purpose, but is placed in the charm-box of the household shrine. As these magical materials are specific for certain ills, and the real or imagined maladies of the people are many, the charm-box is usually full to overflowing. The magical packets are so numerous that people forget what their purposes were and fear to use them again. While the natives are very vague on this point, we can only assume that the idea in retaining all the old magical materials is that their presence in the charm-box, before which the body rituals are conducted, will in some way protect the worshipper.

Beneath the charm-box is a small font. Each day every member of the family, in succession, enters the shrine room, bows his head before the charmbox, mingles different sorts of holy water in the font, and proceeds with a brief rite of ablution. The holy waters are secured from the Water Temple of the community, where the priests conduct elaborate ceremonies to make the liquid ritually pure.

In the hierarchy of magical practitioners, and below the medicine men in prestige, are specialists whose designation is best translated "holy-mouth-men." The Nacirema have an almost pathological horror of and fascination with the mouth, the condition of which is believed to have a supernatural influence on all social relationships. Were it not for the rituals of the mouth, they believe that their teeth would fall out, their gums bleed, their jaws shrink, their friends desert them, and their lovers reject them. They also believe that a strong relationship exists between oral and moral characteristics. For example, there is a ritual ablution of the mouth for children which is supposed to improve their moral fiber.

The daily body ritual performed by everyone includes a mouth-rite. Despite the fact that these people are so punctilious about care of the mouth, this rite involves a practice which strikes the uninitiated stranger as revolting. It was reported to me that the ritual consists of inserting a small bundle of hog hairs into the mouth, along with certain magical powders, and then moving the bundle in a highly formalized series of gestures.

In addition to the private mouth-rite, the people seek out a holy-mouth-man once or twice a year. These practitioners have an impressive set of paraphernalia, consisting of a variety of augers, awls, probes, and prods. The use of these objects in the exorcism of the evils of the mouth involves almost unbelievable ritual torture of the client. The holy-mouth-man opens the client's mouth and, using the above mentioned tools, enlarges any holes which decay may have created in the teeth. Magical materials are put into these holes. If there are no naturally occurring holes in the teeth, large sections of one or more teeth are gouged out so that the supernatural substance can be applied. In the client's view, the purpose of these ministrations is to arrest decay and to draw friends. The extremely sacred and traditional character of the rite is evident in the fact that the natives return to the holy-mouth-men year after year, despite the fact that their teeth continue to decay.

It is to be hoped that, when a thorough study of the Nacirema is made, there will be careful inquiry into the personality structure of these people. One has but to watch the gleam in the eye of a holy-mouth-man, as he jabs an awl into an exposed nerve, to suspect that a certain amount of sadism is involved. If this can be established, a very interesting pattern emerges, for most of the population shows definite masochistic tendencies. It was to these that Professor Linton referred in discussing a distinctive part of the daily body ritual which is performed only by men. This part of the rite involves scraping and lacerating the surface of the face with a sharp instrument. Special women's rites are performed only four times during each lunar month, but what they lack in frequency is made up in barbarity. As part of this ceremony, women bake their heads in small ovens for about an hour. The theoretically interesting point is that what seems to be a preponderantly masochistic people have developed sadistic specialists.

The medicine men have an imposing temple, or *latipso,* in every community of any size. The more elaborate ceremonies required to treat very sick patients can only be performed at this temple. These ceremonies involve not only the thaumaturge but a permanent group of vestal maidens who move sedately about the temple chambers in distinctive costume and headdress.

The *latipso* ceremonies are so harsh that it is phenomenal that a fair proportion of the really sick natives who enter the temple ever recover. Small children whose indoctrination is still incomplete have been known to resist attempts to take them to the temple because "that is where you go to die." Despite this fact, sick adults are not only willing but eager to undergo the protracted ritual purification, if they can afford to do so. No matter how ill the supplicant or how grave the emergency, the guardians of many temples will not admit a client if he cannot give a rich gift to the custodian. Even after one has gained admission and survived the ceremonies, the guardians will not permit the neophyte to leave until he makes still another gift.

The supplicant entering the temple is first stripped of all his or her clothes. In every-day life the Nacirema avoids exposure of his body and its natural functions. Bathing and excretory acts are performed only in the secrecy of the household shrine, where they are ritualized as part of the body-rites. Psychological shock results from the fact that body secrecy is suddenly lost upon entry into the *latipso.* A man, whose own wife has never seen him in an excretory act, suddenly finds himself naked and assisted by a vestal maiden while he performs his natural functions into a sacred vessel. This sort of ceremonial treatment is necessitated by the fact that the excreta are used by a diviner to ascertain the course and nature of the client's sickness. Female clients, on the other hand, find their naked bodies are subjected to the scrutiny, manipulation and prodding of the medicine men.

Few supplicants in the temple are well enough to do anything but lie on their hard beds. The daily ceremonies, like the rites of the holy-mouth-men, involve discomfort and torture. With ritual precision, the vestals awaken their miserable charges each dawn and roll them about on their beds of pain while performing ablutions, in the formal movements of which the maidens are highly trained. At other times they insert magic wands in the supplicant's mouth or force him to eat substances which are supposed to be healing. From time to time the medicine men come to their clients and jab magically treated needles into their flesh. The fact that these temple ceremonies may not cure, and may even kill the neophyte, in no way decreases the people's faith in the medicine men.

There remains one other kind of practitioner, known as a "listener." This witch-doctor has the power to exorcise the devils that lodge in the heads of people who have been bewitched. The Nacirema believe that parents bewitch their own children. Mothers are particularly suspected of putting a curse on children while teaching them the secret body rituals. The counter-magic of the witch-doctor is unusual in its lack of ritual. The patient simply tells the "listener" all his troubles and fears, beginning with the earliest difficulties he can remember. The memory displayed by the Nacirema in these exorcism sessions is truly remarkable. It is not uncommon for the patient to bemoan the rejection he felt being weaned as a babe, and a few individuals even see their troubles going back to the traumatic effects of their own birth.

In conclusion, mention must be made of certain practices which have their base in native esthetics but which depend upon the pervasive aversion to the natural body and its functions. There are ritual fasts to make fat people thin and ceremonial feasts to make thin people fat. Still other rites are used to make women's breasts larger if they are small, and smaller if they are large. General dissatisfaction with breast shape is symbolized in the fact that the ideal form is virtually outside the range of human variation. A few women afflicted with almost inhuman hypermammary development are so idolized that they make a handsome living by simply going from village to village and permitting the natives to stare at them for a fee.

Reference has already been made to the fact that excretory functions are ritualized, routinized, and relegated to secrecy. Natural reproductive functions are similarly distorted. Intercourse is taboo as a topic and scheduled as an act. Efforts are made to avoid pregnancy by the use of magical material or by limiting intercourse to certain phases of the moon. Conception is actually very infrequent. When pregnant, women dress so as to hide their condition. Parturition takes place in secret, without friends or relatives to assist, and the majority of women do not nurse their infants.

Our review of the ritual life of the Nacirema has certainly shown them to be a magic-ridden people. It is hard to understand how they have managed to exist so long under the burdens which they have imposed upon themselves. But even such exotic customs as these take on real meaning when they are viewed with the insight provided by Malinowski when he wrote (1948:70):

> Looking from far and above, from our high places of safety in the developed civilization, it is easy to see all the crudity and irrelevance of magic. But without its power and guidance early man could not have mastered his practical difficulties as he has done, nor could man have advanced to the higher stages of civilization.

REFERENCES CITED

Linton, Ralph
    1936   The Study of Man. New York, D. Appleton-Century Co.
Malinowski, Bronislaw
    1948   Magic, Science, and Religion. Glencoe, The Free Press.
Murdock, George P.
    1949   Social Structure. New York, The Macmillan Co.

The native speaks
for himself

$\mathcal{T}$here is something frustrating about reading about the members of culture X as reported by a member of culture Y. It's not that we don't trust the member of culture Y, since in most instances he is a reliable, trained ethnographer and usually the reader himself is also a member of culture Y. Still, one can't help wondering whether the ethnographer's informants would agree with everything the ethnographer says. (The fact that they might not, of course, would not necessarily invalidate what the ethnographer said. People do not always have insight into their own culture and, in any case, there are healthy differences of opinion even within a culture.) Some ethnographers have the policy of allowing their informants to see what they have written and to comment critically, but most of the writing up of field notes takes place back at the ethnographer's home.

One healthy sign that anthropologists are becoming more interested in individual natives and in these individuals' personal views has been the increase in the number of life histories collected. However, the life history is still written by the ethnographer and hence it is in one way or another filtered through

439

his mind and culture before it reaches the written stage and finally the printed page. A method of eliminating the ethnographer's inevitable editorial bias is to inspire natives to write autobiographical statements. Naturally, there will still be bias, but it will be of a different sort. If the native is writing the autobiographical essay for a missionary or for a teacher of a European language, certain content and/or stylistic features will be altered accordingly. Nevertheless, the native does write from the vantage point of a full-fledged member of the culture being described, whereas the ethnographer, no matter how competent he may be, cannot do this. For this reason, native statements are extremely valuable. Even if there is what the ethnographer considers to be distortion, the distortion itself can be invaluable raw data. How and, more importantly, what an individual distorts can tell the sensitive ethnographer a great deal about how that individual thinks about himself and about different aspects of his culture.

The following statements by a Hopi Indian from the southwest United States, a Malinké from West Africa, a young Siamese woman from northeastern Thailand, a Pomo Indian from northern California, and a Kipsigis storyteller from Kenya all reveal important facets of their respective cultures. But of greater significance is the fact that through these fragments, which remain vivid despite the losses of meaning inevitable in translation, the reader can almost see the people behind the ethnography, and in a small way he can come to know individuals of another culture directly, untroubled by an intervening variable in the form of a professional anthropologist. The unusual experience of seeing another culture from the inside-out rather than from the usual outside-in is a rich and rewarding one.

Don C. Talayesva

TWINS TWISTED INTO ONE

One of the classics of autobiographical ethnography is *Sun Chief: The Autobiography of a Hopi Indian.* In this work Don C. Talayesva, a Hopi Indian from Oraibi, Arizona, gives a chronological diary of fifty years of his life. The first chapter, in which he reconstructs his earliest infanthood, is presented here. Despite the fact that the account was written in English rather than Hopi and that there was an editor, the picture of

Reprinted from *Sun Chief: The Autobiography of a Hopi Indian,* ed. Leo W. Simmons (New Haven, 1942), pp. 25–34, by permission of the Yale University Press. Copyright 1942 by Yale University Press.

Hopi culture which emerges is clearly quite different in content and style from conventional ethnographic writing. Of particular interest are the numerous illustrations of the principles of sympathetic magic as outlined by James George Frazer. Also valuable are the details of infant care and the general nature of infant-parent and sibling relationships in Hopi culture.

For further readings on the Hopi, one should consult the standard bibliographical guide for North American Indian studies, George Peter Murdock, *Ethnographic Bibliography of North America,* 3rd ed. (New Haven, 1960). Hopi references may be found on pp. 314–22.

When we were within our mother's womb, we happened to hurt her. She has told me how she went to a medicine man in her pain. He worked on her, felt her breasts and belly, and told her that we were twins. She was surprised and afraid. She said, "But I want only one baby." "Then I will put them together," replied the doctor. He took some corn meal outside the door and sprinkled it to the sun. Then he spun some black and white wool, twisted the threads into a string, and tied it around my mother's left wrist. It is a powerful way to unite babies. We twins began, likewise, to twist ourselves into one child. My mother also helped to bring us together by her strong wish for only one baby.

My mother has described how carefully she carried me. She slept with my father right along, so that he could have intercourse with her and make me grow. It is like irrigating a crop: if a man starts to make a baby and then stops, his wife has a hard time. She had intercourse only with my father so that I could have an easy birth and resemble him.

She refused to hold another woman's child on her lap and took care not to breathe into the face of small children and cause them to waste away. She had nothing to do with the tanning of skins or the dyeing of anything lest she spoil the goods and also injure me. When she grew big, she was careful to sit in such a way that other people would not walk in front of her and thus make my birth difficult. She would not look at the serpent images displayed in the ceremonies, lest I turn myself into a water snake while still in her womb and raise up my head at the time of birth, instead of lying with head down seeking a way out.

My father has related how he took care to injure no animal and thus damage my body. If he had cut off the foot of any living creature, I might have been born without a hand or with a clubfoot. Any cruel treatment of a dumb beast would have endangered my life. If he had drawn a rope too tightly around the neck of a sheep or burro, it might have caused my navel cord to loop itself about my neck and strangle me in birth. Even if I had been able to free myself from the cord, I might have remained half choked and short of breath for a long time.

Whenever I made movements in the womb, my mother was encouraged to expect an early and easy birth. She worked hard at cooking, grinding corn, and bringing water, so that her body would be in trim for labor. My father fed her the raw flesh of a weasel and rubbed the skin on her body so that I could be active and come out swiftly, in the way that sly little animal slips through a hole.

I have heard that I had a hard birth. It began in the early evening of a day in March, 1890. Since the exact date was not remembered, I could never have a birthday. When my mother's face darkened and she felt the expected pains, she settled down on the earthen floor in the third-story room of her Sun Clan house. She had sent my five-year-old sister Tuva-mainim with my little brother Namostewa to a neighbor's house. Namostewa was about two years old and still nursing.

My grandfather (mother's father, Homikniwa of the Lizard Clan), who lived in the same house with my mother and father, has told me how he climbed the ladder to the third floor where my mother lay. There he rubbed her belly and turned me straight to come out. The power in his hands helped her womb. His presence encouraged her, too, because he was the best medicine man in Oraibi. My father, Tuvanimptewa of the Sand Clan, also came in to help, which was rather unusual for a Hopi husband. He soon sent for Nuvaiumsie, an experienced old midwife and a member of his father's linked Water-Coyote Clan. As soon as she came, she heated water in a clay pot over coals in an old-fashioned fireplace in the southwest corner of the room.

In labor, according to all reports, my mother moved over on a pile of sand which was especially prepared for my birth, rested herself on hands and knees, raised her head a little, and began to strain downward. My father and her father took turns standing over her with their arms around her belly, pressing down gently and trying to force and shake me out. If I had refused to come, more and more pressure would have been applied, but no Hopi doctor would have opened her body to get me.

I was a big baby. I caused a lot of trouble and took a long time coming out—head first. Old Nuvaiumsie is said to have taken me fresh and crying from my mother. She cut my navel cord on an arrow to make me a good hunter, folded back my end of the cord, and tied it about a finger's length from the navel to keep out any fresh air. She used a piece of string from my mother's hair, which was the proper thing to do. If she had not tied the cord securely, fresh air would have entered my belly and killed me. My mother was given some small twigs of juniper to chew and some juniper tea, in order to strengthen her and to hasten the discharge of the afterbirth.

My grandfather, my father, and Nuvaiumsie examined me closely. Sure enough, I was twins twisted into one. They could see that I was an oversize baby, that my hair curled itself into two little whorls instead of one at the back of my head, and that in front of my body I was a boy but at the back there was the sure trace of a girl—the imprint of a little vulva that slowly disappeared. They have told me time after time that I was twice lucky—lucky to be born twins and lucky to just miss becoming a girl.

Wrapping me in a cloth, they laid me near the fire and waited for my mother to free herself from the afterbirth. Nuvaiumsie is reported to have taken hold of the free end of the placenta cord and pulled gently, while my father stood behind my mother, held her around the waist, and shook her. She was told to stick her fingers down her throat and gag until she expelled the afterbirth. Finally it came out. Then my mother was placed near the fire in a squatting position on a low stool—perhaps the Hopi birth stool—so that the blood could drip upon the sand. She was given a drink of warm juniper tea to clear out the womb. A little later Nuvaiumsie bathed her in warm yucca suds, wrapped her in a blanket, fed her some warm corn mush, and had her lie on her side before the fire so that the bones could fit back into place. The old lady carefully swept up the sand and blood from the floor with a little broom, placed them with the placenta, the dirty rags, and the broom in an old basket, sprinkled the whole with corn meal, and gave them to my father to throw on the placenta pile. This he did at a special place near the southeast edge of the village, so that no person would step upon them and cause his feet to become sore and chapped, his eyes yellow, and his urine thick.

When all bloody traces of the birth were removed, my father hastened to the house of his mother's sister, Masenimka. He would have fetched his own mother, had she been alive. Masenimka came quickly, bringing a bowl of water, some corn meal, a piece of yucca root, two white corn ears, and some baby wrappings. She came with a smiling face and a happy heart, hoping thereby to bring me good luck and to insure my having a cheerful spirit.

Masenimka has related how she greeted me with tender words, washed my head in warm yucca suds, rinsed it with clear water, and bathed me from head to foot. She rubbed the ashes of juniper or sage bush over my skin to make it smooth and to cause hair to grow only in the right places. Then she pulled up her black dress (*manta*) to her thighs, rested me on her naked knees, and announced that I was her boy and a child of her clan. Chewing some juniper twigs, she spat upon my ear lobes and rubbed them to numbness. Then she pierced them with a sharp instrument and passed a thread through the holes to keep them open. She placed my arms by my sides, wrapped me in a warm baby blanket, and laid me on a wicker cradle made of a frame of bent juniper branches which was filled in with a network of small lemonberry stems and other twigs. There was a face guard of the same material. The cradle was padded with cedar bark or old clothes. A larger blanket was wrapped about me and the cradle and bound tightly with a string. Masenimka sat before the fire with me in the cradle upon her knees for a long time. Then she placed me on the floor near my mother and put an ear of corn on either side, one to represent me and the other my mother.

In the early morning hours when the cocks began to crow, Masenimka took a little finely ground corn meal and rubbed four horizontal lines, one inch wide and six or seven inches long, one above the other, on the four walls of the room. Then she resumed her seat by my mother and me and said, "Now, thus I have made a house for you. You shall stay here while we wait for you twenty days." Soon after she went to her own home and brought over some corn which she cooked with a few small twigs of juniper. This food was to make my mother's milk flow freely. Masenimka might have given her some unsalted gravy and some milkweed for the same purpose, since when that weed is broken the milk runs out.

Before the eastern sky had turned gray, the Sun Clan women propped two poles against the door that faced the rising sun and draped a blanket over them. This was to keep out the sun's rays from the birth chamber, for they were considered harmful until I had been properly presented to the Sun god. By breakfast many neighbors are said to have dropped in, taken a little food, looked me over, congratulated my mother, and expressed best wishes for my life.

I was bathed again by my godmother, Masenimka, who rubbed me anew with juniper ashes or the powder of a special clay found near the village. After my bath I was fastened back in my cradle and given the breast. My brother may have thought that I was stealing his milk, but he could do nothing about it. If my mother had been dry, I would have received the breast of a relative, fed upon finely ground sweet corn mixed with the juice of stewed peaches, been given a little gravy without salt, or perhaps some milk from the cows of the missionaries. If I had taken the breast of another woman, her own nursing baby might have discovered the theft of milk, worried, and even become nervous or sick. Babies are pretty wise about these things and quickly learn what is going on. I could not have taken the breast of another pregnant woman, for that might have caused my death.

For twenty days my mother was not allowed to eat or drink anything cold or salty, lest blood clot in her womb. All her food was cooked with juniper leaves. The fire in our room was kept going. No one was permitted to kindle other fires from it, for this fire belonged to me and such a theft would have made me unhappy. If it had become extinguished through accident, it would have been rekindled immediately, and that day would have gone uncounted. No food could be cooked on the coals themselves, although it might be cooked in a vessel over the fire. Neglect of this rule would have made me a "fire meddler" and caused me to play with fire carelessly in childhood. My father could not have intercourse with my mother during those twenty days, nor for twenty days thereafter. If he had done so before all the blood had drained from my mother's womb, a new baby would have been started which would have worried me, brought on sickness and nervous spells, and perhaps spoiled me for life. Had he attempted intercourse, the sisters and clan sisters of my mother would have interfered. If he had had intercourse with some other woman and then had an argument with my mother over it, that would have been almost as hard on me, for I would have sensed that something was wrong.

A routine was set up for me. Every morning I was unbound, bathed, rubbed with "baby ashes," and put back on the cradle. A little pad of cloth was placed at the back of my neck to keep me from becoming bull-necked and soft cedar bark was placed under my buttocks to drain off the urine. Someone probably cleaned me three or four times a day. I was always fed in the cradle and could move only my head a little in nursing. I do not know that anyone took saliva from my mouth and rubbed it on the nape of my neck to conceal my crying from the evil spirits, as is done with many Hopi babies.

When my navel cord dried and dropped off, it was tied to an arrow and stuck beside a beam overhead in the room. This was to make me a good hunter and to provide a "house" for my infant spirit in case I died, for my soul could then stay by the arrow in the ceiling and quickly slip back into my mother's womb for an early rebirth.

On the fifth morning I was bathed as usual, but with a special application of yucca suds to my head. My mother's head also was washed with the suds, and her body bathed with warm water in which juniper leaves had been boiled. Her clothes were changed and the soiled ones were taken to a near-by rock cistern and washed. After our bath my mother scraped off the lowermost of the four lines of meal from the walls of the room. She took the scrapings in her hand, and going to the edge of the mesa, held them to her lips, prayed for my long life, and sprinkled the meal to the rising sun. On the tenth and fifteenth days the same ceremony of bathing and prayers to the sun was repeated. If I had been the first baby, my mother could not have gone out before the sun on the fifth day and thereafter. Had she been too sick or weak to go, my godmother would have gone for her. The water with which our bodies had been bathed was carried to the placenta pile and emptied there.

On the twentieth day of my life I was named according to strict custom. About four o'clock in the morning Masenimka and her sisters, Kewanmainim and Iswuhti, and many other clan aunts—any woman of my father's clan and linked clans—came to our house to wash our heads again. Masenimka first washed the two "mother corn" ears in the yucca suds, rinsing them with fresh water. These were the ears that had been by my side since the night of my birth. Then she washed my mother's head, as did all her sisters in turn. Fresh water was poured over it, after which her hair was wrung out dry. They also bathed her arms and shoulders with warm water which had a few sprigs of juniper in it. Sweeping a little sand from the corner into the center of the room, they heated a stone, set it upon the sand, and laid yucca roots and juniper leaves on top of it. My mother stood with her right foot and then her left resting upon this heap of sand, stones, roots, and leaves while Masenimka bathed them. The entire heap was then placed in a tray along with the broom that was used to sweep the floor. The last of the corn-meal lines from each wall was scraped off and the dust thrown on the tray. A live ember from the fireplace was put on top and the fire permitted to go out. One of the women took the tray and its contents and some of the bath water and carried them to the placenta pile.

Within a few minutes the customary naming ceremony began. Masenimka unfastened the wrappings that bound me to the cradle, stripped me bare, and washed my head in a bowl of yucca suds. Then she bathed me from head to foot, rubbing on the "baby ashes." My head was rinsed in fresh water and each of my many aunts bathed me in the same manner, one after the other. The last one handed me back to Masenimka, who wrapped me in a blanket that had been warmed by the fire. My bath water—like my mother's—was handled with care and carried out to the placenta pile. During so many baths I probably cried a little, but no one has reported it.

Masenimka took me again on her left arm, picked up my "mother corn" ears with her right hand, waved them forward over my chest, and said, "May you live always without sickness, travel along the Sun Trail to old age, and pass away in sleep without pain. And your name shall be Chuka." Chuka means mud, a mixture of sand and clay. Masenimka and my father are of the Sand Clan, which made my name appropriate. This name was a sign to everyone that although I was born into the Sun Clan of my mother I was also a "child of the Sand Clan" and that my father and all his clan relatives had a claim on me. Each aunt repeated the ceremony and each gave me another Sand, Lizard, Earth, or Snake Clan name, but they have been forgotten. Even if I had never been told these things about myself I could be sure that they happened, for there is no other way for a new child to get a good name among the Hopi.

After the naming ceremony most of the women went back to their houses. But just before sunrise Masenimka placed me in a blanket upon her back and started with my mother to the edge of the mesa where they were to present me to the Sun god. Each took along a pinch of corn meal, and my mother carried my pair of mother-corn ears. They stopped with me southeast of the village where the trail leaves the mesa. This is a kind of "highway" of the Sun god, the main Sun Trail for the Oraibi people.

My mother took me with the cradle and blanket from Masenimka's back and placed me on the right arm of my godmother. Masenimka, thus holding me before the Sun god, breathed a silent prayer on a pinch of meal which she held in her right hand. Then she uncovered my face to the early dawn with her left hand in the proper way, rubbed some of the sacred corn meal between my lips, and threw the rest to the rising sun. She then sucked the meal from my lips with her mouth and blew it toward the east four times. Taking the ears of corn from my mother, she extended them toward the east with a circular motion from right to left and brought them close up to my chest four times. As she concluded she prayed again for my long life and called out to the Sun god the different names that I had received, in order that he might hear them and recognize me. It was my mother's privilege to take me in her arms and repeat the same ceremony, but it is not required by Hopi rules, and I have never learned whether she did it or not.

When we returned to the house where my father had just washed his own head in yucca suds, a big breakfast feast was served to relatives and friends. They were invited to eat *piki* (native wafer bread), boiled meat mixed with hominy, puddings, and other choice foods. Masenimka received a big load of food in payment for her services as my godmother and carried it home on her back. Many of my mother's sisters and clan sisters were present and were all called my "mothers," while the sisters and clan sisters of my father were called my "aunts." The Sun Clan men who came and ate were called my "uncles," while my father's brothers and clan brothers were all called my "fathers." Almost everyone praised my mother, made hopeful remarks about me, and predicted that I would become a good hunter, a fine herder, and perhaps a powerful healer, for I was a special baby—twins twisted into one. There was no doubt about this, for they could see the two whorls of hair on the back of my head, and those present at my birth told others how large and double-sexed I looked when fresh from the womb. All knew that such babies are called antelopes because these animals are usually born twins. It was anticipated, therefore, that I would have a special power to protect myself, do many strange things before the people, and be able to heal certain diseases, even as a boy. My mother, father, and grandfather made careful note of these signs and sayings and were prepared to fill my mind with them as soon as I could know anything.

I have learned little about my babyhood, except such treatment as is shared by all Hopi children. The first three or four months of my life were spent on my back on the cradle. Like other babies, my hands were bound securely so that I could not awaken myself by movements, and it is reported that I was a good sleeper. Even when awake I rarely had a chance to touch my face or body, and my legs were wrapped in blankets which prevented much kicking. The cradle was placed flat on the floor and the face guard was usually covered with a cloth to exclude flies, but this also kept me in semidarkness. The back of my head flattened itself against the cradle.

I had many kinds of soft food stuck into my mouth and I could get the breast almost any time I cried. My mother was almost always present but I could touch or nestle up to her very little, for I was off the cradle only to be cleaned or for a morning bath, and was rebound before nursing. Of course the people talked baby talk to me, passed me from lap to lap on the cradle, rocked or shook me to sleep on their knees, and often sang to me. I am sure my father and grandfather sang many songs with me on their laps at the close of the day, and before I could remember anything.

At mealtime my cradle was placed on the floor near the food, and first one and then another member of the family would chew up a morsel—piki, stewed meat, dried peaches, corn mush, cantaloupe or watermelon—and feed me from their fingers.

By early fall I was permitted off the cradle during the day and crawled naked over the earthen floor or rolled about in the sunshine on the roof of our winter house. I urinated any time and at any place, but whenever I started to defecate, someone picked me up and held me just outside the door. Dogs, cats, and my brother were my constant playmates. My sister became my nurse and often carried me wrapped in a blanket on her back. On other occasions my mother ground corn with me fastened to her back, or took me with her to the spring or rock cisterns for water. But she often left me to play on the ground under the watchful eye of her crippled brother, Naquima, who lived with us. I had now learned to suck my thumb, my "whole fist," reports my father. I had probably discovered pleasure in my penis, too, for every male child was tickled in his private parts by adults who wished to win smiles and sometimes to stop crying. No doubt other children, including my brother and sister, played with me in the same way.

Whenever the Katcinas danced in the plaza,[1] my mother or some relative sat on the ground with me on their laps and held out my infant hands to receive gifts—peaches, apples, sweet corn, and other blessings.

Before the snows came, we moved down the ladder to our winter house, where I could play on the floor all day and stay up by the fire at night until I wished to sleep. I still slept on my cradle after I had begun to walk and talk at about two. It seemed that I was restless without it. My mother has told me how I would drag it to her crying, "Ache," which means sleep. But several people have agreed that I was never a cry baby. I was healthy, grew rapidly, and surpassed other babies in size. I was still nursing when my mother gave birth to another child. This baby died, so I kept on getting the breast.

Camara Laye

A MALINKÉ REMEMBERS HIS MOTHER

In our culture education is considered a solution for many problems. Through education, we argue, comes progress and a better life. Yet education also causes new problems. It may estrange an individual from his original culture, making it impossible for him to live as happily as he might have without such education. Camara Laye, a Malinké born in Kouroussa, French Guinea in West Africa, was educated at a French school in Conakry (a major city about four hundred miles from Kouroussa) and eventually at a school at Argenteuil, not far from Paris. In this selection from his autobiography we can see how he has been taught to doubt his own culture. In one sense it is sad to see someone apologetic about the values and beliefs of his people. If the price of Western education includes dis-

[1][Katcinas are beneficent supernatural beings, presumably mythical ancestors of the present Hopi people. The term also refers to the small wooden doll-like figures which adults carve and decorate to represent individual katcina beings. The katcina dolls are given to the children during the season when the katcina spirits are above ground. These spirits are worshipped through ritual dances, often involving masks. The uninitiated—that is, most women and all children,—believe that the dancers are the actual katcina spirits. For a sample of the considerable literature on this subject, see J. W. Fewkes, *Hopi Katcinas,* Annual Report of the Bureau of American Ethnology 21 (Washington, 1903), E. A. Kennard, *Hopi Kachinas* (New York, 1938), Elsie Clews Parson, *Pueblo Indian Religion,* 2 vols (Chicago, 1939), and H. S. Colton, *Hopi Kachina Dolls* (Albuquerque, 1959).—*Ed. Note.*]

illusion with one's family and life, then one must proceed cautiously with well intentioned plans to bring Western ideologies to those without it. Otherwise, a Western education in fact creates marginal men, men who cannot truly compete with the Europeans who provided the education and who can no longer live happily among their own people. Such men, regarded as second-class citizens by the European colonial overlords and regarded as not-to-be-trusted Europeanized turncoats by their own society, are often doomed to frustration-filled lives.

For a number of sensitive sketches of Africans trapped between two worlds, see Colin M. Turnbull, *The Lonely African* (New York, 1962). For other African autobiographies, see Rupert East, ed., *Akiga's Story: The Tiv Tribe as Seen by One of Its Members* (London, 1939), and R. Mugo Gatheru, *Child of Two Worlds: A Kikuyu's Story* (New York, 1964). For further information about the Malinké, see the references (most of which are in French) in Ruth Jones, comp., *Africa Bibliography Series: West Africa* (London, 1958), pp. 64–65.

At Kouroussa I lived in my mother's hut. But, since the huts were so small, my brothers and sisters, all of whom were younger than I, slept in my father's mother's hut. My mother kept my brothers and sisters in her hut while nursing them. But as soon as they were weaned—among my people children are weaned very late—she turned them over to my grandmother. I was the only one of her children who lived with her. But I did not have the second bed to myself: I shared it with my father's youngest apprentices.

My father always had lots of apprentices in his workshop; they came from far and near, often from very remote districts, mainly, I think, because he treated them well, but above all because his skill as a craftsman was widely acknowledged, and also, I imagine, because there was always plenty of work at his forge. But these apprentices had to have somewhere to sleep.

Those who had reached manhood had their own hut. The youngest, those who, like me, were still uncircumcised, slept in my mother's hut. My father certainly thought they could have no better lodging. My mother was very kind, very correct. She also had great authority, and kept an eye on everything we did; so that her kindness was not altogether untempered by severity. But how could it have been otherwise, when there were at that time, apart from the apprentices, a dozen children running about the concession, children who were not good all the time, but always so full of life that they must often have sorely tried their mother's patience—and my mother was not a very patient woman.

I see now that she was more patient with the apprentices than she was with her own children. She put herself out for them more than she did for us. These apprentices were far from home, and both my mother and father were very affectionate with them, coddling them like babies, and indulging them more than they did their own children. My mother's chief concern I certainly was, but she did not show it. The apprentices were encouraged to believe themselves on an equal footing with the master's children. I thought of them as elder brothers.

I remember one of them particularly: Sidafa. He was a little older than myself, very lively, thin but vigorous, hot-blooded, always full of projects and ideas of every kind. As my days were spent at school, and his in the workshop, the only time we had for chattering was when we went to bed. The air in the hut was warm, and the oil lamps at the side of the bed cast a dim light. I would repeat to Sidafa what I had been learning at school: and he for his part would recount in detail all that had gone on in the workshop. My mother, whose bed was separated from ours only by the width of the hearth, had of necessity to listen to our chatter. At least she listened for a while but soon wearied of it.

"Have you gone to bed to chatter or to sleep?" she would say. "Go to sleep!"

"Just a minute. I haven't finished my story," I would plead.

Or I would get up and take a drink of water to the canary who had gone dry as he perched over his bed of gravel. But the reprieve I asked for was not always granted, and, when it was, we took such advantage of it that my mother would interrupt us sharply:

"Now that's enough!" she would say. "I don't want to hear another word! You'll neither of you be able to get up in the morning."

Which was true: if we were never in any great hurry to go to sleep, neither were we ever in any great hurry to get up. We would stop chattering. The beds were too near to my mother's sharp ears for us to be able to talk in whispers. And, then, as soon as we were quiet, we very quickly felt our eyes grow weary; the cozy crackling of the fire and the warmth of the bedclothes did the rest: we gradually drifted into sleep.

In the morning when, after some persuasion, we rose, we found the breakfast ready. My mother awoke at dawn to prepare it. We all sat around the great steaming dishes: my parents, sisters, brothers, and the apprentices, those who shared my bed as well as those who had their own hut. There was one dish for the men, and another for my mother and my sisters.

It would not be exactly right for me to say that my mother presided over the meal: my father presided over it. Nevertheless, it was the presence of my mother that made itself felt first of all. Was that because she had prepared the food, because meals are things which are mainly a woman's business? Maybe. But there was something more: my mother, by the mere fact of her presence, and even though she was not seated directly in front of the men's dish, saw to it that everything was done according to her own rules; and those rules were strict.

Thus it was forbidden to cast my gaze upon guests older than myself, and I was also forbidden to talk: my whole attention had to be fixed on the food before me. In fact, it would have been most impolite to chatter at that moment. Even my younger brothers knew that this was no time to jabber: this was the hour to pay honor to the food. Older people observed more or less the same silence. This was not the only rule: those concerning cleanliness were no less important. Finally, if there was meat on the dish, I was not allowed to take it from the centre of the dish, but only from the part directly in front of me, and my father would put more within my reach if he saw I needed it. Any other behavior would have been frowned upon and quickly reprimanded. In any case, my portion was always so plentiful that I should never have been tempted to take more than I was given.

When the meal was over, I would say: "Thank you, Father."

The apprentices would say: "Thank you, master."

Then I would bow to my mother and say: "The meal was good, Mother."

My brothers, my sisters, the apprentices did likewise. My parents replied, "Thank you," to each one of them. Such was the rule. My father would certainly have been offended to see it broken, but it was my mother, with her quicker temper, who rebuked any transgression. My father's mind was with his work, and he left these prerogatives to her.

I realize that my mother's authoritarian attitudes may appear surprising; generally the role of the Africa woman is thought to be a ridiculously humble one, and indeed there are parts of the continent where it is insignificant; but Africa is vast, with a diversity equal to its vastness. The woman's role in our country is one of fundamental independence, of great inner pride. We despise only those who allow themselves to be despised; and our women very seldom give cause for that. My father would never have dreamed of despising anyone, least of all my mother. He had the greatest respect for her too, and so did our friends and neighbors. That was due, I am sure, to my mother's character, which was impressive; it was due also to the strange powers she possessed.

I hesitate to say what these powers were, and I do not wish to describe them all. I know that what I say will be greeted with skeptical smiles. And today, now that I come to remember them, even I hardly know how I should regard them. They seem to be unbelievable; they *are* unbelievable. Nevertheless I can only tell you what I saw with my own eyes. How can I disown the testimony of my own eyes? Those unbelievable things. I saw them. I see them again as I saw them then. Are there not things around us, everywhere, which are inexplicable? In our country there were mysteries without number, and my mother was familiar with them all.

One day—it was toward evening—I saw some men request her to use her powers to get a horse on his feet after he had resisted all attempts to make him rise. He was out at pasture, but he was lying down, and his owner wanted to bring him back to the stable before nightfall. The horse obstinately refused to move, although there was no apparent reason why he should disobey. But his inclination was otherwise, though it might have been a magic spell that immobilized him. I heard the men telling my mother about it, and asking her help.

"Well, then, let's go and have a look at this horse," said my mother. She called the eldest of my sisters and told her to look after the cooking of the evening meal, and then went off with the men. I followed her. When we arrived at the pasture, we saw the horse: he was lying in the grass, gazing at us unconcernedly. His owner tried again to make him get up and spoke to him in honeyed tones, but the horse remained deaf to all entreaty. His master raised a hand to strike him.

"Do not strike him," said my mother. "It won't do any good."

She went up to the horse and, lifting her own hand, declaimed in a solemn tone: "If it is true that from the day of my birth I had knowledge of no man until the day of my marriage: and if it is true that from the day of my marriage I have had knowledge of no man other than my lawful husband—if these things be true, then I command you, horse, rise up!"

And we all saw the horse get up at once and follow his master quietly away. I have told in very simple words, and very exact words, what I saw then, with my own eyes, and to my mind it is unbelievable; but the event was just as I have described it: the horse got up without any further delay and followed his master: if he had refused to follow him, my mother's intervention would once more have had its effect.

Where did these powers come from? Well, my mother was the next child born after my twin uncles in Tindican. Now, they say that twin brothers are wiser than other children, and are practically magicians. As for the child that follows them, and who receives the name *sayon*, that is, the younger brother of twins, he too is endowed with the gift of magic, and he is even considered to be more powerful and more mysterious than the twins in whose lives he plays a very important role. So if twins fall out, it is to the *sayon's* authority that one appeals to settle the matter; indeed, he is accredited with a wisdom greater than that of the twins, and is given a superior position. It goes without saying that his intervention is conducted, must be conducted, in the most tactful way.

It is the custom with us for twins to agree about everything, and they are to have by right a more precise equality of treatment than is accorded to other children: if something is given to one the other must be given the same thing also. It is an obligation which must never be disregarded; if it is, the twins are equally hurt, settle the matter between themselves, and in certain cases cast a spell upon the person who has injured them. If any kind of dispute should arise between them—if one, for example, has a plan which the other thinks is foolish—they make an appeal to their younger brother and are happy to accept his decision.

I don't know if my mother had often had to intervene between my twin uncles, but even if she did so infrequently it was still enough to lead her, very early in life, to weigh the pros and cons of things and to make her own judgments. If it was said of the *sayon* that he was wiser than his twin brothers, the reason was clear: the *sayon* assumed heavier responsibilities than the twins.

I have given one example of my mother's supernatural powers; I could give many others, equally strange, equally mysterious. How many times I have seen her, at daybreak, walk a few steps into the yard and turn her head in one direction or another to shout at the top of her voice:

"If this business goes any further, I shall not hesitate to expose you. That's my final word!"

In the early morning her voice traveled far: it was intended to reach the ears of the witch-doctor, for whom the warning had been uttered. He understood that if he did not stop his nocturnal activities, my mother would denounce him in public; and this threat always worked: from then on, the witch-doctor kept quiet. My mother used to receive warning of these activities while she was asleep. We never wakened her, for fear of interrupting the course of the revelations that flowed through her dreams. This power was well known by our neighbors and by the whole community: no one ever doubted it.

Though my mother could see what evil was being hatched and could denounce the author of it, her power went no further. Even if she had wished, her power to cast spells did not allow her to do any evil on her own account. She was never suspect. If people made themselves pleasant to her, it was not at all out of fear. They were pleasant because they thought she deserved it, and because they respected her power to cast spells from which nothing was to be feared. On the contrary, much was to be hoped from them.

As well as this gift, or rather part-gift, of magic, my mother had other powers that she had inherited in the same way. At Tindican her father had been a skillful blacksmith, and my mother possessed the usual powers of that caste from which the majority of circumcisers and many soothsayers are drawn. My mother's brothers had chosen to be farmers, but if they had not followed their father's trade that was their own affair. Perhaps my Uncle Lansana, the silent one who was a great dreamer, in fixing his choice upon a farm-worker's life, upon the immense peace of the fields, had led his brothers away from the paternal forge. Was he, also, a soothsayer? I am inclined to think he was. He had the customary powers of a twin, and the powers of his caste; only I do not think that he exhibited them very often. I have already spoken of how reserved his manner was, of how much he liked to be alone with his thoughts, of how absent-minded he seemed. No. He was not the man to make a display of these powers. It was in my mother that the spirit of her caste was most visibly—I was going to say ostensibly—manifested. I don't pretend that she was more faithful to it than my uncles were, but she alone demonstrated her fidelity. Finally, she had inherited, as a matter of course, my grandfather's totem which is the crocodile. This totem allowed all Damans to draw water from the Niger without running any danger of harm.

Normally, everyone draws water from the river. The Niger flows slowly and abundantly; it can be forded; and the crocodiles, which keep to the deep water upstream or downstream from where the water is drawn, are not to be feared. You can bathe quite freely on the banks of pale sand and do your washing there.

But when the water rises, the volume of the river is increased three-fold. The water is deep, and the crocodiles are dangerous. One can see their triangular heads breaking the surface. Everyone, therefore, keeps away from the river and instead draws water from the little streams.

My mother used to continue to draw water from the river. I watched her draw it from the place where the crocodiles were. Naturally I watched her from a distance, for my totem is not my mother's. And I had every reason to fear those voracious beasts; but my mother could draw water without fear, and no one warned her of the danger, because everyone knew that the danger did not exist for her. Whoever else had ventured to do what my mother used to do would inevitably have been knocked down by a blow from a powerful tail, seized in the terrible jaws and dragged into deep water. But the crocodiles could do no harm to my mother; and this privilege is quite understandable: the totem is identified with its possessor: this identification is absolute, and of such a nature that its possessor has the power to take on the form of the totem itself; it follows quite obviously that the totem can not devour itself. My uncles at Tindican enjoyed the same prerogative.

I do not wish to say more, and I have told you only what I saw with my own eyes. These miracles—they were miracles indeed—I think about now as if they were the fabulous events of a far-off past. That past is, however, still quite near: it was only yesterday. But the world rolls on, the world changes, my own world perhaps more rapidly than anyone else's; so that it appears as if we are ceasing to be what we were, and that truly we are no longer what we were, and that we were not exactly ourselves even at the time when these miracles took place before our eyes. Yes, the world rolls on, the world changes; it rolls on and changes, and the proof of it is that my own totem—I too have my totem—is still unknown to me.

Prajuab Tirabutana

RECOLLECTIONS
FROM A SIAMESE GIRLHOOD

The majority of anthropologically useful autobiographies and life histories are about males. However, there are a few female autobiographies and hopefully there will be more. The author of this autobiography is a modern young Siamese woman— Prajuab Tirabutana. Born in the late thirties in a provincial town in northeastern Thailand, she is not a professional writer at all. While operating a small dress shop in the town of Ubol in 1957, she attended classes in English taught by Mr. Clifford John Allen who had come from England to teach in a Thailand UNESCO center. As it happened, anthropologist Lauriston Sharp of Cornell University came to Ubol in the fall of 1957 to conduct fieldwork there. During his stay, he met Mr. Allen and suggested that he encourage his Siamese students to write autobiographies. One of the autobiographies was written by

Reprinted in abridged form from Prajuab Tirabutana, *A Simple One: The Story of a Siamese Girlhood,* Papers of the Cornell University Southeast Asia Program No. 30 (Ithaca, 1958), by permission of Lauriston Sharp.

Miss Tirabutana and it was published as one of the Cornell University Southeast Asia Program Data Papers.

In the following selected excerpts from the forty-page autobiography, the reader may learn of Miss Tirabutana's attitudes toward Christianity, the English language, and many other aspects of culture. But most important of all are the valuable insights into portions of Thai culture, which might be overlooked by the inexperienced observer. One such aspect of Thai culture is eye contact. It is extremely difficult to study eye expression, but it is certainly a significant part of a cultural communications system and it is a crucial one in Thai interpersonal relations, judging from the evidence provided by this unique, sensitive autobiographical fragment.

For further information about Thai culture, see Lauriston Sharp, Frank J. Moore, Walter F. Vella, *et. al.*, *Thailand* (New Haven, 1956).

My English is not good enough to write at all, but Mr. Clifford John Allen encouraged his students to write. When I had finished, nobody could make head or tail out of it if he did not correct the spelling and the grammars of what I had written. So if anybody sees any good of this story, please give it all to him.

Ubol, Thailand   Prajuab Tirabutana
May, 1958

The first year in this school we had to study the English language. One day the teacher called me up to read English in front of the class. I could read it well. The teacher admired me a lot but when the other pupils could not read some words in the middle of the page, she told me to read it for them but I could not either. So she found that I could only say those words by heart but if she pointed to the same word in another place I could not read it. She took all her admiration back by the look of her eyes.

In the last term in my first year in this school grandfather died. All I remember was there were so many people in our house and I could not go near grandmother. She was busy doing something all the time and told the servant to take me away from her. One day, a few days after grandfather's death, I came home and saw grandmother and mother had shaved their heads and dressed in white. It was so strange. I felt uneasy. After grandfather's funeral, at night grandmother told me to come to sit in front of her. She held my head with her both hands and looked deep into my eyes for a while, stroked my hair and said: "Tomorrow when you come back from school you won't see mother and grandmother." She always called herself grandmother [jaaj] with us, she had never called herself "I." I started to cry: "No, no, no tears darling, you must be brave. Grandmother will just go to stay in the temple. You can go to see grandmother now and then, and your sister will stay here with you, too, so it won't be so bad. She would play with you and you won't be lonely. Grandmother can't live with you for ever. Grandmother has to die some day, and that day won't be long. So you must make your heart used to it and be a good girl as you used to be when grandmother was with you". All these words called more tears.

Next morning I did not want to go to school so I made a lot of fuss with the servant who took care of me. Grandmother had to do everything for me and saw my sister and I off to school. All day long the thought that one day grandmother had to die haunted me. Oh! Why had a precious, gentle, sweet person like that to die? And then the tears ran down quickly and I was ready to quarrel and fight with anybody who was in my way. . . .

The end of the first term of the second year in school something happened. One night I was holding a long stick when my niece (two years younger than me) pushed the other end of that stick. The other end knocked a few glasses down from the shelves and all were broken. Brother-in-law threw all the blame on me without asking a word. He said I was the naughtiest girl in the world and hit my hand. I could not bear such injustice. I waited till they did not pay attention to me. I went to the backyard without anybody seeing me. I climbed over the back fence to the dark lane. I did not know how late it was but it seemed everything was so quiet. At first the spirits which the servant had told me about came to my thought, I was so afraid. But on the other hand I remembered that grandmother said there were no spirits, I felt quite sure of myself. So I walked along in the desolate, dark street. When I reached the place where grandmother and mother lived in the temple, there was no light inside, every body had gone to sleep. I called grandmother many times before she could hear me, everyone woke up too. Grandmother came to open the door for me. She was so surprised, I ran with tears to embrace her. She pushed me out and asked what was the matter and did I tell my sister when I came out here. I told her every thing. She sent someone to tell my big sister about me right away, and scolded me and said that what I did was completely wrong. But when I looked into her eyes I knew that she was not angry with me. Well, it did not matter what she said then. The person whom grandmother sent to the sister came back while I was in bed but I was not asleep yet. So I heard her tell grandmother that they both were very much frightened and worried, they went to look for me all round that area, but they did not think a bit that I would be brave enough to come out here. Most of the people at that time still were afraid of spirits so when they heard about this event they stared at me with surprise. Grandmother let me stay with her and the happiest thing was that there were not many beds there so she had to let me sleep in the same bed with her and how comfortable and happy it was to cuddle in her warm chest and go to sleep. . . .

While I was here I had dreamt twice that grandmother died. I woke up startled in the middle of the night and cried out loud with sorrow and fright and kept saying: "Grandmother don't you die, don't go away from me". It took a long time for them to soothe me down.

The teacher who was the mistress in our class was very fond of me. One day she asked me to return an exercise book to a pupil in the fifth year class which was up stairs. I went up and saw that I did not want to disturb them so I passed by and looked at that student [and] told her by the eyes that this book was hers. And then I placed the book down on the floor outside the room. As I was descending the stairs that teacher called me with a cross voice. I returned to her in the room. She asked me what I was doing. I did not like the way she made her voice and her acting. So I said, "Putting the book on the floor." She asked that I did so if it was because I wanted to give the book to some one in the room. I said yes. She said then I had to take the book and come in and ask for her permission. I did as she ordered but abruptly. She told me to say it again as she told me. Why, what was wrong with her, what did she eat today that made her be so cross? You did not say nicely yourself, why should I? I talked to myself. So I did it in my own way, which meant the same. She was mad and told me with a loud and sharp voice to say it again. I lost my patience. Why, I had done that because I meant good, I did not want to stir their concentration. I threw the book on the floor and walked away quickly.[1] She was burst out, her face was red with anger. She screamed out hysterically and told her two pupils to run after and catch me. I did not let them touch me and came down to my classroom with rage. A few minutes later a pupil came in our room and gave a note to our mistress. She read it and asked me what had happened. I told her. She said that teacher had asked her to spank me three times and she said she sympathized me but she had to spank me. I held out my hand, she just dropped the ruler on my hand slightly. It was terrible to be punished by the one you loved and thought that one loved you all the time. I could not bear it, I came back to the seat with the tears dropping down like rains. Packing up my things and went right home. Next day the news was spread all over the school, but fortunately all of the teachers hated that teacher because of her bad temper so they looked at me with sympathetic eyes, that soothed me down. . . .

The end of year holiday my brother came home again with the books. Some were medical books. They were written in English. I could not read them but there were many pictures in them. They were curious pictures so I started to ask him about them. At first he thought I asked just for fun

[1][In his review of Miss Tirabutana's autobiography, Herbert Phillips observes that her running away from trouble rather than attempting to deal with it was characteristic of Thai culture. (Note her running away after being punished unjustly by her brother-in-law.) However, he cautions that she is not a typical Thai insofar as she tends to be more introspective, candid, and emotionally articulate than most Siamese. See Herbert P. Phillips, "Review of *A Simple One*," *American Anthropologist*, 62 (1960), 536–37. Those interested in learning more about Thai psychology should read Phillips, *Thai Peasant Personality: The Patterning of Interpersonal Behavior in the Village of Bang Chan* (Berkeley, 1965).—*Ed. Note.*]

so he explained shortly. But I bestowed question after question to him earnestly, so he explained on and on and when he got tired, he wanted to stop but he saw the eagerness in my eyes, he could not stop. It was like this night after night till the holiday was over. We began to be close to each other. . . .

Grandmother died shortly after we came home. She went easily and quickly by fainting at five o'clock in the early morning. When the seventh sister tortured me I used to go to grandmother and cry it out with her. She always said I was grown up now and had to be patient and try hard to hold in my tears because it would show my weakness. All the people had to suffer from one thing or another, she added. So the first day and the second day that she had gone, I tried very hard not to let the tears come out. "I must be brave, I must be brave." I kept saying to myself, But oh, it was terrible when the tears dropped inside, grandmother. I could not bear such feeling anymore. So the tears burst out like a broken dam on the third day. . . .

The oldest sister owned a bus and sometimes the bus had to go to the villages where there was no road to lead in to them. She knew that I loved to see different places so she invited me to go often. One time mother went into a deep village which was surrounded by mountains far from our town. She was sick of malaria, the oldest sister and I had to go to fetch her home. It was about fifty kilometres from the road. We had to go by ox-cart on foot through the green forest. I liked to see various kinds of trees and the plants near by the mountains, it just full of many kinds of ferns and watched those villagers' children, their eyes were so innocent. I got much experience out of that trip.

My sister had a friend who lived close by at an American Christian Pastor's house. I had been thinking about learning English all the time and kept saying so to my sister. My oldest sister said I should learn Chinese which would be useful to my job, but my father did not approve, he said it was useful all right but you had to learn more than ten years before you could use it in writing and reading, English was better, he added. So my sister asked her friend if the Pastor's wife had time and would like to teach English. When we got word from her that she did not mind, we went to study together. She could talk Thai so she talked Thai to us all the time. And the book that she used to teach us was the Bible. She kept talking just about God and Jesus and the miracles that He did. Well, I did not see that all those miracles He had done were any better than those miracles of the spirits which I had read about since I was a child or those of the spirits which some of the villages believed in. After she had told us all of Jesus and God, tried hard to persuade us to be Christians to which we listened with disinterest, she threw out her last card by emphasizing that "All the people who don't believe in God and Jesus the Redeemer will be sent to the deep hot hell." I came home with an agitated and rather frightened mind. I told father all about what she had said. Father popped his eyes with great surprise and said, "Why, I had thought that white people were clever. Who can help you out of hell if you do just bad things. And who can draw you to hell if you do just good and proper things. I don't believe that Jesus would say so. It sounds like dictatorship to me, may be it's the pastor's wife who made that expression up. Why don't you ask her what Jesus told the people to do?" Next time I went to see her I came back to tell father that, "She said, Jesus said, God said, don't steal, don't lie, don't kill *man,* don't have any things that will make you drunk, don't make love to other people's wives or husbands, don't mention other god's name in front of Him, honour your parents, don't worship any idol except Him because He is the only true God, don't have doubts at what He said, don't covet your neighbour's house, don't be fault witness, don't say His name in vain, don't find reason in what He said, and be the good sheep for Him to lead because one who follows His track will never be in danger. And he said don't be angry easily, if some one slaps your right cheek turn your left cheek for them to slap it again. And love your neighbour like you love yourself, and God will give everything to the one who has faith in Him, but He will help just the one who help themselves." Father said, "That was not bad, but you might want to know what Buddha said." He said, don't steal, don't lie, don't *kill,* don't have any thing that will make you drunk, don't make love to other people's wives or husbands. And if you are going to do or to say anything, think it over first so that if the other people do or say the same thing to you, you will approve or you will like it or not. If you like it, all right go ahead say or do it. If you think, no you won't like it, then stop your statement or your action, and avoid every thing that will lead you into a quarrel but if you can't avoid it you must bear the consequences bravely and calmly. And every body has to be sad or suffer for one thing or other, we are the same all over the world so be kind, be sympathetic to every body, don't be jealous, be glad when others get better than you. And you must train your heart to be neutral. The one whom you can and you must depend on is yourself. And for the believing, one day when Buddha was going to preach in Kalama, the people there asked him "You see, our town is near by the high way so there are many preachers who come to preach to us, one said this, the other said that. What will we do? What should we believe?" Buddha said, "Oh yes, it is natural for you to be confused and doubtful, the belief that you don't approve it by yourself should not be in your mind. You should not decide to believe it because of these causes:

Because you have heard it is so.
Because it is the traditions, or old saying.
Because it is spoken by many people.
Because it is in the books.
Because you guess it should be so.
Because of your assumption.
Because you anticipate that it should be so.
Because it was the same as what you have believed before.

Because the speaker is the one you should trust.
Because this speaker, this preacher, is your teacher.

When you have thought carefully and are sure yourself that this preaching is good, this preaching has no bad effect on the one who does it, if you do it, noble people will admire you, if you do it completely it will be good, it will be happiness for yourself and for other people. There, then you should believe it."

She persuaded us to go to her church every Sunday. The Thai preachers who had preached there were all stupid, they said something that, by looking at their faces we could see clearly that they did not even understand what they said themselves. When they prayed, they did like this, "Oh Father, you are the only God, the only Almighty, the only Light of the world, the only Good Shepherd, be kind to us sinful people, give me this and that and these and those, and oh, Father, give us this and that and these and those. And thank you for your kindness that you have given us this and that and these and those. We'll be good sheep for you to lead. And there are so many hard headed people who don't believe in you, forgive them and don't throw them in hell yet, give them a chance, be kind to them by inspiring them to believe that you are the only God, Amen." Oh dear me! if there is God I was sure that He would be bored to death with these flatterers who praised Him because they wanted to beg and beg and beg for many things from Him....

By now I became acquainted with quite a few American people. I liked many things about them, I liked their easy-going ways, some of their straight forward manners, their talkativeness. Talking about their eloquence it reminds me of a remark my sister made about my English. One day an American woman came to see me. She was very, very talkative person. She told me about an event in her home town in the States, she talked quickly and fluently and surely in this case I need not say much. So I just said, yes, when she stopped to breathe and, oh no, when the story seemed impossible. The story was quite long when she left my sister said, "Oh, it was fortunate for me that I did not bother to learn English which you had to learn for so long and all that you can say was "yes and no."

But it stupefied me when I heard some of these well educated Americans talk. One of them said that their dollar was big, had great value, who in the world did not want it? Every body asked for it. I always saw that a child of an American rarely wore clothes in the hot day but one day I did not know what was the matter with the mother she scolded her child in front of me, "Do you want to be naked like Thai children?" Oh yes, she was ashamed that a one or two years old child was naked in a temperature of 100°F. But when a grown up woman was almost naked in a bikini bathing suit in 50°F, that was all right, "Her shape is nice, isn't it?" And one time an American boy when he heard our classical music said, "Oh, it seemed as if she is having a headache and groans and is going to die." I did not know what he would think about the opera because they had the same style of singing, may be he had never heard of it.

And it seemed these people did not understand how we loved and how highly we respected our king at all. Let me explain it in an easy way like this. The most respected persons in all Thai families are the parents. In children's groups the major cause of fighting is calling each other's parents bad names. I remembered that when I was in the fourth year of the primary school I had fought with a friend who was much, much bigger than me because she called my mother bad names and I never talked to her again until we had finished from school. Even a drunken man, if his parents were mentioned in the bad way, he would start up and became sober and the one who mentioned it had to be careful if he did not want any injury. A prostitute stabbed another girl to death and told the police that it was because that girl called her mother a prostitute, "Yes, I am a prostitute but my mother was not, I do not let any body call her by that name."

And all the parents are gathered together in our king and then we put him high up on the highest place in the house. And from there he will watch and take care of us and will not let danger come to us, who have to turn our faces down to work for our own livelihoods. We really have high respect on our king. . . .

About one month later, the teacher came to call us to go to study. It was three weeks before the examination took place, the class was three hours a week so it was quite a short time, but we did not hope to pass the examination in the first time, so it was all right. The class room was decorated nicely. I liked the way of decorating those stamps and coins and flowers very much. When we sat down the teacher distributed to us the papers. I was stunned. I found that if I let the light come in on the left side when I read or write I could see it better so I arrange the light accordingly. But the light in this room came from the right side. I could hardly read and it hurts my eyes so much. It took me quite a long time to get used to it. In the first hour I could not catch some words that he said even though he spoke slowly, but still I knew that he was a real good teacher. The second hour he told me to pronounce the word "A" which I thought I could imitate exactly as he had pronounced it. But he said it was wrong, and told me to do it again. Really I did not see the difference at that time. When he saw that I could not do it he looked at me with eyes that reminded me of when I was a small girl and I was playing with my sister. I broke one of her clay pots. She dared not spank me because grandmother forbade her so she looked at me with eyes which made me sob out loud. Grandmother came to ask what was the matter. I told her, "She scolded me, grandmother." My sister cried out, "What in the world, I didn't say a word." "Oh yes, you didn't say it out loud but you said it in your mind." They all laughed at me. And that expression became a subject of teasing me for a long time. The next week he came to this "A" again, this time I had caught it. And now I had noticed the difference in pronunciation between the American and English language too. At the end of some words and some sentences the English twisted them down in an artful way, and make more space in the mouth when they were speaking. It sounded nice to the ears. I wrote to my brother about it, he said he liked American better. Well, I understood American better though.

My friend and I had never expected that we would pass the examination. But I had read the "Doctor in the House" by Richard Gordon, who said that when you took an examination you need not worry because the examiner could not possibly look at every paper, what he did was, to throw away all the papers down the stair case, the ones that fell down the stairs were the ones that failed, the ones that stayed up stairs were the ones that passed.[2] The author was just joking of course. But fortunately my paper was one among those that stayed up stairs. The more I studied with this teacher the more I liked his teaching. The way he taught and repeated things even the biggest dumb bell could learn English if they tried to help themselves a bit. It was rather slow though but effective. So my English improved a lot.

By now I saw quite a few English people. Even though they talk the same language as the American people but their manners and characters were quite different. The Americans walked with free and easy steps but the English walked with neat and careful steps; some of them were too careful and it made them look as if they were walking on a stage. But if grandmother saw their manners, she would be satisfied. The Americans could talk to other people a lot more than the English. But some times the way that some of them talked about their tremendous prosperity reminded me of the very poor teen ager who became rich suddenly. It was very good that they came to stay in our country and knew each other because when they saw us live in huts and without furniture they felt proud of their country. And when we saw the people of such manners lived in such pretty houses, such lovely furnitures and those convenient things we felt proud of our people and country. But generally I liked them because after knowing each other for a while, we could talk intimately as if we had been acquainted for a long time which could suit the customs of the people in this part of Thailand. "Don't make anybody feel that they are strangers in our house," grandmother would say if I did not speak to some one I did not know before who came to our house. And when I went to those remote villages they treated me just as grandmother had taught me. I just walked pass their houses, they would say, "You have travelled a long way, of course, don't you feel tired? Drop in and rest a while, have some cool water and chew some betel nuts before you go on. Is your destination a long way off?" But the English people were different, their manners were perfect and they talked nicely of course but the way they talked even though you knew them for ages, I did not think you could intimate to one. This was my personal opinion, nobody count on it,

[2][This bit of academic folklore is widespread in American campus oral tradition. See Richard M. Dorson, *American Folklore* (Chicago, 1959), p. 256, for a version in which the bluebooks at the foot of the stairs receive the highest grade A while the ones at the head of the stairs (which didn't fly as far) earn failing F grades.— *Ed. Note.*]

because all these I observed out of just a few people of both countries who came to our town. The majority of people in their countries might be different.

Between us, in our country we call every body even people whom we have never seen before as relative, in the first meeting which naturally we do not know each other's name (introduction is not necessary) so we call them, grandfather, grandmother, uncle, aunt, older brother, or older sister, according to their ages, after we know their names we add the names in, and the older call the younger, little one or some other words that mean younger or just their names; and we never call any body by their families names. So we absolutely have no stranger especially in our town. How can one be a stranger though if one who speaks to you calls you as one of her or his relatives.

One thing that every foreigner who came to stay in our town complained of was the loud noise of the neighbour's radio, which I did not like it either. But I remembered that when we first had radios, at that time there were just a few people who could have them. Every time we turned on our radios, our neighbours would say, "Turn it on loud so we can hear it too." So even though it almost split our ears off still we had to make it loud for our neighbours' sakes. And when almost all of our neighbours had radios still each house had a radio. When we were cooking or washing the clothes and we wanted to listen to some programme that we followed for a long time, what should we do if we did not turn it on loud. Every house was like that. So every body became tolerant towards each other. Money can not buy every thing in our town. The neighbours were very precious, if it is not really necessary we would never do or say any thing to hurt our neighbour's feelings. I think in the future if every house could afford to buy radios and put one in the sitting room, one in the bed room, and one in the kitchen we all will turn it down softly automatically. . . .

I really appreciate the western people coming to our country. We learnt many good and useful things from them. But what I wish with my whole heart is I would like them to learn, to understand us too. And the way to do it is to communicate with as many people as possible or to read our books, and I can assure them that they will find many interesting things in us. And that way they will understand us and will not look down on us as most of them are doing now. When they came to our country what most of them did was to do their duties and learnt a little Thai language, just enough to tell the servants to do what they wanted to do in the house and the drivers to go left or right or straight, if they were doctors they would learn just the sentences that deal with patients such as, "Open your mouth, take a deep breath, is it painful here?" And if they were Pastors, they would learn how to say, "Lord, Almighty, The Glory, The Redeemer, the only Light of the world," and so on in Thai. So their communications were limited to the servants, the drivers and a few people who could talk (mostly a little) English. If these few people failed them, they hated us and looked down on us all. Our language is not hard to study, if they do not try to be too clever and really want to learn they can learn enough to read in six months.

There are just two main differences between these two languages, in English, each word we have to remember which syllable we have to stress, but it has not certain tone at all, each word can speak in many different tones according to the mood of the speaker, and some words have many ways of pronunciation, that way is the way of low class or uneducated people's pronunciation, you have to pronounce it this way so the people will know that you are high class or educated.

Thai language has intonation marks fix for each word, that educated or uneducated, high or low class, if you know that word or can read it you have to pronounce it exactly the same. The way of speaking it abruptly or politely and the manners that you act along with it that will tell the people what class you come from. Most of the foreigners look over the important of these intonation marks which when they speak Thai it sounds horrible and the listener can hardly understand.

For me whom our language, the verbs do not change according to the time, it is very hard when I speak English. I have to worry and have to think for a long time before I can judge what time it is going to be for the sentence I am going to speak, if that sentence has "yesterday, now, tomorrow or next," it is all right I can choose the right form of verb for it quicker. But if the sentence has not those words to go with, I am so confused, I can hardly judge what time it is going to be. Why you have to change the form of the verbs anyway when you say yesterday everybody knows it is the past, and now, every body knows it is present, and tomorrow or next, every body knows it is future. In our language the verbs do not change at all, if we want the listeners to know the time we just add a single word in the sentence, that is all. I think it is much easier than English. But I think the way of thinking about things of all kinds of people is according to the weather and the surrounding, when one does or says about something which you think is absurd if you follow to the real cause you will see there is some reason in it. And if people try to understand each other, all will feel happier, and can be friend to each other easier. . . .

I did not know my face would look like when I was thinking about all these. I was started up when the teacher asked what I was worrying about. It was not the way of the speaking that cut in me but the flash understanding in the eyes that made me miss my grandmother so much. I became distract. Oh, grandmother I needed you very much, I would like to go to you when I was distressed as I used to go, you would understand what was wrong with me the first minute you saw me, then stroke my head and soothed me with your soft voice, "Don't worry, tell grandmother what was it and grandmother will be on your side." Something cut short in front of me. It was a bicycle trying to turn the corner before me, I turned my scooter down to the sandy side of the road quickly and off balance and fell down quite hard. Fortunately, I did fall into the deep ditch beside the road, I got just the bruise. It would be nice to go where you had gone to be with you, grandmother, but if I can not go yet but have to stay alive cripple it would be a pity. I must stop thinking of you, on the road at least.

Burt W. Aginsky

A POMO'S SOLILOQUY

Although the following brief example of American Indian ora-
torical eloquence is clearly not an informant's exact words, the
gist of the argument remains forceful enough. Not only is this
a cogent aperçu of the importance of the family in Pomo
culture, but it is a striking comparative study of two cultures
in which it is our culture that is found wanting. (Here, incidentally, is an excellent example of ethnocentrism, in this case,
Pomo ethnocentrism.) This is precisely the kind of statement
which ought to be made to those among us who have the idea
that the "other" peoples of the world surely envy our "better"
way of life.

For further readings on the Pomo, who are widely known
for their exceptionally beautiful basketry, see the references in
George Peter Murdock, *Ethnographic Bibliography of North
America,* 3rd ed. (New Haven, 1960), pp. 90–92.

While doing field research in northern
California with an Indian group which had suffered a great deal under
the disruptive influences of Spanish and Americans, I became familiar with
an old Indian man well over one hundred years of age. He had lived
through a period which encompassed the days before any whites had come
into his territory, the Spanish raids, the white massacres, the herding of
his people upon reservations, and the variegated civilized tortures accompanying these deprivations. One day after a long period of discussion concerning the changing family situation he talked eloquently for a period of
about two hours. As soon as it was possible I returned to my headquarters
and recorded what he had said in as close an approximation as I could.

An old Pomo Indian once said to me: "What is a man? A man is nothing. Without his family he is of less importance than that bug crossing the
trail, of less importance than the sputum or exuviae. At least they can
be used to help poison[1] a man. A man must be with his family to amount

[1]Sorcery—black magic. [For a more elaborate description of the use of "poison," the
reader should consult Jaime de Angulo's "Singing for *Damaagomes* Among the Pit
River Indians" in this volume. The Pit River Indians or Achomawi and the Pomo are
both northern California peoples and thus it is not surprising that there are a good
many cultural parallels. For further information on Pomo poisoning in particular,
see L. S. Freeland (Mrs. Jaime de Angulo), "Pomo Doctors and Poisoners,"
University of California Publications in American Archaeology and Ethnology, **20**
(1923), 57–73.—*Ed. Note.*]

Reprinted from Burt W. Aginsky, "An Indian's Soliloquy," *American Journal of
Sociology,* **46** (1940), 43–44, by permission of the author and the University of
Chicago Press.

to anything with us. If he had nobody else to help him, the first trouble he got into he would be killed by his enemies because there would be no relatives to help him fight the poison of the other group. No woman would marry him because her family would not let her marry a man with no family. He would be poorer than a newborn child; he would be poorer than a worm, and the family would not consider him worth anything. He would not bring renown or glory with him. He would not bring support of other relatives either. The family is important. If a man has a large family and a profession[2] and upbringing by a family that is known to pro- duce good children, then he is somebody and every family is willing to have him marry a woman of their group. It is the family that is important. In the white ways of doing things the family is not so important. The police and soldiers take care of protecting you, the courts give you justice, the post office carries messages for you, the school teaches you. Everything is taken care of, even your children, if you die; but with us the family must do all of that.

"Without the family we are nothing, and in the old days before the white people came the family was given the first consideration by anyone who was about to do anything at all. That is why we got along. We had no courts, judges, schools, and the other things you have, but we got along better than you. We had poison, but if we minded our own business and restrained ourselves we lived well. We were taught to leave people alone. We were taught to consider that other people had to live. We were taught that we would suffer from the devil, spirits, ghosts, or other people if we did not support one another. The family was everything, and no man ever forgot that. Each person was nothing, but as a group joined by blood the individual knew that he would get the support of all his relatives if any- thing happened. He also knew that if he was a bad person the head man of his family would pay another tribe to kill him so that there would be no trouble afterward and so that he would not get the family into trouble all of the time.

"That is why we were good people and why we were friends with the white people when they came. But the white people were different from us. They wanted to take the world for themselves. My grandfather told me that the white people were homeless and had no families. They came by themselves and settled on our property. They had no manners. They did not know how to get along with other people. They were strangers who were rough and common and did not know how to behave. But I have seen that these people of yours are even worse. They have taken everything away from the Indians, and they take everything away from one another. They do not help one another when they are in trouble, and they do not care what happens to other people. We were not like that. We would not let a person die of starvation when we had plenty of food. We would not bury our dead with no show. We would kill another person by poisoning him if he was an enemy, but we would not treat a stranger the way they

[2]Specialized occupation requiring years of training and preparation. Some of the specializations are deer-hunter, gambler, doctor, and money manufacturers.

treat their own brothers and sisters. Your people are hard to understand. My brother lived with your people for twenty years, and he said that he was used to you; but he cannot understand yet why you people act as you do. You are all the same in one way. We are all the same in another. What is wrong with you? The white people have the land. They own the courts, they own everything, but they will not give the Indians enough money to live on. It is hard to understand.

"With us the family was everything. Now it is nothing. We are getting like the white people, and it is bad for the old people. We had no old peoples' homes like you. The old people were important. They were wise. Your old people must be fools."

A Kipsigis Tale

DEATH AND AN OLD WOMAN

There is another way that the native speaks for himself and that is through his art, folklore, and music. In these creative forms, peoples the world over bare their souls. Ideally, these materials should be recorded in the native language (with a word-for-word interlinear translation) and *in situ*. Moreover, interpretations of these materials by natives should also be elicited. Both the natives performing and the natives in the audience should be asked for "oral literary criticism." For most of the thousands of song and folktale texts recorded in the ethnographic literature, there is either no interpretation at all or else a passing speculative comment or two provided by the collector, who tells what *he* thinks the song or tale means.

This short tale is a remarkable specimen from the oral literature of the Kipsigis, a people who live in the western part of Kenya in East Africa. With a few deft strokes, a perfect picture is painted. The impression of a miserly old woman is skillfully created by allusions to a house that is lonely despite its being filled with many goods. The philosophical implications of an attempt to escape death, an attempt in which the means to one end bring about another, are profound and are perhaps more characteristic of the proverb genre than the folktale. For those who might have been laboring under the misconception that peoples without writing had no literature, this infinitesimal fragment of African oral tradition may prove enlightening. In a way it is sad that while hundreds upon hundreds of students pour through the written literature of our elite, trying to squeeze another term paper or thesis out of Chaucer and Hawthorne,

Collected by Kipsigie A. Marindany in 1959 at the request of Eva E. Gilger. Trans. by Ezekiel A. Kerich.

most of the oral literature of the world lies unnoticed and unstudied.

For an introduction to folklore, see Alan Dundes, ed., *The Study of Folklore* (Englewood Cliffs, N. J., 1965). For examples of native or oral literary criticism, see Alan Dundes, "Metafolklore and Oral Literary Criticism," *The Monist,* 50 (1966), 505–16. For studies of folktales in particular, see J. L. Fischer, "The Sociopsychological Analysis of Folktales," *Current Anthropology,* 4 (1963), 235–95, and such works as Stith Thompson, *The Folktale* (New York, 1946), and Melville Jacobs, *The Content and Style of an Oral Literature* (Chicago, 1959). For a survey of the major African folktale collections, see William Bascom, "Folklore Research in Africa," *Journal of American Folklore,* 77 (1964), 12–31. For a convenient, inexpensive paperback anthology of African narratives, see Susan Feldmann, *African Myths and Tales* (New York, 1963). For African narratives about death, see H. Abrahamsson, *The Origin of Death: Studies in African Mythology* (Uppsala, 1951). The Kipsigis tale presented here was collected in 1959 by Kipsigie A. Marindany at the request of Miss Eva E. Gilger, who was then principal of Tenwek High School, Tenwek, Sotik, Kenya. The tale was translated into English by Ezekiel A. Kerich, another student of Miss Gilger's (The bracketed portions were added by the present editor.) I am indebted to Mrs. Margaret Estes of Lawrence, Kansas, for bringing Miss Gilger's excellent manuscript collection of Kipsigis folktales to my attention. For further information about the Kipsigis, see J. G. Peristiany, *The Social Institutions of the Kipsigis* (London, 1939).

When an old woman back in the passed centuries had stayed long, and having not been sick since birth, stayed in her lonely house, [lonely] though [it was] full of goods and other wealth, [she] was thinking where a death would come from.

"My house is well plastered; I feel no cold at day or night time where could death comes through," she thought.

"I will now go to the attic and sleep there and it will be even harder for the death to find me."

As she was about to get to the attic by the ladder, the ladder broke and there she was on the floor again and the death was with her.

"I heard you mentioning my name from where I was wandering. Here, I am!" roared the death.

"Oh! leave me. I want to live. I don't want you yet," cried the woman. But the death could not take heed.

Cultures
in contact

$\mathcal{E}$ver since the heyday of the great voyages of exploration, there has been considerable interest in the topic of culture contact. What happens when two cultures hitherto unknown to one another suddenly come into contact? There is also the less dramatic question of what happens when there is continuous contact between two distinct cultures that share a common geographical border. However, cultural anthropologists have been slow to study this topic and there are several reasons for this.

The nineteenth-century anthropologist was greatly preoccupied with origins and his techniques of searching for them consisted of variations on the theme of historical reconstruction. Even in the early fieldwork done by the first professional anthropologists to go into the field, the emphasis was definitely upon "pre-contact" culture. An American anthropologist working with American Indians, for example, would practice "salvage" anthropology. The Indian informant might be living off the reservation, away from other members of his tribe, and the anthropologist would record primarily "memory culture," that is, what his Indian informants told him about the way they *remembered* things had been done in the past. By recording this information, the anthropologist hoped to "salvage" what little there was left of pre-contact culture. With this bias, almost all the signs of culture contact (e.g., acculturation) were ignored. The anthropologist essentially pretended that he was studying the culture as it was before the white man came upon the scene. (One device was to describe the people in what is termed the "ethnographic present." In other words, memory culture and, in some cases, practices and peoples which have died out are described using the present tense so as to convey the impression that they still exist.) One collector of American Indian folktales remarked at the turn of the century that he did not even bother to write down what were obviously European tales from his Cherokee informants. Yet the types and amounts of changes in European tales borrowed by American Indians can provide important clues as to cultural values. This attitude was typical.

In the twentieth century, intellectual currents in anthropology moved away from historical reconstruction, the search for origins, and other allied aims of a past-oriented approach. Instead, anthropologists turned to questions of form, function, and problems generally related to a present-oriented approach. Any realistic study of present as opposed to past cultures had to take acculturation and Western influence into account. In addition, the notion of culture as a more or less static entity (consisting of lists of culture traits) gave way to the more dynamic conception of culture as consisting of patterns in a constant state of flux. The study of culture change began to interest anthropologists. The shift then was from almost totally ignoring culture change, especially acculturative changes, to recording and even specializing in the study of the nature and direction of culture change.

Another critical aspect of the study of cultures in contact concerns the controversial matter of applied anthropology. Most of the missionaries and colonial administrators who first recorded ethnographic data did so with a definite ulterior motive. Generally speaking, they wanted to get firsthand information about the culture they were going to seek to change. Administrators figured that a knowledge of native customs would make it easier to govern the natives; Columbus left a priest, Ramon Pane, on the island of Hispaniola where he recorded several Taino myths as a means of learning the nature of the native religion that Christianity was to replace. Even now, dedicated missionary linguists study native languages for the purpose of translating the Bible into these languages. (They even study the linguistic style of native myths in order to use it for their work, the idea being to ensure that the Bible, even in translation,

will have some of the desirable archaic "mythopoeic" qualities.)
This is applied anthropology. It is applying the knowledge gained
from ethnographic fieldwork to help solve a particular problem.

Most cultural anthropologists shy away from applied anthropology. They want to study cultures, not change them. They
want to study culture change, not cause it. Part of this attitude
may be attributable to the older notion of investigating only
pre-contact cultures—the less influenced by Western civilization
the better. On the other hand, there is a fundamental ethical
question involved here. The anthropologist, intellectually committed to the principle of cultural relativism, feels that he has
no moral right to interfere with the workings of another culture.
Of course, he realizes that his very presence in the field and
his very acts of gathering data are irrevocable causes of change
in that culture. However, this is deemed to be an unavoidable
consequence of the nature of the inquiry. It is impossible to
observe the daily life of a people without the observer being
present. No two-way false mirror through which an ethnographer
can observe a people without being observed by them has yet
been devised. But although the anthropologist may in fact be
responsible for minor changes or even major ones, this is not
the same thing as working for a governmental agency or a
religious order to help create or implement a new program or
ideology. The anthropologist is thus caught on the horns of a
nasty dilemma. Normally he comes to be very closely attached to
the people with whom he works and would be glad to help
them. On the other hand, he is far too sophisticated about the
nature of culture not to know what some of the dire consequences
of outside help might be. Obviously, he cannot control any use
made of his published data. If it is in print, it is available to
anyone (although an anthropologist may be saddened by the
thought that the fruits of his long years of fieldwork might be
used by a reactionary colonialist power in a program which he
considers detrimental to his original informants). But when it
comes to taking an active role in designing or executing planned
culture change, the anthropologist may feel that he cannot in all
conscience participate. What is a clear-cut black and white
decision for an anthropologically naïve do-gooder from the
anthropologist's society may be an agonizing one for the anthropologist. Who is to decide and upon what basis that a given
culture needs help? And having decided that, who determines
what form that help should take and how and when it should
be offered or imposed.

It is for this reason that most anthropologists eschew applied
anthropology. Like so many members of the academic community,
their hearts are in pure, not applied, research. The unending
quest for knowledge, the pleasure in paradox and problem, and
the occasional thrill of insight are their own reward. Yet, there

are a few who believe that pure research is not enough. Since attempts at directed culture change are going on anyway (with or without the anthropologist's help), the anthropologist has nothing to lose by offering his knowledge and expertise. Presumably, he could do no harm and he might conceivably do a great deal of good. (Of course, the native people concerned, when they see their friendly anthropologist enrolled in the ranks of their government, may not be so anxious to have that anthropologist visit them again to do further fieldwork.) But in the final analysis, it is the central question of values which remains. Do we have the right to intervene in the cultures of others? Do other cultures have the right to decide their own course of development free from outside influence? Benevolent despotism is one solution. We know what's best for others and we're going to see that they get it, whether they like it or not. Or do we sit back and allow people to continue to have short lifespans and to die from diseases for which we have effective cures? It is a difficult question and it is one which every anthropologist and student of anthropology has to answer for himself.

David Livingstone

CONVERSATION ON RAIN-MAKING

Not all missionaries were intolerant of native points of view. Years of residence among a people often afforded better understanding of native philosophy than is possible for even the best trained modern anthropologist who spends one or two years in the field. Medical missionary David Livingstone (1813–1873), forever immortalized by explorer Sir Henry Morton Stanley's alleged lines upon meeting him deep in Africa, "Dr. Livingstone, I presume," was a careful observer of native life. In reconstructing a typical debate between doctors from two cultures, Livingstone displays remarkable ethnographic acumen. Though the words may not be exact, the gist of the native argument seems to be presented fairly. One might profitably compare Livingstone's account with Darwin's description of the Tierra del Fuegians, as both were written about the same time. The difference between a casual description made by a traveler passing through and one made on the basis of extended residence and study is immense. From Livingstone's unusual report one can see that the first step in intercultural communication is understanding the other culture's interpretation of itself, with special reference to one's own.

Reprinted from David Livingstone, *Missionary Travels and Researches in South Africa* (New York, 1858), pp. 22–27, by permission of Harper and Row.

For more modern information on the Kwena, who numbered nearly 40,000 in 1946, see I. Schapera, *The Ethnic Composition of Tswana Tribes* (London, 1952), and for the general area, see V. G. J. Sheddick, *The Southern Sotho* (London, 1953).

The place where we first settled with the Bakwains is called Chonuane, and it happened to be visited, during the first year of our residence there, by one of those droughts which occur from time to time in even the most favored districts of Africa.

The belief in the gift or power of *rain-making* is one of the most deeply-rooted articles of faith in this country. The chief Sechele was himself a noted rain-doctor, and believed in it implicitly. He has often assured me that he found it more difficult to give up his faith in that than in any thing else which Christianity required him to abjure. I pointed out to him that the only feasible way of watering the gardens was to select some good, never-failing river, make a canal, and irrigate the adjacent lands. This suggestion was immediately adopted, and soon the whole tribe was on the move to the Kolobeng, a stream about forty miles distant. The experiment succeeded admirably during the first year. The Bakwains made the canal and dam in exchange for my labor in assisting to build a square house for their chief. They also built their own school under my superintendence. Our house at the River Kolobeng, which gave a name to the settlement, was the third which I had reared with my own hands. A native smith taught me to weld iron; and having improved by scraps of information in that line from Mr. Moffat, and also in carpentering and gardening, I was becoming handy at almost any trade, besides doctoring and preaching; and as my wife could make candles, soap, and clothes, we came nearly up to what may be considered as indispensable in the accomplishments of a missionary family in Central Africa, namely, the husband to be a jack-of-all-trades without doors, and the wife a maid-of-all-work within. But in our second year again no rain fell. In the third the same extraordinary drought followed. Indeed, not ten inches of water fell during these two years, and the Kolobeng ran dry; so many fish were killed that the hyænas from the whole country round collected to the feast, and were unable to finish the putrid masses. A large old alligator, which had never been known to commit any depredations, was found left high and dry in the mud among the victims. The fourth year was equally unpropitious, the fall of rain being insufficient to bring the grain to maturity. Nothing could be more trying. We dug down in the bed of the river deeper and deeper as the water receded, striving to get a little to keep the fruit-trees alive for better times, but in vain. Needles lying out of doors for months did not rust; and a mixture of sulphuric acid and water, used in a galvanic battery, parted with all its water to the air, instead of imbibing more from it, as it would have done in England. The leaves of indigenous trees were all drooping, soft, and shriveled, though not dead; and those of the mimosæ were closed at midday, the same as they are at night. In the midst of this dreary drought, it was wonderful to see those tiny creatures, the ants, running about with their accustomed vivacity. I put the bulb of a thermometer three inches under the soil, in the sun, at midday, and found the mercury to stand at 132° to134°; and if certain kinds of beetles were placed on the surface, they ran about a few seconds and expired. But this broiling heat only augmented the activity of the long-legged black ants: they never tire; their organs of motion seem endowed with the same power as is ascribed by physiologists to the muscles of the human heart, by which that part of the frame never becomes fatigued, and which may be imparted to all our bodily organs in that higher sphere to which we fondly hope to rise. Where do these ants get their moisture? Our house was built on a hard ferruginous conglomerate, in order to be out of the way of the white ant, but they came in despite the precaution; and not only were they, in this sultry weather, able individually to moisten soil to the consistency of mortar for the formation of galleries, which, in their way of working, is done by night (so that they are screened from the observation of birds by day in passing and repassing toward any vegetable matter they may wish to devour), but, when their inner chambers were laid open, these were also surprisingly humid. Yet there was no dew, and, the house being placed on a rock, they could have no subterranean passage to the bed of the river, which ran about three hundred yards below the hill. Can it be that they have the power of combining the oxygen and hydrogen of their vegetable food by vital force so as to form water?[1]

Rain, however, would not fall. The Bakwains believed that I had bound Sechele with some magic spell, and I received deputations, in the evenings, of the old counselors, entreating me to allow him to make only a few showers: "The corn will die if you refuse, and we shall become scattered. Only let him make rain this once, and we shall all, men, women, and children, come to the school, and sing and pray as long as you please." It was in vain to protest that I wished Sechele to act just according to his own ideas of what was right, as he found the law laid down in the Bible, and it was distressing to appear hard-hearted to them. The clouds often collected promisingly over us, and rolling thunder seemed to portend refreshing showers, but next morning the sun would rise in a clear, cloudless sky; indeed, even these lowering appearances were less frequent by far than days of sunshine are in London.

The natives, finding it irksome to sit and wait helplessly until God gives them rain from heaven, entertain the more comfortable idea that they can help themselves by a variety of preparations, such as charcoal made of burned bats, inspissated renal deposit of the mountain cony—*Hyrax capensis*—(which, by the way, is used, in the form of pills, as a good antispasmodic, under the name of "stone-sweat"[2]), the internal parts of different animals—as jackals' livers, baboons' and lions' hearts, and hairy calculi from the bowels of old cows—serpents' skins and vertebræ, and

---

[1]When we come to Angola, I shall describe an insect there which distills several pints of water every night.

[2]The name arises from its being always voided on one spot, in the manner practiced by others of the rhinocerontine family; and, by the action of the sun, it becomes a black, pitchy substance.

every kind of tuber, bulb, root, and plant to be found in the country. Although you disbelieve their efficacy in charming the clouds to pour out their refreshing treasures, yet, conscious that civility is useful everywhere, you kindly state that you think they are mistaken as to their power. The rain-doctor selects a particular bulbous root, pounds it, and administers a cold infusion to a sheep, which in five minutes afterward expires in convulsions. Part of the same bulb is converted into smoke, and ascends toward the sky; rain follows in a day or two. The inference is obvious. Were we as much harassed by droughts, the logic would be irresistible in England in 1857.

As the Bakwains believed that there must be some connection between the presence of "God's Word" in their town and these successive and distressing droughts, they looked with no good will at the church bell, but still they invariably treated us with kindness and respect. I am not aware of ever having had an enemy in the tribe. The only avowed cause of dislike was expressed by a very influential and sensible man, the uncle of Sechele. "We like you as well as if you had been born among us; you are the only white man we can become familiar with (*thoaéla*); but we wish you to give up that everlasting preaching and praying; we can not become familiar with that at all. You see we never get rain, while those tribes who never pray as we do obtain abundance." This was a fact; and we often saw it raining on the hills ten miles off, while it would not look at us "even with one eye." If the Prince of the power of the air had no hand in scorching us up, I fear I often gave him the credit of doing so.

As for the rain-makers, they carried the sympathies of the people along with them, and not without reason. With the following arguments they were all acquainted, and in order to understand their force, we must place ourselves in their position, and believe, as they do, that all medicines act by a mysterious charm. The term for cure may be translated "charm" (*alaha*).

Medical Doctor. Hail, friend! How very many medicines you have about you this morning! Why, you have every medicine in the country here.

Rain Doctor. Very true, my friend; and I ought; for the whole country needs the rain which I am making.

M. D. So you really believe that you can command the clouds? I think that can be done by God alone.

R. D. We both believe the very same thing. It is God that makes the rain, but I pray to him by means of these medicines, and, the rain coming, of course it is then mine. It was I who made it for the Bakwains for many years, when they were at Shokuane; through my wisdom, too, their women became fat and shining. Ask them; they will tell you the same as I do.

M. D. But we are distinctly told in the parting words of our Savior that we can pray to God acceptably in his name alone, and not by means of medicines.

R. D. Truly! but God told us differently. He made black men first, and did not love us as he did the white men. He made you beautiful, and gave you clothing, and guns, and gunpowder, and horses, and wagons, and many other things about which we know nothing. But toward us he had no heart. He gave us nothing except the assegai, and cattle, and rain-making; and he did not give us hearts like yours. We never love each other. Other tribes place medicines about our country to prevent the rain, so that we may be dispersed by hunger, and go to them, and augment their power. We must dissolve their charms by our medicines. God has given us one little thing, which you know nothing of. He has given us the knowledge of certain medicines by which we can make rain. *We* do not despise those things which you possess, though we are ignorant of them. We don't understand your book, yet we don't despise it. *You* ought not to despise our little knowledge, though you are ignorant of it.

M. D. I don't despise what I am ignorant of; I only think you are mistaken in saying that you have medicines which can influence the rain at all.

R. D. That's just the way people speak when they talk on a subject of which they have no knowledge. When we first opened our eyes, we found our forefathers making rain, and we follow in their footsteps. You, who send to Kuruman for corn, and irrigate your garden, may do without rain; *we* can not manage in that way. If we had not rain, the cattle would have no pasture, the cows give no milk, our children become lean and die, our wives run away to other tribes who do make rain and have corn, and the whole tribe become dispersed and lost; our fire would go out.

M. D. I quite agree with you as to the value of the rain; but you can not charm the clouds by medicines. You wait till you see the clouds come, then you use your medicines, and take the credit which belongs to God only.

R. D. I use my medicines, and you employ yours; we are both doctors, and doctors are not deceivers. You give a patient medicine. Sometimes God is pleased to heal him by means of your medicine; sometimes not—he dies. When he is cured, you take the credit of what God does. I do the same. Sometimes God grants us rain, sometimes not. When he does, we take the credit of the charm. When a patient dies, you don't give up trust in your medicine, neither do I when rain fails. If you wish me to leave off my medicines, why continue your own?

M. D. I give medicine to living creatures within my reach, and can see the effects, though no cure follows; you pretend to charm the clouds, which are so far above us that your medicines never reach them. The clouds usually lie in one direction, and your smoke goes in another. God alone can command the clouds. Only try and wait patiently; God will give us rain without your medicines.

R. D. Mahala-ma-kapa-a-a!! Well, I always thought white men were wise till this morning. Who ever thought of making trial of starvation? Is death pleasant, then?

M. D. Could you make it rain on one spot and not on another?

R. D. I wouldn't think of trying. I like to see the whole country green, and all the people glad; the women clapping their hands, and giving me their ornaments for thankfulness, and lullilooing for joy.

M. D. I think you deceive both them and yourself.

R. D. Well, then, there is a pair of us (meaning both are rogues).

The above is only a specimen of their way of reasoning, in which, when the language is well understood, they are perceived to be remarkably acute.

These arguments are generally known, and I never succeeded in convincing a single individual of their fallacy, though I tried to do so in every way I could think of. Their faith in medicines as charms is unbounded. The general effect of argument is to produce the impression that you are not anxious for rain at all; and it is very undesirable to allow the idea to spread that you do not take a generous interest in their welfare. An angry opponent of rain-making in a tribe would be looked upon as were some Greek merchants in England during the Russian war.

Laura Bohannan

SHAKESPEARE IN THE BUSH

One of the by-products of anthropological fieldwork is that the ethnographer is afforded an opportunity to see his own culture from a different perspective. The self-evident and the common-place become terribly difficult to explain and justify when one discusses them with a member of another culture. (Just try explaining the American game of baseball, or even just the concept of a "strike," to someone not from the United States and see what happens.) Moreover, the way in which members of another culture understand or *misunderstand* materials from the ethnographer's culture may prove extremely illuminating.

In theory, a thorough comparative study of two cultures should provide sufficient data to predict with some accuracy what misunderstandings are likely to occur when a member of culture A discusses a given topic with a member of culture B. Perhaps an analogy from comparative linguistics will illustrate this point. A native speaker of French will normally not be able to articulate the initial consonantal phonemes in the English words "thigh" and "thy." The "th" sounds, both voiced (with the vocal cords vibrating) and voiceless, simply do not occur in the French inventory of phonemes (linguistic units of sound). To understand the difference between voiced and voiceless sounds in English, try to whisper the word "thy." It can't be done. If you whisper "thy," you get "thigh" because the initial phoneme in "thigh" is the voiceless $[\theta]$. Try dip/tip or zip/sip, other pairs of words which reflect the same voiced/voiceless distinction.

A knowledge of French phonology would show not only that neither "th" sound occurs, but also that the nearest sounds in French are the [s] and [z] phonemes. Thus one could predict that for the English voiced "th" sound [ð], the French native will substitute the voiced sound [z]. "This'll" becomes "Zees'll," while the voiceless substitution transforms "thistle" into "seesle."

Reprinted from *Natural History*, 75 (1966), 28–33, by permission of the author.

(Since French does not have the vowel [ɪ] as in "this," the substitution of [i] results in "thees," as it also does when a native speaker of Spanish speaks English.) The point is that these substitutions are predictable, recurrent phenomena and this insight is by no means limited to problems of language learning. Mistakes in any aspect of culture resulting when a member of one culture attempts to employ an element of another culture are often *predictable*. This has important implications for the comparative study of politics with respect to international diplomacy. Possibly, one could predict how the policy of nation *A* would be misunderstood by the citizens of nation *B* and moreover one could explain *why* it was thus misunderstood!

When Laura Bohannan introduced Shakespeare's *Hamlet* to the Tiv of West Africa, she found that they interpreted it in the light of their own culture. Obviously, this is what all peoples do the world over, that is, interpret new ideas in the light of their own culture. This is why it is the height of naïveté for an anthropologically uninformed do-gooder or a governmental representative (the categories are not mutually exclusive) to think that merely introducing a new "helpful" element to a particular group will cause it to "take" in this group. It never occurs to some that perhaps democracy, Christianity, and the capitalist ethic are not for export. But even if they are for export, such ideas are bound to be interpreted in ways different from the ways they are interpreted in the United States. Note the use of the plural, way*s*, for each culture may interpret these ideas differently. The question is thus not just what Hamlet means to the Tiv, but what does Hamlet mean to a Hindu, to an Arab, or to a Trobriand Islander? In the study of culture it is not enough to know the native elements of the other culture and to interpret *their* culture, e.g., their literature (folklore); we must also know how members of other cultures interpret *our* literature and culture. For this reason, Laura Bohannan's essay is a most interesting one.

For an entertaining fictionalized account of her entire field experience among the Tiv, see her novel, *Return to Laughter* (Garden City, 1964). For more conventional ethnographic descriptions of the Tiv, see any of the numerous works written by Laura Bohannan or her husband Paul Bohannan, who is also a professional anthropologist; for example, Laura and Paul Bohannan, *The Tiv of Central Nigeria* (London, 1953), or Paul Bohannan, "The Tiv of Nigeria," in James L. Gibbs, Jr., ed., *Peoples of Africa* (New York, 1965), pp. 515–46.

Just before I left Oxford for the Tiv in West Africa, conversation turned to the season at Stratford. "You Americans," said a friend, "often have difficulty with Shakespeare. He was, after all, a very English poet, and one can easily misinterpret the universal by misunderstanding the particular."

I protested that human nature is pretty much the same the whole world over; at least the general plot and motivation of the greater tragedies would always be clear—everywhere—although some details of custom might have to be explained and difficulties of translation might produce other slight changes. To end an argument we could not conclude, my friend gave me a copy of *Hamlet* to study in the African bush: it would, he hoped, lift my mind above its primitive surroundings, and possibly I might, by prolonged meditation, achieve the grace of correct interpretation.

It was my second field trip to the African tribe, and I thought myself ready to live in one of its remote sections—an area difficult to cross even on foot. I eventually settled on the hillock of a very knowledgeable old man, the head of a homestead of some hundred and forty people, all of whom were either his close relatives or their wives and children. Like the other elders of the vicinity, the old man spent most of his time performing ceremonies seldom seen these days in the more accessible parts of the tribe. I was delighted. Soon there would be three months of enforced isolation and leisure, between the harvest that takes place just before the rising of the swamps and the clearing of new farms when the water goes down. Then, I thought, they would have even more time to perform ceremonies and explain them to me.

I was quite mistaken. Most of the ceremonies demanded the presence of elders from several homesteads. As the swamps rose, the old men found it too difficult to walk from one homestead to the next, and the ceremonies gradually ceased. As the swamps rose even higher, all activities but one came to an end. The women brewed beer from maize and millet. Men, women, and children sat on their hillocks and drank it.

People began to drink at dawn. By midmorning the whole homestead was singing, dancing, and drumming. When it rained, people had to sit inside their huts: there they drank and sang or they drank and told stories. In any case, by noon or before, I either had to join the party or retire to my own hut and my books. "One does not discuss serious matters when there is beer. Come, drink with us." Since I lacked their capacity for the thick native beer, I spent more and more time with *Hamlet*. Before the end of the second month, grace descended on me. I was quite sure that *Hamlet* had only one possible interpretation, and that one universally obvious.

Early every morning, in the hope of having some serious talk before the beer party, I used to call on the old man at his reception hut—a circle of posts supporting a thatched roof above a low mud wall to keep out wind and rain. One day I crawled through the low doorway and found most of the men of the homestead sitting huddled in their ragged cloths on stools, low plank beds, and reclining chairs, warming themselves against the chill of the rain around a smoky fire. In the center were three pots of beer. The party had started.

The old man greeted me cordially. "Sit down and drink." I accepted a large calabash full of beer, poured some into a small drinking gourd, and tossed it down. Then I poured some more into the same gourd for the man second in seniority to my host before I handed my calabash over to a young man for further distribution. Important people shouldn't ladle beer themselves.

"It is better like this," the old man said, looking at me approvingly and plucking at the thatch that had caught in my hair. "You should sit and drink with us more often. Your servants tell me that when you are not with us, you sit inside your hut looking at a paper."

The old man was acquainted with four kinds of "papers": tax receipts, bride price receipts, court fee receipts, and letters. The messenger who brought him letters from the chief used them mainly as a badge of office, for he always knew what was in them and told the old man. Personal letters for the few who had relatives in the government or mission stations were kept until someone went to a large market where there was a letter writer and reader. Since my arrival, letters were brought to me to be read. A few men also brought me bride price receipts, privately, with requests to change the figures to a higher sum. I found moral arguments were of no avail, since in-laws are fair game, and the technical hazards of forgery difficult to explain to an illiterate people. I did not wish them to think me silly enough to look at any such papers for days on end, and I hastily explained that my "paper" was one of the "things of long ago" of my country.

"Ah," said the old man. "Tell us."

I protested that I was not a storyteller. Storytelling is a skilled art among them; their standards are high, and the audiences critical—and vocal in their criticism. I protested in vain. This morning they wanted to hear a story while they drank. They threatened to tell me no more stories until I told them one of mine. Finally, the old man promised that no one would criticize my style "for we know you are struggling with our language." "But," put in one of the elders, "you must explain what we do not understand, as we do when we tell you our stories." Realizing that here was my chance to prove *Hamlet* universally intelligible, I agreed.

The old man handed me some more beer to help me on with my storytelling. Men filled their long wooden pipes and knocked coals from the fire to place in the pipe bowls; then, puffing contentedly, they sat back to listen. I began in the proper style, "Not yesterday, not yesterday, but long ago, a thing occurred. One night three men were keeping watch outside the homestead of the great chief, when suddenly they saw the former chief approach them."

"Why was he no longer their chief?"

"He was dead," I explained. "That is why they were troubled and afraid when they saw him."

"Impossible," began one of the elders, handing his pipe on to his neighbor, who interrupted, "Of course it wasn't the dead chief. It was an omen sent by a witch. Go on."

Slightly shaken, I continued. "One of these three was a man who knew things"—the closest translation for scholar, but unfortunately it also meant witch. The second elder looked triumphantly at the first. "So he spoke to the dead chief saying, 'Tell us what we must do so you may rest in your grave,' but the dead chief did not answer. He vanished, and they could see him no more. Then the man who knew things—his name was Horatio—said this event was the affair of the dead chief's son, Hamlet."

There was a general shaking of heads round the circle. "Had the dead chief no living brothers? Or was this son the chief?"

"No," I replied. "That is, he had one living brother who became the chief when the elder brother died."

The old man muttered: such omens were matters for chiefs and elders, not for youngsters; no good could come of going behind a chief's back; clearly Horatio was not a man who knew things.

"Yes, he was," I insisted, shooing a chicken away from my beer. "In our country the son is next to the father. The dead chief's younger brother had become the great chief. He had also married his elder brother's widow only about a month after the funeral."

"He did well," the old man beamed and announced to the others, "I told you that if we knew more about Europeans, we would find they really were very like us. In our country also," he added to me, "the younger brother marries the elder brother's widow and becomes the father of his children. Now, if your uncle, who married your widowed mother, is your father's full brother, then he will be a real father to you. Did Hamlet's father and uncle have one mother?"

His question barely penetrated my mind; I was too upset and thrown too far off balance by having one of the most important elements of *Hamlet* knocked straight out of the picture. Rather uncertainly I said that I thought they had the same mother, but I wasn't sure—the story didn't say. The old man told me severely that these genealogical details made all the difference and that when I got home I must ask the elders about it. He shouted out the door to one of his younger wives to bring his goatskin bag.

Determined to save what I could of the mother motif, I took a deep breath and began again. "The son Hamlet was very sad because his mother had married again so quickly. There was no need for her to do so, and it is our custom for a widow not to go to her next husband until she has mourned for two years."

"Two years is too long," objected the wife, who had appeared with the old man's battered goatskin bag. "Who will hoe your farms for you while you have no husband?"

"Hamlet," I retorted without thinking, "was old enough to hoe his mother's farms himself. There was no need for her to remarry." No one looked convinced. I gave up. "His mother and the great chief told Hamlet not to be sad, for the great chief himself would be a father to Hamlet. Furthermore, Hamlet would be the next chief: therefore he must stay to learn the things of a chief. Hamlet agreed to remain, and all the rest went off to drink beer."

While I paused, perplexed at how to render Hamlet's disgusted soliloquy to an audience convinced that Claudius and Gertrude had behaved in the best possible manner, one of the younger men asked me who had married the other wives of the dead chief.

"He had no other wives," I told him.

"But a chief must have many wives! How else can he brew beer and prepare food for all his guests?"

I said firmly that in our country even chiefs had only one wife, that they had servants to do their work, and that they paid them from tax money.

It was better, they returned, for a chief to have many wives and sons who would help him hoe his farms and feed his people; then everyone loved the chief who gave much and took nothing—taxes were a bad thing.

I agreed with the last comment, but for the rest fell back on their favorite way of fobbing off my questions: "That is the way it is done, so that is how we do it."

I decided to skip the soliloquy. Even if Claudius was here thought quite right to marry his brother's widow, there remained the poison motif, and I knew they would disapprove of fratricide. More hopefully I resumed, "That night Hamlet kept watch with the three who had seen his dead father. The dead chief again appeared, and although the others were afraid, Hamlet followed his dead father off to one side. When they were alone, Hamlet's dead father spoke."

"Omens can't talk!" The old man was emphatic.

"Hamlet's dead father wasn't an omen. Seeing him might have been an omen, but he was not." My audience looked as confused as I sounded. "It *was* Hamlet's dead father. It was a thing we call a 'ghost.' " I had to use the English word, for unlike many of the neighboring tribes, these people didn't believe in the survival after death of any individuating part of the personality.

"What is a 'ghost?' An omen?"

"No, a 'ghost' is someone who is dead but who walks around and can talk, and people can hear him and see him but not touch him."

They objected. "One can touch zombis."

"No, no! It was not a dead body the witches had animated to sacrifice and eat. No one else made Hamlet's dead father walk. He did it himself."

"Dead men can't walk," protested my audience as one man.

I was quite willing to compromise. "A 'ghost' is the dead man's shadow."

But again they objected. "Dead men cast no shadows."

"They do in my country," I snapped.

The old man quelled the babble of disbelief that arose immediately and told me with that insincere, but courteous, agreement one extends to the fancies of the young, ignorant, and superstitious, "No doubt in your country the dead can also walk without being zombis." From the depths of his bag he produced a withered fragment of kola nut, bit off one end to show it wasn't poisoned, and handed me the rest as a peace offering.

"Anyhow," I resumed, "Hamlet's dead father said that his own brother, the one who became chief, had poisoned him. He wanted Hamlet to avenge him. Hamlet believed this in his heart, for he did not like his father's brother." I took another swallow of beer. "In the country of the great chief, living in the same homestead, for it was a very large one, was an important elder who was often with the chief to advise and help him. His name was Polonius. Hamlet was courting his daughter, but her father and her brother

...[I cast hastily about for some tribal analogy] warned her not to let Hamlet visit her when she was alone on her farm, for he would be a great chief and so could not marry her."

"Why not?" asked the wife, who had settled down on the edge of the old man's chair. He frowned at her for asking stupid questions and growled, "They lived in the same homestead."

"That was not the reason," I informed them. "Polonius was a stranger who lived in the homestead because he helped the chief, not because he was a relative."

"Then why couldn't Hamlet marry her?"

"He could have," I explained, "but Polonius didn't think he would. After all, Hamlet was a man of great importance who ought to marry a chief's daughter, for in his country a man could have only one wife. Polonius was afraid that if Hamlet made love to his daughter, then no one else would give a high price for her."

"That might be true," remarked one of the shrewder elders, "but a chief's son would give his mistress's father enough presents and patronage to more than make up the difference. Polonius sounds like a fool to me."

"Many people think he was," I agreed. "Meanwhile Polonius sent his son Laertes off to Paris to learn the things of that country, for it was the homestead of a very great chief indeed. Because he was afraid that Laertes might waste a lot of money on beer and women and gambling, or get into trouble by fighting, he sent one of his servants to Paris secretly, to spy out what Laertes was doing. One day Hamlet came upon Polonius's daughter Ophelia. He behaved so oddly he frightened her. Indeed"—I was fumbling for words to express the dubious quality of Hamlet's madness—"the chief and many others had also noticed that when Hamlet talked one could understand the words but not what they meant. Many people thought that he had become mad." My audience suddenly became much more attentive. "The great chief wanted to know what was wrong with Hamlet, so he sent for two of Hamlet's age mates [school friends would have taken long explanation] to talk to Hamlet and find out what troubled his heart. Hamlet, seeing that they had been bribed by the chief to betray him, told them nothing. Polonius, however, insisted that Hamlet was mad because he had been forbidden to see Ophelia, whom he loved."

"Why," inquired a bewildered voice, "should anyone bewitch Hamlet on that account?"

"Bewitch him?"

"Yes, only witchcraft can make anyone mad, unless, of course, one sees the beings that lurk in the forest."

I stopped being a storyteller, took out my notebook and demanded to be told more about these two causes of madness. Even while they spoke and I jotted notes, I tried to calculate the effect of this new factor on the plot. Hamlet had not been exposed to the beings that lurk in the forests. Only his relatives in the male line could bewitch him. Barring relatives not mentioned by Shakespeare, it had to be Claudius who was attempting to harm him. And, of course, it was.

For the moment I staved off questions by saying that the great chief also refused to believe that Hamlet was mad for the love of Ophelia and nothing else. "He was sure that something much more important was troubling Hamlet's heart."

"Now Hamlet's age mates," I continued, "had brought with them a famous storyteller. Hamlet decided to have this man tell the chief and all his homestead a story about a man who had poisoned his brother because he desired his brother's wife and wished to be chief himself. Hamlet was sure the great chief could not hear the story without making a sign if he was indeed guilty, and then he would discover whether his dead father had told him the truth."

The old man interrupted, with deep cunning, "Why should a father lie to his son?" he asked.

I hedged: "Hamlet wasn't sure that it really was his dead father." It was impossible to say anything, in that language, about devil-inspired visions.

"You mean," he said, "it actually was an omen, and he knew witches sometimes send false ones. Hamlet was a fool not to go to one skilled in reading omens and divining the truth in the first place. A man-who-sees-the-truth could have told him how his father died, if he really had been poisoned, and if there was witchcraft in it; then Hamlet could have called the elders to settle the matter."

The shrewd elder ventured to disagree. "Because his father's brother was a great chief, one-who-sees-the-truth might therefore have been afraid to tell it. I think it was for that reason that a friend of Hamlet's father—a witch and an elder—sent an omen so his friend's son would know. Was the omen true?"

"Yes," I said, abandoning ghosts and the devil; a witch-sent omen it would have to be. "It was true, for when the storyteller was telling his tale before all the homestead, the great chief rose in fear. Afraid that Hamlet knew his secret he planned to have him killed."

The stage set of the next bit presented some difficulties of translation. I began cautiously. "The great chief told Hamlet's mother to find out from her son what he knew. But because a woman's children are always first in her heart, he had the important elder Polonius hide behind a cloth that hung against the wall of Hamlet's mother's sleeping hut. Hamlet started to scold his mother for what she had done."

There was a shocked murmur from everyone. A man should never scold his mother.

"She called out in fear, and Polonius moved behind the cloth. Shouting, 'A rat!' Hamlet took his machete and slashed through the cloth." I paused for dramatic effect. "He had killed Polonius!"

The old men looked as each other in supreme disgust. "That Polonius truly was a fool and a man who knew nothing! What child would not know enough to shout, 'It's me!'" With a pang, I remembered that these people are ardent hunters, always armed with bow, arrow, and machete; at the first rustle in the grass an arrow is aimed and ready, and the hunter shouts "Game!" If no human voice answers immediately, the arrow speeds on its way. Like a good hunter Hamlet had shouted, "A rat!"

I rushed in to save Polonius's reputation. "Polonius did speak. Hamlet heard him. But he thought it was the chief and wished to kill him to avenge his father. He had meant to kill him earlier that evening. . . ." I broke down, unable to describe to these pagans, who had no belief in individual afterlife, the difference between dying at one's prayers and dying "unhousell'd, disappointed, unaneled."

This time I had shocked my audience seriously. "For a man to raise his hand against his father's brother and the one who has become his father— that is a terrible thing. The elders ought to let such a man be bewitched."

I nibbled at my kola nut in some perplexity, then pointed out that after all the man had killed Hamlet's father.

"No," pronounced the old man, speaking less to me than to the young men sitting behind the elders. "If your father's brother has killed your father, you must appeal to your father's age mates; *they* may avenge him. No man may use violence against his senior relatives." Another thought struck him. "But if his father's brother had indeed been wicked enough to bewitch Hamlet and make him mad that would be a good story indeed, for it would be his fault that Hamlet, being mad, no longer had any sense and thus was ready to kill his father's brother."

There was a murmur of applause. *Hamlet* was again a good story to them, but it no longer seemed quite the same story to me. As I thought over the coming complications of plot and motive, I lost courage and decided to skim over dangerous ground quickly.

"The great chief," I went on, "was not sorry that Hamlet had killed Polonius. It gave him a reason to send Hamlet away, with his two treacherous age mates, with letters to a chief of a far country, saying that Hamlet should be killed. But Hamlet changed the writing on their papers, so that the chief killed his age mates instead." I encountered a reproachful glare from one of the men whom I had told undetectable forgery was not merely immoral but beyond human skill. I looked the other way.

"Before Hamlet could return, Laertes came back for his father's funeral. The great chief told him Hamlet had killed Polonius. Laertes swore to kill Hamlet because of this, and because his sister Ophelia, hearing her father had been killed by the man she loved, went mad and drowned in the river."

"Have you already forgotten what we told you?" The old man was reproachful. "One cannot take vengeance on a madman; Hamlet killed Polonius in his madness. As for the girl, she not only went mad, she was drowned. Only witches can make people drown. Water itself can't hurt anything. It is merely something one drinks and bathes in."

I began to get cross. "If you don't like the story, I'll stop."

The old man made soothing noises and himself poured me some more beer. "You tell the story well, and we are listening. But it is clear that the elders of your country have never told you what the story really means. No, don't interrupt! We believe you when you say your marriage customs are different, or your clothes and weapons. But people are the same everywhere; therefore, there are always witches and it is we, the elders, who know how witches work. We told you it was the great chief who wished to kill Hamlet, and now your own words have proved us right. Who were Ophelia's male relatives?"

"There were only her father and her brother." Hamlet was clearly out of my hands.

"There must have been many more; this also you must ask of your elders when you get back to your country. From what you tell us, since Polonius was dead, it must have been Laertes who killed Ophelia, although I do not see the reason for it."

We had emptied one pot of beer, and the old men argued the point with slightly tipsy interest. Finally one of them demanded of me, "What did the servant of Polonius say on his return?"

With difficulty I recollected Reynaldo and his mission. "I don't think he did return before Polonius was killed."

"Listen," said the older, "and I will tell you how it was and how your story will go, then you may tell me if I am right. Polonius knew his son would get into trouble, and so he did. He had many fines to pay for fighting, and debts from gambling. But he had only two ways of getting money quickly. One was to marry off his sister at once, but it is difficult to find a man who will marry a woman desired by the son of a chief. For if the chief's heir commits adultery with your wife, what can you do? Only a fool calls a case against a man who will someday be his judge. Therefore Laertes had to take the second way: he killed his sister by witchcraft, drowning her so he could secretly sell her body to the witches."

I raised an objection. "They found her body and buried it. Indeed Laertes jumped into the grave to see his sister once more—so, you see, the body was truly there. Hamlet, who had just come back, jumped in after him."

"What did I tell you?" The elder appealed to the others. "Laertes was up to no good with his sister's body. Hamlet prevented him, because the chief's heir, like a chief, does not wish any other man to grow rich and powerful. Laertes would be angry, because he would have killed his sister without benefit to himself. In our country he would try to kill Hamlet for that reason. Is this not what happened?"

"More or less," I admitted. "When the great chief found Hamlet was still alive, he encouraged Laertes to try to kill Hamlet and arranged a fight with machetes between them. In the fight both the young men were wounded to death. Hamlet's mother drank the poisoned beer that the chief meant for Hamlet in case he won the fight. When he saw his mother die of poison, Hamlet, dying, managed to kill his father's brother with his machete."

"You see, I was right!" exclaimed the elder.

'That was a very good story," added the old man, "and you told it with very few mistakes. There was just one more error, at the very end. The poison Hamlet's mother drank was obviously meant for the survivor of the fight, whichever it was. If Laertes had won, the great chief would have poisoned him, for no one would know that he arranged Hamlet's death. Then, too, he need not fear Laertes' witchcraft; it takes a strong heart to kill one's only sister by witchcraft.

"Sometime," concluded the old man, gathering his ragged toga about him, "you must tell us some more stories of your country. We, who are elders, will instruct you in their true meaning, so that when you return to your own land your elders will see that you have not been sitting in the bush, but among those who know things and who have taught you wisdom."

William W. Stein

THE CASE OF THE HUNGRY CALVES

This is the story of a mistake, an honest mistake. Not all mistakes anthropologists make get reported, though more of them should be for they could be instructive. If we can learn from the mistakes made by others, then perhaps the chances of our making a similar mistake may be reduced.

A young anthropologist who has just gone into the field, like an enthusiastic member of the Peace Corps who has just arrived at the scene of his assigned service, sees something he "knows" to be "wrong." What is more natural (and praiseworthy) in terms of our cultural values than to try to right that wrong. Presumably, an individual wouldn't volunteer for Peace Corps service if he didn't want to help his fellow man. In this case, the anthropologist was not visiting the Hualcainos in Peru specifically to help them, but to study them. Nevertheless, he couldn't refrain from making what he thought was a helpful suggestion to alleviate what he saw to be a serious problem, namely, calves suffering from malnutrition. His specific suggestion, entirely logical from our point of view, was a complete flop. It is not always easy to learn why a "good" idea wasn't such a good idea. Professor Stein's account of his discovery of why his well intentioned "experiment" failed and his closing remark to the effect that if he had known enough about the culture he never would have made the suggestion in the first place should give pause to self-confident Peace Corpsmen who are certain that they know what help the natives need and who plan to march in and give them that "needed" help.

For further information on this Peruvian people, see William W. Stein, *Hualcan: Life in the Highlands of Peru* (Ithaca, 1961).

The Community of Hualcan

Hualcan is a Quechua-speaking Andean Highland Indian village in the District of Carhuaz, Department of

Reprinted from *Human Organization,* 15 (1956), 15–21, by permission of the author and the Society for Applied Anthropology.
The material presented in this paper was gathered while the writer was in Peru as an Area Research Fellow of the Social Science Research Council and a Pre-Doctoral Fellow in Anthropology of the Wenner-Gren Foundation for Anthropological Research during 1951–52. This case has been more briefly described in William W. Stein, "Hualcan: An Andean Indian Estancia," Cornell University Ph.D. Thesis. Ithaca, 1955, pp. 393–396. Dr. Stein was with the Human Relations Area Files in New Haven, Conn. [He is now a member of the anthropology department at the State University of New York at Buffalo.—*Ed. Note.*]

Ancash, Peru. The settlement is located in a narrow valley, the Chucchun, which opens into the Callejon de Huaylas just south of the town of Carhuaz, a little over six miles west of the village. The Hualcan lands belong to the Indians who live there, and on the basis of this fact the settlement is locally classified as an *estancia,* an independent land-owning community, as distinguished from an *hacienda,* or estate, which is often in the hands of an overseer appointed by an absentee landlord.

The Hualcan houses are dispersed over the valley bottom-lands and on the low slopes of the hills which surround the village on three sides. The bottom-lands, at an altitude of 9–10,000 feet, are irrigable and in use throughout the year: in the dry season, from May to October, and the rainy season, from November to April. Other Hualcan lands, both single-crop fields and pastures, extend up to the "puna" at about 13,000 feet. The territory of Hualcan actually goes beyond this altitude to the lakes and glaciers of the Cordillera Blanca, a mountain range with peaks of over 20,000 feet.

The economic condition of Hualcan is somewhat better than that of many other *estancias* in the area mainly because the Hualcainos, the people of Hualcan, have a source of water: several small glacial lakes from which water is carried to the fields in the dry season by means of a system of irrigation ditches. Moreover, Hualcainos own both bottom-lands for intensive agriculture and higher, non-irrigable slopes for hardy grain crops and pasture. Larger tracts of pasture land on the hills and the "puna" are also brought into use. Subsistence activity is thus fairly well distributed between farming and herding.

The agricultural capital of Hualcan is not really sufficient to produce adequately for the more than 700 Hualcainos. About half of the households in the village find it necessary to maintain a status of dependency on the Mestizo *haciendas* across the valley. Such households are obligated to furnish *hacienda* labor on three or four days per week in return for fields and pasture which they can use for their own needs. Almost all of the "free" households, the other half of the community, send members to work for periods ranging from a week or two to several months on the Peruvian coastal plantations, a day's journey away. Coastal wages are good and regular migrations of male laborers to centers such as Paramonga and San Jacinto occur during lulls in the agricultural cycle when household supplies can be reduced. Only a very few households are self-sufficient, in the sense of not having to depend on one outside agency or another to supplement production. Even these few fortunate families, however, must trade their surplus products outside the village for the household necessities and luxuries which cannot be produced in Hualcan. In this context, self-sufficiency and accumulation are such highly desirable goals for the Hualcaino that he can seldom bring himself to part easily with even a poor and inferior item of property.

All Hualcainos are agriculturists and herders, although many of them practice some specialty: ceramics, weaving, tailoring, petty trading, or curing. Every Hualcaino owns at least a small piece of land. Without this minimum there is little self-esteem for the individual and no social status in the community. Similarly, every person who belongs to Hualcan, including even infants, will own at least one grazing animal. The fields furnish a variety of grain, root, and garden produce: maize, wheat, barley, quinoa, potatoes, oca, ullocu, squash, pumpkin, cabbage, peppers, and many other minor food plants and herbs. The animals (chickens, guinea pigs, sheep, goats, burros, and cattle) furnish meat almost incidentally, except for the excessive quantities which are consumed at fiestas. The sheep is one of the most important animals in Hualcan since it provides wool for most of the clothing. Cattle, too, are important: they serve as draft animals in agriculture. Cattle also furnish milk which, when it is available, the Hualcainos regard as an interesting if not a staple dietary item.

Getting a living in Hualcan is at best a difficult art. Agricultural capital, land and livestock, is constantly threatened by a host of natural and human forces. Crops are attacked by blights, hail, frost, heavy rains, or drought. Animals are pest-ridden and malnourished because good lands simply cannot be spared for fodder crops. Humans steal from each other and involve themselves in expensive litigation over property. The result is that Hualcainos do not get enough to eat for most of the year. Food is consequently an important item in Hualcan, a source of gratification, anxiety, and violence. Food figures in ritual gift-giving. It is consumed in enormous quantities at fiestas which are periods of food "license." Damages to crops, animals, or food stores, and counter-accusations are bases for verbal and physical aggression.

In Hualcan terms, man is enjoined to seek his living with all the force he can muster. An important principle, or "theme,"[1] of Hualcan culture affirms that all gratification is to be achieved only with effort and that man therefore has to exert himself. The Hualcan approach to the world, especially in the subsistence sphere, is frenetic. Man's relations with nature and with his fellow man are tinged with violence. At the same time, peace and harmony do exist as important goals for the Hualcaino.

The "Experiment"

The field work on which this paper is based was carried on in Hualcan for six months, from December, 1951, to June, 1952. Residence was established in the household of Miguel Paucar, a ,Hualcaino of about 55 years of age who had passed through a long series of ritual offices and thus commanded considerable respect throughout the community.

Miguel Paucar's household was one of the more self-sufficient family groups in Hualcan. It was not among the community's three richest households, the members of which owned large amounts of property and carried on extensive trade outside Hualcan with their surplus produce. However, both Miguel and his wife, Nicolasa, owned enough fields to furnish an

---

[1]Morris E. Opler ("Themes as Dynamic Forces in Culture," *American Journal of Sociology,* 51, 198–206, 1945, p. 198) defines "themes" as follows: "The term 'theme' is used here in a technical sense to denote a postulate or position, declared or implied, and usually controlling behavior or stimulating activity which is tacitly approved or openly promoted in a society." Hualcan themes have been discussed at length in Stein, *ibid.,* pp. 360–398.

adequate diet for most of the year. They owned enough sheep to clothe themselves. Miguel was a specialist in weaving and tailoring. He owned a loom and one of Hualcan's half-dozen sewing machines. With these he was able to add some grain or potatoes to the household income now and then, and even occasionally a few coppers. Nicolasa raised a surplus of hot peppers in her garden and collected the eggs from the household chickens. She would take these to the market in town on Sundays to sell for cash which she then used to buy salt, matches, and sweetening. When Miguel had a free day, he would go to town to work for a townsman in the fields or in construction. With his earnings he purchased coca and, once in a while, a new blade for an agricultural implement. The surplus wool from the flock of about 40 sheep was sold for cash or bartered for coastal products when the traders came to Hualcan every year in July.

Miguel's son, Manuel, and daughter-in-law, Victoria, did not own as much property as their elders but were gradually accumulating things. They expected eventually to inherit from their parents. When Miguel was a young man he made several trips to the coast to earn money for the purchase of much of his present property. He had not been on the coast for several years, however, because his agricultural and ritual responsibilities did not give him the time. Manuel, on the other hand, had been going to the coast from time to time, although since Victoria had had a baby the frequency and duration of these trips were diminishing.

Early during the writer's stay in Hualcan, two of Miguel's cows calved: one early in January and the other toward the end of that month. Shortly after the second calf was born, the two young animals were brought down to the house from the pasture. This action coincided with the onset of a rather cold and rainy period with frequent afternoon and evening hail storms. Miguel explained that keeping the calves at home would protect them from the weather and would give them a chance to suckle peacefully. They were tethered under a shelter in the courtyard of the house. The cows were kept with the other animals in a pen, about 100 yards removed from the house. East morning, the women whose job it was to herd the animals would bring the cows to the calves, let them suckle for a while, and then drive all the animals together up to the pasture where they spent a good part of the day. They often called upon Modista, Miguel's daughter of about eight years, and Deunicia, an older girl whose mother was a poor dependent in the household, to take charge of the animals while the older women went about their other duties.

About a week after the calves were first brought to the house, a change in the morning routine was observed. When the cows were brought from the animal pen they were staked in front of the house. The two girls, Modista and Deunicia, would get the calves from the courtyard and hold them in front of the cows while Nicolasa and Victoria milked. After the women had got perhaps two or three quarts, the calves were let loose and allowed to suckle for a while. Then the animals were taken to the pasture. When this morning milking began, the household diet changed. The milk was used often for the evening meal in the preparation of grain pudding. Immediately, too, the women began to set aside a quantity of milk each day for making into cheese. When the cheese was ripe it was used as a condiment in the flavoring of soups and stews. Both pudding and cheese, incidentally, are considered great dietary luxuries and indices of economic well-being.

The calves, on the other hand, appeared to be receiving an inadequate diet. Hualcan animals are in poor condition to begin with. There are many animal parasites, and fodder is scanty and of poor quality. Hualcainos' knowledge of animal husbandry is not "scientific" but traditional. Folk remedies, charms, divination, and prayers to the Saints are all parts of the Hualcan herding complex. The idea of human control would not apply. Often Hualcainos watch their animals die and are impotent to take any course of action beyond the philosophic comment that at least they will be able to have a little fresh meat for a few days.

The household milking was observed for two weeks. At the end of that period the writer suggested to Miguel that stronger animals might be raised if the calves were allowed to suckle freely for a while. The writer pointed out to Miguel that perhaps one of the reasons for the poor quality of the local cattle was that their milk was taken away from them too soon. He explained that he was no animal doctor but that the additional milk might conceivably produce a better animal in the end. The writer also offered to take the responsibility for the loss of the milk supply to the household by purchasing the cows' milk production for six weeks. At the end of that time, an assessment of the calves' development was to be made. Miguel did not appear too enthusiastic about the idea, but he agreed to go along with it mainly because of the extra cash income which it would afford.

The Problem

When a new technical idea is presented to the members of a community, it is assessed in terms of a field of the relevant features of the way of life of that community in the innovative situation. A wide range of cultural "facts" structures the situation for the culture-carriers. Similarly, such "facts" place certain limits on the action of the innovator and on the nature of the innovation. The new idea has to be conceived on the basis of a pre-existing system of thoughtways. Its meaning to the culture-carriers becomes, therefore, something quite different from its meaning to the foreign innovators who present the idea, who view the technique or the tool from the standpoint of their own cultural system of logic. The problem would appear ultimately to rest in uncovering and understanding the meanings behind differing systems of premises relating to the nature of man and the universe which are to be found among both donors and recipients. On such a groundwork it might be possible to predict what both donors and recipients will do in the situation. This approach would appear to have significance for even so mundane a problem as getting milk to feed hungry calves in the village of Hualcan.

The calf "experiment" was no experiment. Beyond the methodological considerations of supervision and measurement of both experimental and control groups, no control was achieved over situational factors of human relationships and meanings. A trait, such as calf-feeding, may be taken as a kind of point around which are focused a variety of cultural patterns. The system of logic which is inferred to underlie these more immediate systems of belief and action connects them with patterns relating to other avenues of life which appear to be based on the same set of fundamental cultural principles. Thus, from the trait, which is itself a nexus of immediate patterns, it appears to be possible to trace relationships throughout the cultural system, to view the whole culture as a matrix for the trait. The innovative situation in a sense furnishes a challenge to the culture-carriers to assess the new trait in terms of all relevant features which can be defined from the totality of past experience.

It is the aim of this paper to describe and interpret the failure of an attempted technical innovation. The course of events will be shown to involve a network of cultural factors which ramify into all important aspects of the life of the community. Spicer's recent casebook[2] of attempted technical innovations and their successes and failures has clearly pointed out the role of cultural factors which lead to unanticipated consequences in programs of technical "aid."

In the case to be described here, the problem was initially viewed as one of demonstrating the economic consequences of furnishing calves with a better diet. No attempt was made to ascertain the probable social consequences of the manner in which this goal was to be achieved. The human subjects were not consulted with regard to the desirability of such consequences. Fortunately for the household and the community there were no significant consequences since the attempted innovation was patently unfeasible in terms of the viewpoint of the Hualcainos. The observer was able to take a relatively objective position due to the nature of his role in the field: that of an anthropologist who had no strong emotional or economic investment in the outcome of the proposed change in dairying practices. There was neither hostility toward the innovator nor social disruption as by-products of the "experiment." Rather, the subjects were furnished with a humorous subject for leisure-time conversation.

This case illustrates some of the types of problems which a technician might have to face in Hualcan were he to inaugurate a serious attempt at technological change. It will also serve to point out how ignorance of local conditions can lead to an unrealistic demand on people when an innovator from another culture brings with him little more than his own cultural premises to help him assess the situation.

The Human Factors

For a week the cows were not milked in the writer's presence and they were allowed to suckle their calves freely. Suddenly, the women resumed their morning milkings and no explanation was volunteered. When the

---

[2]Edward H. Spicer, ed., *Human Problems in Technological Change; A Casebook.* New York: Russell Sage Foundation, 1952.

family members were asked about it a few days later, they explained that the children of the household were taking the milk while the animals were pastured on the hills, and that they also were stealing into the animal pen at night to get it. Moreover, they added, the women of the household needed it.

It did not seem at the beginning that the proposal was an unreasonable request, except with regard to the fact that no veterinarian had given an opinion on its validity based on technical knowledge. It was unknown whether or not more milk for calves was a significant variable in such an attempt to improve livestock quality. Cattle diseases and parasites plus poor fodder for grown animals appeared to be mainly responsible for the condition of the Hualcan livestock. However, it was hoped that more milk for calves might help a little. There could, of course, be no way of prediction of success or explanation of failure of the milk to produce better animals. Furthermore, the writer understood that while he could take the responsibility of paying for the milk, others would have to take responsibility for the supervision of the "experiment." Even if the family did not believe in a successful outcome, the writer felt that they would accept the money and wait for proof.

The writer ignored practically all of the factors which invalidated the whole "experiment." First, the milk was not paid for in advance. He assumed that a payment could be made weekly for the milk production. However, in this way no compact was made with Miguel. In Hualcan there appears to be an idea or premise which is basic to interpersonal relations and which may be called the principle of compactual responsibility. In practically all transactions which partake of the nature of a contract, a situationally-structuring gift, the DERECHUN,[3] is made in advance. This negotiation is a necessary preliminary. If the subject of a DERECHUN, that is, the one who is approached by another who has a request to make, wishes to avoid responsibility he has but to refuse the gift. If he accepts the DERECHUN he is thereby obligated to perform according to the agreement which is made. This kind of preliminary gift structures the situation for planting a field on shares, for betrothals, for accepting a politico-religious office, and even for relations with demons who cannot get power over one until one accepts the DERECHUN. In effect, then, the writer did not really force anyone to accept compactual responsibility for the supervision of the "experiment" since no preliminary and situationally-structuring gift was made. Miguel was free to promise to *try* to feed the calves more milk but he did not obligate himself to superintend the "experiment" and, indeed, he was not free to perform in accordance with the writer's proposal, as was later discovered. Miguel put as much pressure as he could reasonably be expected to exert on the older members of his household. However, in Hualcan a household head functions in this type of situation more as a mediator than as a director.

[3] The orthographic convention used here is suggested by John H. Rowe ("Inca Culture at the Time of the Spanish Conquest," *Handbook of South American Indians,* ed. Julian Steward. Bureau of American Ethnology Bulletin No. 143, Vol. 2, pp. 183–330. Washington, 1946, pp. 185–186.) The use of capitals for Quechua material distinguishes it from Spanish, which is written in italicized lower-case letters.

Had the writer attempted to make a compact with Miguel he would have been told, as he later found out, that Miguel actually owned only one of the cows. The other belonged to Nicolasa. The writer had assumed that Miguel, as head of the household, had control over the other household members. While this was an essential fact of Hualcan family organization, based on principles of age and maleness as validations of status, there were at least two other important principles involved as regulators of the household economy. Individuals are enjoined to be self-sufficient. They are also enjoined to share with others with whom they have "holy" relationships, that is, relatives. Personal property is inviolable but has to be shared with those who "count." The resources and income of all the members of a household, although they are owned separately, are pooled. A field, for example, is always owned by an individual but the other members of his household help him operate it. The products from the field are divided at the harvest and each individual has his own section of the household storeroom and his own storage jars to hold his share. While it might be said theoretically that Miguel "owned" his cow's milk supply, it belonged to the whole household in fact.

Had Miguel been asked he would have explained further that he really had no say at all in the disposal of his cow's milk since the women of the household were pasturing them. Hualcan women, as "gatekeepers" of gratification, have a general control of the household larder and dispose of the products as they see fit. While Miguel "owned" a number of grain jars, for example, Nicolasa always saw to it that Miguel's grain was used proportionately in the preparation of meals. In the case of the milk, Nicolasa and Victoria were using that product in their cooking. Some of the cheese they made was taken to town to be sold for cash which was then used for the purchase of household items like salt, matches, aspirin, and sweetening.

Also, it was observed that a good portion of the milk was being given away. The women were sharing it with the relatives of every other member of the household. It would be unforgivable for a family to have a milk supply and not share it with relatives. Although the family relationship is a "holy" relationship and a source of stability for the individual, family status has to be validated constantly. In Hualcan perhaps the most important type of status validation is by contribution. Thus Nicolasa and Victoria were validating the status of the other household members as well as their own as relatives to other persons by utilizing the means at their disposal to share something good with those others. In this way, too, the household members affirmed their own dependence on their relatives by offering a symbol of honor and respect, and they fulfilled their obligations for past favors given by those to whom they gave the milk.

Had Nicolasa been approached with the proposal, and had a formal attempt been made to obligate her, she would have pointed out that she could only assume responsibility for her "own" cow, which was really Miguel's. She had lent the cow which was technically hers to Victoria to care for and to milk. In a broad sense, the second cow "belonged" to Victoria while she was taking care of it. It was Nicolasa's alone, with regard to ultimate disposal, since Nicolasa held formal title to it. However, if it had been possible to approach both Nicolasa and Victoria properly, they would no doubt have repeated that the children would take milk from cows in the pens and on the hills, in any case, and that little could be done about it.

Unattended property in Hualcan appears to be "fair game" for any passerby. Hualcainos are constantly on guard against theft. Their expectations are fulfilled frequently when valuable portions of their crops are taken. The people are poor, and many steal because of necessity. Others steal maliciously, in order to hurt their victims in return for real or supposed wrongs. Still others steal because they have been stolen from, and this method is the only way of assuring a return for their labors. A few, perhaps, steal "habitually" because they have always done so.

Hualcainos are not without protective devices against stealing. Houses, for example, are built in such a way that the courtyard cannot be seen from the outside. The would-be thief often does not know whether or not someone is at home. Every family owns one or more dogs which set up a tremendous racket at the approach of someone other than a neighbor and will go on to the attack unless called off by one of the household members. Both harvests and animals are protected by means of CUKLLA, little portable brush huts, which may be moved from a harvested field to one which is ripe or from one pasture to another. Few families, of course, have the personnel to install a guard in a CUKLLA in every field, but it is hoped by the Hualcainos that the presence of such a hut will indicate to the thief the possibility that someone *might* be inside.

If Nicolasa and Victoria had thought about the problem objectively, they would have had to admit that the idea of guarding property, such as the milk supply, from violation was indeed precedented in Hualcan. A family member always takes a turn regularly at staying with the animals when they are pastured on the hill, far away. An arrangement could have been made with a responsible adult to watch over the cows and their calves to see that the latter received their milk.

It must be remembered that the milk thieves were children, not malicious strangers. While children are cherished, in Hualcan terms, they are not in a favorable status of life. Since they are not great contributors they are consequently able to assert no greater status than that of dependents. The infant is fondled and loved demonstrably as long as he is helpless. At the age of about one year, property is heaped upon him at his hair-cutting ceremony, at which time he becomes a property-holding member of the community. As soon as he passes beyond the toddler stage, however, especially when another baby has entered the household, he is thrust into the care of his siblings or other household children. As quickly as possible he is introduced to the hard business of getting a living. Emphasis is placed on making the individual self-sufficient early. Until children are strong enough to "count" in agricultural production, they are generally accorded a scant share of the products. They are clothed in ragged cast-offs in a community where clothing is an important status symbol. They often have to be satisfied with scraps and cold left-overs from meals where food patterns are also integrated with status. Sometimes, children are even sent off on errands when there is something good in limited quantity to be divided among the older members of a household.

Hualcan children, like the dogs, are always hungry. As a consequence, patterns of stealing food are included in childhood activities. Children raid their own and neighbors' household larders for food, just as their parents steal from their *patrones,* the Mestizo land-owners. These patterns of stealing are expected and householders do their best to guard against the raids of children. In the case of the milk supply, Nicolasa and Victoria were satisfied as long as they took a reasonable quantity of milk from the cows each morning. However, it would have been difficult to protect the milk supply from more serious violation from time to time if the women had not been measuring it daily.

Another set of factors relating to herding practices must also be taken into consideration. Children often have sole charge of the household animals away from the house. One of the tasks which is given to children as early as possible is that of herding. While this is generally considered women's work, the women are not always free of other responsibilities in the household economy. Consequently they assign herding tasks to the children. When there is a milk supply among the cows, it is expected that the herders, children or even adults, will take some during the day as a kind of *temple,* a form of additional compensation for labor, like a "tip." *Temple* is always expected to accompany exchange transactions which involve the payment of goods or cash for services. In effect, then, the herders would be denied their *temple* if the milk were forbidden them.

When the scheme for more milk for calves was proposed, the writer had begun to achieve a vague conception of the importance of the principle of the necessity for self-sufficiency in Hualcan. This principle was unconsciously used as a part of the presentation of the argument for the "experiment" to Miguel when the proposal was phrased in terms of allowing the calves to have their due and not withholding from them the means to cope with the world on their own terms. However, the writer did not adequately understand the female principle in Hualcan. As has been pointed out, the female is the "gatekeeper" of gratification. If this principle can be applied to cows, then the cows themselves were the "gatekeepers" to their own milk supply. In no sense could the milk be said to "belong" to the calves. Rather, by applying the principle which enjoins sharing with those who "count," the cows were obligated to their human caretakers who protected them from predatory animals, nursed them when they were sick, and furnished them with food in the form of pasture. Cows, after all, do not own land. Consequently, if anyone is "due" the milk, it is the people who take care of the cows.

Yet the principle of self-sufficiency is not without applicability to the growth and development of calves. It is simply applied in a way which was unanticipated. The call to action is applied to calves as it is to humans, parallel with self-sufficiency, and calves are enjoined to seek independence early. As the calves grew older, it was observed that the household members made systematic and successful attempts to wean the calves. For the first weeks the calves were allowed free access to their mothers. At the end of this period morning milkings were begun. At the same time, the calves were encouraged to eat more grass, and choice leaves and blades were offered to them. It cannot be said that Hualcainos are lacking in concern for the well-being of their cattle. The family members pointed out that it was advisable to get the calf used to taking care of itself early, that it was not good for it to be too dependent upon its mother. Anything can happen to a cow. For the calf ultimate satisfaction and service lies precisely in self-sufficiency within the rules of the system.

In the context of Hualcan culture, the proposal as it was originally stated was meaningless. The subjects of the "experiment" worked out a resolution of the problem which was set before them: they ignored it. Miguel and his family were frank in explaining, to the best of their ability, why they did not wish to continue attempting the impossible. While the writer had some prestige in their eyes he had no power. If coercion had been possible and had been attempted, the family would have conformed openly but they would have continued their traditional practices in secret, and they would have been amused at the trick they were playing on the outsider. The Hualcan ethical system does not apply completely to the outsider and Hualcainos feel their greatest solidarity in many situations where relationships with outsiders are involved. Since they fear outsiders and feel themselves to be powerless and ineffective in dealings with them, Hualcainos find it difficult to be direct. Instead, they tend to assume confusion and lack of understanding.[4] They try to take advantage of the outsider, stealing from him if possible.

This type of behavior is in conformity to another organizing principle of Hualcan culture, that of the supernatural danger of the outside world. Some of this evil power adheres to the Hualcaino who visits the outside. An outsider brings it into the community. While outsiders effectively control Hualcan and the Hualcainos, as *hacienda*-owners who control the household economies of their *peones,* as townsmen who exact labor tribute, or as political authorities with the means of physical coercion, they are also believed to be dangerous in a supernatural sense. Many outsiders are conceived as demons of one type or another, or they are thought to bear evil powers which make people sick with tuberculosis or syphilis. It is only after social interaction has gone on, when the stranger is no longer strange, that most Hualcainos are able to assess the outsider as a fellow human being who, if slightly contaminated, is not particularly dangerous.

Matters relating to the supernatural are not irrelevant to the context of animal husbandry. God is conceived in Hualcan as the supreme power who has arranged the world in its present form for His own reasons. He has placed good and evil forces in the world in a kind of balance. His relatives, the Saints, are more approachable and are in fact the mediators between man and God. The Hualcaino therefore prays not to God but to Santa Ursula, the patroness of Hualcan. The household economy of any family depends upon destiny which is equated with God's will. If the fields produce

---

[4]As a case in point: Once one of the writer's colleagues in the field came to Hualcan for a visit. When he presented himself at the house, the family at first denied all knowledge of the writer. When pressed, they denied knowledge of his whereabouts. Finally they sent the visitor off in the opposite direction from the house where they knew the writer to be.

well, for example, it is a sign that one has fulfilled one's obligations to the supernatural powers and has achieved harmony with the field of forces of the universe. Bad luck in agriculture is a sign that something is lacking in one's obligations or that one has become contaminated with evil power. Blasphemy brings as a supernatural sanction contamination with holy power. Therefore, if one's animals are poor, the matter is between oneself and God, to be mediated by God's representatives, the priests, or by Santa Ursula. The condition of the livestock varies according to God's will and not according to man's efforts. Livestock can be protected and one's herds can become numerous and healthy through devotion to God's will, by serving Him and His relatives through ritual practices and labor. It would be presumptuous for a human to pretend to assume control over the destiny of his own livestock. It is man's duty to accept the destiny which God gives him and to try to achieve harmony within these limits. At the same time, if one fulfills the letter of one's compact with God, if one devotes oneself to labor and to the honor of God and the Saints, one's destiny can be changed. However, this is a matter of appeal to the supernatural and not one of human action. In a religious sense, therefore, the avenue to the control over the condition of the livestock is defined as supernatural. God, not more milk, is the deciding factor in the maturation of calves.

Conclusion

The "experiment" failed because of the lack of control over a multitude of human factors which have been outlined in the preceding section. These factors make sense in Hualcan terms, despite superficial inconsistencies. It would be apparent in terms of Western logic that one cannot be at the same time self-sufficient economically, a good relative who shares his things freely, and an honorable man in terms of compactual responsibility. The principle of the call to action is hardly compatible with the idea of the acceptance of destiny, or God's will, and the principle behind the procedure of enlisting God's aid through service and ingratiation is a contradiction of both. Yet in the Hualcan system these principles are not contradictory; rather, they are applied in any real situation in different ways. No Hualcaino senses tension or feels disturbed.[5]

There is little conflict or ambivalence in the decisions which are made with regard to problems of milk supply for Hualcan calves. Similar assessments of situations occur regularly in Hualcan, based on the Hualcan system

[5]The criteria of tension and disturbance are used in a definition of cultural integration by Albert K. Cohen as follows: "...integration, in the cultural sense, is a matter of tension on the level of action...whether or not two norms [give] rise to felt disturbances or tensions [is] a function of situations. That is, if norm "A" prescribes a certain mode of action towards objects and situations with the characteristic "a," and norm "B" prescribes a different mode of action towards objects and situations with the characteristic "b," the consistency of the two norms or their capacity to generate tension depends on the extent to which the social system generates situations which combine both characteristics "a" and "b"." ("On Definitions of Integration," Social Science Research Council Social Integration Seminar. MS., 1952, p. 4.)

of thought. It is not so much a matter of *which* principles are applied to a situation but *how* they are applied. Such integration is dynamic: situations can change, and some principles may become emphasized, while the integrative significance of others diminishes.

The terms of the original proposal which called for a change in Hualcan dairying practices would have created conflict by bringing about an abnormal situation, or series of situations, relating to the several aspects of milk-handling and calf-care, had the Hualcainos accepted the goal and the means. Fortunately, they accepted neither. The Hualcainos might have been favorably influenced in their assessment of the new idea if the potential conflicts which accompanied the proposed means could have been resolved. In daily life Hualcainos dispose of countless complex problems in terms of their own definitions of the nature of the social and physical world. If an innovator had introduced the idea of more milk for calves and had made the goal of greater control over the destiny of livestock understandable, attractive, and feasible, and if objective evidence of the utility of the means could have been furnished, many Hualcainos would no doubt have made the attempt to incorporate the new trait into their lives. If the innovator had been equipped to phrase the proposal in accord with the principles of Hualcan culture the "experiment" would have had more chance of success. This would have meant the achievement of an understanding of Hualcan principles and their integration in order to gain some basis for making reasonable predictions of how the situation would be assessed by the Hualcainos. The evidence suggests that some substitute for milk would have been required in the relevant contexts in order to avoid disruptions of patterns of milk production, distribution, and consumption, and repercussions in the wider social context. The writer, with limited means, would not have been able to furnish a milk substitute had he understood its necessity. Therefore, from both methodological and ethical standpoints, the "experiment" should never have been attempted.

Anacleto Apodaca

> CORN AND CUSTOM:
> THE INTRODUCTION OF HYBRID CORN
> TO SPANISH AMERICAN FARMERS
> IN NEW MEXICO
>
> In American culture a high value is placed upon efficiency and productivity and this tends to bias the kinds of counsel we offer other peoples. We try to make them more productive and more

Reprinted from Edward H. Spicer, ed., *Human Problems in Technological Change: A Casebook* (New York, 1952), pp. 35–39, by permission of the Russell Sage Foundation.

efficient. Rarely does it occur to us that there could be factors which might take precedence over our brands of scientific and technological progress. The following brief study is a classic example of what can happen when "brute technological force" is introduced without sophisticated cultural know-how. Note that this was no casual suggestion made by a passing anthropologist or Peace Corpsman. This was a "scientifically" planned experiment in culture change administered by a county extension agricultural agent who resided in the area. It is important to realize that technological breakthroughs are not enough to solve the problems of the world. Inevitably, one comes to people, and with people one has culture. Immunization by inoculation can't work unless people are willing to be inoculated. The latest surgical innovation cannot save lives unless people are willing to submit to surgery. It may well be that the reasons why different peoples reject a given "improvement" appear to be trivial or unimportant *to us*. The point is that the reasons are not trivial or unimportant *to them*.

One of the best introductions to the problems of applied anthropology with regard to introducing technological change is George M. Foster, *Traditional Cultures: and the Impact of Technological Change* (New York, 1962). Also useful is Margaret Mead, ed., *Cultural Patterns and Technical Change* (New York, 1955). For other case studies, see Edward H. Spicer, ed., *Human Problems in Technological Change* (New York, 1952), and Benjamin D. Paul, ed., *Health, Culture and Community: Case Studies of Public Reactions to Health Programs* (New York, 1955).

1. The Problem

For generations Spanish American farmers in the Rio Grande Valley of New Mexico have grown corn as an important crop. As compared with midwestern United States farmers their yields are very low, and the quality of the corn is poor by any ordinary standards. In one community recently, a county extension agent of the United States Department of Agriculture succeeded in introducing hybrid corn which gave about three times the yield of that grown traditionally. Once the results of the new seed were seen, a majority of the growers adopted the hybrid variety. Four years after the first introduction, however, nearly all the farmers had ceased to plant the hybrid and were again using the old corn. Why did a seemingly successful introduction not ensure the establishment of an improved seed? What factors had the county agent failed to take into consideration?

2. The Course of Events

1. In 1946 the county extension agent in...County, New Mexico, decided to try hybrid seed corn as a way of improving the corn yield of farmers in his jurisdiction.

2. He persuaded leaders in one village to allow him to present information concerning a hybrid variety. Discussions with the farmers proved more successful than he had hoped. Forty of the 84 growers in the village planted small amounts of the hybrid and doubled the production per acre of the preceding year.

3. The following year 60 growers planted hybrid corn, and the county agent felt that the introduction had been successful.

4. In 1948, however, although the high yield had continued, only 30 farmers planted hybrid. The other 30 who had planted it the year before went back to the traditional variety.

5. In 1949 the decline in number of farmers planting the hybrid was even greater. Only three in the whole village planted it. They were farmers whom the county agent had long regarded as progressive. All the rest were growing the old corn, and the planting of hybrid had not spread to any other village.

3. Relevant Factors

Originally borrowed from the Indians, corn has long been a staple crop among Spanish American farmers of...County. They grow it for their own consumption, selling none of it outside the villages. Formerly, like the Indian women of the region, the Spanish American women ground the corn on stone slabs. Now it is made into meal at local mills. From the meal thin, round cakes, called tortillas, are prepared which serve as a major item in the diet. Also when crops are relatively abundant, corn is fed to the stock, and the stalks are used as roughage for the animals.

The corn grown prior to 1946 is a variety developed locally, which the farmers call "Indian corn." It attains medium height, producing a minimum of roughage. Its average yield is 25 bushels to the acre and the farmers save their own seed from year to year, mostly without benefit of selection. The corn is planted in small irrigated fields, for which there is usually a plentiful supply of water.

The county agent's relations with the farmers were good. He spoke Spanish in the same manner, was familiar with their background and agricultural practices, and had served as agent for several years immediately preceding this venture. The seed corn, he felt, had degenerated and he suspected that this was an important factor in keeping production low. He decided to introduce a hybrid seed that was known for high yield and proceeded carefully, consulting with the college agronomist, who selected a variety—Hybrid U.S. 30—that had been tested in the immediate area. It was considered disease-resistant and capable of producing a good growth, averaging 100 bushels to the acre.

Then the agent discussed the problem of low corn yields with the leaders of the village, having chosen this particular community as a likely place for a good response. The men readily recognized the need for better production and were willing to think that, perhaps, their seed strain was weakening after long continuous propagation.

The soils of the fields used by this village were tested and found to be of good fertility, since here, as elsewhere in the area, it had been customary to use some manure yearly. After discussion with the leaders of the various problems involved, a meeting was called in order to present the county agent's plan.

Everyone in the village was invited to the meeting. The agent showed movies of the hybrid corn and cartoons to enliven the demonstration. Then the leaders took over the meeting and explained in their own words the plan for introducing hybrid corn. All those present seemed to agree that the new seed was the answer to many of their problems and that they would be well able to afford the price of the seed, once it was available locally.

By special arrangement with a grower of seed, the new hybrid was furnished in exchange for the old seed. A demonstration plot which clearly showed a tripled crop was set up near the village, with the result that 40 farmers planted hybrid and each doubled his production the first year.

The whole procedure seemed to have been soundly based and to have got unusually rapid results. There was confirmation of this, when, in the following year, the county agent was able to report that 60 farmers, about three-fourths of all the growers in the village, had accepted the new seed. The seed was producing admirably; it was within their means and seemed a very profitable innovation.

4. The Outcome

Inquiry during 1949, after nearly all the farmers had gone back to planting "Indian corn," revealed the reasons for their rejecting the hybrid. The feeling of need for better yields was still strongly present. No one complained of lack of market for surpluses, which the extension agent had feared might be a factor. There had not, in fact, been any real surplus over the requirements of people and livestock. No one had had any particular difficulty in producing the new crop. All those who had grown it were still much impressed with the large yields, and some said it confirmed their belief that their own seed had become weakened through generations of in-breeding. Owing to increased production, there had been no difficulty in obtaining seed.

Gradually the agent secured responses to direct questions as to why those who had tried hybrid had not continued to plant it. The answer was simple. As one farmer said, "My wife doesn't like that hybrid, that's all." He and others explained that the new corn had not been popular from the first harvest. All the wives had complained. Some did not like its texture; it did not hang together well for tortillas; the tortillas were not the color of nixtamal (the corn flour dough to which they were accustomed). Few had cared for the flavor, but the farmers who persisted in planting it after the first year had hoped that they would get used to it. It made abundant food for the stock and they were reluctant to drop it for that reason. However, after three years they had not become accustomed to the flavor or texture, and their wives were up in arms.

5. Analysis

This is an instance of careful procedure, up to a point, in the best tradition of agricultural extension in the United States. The agent moved slowly and carefully, and then only after a considerable period of observation and analysis of the specific local situation. He examined all the technical aspects of soil, growing conditions, and existing practices. A real need was felt for the new crop and he was able to induce farmers to formulate that need among themselves. He utilized local leadership and made no start until the people thoroughly understood what was to be done. He demonstrated procedure and results. It cannot be said that he ignored any of the well-tried, and often reiterated, rules of extension procedure.

Nevertheless, the agent's exploration of the context of the change sought did not go quite far enough. He had paid attention to the relations between the agricultural technology and the environmental conditions, and to those between farming practices and the social organization of the community. He failed, however, to inquire into the food habits and their influence on the selection of crops. By experiment, as it were, he found that food habits could not be ignored. He learned that the interests and wishes of the village women had to be taken into account as an important factor in the agricultural economy. Finally, he found that in the system of values of the community, corn quality was more important than corn quantity.

The agent had proceeded on the belief that increased farm production was the only important factor involved. He had not gone into the uses of the crop, nor had he tested it as a food prepared by the farmers in the usual manner.

He failed also to make allowance for the customary courtesy of the people, who were not used to correcting "experts" or to expressing themselves freely in the presence of the latter. On reflection the agent realized that some of the farmers had had doubts about the introduction, but had not felt that they should discourage his efforts.

It is probable that a successful procedure would have included the following steps:

1. Trial of several varieties of hybrid corn and the selection of one
2. More thorough testing of the corn to see how it fitted into the culture patterns
3. Continued demonstration of the advantages of the new seed

4. Close contact with the growers to detect any difficulties and to make modifications in the plan as needed

By these means the taste problem might have been detected earlier and met through the use of a more suitable type of hybrid.

REFERENCES

Harper, Allan G., Andrew R. Cordova, and Kalervo Oberg, *Man and Resources in the Middle Rio Grande Valley.* University of New Mexico Press, Albuquerque, 1943.

Leonard, Olen, and C.P. Loomis, *Culture of a Contemporary Rural Community, El Cerrito, New Mexico.* Rural Life Studies : 1. United States Department of Agriculture, Washington, 1941.

Sanchez., George I., *Forgotten People: A Study of New Mexicans.* University of New Mexico Press, Albuquerque, 1940.

Don Adams

THE MONKEY AND THE FISH:
CULTURAL PITFALLS
OF AN EDUCATIONAL ADVISER

It is easy for members of our society to criticize, and it is only slightly more difficult to offer advice. Thus one technique, which seems reasonable to us for helping to solve the problems of other peoples of the world, is to visit those peoples, offer them helpful criticisms, and provide sound advice. The anthropological rub is that the criticisms and advice are too often made from our cultural perspective without regard for the cultural context in which these criticisms and well meant advice are to be applied. We have seen how a casual suggestion made by an anthropologist in the field led to failure and how a more elaborate plan for agricultural reform also failed. Is there no way in which meaningful assistance may be offered and utilized?

There is also a crucial ethical problem. First of all, the very notion of offering help to members of another culture is a value-oriented concept. Then, what if the people allegedly in need of help don't want our help. Does our culture-bound confidence that "we know what's best for them even if they don't have sense enough to realize it" give us the moral right to ram this help down their protesting throats? Or even if we want to offer advice and the other culture is willing or indeed anxious to

Reprinted from the *International Development Review,* **2** (1960), 22–24, by permission of the author and the Society for International Development.

accept it, do we have the ethical right to interfere with the culture pattern of other peoples? One answer to these vexing problems is proposed by Professor Don Adams of the Syracuse University School of Education, who discusses the difficulties in introducing education reform in Korea. The adviser serves as a catalytic agent who provides alternatives, but which alternative is selected is decided by the people concerned. Of course, it can be argued that the mere suggestion of alternatives constitutes unwarrantable interference with another culture. Frequently, the presentation of alternatives accomplishes little more than making people discontent with what they have. However, there is no culture which does not change in some way and many of these culture changes entail something new replacing something old. Since culture change occurs in any case, one can be content that, at least within our cultural framework, there is nothing wrong with human intelligence consciously affecting the speed, direction, and nature of culture change. In a way, one of the best reasons for studying the nature of culture is so that man can exercise more control *over* it rather than be unconsciously controlled *by* it. Admittedly this depends upon a philosophical position which is not necessarily universal.

For considerations of the ways cultural anthropology can illuminate the problems facing specialists in education, see George D. Spindler, ed., *Education and Anthropology* (Stanford, 1955), Theodore Brameld, *Cultural Foundations of Education* (New York, 1957), Frederick C. Gruber, *Anthropology and Education* (Philadelphia, 1961), and George D. Spindler, ed., *Education and Culture: Anthropological Approaches* (New York, 1964). A useful survey article is Jules Henry, "A Cross-Cultural Outline of Education," *Current Anthropology,* 1 (1960), 267–305. For further references on Korean culture, see Cornelius Osgood, *The Koreans and Their Culture* (New York, 1951), B. H. Hazard, Jr., *et al., Korean Studies Guide* (Berkeley and Los Angeles, 1954), and Bernard S. Silberman, *Japan and Korea: A Critical Bibliography* (Tucson, 1962).

There is an old oriental story that accurately depicts the plight of an unwary foreign educational adviser: Once upon a time there was a great flood, and involved in this flood were two creatures, a monkey and a fish. The monkey, being agile and experienced, was lucky enough to scramble up a tree and escape the raging waters. As he looked down from his safe perch, he saw the poor fish struggling against the swift current. With the very best of intentions, he reached down and lifted the fish from the water. The result was inevitable.

The educational adviser, unless he is a careful student of his own culture and the culture in which he works, will be acting much like the monkey; and, with the most laudable intentions, he may make decisions equally disastrous. Using Korea as a case in point, I shall describe some of the cultural pitfalls facing an American working in that country. The description will involve examining some of the basic assumptions, or "unconscious canons of choice" as the distinguished anthropologist Ruth Benedict called them, of the Korean people. This analysis will be made in terms of the behavior promoted by such assumptions in order to indicate how such behavior may appear to be illogical or even unintelligible to a Western adviser. Many of the° value orientations described here also appear in other East Asian countries where similar cultural roots may be found. Japan and Korea, for example, were both greatly influenced by a variety of cultural forces emanating from China, the most profound of which has been called Confucianism. But sharply contrasting twentieth century forces of militarism, communism, and democracy have brought elements of noticeable dissimilarity among Asian countries that make extensive generalizations dangerous.

Time Orientation

The first obvious cultural difference noted by the American in Korea is regarded by some to be an especially important element in differentiating cultures. This is *time orientation,* the perspective with which a nation views the process of time. All peoples must examine problems rooted in the present or past and yet must try to anticipate the future. The differences in the view of time pointed out here are related to the degree of precedence given.

The American, for example, has historically looked with pleasant anticipation toward the future. Tomorrow is expected to be brighter than today, and, with minor exceptions, only things bigger and better can be envisioned for the future. History itself is often viewed as a continuum of progress, with each succeeding generation more advanced than the former. American schools consider that one of their major functions is the examination of the present so that their products may better plan the future.

Contrast this with the Korean culture, which historically has been oriented to the past; where the Good Life has been defined completely in terms of past living; where history has largely been viewed as cyclical, with the future regarded as a mere repetition of some portion of the past; and where innovations in terms of things bigger and better may be disrespectful to one's ancestors. The American technical adviser, geared to "getting things done" and "getting things moving," is often frustrated by situations in which his Korean colleagues appear to be acting too slowly or even stalling. Conversely, the American may by his direct approach appear exceedingly rude to the Korean, who sees no reason to be upset over current ills since the good times of the past are bound to reappear.

Historically, then, Korea has not viewed its institutions as developmental to the same degree as is done in the USA. While not adept at operation thinking, however, Korean students often pursue with skill the more purely academic and aesthetic interests. In so doing they exhibit characteristics that make the current-and-future-oriented American often seem superficial, even at times crude. Education in this cloistered setting could not be expected to be dynamic or experimental, and until the Japanese introduced colonial-flavored modern education in the twentieth century, the Korean school system was designed only to perpetuate the best of the past in an unaltered form. From ancient times the prescribed curriculum was the written wisdom of the Chinese sages and constituted what might be called a series of Asian Great Books. From the tender age when he memorized his first Chinese character until many years later when, if exceptionally able, he might pass the royal examination and become a government official, the curriculum of the scholar was the literature of the past. He studied not only the ideas involved but the author's phraseology and his technique of calligraphy. As the ancient texts assumed the proportions of canons, he studied to imitate rather than to exceed, to conform rather than to create. Education that was prized was divorced entirely from the social, economic, and scientific problems of the present.

The Man-Nature Orientation

A second cultural difference lies in the relation of man and nature or what might be called *man-nature orientation.* In America man has increasingly expected to gain mastery over nature and he has watched his wildest expectations come true. Mountains he crossed, tunneled through, or even pulverized. Rivers proved no obstacle to his energy, for these were easily dammed or bridged. In the East Asian culture, man typically has not been so concerned with gaining mastery over his environment as he has been in living in harmony with it. Mountains that might obstruct travel and rivers that might be impassable during certain seasons have not been viewed as merely frustrating inconveniences. Rather, these are historical facts to which man must discipline himself. The challenge lies not in constructing new weapons for mastery but in developing a higher degree of resignation.

As with time orientation the traditional view held by Koreans with respect to nature has not contributed to a dynamic educational system. If man does not seek mastery over nature, there is little need for the schools to be concerned with the tools and skills for manipulating the physical universe. Rather, schools should be concerned with developing not the active but the passive person, one who seeks to avoid the common, tedious, daily environment by finding and developing problems in a more aesthetic realm. The educated man is the man of contemplation who carries about him at all times an air of peace and tranquillity. His view toward the natural environment is shown in many and diverse ways but perhaps is best expressed in his works of art, in which he so often chooses as his subject the essential harmoniousness of the universe and avoids portraying the raucous world of change and discord.

This view of man's relation to nature coupled with his orientation to time has created what Thorstein Veblen once called "a poverty of wants." Until recent years little need was felt among the great bulk of the population of Korea for the fruits of an educational system geared to produce the wide variety of skills and understandings needed to revamp and improve the existing mode of life. This does not mean that the less sophisticated people lack educational drive. On the contrary, individual families willingly make tremendous sacrifice to obtain schooling for their children. Yet these same families exert no pressure toward making the school an economically oriented institution capable of teaching functional knowledge. The urgency of keeping up to date lest history leave you behind or nature overwhelm you is not present to the same extent in the Korean culture as in the American. The goal of Korean education was, until the recent impact of Western culture, adjustment rather than improvement.

The Power and Status Orientation

A third cultural difference could be called *power and status orientation*. The USA has been proud of its decentralization of political and educational responsibilities. Under a system where considerable power is exercised at the state and local levels, every citizen becomes a leader, inasmuch as he has the right to share in decision-making. The town meeting, the school board, and all the trappings of direct and representative democracy have been widely eulogized. Because of these opportunities the American citizen, it has been said, is a more sophisticated voter than his foreign brother, and the American student a more independent learner, as well as a better team man. Obviously there is more than a little jingoism mixed in these interpretations. Nevertheless, the fact remains that Americans are still committed largely to the belief in shared decision-making.

A power structure has existed in Korea that has equated position with authority while social custom has further equated authority with validity. This hierarchal structure and manner of decision-making are also reflected in the classroom and in the family. The teacher and the father both occupy positions of ultimate trust, respect, power. Their word is law. The obvious difficulty of using modern educational methods within this framework is readily seen. The school in both fostering cooperation and stressing at the same time reliance on the individual's ability to solve his own problems runs into conflict with family and societal tradition. Moreover, it is difficult to break down the school's authoritarian structure because of the fear that the teacher may lose the traditional respect felt for him.

The organization and administration of Korean education reflects the power structure found elsewhere in Korean society. Until 1948 and to a gradually modifying degree since then, Korean education has operated within a framework that was highly centralized. Major decisions emanated from the Ministry of Education. Even though opportunities for local control have been provided, they have not been taken advantage of, and lesser educational officials invariably refuse to take responsibility for decisions clearly within their jurisdiction but prefer the decisions to be made "higher

up." The danger, in addition to the perpetuation of authoritarian procedures, is that the bases for determining professional action are largely
founded on judgmental evidence as represented by the expressions of a
status person rather than on factual evidence.

There are further and widespread educational implications of this
lineally organized society. As with individuals in an organization, the
schools have a definite order of rank, as do the courses of study within the
school. Since academic subjects carry the most prestige, the technical and
vocational schools, in attempting to gain recognition, tend to deemphasize
the applied parts of their curriculum. There is so much status value
attached to abstract and difficult works that Korean students enjoy being
immersed in little understood concepts and often rebel in studying subjects
within their comprehension.

Language is another major curriculum problem which is rooted partly
in status factors. Although a simple phonetic alphabet, Hangul, had been
developed in Korea in the fifteenth century, it had never been widely
accepted by scholars. Government officials historically have used a written
script based on Chinese characters, which has served to create and perpetuate the gulf between the Korean people and their culture. During the latter
part of the Japanese annexation, to further complicate matters, the Koreans
were required to use the Japanese language on all occasions. After being
freed from colonial status, Korea erased most traces of the Japanese
language, and the vernacular was not only re-introduced into the schools
but also increasingly stressed in all literature.

The net result of this complex language situation is that Korea in 1959
finds itself with very little professional literature appropriate for students
at the secondary school and college levels. There are few modern technical
or professional books written in Chinese, and the children entering school
after 1945 have been receiving only limited work with Chinese characters
anyway. Most of the books written in Japanese (and all educated Korean
adults are fluent in this language) have been destroyed. Moreover, the
generation of Koreans now in school have no familiarity with the Japanese
language. And at the present time, in spite of official government urgings,
newspapers and most professional periodicals are being made incomprehensible to a major part of the Korean population by the inclusion of a
large number of Chinese characters rather than relying on the vernacular.
(It is interesting to note that under communism North Korea has made
great strides in eliminating the use of Chinese characters, simplifying and
refining the pure Korean. It appears that all literature being published in
North Korea uses only the simple, practical Hangul script.)

The indirect influences of the West through Japanese colonialism and
the direct contacts since 1945 have forced a re-examination of Korean
value orientations. The sincere if awkward attempts to industrialize and
democratize a nation with a long agrarian and authoritarian heritage have
produced a considerable number of inconsistencies within the Korean
society. For example, the political party in power one day exalts democratic
freedoms, yet on the next may order all students to participate in "spontaneous demonstration" to promote a particular party bias. Police in one

section of the country initiate youth clubs to combat delinquency yet themselves may at times use extremely harsh methods. The government through all avenues of propaganda promotes moral education, yet, as in older times, the bribe may often be the easiest recourse for the Korean citizen who attempts to get action through official channels. Such discrepancies indicate not only policy incongruities and personal confusion but also identify a major obstacle to a smooth cultural transition. Unity, loyalty, and morality are well defined and practiced in the family, making this an institution long admired in the West, but these qualities are yet to be raised to the societal level.

The Adviser as Catalyst

The role of the foreign educational adviser in this setting is, then, both sensitive and difficult. His own knowledge and skills are to a certain extent culture-bound and unintelligible or incongruous in new surroundings. Yet it may be precisely his new perspective that is badly needed. The task of technical assistance can obviously not be defined as "teaching them to do it our way." But neither is the counter alternative, "helping them to do what they wish to do better," completely satisfactory. The former runs the danger of technical inapplicability or of cultural resistance while the latter may involve no substantial progress toward the newer and only partially defined goals. The adviser by his increased technical knowledge sheds light on possible alternatives, but neither through coercion nor through persuasion does he determine the direction of change.

Perhaps the adviser can best be likened to a catalyst. By bringing his knowledge and experience and points of view to the new situation, his role is to speed desirable change. To fulfill this role adequately the adviser must be a student of the culture and metaculture. He must establish guidelines that will determine in broad outline educational priorities acceptable to the host nation. He must face up to the enigmatic problem of focusing attention on grassroots education—for example, increasing literacy, helping the farmer to eke out a slightly bigger yield per acre—or striking out on a broad scale to teach the highly developed skills and understandings needed by a nation moving toward industrialization. Since it is extremely difficult or impossible to change a cultural pattern by attacking its isolated parts, he must answer the question whether the establishment of a few model projects can be justified in hopes that their influence will spread.

Korea is a nation in the throes of a rapid but uneven cultural change. While members of the older generation may still cling to the belief that "the scholar should neither shoulder a carrying pole nor lift a basket," young students are beginning to seek the skills requisite for nudging an ancient culture toward new directions. In Korea, as in any developing country, cultural modification depends primarily on the initiative and drive of the people. Through his minor but vital role, the adviser, by participating from the beginning with the people whose lives are being affected, may be able to lessen the traumatic effects of such change.

Edward T. Hall, Jr.

THE ANTHROPOLOGY OF MANNERS

It is all very well for anthropologists to confess their own mistakes
or to analyze the mistakes made by government administrators,
but if there is only hindsight analysis, what can cultural anthropology constructively contribute toward the betterment of intercultural relations (assuming for the moment that this is a
desideratum)? The answer is that there is a great deal that
cultural anthropologists can do, but there are at least two
preconditions for progress. One is that cultural anthropologists
have to work in the area of applied anthropology and attempt
to provide the specific kinds of information that could be
profitably utilized by individuals visiting particular cultures.
Actually, much of the conventional field data gathered by
anthropologists could be of use. The second is that the general
public be educated about the nature of culture and the kinds
of analysis made available by cultural anthropologists. The finest
research in the world won't do much good if the diplomatic
corps and the international business representatives are totally
unaware of it.

The following article by Edward T. Hall, Jr., who is a
specialist in applied cultural anthropology, gives some striking
examples of how the research of cultural anthropologists can be
of enormous assistance in improving international relations.
Although the article tends to depend upon what is termed
"anecdotal anthropology," in that numerous cases are cited from
diverse cultures in order to illustrate points, the examples are
fascinating and they do demonstrate quite convincingly the
exciting possibilities of using the data gathered painstakingly by
anthropologists in the field for eminently practical purposes.

Ivory tower academics sometimes tend to sneer at tourism
and commercialism, but the fact is that they are an important
part of the modern world. If cultural anthropology is really
relevant to the problems of our day, then it ought to be relevant
to these topics. Actually no one could possibly object to an
individual's using the information gained from a study of
cultural anthropology to enjoy visiting a foreign culture more
than he would have otherwise, especially if the wake of misunderstanding and mistrust in the country visited, which all
too frequently follows such visits, can be reduced or even eliminated. Hall's study should make it abundantly clear that any
diplomat or other government official serving overseas could

benefit greatly from exposure to the methods and materials of cultural anthropology.

For a fuller treatment of Hall's comparative analyses of time and space, see his book *The Silent Language* (New York, 1959). For further reading in applied anthropology, see Warren Bennis, Kenneth Benne, and Robert Chin, eds., *The Planning of Change: Readings in the Applied Behavioral Sciences* (New York, 1962), and many of the articles in the periodical *Human Organization* (formerly titled *Applied Anthropology*), which is the organ of the Society for Applied Anthropology. For earlier references, see Arlene Fonaroff, "Applied Anthropology: A Selected Bibliography," *Davidson Journal of Anthropology*, 3 (1957), 59–137.

The Goops they lick their fingers
　and the Goops they lick their knives;
They spill their broth on the table cloth—
　Oh, they lead disgusting lives.
The Goops they talk while eating,
　and loud and fast they chew;
And that is why I'm glad that I
　am not a Goop—are you?

In Gelett Burgess' classic on the Goops we have an example of what anthropologists call "an enculturating device"—a means of conditioning the young of life in our society. Having been taught the lesson of the goops from childhood (with or without the aid of Mr. Burgess) Americans are shocked when they go abroad and discover whole groups of people behaving like goops—eating with their fingers, making noises and talking while eating. When this happens, we may (1) remark on the barbarousness or quaintness of the "natives" (a term cordially disliked all over the world) or (2) try to discover the nature and meaning of the differences in behavior. One rather quickly discovers that what is good manners in one context may be bad in the next. It is to this point that I would like to address myself.

The subject of manners is complex; if it were not, there would not be so many injured feelings and so much misunderstanding in international circles everywhere. In any society the code of manners tends to sum up the culture—to be a frame of reference for all behavior. Emily Post goes so far as to say: "There is not a single thing that we do, or say, or choose, or use, or even think, that does not follow or break one of the exactions of taste, or tact, or ethics of good manners, or etiquette—call it what you will." Unfortunately many of the most important standards of acceptable behavior in different cultures are elusive: they are intangible, undefined and unwritten.

An Arab diplomat who recently arrived in the U. S. from the Middle

East attended a banquet which lasted several hours. When it was over, he met a fellow countryman outside and suggested they go get something to eat, as he was starving. His friend, who had been in this country for some time, laughed and said: "But, Habib, didn't you know that if you say, 'No, thank you,' they think you really don't want any?" In an Arab country etiquette dictates that the person being served must refuse the proffered dish several times, while his host urges him repeatedly to partake. The other side of the coin is that Americans in the Middle East, until they learn better, stagger away from banquets having eaten more than they want or is good for them.

When a public-health movie of a baby being bathed in a bathinette was shown in India recently, the Indian women who saw it were visibly offended. They wondered how people could be so inhuman as to bathe a child in stagnant (not running) water. Americans in Iran soon learn not to indulge themselves in their penchant for chucking infants under the chin and remarking on the color of their eyes, for the mother has to pay to have the "evil eye" removed. We also learn that in the Middle East you don't hand people things with your left hand, because it is unclean. In India we learn not to touch another person, and in Southeast Asia we learn that the head is sacred.

In the interest of intercultural understanding various U. S. Government agencies have hired anthropologists from time to time as technical experts. The State Department especially has pioneered in the attempt to bring science to bear on this difficult and complex problem. It began by offering at the Foreign Service Institute an intensive four-week course for Point 4 technicians. Later these facilities were expanded to include other foreign service personnel.

The anthropologist's job here is not merely to call attention to obvious taboos or to coach people about types of thoughtless behavior that have very little to do with culture. One should not need an anthropologist to point out, for instance, that it is insulting to ask a foreigner: "How much is this in real money?" Where technical advice is most needed is in the interpretation of the unconscious aspects of a culture—the things people do automatically without being aware of the full implications of what they have done. For example, an ambassador who has been kept waiting for more than half an hour by a foreign visitor needs to understand that if his visitor "just mutters an apology" this is not necessarily an insult. The time system in the foreign country may be composed of different basic units, so that the visitor is not as late as he may appear to us. You must know the time system of the country to know at what point apologies are really due.

Twenty years of experience in working with Americans in foreign lands convinces me that the real problem in preparing them to work overseas is not with taboos, which they catch on to rather quickly, but rather with whole congeries of habits and attitudes which anthropologists have only recently begun to describe systematically.

Can you remember tying your shoes this morning? Could you give the rules for when it is proper to call another person by his first name? Could you describe the gestures you make in conversation? These examples illustrate how much of our behavior is "out of awareness," and how easy it is to get into trouble in another culture.

Nobody is continually aware of the quality of his own voice, the subtleties of stress and intonation that color the meaning of his words or the posture and distance he assumes in talking to another person. Yet all these are taken as cues to the real nature of an utterance, regardless of what the words say. A simple illustration is the meaning in the tone of voice. In the U. S. we raise our voices not only when we are angry but also when we want to emphasize a point, when we are more than a certain distance from another person, when we are concluding a meeting and so on. But to the Chinese, for instance, overloudness of the voice is most character-istically associated with anger and loss of self-control. Whenever we become really interested in something, they are apt to have the feeling we are angry, in spite of many years' experience with us. Very likely most of their interviews with us, however cordial, seem to end on a sour note when we exclaim heartily: "WELL, I'M CERTAINLY GLAD YOU DROPPED IN, MR. WONG."

The Latin Americans, who as a rule take business seriously, do not under-stand our mixing business with informality and recreation. We like to put our feet up on the desk. If a stranger enters the office, we take our feet down. If it turns out that the stranger and we have a lot in common, up go the feet again—a cue to the other fellow that we feel at ease. If the office boy enters, the feet stay up; if the boss enters and our relationship with him is a little strained at the moment, they go down. To a Latin American this whole behavior is shocking. All he sees in it is insult or just plain rudeness.

Differences in attitudes toward space—what would be territoriality in lower forms of life—raise a number of other interesting points. U. S. women who go to live in Latin America all complain about the "waste" of space in the houses. On the other hand, U. S. visitors to the Middle East complain about crowding, in the houses and on the street cars and buses. Everywhere we go space seems to be distorted. When we see a gardener in the mountains of Italy planting a single row on each of six separate terraces, we wonder why he spreads out his crop so that he has to spend half his time climbing up and down. We overlook the complex chain of communication that would be broken if he didn't cultivate alongside his brothers and his cousin and if he didn't pass his neighbors and talk to them as he moves from one terrace to the next.

A colleague of mine was caught in a snowstorm while traveling with companions in the mountains of Lebanon. They stopped at the next house and asked to be put up for the night. The house had only one room. Instead of distributing the guests around the room, their host placed them next to the pallet where he slept with his wife—so close that they almost touched the couple. To have done otherwise in that country would have been unnatural and unfriendly. In the U. S. we distribute ourselves more evenly than many other people. We have strong feelings about touching and being crowded; in a street-car, bus or elevator we draw ourselves in. Toward a person who relaxes and lets himself come into full contact with others in a crowded place we usually feel reactions that could not be printed on this page. It takes years for us to train our children not to crowd and lean on us. We tell them to stand up, that it is rude to slouch, not to sit so close or not to "breathe down our necks." After a while they get the point. By the time we Americans are in our teens we can tell what relationship exists between a man and woman by how they walk or sit together.

In Latin America, where touching is more common and the basic units of space seem to be smaller, the wide automobiles made in the U.S. pose problems. People don't know where to sit. North Americans are disturbed by how close the Latin Americans stand when they converse. "Why do they have to get so close when they talk to you?" "They're so pushy." "I don't know what it is, but it's something in the way they stand next to you." And so on. The Latin Americans, for their part, complain that people in the U. S. are distant and cold—*retraídos* (withdrawing and uncommunicative.)

An analysis of the handling of space during conversations shows the following: A U. S. male brought up in the Northeast stands 18 to 20 inches away when talking face to face to a man he does not know very well; talking to a woman under similar circumstances, he increases the distance about four inches. A distance of only eight to 13 inches between males is considered either very aggressive or indicative of a closeness of a type we do not ordinarily want to think about. Yet in many parts of Latin America and the Middle East distances which are almost sexual in connotation are the only ones at which people can talk comfortably. In Cuba, for instance, there is nothing suggestive in a man's talking to an educated woman at a distance of 13 inches. If you are a Latin American, talking to a North American at the distance he insists on maintaining is like trying to talk across a room.

To get a more vivid idea of this problem of the comfortable distance, try starting a conversation with a person eight or 10 feet away or one separated from you by a wide obstruction in a store or other public place. Any normally enculturated person can't help trying to close up the space, even to the extent of climbing over benches or walking around tables to arrive within comfortable distance. U. S. businessmen working in Latin America try to prevent people from getting uncomfortably close by barricading themselves behind desks, typewriters or the like, but their Latin American office visitors will often climb up on desks or over chairs and put up with loss of dignity in order to establish a spatial context in which interaction can take place for them.

The interesting thing is that neither party is specifically aware of what is wrong when the distance is not right. They merely have vague feelings of discomfort or anxiety. As the Latin American approaches and the North American backs away, both parties take offense without knowing why. When a North American, having had the problem pointed out to him, permits the Latin American to get close enough, he will immediately notice that the latter seems much more at ease.

My own studies of space and time have engendered considerable cooperation and interest on the part of friends and colleagues. One case recently reported to me had to do with a group of seven-year-olds in a crowded Sunday-school classroom. The children kept fighting. Without knowing quite what was involved, the teacher had them moved to a larger room. The fighting stopped. It is interesting to speculate as to what would have happened had the children been moved to a smaller room.

The embarrassment about intimacy in space applies also to the matter of addressing people by name. Finding the proper distance in the use of names is even more difficult than in space, because the rules for first-naming are unbelievably complex. As a rule we tend to stay on the "mister" level too long with Latins and some others, but very often we swing into first-naming too quickly, which amounts to talking down to them. Whereas in the U. S. we use Mr. with the surname, in Latin America the first and last names are used together and señor (Sr.) is a title. Thus when one says, "My name is Sr. So-and-So," it is interpreted to mean, "I am the Honorable, his Excellency So-and-So." It is no wonder that when we stand away, barricade ourselves behind our desks (usually a reflection of status) and call ourselves mister, our friends to the south wonder about our so-called "good-neighbor" policy and think of us as either high-hat or unbelievably rude. Fortunately most North Americans learn some of these things after living in Latin America for a while, but the aversion to being touched and to touching sometimes persists after 15 or more years of residence and even under such conditions as intermarriage.

The difference in sense of time is another thing of which we are not aware. An Iranian, for instance, is not taught that it is rude to be late in the same way that we in the U. S. are. In a general way we are conscious of this, but we fail to realize that their time system is structured differently from ours. The different cultures simply place different values on the time units.

Thus let us take as a typical case of the North European time system (which has regional variations) the situation in the urban eastern U. S. A middle-class business man meeting another of equivalent rank will ordinarily be aware of being two minutes early or late. If he is three minutes late, it will be noted as significant but usually neither will say anything. If four minutes late, he will mutter something by way of apology; at five minutes he will utter a full sentence of apology. In other words, the major unit is a five-minute block. Fifteen minutes is the smallest significant period for all sorts of arrangements and it is used very commonly. A half hour of course is very significant, and if you spend three quarters of an hour or an hour, either the business you transact or the relationship must be important. Normally it is an insult to keep a public figure or a person of significantly higher status than yourself waiting even two or three minutes, though the person of higher position can keep you waiting or even break an appointment.

Now among urban Arabs in the Eastern Mediterranean, to take an illustrative case of another time system, the unit that corresponds to our five-minute period is 15 minutes. Thus when an Arab arrives nearly 30 minutes after the set time, by his reckoning he isn't even "10 minutes" late yet (in our time units). Stated differently, the Arab's tardiness will not amount to one significant period (15 minutes in our system). An American normally will wait no longer than 30 minutes (two significant periods) for another person to turn up in the middle of the day. Thereby he often unwittingly insults people in the Middle East who want to be his friends.

How long is one expected to stay when making a duty call at a friend's house in the U. S.? While there are regional variations, I have observed that the minimum is very close to 45 minutes, even in the face of pressing commitments elsewhere, such as a roast in the oven. We may think we can get away in 30 minutes by saying something about only stopping for "a minute," but usually we discover that we don't feel comfortable about leaving until 45 minutes have elapsed. I am referring to afternoon social calls; evening calls last much longer and operate according to a different system. In Arab countries an American paying a duty call at the house of a desert sheik causes consternation if he gets up to leave after half a day. There a duty call lasts three days—the first day to prepare the feast, the second for the feast itself and the third to taper off and say farewell. In the first half day the sheik has barely had time to slaughter the sheep for the feast. The guest's departure would leave the host frustrated.

There is a well-known story of a tribesman who came to Kabul, the capital of Afghanistan, to meet his brother. Failing to find him, he asked the merchants in the market place to tell his brother where he could be found if the brother showed up. A year later the tribesman returned and looked again. It developed that he and his brother had agreed to meet in Kabul but had failed to specify what year! If the Afghan time system were structured similarly to our own, which it apparently is not, the brother would not offer a full sentence of apology until he was five years late.

Informal units of time such as "just a minute," "a while," "later," "a long time," "a spell," "a long, long time," "years" and so on provide us with the culturological equivalent of Evil-Eye Fleegle's "double-whammy" (in *Li'l Abner*). Yet these expressions are not as imprecise as they seem. Any American who has worked in an office with someone else for six months can usually tell within five minutes when that person will be back if he says, "I'll be gone for a while." It is simply a matter of learning from experience the individual's system of time indicators. A reader who is interested in communications theory can fruitfully speculate for a while on the very wonderful way in which culture provides the means whereby the receiver puts back all the redundant material that was stripped from such a message. Spelled out, the message might go somewhat as follows: "I am going downtown to see So-and-So about the Such-and-Such contract, but I don't know what the traffic conditions will be like or how long it will take me to get a place to park nor do I know what shape So-and-So will be in today, but taking all this into account I think I will be out of the office about an hour but don't like to commit myself, so if anyone calls you can say I'm not sure how long I will be; in any event I expect to be back before 4 o'clock."

Few of us realize how much we rely on built-in patterns to interpret messages of this sort. An Iranian friend of mine who came to live in the

U. S. was hurt and puzzled for the first few years. The new friends he met and liked would say on parting: "Well, I'll see you later." He mournfully complained: "I kept expecting to see them, but the 'later' never came." Strangely enough we ourselves are exasperated when a Mexican can't tell us precisely what he means when he uses the expression *mañana*.

The role of the anthropologist in preparing people for service overseas is to open their eyes and sensitize them to the subtle qualities of behavior —tone of voice, gestures, space and time relationships—that so often build up feelings of frustration and hostility in other people with a different culture. Whether we are going to live in a particular foreign country or travel in many, we need a frame of reference that will enable us to observe and learn the significance of differences in manners. Progress is being made in this anthropological study, but it is also showing us how little is known about human behavior.

Margaret Mead

THE APPLICATION OF
ANTHROPOLOGICAL TECHNIQUES
TO CROSS-NATIONAL COMMUNICATION

The problems of inter- or cross-national communication are culturally relative. If Americans and Russians wish to understand one another better, the relevant data would not be the same as that which would be useful in improving the relations between Americans and Chinese or between Russians and Germans. This is why it is absurdly naïve to speak of *the* foreign policy of the United States, as if there could or should be only one. In theory there would have to be as many versions of policy as there are separate cultures with whom the United States must concern itself. The same holds for other cultures and countries. A political posture which would strengthen bonds with one culture might seriously jeopardize ties with another. This all seems obvious enough, yet there is unfortunately plenty of good evidence that cultural relativism is not taken into account in such matters as making diplomatic appointment and foreign policy decisions.

Evidence for the lack of awareness of the cultural relativistic factors in intercultural communication may be found in both domestic and foreign government service appointments. A man who serves as Indian agent for the Florida Seminoles is suddenly

Reprinted from *Transactions of the New York Academy of Sciences*, Series II, **9**, No. 4 (1947), 133–52, by permission of the author and the New York Academy of Sciences.

transferred to a Plains Indian reservation. The assumption here is that anyone who knows the government regulations applicable to Indian affairs can be equally effective in any post. This is taking account of *our* culture only. Florida Seminole languages and culture are very different from Sioux languages and cultures. An agent who spoke Mikasuki (one of the two languages spoken by the Seminoles)—assuming that government employees master the language of the people with whom they work—would not be able to communicate with Sioux Indians in their native language. In other words, appointments and policies should take account of *their* culture too.

Similarly, in the diplomatic corps, a man who serves as ambassador to Nigeria may be "promoted" to a post in India. Assuming the man knew something about Ibo, Ibibio, Ijaw, Nupe, Tiv, and Yoruba cultures *among others,* how would this equip him to deal effectively with the various peoples of India? To use some of the several *hundred* languages spoken in India as an example, suppose he could speak the major languages spoken by 150 million people, e.g., Hindi, Urdu, Punjabi. Could he communicate easily with the more than 30 million speakers of Telegu? What about the 27 million Marathi speakers, 26 million Tamil speakers, 25 million Bengali speakers, 16 million Gujarati, 14 million Kannada, and 13 million Malayalam speakers to mention some of the larger linguistic-cultural groups? It would take a lifetime to master just a portion of these, and these are languages only. What of the cultures as a whole? No wonder Americans (and others) are misunderstood all over the world. Thus far our intercultural communications are barely in an embryonic stage of development.

As a fairly detailed example of the ways in which cultural anthropologists can facilitate and markedly improve inter-cultural communications, the following comparative analysis of English and American national characters by Margaret Mead is presented. Margaret Mead, one of the most prolific and well-known anthropologists of our day, is very much interested in making the findings of cultural anthropology available to a wider audience and she has for some years devoted considerable professional energies to the area of applied anthropology.

In this particular research, which grew out of projects initiated during World War II, Margaret Mead discusses British and American characteristics with an eye toward revealing what misconceptions the one group has about the other and how these misconceptions come about. This is no mere delineation of stereotypes; it is a serious attempt to explain the underlying reasons for the existence of the stereotypes. Even if she were not correct in every detail, the paper would still provide an important model for future research. It is hard to imagine that any Englishman who read this paper would not be better able to deal more intelligently with Americans. Similarly, an American reader of the study ought to be more sensitive and skillful in his dealings with British friends. If this is true, then what is needed are a host of similar comparative bi-national studies to improve intercultural communications all over the world. Such studies would appear to represent some progress since the time Herodotus described the cultures of the Scythians and the Persians as one describes mere curiosities, for here cultures are described in terms designed to maximize meaningful communication and to minimize mistrust. The point is thus not just that every man has his way, but that by understanding these ways, men can make their world a safer, happier, and generally better place in which to live.

For references to the considerable national character literature, see Alex Inkeles and Daniel J. Levinson, "National Character: The Study of Modal Personality and Sociocultural Systems," in Gardner Lindzey, ed., *Handbook of Social Psychology*, **II** (Cambridge, 1954), pp. 977–1020, and H.C.J. Duijker and N. H. Frijda, *National Character and National Stereotypes*, Confluence: Surveys of Research in the Social Sciences, Vol. 1 (Amsterdam, 1960), which includes a bibliography of nearly one thousand references. For some consideration of intercultural communication, see Alfred G. Smith, ed., *Communication and Culture: Readings in the Codes of Human Interaction* (New York, 1966), pp. 565–608.

During the war, anthropologists addressed themselves to various ways in which their discipline could be put at the direct service of their society, attempting to short-cut the lag which normally obtains between the development of abstractions based upon laboratory and field research and their application to contemporary problems. One part of this anthropological effort was concerned with delineating significant aspects of the national character, or culture pattern, of enemy peoples or peoples of occupied countries about whom our knowledge was wholly inadequate.[1]

A second use of anthropological techniques was found in the attempt to select salient aspects of our own cultures and describe them in such a

[1]The most significant work was done on Japan and Germany. Reference may be made particularly to Gorer (8), Benedict (5), Round Table on Germany after the War (26), Parsons (24), and to unpublished work by Gregory Bateson, Ruth Benedict, Geoffrey Gorer, Douglas Haring, Frederick Hulse, Clyde Kluckhohn, Alexander Leighton, David Mandelbaum, Arnold Meadow, Rhoda Metraux, Marian Smith, and others. Some of the general implications of this work are described by Mead (15) and Benedict (4).

way that they could be used for various sorts of rapid training or morale building.[2]

The use of anthropological knowledge in operations directed towards the enemy involved only a limited analysis of our own culture, except when a policy had to be carried out by large numbers of Americans whom it was impossible to train in detail to act in any way antithetical to their usual behavior, or when, as in our formal treatment of the Japanese emperor, widespread public support of a national policy was necessary. The use of similar anthropological knowledge within the limits of our own culture raised all the ethical problems of the responsibility of leaders of a democratic society not simply to manipulate, but to appeal openly to existing and cherished strengths.

When an attempt is made to use the anthropological methods to strengthen a relationship between peoples of two contemporary cultures, still different problems arise. Here, the focus is not upon points of vulnerability (which may be breached, as with the enemy, or strengthened, as for members of occupied countries), nor upon traditional strengths and coherencies to be enhanced and weaknesses and contradictions to be guarded against, as in work in one's own culture. Instead, our efforts have to be directed towards finding areas of agreement which can be used as a background for the acceptance of differences which are causing specific friction and tension. Research and resulting communications are focused upon a relationship, and the nodes selected for emphasis are defined in terms of that relationship, not in terms of the emphasis within the whole culture pattern of each society. For instance, if foreign policy is to be discussed and the foreign policy of one culture is most congruent with upper class values, while in the other it is most congruent with middle class values, this asymmetry would be consciously explored, perhaps to the neglect of any exploration of the exactly corresponding class in the other country, because of its lack of immediate relevance to the problem in hand.

As illustrative material for such an operation, I shall draw upon my own experiences in working on Anglo-American relations. I particularly propose to use data upon the areas of friction and misunderstanding between American troops and British civilians in Britain in 1943. My case is unusual because I had the opportunity to participate in framing the hypotheses with which I went to Britain, to combine field work on these hypotheses with lecturing all over Britain, under the auspices of the Ministry of Information and, later, through the United States Office of War Information in London, to prepare various sorts of materials, both as background and immediate communication, for circulation among Americans and Britons. Thus, activities which would more usually be divided among a large number of individuals with different skills—research, field work, analysis, interpretation, preparation of directives, writing, rewriting,

---

[2]Some of the principles for such a treatment of our own culture were discussed in Bateson & Mead (3). The method was exemplified by the work of the Committee on Food Habits (25), particularly by the methods of pattern analysis of verbal materials on attitudes to current situations developed by Metraux (22) and Mead (9).

broadcasting, presentations, etc.—and which would be subject to all the hazards which attend communication within such a diversified group, were embodied in the work that I did. This is an accident which we have no reason to believe will be repeated often. Analysis of such an experience bears the same relationship to thinking about cooperative operations that an analysis of the functions of the vanishing general practitioner bears to an attempt at constructing modern medical services in which many disciplines participate. This experience also provided a unique opportunity to explore some of the problems involved, and to test our hypotheses on the spot.

I plan to discuss examples of a variety of the procedures and problems which arose, so as to give as broad a picture as possible of the way in which anthropological methods may be applied to relationships between any pair of peoples. The analysis of such binary relationships is a necessary step towards an understanding of more complicated patterns of relationship on which a world order will have to be built.

I have used the term, cross-national, deliberately, to indicate that I am dealing not with relationships between *nations*, self-maximating competitive national units, but between the *peoples* of different nations, whose effective communication is a compromise of both differences in culture and the circumstance of different nationality which gives a special competitive coloring and significance to these differences. To the extent that local allegiance is an important ingredient of the picture of the own group, the acceptance of differences in culture will vary enormously, according to whether any sort of boundary, even a state or county line, intervenes. In wartime, uniforms and all the paraphernalia of nationalistic warfare exacerbate the sensitivities of the populations involved.

Application of General Theoretical Formulations to a Particular Case

In the initial steps, I depended upon the formulations of symmetrical and complementary schismogenesis, developed by Gregory Bateson (1, 2), in which the United States and Britain were both diagnosed as relying upon the stimulus provided by greater strength in the opponent, while Germany seemed to rely upon greater weakness. With this approval of symmetrical relationships shared by both countries, there was associated a common moral disapprobation of bullying, picking on someone who was smaller, throwing one's weight around, etc. In addition to the original statement of this diagnosis, I had elaborated, before going to England, the American version of adequate provocation to attack, under the formulation of "the chip on the shoulder" (12). In this, I stressed that the American boy, reared by women, was given a deep doubt of his essential aggressiveness, combined with a lack of pattern for exercising it, in contrast to the British boy, reared by older boys and men to combine a belief in his innate aggressiveness with an obligation never to use his full strength unless pushed into an extreme position in which he could turn at bay. The famous "Back to the Wall" order of Haig in World War I to the British, and reported exhortations of General Patton to his men, emphasizing the difficulty of the task but also the fact that the enemy was on the run and the United States Army had the best equipment in the world, are conspicuous examples of the way in which military leaders have intuitively relied upon these different patternings of a basically symmetrical schismogenic attitude. Phrased colloquially, the underlying similarity became, "Both British and Americans believe that the strong have an obligation not to abuse their strength. We both hate bullies and, conversely, those who cringe to bullies."

The second theoretical formulation was the hypothesis of *end linkage* (Bateson [2]) that the way in which parent-child relationships are patterned in respect to succouring-dependence, dominance-submission, and exhibitionism-spectatorship, provides a learning situation for the child which patterns his subsequent behavior in situations where these behaviors are involved. Specifically, in Anglo-American relationships, the exhibitionism is reversed. In Britain it is Father who exhibits to his children: he is the model for their future behavior. Father does the talking and provides the model, before a very quiet and submissive audience, in accordance with the deep ethical disapproval of over-use of strength. He underplays his strength, understates his position, speaks with a slight appearance of hesitation in his manner, but with the cool assurance of one who knows. In the United States, this position is reversed: at the American breakfast table, it is not Father but Junior who talks, exhibits his successes and skills, and demands parental spectatorship and applause with an insistence that can be clamoring and assertive because, after all, he is speaking from weakness to strength. The American background for this reversal was explored (9) and, in the spring of 1943, we tried an experiment of using the contrast in a radio program in which samples of parent-child behavior at the breakfast table were followed by excerpts from American and British public speeches.[3]

These two formulations, of symmetrical schismogenesis and end linkage, provide both a theoretical background for understanding and material for

---

[3]This program was given as part of the series, *Science at Work,* of the American School of the Air of the Columbia Broadcasting System (7) and was published in *Education* (7). The two speeches ran as follows:

British Lecturer: "Ladies and Gentlemen—I have been asked to talk to you tonight about British war production. We have, of course, improved. Our over-all figures for the past year show a definite increase. But it is, I think, in planes that the picture is most striking. Our largest bombers, which incidentally carry four times the bomb load of yours, are now coming quite satisfactorily into production."

American Lecturer: "Well, ladies and gentlemen—I see I'm down on the program to talk to you tonight about Alaska. I can think of one good reason why I know something about that country. It's because I've had to make upwards of 20 to 30 trips there, Summer and Winter in the past fifteen years.

Two or three of these trips, I might add, were by dog sled, far off the beaten track. On at least one of them, I nearly lost my life. But the thing I want to tell you folks about tonight, is the change that's come over Alaska since our boys went in there. Yes sir...mass production methods and the Good Old American qualities of hard work and initiative are showing results up there these days. (fading) I predict that five years after this war finishes, we'll be spending Summers in Alaska the way we used to spend Winters down in Florida. That's a tip, folks."

interpreting one of the acute points of friction between British and Americans. This point of friction was the British repudiation of American "boasting" and the American repudiation of British "arrogance." It lent itself particularly well to use on the lecture platform and over the radio, as tone of voice was the principle medium in the demonstration. By a little careful interviewing in each new area in Britain, I could get *verbatim* (and, therefore, acceptable) statements of the British objections: "The trouble with the Americans is that when they are good at something they *say* so", or "The trouble with the Americans is that they talk so much about what they are going to do; we don't talk, we just *do* it" (from the Scots), etc. I could then rely upon the lecture situation, itself one in which the exhibitionistic role of the lecturer and the spectatorship role of the audience was defined, to provide me with additional illustrative material. I could quote from the chairman who, in presenting me—putatively in the parental role on a British stage—to a great tired audience who had come out in the blackout on a freezing Sunday night in Scotland, said: "Be as kind to the audience as you can, Dr. Mead." Or I could refer to the whole institution of the "vote of thanks," in which the British audience, after sitting docile and respectful while the lecturer plays Father, reestablishes the balance by the paternalistic tone in which the proposer of the vote of thanks addresses the now seated lecturer. Explanations of behavioral differences which stressed upbringing were easily acceptable to the British, because of the strong cultural emphasis upon "character" as something which is acquired in the course of the right education rather than as an innate possession of any individual or class of individuals. It was possible to show that, whenever an American spoke, he spoke as he had learned to speak when he was small, and so would put that irritating overstatement into his voice which the British called "boasting"; while, whenever a Briton spoke, he spoke as he had heard his father and other elders speak, as the strong and assured, carefully pulling his punches, with that irritating understatement in his voice which the American called "arrogance." It was possible to show how the words *understatement* applied to the British and *boasting* applied to the Americans, emphasized the virtues of British behavior and devalued American, while by using the parallel words *understatement* and *overstatement,* both British and American behavior could be put in a common frame, *viz.,* that of habits learned in childhood.

Exploration of a Friction Point

When I reached Britain, our troops were still pouring into the country, there were still many British troops around, and very few American girls had, as yet, reached Britain. The relationships between American men and British girls were providing an acute point of misunderstanding among both nationalities.

The friction took many forms, which required quite different types of treatment. It was necessary to explain to British authorities that an American boy would have difficulty in judging the age and degree of discretion of a girl who told him she had been out of school and working for two years, and to construct ways in which the Americans could spend their disproportionately large pay on British girls without using up goods or creating new social problems. But there was the much more basic problem of the way in which disturbed heterosexual relationships were festering beneath the surface of Anglo-American relationships in general. The problem was not primarily a police problem involving the reduction of illegitimate births, which seemed to be following a pretty uniform curve whichever troops and nationalities were involved, but rather to reduce the disorientation which expressed itself in the British statement that the American men were "immoral" and the American insistence that the British girls "had no morals." Accusations of this sort might, of course, have been mere expressions of symmetrical friction, in which case it would have been necessary to look elsewhere for more basic areas of discrepancy. However, there is always a good possibility that, under identical accusations, there will be expressed some profound and unrealized difference which has become the more dangerous because it is so completely masked.[4]

I set about to explore the relationships between American men and British girls. A key to the misunderstanding lay in the differences in the location of responsibility for sex advances and sex refusals; in fact, for the whole modulation of sex behavior. The American girl is trained to look after herself, unchaperoned and without any insistence upon rules of etiquette which will insure her person immunity from physical advances. She is taught that her behavior is in her own keeping, and the boy learns to make advances and rely upon the girl to repulse them whenever they are inappropriate to the state of feeling between the pair. In Britain, the situation is reversed: the girl is reared to depend upon a slight barrier of chilliness and frostiness which the boys learn to respect, and for the rest to rely upon the men to approach or advance, as warranted by the situation. Both systems give about the degree of satisfaction which can be expected in any pattern which locates initiative formally in one sex, without reference to temperament, in the respective countries concerned. In wartime Britain, however, it meant that American boys, taught to ask with a full expectation of being refused effectively most of the time, were confronted by British girls, taught to accede to every forceful invitation. Several characteristic patterns of response developed. Some British girls became even chillier and, repelling even American optimism, succeeded in keeping the Americans at arm's length and sending them away to complain about everything in Britain. Some responded to the first stylized wisecrack with an impassioned surrender which was thoroughly disconcerting to the American in its intensity and implications. Some, finally, succeeded in maneuvering a middle

---

[4]Early in the war, the British were frequently advised, by American expatriates and Anglophiles, to retaliate against American comments about India by remarks about the treatment of Negro Americans in the United States. This *tu quoque* phrasing only increased the bitterness and intolerance on both sides, as the two cases were felt as basically dissimilar by the Americans, who equated Indian problems with American pre-revolutionary problems as a country, and racial problems in the U. S. as equivalent to the slum problem inside Britain, a purely domestic matter.

course for a few hours, until the Americans who seemed to be "serious" could be presented at home as future sons-in-law—which annoyed a great many Americans very much. The interpretation of this difference to the men themselves, and to those who were charged with youth and protection programs, gave a working basis for improved relationships,[5] and a phrasing under which the mutual accusations of immorality could be reduced.

Problems of Phrasing and Translation

The problem of communication in a language which was theoretically mutually intelligible and "one language," presented a number of difficulties which could be partially resolved by reference to cultural differences. In all probability, the greater the difference between the languages of the pair of cultures with which one is attempting to work, the more automatic warnings are provided to the translator. Between English and American, however, and between other cultures similarly related through a common tradition and a still somewhat intelligible pair of languages, language confuses rather than clarifies, and other sorts of clues are necessary. Two systematic observations made it possible to communicate better. The first was analysis of the difference between the American and British sense of a scale of values. Americans tend to arrange objects on a single scale of value, from best to worst, biggest to smallest, cheapest to most expensive, etc., and are able to express a preference among very complex objects on such a single scale. The question, "What is your favorite color?" so intelligible to an American, is meaningless in Britain, and such a question is countered by: "Favorite color for what? A flower? A necktie?" Each object is thought of as having a most complex set of qualities, and color is merely a quality of an object, not something from a color chart on which one can make a choice which is transferable to a large number of different sorts of objects. The American reduction of complexities to single scales is entirely comprehensible in terms of the great diversity of value systems which different immigrant groups brought to the American scene. Some common denominator among the incommensurables was very much needed, and over-simplification was almost inevitable (Mead [12]). But, as a result, Americans think in terms of qualities which have uni-dimensional scales, while the British, when they think of a complex object or event, even if they reduce it to parts, think of each part as retaining all of the complexities of the whole. Americans subdivide the scale; the British subdivide the object. Americans are able to describe a room in terms of its "color scheme," where the British eye would retain a sense of some fifty elements involved in the whole interior pattern, even when speaking of a square inch of the rug. From this British insistence on complexity there flows, naturally enough, an insistence upon uniqueness and an unwillingness to make comparisons. Discussions as to the relative virtues of cities, which Americans make

[5]All of the material outlined in this and preceding sections was used as a background for various educational pamphlets, Mead (16) and (19) ("What is a Date?").

happily in terms of size, wealth, or some other common denominator, appear to the British either as meaningless or as irrelevant boasting. In turn, the British refusal to provide statistics on the size or wealth of a city seemed to the Americans to be either obscurantist or unfriendly. In Anglo-American contacts of all sorts, committee meetings, teaching situations, etc., it was important to watch the misunderstandings which arose along these lines, since the British voted the Americans as oversimplifying when they harped on some exact statement of a position on a numerical scale, and the Americans voted the British as inaccurate, if not engaged in deliberate falsification, when they quoted the population of Bengal with an error of ten million, with the statement that it "didn't matter," because they were concerned with the relative, not the absolute size of one Indian province.

Another sort of misunderstanding which influenced communication was the difference between the British and American sense of the real world. The Americans see the world as man-controlled, a vast malleable space on which one builds what one wishes, from blueprints one has drawn, and, when dissatisfied, simply tears the structure down and starts anew. The great sense of mechanical control of the environment—product, at least in part, of an empty continent and the machine age—extends to American attitudes towards crops and animals, which are again something to be planned for, streamlined, increased or decreased at will, and even, to a certain degree, to human beings, who can be, if not completely molded by man-made devices, at least sorted mechanically into simply defined pigeon-holes. The British, in contrast, see the world as a natural world to which man adapts himself, in which he assumes no control over the future but only the experienced foresight of the husbandman or the gardener, who plants the best seed and watches carefully over the first green blades. Man is seen as the junior partner of God (expressed in either conventional or more contemporary forms, but still as the junior partner of forces to which he can adapt himself but which he cannot control). He can "only handle one link in the chain of destiny at a time." The humility of this phrasing has its own forms of arrogance, as in Milton's: "God is decreeing to begin some new and great period...what does he then but reveal Himself to his servants, and as his manner is, first to his English-men." *Vis à vis* this state of mind, ordinary American figures of speech implying control and mechanism not only fail to communicate but actually establish barriers. It was necessary to drop the familiar figures of an America converting for full production, laying down blueprinted acres of factories, six months ahead of schedules, and streamlining labor-management relations, and to use instead the figures of speech of horticulture, to speak of "planting the seed" in "carefully prepared ground," of an effort which, even when skill and experience were used to their utmost, still depended in final outcome on forces with which man could cooperate but which he could not control.

Roads and buildings in Britain which have been there a long time, become part of the natural world, not something to be swept aside lightly for a new plan. This was difficult to understand for Americans who often found that a badly bombed city, which was still a wounded landscape to the British once the rubble had been cleared away, looked to them very much like any American city, in the eternal process of rapid transformation in which the old was torn down with hardly a sigh of regret.

The very different sorts of selfconsciousness about all social process also had to be analyzed and allowed for: the American's willingness to think about the immediate future and his unwillingness to think very far ahead; the British unwillingness to let too great a degree of selfconsciousness interfere with the smooth flow of highly disciplined habitual behavior but their greater willingness to think ten years ahead; the sudden shift in British attention which permitted them to attribute to themselves, retrospectively, a degree of planfulness which they would have repudiated, at the time, as paralyzing. I was at first confused by these contradictions, by being told in one breath that to think about next week's plan would be unthinkable, and that, in some earlier operation of exactly the same nature, "we were very clever" and infinitely cunning. Once the contrast was clear, it was possible to discuss the past when any detailed dissection of motive and behavior was desired and the far future if articulate goals came into question.

The Interpretation of British Behavior to Americans

My formal mandate in 1943 had included only the British side of the task, and work which I did in the United States was under various scattered auspices and not a part of the Office of War Information program. During the next two years, however, I had occasion to lecture on Britain to various types of professional and popular audiences, to write, and to teach selected groups of personnel destined for the Far East where they would come into frequent and friction-laden contact with the British. The problems of addressing members of one's own culture about their relations with members of another culture presented some distinct features and led to formulations of significant differences which had not been pointed out during my British experience. These differences in insight are to be laid primarily, I think, to the inevitable shift in one's type of participation under the two circumstances. In Britain, I was a friendly visitor, using my professional skill to facilitate relationships between two wartime allies. In the United States, particularly in my teaching role in the various outpost schools, I was concerned with the strengths and weaknesses of Americans for the tasks of cross-cultural understanding which they were going to face. I had to find, if possible, approaches which, in clarifying their own cultural attitudes, would make it possible for them not merely to be more understanding but to act in cross-cultural situations. Furthermore, one faces, in discussing one's own culture with fellow members, a different sort of cross-fire of criticism and is likely, occasionally, to abandon sympathetic impartiality for a note of urgency, if not astringency. In closed classes, designed for war purposes, there were no members of other nationalities, and it was sometimes difficult to convince the students that I would have used the same words and made the same points had there been British in the audience. In all work of this sort, it is essential to speak in terms which envelop the two or more peoples being discussed, and which represent the differences in ways acceptable to both. However, this necessity is more vividly demonstrated if actual human beings of each group are present in the flesh.

Rapport Difficulties

An American addressing an American audience about Britain is speaking to people who have strong and partly unconscious attitudes about Britain which go very deep,—much deeper than any attitudes which the British, as a group, had about America in 1943. The American sense of national identity contains the earlier and severed relationship with Britain as an intrinsic part, while the British do not use the loss of America as a component of their sense of national identity. Furthermore, in the United States the Anglophile position is traditionally associated with that of the upper-class, the conservative, the wealthy, and the more easterly part of our population—added to the circumstance that the bulk of American tourists before the war were women devoutly following the footsteps of one or another bard. The Anglophobe position contains a mass of assorted elements, Middle West against the East, European ancestry against the older Anglo-Saxon stock, the plain man against the would-be aristocrat, etc. To discuss Britain dispassionately, it was necessary for the lecturer to face and deal with these strong currents of feeling, sometimes existing simultaneously in the same individual. I finally solved this problem, satisfactorily for myself at least, by beginning a lecture with a caricature[6] of the pro-American British woman, who represents, in capsule form, a way of repudiating the snobbish note which over-sweetened the voice of the Anglophile and of startling the Anglophobe into a provisional (British) identification with the kind of Britons who would not like the type of Americanphile whom I presented. This produced a loosening of traditional identifications, which permitted the clarification material to get a hearing.

A second difficulty arose from the inveterate American habit of asking about every piece of behavior, "Is it better or worse than ours?" This contrast with the British insistence on complexity and, hence, uniqueness, has been discussed above, but it presented itself in a new form as I lectured on British wartime arrangements for community feeding, advising disoriented citizens through the Citizens' Advice Bureaus, or caring for the children of working mothers. Invariably, the American audience wanted to know, "Is their system better or worse than ours?" Behind this question were two unexpressed attitudes: one, the hope that ours would be better and, second, the tacit acceptance of the obligation to copy theirs if ours was worse. As most of the audience vigorously resented any suggestion that they copy Britain, these presentations were always charged with rapport dangers. It was necessary to stress, over and over again, that the British

---

[6]It should be noted that caricatures contain a strong hostile element, which has to be recognized whenever they are used.

solution was different, not better or worse. While this point might be surmounted temporarily in a lecture, it usually did not survive in next day's newspaper headlines, and actually represents one of the most serious hazards to any sort of comprehension of other peoples by Americans. A simple sense of either inferiority or superiority would be easier to deal with than this belief that all institutions can be placed on a single scale, and that it becomes the American's obligation to choose the best. The pleasure derived from the study of foreign behaviors which can be voted as inferior is alloyed by the discomfort of encountering those which are superior.

Attitude Towards Compromise

American audiences raised a question whose counterpart I never met in Britain. It illustrates how valuable each side of such a relationship is in drawing attention to parts of the whole which the other side might neglect. "Why is it the British always insist on their own way in international affairs and we always lose?" "Why do the British always pull the wool over American eyes?" were frequent questions. In comments upon our international negotiations, the terms "the poor little United States" cropped up with amazing frequency. In working out a clarification of these questions, of this American belief that we always lost, I again sought for a common element in the two cultures against which the differences could be highlighted. Americans share with the British a common tradition in regard to the appropriate behavior of minorities who are minorities because they are in some way more right than the majority. Such minorities, best represented by the long line of dissident Protestant sects, but today also represented by the Roman Catholic minority in England, have been accorded, as part of the whole picture of our form of government, the right to differ and the duty to stand up for their positions. A virtuous minority in both countries is virtuous just because it does not compromise. Here, however, the parallel ends, because the British, speaking from strength, from the paternal position, do not identify government negotiations as made from a minority position. The government acts from strength and, being strong, can *include* some of the minority demands in any proposal. To compromise is the act of the strong and the entrenched, an act of graciousness, expediency, and a recognition that the heresies of today become the orthodoxies of tomorrow. Thus, in Britain, the word "compromise" is a good word, and one may speak approvingly of any arrangement which has been a compromise, including, very often, one in which the other side has gained more than fifty per cent of the points at issue. On the other hand, in the United States, the minority position is still the position from which everyone speaks: the President *versus* Congress, Congress *versus* the President, the State government *versus* the metropolis, and the metropolis *versus* the State government. This is congruent with the American doctrine of checks and balances, but it does not permit the word "compromise" to gain the same ethical halo which it has in Britain. Where, in Britain, to compromise means to work out a good solution, in America it usually means to work out a bad one, a solution in which all the points of importance (to both sides) are lost. Thus, in negotiations between the United States and Britain, all of which had, in the nature of the case, to be compromises, as two sovereignties were involved, the British could always speak approvingly and proudly of the result, while the Americans had to emphasize their losses. Out of the same ethic, but as contrasting interpretations of our position, came these mutually reinforcing estimates of a document or treaty.

Closely related to this sense of being weak but on the side of the right, and therefore committed to demanding a hundred per cent victories, is the American fear of being exploited by other groups, best summed up in the vernacular phrase, "Don't be a sucker." This is so deeply seated and has been so heavily exploited in discussions of our relationship to other countries, both those who are believed to outwit us in the diplomatic game and those who ask us for help, that it seemed important to analyze it. First, it was necessary to work out the interpersonal dynamics of the conception. A "sucker" in America, who is not to be given an even break, is anyone who enters a game in which he does not have the skill, or wit, or strength, to compete. Superficially, the American ethic that a sucker should be trimmed seems discrepant with the ethic that it is wrong to bully. However, seen against the way in which American boys are reared it becomes intelligible. Instead of the British father who supports the eldest son, as a surrogate of himself, against the competition of the younger sons, and at the same time exhorts the eldest to be gentle but firm, the American boy is reared by a mother who defends the younger against the elder and continually uses the success of the younger to goad the elder towards achievement. The slightly younger brother, backed up by the mother, becomes a threat, especially to the young boy whose games are continually subject to the intrusion of the younger. This contemporary child-rearing tradition combines with the frontier tradition in which the tenderfoot is a threat to the whole community. Older frontiersmen, alert to the dangers which one careless act may precipitate, and older brothers alert to the way in which the younger may spoil their games, both find refuge in the ethic, "Never give a sucker an even break," an ethic which is also honored by the admission of the American who loses, "I was a sucker, I asked for it." The extent to which this treatment of the sucker may justifiably be classified as a deeply-rooted ethical attitude is illustrated by the report in *Time* (November 6, 1944) in which Oldendorf is pictured with the slogan "never give a sucker an even break," and his adherence to the slogan is then described as accounting for the way in which a successful ambush of Japanese ships was conducted. Stated for American consumption, the havoc was justifiably wrought among the Japanese because they had "asked for it."

At the same time, the word, sucker, is used in another and positively toned sense, to describe the man who is generous, enthusiastic, willing to give of his time and energy, as when a physician remarks in a public speech, "You know doctors always head the sucker list." This is said with approval of the doctor's kind heart and is tantamount to saying, "We are admirably tenderhearted people." Or, the student, cited in a psychological study as a normal, well-adjusted young American, will remark on the offices which he has held in organizations and adds "I'm a sucker for work." This dual attitude towards the sucker position further complicates the American attitude towards other peoples, because it is just when Americans are behaving well that they are most likely to suspect that they are being made suckers against their will. Then the whole negative set of sanctions comes into play, and the ethic of never giving a sucker an even break is projected on to the other national group. The formula reads that we are suckers in the international game, either when we compete or when we are generous, that we aren't up to it, either way, that we are playing a game we do not understand and that, therefore, we will be trimmed. A perfect instance of this interpretation when confronted by the British insistence on the assumption of an appearance of model, self-controlled parental behavior, was provided in an article by Senator Brewster (6):

> A number of different diplomatic, commercial, and financial moves will be necessary if we are to hold our rightful place in world commerce, but one of the most important is this: We must stop being out-traded by our good friends the British, the world's greatest experts in economic diplomacy.
> "One day I was talking with Sir Gerald Campbell, Lord Halifax's right hand man in the British Embassy in Washington, and I told him I believed our statesmanship is so bad that in nearly every negotiation with the British we came out second best.
> "Sir Gerald smiled. 'Of course, we put it over on you,' he said. 'But not half as often as we could!'. . .

This passage sums up the whole position, the American fear of being trimmed as suckers who do not know the game, the British failure to recognize the issue which is being raised, and their response first with a jocular acceptance of the stated inferiority, which from their point of view takes the sting out, coupled with a statement of the high ethical behavior which all fathers, governors, and persons in authority are supposed to display. The unpalatability of the British reply to the ordinary American can best be stated by referring to the Fijian form of insult in which most enemies were eaten but those who were to be most insulted were cooked and left uneaten. The jocular, Olympian assumption of restraint in the British answer simply exacerbates the American feeling of being treated negligently and condescendingly.

Another pretty example occurred in an article in the *Washington Star,* in 1945 (23), under the heading, "Critics Air U.S.-British Views." One author, Sir John Wardlaw Milne, writes: "In this country we are thankful and *indeed proud* of the great United States, but we heartily dislike the tendency to suggest that America's intervention is a kind of act of grace from some superior beings who need not have engaged in the war at all." (The italics are mine.) Senator Burton Wheeler writes, in the other column: "America wants no more deceptive slogans such as 'Give us the tools, we'll finish the job.' We are not going to tolerate any condescending attitude on the part of anyone that implies or assigns us the status of 'poor relations'." Here, we see the British tone of speaking from an established position, and discouraging any upstart claims, the American tone of maintaining their rights against those who would put them down.

The phrase *proud* of, so galling to American ears, was a British way of boasting on behalf of the Americans. The whole problem of how Americans should speak of British achievement and British of American was a particulary ticklish one all through the war. After repeated instances of the degree of misunderstanding which was generated by the way in which each ally spoke of its own and allied efforts, Geoffrey Gorer and I worked out a phrasing in terms of the conceptions of partnership which provided a form of clarification suitable for lecturing and teaching. All through the war, the United States and Britain were spoken of as "partners," a word which is common to both languages. But the British associated the word, when applied to international affairs, with a sports concept, with the tennis partner who, for the duration of the game, is treated as like oneself, whose successes one acclaims and whose failures one grieves over. It was possible to invoke from the memories of anyone who had played deck tennis with British partners the continuous, "Good shot, partner!" "Hard luck, partner!" which is an inseparable part of the verbal etiquette of the game. The American, however, seeing international relationships primarily in a business context, associated the word with a business partnership, in which the relationship is conventionally asymmetrical—one partner putting up the funds, the other providing the brains or the entry, but neither committed to a social relationship with the other, with an expectation of the partnership lasting until it is disrupted by disagreement or death, and with no obligation on either to boast or grieve for the other partner. Therefore, a careful British attempt to boast for their partners (as in the case of the great emphasis given to the American contribution to bringing down the buzz bombs) was met by the Americans, not by a little piece of symmetrical vicarious boasting, about, say, the landing platforms, but instead by blow-ups in the American papers of what the British had said about the buzz bombs. This produced inevitable confusion, and even some abortive attempts on the part of the British to do their own boasting.

Conclusion

The methods described in this paper are anthropological methods. That is, they rely upon an understanding of the cultural patterns of the peoples involved, and they invoke regularities for purposes of clarification. It is, however, important to recognize that clarification alone will not promote understanding,—that it is still necessary to set some tone within which feeling may flow freely. In the presentations and teaching described in this paper, I relied on several methods which invoked feeling: first, emphasizing symmetries and, when possible, reducing to symmetrical terms what looked like complementary contrasts; second, giving a description of the other peoples' behavior in terms which made *identification* possible (*e.g.*, in the description of the breakfast table, it is possible for listeners of each nationality to imagine what it would be like to be in the reciprocal exhibitionist position) ; and, third, on arousing the kind of laughter which comes from the exactitude of the cultural statement. Members of an audience invariably laughed at the description of their own cultural behavior, not at that of the others. To obtain this effect, it is very important to avoid caricature, which is self-defeating. The device also fails if there are many expatriates in an audience, since these are likely to see their home culture with a degree of distortion that makes any exact description, which will invoke the laughter of recognition from others, seem to them a caricature,—usually a hostile caricature. In other words, the method failed when it was used with those who were themselves highly ambivalent about their own culture, and overaccepting of the other. Significantly enough, attempts to give equally exact descriptions of German behavior have usually failed to evoke the same sort of recognition from Germans in this country. It is possible that this method is best suited to cultures and situations in which ambivalence towards the own culture is least in evidence.

Undoubtedly, in other interpretative hands or in different media, other ways of evoking feeling would be more appropriate than the deliberate attempt to embody the clarifying statement in exact, laughter-producing *verbatim* vignettes. That the method is suitable for more than one culture is evidenced by the very similar response which I received from British and American audiences when I gave the same material, in the same way. At the same time, the evocation of pity, or eager purposive aspiration, may also be feeling states which might appropriately accompany the type of clarification which an initial objective anthropological analysis of cultural patterns provides. Evoking either fear or anger runs, I believe, into the danger of stirring up, in the audience, feelings which interfere with acceptance of the clarification. Strong identification is possible with an evocation of fear or anger, but the identification tends to be so strong as to interfere with the degree of distance which is necessary both for laughter and for an understanding of difference.

If we are to build a world in which a variety of cultures are orchestrated together so as to produce a viable social order, we need intensive exploration of the types of clarification and types of presentation which will increase understanding between pairs of cultural groups and then among more complicated groupings.

LITERATURE CITED

1. Bateson, G.
   1942. Some systematic approaches to the study of culture and personality. Character and Personality XI, 1 : 76–84.
2. Bateson, G.
   1942. Morale and National Character. In, *Civilian Morale,* 2nd. yearbook of S.P.S.S.I. : 71–91.   Houghton Mifflin Co. Boston.
3. Bateson, G., & M. Mead
   1941. Principles of morale building.   J. Educ. Sociol. 15(4) : 206–220.

4. Benedict, R.
   1946. The study of cultural patterns in European nations. Trans. N. Y. Acad.
   Sci., Ser. II, 8(8) : 274–279.
5. Benedict, R.
   1947. The Chrysanthemum and the Sword. Houghton Mifflin Co. Boston.
6. Brewster, O.
   1945. Let's not be suckers again. American Magazine, January issue : 24–26,
   93–98.
7. Dyer, A. M., & M. Mead
   1944. It's human nature. CBS Broadcast. Education 65(4) : 228–239.
8. Gorer, G.
   1943. Themes in Japanese culture. Trans. N. Y. Acad. Sci., Ser. II, 5(5) : 105–
   124.
9. Mead, M.
   1942. And Keep your Powder Dry. William Morrow & Co. New York.
10. Mead, M.
   1942. Preface From England. Preface to : *The American Character*, vii–xi.
   Pelican Books. Harmondsworth, England.
11. Mead, M.
   1942. Brothers and Sisters and Success. VII : 54–70 in : *And Keep your Powder
   Dry.* William Morrow & Co. New York.
12. Mead, M.
   1942. The Chip on the Shoulder. IX : 138–158 in : *And Keep your Powder Dry.*
   William Morrow & Co. New York.
13. Mead, M.
   1943. Why we Americans talk big. The Listener 30 : 772. B. B. C., London.
14. Mead, M.
   1943. Can you tell one American from another ?   The Listener 30 : 772.
   B. B. C., London.
15. Mead, M.
   1943. Anthropological techniques in war psychology. Bull. Menninger Clinic
   7 : 137–140.
16. Mead, M.
   1944. The American Troops and the British Community. Pamphlet. Hutchinson.
   London.
17. Mead, M.
   1944. Ferment in British education : some impressions of educational thinking in
   England. J. Am. Assoc. Univ. Women 37(3) : 131–133.
18. Mead, M.
   1944. A G.I. View of Britain. New York Times Magazine, March 19 : 18–19,
   34.
19. Mead, M.
   1944. What is a date ? Transatlantic 10 : 54, 57–60.
20. Mead, M.
   1944. A Bread and Butter Letter from a Lecturer. (Washington.) Occidental
   College, Los Angeles.
21. Mead, M.
   1944. The American Troops and the British Community. An Examination of the
   Relationship between the American Troops and British. Hutchinson. London.
22. Metraux, R.
   1943. Qualitative attitude analysis—a technique for the study of verbal behavior.
   Bull. Nat. Res. Council 108 : 86–95.

23. Wheeler, B. K.
     1945. Critics air U.S.-British views. Washington Star, January 14.
24. Parsons, T.
     1945. The problem of controlled institutional change : an essay in applied social
     science. Psychiat. 8(1) : 79–101.
25. Committee Report
     1943. The Problem of Changing Food Habits. Report of the Committee on Food
     Habits, 1941–1943. Bull. Nat. Res. Council 108.
26. Round Table
     1945. Germany after the war. Am. J. Orthopsychiat. 15(3) : 381–441.

Guide to research in cultural anthropology

ALAN DUNDES and ROBERT E. PFEIFFER

*T*here are thousands of books and articles dealing with various aspects of cultural anthropology. The following bibliographical essay is intended only to provide a few clues for those who may wish to explore this fascinating field in more depth. At the same time, the beginner may get some idea of the immensity of the scholarship and how anthropologists in different times and in different places contribute to our knowledge of man.

Introductions to Cultural Anthropology

Those especially interested in the historical development of cultural anthropology as a discipline may consult such works as Alfred C. Haddon, *History of Anthropology* (London, 1910; 2nd ed. 1934); Thomas K. Penniman, *A Hundred Years of Anthropology* (London, 1935; 3rd ed. 1965); Robert H. Lowie, *The History of Ethnological Theory* (New York, 1937); Margaret T. Hodgen, *Early Anthropology in the Sixteenth and Seventeenth Centuries* (Philadelphia, 1964); or Paul Mercier, *Histoire de l'anthropologie* (Paris, 1966). There are also useful studies of the development of anthropology in one or more individual countries or regions, e.g., Meyer Fortes, *Social Anthropology at Cambridge Since 1900* (Cambridge, 1953) and Robert Heine-Geldern, "One Hundred Years of Ethnological Theory in the German-Speaking Countries: Some Milestones," *Current Anthropology*, 5 (1964), 407–18.

For introductions to theory and method, one may look at Paul Radin, *The Method and Theory of Ethnology* (New York, 1933); David Bidney, *Theoretical Anthropology* (New York, 1953); Robert F. Spencer, ed., *Method and Perspective in Anthropology* (Minneapolis, 1954); or Alfred R. Radcliffe-Brown, *Method in Social Anthropology* (Chicago, 1958).

The beginning student of cultural anthropology may want to know where to find basic definitions of key terms and concepts. One valuable source is the *Encyclopaedia of the Social Sciences*, 15 vols. (London and New York, 1930–35), an updated international revision of which was published in 1968. Among specialized dictionaries are Charles Winick, *Dictionary of Anthropology* (Paterson, N.J.; 1964) and Carleton S. Coon and Edward E. Hunt, *Anthropology A to Z* (New York, 1963). Perhaps one of the best sources is the Swedish anthropologist Åke Hultkrantz's excellent *General Ethnological Concepts* (Copenhagen, 1960), Volume I of a series entitled *International Dictionary of Regional European Ethnology and Folklore,* in which may be found concise definitions of most of the central concepts employed by American and European cultural anthropologists as well as bibliographical suggestions for further discussion. Some concepts have had books devoted to them. For the concept of culture, one may wade through Alfred L. Kroeber and Clyde Kluckhohn, *Culture: A Critical Review of Concepts and Definitions* (Cambridge, Mass., 1952).

Readers in search of definitions may also profit from examining textbooks in cultural anthropology. Among the numerous books of this kind, one may well elect to choose from the older ones, e.g., Ralph Linton, *The Study of Man* (New York, 1936), Alfred L. Kroeber, *Anthropology,* 2nd ed. (New York, 1948), and Melville J. Herskovits, *Man and His Works: The Science of Cultural Anthropology* (New York, 1948). Many of the more recent textbooks are introductions to social anthropology rather than to cultural anthropology. Social anthropology in England (and in Europe generally) differs somewhat from cultural anthropology in the United States, although the difference is not always well defined. From the perspective of a cultural anthropologist, social anthropology is a large and important division of cultural anthropology, a division which is primarily concerned with institutions. Normally the institutions studied are those of a political, economic, religious, or social organizational nature. Insofar as social anthropologists emphasize individual social *institutions* rather than concentrating upon descriptions of *cultures* as wholes, they are not the same as cultural anthropologists. In any event, the beginner may prefer to consult one of the many modern guides to social anthropology:

J. H. M. Beattie, *Other Cultures: Aims, Methods and Achievements in Social Anthropology* (London, 1964)
Paul Bohannan, *Social Anthropology* (New York, 1963)

E. E. Evans-Pritchard, *Social Anthropology* (London, 1951)
Godfrey Lienhardt, *Social Anthropology,* 2nd ed. (London, 1966)
Lucy P. Mair, *An Introduction to Social Anthropology* (Oxford, 1965)
S. F. Nadel, *The Foundations of Social Anthropology* (London, 1951)
D. F. Pocock, *Social Anthropology* (London, 1961)

There are, of course, a large number of conventional introductions to cultural anthropology. For a list of these as well as other aids for the beginner, see Rexford S. Beckham, "A Basic List of Books and Periodicals for College Libraries," in David G. Mandelbaum et al., eds., *Resources for the Teaching of Anthropology,* Memoir 95 of the American Anthropological Association (1963), pp. 77–316. One should realize that there are numerous introductory books in languages other than English and students controlling these languages might find it fruitful to acquaint themselves with other orientations in cultural anthropology. A reader of French might examine such works as Marcel Mauss, *Manuel d'ethnographie* (Paris, 1947) and Marcel Griaule, *Méthode de l'ethnographie* (Paris, 1957), while a reader of German might look at Kunz Dittmer, *Allgemeine Völkerkunde, Formen und Entwicklung der Kultur* (Braunschweig, 1954) or Leonhard Adam and Hermann Trimborn, eds., *Lehrbuch der Völkerkunde,* 3rd ed. (Stuttgart, 1958). For those who would prefer less "textbookish" introductions to cultural anthropology, Ruth Benedict's classic *Patterns of Culture* (New York, 1934), readily available in paperback, or Clyde Kluckhohn's *Mirror for Man* (New York, 1949) or Ina Corinne Brown's *Understanding Other Cultures* (Englewood Cliffs, N. J., 1963) can be recommended.

One must realize that there are also numerous book-length introductions to the other branches of anthropology, i.e., to physical anthropology and to archaeology. A few textbooks attempt to cover all of anthropology. One of the more successful of these is Ralph L. Beals and Harry Hoijer, *An Introduction to Anthropology,* 3rd ed. (New York, 1965), available in paperback. However, the beginner may wish to pursue cultural anthropology in a book devoted entirely to that subject rather than in a necessarily more abbreviated version appearing as a part of a general survey volume. The real problem, of course, with textbooks is that invariably in any vital discipline they become obsolete almost as soon as they are published. One way of learning about new textbooks and how they are evaluated by the professionals in the field is to check the book review sections of leading anthropology periodicals, for example, *American Anthropologist.*

Journals and Monographs

The average reader has little idea of the incredible wealth of professional literature which exists in most disciplines. Yet one of the best ways of finding out what is happening in a field of inquiry is to read the current leading journals in that discipline. It is in the journals that new ideas and methods are debated. In anthropology, there are important periodicals published in a wide variety of countries (and languages). The following small but representative sampling of some of these journals may illustrate the variety.

Argentina
  Revista del Museo de La Plata (nueva serie) Sección anthropología
    (1936), continuation of *Revista del Museo de La Plata* (1890)
  Runa, Archivio para las Ciencas del Hombre (1948)
Australia
  Anthropological Forum (1963)
  Journal of the Anthropological Society of South Australia (1963)
Austria
  *Bulletin of the International Committee on Urgent Anthropological
    and Ethnological Research* (1958)
  Mitteilungen der Anthropologischen Gesellschaft in Wien (1871)
Brazil
  Revista de Antropologia (1953)
Canada
  Anthropologica (1955)
  The Canadian Review of Sociology and Anthropology (1964)
Colombia
  Divulgaciones Etnológicas (1950)
  Revista Colombiana de Antropología (1953)
Czechoslovakia
  Ethnographica (1959)
Denmark
  Folk (1959)
France
  L'Anthropologie (1890)
  Revue Anthropologique (1891)
  L'Homme (1961)
Germany
  Archiv für Anthropologie (1866–1943)
  Baessler-Archiv; Beiträge zur Völkerkunde (1910)
  Ethnologica (1909)
  Zeitschrift für Ethnologie (1869)
Great Britain
  Man, 2nd series (1966), continuation of both *Man*, 1st series (1901)
    and the *Journal of the Royal Anthropological Institute of Great
    Britain and Ireland* (1872)
Hungary
  Acta Ethnographica (1950)
India
  The Anthropologist (1954)
  Eastern Anthropologist (1947)
  Journal of the Anthropological Society of Bombay (1886)
  Journal of the Indian Anthropological Society (1966)
  Man in India (1921)
Italy
  Archivio per l'Antropologia et la Etnologia (1871)

Rivista di Antropologia (1893)

Mexico
    Acta Anthropologica (1956)
    América Indígena (1941)
    Revista Mexicana de Estudios Antropológicos (1927)

The Netherlands
    Bijdragen Tot de Taal-, Land- en Volkenkunde (1853)
    Internationales Archiv für Ethnographie (1888)

Spain
    Antropología y Etnología (1949)
    Revista Española de Indigenismo (1964)

Sweden
    Ethnos (1936)
    Ymer (1881)

Switzerland
    Anthropos (1906)

Union of South Africa
    African Studies (1942), continuation of *Bantu Studies* (1921)

United States of America
    American Anthropologist (1888)
    Anthropological Quarterly (1953), continuation of *Primitive Man* (1928)
    Current Anthropology (1960)
    Ethnology (1962)
    Human Organization (1948), continuation of *Applied Anthropology* (1941)
    Southwestern Journal of Anthropology (1945)

U.S.S.R.
    Sovetskaia Etnografiia (1949), continuation of *Etnografiia* (1926)

Zambia
    African Social Research (1966), continuation of *The Rhodes-Livingstone Journal: Human Problems in British Central Africa* (1944)

Most of the journals cited above serve as general forums for a large number of anthropological topics and areas. In addition to these, there are various specialized journals for individual topics and for particular areas. Examples of area journals are:

    Africa (1928)
    Arctic Anthropology (1962)
    Journal of the Polynesian Society (1892)
    Oceania (1930)

Examples of special topic journals include:

    Ethnohistory (1954)
    Ethnomusicology (1957)
    Temenos: Studies in Comparative Religion (1965)

There are even journals which combine area and topic. For example, a key publication for the study of American Indian languages is:

International Journal of American Linguistics (1917)

In addition to the many periodicals, there are also a great number of monograph series. In such series, one frequently finds book-length discussions of anthropological subjects. Monograph series are issued by museums, by university presses, and by governmental agencies. Some of the more important monograph series in the United States—there are similar series in other countries—include:

Annual Report of the Bureau of American Ethnology (1879/1880)
Anthropological Papers of the American Museum of Natural History (1908)
Anthropological Papers of the University of Alaska (1952)
Anthropological Papers of the University of Arizona (1959)
Anthropology Papers of the University of Michigan Museum of Anthropology (1949)
Anthropological Papers of the University of Utah (1939)
Anthropological Records (University of California Publications) (1937)
Anthropological Series of the Catholic University of America (1930)
Bulletin of the Bernice P. Bishop Museum, Honolulu (1922)
Bulletin of the Bureau of American Ethnology (1887)
Columbia University Contributions to Anthropology (1913)
Contributions of the Museum of the American Indian, Heye Foundation (1913)
Fieldiana: The Anthropological Series of the Chicago (Field Columbian) Museum of Natural History (1895)
Logan Museum Publications in Anthropology (1928)
Memoirs of the American Anthropological Association (1905)
Memoirs of the Bernice P. Bishop Museum, Honolulu (1899)
Monographs of the American Ethnological Society (1940)
Monographs of the Society for Applied Anthropology (1959)
Papers in Anthropology of the Museum of New Mexico (1958)
Papers of the Peabody Museum of Archaeology and Ethnology, Harvard University (1888)
Publications in Anthropology of the University of New Mexico (1945)
Smithsonian Contributions to Anthropology (1965)
Stanford Anthropological Series (1953)
University of California Publications in American Archaeology and Ethnology (1903–1964)
University of California Publications in Anthropology (1964)
University of Colorado Studies: Series in Anthropology (1948)
University of Illinois Studies in Anthropology (1961)
University of Kentucky Studies in Anthropology (1961)
University of Washington Publications in Anthropology (1920)
Viking Fund Publications in Anthropology (1943)
Yale University Publications in Anthropology (1936)

How to Find Cultural Anthropology Books in a Library

Typically, a beginning student wants to learn how he can determine what is known about a particular people or a particular topic. Such a student should visit the nearest and largest public or university library to try to obtain the information he desires. If he already has the name of an author or a title—which his instructor may have given him or which he found as a suggested source in a textbook—it should not be difficult to find out if the book is in the library. He should look in the alphabetically arranged "author-title" card catalog for the last name of his author or the first (key) word of his title. If the library does have the book, the student should easily be able to discover this, unless the book happens to be one of those published by a government agency, an international congress, a museum or some other corporate body. Books published by such "corporate" institutions may well be listed under a "corporate entry" such as:

International Congress of Americanists, 28th, Paris, 1947
New York (City) Museum of Primitive Art
U.S. Bureau of American Ethnology
Wenner-Gren Foundation for Anthropological Research, New York
Bogotá (City) Universidad de los Andes

Fortunately, most libraries provide "added entries" under the names of authors or editors, as well as the title if it is distinctive.

But what if the student does not begin with knowledge of a specific author or title? Suppose he starts only with some intellectual curiosity about a particular people or topic. In this case, the student would use the subject card catalog rather than the author-title catalog (at least in libraries which have both types of catalogs). However, he should be aware that subject headings are neither perfect nor encyclopaedic in coverage. If a book is about a single tribe in Africa, it may be listed under the name of the tribe. Yet works which may include definitive information about that tribe may also cover other tribes, and the subject heading then may be as broad as "Ethnology—Kenya" or even "Ethnology—Africa" without any entry under the tribal names. Library subject headings, although somewhat curiously called "specific" subject headings, are assigned by catalogers according to the theory that whatever subject heading is the most specific for the *entire* book being cataloged is the one used. Sometimes, more than one subject heading may be assigned, e.g., "Law—Zambia" and "Zambia—Social life and customs" when the book is about both and no more specific single subject heading is available that includes both. Anyone interested in the theory and practice of assigning library subject headings may consult David J. Haykin's *Subject Headings: A Practical Guide* (Washington, D.C., 1951).

The important point for beginners to remember is that rarely are enough subject headings for any book assigned and consequently one should not expect to be able to find all of the available materials by looking under just one subject heading. For example, to find out about a lawsuit involving the Yana, a California Indian tribe, you may need to consult such headings

as "Indians of North America—California," "Indians of North America—
Legal status, laws, etc.," "Law—California," "Indians of North America—
Government relations," "Yana Indians," and perhaps many more. (Research-
ing legal proceedings is more complicated in practice, involving as it
sometimes does government documents, reports, legislative bills, laws, etc.,
which are in many cases not cataloged and which may be found arranged
in various ways in a Government Documents department of the library
or in a Law School library.) A great deal of time and trouble is necessary
not only to ascertain what is available, but also what is not. Proving to one's
own satisfaction that very little of importance has been written about
a particular subject is often much more difficult than finding what is in
the library.

Still another problem with subject headings in the United States is that
so many, particularly in the field of anthropology, were originally formulated
by catalogers in the Library of Congress in the early decades of this century
and consequently they may not be especially appropriate for some of the
newer concepts and subdisciplines of anthropology. For example, most of the
books describing the results of archaeological expeditions are still under the
subject headings "Antiquities" or "Excavations (Archaeology)" subdivided
by place, e.g., "Antiquities—Brazil—Amazon" or "Excavations (Archaeology)—Southwest, New," even though today we do not ordinarily think of
those artifacts uncovered by archaeological excavation as "antiquities."
Similarly, the student searching for "Latin America" in the subject card
catalog in older libraries may have to look under the more archaic "Spanish
America" heading. Though it is time-consuming to use, a large volume
almost always available near a library catalog, *Subject Headings Used in the
Dictionary Catalogs of the Library of Congress,* the 7th edition of which was
published in 1966, will often provide clues in using subject headings and
classification categories that would not have occurred to the beginner without help.

The student may also learn the relevant portions of the general classification system which in most American libraries is either the Dewey Decimal
Classification or the Library of Congress system. Unfortunately, these may
be of only limited value. In the Dewey system, cultural anthropology books
may be under "Social Science" (300), but also under "The Arts" (700),
"Travel" (910), and many other headings. The Library of Congress system
is a little more helpful. Many books will have GN (Anthropology) call
numbers, some of which are quite specific: GN 1 includes anthropology
periodicals; GN 408 is reserved for books on Geophagy (dirt eating), while
GN 409, another category of "Food" is designated for works on Anthro-
pophagy (cannibalism). However, many cultural anthropology books have
non GN labels. For example, many books dealing with American Indians are
in the E 51–99 range inasmuch as E is for "American (North America)."
Similarly, one may discover that Africa is DT, Latin American is F, etc.
Students who have access to the book stacks or who are using an "open
shelf" library may wish to browse in a particular section. One technique
is to look up the call number of one relevant book and then look on the
shelf in the general vicinity of that one book. Unexpected but valuable

sources can often be found in this way. Of course, one should not rely solely on this technique or upon the general classification systems either inasmuch as books which anthropologists would consider anthropological will be found scattered throughout the gamut of library classifications, e.g., in linguistics, economics, sociology, art, music, etc.

If the student expects to be a detective in the library, it will make his use of it more pleasant and rewarding than if he approaches the card catalog expecting to find exactly what he wants at once—especially if there has never been anything published on what he wants. Another general rule is that there is no substitute for the work of a subject specialist. That is, no library catalog, compiled as it is by non-specialists, can be expected to show all those items that an expert in a particular subject might turn up for a special bibliography. A bibliography is a list of books and articles written on a particular subject. The beginner who can put his hands on a specialized bibliography relevant to the subject he wishes to investigate may save hours of frustration caused by the obscurities and incongruities of library catalogs.

Indexes and Bibliographies

As more and more books and articles are written on anthropology, it becomes more difficult for even dedicated professional anthropologists to keep up with their subdisciplinary specialties. With all the journals and monograph series in anthropology, not to mention all the studies of anthropological topics which appear in non-anthropological publications, it is obvious that a professional anthropologist must depend upon the special indexes and other bibliographical aids designed to assist him in finding the materials published on subjects in which he has a research and teaching interest. Such indispensable tools of the trade can also prove invaluable to the beginning student of cultural anthropology who becomes especially intrigued by a particular people or problem.

Let us take the matter of anthropological periodicals. While most anthropology journals have an annual index, many have not yet published cumulative indexes. Thus someone searching through articles in *Ethnology, Man,* or *Oceania* would have to look through the indexes of each individual volume (year). Fortunately, in 1963, partly in order to alleviate the lack of a comprehensive cumulative periodical index in anthropology, the Library of Harvard University's Peabody Museum published in book form its card catalog, complete to the year 1962. The catalog had included analytic cards by author and by subject for journal articles for over fifty years. Though limited to the periodicals received in that particular library, this catalog is the best retroactive index now available for anthropology periodicals. The full title is: *Catalog of the Library of the Peabody Museum of Archaeology and Ethnology, Harvard University.* The section for *Authors* consists of 26 volumes and the section for *Subjects,* 27 volumes, along with an additional index volume to the subject headings, which are unique to this library and which are primarily geographical, with subdivisions by topic, e.g., "Germany —Archaeology—Copper." Although no supplement has been issued to keep this excellent catalog current, there is another index which may be used. In

1963, publication was begun of a quarterly *Index to Current Periodicals Received in the Library of the Royal Anthropological Institute* (London). Primarily geographical in its orientation, this index is of course limited to those periodicals received in the Institute's library.

It is true that bibliographies, like textbooks, soon become outdated. Nevertheless, until superseded by a more inclusive, newer version, they may still serve. For instance, some of the earlier bibliographical aids in anthropology, William Z. Ripley, *A Selected Bibliography of the Anthropology and Ethnology of Europe* (Boston, 1899); Juul Dieserud, *The Scope and Content of the Science of Anthropology* (Chicago, 1908), especially Part III, Bibliography, pp. 91–186; Sebald Rudolf Steinmetz, *Essai d'une Bibliographie Systematique de L'Ethnologie jusqu'à l'année 1911* (Brussels, 1911); or Martin Heydrich, ed., *Ethnologischer Anzeiger*, 4 vols. (Stuttgart, 1926/28–1935/44) continue to provide access to materials not included in recent compendia, which, because of the great volume of publishing, have necessarily been limited to annual or current rather than comprehensive cumulative coverage. The majority of the latter have begun only in the middle of the twentieth century, for example, *Sociological Abstracts* (1952) and the especially valuable *International Bibliography of Social and Cultural Anthropology* (1955) published by UNESCO.

An excellent example of the utility of bibliographies is provided by indexes to the papers presented at international congresses or conferences. For instance, there is a Society of Americanists which consists of diverse scholars who share a common interest in the Americas, North and South. These historians, linguists, and anthropologists, among others, have been meeting every two years or so ever since the first International Congress of Americanists was held in Nancy, France, in 1875. Although a *Journal de la Société des Américanistes de Paris* was founded in 1895, the various papers presented at the congresses have been published separately as acts or proceedings of the individual congresses. How can the student (or the professional anthropologist, for that matter) locate those papers which are germane to his interests? One could, of course, plow patiently through the table of contents of each volume looking for relevant papers or one could hope that such papers were already listed in appropriate regional or topical bibliographies. However, the fact is that many of the papers given at international congresses are effectively "lost." Fortunately for students of the Americas, there is a cumulative index to the early papers presented at meetings of the International Congress of Americanists: Juan Comas, *Los Congresos Internacionales de Americanistas, Síntesis Histórica e Índice Bibliográfico General 1875–1952* (Mexico City, 1954). For an entrée into the proceedings of some of the other international anthropological congresses, see Juan Comas, *Historia y Bibliografía de los Congresos Internacionales de Ciencias Antropológicas: 1865–1954* (Mexico City, 1956).

Now let us see how indexes and bibliography can help transform the beginning student's quest for information into a relatively easy mechanical task. Suppose someone wanted to know what had been written about the Crow Indians. How would he find out? First of all, as previously explained, he could consult the subject card catalog of the nearest large library. If he wanted to discover whether his library had the most recent books on the Crow, he might look at the published catalogs from larger libraries or from libraries with extensive specialized holdings in anthropology. Thus he could look up "Crow Indians" in the *Library of Congress Catalog: Books: Subjects,* an important reference tool, published in five-year cumulations beginning with 1950 (Ann Arbor, 1955 ff), or he could look in the above mentioned Peabody Museum catalog in the appropriate one of the 27 volumes devoted to *Subjects.* In the unlikely event that he found nothing by the above means, he should then try again using larger subject headings which hopefully might include his original subject. For example, if he looked in a library subject card catalog under "Indians of North America" and in that subsection of cards labelled "Bibliography," he would probably find George P. Murdock's *Ethnographic Bibliography of North America,* 3rd ed. (New Haven, 1960), the basic bibliographical source for American Indian studies, which in fact has a substantial section devoted to Crow Indian materials.

Another bibliographical technique may be used *after* the inquiring student has learned that a particular author appears to have written several works about the people in question. Thus the student in search of information concerning the Crow Indians should soon discover that anthropologist Robert Lowie had written extensively on the Crow. The obvious thing for the student to do would be to locate a bibliography of Robert Lowie's writings to see if he had read all of what Lowie had to say. about the Crow. To find such a bibliography, the student should first look up the author in the card catalog in a library. If there is no separately published bibliography of an author's writings, the student will have to look elsewhere such as in a book of the author's collected papers or in a *festschrift* volume. A *festschrift* is a book of essays written by a group of a scholar's friends and former students which is presented to honor him on a special day (e.g., a seventieth birthday) or on the eve of his retirement or on some comparable occasion. Normally a bibliography of the scholar's works is included in the volume. If these leads fail and if the author is no longer living, the student may check his obituary in one of the professional journals, e.g., in the *American Anthropologist.* Often obituaries will contain bibliographical details. If the author is living, the student may look in indexes to professional journals or other standard bibliographical aids, beginning with the most recent and working back through time, to find the most recent article or book on the subject by the author. The reason for looking in, say, the most recent ten year cumulative index to the *American Anthropologist,* for example, is that a recent article or book is likely to contain references to the author's earlier studies. If one found the earlier study first, it would not necessarily aid in finding the more recent work (where the author may have corrected or altered a view expressed in his early works). In this particular hypothetical case, the student would presumably be fortunate enough to have come upon *The Complete Bibliography of Robert H. Lowie* (Berkeley, 1966) where Lowie's many writings on the Crow are listed.

Some of this information may bewilder the student unfamiliar with such aids for research, but he should realize that an individual interested in a particular region or people makes it his business to know about the appropriate bibliographical tools. Thus the student interested in a particular Brazilian Indian tribe might not need to consult the *Boletín Bibliográfico de Antropología Americana* (1937ff) or the general survey work, Julian H. Steward, ed., *Handbook of South American Indians,* 7 vols. (Washington, D.C., 1946–59). Such a student would probably go directly to Timothy J. O'Leary, *Ethnographic Bibliography of South America* (New Haven, 1963) or Herbert Baldus, *Bibliografia Crítica da Etnologia Brasileira* (São Paulo, 1954). Similarly, the student who had already looked up sources on Burma would know that Burma was not included in Elizabeth Von Fürer-Haimendorf, *An Anthropological Bibliography of South Asia,* 2 vols. (Paris, The Hague, 1958–1964) which is primarily concerned with India, but rather that it, along with Cambodia, Laos, Thailand, and Vietnam, was covered in John F. Embree and Lillian Ota Dotson, *Bibliography of the Peoples and Cultures of Mainland Southeast Asia* (New Haven, 1950). In fact, if he knew his way around the library, chances are that he would go immediately to the relevant section of Frank N. Trager, ed., *Annotated Bibliography of Burma* (New Haven, 1956).

One problem is that not all of the areas of the world are equally well indexed bibliographically and, of course, not all of the world's peoples have been equally well studied. The point is simply that the conscientious student makes a concerted effort to familiarize himself with whatever bibliographical tools there may be for his area of interest. If he is interested in Africa or a region in Africa or one culture in a region, he would no doubt consult such general works as Norbert Mylius, *Afrika Bibliographie, 1943–51* (Vienna, 1952); Heinrich A. Wieschoff, *Anthropological Bibliography of Negro Africa* (New Haven, 1948) or the appropriate regional African ethnographic bibliography in the *Africa Bibliography Series* of the International African Institute (London, 1958ff) compiled by Ruth Jones. He might also look at the indexes to such major journals as *Africa* (1928), *Journal of the African Society* (1910) presently titled *African Affairs, Journal de la Société des Africanistes* (1931), or any of the periodicals included in Helen F. Conover's 163 page *Serials for African Studies* (Washington, D.C., 1961). For the recent scholarship, he would read *African Abstracts* (1950ff) which gives not only references but brief synopses of articles in the vast current African literature, including materials not originally written in English.

So far, only tribal or regional bibliographies have been discussed. There are also a few excellent·topic or subject bibliographies. For example, someone interested in culture change might want to check Felix M. Keesing, *Culture Change: An Analysis and Bibliography of Anthropological Sources to 1952* (Stanford, 1952). Incidentally, one must be alert for the coverage time cut-off in bibliographies. Usually there is a considerable time lag between the completion of the compilation of the bibliography and its publication, e.g., John Greenway, *Bibliography of the Australian Aborigines and the Native Peoples of Torres Strait to 1959* (Sydney, 1963). Generally, topic bibliographies or bibliographic surveys such as Roger Goodland, *A Bibliography of Sex Rites and Customs* (London, 1931) or Gertrude P. Kurath's "Panorama of Dance Ethnology," *Current Anthropology,* 1 (1960), 233–54, may be found by the same techniques as those employed in locating areal bibliographies.

One can easily see that useful as bibliographies are, there is the critical matter of locating the appropriate bibliography—if indeed there is an appropriate one—for a particular research problem. One way of checking to see if a relevant area or subject bibliography exists is to consult a bibliography of bibliographies! Examples of reference works of this kind are: Constance M. Winchell, *Guide to Reference Books,* 8th ed. (Chicago, 1967), Hanns Bohatta and Franz Hodes, *Internationale Bibliographie der Bibliographien* (Frankfurt, 1950), and Theodore Besterman, *A World Bibliography of Bibliographies and of Bibliographical Catalogues, Abstracts, Digests, Indexes, and the Like,* 3rd ed., 4 vols. (Geneva, 1955–56). There are also such guides as Robert L. Collison, *Bibliographies, Subject and National: A Guide to Their Contents, Arrangement, and Use,* 2nd ed. (New York, 1962), and Carl M. White, et al., *Sources of Information in the Social Sciences: A Guide to the Literature* (Totowa, N.J., 1964). Here the beginning student is best advised to check with a professional reference librarian, skilled in the techniques of library science, who can help find the most up-to-date aid of this kind. It should be noted also that there are "bibliographies of bibliographies" in anthropology proper, e.g., Gordon D. Gibson, "A Bibliography of Anthropological Bibliographies: The Americas," *Current Anthropology,* 1 (1960), 61–75, and Ida E. Leeson, *A Bibliography of Bibliographies of the South Pacific* (Melbourne and New York, 1954). While the majority of students will never need to come into contact with these reference works, they may at least realize that the serious student of anthropology finds them indispensable. As the proliferation of printed materials continues at an incredible pace, the importance of such information retrieval systems as comprehensive bibliographies increases.

Another way professionals try to keep abreast of developments in their field is through survey articles or books. These surveys, often of a subdiscipline of cultural anthropology, can be of enormous assistance to a beginning student who is searching for clues to contemporary trends. Recommended surveys in cultural anthropology include Alfred L. Kroeber, ed., *Anthropology Today* (Chicago, 1953) and William L. Thomas, Jr., ed., *Current Anthropology, A Supplement to Anthropology Today* (Chicago, 1956). Especially valuable are the volumes in the series *Biennial Review of Anthropology,* edited by Bernard J. Siegel, the first one of which was published in 1959. Each volume surveys a different series of topics, e.g., medical anthropology, economic anthropology, and peasant life studies. The six or more survey articles in each volume are written by different specialists.

Ethnographic Films

Traditionally, one of the ways of showing a beginner what cultural anthropology is all about has been to send him to some of the "classic" examples of ethnographic description. Thus the new student is advised to read such works as Bronislaw Malinowski, *Argonauts of the Western Pacific* (London, 1922); Alfred R. Radcliffe-Brown, *The Andaman*

Islanders (Cambridge, 1922) ; Raymond W. Firth, *We, the Tikopia* (London, 1936) ; or E. E. Evans-Pritchard, *The Nuer* (Oxford, 1940), among others. This is still a good plan. However, in addition, the beginner may be greatly helped by actually seeing other cultures in action. Ideally, the student should visit other peoples and see for himself the problems and excitement of trying to understand the nature of culture. Unfortunately, such experiences are not easy to arrange. As a poor but reasonable substitute, ethnographic films may communicate to the novice that it is people and how they live which is the subject matter of cultural anthropology. Opinions differ as to which films are best. Recommended by many are *Nanook of the North* (1925), a pioneering ethnographic documentary by Robert Flaherty which shows the hard daily life of the Eskimo; *The Hunters* (1956) which despite some "staging" shows some of the rigors of the food quest among the African Bushmen as a small group of men seek a giraffe quarry, and *Dead Birds* (1964), a truly extraordinary and beautiful color film which captures many details of the culture of a New Guinea people including actual "warfare" with a neighboring group.

There are a number of sources of information about ethnographic films. Some of these include Anthony R. Michaelis, *Research Films in Biology, Anthropology, Psychology and Medicine* (New York, 1955) ; the *Educational Film Guide, 1954–58* (New York, 1958) and its supplements (1959ff) ; and the *EFLA* (Educational Films Library Association) *Film Evaluation Guide, 1946–64* (New York, 1965). An especially helpful list is "Films for Anthropological Teaching" (Revised Edition, June, 1967) prepared by Karl G. Heider and available from the Program in Ethnographic Film, Film Study Center, 19 Prescott Street, Cambridge, Massachusetts 02138. For access to the numerous ethnographic films made by German and other European ethnographers, one might consult the various publications of the Institut für den Wissenschaftlichen Film, Nonnensteig 72, Göttingen, Germany. For example, this institute's *Gesamtverzeichnis der Wissenschaftlichen Filme* published in 1962 as well as Sektion B Völkerkunde-Volkskunde of the somewhat irregularly appearing *Publikationen zu Wissenschaftlichen Filmen* (1963ff) provide useful film summaries and descriptions. For a brief history of the development of the art of ethnographic cinematography, see Luc de Heusch, *The Cinema and Social Science: A Survey of Ethnographic and Sociological Films,* Reports and Papers in the Social Sciences, No. 16, published by UNESCO (Paris, 1962). The increasing importance of such films is indicated by the fact that some professional anthropology journals, e.g., *American Anthropologist,* have instituted a film review section in which new ethnographic films are reviewed in the same manner as new books.

Anthropologists and Anthropological Institutions

Some readers might want to know where the nearest institutions concerned with anthropological research are located. To find out, they might look at the "Fourth International Directory of Anthropological Institutions," *Current Anthropology,* 8, no. 5, Part II (1967), 647–751. One type of institution is the anthropological or ethnographic museum. For a convenient list of some of the principal European ethnographic museums, see Leonhard Adam and Hermann Trimborn, eds., *Lehrbuch der Völkerkunde,* 3rd ed. (Stuttgart, 1958), pp. 293–97. For museums in North America, see John E. Hunter, *Inventory of Ethnological Collections in Museums of the United States and Canada* (Milwaukee, 1967).

There are also lists of anthropologists, e.g., "Fourth International Directory of Anthropologists," *Current Anthropology,* 8, no. 5, Part II (1967), 549–646. Also useful is an annual *Guide to Graduate Departments of Anthropology* published by the American Anthropological Association, Suite 112, 3700 Massachusetts Ave., N. W., Washington, D. C. 20016. This *Guide* lists all departments of anthropology at colleges and universities in the United States which offer graduate degrees (i.e., an M.A. or a Ph.D.) in anthropology. The *Guide,* which also gives the names of the individual staff members of these departments together with their teaching and research interests, may be obtained at a nominal cost by writing the Association. Students interested in learning more about the vocational aspects of anthropology may read William C. Sturtevant's "Anthropology as a Career," the Smithsonian Institution's Publication 4343, revised (Washington, D.C., 1963). Sturtevant's essay has been reprinted in Morton H. Fried, ed., *Readings in Anthropology,* 2nd ed. 2 Vols. (New York, 1968).